Sources of English Legal History
Private Law to 1750

ONE WEEK LOAN

Sources of English Legal History
Private Law to 1750

J. H. Baker, LL.D., F.B.A.
Reader in English Legal History and
Fellow of St Catharine's College,
Cambridge

S. F. C. Milsom, Q.C., F.B.A.
Professor of Law and
Fellow of St John's College,
Cambridge

London · Butterworths · 1986

United Kingdom	Butterworth & Co (Publishers) Ltd, 88 Kingsway, LONDON WC2B 6AB and 6/A North Castle Street, EDINBURGH EH2 3LJ
Australia	Butterworths Pty Ltd, SYDNEY, MELBOURNE, BRISBANE, ADELAIDE, PERTH, CANBERRA and HOBART
Canada	Butterworths, A division of Reed Inc., TORONTO and VANCOUVER
New Zealand	Butterworths of New Zealand Ltd, WELLINGTON and AUCKLAND
Singapore	Butterworth & Co (Asia) Pte Ltd, SINGAPORE
South Africa	Butterworth Publishers (Pty) Ltd, DURBAN and PRETORIA
USA	Butterworth Legal Publishers, ST PAUL, Minnesota, SEATTLE, Washington, BOSTON, Massachusetts, AUSTIN, Texas and D & S Publishers, CLEARWATER, Florida

British Library Cataloguing in Publication Data

Source of English legal history : private
  law to 1750
  1. Civil Law—England—History—Sources
  I. Baker, J.H.   II. Milsom, S.F.C.
  344.206′09   KD720

ISBN Hardcover 0 406 01640 2
     Softcover   0 406 01641 0

1170653 8

Learning Resources
Centre

Printed and bound in Great Britain by Biddles Ltd, Guildford and King's Lynn

The cover of the limp edition shows the illuminated first membrane of the plea rolls of the Queen's Bench for Easter term 1584, with a miniature of Queen Elizabeth I: Public Record Office, KB 27/1289, m. 1.

Preface

The notion of a 'leading case' is not new: Lord Keeper Egerton, in the time of Elizabeth I, said that a leading case was not to be questioned. Some of the cases in this volume were evidently seen as significant in their own day, though it is important—and sometimes difficult—not to imagine a court as consciously choosing all the consequences attributed to its decision by later contemporaries, let alone by the legal historians of a later time. One of our aims has been to give students (at every level including the professorial) the chance to sink deep enough into past discussions to lose the misleading perspectives of hindsight. Historians tend to regard their 'ifs' as a game: but the legal historian who does not listen for the arguments of his losers is not doing justice to his winners. Not infrequently he is also misunderstanding the question at issue; and the changing focus of discussion—in general from procedural to substantive—often appears most clearly from cases that were in no way 'leading'.

Indeed, the further back one goes in time, the harder it is to reconstruct not just the 'legal' question but also the underlying facts. Did this action for battery grow out of a malicious attack or unsuccessful surgery or a road accident? Did that assize of novel disseisin grow out of a mistake in unenclosed land or plain grabbing or an exercise of lawful authority by the plaintiff's lord? Such questions are about the conditions of daily life as much as about 'the law'; and since the legal materials form an important proportion of the surviving social evidence, the legal historian has a special responsibility to point out ambiguities which tradition has overlooked.

But a book like this can provide no more than pointers for social and economic historians, in the hope that they may be moved to make larger and more systematic use of the legal sources. And of course they will need to exploit a wider range of such materials than are represented here, especially the records of local courts. Our concern has been to illustrate the development of the common law. A few Chancery cases will be found, and one from the Star Chamber, but only as necessary supplements to an otherwise misleading picture. And even within the ambit of the common law, only a general qualitative impression is possible for the medieval period. The action of debt, for example, generated much systematic and often subtle learning: but it was all about proof rather than substance, and all we can hope to do is to give some idea of the ways in which substantial questions could arise.

It is this, as much as the greater prolixity of the later materials, that has dictated the chronological balance of the collection. But this may be the appropriate place to state what will be obvious to those who know our respective works: that the book is very much more Dr. Baker's than Professor Milsom's. We had made independent approaches to the publishers; and after 22 years as fellow students of the subject we were both attracted by their suggestion that we should work together. But Dr. Baker has done most of it. (It is proper for the younger student to add for himself what will be still more obvious, that his master's contribution is not to be measured in pages.)

All the texts are new editions, and even when there is a modern edition we have translated for ourselves. Where old printed texts have been used, we have usually tried to compare at least one manuscript version; and we have usually made reasonable efforts to trace records in the plea rolls. The names of parties follow the record, where found, unless otherwise stated. Place-names have been modernised, and the names of judges and counsel standardised. (Judges' names are printed in capitals, those of counsel in italics.) Dates in the text are given as they occur, but in the notes they have been converted into modern style. Texts originally in English—marked 'untr.' unless later than 1700—have been rendered into modern spelling, and repunctuated in accordance with the conventions used for the translations.

June 1986   J. H. Baker
                                                              S. F. C. Milsom

Contents

Acknowledgements

For permission to use manuscript material, we are grateful to the following:

Bodleian Library, Oxford
British Library
Harvard Law School
Henry E. Huntington Library, San Marino, California
Library of Congress (American-British Law Division), Washington D.C.
The Master and Fellows of University College, Oxford
The Rector and Fellows of Exeter College, Oxford
Spencer Research Library, University of Kansas at Lawrence
The Syndics of Cambridge University Library
The Treasurer and Masters of the Bench of Gray's Inn
The Treasurer and Masters of the Bench of Lincoln's Inn
The Treasurer and Masters of the Bench of the Middle Temple
Yale Law School (manuscripts deposited in the Beinecke Library)

For permission to use published material, we are also grateful to the following:

The Ames Foundation (year books of Richard II)
Cambridge University Press (extracts from *Lord Nottingham's Two Treatises*, Yale, ed.)
Oxford University Press (extract from Treharne and Saunders, *Documents of the Baronial Movement*)
The Selden Society.

Table of Statutes

Alphabetical Table of Named Cases

Table of Cases cited by Year

Table of Extracts from Treatises and other Texts

(1) Treatises

(4) Miscellaneous notes

Notes from the year books will be found in the Table of Cases cited by Year.

List of Abbreviations

A.-G.	Attorney General.
Ames Fdn	Publications of the Ames Foundation: Year Books of Richard II (1914–).
And.	Reports by Sir Edmund Anderson (d. 1605), C.J.C.P. Printed in 1664, 2 vols.; reprinted in 123 E.R. There is no English ed.
Atk.	Chancery reports by John Tracy Atkyns (d. 1773), cursitor Baron of the Exchequer. 1st ed. 1765–68, 3 vols.; 3rd ed. reprinted in 26 E.R.
B.	Baron of the Exchequer.
Beare's reports	Unpublished reports by George Beare (d. 1662) of MT, later K.Sjt.
Benl.	Reports of William Bendlowes (d. 1584), Sjt. Printed in 1689; reprinted in 123 E.R. There is no English ed.
BL	British Library (Department of Manuscripts).
Bla. (Wm)	Reports by Sir William Blackstone (d. 1780), J.C.P. 1st ed. 1780; reprinted from 1828 ed. in 96 E.R.
Bod. Lib.	Bodleian Library, Oxford.
Bracton	*Bracton on the Laws and Customs of England:* Latin text ed. G. E. Woodbine (1915–42), reissued with translation and notes by S. E. Thorne (1968–77), 4 vols. The treatise has long been associated with the name of Henry de Bracton (d. 1268) J.K.B., but it now seems that he was not the author.
Bracton's Note Book	*Bracton's Note-Book*, ed. F. W. Maitland (1887), 3 vols. A collection of cases from the plea rolls, now thought to have no connection with Bracton.
Bridgman (J.)	Reports by John Bridgman (d. 1638), Sjt., C.J. of Chester. Printed in 1659; reprinted in 123 E.R.
Bro. & Golds.	Reports attributed to Richard Brownlow (d. 1638), chief prothonotary of C.P., and John Goldesborough (d. 1618), second prothonotary of C.P. 1st ed. 1651, 2 vols; reprinted from 1675 ed. in 123 E.R.
Brooke Abr.	Sir Robert Brooke, *La Graunde Abridgement* (1573). The compiler (d. 1558) was C.J.C.P. There is no English ed.

Brown P.C.	Reports of cases in Parliament by Josiah Brown of IT. 1st ed 1779–83, 7 vols.; reprinted from 1803 ed. in 1–3 E.R.
Buls.	Reports by Edward Bulstrode (d. 1659) of IT, Welsh judge. 1st ed. 1657–59; 3 vols; reprinted from 1688 ed. in 81 E.R.
Burr.	Reports by Sir James Burrows (d. 1782), master of the Crown Office. Printed in 1766–71; reprinted from 1812 ed. in 97–98 E.R.
C1	Public Records Office, 'Early Chancery Proceedings'.
C33	Public Record Office, 'Chancery Decree and Order Books'.
Car.	(King) Charles.
Carthew	Reports by Thomas Carthew (d. 1704) of MT, later Sjt. 1st ed. 1728; reprinted from 1741 ed. in 90 E.R.
Caryll's reports	Reports by John Caryll (d. 1523) of IT, later K. Sjt. Some were printed in Keil. (q.v.), but the remainder are unpublished.
C.B.	Chief Baron of the Exchequer.
Ch. Cas.	*Cases argued and decreed in the High Court of Chancery.* Anonymous, though part has been attributed to Sir Anthony Keck (d. 1695) of IT. 1st ed. 1697–1700, 2 parts; reprinted in 22 E.R.
C.J.	Chief Justice.
C.J.C.P.	Chief Justice of the Common Pleas.
C.J.K.B. (or Q.B.)	Chief Justice of the King's Bench (Queen's Bench).
C.L.J.	Cambridge Law Journal.
Co. Entr.	Sir Edward Coke, *A Booke of Entries* (1614). The author (d. 1634) was C.J.K.B. at the time of publication. Published in Latin.
Co. Litt.	Sir Edward Coke, *First Part of the Institutes of the Laws of England* (1628), a commentary on Littleton, *Tenures* (q.v.). Written after Coke's dismissal as C.J.K.B. in 1616.
Co. Rep.	The reports of Sir Edward Coke (d. 1634), A.-G., C.J.C.P. and C.J.K.B. 1st eds. (in French) 1600–15, 11 vols., with 2 further posthumous vols. in 1658–59; reprinted (in translation) from the 1826 ed. in 76–77 E.R. Some of the original notebooks containing Coke's reports survive in BL and CUL.
Comb.	Reports by Roger Comberbach (d. 1720) of IT, Welsh judge. Printed in 1724; reprinted in 90 E.R.
Comyns	Reports by Sir John Comyns (d. 1740), C.B. 1st ed. 1744; reprinted from 1792 ed. in 92 E.R.
C.P.	Court of Common Pleas.
CP 40	Public Record Office, 'De Banco Rolls'; i.e., the plea rolls of C.P.
Cro. Eliz. (Jac., Car.)	Reports by Sir George Croke (d. 1642) of IT, later J.K.B. 1st eds. 1657 (*temp.* Car. I), 1658 (*temp.* Jac. I) and 1661 (*temp.* Eliz. I); reprinted from 1790–92 ed. in 78–79 E.R.
CUL	Cambridge University Library.
Curia Regis Rolls	*Curia Regis Rolls* (1922–), by various editors.

D.	Digest (of Justinian).
Dalison	Reports attributed (some falsely) to William Dalison (d. 1559), J.Q.B. Printed in 1689; reprinted in 123 E.R. There is no English ed.
Danv.	D'Anvers: see Rolle Abr.
Dyer	Reports by Sir James Dyer (d. 1582), C.J.C.P. 1st ed. (in French) 1585; reprinted from the 1794 ed. (in translation) in 73 E.R.
E 13	Public Record Office, 'Plea Rolls of the Exchequer of Pleas'.
ECO	Exeter College, Oxford.
ed.	edition, edited by.
E.H.R.	English Historical Review.
Eq. Cas. Abr.	*A General Abridgment of Cases in Equity ... by a gentleman of the Middle Temple*; usually cited as 'Equity Cases Abridged'. 1st ed. 1732; reprinted from the 1792 ed. in 21-22 E.R.
E.R.	*The English Reports.*
Exch. Cha.	Court of Exchequer Chamber.
Fitz. Abr.	Sir Anthony Fitzherbert, *La Graunde Abridgement* (1577). The author (d. 1538) was J.C.P. He was a Sjt. at the time of the 1st ed. (1514–16).
Fo.	Folio (leaf of a book).
Fort.	Reports by John Fortescue Aland (d. 1746), 1st Baron Fortescue of Credan, J.C.P. Printed in 1748; reprinted in 92 E.R.
Freem.	Reports by Richard Freeman (d. 1710) of MT, later L.C. of Ireland. 1st ed. 1742; reprinted from 1826 ed. in 89 E.R.
Gell's reports	Unpublished reports by Anthony Gell (d. 1583) of IT.
GI	Gray's Inn.
Gilb. Cas.	*Cases in Law and Equity ... during the time of Lord Chief Justice Parker ... from the original manuscript of the late Lord Chief Baron Gilbert* (1760). Jeffrey Gilbert C.B. (d. 1726) was probably not the author. Reprinted in 93 E.R.
Godb.	Reports attributed to John Godbold (d. 1648), J.C.P. Printed in 1653; reprinted in 78 E.R.
Goulds.	Reports attributed to John Goldesborough or Gouldsborough (d. 1618), second prothonotary of C.P. 1st ed. 1653; reprinted from 1682 ed. in 75 E.R.
Gundry's notebook	Unpublished notebook of Sir Nathaniel Gundry (d. 1754), J.C.P.
Hardres	Reports by Thomas Hardres (d. 1681) of GI, later K. Sjt. 1st ed. 1693; reprinted from 1792 ed. in 145 E.R.
Harpur's reports	Unpublished reports by Richard Harpur (d. 1573), J.C.P.
Hawarde	*Les Reports del Cases in Camera Stellata 1593 to 1609. From an original MS. of John Hawarde*, ed. W. P. Baildon (1894). The reporter was John Hawarde or Hayward (d. 1631) of IT.

HEHL	Henry E. Huntington Library, San Marino, California.
Herne, *The Pleader*	J. Herne, *The Pleader: containing Perfect Presidents and Forms of Declarations, Pleadings* ... (1657). The compiler was John Herne or Heron of LI (called to the bench 1636).
Hetley	Reports attributed (most doubtfully) to Thomas Hetley (d. 1637), Sjt., sometime official reporter. Printed in 1657; reprinted in 124 E.R.
Hil.	Hilary term.
HLS	Harvard Law School (Treasure Room).
Hob.	Reports by Sir Henry Hobart (d. 1625), C.J.C.P. 1st ed. 1641; reprinted from 1724 ed. in 80 E.R.
Holt	*Cases determined by Sir John Holt ... alphabetically digested* (1738). Anonymous collection; reprinted in 90 E.R.
IT	Inner Temple.
J., JJ.	Justice, Justices.
Jac.	(King) James.
J.C.P.	Justice of the Common Pleas.
J.K.B. (or Q.B.)	Justice of the King's Bench (Queen's Bench).
Jones (T.)	Reports attributed to Sir Thomas Jones (d. 1686), C.J.C.P. 1st ed. 1695; reprinted from 1729 ed. in 84 E.R. There is no English ed.
Jones (Wm)	Reports by Sir William Jones (d. 1640), J.K.B. Printed in 1675; reprinted in 82 E.R. There is no English ed.
J.S.	John Style, an imaginary person used in putting cases.
JUST 1	Public Record Office, 'Rolls of the Justices Itinerant'.
K.B.	Court of King's Bench.
KB 27	Public Record Office, 'Coram Rege Rolls'; i.e. the plea rolls of K.B.
KB 122	Public Record Office, 'Plea or Judgment Rolls of the Court of King's Bench' (from 1702).
Keb.	Reports by Joseph Keble (d. 1710) of GI. Printed in 1685, 3 vols.; reprinted in 83–84 E.R.
Keil.	*Relationes quorundam casuum selectorum ex libris Roberti Keilwey*, ed. J. Croke (1602). These are part of the reports by John Caryll (q.v.). Reprinted from 1688 ed. in 72 E.R. There is no English ed.
Kiralfy, *Source Book*	A.K.R. Kiralfy, *A Source Book of English Law* (1957).
K.Sjt.	King's Serjeant at Law.
KU	Kansas University (Kenneth Spencer Research Library, University of Kansas at Lawrence).
LC	Library of Congress, Washington D.C. (Law Division).
L.C.	Lord Chancellor.
Ld Raym.	See Raym. (Ld)
Leeds' notebook	Unpublished reports by Edward Leeds (d. 1758), K.Sjt.

Leon.	Reports collected (but not written) by William Leonard of GI (called 1585). 1st ed. by William Hughes of GI, 1658–75, 4 vols.; reprinted from 1687 ed. in 74 E.R.
Lev.	Reports attributed to Sir Creswell Levinz (d. 1701), sometime J.C.P. Translated into English by William Salkeld (q.v.). 1st ed. 1701, 3 vols.; reprinted from 1793 ed. in 83 E.R.
LI	Lincoln's Inn.
Lib. Ass.	*Liber Assisarum* (14th century). The reports in this volume are cited by regnal year of Edw III, followed by the case-number. They are not (like the other Y.B.s) divided into terms. Latest ed. 1679 (in French).
Lilly, *Entries*	John Lilly, *A Collection of Modern Entries* (3rd ed., 1758). 1st ed. (in Latin) 1723.
Littleton, *Tenures*	Sir Thomas Littleton, *The New Tenures*. This was probably written in the 1450s; first printed (in French) 1481; printed with parallel French and English texts in Co. Litt. (q.v.). The author (d. 1481) was J.C.P.
L.K.	Lord Keeper of the Great Seal.
L.Q.R.	Law Quarterly Review.
m.	membrane; i.e. rotulet in a bundle of plea rolls.
Mich.	Michaelmas term.
Mod.	*Modern Reports*, by various reporters and editors; first printed in 1682–1738 in 12 separate parts; collected into a series by Thomas Leach (1793–96); reprinted in 86–88 E.R.
Moo. K.B.	Reports by Sir Francis Moore (d. 1616), Sjt. 1st ed. 1663; reprinted from 1688 ed. in 72 E.R. There is no English ed.
M.R.	Master of the Rolls.
MS.	Manuscript.
MT	Middle Temple.
Nelson	A collection of Chancery cases, ed. William Nelson of MT (called 1684). Printed in 1717; reprinted in 21 E.R.
Noy	Reports attributed to William Noy (d. 1634) of LI, A.-G. 1st ed. 1656; reprinted from 1669 ed. in 74 E.R.
Owen	Reports attributed to Thomas Owen (d. 1598), J.C.P. Printed in 1656; reprinted in 74 E.R.
Palm.	Reports attributed to Sir Geoffrey Palmer (d. 1670) of MT, A.-G. 1st ed. 1678; reprinted from 1721 ed. in 81 E.R. There is no English ed.
Pas.	Easter term (*Pascha* in Latin).
P.C.C.	Prerogative Court of Canterbury, registers of wills (now in the Public Record Office, class PROB 11).
pl.	*placitum* (case-number).
Plowd.	Edmund Plowden, *Les Comentaries* (1571–79), 2 parts. The reporter (d. 1585) was of MT. Originally published in French; reprinted (in translation) from 1816 ed. in 75 E.R.

Pollard's reports	Unpublished reports by Richard Pollard (d. 1542) of MT.
Pollex.	Reports attributed to Sir Henry Pollexfen (d. 1691), C.J.C.P. Printed in 1702; reprinted in 86 E.R.
Poph.	Reports by Sir John Popham (d. 1607), C.J.K.B. 1st ed. 1656; reprinted from 1682 ed. in 79 E.R.
Port's notebook	MS. notebook of Sir John Port (d. 1540), J.K.B. An edition of the principal contents will shortly be published by the Selden Soc.
Q.B.	Court of Queen's Bench.
Q.Sjt.	Queen's Serjeant at Law.
Rastell, *Collection of Entrees*	*William Rastell, A Collection of Entrees* (1st ed., 1566; 1596). The compiler (d. 1565) was J.Q.B., and brought together several earlier books of entries. Published in Latin.
Raym. (Ld)	Reports collected (but not all written) by Sir Robert Raymond (d. 1733), 1st Baron Raymond, C.J.K.B. 1st ed. 1743, 3 vols.; reprinted from 1790 ed. in 91-92 E.R.
Raym. (T.)	Reports attributed to Sir Thomas Raymond (d. 1683), J.K.B. 1st ed. 1696; reprinted from 1803 ed. in 83 E.R.
Ridg. *temp.* Hard.	Reports of Chancery cases in the time of Lord Hardwicke L.C., ed. William Ridgeway (d. 1817) of the Irish bar. Printed in 1794; reprinted in 27 E.R.
Rolle Abr.	Henry Rolle, *Un Abridgement des Plusieurs Cases* (1668), 2 vols. The author (d. 1656) was C.J. of the Upper Bench. There is no English ed., except for an enlarged ed. in translation of the titles A to E by Knightley D'Anvers of MT.
Rolle Rep.	Reports by Henry Rolle (d. 1656) of IT, later C.J. of the Upper Bench. Printed in 1675, 2 vols.; reprinted in 81 E.R. There is no English ed.
Rolls Series	Editions of Y.B.s of Edw. I and 11-20 Edw. III published by authority of the Treasury under the direction of the Master of the Rolls (1863-1911). The editors were Alfred John Horwood of MT and Luke Owen Pike (d. 1915) of LI.
Rotuli Curiae Regis	*Rotuli Curiae Regis*, ed. Sir Francis Palgrave (1835), 2 vols.
Salk.	Reports by William Salkeld (d. 1715), Sjt., C.J. of Carmarthen. 1st ed. 1717, 3 vols.; reprinted from 1795 ed. in 91 E.R.
Saund.	Reports of Sir Edmund Saunders (d. 1683) of MT, later C.J.C.P. 1st ed. 1686 (in French); ed. in translation with extensive notes by John Williams Sjt. in 1799; reprinted from 1845 ed. in 85 E.R.
Saund. (Wms)	Williams' ed. of Saund. (q.v.).
Selden Soc.	Publications of the Selden Society (1887–).
Selw. N.P.	W. Selwyn *An Abridgement of the Law of Nisi Prius* (1st ed. 1806–08), in 3 parts. References are to the 3rd ed. (1812).
S.-G.	Solicitor General.

Sheppard Abr.	William Sheppard, *A Grand Abridgment of the Common and Statute Law of England* (1675), 4 parts. The compiler (d. 1675) was of MT, and a Sjt. during the interregnum.
Show. K.B.	Reports by Sir Bartholomew Shower (d. 1701) of MT, recorder of London. 1st ed. 1708–20, 2 vols.; reprinted from 1794 ed. in 89 E.R.
Sid.	Reports by Thomas Siderfin of MT (called 1661). 1st ed. 1683–84; reprinted from 1714 ed. in 82 E.R. There is no English ed.
Sjt.	Serjeant at Law.
Skin.	Reports by Robert Skinner of IT (called 1682). Published by his son, Matthew Skinner K.Sjt., in 1728; reprinted in 90 E.R.
Spelman, *Reports*	*The Reports of Sir John Spelman*, ed. J. H. Baker (Selden Soc. vol. 93, 1977). The reporter (d. 1546) was J.K.B.
Statham Abr.	Abridgment, printed without title at Rouen (*c.* 1490), and traditionally attributed to Nicholas Statham (d. 1472) of LI. There is an English ed. by Miss M. C. Klingelsmith (1915), which is almost as rare as the original and not wholly reliable.
Statutes of the Realm	*Statutes of the Realm* (1810–28), a new ed. in 12 vols. of the statutes from 1235 to 1713.
Stra.	Reports by Sir John Strange (d. 1754), M.R. 1st ed. 1755, 2 vols.; reprinted from 1795 ed. in 93 E.R.
Style	Reports by William Style (d. 1679) of IT. Printed as *Narrationes modernae* (1658); reprinted in 82 E.R.
temp.	in the time of (*tempore* in Latin).
T. Jones	See Jones (T.).
Tothill	Chancery cases collected and ed. by William Tothill of MT (called 1619). 1st ed. 1649; reprinted from 1658 ed. in 82 E.R.
T. Raym.	See Raym. (T).
Treby's reports	Unpublished reports by Sir George Treby (d. 1700), C.J.C.P.
Trin.	Trinity term
Turnor's reports	Unpublished reports by Arthur Turnor (d. 1651), Sjt.
UCO	University College, Oxford.
unfol.	unfoliated.
untr.	untranslated (indicating a text originally in English).
Vaugh.	Reports by Sir John Vaughan (d. 1674), C.J.C.P. Printed in 1677; reprinted in 124 E.R.
Vent.	Reports attributed to Sir Peyton Ventris (d. 1691), J.C.P. 1st ed. 1696, 2 vols.; reprinted from 1726 ed. in 86 E.R.
Vern.	Chancery reports by Thomas Vernon (d. 1721) of MT. 1st ed. 1726–28, 2 vols.; reprinted from 1828 ed. in 23 E.R.
Were's reports	Unpublished reports by Humphrey Were (d. 1625) of IT.

Wils. K.B.	Reports by George Wilson (d. 1778), Sjt. 1st ed. 1770, 3 vols.; reprinted from 1799 ed. in 95 E.R.
Wm Bla.	See Bla. (Wm).
Wm Jones	See Jones (Wm).
Wms Saund.	See Saund. (Wms)
Y.B.	Year Books. Y.B. Edw. I and 11–20 Edw. III are from the Rolls Series; Edw. II from the Selden Soc. series; and Ric. II from the Ames Fdn series. The remainder are from the small folio black-letter editions, in most cases collated with MSS. as cited. There is no English ed. of these last.
Yelv.	Reports attributed to Sir Henry Yelverton (d. 1630), J.C.P. 1st ed. (in French) 1661; reprinted from 1792 ed. (in translation) in 80 E.R.
YLS	Yale Law School (MSS. deposited in the Beinecke Rare Book Library, Yale University). Most of the law reports in this collection belonged to Sir Matthew Hale (d. 1676), C.J.K.B.
Yorke's reports	Unpublished notebook of Roger Yorke (d. 1536), Sjt., containing reports and Gray's Inn notes.

1 Tenure: services and incidents

(1) Services

STANFELD v BREWES (1199)

Rotuli Curiae Regis, I, p. 366.

Surrey. An assize comes to declare whether Simon de Brewes and Luke the clerk and Peter de Brewes unjustly and without judgment disseised Odo de Stanfeld and Juliana his wife of their free tenement in Mitcham within [the limitation period of] the assize.

Simon says the assize should not be taken because he took that land into hand by judgment of his court, which he produces and which attests this, for failure of service.

And it was attested that Odo holds that land of this Simon.

Simon is commanded to replevy that land to Odo together with his chattels, and to deal with him rightly in [Simon's] own court.

LUCY v ADAM SON OF JOHN (1203–04)

(a) *Curia Regis Rolls*, II, p. 273.

Cumberland. Richard de Lucy claims from Adam son of John that he should do the services and customs that he ought to do for him in respect of the free tenement he holds of him in Briscoe, namely . . . [an elaborate recital of services mostly concerning the forest and the collection of tolls].

And Adam comes and expressly acknowledges that he owes [some of these services]; and he puts himself upon the grand assize of the lord king and asks that it be declared whether he ought to hold his tenement just by the services that he acknowledges or by the service that Richard demands . . .

(b) *Curia Regis Rolls*, III, p. 206.

Adam son of John, who placed himself upon the grand assize in a plea concerning the service which Richard de Lucy demanded from him in respect of the free tenement which he held of him in Briscoe, has come and surrendered to [Richard] the tenement from which he demanded the service, and has quitclaimed it for ever for himself and his heirs in favour of Richard and his heirs . . .

(2) Incidents

NEREFORD v WALTER SON OF HUMPHREY (1200–01)

(a) *Curia Regis Rolls*, I, p. 177.

Essex. Peter son of Geoffrey [de Nereford] claims from Walter son of Humphrey that he should do homage and service for one knight's fee in Great Yeldham with the appurtenances, which [Peter's] father Geoffrey and Peter himself granted to Walter's father Humphrey by fine agreed in the king's court.

And Walter comes and says that the earl of Clare has disseised him for the default of this Peter, because Peter has not done homage for this land or paid relief to the earl; and the earl's steward attests this and says the earl still holds the land because of Peter's default.

And Peter says that Walter is not yet disseised because he is still seised . . .

(b) *Curia Regis Rolls*, II, p. 61.

Essex. Walter son of Humphrey, from whom Peter de Nereford claimed homage and relief for one knight's fee in Great Yeldham, has come and done homage and paid him his relief.

VAVASSUR v BEC (1218)

Rolls of the Justices in Eyre for Lincolnshire, 1218–19, and Worcestershire, 1221, Selden Soc. vol. 53, pl. 141.

[Lincolnshire]. An assize comes to declare whether Henry Bec unjustly and without judgment disseised Goda daughter of Gilbert Vavassur of her free tenement in Saltfleetby [within the limitation period of the assize].

And Henry comes and says that she never had seisin because immediately on the death of Goda's brother Robert, who died seised of that land, [Henry] as lord of the fee took the land into hand by reason of the infancy of Robert's son and heir Gilbert.

And Goda says that the same Robert had no son by his wedded wife; and she was herself in seisin of that land for half a year after Robert's death, and behaved as heir and sowed the land and took other issues; and she asks that her assize [be taken].

And Henry says that she never had seisin [of the land]; and thereof he puts himself upon the assize, and Goda likewise.

The jurors say that after Robert's death [Goda] remained in seisin of that land as heir, and was seised of it and took issues; and that, on the order of the same Henry, John Bec unjustly and without judgment disseised her.

And so it is adjudged that [Goda] have her seisin; and Henry is to be amerced. Damages 15 marks.

CLAVERDON v EARL OF WARWICK (1221)

Rolls of the Justices in Eyre for Gloucestershire,
Warwickshire and [Shropshire], 1221–22,
Selden Soc. vol. 59, pl. 406.

[Warwickshire]. An assize comes to declare whether Henry earl of Warwick and Thomas de Hethe unjustly and without judgment disseised Richard son of Richard of Claverdon of his free tenement in Claverdon [within the limitation period of] the assize.

And the earl comes and says the assize should not be taken because he readily acknowledges that the aforesaid Richard's father Richard held the tenement of him and did him homage, and this Richard should be his man; but when the father Richard died his widow stayed on in the house and is still there; and because she would not at [the earl's] summons deliver up the heir Richard to him, he took the land into his own hand by judgment of his court; and [to attest this] he produces his court of Warwick where this was done, namely ... [six names] who record that when [the father] Richard died his widow remained in the land with the aforesaid heir, so that the heir was in seisin with his mother; and the earl ordered the mother to deliver up the heir; and because she would not, he asked his court what was to be done about it, and the court adjudged that she should be summoned to come to his court on a certain [day] to answer; and she was summoned by . . . [two names] who are present and attest this. At that day she neither came nor essoined herself, and the earl asked his court what was to be done about it; and the court adjudged that she should be distrained to come to the next court. At that [next] court, because it was attested that she had no chattels by which she could be distrained, the court adjudged that the earl should betake himself to his fee until the heir should do what he ought to do. And so he took that land into his hand by way of distraint [as well he might].

And Richard who is within age says he was seised of that land for three years after his father's death; and after the disseisin the earl enfeoffed the aforesaid Thomas of nine acres for five shillings to be paid to the earl. And Thomas acknowledges this. And Richard says also that the land is socage and no wardship attaches to it. And he says that on the earl's authority Thomas cultivated the land and took the fruits for four years. And the earl acknowledges that indeed his bailiffs caused the land to be cultivated, but not on his authority.

And so it is adjudged that Richard should recover his seisin, and that the earl should be amerced . . . Damages one mark . . . Afterwards the earl came and made fine of 40 marks for himself and his court.

BISHOP OF CARLISLE v WIGENHALE (1236–37)

(a) *Bracton's Note Book*, pl. 1175.

Norfolk. Adam de Wigenhale was summoned to answer to the lord king by what warrant he holds himself in one carucate of arable with the appurtenances in Garboldisham which [his brother] William de Wigenhale held of John de Jarpenvilla the father of his heir John de Jarpenvilla who is within age and in the king's wardship, which land should escheat to the heir because the aforesaid William was a bastard and died without heir of his body etc.; the bishop of Carlisle has this wardship by grant from the king.

And Adam comes and is unwilling to answer without writ; and he says that he was in seisin of the same land and is disseised of it, and he claims his seisin.

And the bishop, as the king's grantee of the wardship of the aforesaid heir, says that [Adam] never had seisin: it is true that the bishop took Adam's fealty and ordered his bailiff to make seisin to him of the aforesaid land; but before seisin was made, the bishop was given to understand that Adam's brother William was a bastard, because born before his father married his mother.

And Adam as before asks judgment whether he need answer. And because the sheriff has not sent the writ, they are given such a day before the lord king; and meantime let the writ come, and the sheriff is to have the writ on that day . . .

(b) *Curia Regis Rolls*, XV, pl. 1882; also *Bracton's Note Book*, pl. 1181.

Norfolk. Adam de Wigenhale was summoned to answer to the lord king by what warrant he holds himself in one carucate of arable with the appurtenances in Garboldisham, which [his brother] William de Wigenhale held of John de Jarpenvilla the father of his heir John de Jarpenvilla who is within age and in the king's wardship, which land should escheat to the heir because the same William was a bastard and died without heir of his body, so it is said. And as to this the bishop of Carlisle, who sues for the king, says that the land should revert to the aforesaid heir because Adam's brother William was a bastard because born before William's father married his mother.

And Adam comes and says that that William was legitimate; and he asks judgment whether bastardy should be imputed against him after his death. And he says that his dead brother William, on the death of [William's] father, came to the chief lords and did them homage for his father's lands and tenements without any challenge of bastardy. And when William died, [Adam] himself likewise did homage to the chief lords without challenge; and he went to this bishop and offered him homage, and [the bishop] answered that he would not take his homage until [the bishop] knew whether [Adam] was heir or not. And later, having inquired into the matter, [the bishop] took his fealty and made him letters patent telling [the bishop's] bailiff to put [Adam] in seisin; and the bailiff did put him in seisin; and [Adam] says that he is disseised by the bishop, and he asks judgment whether he need answer while disseised. And he will show that the same William was legitimate in whatever way the court shall adjudge.

Afterwards came Adam and acknowledged that William died seised, and claims seisin as [William's] brother and heir . . .

And the bishop comes and says that the same Adam had no seisin and so was not disseised; although indeed it may well be that when William was dead the same Adam intruded himself into that

land. But the same bishop on [William's] death took that land into
his own hand as that of which he was entitled to the wardship
because John de Jarpenvilla's heir was in his hand by the king's
command, and he placed his serjeant [in that land]; and the
aforesaid [Adam] had no seisin except such as [he acquired by] his
own intrusion. But the bishop says that indeed [Adam] came to the
bishop and made an agreement about his relief and did him fealty
and had letters from the bishop to [the bishop's] serjeant ordering
him, if Adam gave him security for that relief, to make seisin to him
of that land. But because Adam did not give security, and also
because [the bishop] heard that the aforesaid William was a bastard
and so could have no heir except of his body, [the bishop] would
not make seisin to [Adam], but he and his serjeant were in seisin
until the lord king took that land into his own hand. And
concerning this, if need be, he puts himself upon the country.

And Adam by his attorney says that he was [put] in seisin by the
bishop's bailiff; but he says that the country knows nothing of the
seisin made by the bishop's bailiff.

Afterwards the bishop comes and says that he ought not to make
seisin to the aforesaid Adam because William was married to a
wife, Agnes de Wigenhale by name, by whom he had an heir who is
clearly heir and who claims William's inheritance; and indeed the
aforesaid Agnes is claiming her dower and if need be is ready to
prove the marriage between herself and William, and so it seems to
[the bishop] that he ought not to make seisin to the same Adam or
anyone else until it is certain who is the right heir. And he says that
the same Adam on another occasion acknowledged that the
aforesaid Agnes was holding herself out as William's wife and had
children by William.

And Adam's attorney acknowledges that indeed this Agnes says
she was married to William, but she says it falsely and to hinder
and bar Adam's right. And because the same attorney acknowledges this, it is adjudged that Agnes is to be summoned to come
[on such a day] to declare whether she is claiming dower from that
land and whether or not she has children who ought to be
William's heirs.

On that day Agnes comes and declares that she was William's
wedded wife and that she has by him a son called Adam who ought
to be William's heir, and that she is claiming her dower as one who
was married to the aforesaid William; and if need be she has
sufficient proof that she was so married.

And Adam says that so far as he knows the aforesaid Agnes was
never married to his brother William; and that she was never

married [to him] appears clearly from the fact that not long ago she was claiming as her husband a certain Nicholas son of Alan de Wigenhale; but [Adam] does not know what became of that claim.

And because it is not known whether or not the same Adam son of William [and of Agnes] intends to claim any right in that land, he is to be summoned to come [on such a day] to declare what right he claims in that land.

DE LA HETHE v LONDON (1241)

Curia Regis Rolls, XVI, pl. 1767.

Herefordshire. Edith de la Hethe claims from Master Gervase de London the wardship of the land and heir of Robert de la Hethe in Cradley, which belongs to her because the aforesaid Robert held his land in socage and because the aforesaid Edith is next of kin to the aforesaid heir.

And Gervase, who at another time vouched the bishop of Hereford to warranty in this matter, comes and says that he has the aforesaid wardship by gift from a certain Roger de Waure by [Roger's] charter, which [Gervase] produces and which attests this; and he says that the aforesaid Roger had it by gift from Ralph, formerly bishop of Hereford, by [bishop Ralph's] charter, which [Gervase] likewise produces and which attests this; and he says the bishop could well give that wardship to whomever he wished, because Robert de la Hethe, the aforesaid heir's father, held of [the bishop] by charter and by knight service and not merely in socage; and as to this he puts himself upon the country.

And the bishop of Hereford comes by his attorney and warrants [Gervase], and likewise puts himself upon the country.

And Edith says that the aforesaid Robert held his land merely in socage and not by knight service; and as to this she puts herself upon the country. And so the sheriff is ordered to hold an inquest . . .

On that day the inquest comes, which is as follows: that the aforesaid Robert held his land merely in socage and not by knight service. And the aforesaid Gervase knows of no other reason why the wardship should not belong to [Edith]. It is adjudged that the aforesaid Edith should recover her seisin, and that Gervase should be amerced.

(3) Legislation protecting lords' interests

ORDINANCE ABOUT ALIENATION BY TENANTS IN CHIEF (1256)

Calendar of Close Rolls, 1254–56, p. 429.

The king to the sheriff of Yorkshire, greeting. Because it is clearly to our most serious loss and to the insupportable harm of [our] crown and royal dignity that anyone should enter baronies and fees which are held of us in chief within our realm and power, at the will of those who hold of us those baronies and fees, so that we lose wardships and escheats, and [so that] our barons and others who hold of us those baronies and fees so decrease [in resources] that they cannot properly do the services due to us [from those baronies and fees], whereby our crown is seriously harmed, which we will bear no longer; we have by our council provided that from henceforth none shall enter a barony or any fee held of us in chief by purchase or in any other way without our consent and special licence.

And so we strictly command you, in the faith by which you are bound to us and as you love yourself and all that you have, that you do not permit anyone from henceforth to enter by purchase or any other way a barony or any fee held of us in chief within your bailiwick without our consent and special licence. And if contrary to this provision anyone enters a barony or any fee held of us in chief within your bailiwick, then you are to take into our hand the land so entered and to keep it safely until we give you some other command concerning it. And you are so to conduct yourself in carrying out this our order that we suffer no damage in this respect and no harm to our crown or dignity through your failure or neglect, for which we should have to betake ourselves seriously to you and yours. Witness the king at Bristol on the 15th day of July [1256].

A like order has been sent to every sheriff in England, witness as above.

STATUTE ABOUT EVASION OF WARDSHIP (1267)

Statute of Marlborough, 52 Hen. III, c. 6;
Statutes of the Realm, vol. I, p. 20.

Concerning those who make feoffment of their inheritance to their first-born sons and heirs under age, so that the lords of the fees thereby lose their wardships: it is provided, agreed and granted that no chief lord shall lose his wardship by reason of such feoffment.

Further concerning those who, wishing to hand over lands for a term of years so that the lords of the fees shall lose their wardships, make up false feoffments which allege that they are satisfied for the service reserved in [those feoffments] up to a stated time, and that after that time the feoffees shall be bound to pay some amount much exceeding the value of those lands, so that after that time the lands will revert to [the grantors] because nobody will want to hold them for so much [service]: it is provided and granted that no chief lord shall lose his wardship by this kind of fraud. But still it shall not be lawful for [such lords] to disseise such feoffees without judgment, but they shall [proceed by] writ to recover such wardships, and by the witnesses named in the charters of such feoffments together with other free and lawful men of the countryside, and by [comparing] the value of the land with the amount of the service reserved after the aforesaid stated time, it shall be determined whether such feoffment was made in good faith or fraudulently to deprive the chief lords of their wardship. And even if the chief lords in such cases recover their wardship by judgment of the court, still there shall be saved to such feoffees their action against the heir when he comes of age to recover their term or their fee.

And if any chief lords maliciously implead any feoffees pretending that it is such a case, when the feoffments were made lawfully and in good faith, then there shall be adjudged to the feoffees their damages and the costs which they incurred by the aforesaid plea, and those claimants shall be heavily punished by amercement.

STATUTE *QUIA EMPTORES* (1290)

Statutes of the Realm, vol. I, p. 106.

Whereas the buyers of lands and tenements belonging to the fees of great men and other [lords] have in times past often entered [those] fees to [the lords'] prejudice, because tenants holding freely of those great men and other [lords] have sold their lands and tenements [to those buyers] to hold in fee to [the buyers] and their heirs of their feoffors and not of the chief lords of the fees, with the result that the same chief lords have often lost the escheats, marriages and wardships of lands and tenements belonging to their fees; and this has seemed to the same great men and other lords [not only] very hard and burdensome [but also] in such a case to their manifest disinheritance:

The lord king in his parliament at Westminster after Easter in the eighteenth year of his reign, namely a fortnight after the feast of St John the Baptist, at the instance of the great men of his realm, has granted, provided and laid down that from henceforth it shall be lawful for any free man at his own pleasure to sell his lands or tenements or [any] part of them; provided however that the feoffee shall hold those lands or tenements of the same chief lord and by the same services and customary dues as his feoffor previously held them. And if he sells to another any part of his same lands or tenements, the feoffee shall hold that [part] directly of the chief lord and shall immediately be burdened with such amount of service as belongs or ought to belong to the same lord for that part according to the amount of the land or tenement [that has been] sold; and so in this case that part of the service falls to the chief lord to be taken by the hand of the [feoffee], so that the feoffee ought to look and answer to the same chief lord for that part of the service owed as [is proportional to] the amount of the land or tenement sold. And be it known that through the aforesaid sales or purchases of lands or tenements or any part of them, those lands or tenements must in no way, in part or in whole, by any scheming or contriving, come into mortmain contrary to the form of the statute lately laid down on this matter. And be it known that this statute applies only to lands to be held in fee simple; and that it applies [only to sales to be made] in the future; and it is to take effect at the feast of St Andrew next coming.

2 Actions concerning land

(1) Writs of right

BAVENT v GARNOISE (1194)

(a) *Rotuli Curiae Regis*, I, p. 5.

Suffolk. Maud de Loudham was ordered to do full right to Adam Bavent concerning 60 acres of arable in Chippenhall which he claims to hold of her for three shillings a year and of which Robert Garnoise deforces him; and if she would not do [right] the sheriff would do it. And by the default of that Maud's court the plea was in the county, and from the county it was placed [on such a day in the king's court] by writ of [the justiciar]. And then came Robert Garnoise and asked for a view of that land because he had several [parcels of arable] in that vill . . .

(b) Ibid., p. 76.

Suffolk. Adam de Bavent claims from Robert Garnoise 60 acres of arable in Chippenhall as his right and inheritance.

And Robert comes and says that he holds that land as his right, and thereof he puts himself upon the grand assize of the lord king . . .

DE MARA v BOHUN (1198–1207)

(a) *Memoranda Roll*, 10 John, Pipe Roll Soc. N.S., vol. 31, p. 105 (*Curia Regis Roll*, 9 Ric. I).

Gloucestershire. Bertram de Mara claims from Roger son of

Nicholas two carucates of arable with the appurtenances in Longford, by writ of right addressed to Margaret de Bohun, as his right
and inheritance of which his uncle Henry was seised in demesne as
of fee in the time of King Henry I, the day and the year when he
died, taking therefrom issues to the value of five shillings or more;
and this he offers to prove by Simon Tirel, who offers to prove it by
the command of his father who was eye-witness.

And Roger comes and denies [Bertram's] right and says that on
another occasion [Bertram] claimed this land from him in the
king's court, and [Roger] then vouched to warranty Margaret de
Bohun on the basis of her ancestors' charters [witnessing] the gift
of the said ancestors; and that Margaret came into court and
warranted him; and then these proceedings were put without day
because he was summoned to military service for the king; and now
he vouches to warranty Henry de Bohun son of the aforesaid
Margaret. They are given their day at the coming of the justices,
and then Roger is to have Henry de Bohun whom he has vouched
to warranty.

(b) *Curia Regis Rolls*, V, p. 18.

Gloucestershire. Bertram de Mara claims from [Roger] son of
Nicholas the fee of half a knight with the appurtenances in
Longford as his right of which his uncle Henry de Mara was seised
in the time of King Henry I etc.

And Roger comes and vouches to warrant Henry earl of Hereford, and he prays the aid of the court . . .

(c) Ibid., p. 57.

Gloucestershire. Bertram de Mara claims from Henry de Bohun
earl of Hereford, whom Roger son of Nicholas vouched to warranty and who warranted him, the fee of half a knight with the
appurtenances in Longford as his right of which his uncle Henry
was seised in his demesne as of fee and of right taking therefrom
issues etc., to the value of half a mark and more; and this he offers
to prove against him by a certain free man of his, Simon Tirel, who
offers this etc. as of the seeing and hearing of [blank for Simon's
father's name never filled in] his father, who commanded etc.

And Henry denies [Bertram's] right and says that he should not
answer to him because that Bertram had an elder brother, namely
Oliver de Mara, whose heir [William] is still alive, [which William]
would have greater right in that fee than this Bertram if either of
them had any right in that fee. [Bertram replied that the same

objection had been made in an earlier action against Nicholas, Roger's father, that William had been summoned and had quit-claimed to Bertram for Bertram's life]. But since this land could not descend to Bertram by hereditary right, it is adjudged that he take nothing by this writ.

ROBERT SON OF RICHARD v NEVILL (1199–1201)

(a) *Pleas before the King or his Justices*, I,
Selden Soc. vol. 67, pl. 3481.

[The justiciar] to the sheriff of Yorkshire, greeting. Command Ralph de Nevill that justly and without delay he deliver up to Robert, son of Richard de Haverford, Filey and Muston and Sloxton with the appurtenances, which the same Robert claims as his right and inheritance and of which he claims that [Ralph] unjustly deforces him. And if [Ralph] will not, then because Robert has given us security to prosecute his claim summon that Ralph by good summoners to be before us at Westminster [on such a day] to show why he will not do it. And have there the summoners and this writ. Witness [etc.]

(b) *Curia Regis Rolls*, II, p. 12.

Yorkshire. Robert son of Richard claims from Ralph de Nevill the manors of Filey and Muston and Sloxton and Reighton as his right and inheritance of which [blank space left] his grandfather was seised in demesne as of fee in the time of King Henry I taking therefrom issues to the value of five shillings and more; and this he offers to prove against [Ralph] by Roger son of Miles, who offers this by the command of his father who was eye-witness etc.

And Ralph denies [Robert's] right and asks the judgment of the court on the basis of [Robert's] claim and [Ralph's] answer.

It is adjudged that Ralph and his heirs may hold in peace for ever, because Robert did not specify in his count the year and the day on which King [Henry I] was alive and dead, and there can be no proof of title concerning a time uncertain, nor did he name his grandfather [upon whose seisin] his claim is based.

ST IVES v OVER (1199–1201)

(a) *Rotuli Curiae Regis*, I, p. 329.

Cambridgeshire. A grand assize comes to declare whether the

tenant Guy of Over has greater right to hold two virgates of arable with the appurtenances [as tenant] of Baldric [of St Ives], son of Baldric, who claims them from him by writ of right, or Baldric [to hold] them in demesne.

The jurors say that Guy has greater right to hold that land of [Baldric] than Baldric in demesne.

Judgment: let Guy hold in peace and Baldric be in mercy for his false claim; and he took Guy's homage [for the land] in court.

(b) Curia Regis Rolls, II, p. 53.

Cambridgeshire. Baldric of St Ives claims from Guy of Over the service of five shillings a year or one mewed hawk a year from half a hide of land with the appurtenances in Over.

And this Guy comes and says that he owes this service, namely the mewing of one hawk if that Baldric delivers one for mewing and nothing else except the forinsec service; and thereof he puts himself on the grand assize and asks that it be declared whether he owes the service that [Baldric] claims or that which [Guy] admits, namely the mewing of a hawk and the forinsec service, [calculated on the basis that] 27 hides make the fee of one knight. . .

DE STAGNO v GEOFFREY SON OF RICHARD (1200)

Rotuli Curiae Regis, II, p. 227.

Cambridgeshire. Gilbert de Stagno claims from Geoffrey son of Richard one virgate of arable with the appurtenances in Horseheath to be held of that Geoffrey as his right of which Ailmer his grandfather was seised in his demesne as of fee in the time of King Henry I etc.

And Geoffrey comes and denies [Gilbert's] right and puts himself upon the grand assize and asks that it be declared whether that Gilbert has greater right to hold that land of [Geoffrey] or this Geoffrey [to have it] in demesne . . .

FAVARCHES v KEINETO (1203)

Curia Regis Rolls, II, p. 286.

Sussex. William de Favarches claims from Richard de Keineto and Muriel his wife, one virgate of arable with the appurtenances in Walberton, which William's grandfather Robert of Walberton gave to [William] and confirmed by his charter and of which the said Robert was seised in his demesne in the reign of King Henry II taking therefrom issues to the value of half a mark etc.; and this he offers [to prove] etc.

And Richard and Muriel come and deny [William's] right; and they ask judgment of the court on the basis of their answer and of William's count.

It is adjudged that Richard and Muriel go quit [of this claim] because that William speaks not of his own seisin but only of the seisin of Robert who, he says, gave him [the land]; and he does not say that it should descend to him from that Robert by hereditary right. And William is to be amerced.

FOLIOT v SELVEIN (1205)

Curia Regis Rolls, IV, p. 58.

Oxfordshire. A grand assize concerning one hide of arable with the appurtenances in Cadwell comes to declare whether Richard Foliot has greater right in the aforesaid land or the tenant William Selvein, which William placed himself on the grand assize.

The jurors, namely. . . [12 names], say that Richard [Foliot] has the greater right in that land because Henry de Oilly the father of Henry de Oilly and chief lord of the aforesaid fee,[1] after he gained seisin of his lands having been in the wardship of the lord King Henry gave the land to Ralph Foliot father of the aforesaid Richard for his homage and service and for 15 marks and a horse; and that Ralph let that land to Gilbert father of the aforesaid William for Gilbert's life for 40s. a year; and when Gilbert died, the same Ralph took that land back in demesne and held it until Humphrey de Bohun, who had wardship of Henry de Oilly with his whole barony, expelled Ralph from that land and handed it over to the aforesaid William Selvein for five marks, which the same William owes to the same Humphrey; and the same William had no entry or right other than through the aforesaid Humphrey, nor [had] Gilbert his father [entry or right] other than the letting for his life from Ralph the father of the aforesaid Richard.

So it is adjudged that Richard is to have his seisin thereof, and William Selvein is to be amerced; and [William] gives one mark for his amercement.

1 The action had been started by writ of right patent directed to Henry de Oilly; *Curia Regis Rolls*, II, p. 296.

MASTER OF THE TEMPLE v WATERBEACH
(1206)

Curia Regis Rolls, IV, p. 304.

Cambridgeshire. The master of the Temple claims from Michael of Waterbeach 15 acres of arable and one messuage with the appurtenances in Waterbeach as his right.

And Michael comes and says that he ought to hold of the Temple; and he puts himself upon the grand assize, namely whether he has greater right to hold of the Temple or they [to have it] in demesne.

And the Templars say that there should be no grand assize, because it has been their custom not to grant land except by charter; and since this is said to concern recent enfeoffment, it does not seem [to them] that the assize should be taken. Day is given . . .

GRENEHILL v PRIOR OF LANTHONY (1206–07)

(a) *Pleas before the King or his Justices*, I
Selden Soc. vol. 67, pl. 3552.

[The justiciar] to the prior of Lanthony, greeting. We command you that without delay you do full right to William de Grenehill concerning one virgate of arable with the appurtenances in Henlow which he claims to hold of you by the free service of six shillings a year for all service of which you yourself deforce him; and if you will not the sheriff of Bedfordshire is to do it . . .

(b) *Curia Regis Rolls*, V, p. 118.

Bedfordshire. William de Grenehill by . . . his attorney claims from the prior of Lanthony one virgate of arable with the appurtenances in Henlow as the same William's right of which the aforesaid William's grandfather Adam Ruffus was seised as of fee and of right the day and the year when King Henry I was alive and dead taking therefrom issues to the value of five shillings and more; and this he offers to prove etc.

The prior comes and vouches John de Merston to warrant . . .

PEVEREL v PUNZUN (1210)

Curia Regis Rolls, VI, p. 77.

Northamptonshire. Robert Peverel claims from William Punzun, whom Richard Punzun vouched to warrant and who warranted him, 48 acres of arable with the appurtenances in Paston and in Werrington as his right, of which Hawise Peverel his grandmother was seised as of fee and of right in the reign of King Henry II taking therefrom issues to the value of half a mark etc.; and from that Hawise the right in that land descended to her son William the father of Robert etc.

And William Punzun comes and denies [Robert's] right to have that land in demesne; and he puts himself on the grand assize of the lord king and asks that it be declared whether he has greater right to hold that land of this Robert as that which properly fell to Hawise's sister Alice as her share and of which Alice's son Eudo was later seised, from which Eudo that land properly descended by inheritance [to William] to be held of that Hawise and her heirs, or whether the same Robert [has greater right] to hold it in demesne. Day is given them . . .

BOLBEC v TUREVILLE (1212)

Curia Regis Rolls, VI, p. 285.

Buckinghamshire. Herbert de Bolbec claims from William de Tureville the fees of seven knights and of the fourth part of one knight with the appurtenances, namely in demesne and in service, in Weston Turville and in Penn and in Taplow as his right and as those [fees] of which Roger son of Anketill his ancestor was seised as of fee and of right in the time of King Henry the grandfather of the lord king's father, namely the year and the day when he died, taking therefrom issues to the value of half a mark and more; and from the same Roger the right descended to [Roger's] daughter Isabel, and from Isabel to her son Herbert de Bolbec who was grandfather of this Herbert, and from that Herbert to his son Gilbert who was father of this Herbert; and that [Roger] was so seised as stated he offers to prove by a certain free man of his, namely William de Copland, who offers to prove this by his body as on the command of his father Ulfkill who was eye-witness.

And William denies [Herbert's] right and the seisin of the aforesaid Roger as it has been stated and all word for word; and he puts himself on the grand assize of the lord king and asks that it be declared which of them has the greater right in that land and whether the same Roger was seised of it in the year and on the day when King Henry I died; and he proffers two palfreys for the assize to be taken in such words. Let it be done, and the assize is to be taken in that way . . .

BECHEHAM v GRAMATICUS (1212)

Curia Regis Rolls, VI, p. 268.

Yorkshire. Thomas son of Robert de Becheham by Alan his brother as attorney claims from William Gramaticus 50 acres of arable with the appurtenances in Becca Hall as his right and as those [acres] of which his father Robert de Becheham was seised as of fee and of right in the time of King Henry II taking therefrom issues to the value of five shillings. And this he offers to prove against [William] by [Thomas's] own body as the court shall adjudge.

And William comes and denies [Thomas's] right and all word for word by the body of a certain free man of his Simon Fot, who offers to deny this etc.

And because Thomas put nothing in his count about the sight and the hearing which a champion of his might have had, it is adjudged that Thomas has lost his claim for ever; and he is to be amerced.

BRACKLEY v BLOIS (1212–14)

(a) *Curia Regis Rolls*, VI, p. 241.

Oxfordshire. W[illiam de Blois] archdeacon of Buckingham on the third day before pleas, namely the Friday after the close of Easter, claimed his jurisdiction concerning four virgates of arable with the appurtenances in Hornton which Richard de Brackley claims from him. And because he claimed [jurisdiction] at the [proper time], he is to have it. And so [he is] without day.

(b) Ibid., p. 286.

Oxfordshire. Richard de Brackley puts his son John in his place [as his attorney] against W[illiam] archdeacon of Buckingham in a plea of land, which plea is [now] in the county [court] of Oxford; and he likewise puts [John] in his place when the plea comes before the king . . .

(c) *Curia Regis Rolls*, VII, p.91.

Oxfordshire. Richard de Brackley claims from William de Blois archdeacon of Buckingham four virgates of arable with the appurtenances in Hornton as his right and as [the virgates] of which his grandmother Goda was seised as of fee and of right in the time of King Henry II taking therefrom issues to the value of five shillings etc., and from that Goda the right in the land descended to [Goda's] son and Richard's father Alfred, and from Alfred to the same Richard; and that this is true etc.

And the archdeacon comes and denies [Richard's] right. And he says it does not seem to him that he need answer to [Richard] because if any right should have descended from Goda no right should have descended from her to [Richard], because that Goda had two sons, namely Alan and Alfred; and from Alan, who was the first-born son, descended his son Robert, and from Robert a certain Richard who is still alive and who would have greater right in that land than Richard de Brackley, if either of them had any right, as the one who issued from the first-born brother Alan. Later the same archdeacon came and put himself upon the grand assize of the lord king; and he asked that it be declared whether he has greater right to hold that land in demesne, as that which belongs to his prebend of King's Sutton, or the same Richard to hold it of this archdeacon and of his prebend of King's Sutton.

Day is given to them . . .; and then let four [knights to elect the grand assize] come. And the archdeacon is to have a writ to summon the aforesaid Richard son of Robert to come at the same time and say whether he claims any right in that land [by descent from] the aforesaid Goda.

PERCY v HAULAY (1218–19)

(a) *Rolls of the Justices in Eyre for Yorkshire, 1218–19*,
Selden Soc. vol. 56, pl. 353.

[Yorkshire]. An assize comes to declare whether Richard de Percy [and eight other named persons] unjustly and without judgment disseised Robert de Haulay of his free tenement in Wansford within the [limitation period of the] assize.

And Richard does not come but his steward comes and says nothing to stay the assize; and the other disseisors do not come.

The jurors say that all the aforesaid persons thus disseised him. And so it is adjudged that Robert is to have his seisin. . . and all the others are to be amerced. Damages, seven marks.

(b) Ibid., pl. 198.

[Yorkshire]. Richard de Percy claims from Robert de Haulay one carucate of arable with the appurtenances in Wansford which he claims to be his right and inheritance and to hold of the lord king in chief, and of which his grandfather William was seised in the time of King Henry II taking issues etc. to the value etc.; and from that William the right in that land descended to his daughter and Richard's mother Agnes, and from that Agnes to this Richard as son and heir; and thereof he produces suit etc.

And Robert comes and denies [Richard's] right. And he says that he recovered seisin of that land from Richard by an assize of novel disseisin, and damages of seven marks were awarded him; and because he still does not have those seven marks he asks judgment of the court whether he need answer before he has his damages.

And Richard by his attorney says it is not his doing that [Robert] has not got his damages; indeed he says that the sheriff distrained on his land for these damages and still keeps his beasts [the entry is unfinished].

(c) Ibid., pl. 287.

[Count as above, but losing in an 'etc.' the assertion that the land is held of the king in chief, and specifying the suit as follows: and this he offers to prove by the body of a certain free man of his Simon Fot, as the court etc.].

And Robert [comes] and denies [Richard's] right and says that Richard's grandfather William de Percy gave that land to [Robert's] father Joelan for homage and service to hold from [William] and his heirs for the service of the tenth part of one knight, by [William's] charter which [Robert] puts forward and which attests this. And for this reason it seems to [Robert] that Richard is bound to warrant him that land etc.

And Richard comes and says that that charter should not harm him, because if the aforesaid William ever made it he did so in the illness from which he died; and indeed he says that Robert's father Joelan never had seisin in the lifetime of the aforesaid William, and if he had any seisin of that land he had it through William's wife Sybil de Valoines. And so it seems to him that [the supposed grant] should not harm him, since [Joelan] had no seisin in the aforesaid William's lifetime.

And Robert comes and puts himself upon the grand assize of the lord king and asks that it be declared whether he has greater right to hold that land of this Richard for the service of the tenth part of one knight, or Richard to have it in demesne.

Day is given them.

(d) Ibid., pl. 1115.

[Count as at pl. 198. No mention of grant or charter].

And Robert comes and denies [Richard's] right and puts himself on the grand assize of the lord king and asks that it be declared whether he has greater right to hold that land of Richard or Richard to have it in demesne.

But because Richard had a first-born brother namely [Henry] father of William de Percy, and no land could descend to Richard by hereditary right from his grandfather William, but only to his first-born brother and his heirs, it is adjudged that the assize does not lie; and so Robert goes without day, and Richard is to be amerced.

LE HEYR v ROBERT SON OF PHILIP (1224)

Bracton's Note Book, pl. 980.

Bedfordshire. Hugh le Heyr in the county court claimed from Robert son of Philip 30 acres of arable in Bolnhurst as his right, of which his grandfather Thurstan was seised as of fee and of right and in demesne in the time of King Henry II taking therefrom issues to the value of five shillings etc.; and from Thurstan the right in that land descended to Gilbert his son, and from Gilbert to this Hugh as his son and heir; and that this was his right he offered to prove by the body of a certain free man of his Stephen Gambun, who offers [to prove this] as of his own seeing.

And Robert comes before the justices and denies, as he had earlier denied in the county by his own body, Hugh's right and the seisin of Thurstan and all ...

And the same Robert made his oath against the aforesaid Stephen; and when the same Stephen should have sworn and did swear to all the words of the duel up to the view of the land, at the point at which he should have said that he saw the aforesaid Thurstan seised as aforesaid, the same Stephen said he would not swear to that because he did not see it, that is to say the same Thurstan seised as aforesaid, but he heard tell that he was seised. And Robert asks that this be allowed him.

And because [Stephen] made himself witness and gave security for the battle to prove Hugh's right and Thurstan's seisin as matters which he saw, and afterwards at the [time of the] oath he retracted that, it is adjudged that Stephen has failed in his proof, and that the same Robert and his heirs should hold for ever quit of this Hugh and his heirs; and Hugh and Stephen are imprisoned.

(2) Writs of entry

ALAN SON OF GUY v PANTON (1210)

Curia Regis Rolls, VI, p. 46.

Lincolnshire. Alan son of Guy claims from William of Panton half a carucate of arable with the appurtenances in Ashby-by-Partney as his right and as that of which Roger Black great-grandfather of this Alan was seised as of fee and of right in the time of King Henry I, namely the day and the year when he died, taking therefrom issues to the value of half a mark and more; and from the same Roger the right descended to his son Warin the grandfather of this Alan, and from Warin to Guy [Alan's] father, and from Guy to this Alan; and that [Roger] was thus seised as has been said [Alan] offers to prove against [William] by a certain free man of his John son of Gunfrid who offers to prove that against [William] as the court shall adjudge as by command of his father Gunfrid who was eye-witness.

And William denies [Alan's] right and everything word for word [and offers proof] by a certain free man of his who offers to prove this by his body as the court shall [adjudge], namely Baldwin of Kirton.

And note that Alan says that [William] has no entry in that land except through Godfrey of Panton great-grandfather of this William who took that land with Oriolda the widow of the aforesaid Roger [Black] who held it in dower by gift of the aforesaid Roger; and he proffers 100s. to have a jury on this . . .

PERCY v PRIORESS OF SINNINGTHWAITE (1218–19)

Rolls of the Justices in Eyre for Yorkshire, 1218–19,
Selden Soc. vol. 56, pl. 1127.

[Yorkshire]. By writ of right.[2] Walter de Percy claims from the prioress of Sinningthwaite two bovates of arable with the appurtenances in Marton-le-Moor as his right etc., and as those [bovates] in which the same prioress has no entry except through John de Birkin and his wife Agnes the mother of this Walter whose inheritance that land was, who made that gift to the prioress while the same Agnes lay on her death-bed in the illness of which she died; and this he offers to prove as the court shall adjudge.

2 A marginal note.

And the prioress denies [Walter's] right now and [will deny it] whenever else she should deny it; and she says that she has that land by the gift of the aforesaid Agnes, whose heir the same Walter is, by [Agnes's] charter which [the prioress] produces and which attests this; and she says that the same Walter is bound to warrant that land to her, and she asks that he should warrant it to her.

And Walter says that that charter should not harm him nor avail the prioress, because if [Agnes] ever made it, she made it on her death-bed in the illness of which she died and while she was under the power of her husband John . . .

CROXBY v TILEBROC (1219)

Rolls of the Justices in Eyre for Lincolnshire, 1218–19, and Worcestershire, 1221, Selden Soc. vol. 53, pl. 655.

[Lincolnshire]. Muriel widow of Adam of Croxby claims from William de Tilebroc three messuages in Barton-on-Humber as her right and as [those messuages] in which the same William has no entry except through her aforesaid former husband Adam who sold them to [William], and whom in his lifetime she could not gainsay; and thereof she has suit etc.

And William says it does not seem to him that he should answer Muriel because the same Adam is fit and well in the parts of Jerusalem, as he believes, and he left his own parts fit and [William] has never since heard anything of his death.

And Muriel says [Adam] is dead; and she says that to prove his death she had two men who were present when he was alive and dead and who were present at his burial; but she says they left the court because for poverty Muriel had nothing with which to maintain them; but if the suit which she does produce is not enough, she will have [the two in court] at the day and hour etc.

And so day is given . . . and then let [Muriel] produce suit which was present at [Adam's] death.

JOFNE v ABBOT OF READING (1248)

Roll and Writ File of the Berkshire Eyre of 1248, Selden Soc. vol. 90, pl. 440.

[Berkshire]. John le Jofne, Adam le Venur and his wife Maud and Maud's sister Margery claim from the abbot of Reading one messuage in Reading, in which the same abbot has no entry other than through Bartholomew the chaplain, to whom Roger Blik, uncle of this John and brother of the aforesaid Maud and Margery whose heirs [John, Maud and Margery] are, granted it while he was not of sound mind etc.

And the abbot comes and denies the right of John, Maud and Margery, and readily acknowledges that he had entry in the aforesaid tenement through the aforesaid Bartholomew; but he says that the aforesaid Roger enfeoffed the aforesaid Bartholomew by his charter, which [the abbot] proffers [in proof] of the enfeoffment, while [Roger] was of good memory and sound mind; and that this is so he puts himself upon a jury of the vill; and John and the others do likewise.

And 12 jurors of the vill say on their oath that when he enfeoffed the aforesaid Bartholomew of the aforesaid messuage the aforesaid Roger was of good memory and sound mind, and made him the aforesaid charter.

And so it is adjudged that the aforesaid abbot [is to go] without day, and that John and the others are to take nothing by this writ but are to be amerced for a false claim.

BENTHALL v PRIOR OF WENLOCK (1256)

Roll of the Shropshire Eyre of 1256,
Selden Soc. vol. 96, pl. 115.

[Shropshire]. Philip de Benthall claims from the prior of Wenlock four messuages, one virgate and six acres of arable with the appurtenances in Benthall as his right, and in which [the prior] has no entry other than through Siward le Champiun to whom Philip's grandfather Robert de Benthall, whose heir [Philip] is, demised them for a term which has run out, that is to say from year to year at [Robert's] will.

And the prior comes and denies [Philip's] right. And he acknowledges that he had entry into the aforesaid land and messuages through the aforesaid Siward, and the same Siward through the aforesaid Robert but not for a term. On the contrary he says that the aforesaid Robert gave and granted that land and those messuages to the aforesaid Siward to hold to himself and his heirs of the aforesaid Robert and his heirs for ever, by Robert's charter which [the prior] puts forward and which witnesses this.

And the aforesaid Philip can not deny the aforesaid charter.

And so it is adjudged that the aforesaid prior is [to go] without day, and Philip is to be amerced.

(3) Assize of mort d'ancestor

WILLIAM SON OF HUMPHREY v SNARING (1199)

(a) *Rotuli Curiae Regis*, I, p. 355.

Hertfordshire. An assize between William son of Humphrey, demandant, and Anketill de Kelshall concerning one virgate with the appurtenances in Kelshall remains [not taken]; and Anketill says that he holds that land only for a term from Philip de Snaring and vouches him to warrant. And Philip comes and acknowledges this.

It is adjudged that [William] should proceed against Philip if he wishes.

(b) *Rotuli Curiae Regis*, II, p. 47.

Hertfordshire. An assize comes to declare whether Humphrey father of William was seised in his demesne as of fee of one virgate of arable with the appurtenances in Kelshall on the day on which he died, and whether he died [since the period of limitation], which land Philip de Snaring holds.

Philip comes and acknowledges [William's] right; and he has taken his homage.

COCKFIELD v ABBOT OF BURY ST EDMUNDS (1201)

Curia Regis Rolls, I, p. 430.

Suffolk. An assize comes to declare whether Adam of Cockfield the father of Margaret who is within age was seised in his demesne as of fee farm of the manor of Cockfield and of the manor of Semer and of the manor of Groton on the day that he died, and whether this Margaret is his nearest heir, which land the abbot and prior of Bury St Edmunds hold.

The abbot comes and says that the assize should not be taken for the aforesaid manors of Semer and Groton, because Robert the father of Adam held them only for his life, by request of the lord king Henry made on [Robert's] behalf to the abbot and convent of Bury St Edmunds; so that at the time when King Henry was going on crusade and that Robert took the cross, he wished to have the tenth of these manors as ordained throughout the kingdom for crusaders[3] and then the abbot of Bury St Edmunds came before the

3   The Saladin tithe of 1188.

justices assigned to collect the tenths and said that [Robert] should hold that land only for his life; and Robert himself admitted that before [the justices]; and he likewise admitted it in his dying moments and forbade that any heir of his should claim right after his death; but it came about after his death that his son Adam persuaded the abbot and monks of Bury St Edmunds to grant him these manors to hold for his life, and thereof they made a chirograph between them which [the abbot] proffers and which attests this. But as to the third manor, namely Cockfield, the abbot says that Robert in his dying moments indeed said that manor, as he thought, was his right and inheritance.

It is adjudged that the assize should proceed for the aforesaid two manors, and that Margaret should have her seisin of Cockfield.

The jurors say that Robert's faTher Adam held the aforesaid two manors for a long time fully and in peace and so died, and Robert his son after him for his whole life, and Robert's son Adam, father of the said Margaret, similarly held them until his death and died in them; but they well know that,[4] and because of the long tenure of the aforesaid [ancestors] they believe that the aforesaid Adam died seised as of fee farm; and they say that Margaret is his nearest heir.

Judgment: it is adjudged that Margaret should have her seisin and the abbot be amerced.

DE LA TUR v EARL OF ESSEX (1220)

Curia Regis Rolls, IX, p. 72; also *Bracton's Note Book*, pl. 1397.

Middlesex. An assize comes to declare whether Jordan de la Tur, uncle of Robert [de la Tur], was seised in his demesne as of fee of 11 acres of meadow and 2s. of rent with the appurtenances in Enfield on the day on which he set out on a journey of pilgrimage to Rome during which [journey he died], and whether the journey [was begun within the limitation period of the assize] . . . and whether [Robert is his next heir], which land William de Mandeville earl of Essex holds.

[And the earl] comes by his attorney and says that the assize should not be taken because the same Robert was in seisin of that land after the aforesaid Jordan set out on his journey and after the same Jordan died, for a period of two [years]; and thereof he

---

4   The phrase 'but they well know that' is a subsequent insertion on the plea roll, no doubt because the mere belief of the jurors would not warrant judgment.

produces suit, and if that is not enough he puts himself upon the jury.

And Robert says that he was never seised of that land after Jordan's death; but indeed, when Jordan set out on his journey he handed the land over to a certain Robert to look after, [and that Robert] made [this Robert] guardian of that land; and he fully denies that he was ever seised after Jordan's death, and thereof he puts himself upon the jury.

And the jurors, asked on the faith which they owe to the lord king whether the same Robert was seised [of the land] after Jordan's death as heir and in fee, say that he was seised of it as of fee after Jordan's death for one year and more, and that he was disseised of it for failure of service.

And so it is adjudged that the [assize should not be taken]; and Robert may sue by writ of right and is to be amerced for his false claim; and the earl goes without day.

KIVELINGEWURTH v L'AIGLE (1219)

Bracton's Note Book, pl. 44.

Sussex. An assize comes to declare whether Ralph de la Roche uncle of Roger de Kivelingewurth was seised in his demesne as of fee of 40 acres of arable with the appurtenances in Chyngton and of one hide of arable with the appurtenances in South Heighton and of one virgate of arable with the appurtenances in Nererock and of one virgate of arable with the appurtenances in Farlegha (West Firle?) and of 13 virgates of arable with the appurtenances in Stockingham and of 20s. of rent with the appurtenances in Beverington on the day on which he died etc., which land Gilbert de Aquila holds.

[Gilbert] comes and says that indeed the aforesaid Ralph died seised as of fee of all the aforesaid land, except the 40 acres of arable and the aforesaid one hide and except the aforesaid 20s. of rent; but because there is a dispute between the aforesaid Roger and a certain Ralph de Wedona about which of them is the aforesaid Ralph's heir, [Gilbert] is holding those lands in his own hand as chief lord until it is determined which of them is nearer heir; and if the court adjudges that Roger is heir, he will willingly yield up those lands to him. About the other lands which he excepts [from this answer] he says that he is not sure whether [Ralph de la Roche] died seised as of fee or not; and he asks for an adjournment so that in the meantime he can find out about that; and the adjournment is allowed because he says that he will willingly yield [the excepted lands] to him if he is heir and if he can make sure that [Ralph de la Roche] did die seised as of fee.[5]

And thereupon comes Ralph de Wedona and says that he is nearer heir, because he was Ralph [de la Roche's] brother's son and Roger is Ralph de la Roche's sister's son, so that it seems to him that the male child of a male should be nearer heir.

And Roger says that that should not harm him because indeed this Ralph was Ralph de la Roche's brother's son; but [this Ralph's] father and Ralph de la Roche were not brothers by one father and one mother but only by one father; and [Roger's] mother and the same Ralph de la Roche were born of one father and one wife; and that land was not of the inheritance of the mother nor of the inheritance of the father but was the purchase of Ralph de la Roche himself, and Ralph de Wedona acknowledges this.

And because the same Ralph de Wedona acknowledges that the land was the purchase of Ralph de la Roche, and not inheritance descending from Ralph de la Roche's father . . ., it is adjudged that Roger is nearer heir as son of a sister by the same father and mother.

BROWN v MUNEVILLE (1221)

Rolls of the Justices in Eyre for Gloucestershire,
Warwickshire and [Shropshire], 1221–22,
Selden Soc. vol. 59, pl. 589.

[Warwickshire]. An assize comes to declare whether Thomas Brown brother of William Brown was seised in his demesne as of fee of one virgate of arable with the appurtenances in Berkswell on the day that he died etc.; which land Richard de Muneville holds.

[Richard] comes and says the assize should not be taken because he claims nothing in the land except through Thomas's daughter Joan, who is within age and whom he produces; and he says that he has her in wardship with that land.

And William says that Joan's mother was never married to the aforesaid Thomas; and he says that Joan is a bastard. So [Joan's mother] is to come. And Christina who was said to be Thomas's wife comes and acknowledges that she was never married to the same Thomas.

And Richard comes and acknowledges that Thomas died seised [of the land] as of fee, and that he died since [the period of

5   Gilbert later contended that Ralph had held these lands only for life; *Curia Regis Rolls*, VIII, p. 221.

limitation], and that William is his next heir since [Christina] acknowledges that she was not married, and that he claims nothing except lordship as chief lord.

And so it is adjudged that William recover his seisin; and that Joan pursue her remedies when she is of age if she wishes.

PULLEY v BRACY (1221)

Rolls of the Justices in Eyre for Gloucestershire,
Warwickshire and [Shropshire], 1221–22,
Selden Soc. vol. 59, pl. 1163.

[Shropshire]. The assize comes to declare whether Stephen of Pulley the father of William who is within age, was seised in his demesne as of fee of one virgate of arable with the appurtenances in Pulley on the day on which he died etc. and whether etc., which land Audulf de Bracy holds.

[And Audulf] comes and says that the assize should not be taken because the same William is a bastard, because he was born before his mother was married to his father, because she was married only during the illness from which [his father] died.

But because his mother is dead and William is under age and cannot plead, it is adjudged that the assize should proceed.

Afterwards Audulf came and acknowledged [the points of the assize] and conceded to the same William his land and delivered it up to him and took his homage for it.

So [William] is to have his seisin.

HALLAGH v GRIMENHALL (1221)

Rolls of the Justices in Eyre for Lincolnshire, 1218–19,
and Worcestershire, 1221, Selden Soc. vol. 53, pl. 981.

[Worcestershire]. Oswaldslow hundred. An assize comes to declare whether Robert de Hallagh, the father of Ingrith and Mabel, was seised in his demesne as of fee of half a virgate and of quarter of a virgate with the appurtenances in Grimes Hill on the day that he died etc. Which land Master Mathew de Grimenhall holds, and as to which he vouches to warranty Robert de Grimenhall, who is present by summons made to him and who warrants and says nothing to stay the assize.

The jurors come and say that the aforesaid Robert [de Hallagh] held that land as his inheritance and handed it into the care of his brother Peter and left the neighbourhood in pursuance of his work as a mason. And afterwards it came about that Peter became a leper and went into a leper-house. And then Robert [de Hallagh] came back and handed over that land to [another] brother Reginald to look after, who held it in his keeping and did the service to the chief lord. And then Reginald abandoned that land and it lay uncultivated; and then came the aforesaid Robert de Grimenhall and took it into his own hand for failure of service, and part of it he cultivated himself and part he handed over to others to cultivate. And then Robert de Hallagh died, and on his death his aforesaid children came and sought to enter that land; but [Robert de Hallagh's] lord the same Robert [de Grimenhall] would not allow it. And since the same Robert [de Hallagh] never gave up [his rights in] that land nor did he lose that land by judgment, it seems to [the jurors] that he died seised of that land as of fee; and they say that [Ingrith and Mabel] are indeed next heirs.

And so it is adjudged that they recover their seisin; and that Robert [de Grimenhall] is to be amerced on the suretyship of Ivo de Grimenhall; and that [Robert de Grimenhall] is to provide Master Mathew with [a tenement] to the same value in exchange ...

(4) Assize of novel disseisin

JOHN SON OF GODRIC v NORFOLK (1200)

Rotuli Curiae Regis, II, p. 194.

Norfolk. An assize comes to declare whether [Gilbert] of Norfolk unjustly and without judgment disseised John son of Godric and Aifled his wife of their free tenement in Creake within [the limitation period of] the assize.

The jurors say that he did not disseise them; and later when questioned they said that Gilbert disseised them by judgment of his court.

HARENG v ROGER, BAILIFF OF THE EARL DE L'ISLE (1202)
MATHEW SON OF GRENE v SAME (1202)

Curia Regis Rolls, II, p. 120.

Surrey. An assize comes to declare whether Roger the clerk, bailiff of the earl de l'Isle, unjustly and without judgment disseised Hugh

Hareng of his free tenement in Mitcham within [the limitation period of] the assize.

The jurors say that Roger thus disseised him.

Judgment: [Hugh] is to have his seisin; and Roger is amerced and is to pay one mark for damages.

Surrey. An assize comes to declare whether the same Roger unjustly and without judgment disseised Mathew son of Grene of his free tenement in Mitcham within [the limitation period of] the assize.

The jurors say that Roger thus disseised him.

Judgment: Mathew is to have his seisin; and Roger is amerced and is to deliver up to [Mathew] the chattels that he took in that land etc.

PORTUBUS v MERY (1204)

Curia Regis Rolls, III, p. 133.

Devonshire. An assize comes to declare whether Ralph de Mery and Margaret his wife unjustly and without judgment disseised Roger de Portubus and Alice his wife of their free tenement in Newton within the [limitation period of the] assize.

And Ralph and Margaret come and say that they took the tenement as distress by judgment of their court for default of customs and service, because they caused Roger and his wife to be summoned once, twice and a third time to come to their court and do what they ought for the same tenement; and when they did not come on any of these summonses, by judgment of their court they took the tenement as distress and offered and still offer to replevy it to them; and they produce their court which warrants this.

And Roger and Alice deny that any service or custom is in arrear.

It is adjudged that the [defendants'] court is to be amerced for a false judgment, because they produced no summoners to attest the summons and moreover proceeded too hastily to take the land as distress, because they should first have made distraints by chattels found on the fee. Ralph de Mery is to be amerced, and Roger and his wife are to have their seisin.

The names of those who are members of the [defendants'] court who were present and warranted, that is to say [six names follow]. The damage sworn by the recognitors is 30 marks, but [the parties] have made fine for 100s. for which the sheriff has sureties. And Ralph is amerced 20 marks; [four names are] Ralph's sureties.

OYSUN v CARDINAN (1204)

Curia Regis Rolls, III, p. 135.

Devonshire. An assize comes to declare whether Robert de Cardinan unjustly and without judgment disseised William Oysun of his free tenement in St Mary Church within the [limitation period of the] assize.

And Robert's bailiff comes and says that Martin Oysun, William's elder brother, had that land as his right; and he married and his wife became pregnant in his lifetime, and he died before she gave birth; and the same William remained in that land as keeper until it should be known what would come of the pregnancy; then [the widow] gave birth to a daughter, whom the same Robert as chief lord has in wardship with the aforesaid land; and he holds the land in wardship with the aforesaid daughter.

And the same William can not deny this.

And so William is amerced for his false claim, and takes nothing by this assize.

BURTUN v VALOINES (1212)

Curia Regis Rolls, VI, p. 335.

Yorkshire. An assize comes to declare whether William de Valoines unjustly and without judgment disseised Henry de Burtun of his free tenement in Burton Leonard within [the limitation period of] the assize.

The jurors say that the vill of Burton Leonard was once a member belonging to the vill of Aldborough which was the lord king's demesne, and that the same Henry's father Uctred and his grandfather Ugge always held that tenement by the underwritten service, namely paying each year a rent of 12 pence for each bovate, and doing each year two ploughings with food provided by the lord and three boon-works with food provided by the lord each autumn, that is to say one mowing for each bovate. They say also that they can, and their ancestors always could, marry their daughters at their own will to free or other men without payment and without licence.

And therefore it is adjudged that this tenement is free, and that for this reason [William] disseised [Henry] of his free tenement. Henry is to have his seisin and William is to be amerced. The damages are half a mark.

Afterwards at William's request the lord king had 24 men summoned to attaint [the 12] of a false oath. And that jury was taken, and the 24 said the same as the 12. And so Henry is to have his seisin, and William is to be amerced. The amercement is 100 marks.

RICHARD SON OF THURSTAN v WILLIAM SON OF LUCY (1222)

Bracton's Note Book, pl. 1792.

[Norfolk]. An assize comes to declare whether William son of Lucy and such-and-such others [including William's wife Mabel] unjustly and without judgment disseised Richard son of Thurstan of his free tenement in Holme after [the limitation period of the assize].

Amd William and the others come and concede [that] the assize [be taken].

The jurors say that the aforesaid Mabel's father Rannulf held six acres in *maritagium* with his wife, and he gave one and a half of those acres to the aforesaid William in *maritagium* with the same Mabel, and promised them the rest after his death. But Rannulf remained in seisin of the four and a half acres and kept with him his daughter Juetta, sister of the aforesaid Mabel. And then came the aforesaid Richard and married [Juetta] with Rannulf's consent and lived [in Rannulf's household] all Rannulf's life. When Rannulf died, there came the aforesaid William and persuaded the chief lord to grant him the four and a half acres; and that was in summertime. Then came Richard with his force in autumn and had the crops reaped. And William came with his force and removed the crops into other land and another fee. And Richard, by night or by day, took away the crops. Afterwards at sowing-time came William and ploughed and sowed that land, and Richard afterwards ploughed and sowed it again; and in the autumn they both came and each carried away as much of the crop as he could. And in the third year came William and sowed all the land and took all the crop, and in the fourth year likewise. So they say they do not know which of them was in seisin as of free tenement, but they say clearly that Rannulf died seised as of fee.

And because William had seisin through the chief lord, and Richard had nothing except by his force and without warrant, it is adjudged that Richard is to take nothing by this assize, because he had no warrant for his seisin; and he is to be amerced for his false claim and also because he sowed [when William had already sowed].

RIPTON v ABBOT OF RAMSEY (1229)

Bracton's Note Book, pl. 360.

Huntingdonshire. An assize comes to declare whether Hugh abbot of Ramsey unjustly and without judgment disseised Richard de Ripton of his common pasture in Abbot's Ripton which belongs to his free tenement in the same vill since [the limitation period of the assize].

And the abbot comes and says nothing to stay the assize.

The jurors say that the aforesaid abbot assarted a certain part of his wood where the same Richard had been accustomed to have common pasture, and raised dykes and built buildings there, and so they say that the aforesaid abbot unjustly disseised him.

And so it is adjudged that Richard is to recover his seisin and the abbot is to be amerced . . .

RENARD v FAY (1234)

Curia Regis Rolls, XV, pl. 1187; also *Bracton's Note Book*, pl. 1118.

Surrey. An assize comes to declare whether John de Fay unjustly and without judgment disseised William Renard of his free tenement in Bramley since the [period of limitation of the assize]; and he complains that he disseised him of about one carucate of arable.

And John comes and says that the assize should not be taken because the land of which he complains belonged to a certain Anxell de Coburg, who went to Normandy; and because this John heard that the same Anxell was dead, he took that land into hand and held it in his own hand; and then, because the same William had in the past served him well, he committed that land to him, handing it over at John's will and as long as it pleased him and as long as William served him well and until [Anxell's] right heirs should come and do what was due from them; and then Anxell himself came to England and found William so seised and sued to the king to have his seisin back [and recovered it] . . . And [John] says that [William] never had that land in fee except at [John's] will; and if indeed he was disseised, it was by Anxell and not by John; and thereof he puts himself upon the country. And he says that William accepted five marks to withdraw from the land.

And William comes and says that he was enfeoffed and was in seisin a long time and that John took his homage and that he was seised until disseised by John . . .; and he denies that he ever accepted money to withdraw from the land. And that he was enfeoffed and so seised he puts himself upon the jury.

The jurors say that the land was Anxell's and that John took it in hand as aforesaid because he believed that Anxell had died in Normandy; and when John had it in hand, he delivered it to William so that William was in seisin for three years and took the issues; and when Anxell came back from Normandy, John came and disseised William of the same land and delivered it to Anxell; but they do not know whether he had the king's command [to do this]. And they say they rather believe that the land was delivered to William at John's will, and for as long as it pleased him, rather than in any other way or in fee.

And so it is adjudged that John go quit, and that William is to be amerced and give surety. He has nothing.

CONSUETUDINES DIVERSARUM CURIARUM
(*c.* 1240)

Select Cases of Procedure without Writ,
Selden Soc. vol. 60, at p. cxix.

The tract is an informal account of various kinds of legal proceeding, ecclesiastical and lay, which its editors thought was written for clerks and court officials in the ten years or more before 1243. The reticence of the plea rolls makes the account of an assize of novel disseisin especially valuable. This extract describes what happens in court between the swearing and the retirement of the recognitors. Compare the story attributed to the defendant with the special verdict in *Bracton's Note Book*, pl. 1792 (p. 33, above).

When the assize has been sworn, the plaintiff makes his plaint against the disseisor like this: 'I complain of B. that unjustly and without judgment he disseised me of my free tenement in C., that is of ten acres of arable with the appurtenances, after the time specified in the writ; and I was in good and peaceful seisin of those ten acres until he disseised me'. And then the justice at once asks the disseisor if he has anything to say against the plaintiff and why the assize should not be taken. He may reply that he never disseised him, but that his father died vested and seised, and the chief lord found that he was vested and seised of that tenement on the day [B.'s father] died and put this B. in seisin of that tenement; and that this is true he will put himself upon the assize to win or lose. Then the justice rehearses what each party has said, telling the assize that they must speak the truth and save their oath. And then the assize goes to discuss this in some private place, which shall be guarded by some keeper . . .

ANON. (1334)

Y. B. Mich. 8 Edw. III, fo. 57, pl. 10.[6]

One John brought an assize of novel disseisin against a woman etc., and made his plaint of a messuage with the appurtenances; and the woman pleaded to the assize, which comes and says that one Robert was seised of the messuage and held it for the term of his life by grant from one Richard, and the reversion belonged to Richard; and they say further that Richard was indicted of a certain felony, and was arrested and imprisoned at Pontefract, and John came to him where he was imprisoned, and said that he would help to secure his release if [Richard] would grant [John] the reversion of the same messuage, and so Richard granted him the reversion by deed made in prison; and John came to Robert and showed him the grant, whereupon Robert paid [John] one penny by way of attornment, but the assize says that no rent was due to the lessor of the messuage [under the terms of the grant for life]. They say further that Richard was arraigned for this felony before justices assigned to deliver the jail, and said he was a clerk, and later by inquest of office he was [found to be so] and delivered to the bishop's prison, and John later helped with his purgation. And they say further that Robert who held the messuage later died, and Richard entered and at once enfeoffed this woman against whom the assize is brought, who was [Richard's] own daughter, and delivered seisin to her; and John came upon the livery, and because he could not enter through the door he entered through a window; and when the one-half of his body was inside the house and the other half outside, he was dragged out, for which he brought the assize.

The assize was asked whether Richard was in prison at John's suit, or in [John's] prison or in his keeping at the time when he made the deed, or whether he did it under duress. The assize says not: he made it of his own good will.

So it was adjudged that [John] is to recover [the messuage] etc. And yet the woman was in by feoffment.

6   Also reported in 8 Lib. Ass., pl. 25.

3 Family interests and settlements at common law

(1) Dower

PEVENSEY v BAVENT (1206)

Curia Regis Rolls, IV, p. 238.

Sussex. Hawis of Pevensey claims from Adam de Bavent 50 acres of arable in Horsey as her dower.

And [Adam] asks that it be allowed in his favour that she claimed those 50 acres by writ of right to be held of Richard de Essec' the chief lord of that land by the service of 30 pence a year for all service, when she has a son and warrant [as] heir of her late husband who is bound to warrant her dower; and if this is not [answer] enough, he asks a view of the land.

And because in her count she has departed from her writ, it is adjudged that Adam [go] without day; and she is to seek another writ if she wants.

GREENFORD v HUGH SON OF WALTER (1211)

Curia Regis Rolls, VI, p. 153.

[Middlesex]. Claricia widow of Walter of Greenford claimed from Hugh son of Walter the third part of two carucates of arable with the appurtenances in Greenford as her dower. And [Hugh] said that she was not married [to Walter], and the plea was sent to court Christian, and she proved the marriage.

And then Hugh came and acknowledged her third part. So she is to have a writ to get her seisin, and Hugh is to be amerced.

KERSIMERE v KERSIMERE (1211)

Curia Regis Rolls, VI, p. 149.

Suffolk. Agatha de la Kersimere by her attorney claims from Gilbert de la Kersimere the third part of ten and a half acres with the appurtenances in Stainsfield as her dower, in respect of which Thomas de Muleton vouched [Gilbert] to warrant who warranted him.

And so it is adjudged that Agatha is to have seisin from Gilbert's tenement to the value of the tenement which she claims from [Thomas], because it is not specified in her count that she was endowed specially of this land but of a third part generally.

The same [Agatha] claims from Peter de Nereford the third part of 26 acres of arable and of ten acres of wood with the appurtenances and the third part of one acre of meadow in Stainsfield as her dower; and Peter vouched to warrant Gilbert de la Kersimere, son and heir of Ralph de la Kersimere, whose charter the same Peter produced.

And Gilbert comes and says that he should not warrant that charter because, if his father made it [at all], he made it on his death-bed and in the illness of which he died, namely within 15 days of his death.

And Peter's attorney denies that the charter was made as [Gilbert] says: [on the contrary] it was made in the first week of Lent, and [Ralph] died after Easter. And as to this he puts himself upon all the witnesses named in the charter; and Gilbert [puts himself] upon all the witnesses except three who are Peter's men. Day is given them . . .

(2) Curtesy

MESSINGHAM v BRETT (1212)

Curia Regis Rolls, VI, p. 333.

Yorkshire. An assize comes to declare whether Henry Brett unjustly and without judgment disseised Henry de Messingham of his free tenement in Etton within [the limitation period of] the assize. And Henry Brett does not come and was not found.

The jurors say that this land was given in *maritagium* to a certain

Olive, who had a certain husband by whom she had the same Henry [Brett]. And afterwards, that husband having died, she was married to this Henry de Messingham, who took her to wife and by whom she had an heir who is still alive. And after Olive's death there came this Henry [Brett], who was Olive's son by her first husband, and thrust himself into that land without judgment. And therefore they say that he did disseise him unjustly and without judgment.

And so it is adjudged that Henry de Messingham is to have seisin, and Henry Brett is to be amerced. Damage, 20 s.; his amercement, 20 s.

NUUEL v WILSTROP (1218–19)

Rolls of the Justices in Eyre for Yorkshire, 1218–19,
Selden Soc. vol. 56, pl. 309.

[Yorkshire]. An assize comes to declare whether Richard son of Robert of Wilstrop unjustly and without judgment disseised Ralph Nuuel of his free tenement in Cowthorpe within the [limitation period of the] assize . . .

The jurors say that that land was the *maritagium* of Richard's mother Helen, and that she was wife of the aforesaid Ralph and it was through her and in no other way that [Ralph] had entry into that land; and on her death the same Richard put himself into that land as Helen's heir, because Ralph had no child by that Helen.

And so it is adjudged that it was not Ralph's free tenement, and so [Richard] goes without day and Ralph is to be amerced for his false claim.

CARLISLE v BOYTHORPE (1218–19)

Rolls of the Justices in Eyre for Yorkshire, 1218–19,
Selden Soc. vol. 56, pl. 22.

[Yorkshire]. An assize comes to declare whether Robert de Boythorpe, William Champenays, William Levinge, Henry de Folkton and Robert son of Peter unjustly and without judgment disseised John of Carlisle of his free tenement in Flotmanby within the summons of the justices' eyre.

And Robert comes and says that the assize should not be taken because he gave the tenement about which this assize is brought to the aforesaid John in *maritagium* with a certain daughter of his, and she died without heir apparent of her body; and on her death [Robert] came and placed himself in that land because his daughter had no heir.

And John says that indeed he took that land in *maritagium* with Robert's daughter; but he says that by her he had one son who was taken to the church alive and baptized and lived from midnight until the hour of prime. And of this he produces suit, who attest that they saw the infant alive.[1]

And Robert, asked when his daughter was married to this John and when she died, says she was married on the vigil of the Invention of the Holy Cross[2] and died on the feast of St Martin in Winter[3] next following. And John acknowledges this. They agree by leave of the justices . . .

NOBLE v ABBOT OF GRIMSBY (1219)

Rolls of the Justices in Eyre for Lincolnshire, 1218–19,
and Worcestershire, 1221, Selden Soc. vol. 53, pl. 357.

[Lincolnshire]. An assize comes to declare whether the abbot of Grimsby and William son of Hawise and Walter nephew of Fulk of South Kelsey unjustly and without judgment disseised Stephen Noble of South Kelsey of his free tenement in South Kelsey within the [limitation period of the] assize.

And no defendant came except the abbot. He came and said that the assize should not be taken because, on the death of Stephen's wife Emma whose inheritance that land was, the same abbot as chief lord took that land into his own hand for lack of any heir of [Emma's] body.

And Stephen says that the assize should not on that account remain [not taken], because, [while] he freely admits that that land was the right and inheritance of his wife, nevertheless on the day that he married that wife the then abbot of Grimsby, at the request of that Emma, granted that land to this Stephen to hold all his life if this Stephen should survive [Emma] whether he had an heir by her or not; and on this he puts himself upon the assize.

The jurors say that the abbot and the others disseised him of his free tenement unjustly etc.

---

1   The three names written in the margin at this point are no doubt those of the witnesses.
2   2 May.
3   11 November.

And so it is adjudged that Stephen [is to have his] seisin, and the abbot and the others are to be amerced. The damages are four shillings.

(3) Transfer to heir *inter vivos*

DUNMERE v DUNMERE (1214)
Curia Regis Rolls, VII, p. 117.

Somerset. An assize came to declare whether Agnes the mother of Robert de Dunmere was seised in her demesne as of fee of one knight's fee with the appurtenances in Penselwood on the day on which she died etc.; which [knight's] fee William de Dunmere holds.

[William] comes and says the assize should not be taken, because he fully acknowledges that the same knight's fee was Agnes's right and inheritance; but she had a certain husband Ralph de Dunmere by whom she had two sons, namely the same William's father Henry and the aforesaid Robert; but Henry was the elder brother. And it came about that when Henry's and Robert's father Ralph died, their mother Agnes allowed Henry to marry a wife; and having married her he brought her [to live] in his mother's house by his mother's permission and desire; and by [that wife, Henry] had this William and two daughters. And then it came about that Henry died, and that Agnes took those children into her own wardship, and delivered dower to Henry's wife out of [Agnes's] own inheritance. And then Agnes fell into old age, and wished to secure Henry's heirs in that land; and she went to the chief lord John de Montague and persuaded the same John to take for the aforesaid land the homage of that William as that Henry's son and heir; and while in her full power she altogether gave up her rights in[4] the aforesaid fee. And afterwards she remained as an old woman in the care of the same William until she died.

And Robert says that the aforesaid Agnes never gave up her rights in the aforesaid land, but died seised of it; and he asks that the assize [be taken]. Day is given . . .

It is adjudged that the assize should remain [not taken], because Robert fully acknowledges that the aforesaid Henry was his first-

---

4   The Latin is *se inde dimisit*.

born brother and that William, who holds the land, was [Henry's] son; and so let him sue in some other way if he wishes.

MARMIUN v ALDITHELEGE (1220)

(a) *Curia Regis Rolls*, VIII, p. 238; also *Bracton's Note Book*, pl. 95.

Staffordshire. Henry de Aldithelege was summoned to answer Aubrey Marmiun by what warrant he holds himself in the manor of Clifton Campville with the appurtenances which she claims as her right and inheritance and which she handed to her son Geoffrey de Campville to look after for so long as it pleased her, which [Geoffrey] is dead as she says.

And Henry comes and denies her right; and he says that he holds that land in wardship with the heir of the aforesaid Geoffrey de Campville, who held that land in fee and not as bailee of this Aubrey because [Geoffrey] did homage to his lord the earl of Chester and died seised of the land as of fee and not as bailee; and so it seems to [Henry] that he should not answer, because [Aubrey] resigned the tenure of that land in the county court.

And [Aubrey] by her attorney says that Geoffrey had nothing except the keeping of the land by bailment from herself; and thereof she produces suit; and if that is not enough she puts herself upon a jury of the countryside; and so does [Henry]. Let a jury be taken thereon; and it is to come on [such a day] to declare whether the aforesaid Geoffrey was on the day on which he died seised of the aforesaid land as of fee or in his keeping as bailee of the aforesaid Aubrey, who handed it to him to look after and to do the service to the chief lords etc... And [five names] are to be summoned, and another ten men, both knights and other free and lawful men of the neighbourhood who are not concerned with this Henry nor related to Aubrey and who do not hold of the fee of the earl of Chester or of Henry.

(b) *Curia Regis Rolls*, VIII, p. 290.

Staffordshire. By consent of the parties a jury comes to declare whether Aubrey Marmiun's son Geoffrey de Campville was on the day on which he died seised of the manor of Clifton Campville with the appurtenances as of fee or in keeping by bailment from the aforesaid Aubrey to do the service to the chief lords.

The jurors say they well know that the aforesaid Geoffrey did homage therefor to his lord the earl of Chester and paid him relief;

and he took homage from the free tenants and reliefs and profits issuing [from the land] and made grants from it and was in seisin and died so seised; and this, as they understand, was all with the agreement of his mother Aubrey, because she never repudiated it.

And so it is adjudged that the land shall remain in the hand of the earl as chief lord, through whom Henry has the wardship, until [Geoffrey's] heir comes [to do homage etc.]; and Aubrey is to take nothing by this jury, and is to be amerced for her false claim.

(4) Gift to younger son

BOSWORTH v BOSWORTH (1206–08)

(a) *Curia Regis Rolls*, IV, p. 187.

Leicestershire. Richard of Bosworth claims from David de Hakelinton six virgates of arable with the appurtenances in Husband's Bosworth as his right. And David comes and vouches to warrant Alexander of Bosworth who comes and has warranted him.

So Richard comes and claims from the same Alexander those six virgates with the appurtenances and from the same Alexander another six virgates with the appurtenances in the same vill as his right and as those of which his grandfather Robert was seised as of fee and of right and in demesne in the time of King Henry I, namely the year and the day etc., taking therefrom issues etc.; and from [Robert] the land descended to Roger [Richard's] father, who was seised of it in the time of King Henry II, and from that Roger it descended to this Richard who was seised of it in the time of King Richard; and that he was thus seised [he offers to prove] etc.

And Alexander comes and denies [Richard's] right to have that land in demesne. But he indeed acknowledges that the aforesaid Robert was seised of that land as his right. And that Robert had three sons, namely [Roger] the father of this Richard and William and Alexander himself. And that Robert gave [the land] to William his son for his homage and service and took [William's] homage for it, so that [William] held it all Robert's life, and when [Robert] was dead [William held it] of Roger [Robert's] eldest son and heir and this Richard's father, who took William's homage, so that [William] held of [Roger] for the rest of [William's] life. And from the same William the right in that land descended to this Alexander as [William's] heir; and he puts himself upon the grand assize of the lord king, and asks that it be declared whether he has greater right to hold that land of this Richard or the same Richard [to have it] in demesne . . .

(b) *Curia Regis Rolls*, V, p. 134.

Leicestershire. [12 names] . . . the 12 knights summoned to make up the grand assize between the demandant Richard of Bosworth and the tenant Alexander of Bosworth concerning 12 virgates of arable with the appurtenances in Husband's Bosworth, in respect of which the same Alexander who is tenant put himself upon the grand assize and asked that it be declared whether he has greater right to hold that land of that Richard, as that which Alexander's father Robert gave to his son William from whom that land ought to descend to [Alexander], or the same Richard [to have it] in demesne, which jurors say that Alexander has greater right to hold of Richard than Richard [to have it] in demesne; because Richard's grandfather Robert gave that land to his son William for [William's] homage, so that [William] was [Robert's] man for [that land] and held it of him all his life; and after [Robert's] death William did homage to Robert's heir Roger, who was this Richard's father, and from that William the land descended to this Alexander.[5]

So it is adjudged that Alexander holds it quit of Richard and his heirs; and Richard is to be amerced for his false claim . . .

BEAUMONT v BEAUMONT (1221)

Rolls of the Justices in Eyre for Gloucestershire,
Warwickshire and [Shropshire], 1221–22,
Selden Soc. vol. 59, pl. 257.

[Gloucestershire]. Felicia the widow of Philip de Beaumont claimed from John de Beaumont the third part of seven virgates [less one-quarter] and of four acres of arable in Dorsington as her dower.

And John came and said that she had dower, namely half a hide of arable in Marston; and if this was not enough he would willingly make it up to the third part [with land] elsewhere.

To this [Felicia] answered that she claimed nothing in that [Marston] land by way of dower, because her former husband Philip while in his full power gave that land to his younger son Walter; and [Walter] has it together with herself, and she is in his care with that land.

---

5   The youngest brother takes because the eldest was lord and so could not be heir.

And to this John replied that [the land] was never given to Walter, because the same Philip died seised of it; and Walter was then in Ireland and had been there for the four years preceding.

And so it was adjudged that Walter should be summoned to say what right he claimed in that land, of which his father had died seised.

And Walter comes and denies that his father had died seised [of the land], because [the father] had given it to [Walter] three years before [Walter] set out for Ireland; and thereof he puts himself upon a jury, and so does John.

Let a jury declare whether Philip died seised of that land as of fee or whether Walter was in seisin while Philip was in his full power as of that land which the same Philip had given him and for which [Walter] had done homage to the chief lord. And let the jury come [on such a day and in such a place].

Afterwards ... the jury was taken, and the jurors say upon their oath that indeed Philip bought various [parcels of] land, this one among others; and he wished to advance his son Walter; and he called together all his neighbours and many others, and in the presence of them all he stood himself down [*dimisit se*] from the aforesaid half hide of arable and gave it to Walter, and asked the chief lord from whom he had bought the land to take Walter's homage for it, so that at Philip's request [the lord] took Walter's homage for it. But then Walter at once asked his father to stay on as his keeper of the aforesaid land, and set sail for Ireland, and stayed there until after his father's death; and [the father] remained in such seisin after the gift as he had before the gift and in such seisin he died.

And because the jurors say that Philip had only the keeping [of the land] after that gift, it is adjudged that Philip did not die seised as of fee; and so [Felicia] is to have her dower and John is to be amerced.

(5) *Maritagium* and fee tail

REGINALD SON OF SAGAR v HATFIELD (1199)

Rotuli Curiae Regis, I, p. 447–448.

Essex. An assize of novel disseisin between Reginald son of Sagar, plaintiff, and Walter of Hatfield concerning [Reginald's] free tenement in Hatfield [Peverel] remains [not taken] because the same Walter says he took that tenement because it was his escheat by judgment of his court. And thereof he vouched his court and produced [ten names] who came and said that the tenement in question was given in *maritagium* by the ancestors of this Walter with a certain woman, and she had an heir Ralph Folenfait who died without heir, and [the ten] adjudged that [Walter] should take his fee [into hand] until there appeared someone with right to demand it from him.

And Reginald says that he was never summoned to that court nor was there any writ of right.

Judgment: Walter is amerced and so are all who were concerned in the making of that false judgment by that court.

COWLEY v COWLEY (1199)

Curia Regis Rolls, I, p. 87.

Oxfordshire. William of Cowley claims from Alice his sister five virgates of arable with the appurtenances in Cowley as his right and inheritance; and he says their father gave her that land in *maritagium* to his disinheritance since he had no more [land]; and he asks the judgment of the court whether his father could give all his land in *maritagium* to his daughter to [William's] disinheritance . . .

TRESGOZ v COLEVILLE (1208)

Curia Regis Rolls, V, p. 137.

Suffolk. William Tresgoz claims from Maud de Coleville the fee of half a knight with the appurtenances in Aspall as his right, of which his father Geoffrey was seised etc.

And Maud comes and denies [William's] right. And she says that the aforesaid Geoffrey gave that fee to Robert de Boseville in *maritagium* with Geoffrey's sister Aubrey who was mother of the said Maud. And she puts herself on the grand assize of the lord king and asks that it be declared whether she has greater right to hold that fee of William Tresgoz, as that which was given to the aforesaid Aubrey in *maritagium* as stated, or the same William [to have it] in demesne . . .

BEAUCHAMP v WAHULL (1212)

Curia Regis Rolls, VI, p. 354.

Buckinghamshire. Ellis de Beauchamp and his wife Constance by their attorney claim from John de Wahull that he should do them homage and [pay] rightful relief in respect of the free tenement that he holds of them in Ravenstone and in Maulden; as to which Ellis and Constance say that [John] should do them the service of two knights and [should pay them] the relief proper to such a tenement.

And John comes and acknowledges that that tenement is part of Ellis's and Constance's barony. And he says that it was given to Walter de Wahull in *maritagium* with [John's] grandmother Rose; and from [Rose] it descended to [John's] father Simon, and from Simon to this John, so he is only the second after her to whom it was given in *maritagium*; and he asks the judgment of the court whether on these facts he owes homage and relief. And he says further that, if he should do homage, he should not do it without Constance's sister Isabel de Bolbec who is [Constance's] parcener of the barony.

And the attorney of Ellis and Constance says that they should not lose their own right if [Isabel] does not wish to sue. Day is given them . . .

LOPPINGTON v LESTRANGE (1221)

Rolls of the Justices in Eyre for Gloucestershire,
Warwickshire and [Shropshire], 1221–22,
Selden Soc. vol. 59, pl. 981.

[Shropshire]. [Four names] summoned to elect 12 to make the grand assize between the demandant Richard of Loppington and the tenant William Lestrange concerning one hide of arable with the appurtenances in Loppington, in respect of which the tenant William has put himself upon the grand assize of the lord king and asked that it be declared whether he has greater right to hold that land of Richard or the same Richard to have it in demesne, come and elect [16 names, of which 4 are cancelled and 12 noted by interlineation as sworn].

And the aforesaid sworn knights say upon their oath that the same William has greater right to hold that land of this Richard (by virtue of the gift which Richard's father made to William's mother, his daughter, when he gave it to her in *maritagium*),[6] than the same Richard to have it in demesne.

And so it is adjudged that William and his heirs shall hold for ever of Richard and his heirs. Pledges for the amercement: [two names].

And be it known that the same Richard acknowledged the gift made to William's mother and asked judgment whether [his father] could give half.[7]

PETITION OF THE BARONS (1258), c. 27

R. E. Treharne and I. J. Sanders, *Documents of the Baronial Movement of Reform and Rebellion, 1258–1267* (1973), at p. 88.

Item, they ask a remedy for *maritagia* alienated, as in this kind of case: if anyone gives to another a carucate of land in *maritagium* with his daughter or his sister to have and to hold to them and to the heirs issuing from the aforesaid daughter or sister, so that if the aforesaid daughter or sister dies without heir of her body the land with the appurtenances is to revert whole to him who gave the land in *maritagium* or to his heirs; and although the aforesaid gift is not absolute but conditional, nevertheless women after the death of their husbands in their widowhood give or sell the aforesaid *maritagia* and enfeoff [grantees] as they wish although they have no heirs of their bodies, and hitherto such feoffments have not been to any degree revoked. And so they ask that, for the sake of the equity of the law, by reason of the aforesaid condition there be provided a remedy to revoke such feoffments whether by writ of entry or by some other effective means, and that in such a case judgment shall be given for the demandant.

STATUTE *DE DONIS CONDITIONALIBUS* (1285)

Statute of Westminster II, c. 1;
Statutes of the Realm, vol. I, p. 71.

First, concerning the frequent gifts of tenements upon condition, namely: when anyone gives his land to a man and his wife and to

---

6   On the roll the words from which the passage within the round brackets is translated are added by interlineation.
7   Memoranda such as this are rare. Without it, and without the addition in fn. 6 above, there would be nothing to indicate the real dispute.

the heirs born of that man and that woman adding the express condition that if such man and woman die without heir born of that man and woman the land so given shall revert to the donor or his heir; and also in the case when anyone gives a tenement in *liberum maritagium*, which gift has an inherent condition, although it may not be expressed in the charter of the [particular] gift, which is as follows, that if the man and woman die without heir born of themselves the tenement so given shall revert to the donor or his heir; and also in the case when anyone gives a tenement to [a donee] and to the heirs issuing from his body, it has seemed and still seems hard to donors and to the heirs of donors that their will [as it is] expressed in their gift has not hitherto been and still is not observed. For in all the aforesaid cases, after issue has been begotten and born of those to whom the tenements were so given conditionally, such feoffees have hitherto had the power of alienating the tenement so given and disinheriting their issue of that tenement against the will of the donors and the express form of the gift. And furthermore whereas upon failure of issue of such feoffees the tenement so given ought to revert to the donor or to his heir according to the form expressed in the charter of the gift, [the donor or his heir] has hitherto been excluded from the reversion of those tenements by the deed and feoffment of those to whom the tenements have so been given upon condition, notwithstanding that any issue [born of them] has died, which was clearly contrary to the form of [the donor's] gift.

And therefore the lord king, considering that it is necessary and useful to supply a remedy in the aforesaid cases, has laid down that the will of the donor, according to the form clearly expressed in the charter of his gift, shall henceforth be observed; so that those to whom a tenement is so given upon condition shall not have the power of alienating the tenement so given in such a way that it will not remain to the issue of those to whom the tenement was so given after their death, or to the donor or to his heir if issue fails, whether because there was no issue at all or [because] there was issue but it failed by death without an heir [of the body] of such issue. Nor from henceforth shall the second husband of such a woman have any [right] in a tenement so given upon condition after the death of his wife by the [curtesy] of England, nor shall the issue of the woman and her second husband [have any right of] hereditary succession. But immediately upon the death of the man and woman to whom a tenement was so given, [the tenement] after their death [shall] either [pass] to their issue or shall revert to the donor or to his heir as is aforesaid.

And because in a new case a new remedy must be supplied, the demandant shall have a writ like this:

Command A. that he is justly etc. to yield up to B. such a manor with the appurtenances which C. gave to such a man and such a woman and to the heirs issuing from that man and that woman; *or*, which C. gave to such a man in *liberum maritagium* with such a woman, and which after the death of the aforesaid man and woman ought to descend to the aforesaid B., the son of the aforesaid man and woman, by the form of the aforesaid gift, as [B] says; *or*, which C. gave to [a donee] and to the heirs issuing from his body, and which after the death of that [donee] ought to descend to the aforesaid B., the son of that [donee] by the form [of the aforesaid gift].

The writ by which the donor may have his recovery upon failure of issue is in common enough use in the Chancery. And be it known that this statute shall apply to the alienation of a tenement contrary to the form of [any such] gift to be made hereafter, and shall not extend to gifts previously made. And if a fine shall hereafter be levied concerning such a tenement, it shall be void by [the operation of] the law itself, and there shall be no need for the heirs or for those to whom the reversion belongs, even though [at the time of the fine] they are of full age and within England and not in prison, to put in their claim.

DANIEL v BERE (1292)

Y.B. 20 & Edw. I, Rolls Series, p. 59.

Richard Daniel, an infant within age, brought a writ of formedon against Richard de Bere, for the reason that one John le Seculer gave so much land to [Richard Daniel's] father John Daniel and to his mother Alice and to the heirs begotten of their two bodies. And he says that his father John Daniel and his mother Alice were seised in their demesne as of fee and of right, and that the land ought to descend to him as to the son and heir begotten of their two bodies according to the form [of the gift].

Spigurnel. Sir, Richard Daniel is an infant within age. [We ask] judgment whether he should be answered on this writ of right.

Louther. Sir, his demand rests wholly upon the form of the gift by reason that the tenements were given etc.; and so he is a purchaser. [We ask] judgment whether he should not be answered concerning his own purchase.

Spigurnel. Sir, if he is entitled to be answered now, and we were to say that John le Seculer enfeoffed his father John and his mother Alice simply and without condition, and that were found [to be so by a jury], he would be barred from his claim for ever when he is under age. And so we ask judgment whether he should be answered.

Louther. Sir, after the gift was made to our father John and our mother Alice, John and Alice had only freehold[8] until they had issue; and the fee and the right remained in the person of the donor until [John and Alice] had issue; and then [when issue was born] at once the fee and the right began to be in the person of the issue and out of the person of the donor; and then for the first time [the issue, Richard Daniel] became a purchaser together with [his mother and father]. And since he became a purchaser within age, [we ask] judgment whether he is not to be answered within age.

Spigurnel. Sir, it seems to us that he should not be answered on the basis of his purchase, because in his count he says that his ancestors were seised as of fee and of right, and that then [the land] descended to him through them as to son and heir; and so he makes his claim rather by descent than on the basis of his purchase.

Louther. The basis of his title is the form of the gift; and although the count says that the ancestors were seised as of fee and of right, and that [the land] ought to descend to him as to son and heir, that is to be understood of the form of the gift; and the end of [our] count says that; so his claim is by reason of the purchase according to the form etc., and not by hereditary descent. [We ask] judgment as before.

Spigurnel. He can demand nothing otherwise than on the basis of the seisin of his ancestors and the descent to himself; because if [the ancestors] had not existed he could claim nothing now; and since he demands nothing except as descending through them to himself, it seems to us that he claims by descent and not as of his own purchase. [We ask] judgment.

Howard. Suppose his father and mother were still alive, and were impleaded for these tenements, and said that the tenements were given to themselves and to their heirs begotten of their bodies and that they had a son [Richard] begotten between them, who was as much a purchaser as themselves, and they prayed aid of him; would they delay the plea until the age of their issue? By God, no. Why then in this case?

Berwick. My companions think that because he is nearly of age, being 20, that he is of age enough to be answered: so answer, [especially] because this is in a way a possessory writ. But I think that if he had been 10 or 12 years old or so, he ought not to have been answered.

8   I.e. tenancy for life.

GLOSS ON *DE DONIS* (*c.* 1310)

CUL MS. Dd. 7. 6(1), fo. 14v.

Be it known that there is fee pure, fee simple and fee tail. Fee pure is when the purchaser is enfeoffed unto himself and his heirs and assigns. Fee simple is unto him and his heirs, but not his assigns. Fee tail is when it is unto him and some (but not all) of his heirs. For just as a stick may be tailed and cut down by someone, and then it is not whole, in the same way the fee is by such gifts tailed in some of the heirs and not in all: for the collateral heirs are cut out (*forsclos*), while the lineal heirs of the purchasers are included. And therein it is to be known that in such gifts the purchasers and their heirs, down to the third degree lineally descending, have nothing except freehold;[9] for if they had the fee they might alienate, and their heir might recover by mort d'ancestor, whereas they (and their lineal heirs) shall recover by writ of formedon. Thus it appears that they have no fee; for they cannot forfeit such tenements for felony, nor may they disclaim. And so it appears that they are not true tenants, but their donors are. (All this appears in the statute, which numbers them among those who hold for life.) Also, if they had a fee the second husband of a woman would hold by the curtesy, and the second wife of a husband would take dower, and none of their heirs would succeed except the issue of the two joint purchasers: as appears by the words of the writ here ordained for their heir, which says 'to the son of the aforesaid man and woman'.

BELYNG v ANON. (1312)

Y.B. 5 Edw. II, Selden Soc. vol. 31, p. 176 (C.P.).

John de Belyng brought his writ of formedon etc., [which said]: 'and those tenements, after the death of the aforesaid Henry and Joan and of John son of those same Henry and Joan, ought to descend to the aforesaid John de Belyng son and heir of the aforesaid John'.

Scrop. At the point at which he has in his writ made John [de Belyng] son and heir of John, he should have made John de Belyng grandson and heir of Henry and Joan to whom the tenements were given. [We ask] judgment of the writ.

Willoughby. There is no need because John survived Henry and Joan and attained estate, so it is to him that we must make the

---

9   I.e. tenancy for life.

demandant heir and not to those to whom the tenements were given etc.

SPIGURNEL.[10] What estate did he attain?

Willoughby. He survived [the donees] and was seised.

Scrop. You have acknowledged that the issue was seised, and so the gift was fulfilled in his person. [We ask] judgment whether you can use such a writ against us.

Willoughby. That is to the action: if you oust us from this writ you take away the action [altogether] because we can not use mort d'ancestor. So do you mean that for your answer?

Herle. This exception does not go to the action, for if you are [not] within the statute[11] you have your recovery at common law; for before the statute the issue could use mort d'ancestor or entry *sur disseisin* or entry *dum infra aetatem.* And so you are at common law, and we ask judgment of this writ which is based upon the statute but is not warranted by the statute.

Scrop to the same effect. At common law as soon as the feoffees had issue they acquired an estate of inheritance and could alienate. And by the statute, nobody is prevented [from alienating] except the original feoffees. And the words of the statute make that clear: 'so that those to whom a tenement is so given shall not have the power of alienating . . .'. But nothing is specified [about the issue alienating]. If the feoffees die without issue, or if their issue die without issue, then the reversion is preserved by the words 'failing an heir of the body of such issue'. But the statute provides nothing to save the descent to the issue, except only that the feoffees can not alienate. [We ask] judgment etc.

BEREFORD. He that made the statute meant the issue in tail to be within the statute as much as the feoffees until the tail should [become fee simple] in the fourth degree. And it was only by his oversight that he did not bring the issue in by express words in the statute. So we shall not abate this writ.

Herle. [The grantor] did not give to John's grandfather Henry nor to [Henry's] wife Joan, ready etc.

And the others said the opposite.

HELTON v KENE (1344)

Record: CP 40/340, m. 368. John, son of William de Helton, brought an assize of novel disseisin in Westmorland against Nicholas le Kene and Joan his wife, Adam de Backworth and Agnes his wife, and six others, in respect of tenements in Brampton. These tenants pleaded in bar of the assize—as to

10 Perhaps a mistake for *Scrop.*
11 Statute of Westminster II (1285), c. 1; see p. 48 above.

part of the tenements—that John de Helton (grandfather of the plaintiff, and of Joan and Agnes) had two sons, William (the elder) and John (the younger),[12] and gave the tenements to John the younger son in fee simple; and this John had issue Thomas, Joan and Agnes; and after the death of John the younger, Thomas entered and then died without issue, and so Joan and Agnes entered as sisters and heirs to Thomas; and the plaintiff intruded on their possession, supposing that the grandfather had given the tenements to John and the heirs of his body; and Joan and Agnes (with their husbands and others) ousted him. To this the plaintiff replied that the grandfather made the gift to John and his heirs male of his body, so that if John should die without heir male of his body the tenements would revert to the donor and his heirs; and John had issue Thomas, who died without heir of his body, and so the plaintiff entered as kinsman [i.e. grandson] and heir of the donor as in his reversion, and was seised until the tenants removed him. The tenants prayed judgment because, while not denying the gift to have been made to John and his heirs male of his body (as the plaintiff alleged), they said that by virtue of the seisin of Thomas after the death of his father the gift was completely fulfilled (*omnino completum*) in the person of Thomas as heir male, and the fee simple is adjudged to be in his person. The plaintiff also prayed judgment, because, the tenants having confessed the gift in tail male, the tenements were 'revertible' on Thomas's death to the donor and by the terms of the gift could in no way descend to Joan and Agnes as Thomas's sisters. The proceedings began at Appleby, Westmorland, on 6 August 1344 (before Basset J.K.B., Fencotes and Blaykeston Sjts.), but because of the difficulty were adjourned to Westminster. The case was argued at Westminster in October 1344.

Y.B. Mich. 18 Edw. III, fo. 45, pl. 52;
18 Lib. Ass., pl. 5; LI MS. Hale 141, fo. 271v.

Skipwith. The point is none other than this: when the land was given to a man, unto him and the heirs male of his body, does the possession by his male issue entitle the daughters of that male issue to inherit, or does the land revert on failure of issue male? It seems that the land should revert, and that the sisters should not inherit; for if the male issue should have an estate other than that which their father had, as the first donee, it would have to be [either] by the gift or by descent: and it cannot be by the gift, for the gift does not extend any further in the issue than in the first donee; and it would be impossible by descent to have a larger estate than one's ancestor had. It is certain that if the ancestor had had no issue male[13] the land would have reverted to the donor, as a consequence of the failure of male issue of the person who is issue in tail. For

---

12   The Y.B., otherwise accurate, gives their names as John and Thomas.
13   Lib. Ass. says 'a thousand female issue', misreading 'nulle' as 'mille' and correcting to take account of it.

who would say that the fee was pure in the first male issue in tail, in that the donor's will should be adjudged to have been performed when the first issue in tail who is male is seised by the form of the gift? By that same argument, where land is given to a man and the heirs of his body begotten, the tail would be adjudged to be performed by the seisin of the first issue. But the law is the reverse of that: for the second, third and fourth issue in line shall have the same advantage as the first, even though they are not begotten of the body of the first donee. It follows that the same law should be applied in this case.

Robert de Thorpe. A female is a stranger to this form of gift. This case is not like *Multon's Case*, which was adjudged in parliament, where the sisters were entitled to inherit; for there the gift was to him and his heirs male, so that collateral heirs as well as heirs [of the body] were inheritable, and so by such a gift he had a fee simple. But it is not so in the case propounded, where a reversion of the fee simple was reserved by the donor.

HILLARY. Would you say, then, that in your present case the daughters (if he had any) are not inheritable?

Robert de Thorpe. They are not, that is certain.[14]

Greene. At common law when the issue in tail had [an assize of] mort d'ancestor, this was because after issue he had a fee simple; and the sisters in this case ought to have inherited. But after the statute,[15] which by express words provides a remedy for the issue of the issue as well as for the first issue, the law is otherwise. Therefore the inheritance of the tail must be adjudged according to the words used in the gift.

Huse. Under the old law the issue in tail had mort d'ancestor but they did not thereby have a fee; for when the tail was continued, if the lineal issue failed a formedon in the reverter was provided, even if the issue had alienated, and the person who was collateral heir never had mort d'ancestor. So in this case, whether the gift was made before or after the statute, when the reversion was reserved in the donor the donee has only a fee tail; and that must be according to the form of the gift, namely for males only.

Sadlingstanes. When the donor gave the land to him and the heirs male of his body, and this first donee had male issue, the tail and the donor's will was in this respect accomplished, so that the female issue of the male issue are entitled to inherit. Therefore the sisters are entitled to inherit, whether the male issue has a fee simple or a fee tail.

14 'Non certum est', which is ambiguous.
15 Statute of Westminster II (1285), c. 1; see p. 48, above.

STONORE.[16] You must look at the statute which gives the estate tail, and this case is not in any of the cases expressly mentioned in the statute: and so it is at common law, and consequently it is fee simple.

Seton. Indeed, sir, we attach much importance (*fichons*[17] *mult*) to that on our side.

Sadlingstanes. We think that in the case of this gift at common law the issue was entitled to inherit as in fee simple, for it is certain that they could have alienated; and although the [power of] alienation is restrained by the statute, the estate is nevertheless continued and remains as it was at common law, namely fee simple.

Mowbray. This tail whereby the gift was made to Thomas and the heirs male of his body is more restrictive, and does not give an inheritance as amply as if the gift had been made to someone and the heirs of his body; and in that case the twentieth in descent has only a fee tail, and for want of issue it will revert. So much the more so in this case.

WILLOUGHBY to the plaintiff. The assize must nevertheless be taken, for another tenant in the same assize has pleaded to the assize with respect to part of the land.[18] So sue the assize as to that for the damages, and the assize also for the rest.[19]

(Thus note that the female issue shall not inherit under such a gift, even if the male issue was seised.)

The record shows that on 27 October 1344 the court held that the tenements were revertible to the donor; and since the tenants confessed that the plaintiff had been seised until they removed him, it was awarded that the assize should be taken with respect to the damages, and that the record should be remitted to the justices of assize. This case was cited and followed in *Carbonel's Case* (1359) Mich. 33 Edw. III, Fitz. Abr., *Taile*, pl. 5.

BLOUNT'S CASE (1387)

Y.B. Trin. 11 Ric. II, p. 70, pl. 20.

Hugh Blount gave a manor to his son H. and his male children (*filiis suis masculis*) lawfully begotten of his body; 'and whichever of them shall live the

16   Misprinted in Lib. Ass. as 'Seton'.
17   LI MS. Reads 'fithomus' in Lib. Ass., 'fauchons' in Y.B. (1679 ed.).
18   This refers to a plea by Master William de Brampton, which for the sake of clarity has been omitted from the above note of the pleadings.
19   Cf. variant report in Fitz. Abr., *Taile*, pl. 16: '... And then WILLOUGHBY *ex assensu sociorum* said that they were advised that Thomas ... had but a tail by the gift, and therefore the women could not inherit this land; and so the assize was awarded in right of the damages ...'.

longest shall enjoy it in fee and inheritance for ever; and if H. [my] son should happen to die without heir male lawfully begotten of his body, then the manor . . . shall thereupon revert to me and my heirs for ever'. The donee H. alienated the manor to the tenants, against whom H.'s son now brought formedon in the descender on the grounds that H. had a fee tail, not a fee simple. The parties pleaded to demurrer.

. . . Now, in the present term, BELKNAP [C.J.] asked the serjeants who were [of counsel] with the tenants whether H. the donee had any male child at the time of the gift, or not.

They said he had not, and that this was part of their demurrer.

BELKNAP said that if he had had a male child at the time of the gift, he would have had a fee simple by reason of survivorship. (Note that.)

HOLT said in this plea that the statute[20] says, 'that the will of the donor shall be observed' in all respects, . . . and in this case the donor's will was that it should be fee tail, as appears from the deed. And he said that if land is given to a man and his heirs of his body begotten, according to the donor's will the issue begotten after the gift should inherit and not the issue before.

But the serjeants at the bar said that it seemed to them that the issue begotten before [the gift] should rather inherit; and they said that there was a case on the same point.

HULCOTE v INGLETON (1493)

Record: CP 40/924, m. 156. Richard Hulcote brought formedon in the remainder for the manor of Hulcote, Northamptonshire, and counted on a gift by John Shotesbroke in the time of Henry VI to Richard and Elizabeth Pekke for life, remainder to John Hulcote in tail male, whose kinsman and heir he was. The tenants pleaded a charter of 1360 (set out below) whereby Richard Wydeville had given the manor to Fulk and Agnes Hulcote and the heirs of their bodies, remainder to the right heirs of Fulk, on condition that if Fulk and Agnes or their heirs alienated in fee (or leased beyond their lives) the donor might re-enter; and said that Fulk and Agnes entered and had issue John Hulcote, senior, the plaintiff's grandfather; and John enfeoffed Shotesbroke, who made the gift in tail as in the count; and after the death without issue of John Hulcote, the first remainderman, Richard Wydeville, earl Rivers,[1] entered as heir of the donor of 1360 [for breach of the condition]; and the tenants had their estate from the earl. To this plea the demandant demurred.

---

20 Statute of Westminster II (1285), c. 1; see p. 48, above.
1 Died without issue in 1491.

(a) The charter of 1360, from the record.[2]

Know all men present and to come that I, Richard Wydeville of Grafton, have given, granted and leased to Fulk of Hulcote and Agnes his wife, and the heirs lawfully begotten of their bodies, my manor of Hulcote with all the appurtenances (which manor I had by the grant of the said Fulk and Agnes by fine levied in the court of our lord king), to have and to hold the said manor with all the appurtenances unto the said Fulk and Agnes and unto the heirs lawfully begotten between them, from the chief lords of the fee by the services due and accustomed; and if it should come to pass that the said Fulk and Agnes should die without heirs lawfully begotten of their bodies, which God forbid, then let the said manor with all the appurtenances remain to the right heirs of the said Fulk; upon this condition, that if the said Fulk and Agnes, or their heirs lawfully begotten between them, or the right heirs of the said Fulk, should alien the said manor in fee, or let it to farm beyond the term of their lives, it should be fully permissible for the said Richard Wydeville and his heirs to re-enter in the said manor and to hold it with all the appurtenances without contradiction from anyone. In witness whereof the abovesaid parties have respectively put their seals to this indented charter, before these witnesses: Ellis Sater, John of Easton Neston, Thomas Ratford, John Robert, James Bydell, and others. Given at Hulcote the Wednesday [1 January[3] 1360] in the vigil of the Circumcision of our Lord in the thirty-third year of the reign of King Edward the third since the conquest.

(b) Caryll's reports, BL MS. Harley 1691, fo. 76v.[4]

... *Fisher.* The condition seems to be void, because a remainder is granted over and nothing remains in the donor; and therefore there lacks privity between the donor and the donee. If rent had been reserved, perhaps such a condition could have been annexed to that rent; or else, if the reversion had been in the donor, the condition would have been good because of the possession of the reversion resting in him. Moreover, if the condition were good it would destroy the remainder, contrary to his own grant, which is not right.

Kebell. The old learning of court[5] has always been that a feoffor

---

2   The original is in French.
3   The *feast* of the Circumcision was 1 January, but in 1360 this was a Wednesday.
4   Also briefly reported in Y.B. Mich. 10 Hen. VII, fo. 11, pl. 28; Mich. 11 Hen. VII, fo. 6, pl. 25. (Both books are misdated.)
5   I.e. of the inns of court.

who conveys the fee simple may not condition with his feoffee that he shall not alienate to anyone, but that it is perfectly good if he conditions that he shall not alienate to a particular person. It seems to me, however, that the condition is perfectly good in both cases; for it is not contrary to his estate, even though a tenant in fee simple has power to alienate, since it may be the feoffor's intention that the land should flow downwards for ever to the feoffee's heirs, for the advancement of his blood: as where a man makes such a feoffment to his younger son. If a man founds a hospital for maintenance of paupers, or founds an abbey, on condition that they should not alienate, this condition seems clearly to be good, because his intention appears plainly upon the feoffment; and if their endowments were alienated, the house, or the maintenance of the paupers, could not be kept up; and therefore it seems clear that the condition fully pursues the intention of the estate. If a feoffment is in fee, however, and the condition is that the feoffee shall not take the profits, or that his heirs should not inherit after his death, this condition is void because of the inconsistency. The present case, however, is better for us, because the condition relates to a thing which may lawfully be done by the feoffee . . . And so the condition is good.

Wode to the same effect. If a man gives lands to his feoffee and to his heirs, without speaking of assigns, upon condition that he should not alienate, the condition is good. But if he says, 'to him, his heirs and assigns', the condition seems to be void because of the inconsistency . . .

Rede.[6] The condition is not good, for it is contrary to the estate, since the gift is not only of an estate tail but also of a fee simple. Now, a feoffment in fee simple on condition that he should not alienate is void, because it is absolutely contrary to the estate. The condition [here] goes in defeasance of his whole estate, and in that case it shall be taken as void with respect to the remainder in fee simple; and so, being void in part, it is void throughout. Suppose I make a lease for life on condition that if I grant the reversion the tenant for life should have the fee: I say that this condition is void, because by the grant of the reversion a third party has a lawful interest before the condition can take effect. So here, by the grant of the remainder in fee simple to the same donee, on account of the interest which he has in the fee simple, the condition annexed to the estate tail cannot take effect because it goes in destruction of both estates. It is clear that this fee simple may be lawfully alienated, despite such a condition, because the condition is contrary to an

6 Perhaps on another occasion.

estate of fee simple. Therefore, because the condition is inconsistent in part and against law in part, it seems to be void in whole.

Kebell to the contrary. It seems to me that a man may condition with his feoffee that he should not alienate.

BRYAN [C.J.] interrupted him and said they would not hear him argue that proposition, because it was absolutely contrary to our old common learning, and contrary to what is now in effect a principle. By this means we would overturn all our old precedents. So speak no more on that point.

Kebell. Sir, it seems to me that the condition is good. There are three kinds of condition which are not allowable: (1) if the condition is impossible, (2) if it is self-contradictory, and (3) if it is against the law. But the condition here is none of these. It follows the estate well, for it greatly reinforces the estate ...

VAVASOUR thought the condition good. I quite agree that such a condition annexed to land in tail at common law was void, because the issue was unsure of having the land except *dubitativè*, for by alienation by the ancestor after issue born the issue was remediless. But that is no longer so, for the issue may recontinue the land by action. Thus it seems that the condition in the present case is good; though such a condition would have been void if annexed to a gift in tail at common law, or if [an estate was granted] to a feoffee in fee simple for so long as John Style had issue.

Query this, however, for TOWNSHEND was against him.

DANVERS to the contrary.[7] It has been said that the condition reinforces the entail, but that is not so: it goes in destruction of the entail; for by his re-entry he is to destroy the entail completely. Therefore the condition is contrary ...

TOWNSHEND to the contrary. Everyone agrees that if the reversion had continued in the donor the condition would have been good. I shall prove that that should not alter the case; for if he had made the condition upon the gift at the outset, and later on another occasion afterwards had granted over the reversion upon the same condition ... no one could deny that these conditions made upon separate grants are good. Why, then, are they not good when both estates pass at the same time? ... As to Danvers' argument that the condition goes in destruction of the entail: sir, that is not so; for it is a penalty in restraint of the donee's alienation, with the purpose that his alienation should be of no force. Thus it is a penalty which depends on the alienation, in order to prevent an alienation, and it does not make the alienation good but void ...

7 Danvers' dissenting opinion is not mentioned in the Y.B.s, which suggest that the judges were unanimous.

BRYAN [C.J.] to the same effect. The remainder in fee simple depends upon the estate tail, which may by no means be executed until the issue in tail have run out.

(c) Port's notebook,
HEHL MS. HM 46980, fo. 126.

If land is given in tail, remainder to the right heirs of the donee, on condition that he should not alienate, this condition is good even though the fee simple is out of the donor. Study this, for it was well argued in the Common Bench in Trinity term 8 Hen. VII.

The second of the Y.B. reports says that in Michaelmas term 1493 the condition was held good by all the justices. The record shows that the court took advisement until Michaelmas term 1493, and then the plaintiff was nonsuited.

A DISCUSSION OF THE COMMON RECOVERY (1531)[8]

St German's Doctor and Student, Selden Soc. vol. 91,
p. 156 (book I, ch. 26, of the 1531 ed.; untr.).

... *Doctor.* I have heard say that when a man that is seised of lands in the tail selleth the land, that it is commonly used that he that buyeth the land shall for his surety and for the avoiding of the tail in that behalf cause some of his friends to recover the said lands against the said tenant in tail; which recovery, as I have been credibly informed, shall be had in this manner: the demandants shall suppose in their writ and declaration that the tenant hath no entry but by such a stranger as the buyer shall list to name and appoint, where indeed the demandants never had possession thereof, nor yet the said stranger; and thereupon the said tenant in tail shall appear in the court and by covin and by assent of the parties shall vouch to warranty one that he knoweth well hath nothing to yield in value, and that vouchee shall appear and the demandants shall declare against him; and thereupon he shall take a day to imparl in the same term; and at that day by assent and covin of the parties he shall make default; upon which default, because it is a default in despite of the court, the demandants shall have judgment to recover against the tenant in tail, and he over in value against the vouchee. And this judgment and recovery in value is taken for a bar of the tail for ever. How may it therefore be taken that that law standeth with

8 For a precedent of 1508, see Selden Soc. vol. 94, p. 270.

conscience that, as it seemeth, alloweth and favoureth such feigned recoveries?

Student. If the tenant in tail sell the land for a certain sum of money, as is agreed betwixt them, at such a price as is commonly used of other lands, and for the surety of the sale suffereth such a recovery as is aforesaid, what is the cause that moveth thee to doubt whether the said contract—or the recovery made thereupon for the surety of the buyer that hath truly paid his money for the same— should stand with conscience?

Doctor. Two things cause me to doubt therein. One is for that that after our Lord had given the land of behest to Abraham and to his seed, that is to say, to his children in possession, always to continue, he said to Moses (as it appeareth [in] *Leviticus*, 25) the land shall not be sold for ever, for it is mine ... [and] it seemeth that he doth against the example of God that alieneth or selleth the land that is given to him and to his children as lands entailed be given. Another cause is this: it appeareth by the commandment of God that thou shalt not covet the house of thy neighbour...

Student. ... it appeareth that the said prohibition was not general for every place ... [or] to all people ... And to thy second reason which is grounded upon the commandment of God, it must needs be granted that it is not lawful to any man unlawfully to covet the house of his neighbour ... but then it remaineth for thee yet to prove how in this case this tailed land that is sold by his ancestor, and whereof a recovery is had of record in the king's court, may be said [to be] the land of the heirs.

Doctor. That may be proved by the law of the realm: that is to say, by the statute of Westminster the second, the first chapter,[9] where it is said [that] the will of the giver expressly contained in the deed of his gift shall be from henceforth observed ... for it is holden commonly by all doctors that the commandments and rules of the law of man, or of a positive law that is lawfully made, bind all that be subjects to that law according to the mind of the maker...

Student. But some hold that the said statute of Westminster the second was made of a singularity and presumption of many that were at the said parliament for exalting and magnifying of their own blood; and therefore they say that that statute, made by such a presumption, bindeth not in conscience.

Doctor. It is very perilous to judge for certain that the said statute was made of such a presumption as thou speakest of ... but it is good and expedient in this case, as it is in other cases that be in doubt, to hold the surer way: and that is that it was made of charity,

9 Statute of Westminster II (1285); see p. 48 above.

to the intent that he nor the heirs of him to whom the land was given should not fall into extreme poverty . . . and certain it is that it is not apparent that there was any such corrupt intent in the makers of the said statute. How may it therefore be said that the law is good or right-wise that not only suffereth such things against the statute but also against the commandment of God?

Student. To that some answer and say that when the land is sold, and a recovery is had thereupon in the king's court of record, that it sufficeth to bar the tail in conscience: for they say that, as the tail was first ordained by the law, so they say that by the law it is annulled again.

Doctor. Be thou thy self judge if in that case there be like authority in the making of the tail as there is in the annulling thereof; for it was ordained by authority of parliament, the which is always taken for the most high court in this realm before any other, and it is annulled by a false supposal . . .

Student. I cannot see but that after the law of the realm [the recovery] is a bar of the tail . . .

Doctor. . . . If thou can yet shew me any other consideration why the said recoveries should stand with conscience, I pray thee let me hear thy conceit therein: for the multitude of the said recoveries is so great that it were great pity that all they should be bound to restitution that have lands by such recoveries, since there is none that (as far as I can hear) disposeth them to restore . . .

Student. This matter is great, for as thou sayest there be so many that have tailed lands by such recoveries that it were great pity and heaviness to condemn so many persons and to judge that they all were bound to restitution; for I think there be but few in this realm that have lands of any notable value but that they or their ancestors, or some other by whom they claim, have had part thereof by such recoveries . . . And so that yet I trust that ignorance may excuse many persons in this behalf.

Doctor. Ignorance of the deed may excuse, but ignorance of the law excuseth not . . .

Student. What then, shall we condemn so many and so notable men?

Doctor. We shall not condemn them, but we shall shew them their peril.

Student. Yet I trust that their danger is not so great that they should be bound to restitution. For John Gerson sayeth . . . *quod communis error facit jus,* that is to say, a common error maketh a right . . .

Doctor. . . . the said recoveries, though they have been long used, may not be taken to have the strength of a custom, for many (as well learned as unlearned) have always spoken against them, and yet do. And furthermore, as I have heard say, a custom or a prescription in this realm against the statutes of the realm prevails not in the law.

Student. Though a custom in this realm prevaileth not against a statute as to the law, yet it seemeth that it may prevail against the statute in conscience: for though ignorance of a statute excuseth not in the law, nevertheless it may excuse in conscience; and so it seemeth that it may do of a custom ...

The Doctor denies this proposition, and the difference is left unresolved, with the Student noting the Doctor's advice that men should refrain from recoveries thereafter.

(6) Remainders

HENRY SON OF TORKIN v KERNEGE (1302)
Y.B. 30 & 31 Edw. I, Rolls Series, p. 181.

Henry the son of Torkin, who is here, lays before you this:[10] that Ralph Kernege, who is there, wrongfully deforces him of a messuage and one acre of land with the appurtenances in N., and wrongfully for this reason: that it is his right because one A. was seised of this messuage and this land in his demesne as of fee and right in time of peace, in the reign etc., taking issues etc., that is to say etc; and this A. gave those tenements to B. and C. for their two lives, and after their deaths the same tenements were to remain to this Henry; and by that gift [B. and C.] were seised in their demesne as of freehold[11] in time [of peace] in the reign of king etc., [taking] issues etc. amounting to etc. as of freehold[11]; and after the deaths of B. and C. those tenements ought to remain to Henry by the form of the aforesaid gift; and if Ralph will deny it, Henry has good suit [to prove] it.

Kyngeshemede. Since he lays no [hereditary] right in his person, [we ask] judgment of this writ, and judgment whether you should be answered on this writ.

Westcote. We can have no other form in the Chancery. If you wish to abate this writ, you must give us another.

Kyngeshemede. In this way any stranger [to the land] can make a claim.

10   The first speech represents the demandant's count.
11   I.e. as tenants for life.

Mutford. You have had a view [of the land] in the bench, and by doing so have affirmed the writ good as a matter of form.

Kyngeshemede. Shame on him who asked for the view. But still you should not be answered, for see here a fine witnessing that A. gave the tenements to B. alone and that after [B.'s] death one-half should remain to G. and the other half should revert to [A.] himself; and you are not G. [We ask] judgment whether you can claim anything.

Mutford. So are you saying that whereas our writ supposes the gift to have been made to B. and C., the gift was made to [B.] alone and on this basis asking for judgment of the writ?

STANTON. He makes the exception to the writ and to the action.

Mutford. We will imparl. And then he lost his writ by non-suit etc.

SUTTON'S CASE (1366)

Y.B. Hil. 40 Edw. III, fo. 9, pl. 18;
LI MS. Hale 187, fo. 67; CUL MS. Hh. 2. 5, fo. 11v;
MS. Hh. 2. 7, fo. 6.

In replevin by Richard Sutton, the provost of Beverley's bailiff avowed for 100s. relief for one knight's fee after the death of John Sutton, claiming that the land had descended to the plaintiff as his brother and heir. The plaintiff replied that John Sutton's father (also John) had levied a fine whereby the land was granted and rendered to himself for life, remainder to John Sutton (his son) and his wife Ellen in tail, remainder to the right heirs of himself (i.e. John Sutton the father); and the father died, and John and Ellen entered; and John and Ellen died without issue; and so the plaintiff entered as heir of the father but by way of remainder, as a purchaser.

... *Cavendish* (for the avowant). Since you have confessed that you are in as heir in which case you should pay relief, we demand judgment and pray return.

Fencotes.[12] You demand relief from us as heir to John the son, and we have said that we cannot be called heir to him because he had but a fee tail, and the remainder was limited (*taillé*) after his decease and the decease of Ellen his wife to the right heirs of our father, and that we are in as purchasers in the remainder: and therefore there is no cause to avow...

THORPE [C.J.]. Is your meaning that he shall not have the avowry for relief, because you are in as a purchaser, or that he ought to avow upon you as heir to John your father?

Fencotes.[12] Sir, we mean that he may not avow upon us for relief as heir to John [the son], who had nothing except in tail ...

WYCHYNGHAM ... It seems the avowry is good, for when he was heir to the father the fee simple descended to him: by the forfeiture or attainder of the father the lord would have had escheat, and that proves that he had a fee simple and was very tenant to the lord. Therefore, since he was his rightful tenant, and the plaintiff is his heir, the avowry seems good.

Fencotes. If tenements are given to a man for life, remainder to the right heirs of John de T., the fee simple remains (*demurt*) in suspense because the remainder cannot take effect in anyone [until the entail has determined, any more than the land descends to him][13] as heir while the ancestor is living, but is suspended.[14] Therefore when the remainder was limited (*taillé*) to John the son and Ellen his wife and the heirs of their bodies, remainder in fee simple to the right heirs of the father, the fee simple was *in nubibus*[15] until after the entail was determined; for, by the wording of the deed, the remainder in fee simple was not to commence until after the tail was extinct, and at that time it was to commence in whomever was right heir to John the father.

Cavendish. If the lease had been to your father for life, remainder to his right heirs, he would have had the fee. When, therefore, it was leased to your father for life, remainder to John his son in tail, remainder over to the right heirs of your father, if you were now under age the lord would have the wardship, and by consequence relief ...

Then they changed their avowry and avowed for two marks according to the usage.[16] And they did this by reason of conscience, for it was said that if judgment were given to have return upon the former avowry the tenancy would have been bound for ever to pay 100s. relief.

Fencotes. He may not avow upon us for relief as heir to John the son, since we are not in as heir to him; for even if we were only of the half-blood to him we should nevertheless have had the remainder.

12 MSS. This is misprinted as 'Fyncheden', who by this date was J.C.P.
13 MS. Hh. 2. 7 only.
14 LI MS. says 'suspendu'; MS. Hh. 2. 5 says 'suspensif'; MS. Hh. 2. 7 says 'suspensist'; and the 1679 ed., 'en suspens'.
15 I.e. in the clouds.
16 That all tenants of the provostship of Beverley should pay only two marks on the death of a tenant for relief.

THORPE. I know full well what you are getting at, but you have pleaded that you ought not to pay relief because you are in as purchaser, in that you are the first person in whom the remainder is to take effect by the words of remainder. You are, however, in as heir to your father, and your father[17] had the freehold before: and during that time, if John his son and Ellen had died while your father was alive, your father would have had fee simple, for which estate he could have had a writ of right. And the remainder was not limited to you by your own name, but as 'heir'.

So it was awarded by advice of all the justices that the avowant should sue for return if he would.

RIKHILL'S CASE (*c.* 1395)

Littleton, *Tenures*, ss. 720–723.

I have heard say that in the time of King Richard II there was a justice of the Common Pleas called Rikhill,[18] living in Kent, who had issue various sons; and his purpose was that his eldest son should have certain lands and tenements unto him and the heirs of his body begotten, and for default of issue remainder to the second son [in tail], and so to the third son, and so forth; and because he wanted none of his sons to alienate or make a warranty to bar or hurt the others in remainder, he caused an indenture to be made to the effect that the lands and tenements were given to the eldest son on condition that if he or any of his sons should alienate in fee or in fee tail, then their estate should cease and be void and that the same lands and tenements should then immediately remain to the second son and the heirs of his body begotten, and so on ... But it seems by reason that all such remainders in the form aforesaid are void and invalid, and that for three causes:

1 Because every remainder which begins by deed must be in the person to whom the remainder is limited (*taylé*) by force of the same deed, before livery of seisin is made to the person who should have the freehold; for in such a case the birth and existence of the remainder is by the livery of seisin to him that shall have the freehold and such remainder was not to the second son at the time of the livery of seisin in the aforesaid case.

2 If the first son alienated the tenements in fee, then the freehold and the fee simple is in the alienee and no one else; and if

17 MSS. Reads 'frere' in the 1679 ed.
18 William Rikhill, J.C.P. 1389–1407, died in 1407 and was buried in Rochester cathedral. Littleton might have confused him with Thirning C.J. (see p. 68, below), though Thirning did not live in Kent.

the donor had any reversion, it would be discontinued by such alienation. How, then, by any reason, can it be that such a remainder shall begin its being and have its birth immediately after such alienation to a stranger, who by the same alienation has a freehold and fee simple? Moreover, if such a remainder were good he might enter upon the alienee, where he had no manner of right before the alienation: which would be absurd (*inconvenient*).

3   When the condition is that if the eldest son should alienate etc. his estate shall cease or be void, then it seems that after such alienation the donor could enter on the basis of such condition; and so the donor or his heirs ought in such case to have the land, rather than the second son, who had no right before such alienation.

And so it seems that such remainders as in the case aforesaid are void.

In his commentary on this case (Co. Litt. 377b), Coke draws the lesson 'that it is not safe for any man (be he never so learned) to be of counsel with himself in his own case', and ends (Co. Litt. 379b): 'In these last three sections, our author hath taught us an excellent point of learning, that when any innovation or new invention starts up to try it with the rules of the common law (as our author here hath done), for these be true touchstones to sever the pure gold from the dross and sophistications of novelties and new inventions ... and commonly a new invention doth offend against many rules and reasons (as here it appeareth) of the common law, and the ancient judges and sages of the law have ever (as it appeareth in our books) suppressed innovations and novelties in the beginning, as soon as they have offered to creep up, lest the quiet of the common law might be disturbed'.

THIRNING'S CASE (*c.* 1400)

This may be a garbled recollection of Rikhill's case, or vice versa. Neither has been verified from a contemporary source, though Paston J. seems to speak from personal memory here and would have been in his 20s or early 30s at the time.

Y.B. Hil. 21 Hen. VI, fo. 33v, pl. 21.

... FULTHORPE. Suppose someone gives land in tail on condition that the donee should not discontinue the tail. Is that condition void? I do not think so, because Thirning (who was chief justice here[19]) gave his land to his eldest son on condition that if he alienated it should remain to his younger son, and he made similar remainders to two or three others.

19   William Thirning C.J.C.P. 1396–1413; died in 1413.

AYSCOUGH. I think such a gift in tail, with the condition, is good and effectual; for Thirning made the gift with the advice of those who were justices in those times.

PASTON. Truly it is not so, and I know well that it was not done by assent of the justices; but he said he would have the gift openly notified in the place, and Hankford[20] said he could, but smiled and said that the whole condition was void: and so it seems to me.

BLAKETT'S CASE (1410)

Y.B. Trin. 11 Hen. IV, fo. 74, pl. 14.

Scire facias was brought on a fine against J. Blakett and his wife E.

[*Skrene*] showed that the land of which execution is demanded was given to the wife against whom the writ is brought for the term of her life, remainder to the right heirs of one W. Worcester, who had died before the remainder was granted; and so the remainder is in one J. as right heir of that same W. and we pray aid of him; and since he is within age, we pray that the plea shall await [his age].

Norton. He should not have his age because in this case the infant is a purchaser just as if the remainder had been granted to him by his proper name; and so etc.

Skrene. If he was not heir the remainder could not be his. And if he brought *scire facias* to get the remainder, bastardy would be a good plea against him. And suppose there is a grant to a man for life, remainder to the right heir of one W. who is alive: the remainder can not vest until W. dies, and the death of W. will make the remainder vest because then the remainderman has become heir; and in that case he must have his age, and so here.

HANKFORD. In the case you have put, I would hold the remainder void. But if the land were given to a man for the term of his life, remainder in tail, and for default of issue remainder to the right heir of the first tenant, in such a case the [second] remainder is effective; and the remainder in fee simple has effect because of the possession which the first tenant had.

THIRNING. It has been said that the fee simple is 'in the clouds'[1] and is put in suspense.

HANKFORD. I could never see how in reason or in law such a remainder can be effective, because it is necessary that the fee should pass at once to the grantee immediately upon the death of the tenant for life; and if it does not pass to him, it must stay with

20   J.C.P. 1398–1413.
1   See *Sutton's Case* (1366), p. 65 above.

the donor, because land can not pass from any person [and be] 'in the clouds'.

HILL said the same, and said also that if such a remainder does not take effect from the beginning at the time of livery [of seisin], it is hard to make out how it can ever take effect.

THIRNING. He who is now prayed in aid should not have his age, because he is the first in whom the remainder was to take effect, and [his estate] began by purchase, and there was no previous descent to him which would entitle him to have his age. And although he is named as heir he is purchaser of the remainder, and would not fall into wardship or pay relief . . .

FARYNGTON v DARELL (1431)

Record: CP 40/678, m. 312; abstracted in Kiralfy, *Source Book*, p. 100. John Faryngton brought trespass against John Darell for breaking his close and house in the parish of St John Walbrook, London, on 28 June 1429. The defendant pleaded that by the custom of the city of London all tenements there were devisable by will; and that one Reynold de Conduyt in 1346 had devised the house to his wife Lettice[2] for life, remainder to his son John and the heirs male of his body, remainder to the next heir male of Reynold and the heirs male of his body; and on Reynold's death Lettice entered; and John died without issue during Lettice's lifetime; then Lettice died seised, and Joan Burton (daughter of Reynold's daughter Isabel, now the wife of Philip Burton) and her husband entered as heir general and had issue Giles; then in 1419 Joan and Philip gave the house to the plaintiff; afterwards Giles, claiming the house as Reynold's next heir male, entered upon the plaintiff and was seised by virtue of the devise; and Giles's estate came to the defendant, upon whom the plaintiff re-entered, and the defendant re-entered upon him. To this plea the plaintiff demurred on the express ground that the defendant had admitted that on Lettice's death John had no male issue, and therefore the next remainder (to the next heir male of Reynold) was extinct and determined, so that the house reverted to Joan as Reynold's heir in fee simple. The first reported argument of the demurrer is in Trinity term 1431.

(a) Y.B. Trin. 9 Hen. VI, fo. 23, pl. 19;
CUL MS. Gg. 5.8, fo. 66v.

. . . *Rolf*. It seems to me that the plaintiff should have his damages, for it is confessed that at the time of the devise and when the remainder fell in (*eschut*) the said Reynold, the devisor, had no heir male; and this Giles, who claims as heir male, was born after the remainder fell in, and so the remainder is void.[3] For if land is given

---

2　'Sybil' in the Y.B.
3　This is not the point of the demurrer.

to a man for life, remainder to the right heirs of my lord Babington, and then the tenant for life dies in the lifetime of my lord Babington, this remainder is void because Babington cannot have an heir while he is living. In the same way here, it is not alleged that Joan, who was Reynold's kinswoman and heir, was dead at the time when the remainder fell in. Moreover, I think that when an estate tail or remainder is absolutely void it cannot be revived afterwards. For instance, if land is given to a man unto him and his heirs male of his body begotten, and he has issue a daughter and dies without male issue; and the donor enters; and then the daughter has male issue and dies: her male issue shall never have his land, and yet he is now heir male of [the donee's] body. Likewise here.

Newton. I think the contrary. I quite agree that in the case which Rolf has put the son of the donee's daughter shall not inherit by virtue of such a special gift.

Martin. You do not concede that?

Newton. Yes, sir, I will concede it. The reason for that case is that the demandant ought to trace [his title] through a lineal descent, and land entailed to heirs male cannot descend through a daughter. But in this case at the bar the said Giles claims through a remainder, and he is in effect a purchaser because he is the first person to whom the remainder comes; and he is heir male by virtue of the gift even though his mother is alive. Similarly, if land is given to a man and his heirs female of his body, and he has issue a son and a daughter and dies, his daughter shall have formedon as heir female by virtue of the gift; and yet she is not heir, since she has a brother.

Fulthorpe. A devise is stronger than a grant at common law, because everyone is bound to carry out the last will. In this case, then, the said Giles is heir male to the said Reynold by virtue of the gift. If a man devises or grants that his executors may alienate his land after his death, and the land is not devisable, all is void, for it is against common reason that each executor should be able to sell land in which he has no [property] (*riens*); but by the custom he may well do so, and may sell and put the alienee in possession even though the heir is in by disseisin. Thus a devise is stronger than a grant. Therefore it seems to me that it should be carried out as far as possible. As to the point that this remainder[4] was once absolutely void, since he had no capacity, because there was no male heir

---

4 MS. Reads 'reversion' in print.

at the time when the remainder fell in, [compare this case:] if a man is seised of land in fee simple or in fee tail, and dies without heir except that his wife is pregnant, and the lord or donor enters, and then the woman has issue, the issue shall have this land—and yet at the time of his death he had no issue and no heir. In the same way here.

Ellerker. This remainder was determined at one time, as has been said, and in my view it cannot be revived. If someone devises that his executors should sell his land to the person who would give the most for it, and they sell the land to one man, and then another comes to them and offers more, they cannot sell the land to him because their power is determined by the first sale. Likewise here, his remainder was determined at one time. And, sir, I think that if land is given to a man for life, remainder to the right heirs female of a stranger who is dead and has issue a son and daughter, and the tenant for life dies, the stranger's daughter shall not have the land because she is not the stranger's heir. Likewise here.

PASTON. I am fully aware that the custom of devising enables the executors to sell, and the sale will be effectual by the devise even though the executors have nothing in the freehold: but the custom of devising does not make a man inheritable as heir where he is not heir. Moreover it would be absurd (*inconvenient*) that when an estate tail has been defeated many years and days ago it should be revived by reason of someone's birth ten years afterwards. There are many cases, sir, where even though a man has issue male of his body he ought nevertheless not to inherit by virtue of the tail. For instance, if land is given to a man and his heirs male of his body, and he has issue a son and a daughter and dies, the son enters, and the daughter has issue a son and dies, and then the donee's son dies without issue, the daughter's son shall not have the land: and yet he is heir male to the donee, and of his body. (This was conceded by all, except MARTIN.) As to the argument that if a man dies without heir except that his wife is pregnant, and then the woman has issue, his issue shall have the land even though he was once dead without issue: it is true that the issue shall inherit, and the reason is because in this case the inheritance was not absolutely determined, for even though he had no heir apparent *quoad mundum* he nevertheless had an heir *in esse* at the time of his death, for although the heir was not born at the time of his father's death he was nevertheless *in esse*, and in such a case he shall be vouched in his mother's womb.

MARTIN. It has been adjudged that if land is given to a man for life, remainder to the right heirs of one A., and A. is alive, and then A. has issue and dies, and then the tenant for life dies, the stranger's heir shall have this land, and yet at the time of the grant the remainder was in manner void.

This was not denied, although PASTON said it could not be proved by reason.

BABINGTON [C.J.]. It has been the point of a moot case.

MARTIN. In an even stronger case it has been adjudged that if a man devises that his executor or his executor's executor may sell his land, and at the time of this devise the executor's executors were not in existence, a sale by them has nevertheless been held good and sufficient.

PASTON. That may well be, for they were *in esse* at the time when the first executors died.

MARTIN. If [a] tenant in tail has issue who is attainted of felony in his father's lifetime, and alienates, and dies, and the son who was attainted dies, the son of the one who committed the felony shall have his land: and yet the right to his land never descended to his father, because of the aforementioned felony. This proves well that even though a man cannot make out a lineal descent he may nevertheless inherit, as in the case put by Rolf.

PASTON. There is a great difference between the case which Rolf put and your case; for when the land was entailed to the heirs male, and the donee died without heir male, the entail was forthwith determined because neither the land nor the right could descend to the heir female, and the heir female could not by any possibility inherit. But in your case the person who committed the felony was capable of inheriting before the felony was committed. Moreover, the statute says [that an entail shall not be barred] by deed or feoffment,[5] and if the heir of the person who committed the felony should be disinherited it would be by his father's misdeed, which would be expressly contrary to the form of the statute.

Godered. A devise is stronger than a grant by deed, for if a man leases land for life to someone who is professed [as a monk] and not capable (*persona capax*) [of taking], remainder over in fee, or leases land for life to someone who does not exist, remainder over in fee, this remainder and everything else is void: for *debile fundamentum fallat opus*. But if a man devises for life to a party who is incapable, or to a man who is not in existence, remainder over in fee, the remainder is nevertheless good. Likewise in this case, although this might perhaps have been void [if done] by deed, it is good by devise.

---

5   The preamble to *De donis conditionalibus* (see p. 49, above) refers to a deed or feoffment which bars the reversion rather than the issue.

BABINGTON. The nature of a devise, where land is devisable, is [such] that a man may devise that the land shall be sold by the executors; and this is good, as has already been said. And this is an amazing proposition in law,[6] but it seems to me that it is the nature of a devise, and devises have always been used in that way. Thus may a man lawfully acquire a freehold from someone who has nothing, in the same way as a man can get fire from a flintstone even though there is no fire inside the flint. This is in order to carry out the last will of the devisor. Also, a guardian in chivalry may endow a woman, and a writ of dower lies against him, even though he has no freehold. But I think a devise must be good and effectual at the time of the devisor's death, or else it is void; for if it is void at the time of his death it cannot be effectual afterwards. For instance, if a man devises lands to the priests of a chantry or college in the church of A. and dies, and at that time there is no chantry or college of A., this devise is void even if it is made by the king's licence; and if afterwards a chantry or college is made in the same place they shall not have this land, because at the time of the devise there was no corporation in which the devise could take effect.

PASTON. A devise is inherently peculiar[7] as to when it may take effect; for if a man devises in London that his executors should sell his lands, and dies seised, his heir is in by descent, and yet he shall be ousted by a sale made by the executors—and in the same way shall his heir after him. But if a man devises his lands to his executors, so that the freehold passes to them by the devise, and then the devisor's heir intrudes and dies seised, and his heir is in by descent, in this case the executors cannot oust him who is in by descent.

BABINGTON. If a man has issue a daughter and dies, his wife being pregnant, the daughter may lawfully enter; and if she dies, her heir may enter and take the profits for the time being; but if then the woman who was pregnant by the ancestor paramount is delivered of a son, the son may enter even though his sister's heir is in by descent, but he shall not have an action of account or any remedy for the profits in the meantime before his birth because her entry was permissible until he was born. And if a church becomes vacant, and the sister or her heir presents, and their presentee is instituted and inducted before the son's birth, the son

---

6   Reads 'est merveilous ley de reason' in print, 'est merveilous reson per ley' in MS.

7   Reads 'merveilous en luy mesme' in print, 'un mervailous cas en luy mesme' in MS.

shall not have advantage of this avoidance;[8] and yet he shall not be adjudged out of possession [of the advowson] by reason of this presentation. I think that if this matter had been well pleaded the matter in law should have come in from the plaintiff's side, in which case perhaps the defendant could have had a better advantage than he now has.

Then PASTON said that if land is given to a man and his heirs male or his heirs female, he has a fee simple (which was agreed); but if he gives it to him and his heirs male or female of his body he has a good tail. Likewise in the case at the bar, the remainder was to the right heirs male of the devisor, and not the heirs male of the body of the devisor, and therefore it is fee simple.

Rolf. If there are a grandfather, father and son, and the father is executed for felony, nevertheless in formedon the son should trace the descent through the father according to the form of the gift, for the tail was not determined at any time.

STRANGEWAYS. As I see it, Joan had a fee simple at one stage, and so if she has male issue afterwards that does not change her estate, notwithstanding the express words in the devise. For if a man devises his lands to his son, unto him and his heirs male of his body, and for want of issue male remainder to one B. in fee, and devises that if the son dies without heir male and afterwards has an heir male his heir male shall inherit by virtue of the tail; and then his son has issue a daughter and dies without heir male, and the remainderman in fee enters, and then the daughter has issue male and dies, I say that his issue male shall not have this land: for then this land would be at one time fee simple in one person, and at another time fee tail in another, and so on infinitely.

PASTON. If land is given to a man and his heirs male or his heirs female, he has a fee simple; and even though he goes on to say 'and the heirs begotten on the body of his heir' there is still no estate tail in my view, because he may not have fee simple and fee tail. In the same way in this case, when he said 'remainder to the right heirs male' this word 'male' was void because he has not said 'begotten of his body', and therefore the remainder shall be understood as being to his right heirs, and therefore Joan (who was his right heir) had fee simple, and therefore she could well alienate.

MARTIN. But since Joan has male issue, her male issue is heir male to the devisor by the form of the gift. For if land is given to a man and his heirs female, and he has issue a son and a daughter, his daughter shall have formedon as 'heir by the form [of the gift]'.

---

8 I.e. shall not himself present as if the church were still vacant. The MS. has 'presentation' for 'avoidance'.

COTTESMORE. As has been said before, this remainder cannot be called an estate tail. And even if such a remainder could be called an estate tail, nevertheless Joan in this case had a fee simple; for the plea says that the tenant for life died and Joan entered and had issue male, and so it is not alleged that she had issue male at the time when the remainder fell in.

PASTON. Entailed land must always descend or resort in line. Thus, if land is given to a man and his heirs male or female of his body, none of his blood ought to inherit except those who come of his body. In this case at the bar when the remainder was to the nearest heir male of the devisor, this word 'male' was void, and by virtue of this remainder the devisor's brother [or sister][9] ought to have this land as heir general, even though he is not heir of his body. Therefore this remainder is fee simple and not fee tail.

(b) Y.B. Mich. 11 Hen. VI, fo. 12, pl. 28.

Rolf came to the bar and [stated the case]. Sir, it seems to me that Giles's entry was not good, for Giles cannot be heir male to Reynold. If land is given to a man and the heirs male begotten of his body, and the donee's daughter has issue a son and dies in the lifetime of the donee, and the donee dies, the daughter's son shall nevertheless not have the land, because he cannot be called 'heir male' by that line: for it was interrupted, inasmuch as he did not come from a male. Likewise here, since Giles came from a female he cannot be called heir male to Reynold. Moreover, when Sybil died, Joan's entry was permissible as heir general to Reynold because of the reversion in fee simple which was reserved to him, in that Giles was not born at that time but afterwards: therefore Joan's entry was good, because there was no heir male to Reynold *in esse* who should take the remainder, and so when Joan was lawfully seised as of fee simple she should not be ousted by the birth of Giles afterwards . . .

PASTON [to the same effect].

COTTESMORE. I think the contrary. For if land is given to a man and his wife and to their heirs male begotten of their two bodies, and the husband has issue male by this wife, then even though the husband had older issue by a former wife who is his heir general yet by the special gift the issue begotten between the husband and wife shall have the land. In the same way, if it had been given to him and his wife and their heirs female of their two bodies, and there was an

9   MS. The pedigree in the case is unclear, but the pleadings suppose Joan to be granddaughter and heir.

heir male before, yet by this special gift the female shall inherit and shall be called heir notwithstanding the elder brother. Likewise shall Giles be here, while his mother is living, by virtue of the devise. As to the argument that where land is given to someone and the heirs male of his body, the issue of his daughter shall not inherit: sir, that is not like the present case. For by that gift a special line is limited, which line is interrupted in that one of the line is female. But in this case the remainder was to the nearest heir male of Reynold, and so no line is limited, but it is limited generally, and so there cannot be said to be any interruption even though Giles comes of a female.

BABINGTON. I am of the same view. And I say that this case is not like other gifts in tail, for this is a devise and a testamentary cause and should be adjudged according to the devisor's will and according to what one may adjudge his intention to have been. Thus, if a man devises his land for life, remainder to John Cottesmore, and there are two John Cottesmores (namely the father and the son, or two brothers), which of them shall have this remainder? I say that his will shall be tried by the discretion of an inquest. And it has been adjudged good to make a devise to the devisor's child who was in his mother's womb, even though the issue was born after his death and was not *in esse* at the time of his father's death. Likewise here, even though Giles was not born at the time when the remainder fell in, he shall still have the land by reason of the devise.

PASTON. This plea was pleaded here by Darell, and so inasmuch as he does not plead specifically whether Joan had issue when Sybil died or afterwards, it shall be taken most strongly against him: namely, that she had Giles afterwards. Moreover, the pleading proves as much according to common understanding. Therefore, when a lawful estate was in Joan, the birth of Giles afterwards does not give him a right of entry. For if land is given to a man for life, remainder in tail to someone who does not exist, remainder over in fee, after the death of the tenant for life the remainderman in fee shall enter. Likewise here. As to the argument that a devise made to someone in his mother's womb is good, I say that it cannot be good, because he was not *in rerum natura* when the devisor died. (BABINGTON denied this.) As to the question of the remainder to John Cottesmore, where there are two, I say that the elder shall have this remainder; for he has the name without addition, and the younger only with addition ['the younger']. But here, since the remainder is generally to the right heirs male of Reynold, and because when Sybil died there was no one who was the right heir male of Reynold in whom the remainder could vest by virtue of the devise, Joan's entry by reason of the reversion in fee was good. Suppose Reynold had had issue two daughters, and each of them had a son, which of the sons should have had this land by the remainder? For either is as near as the other. Therefore neither of them should have the land, but the remainder would be void. Likewise here, since there is no nearest heir male, because he is not heir while his mother is living.

After further argument as to whether wills should be construed according to the devisor's intention, the case was adjourned. No more is reported. The case was continued on the roll until 1435, but no judgment was entered.

COLTHIRST v BEJUSHIN (1550)

Record: CP 40/1141, m. 441; Plowd. 21. Matthias Colthirst[10] brought trespass against Peter Bejushin[11] for breaking his close and house at Barton and Walcot, Somerset, on 18 December 1548 and continuing the trespass until 3 January 1549 (when the writ was purchased). The defendant pleaded in bar that the place in question was called The Grange in Barton, next Bath, which in 1529 had been demised by the prior of Bath to Henry Bejushin and Eleanor his wife, to have and to hold unto them for their lives and for the life of the survivor, remainder to their son William for life if he should reside in The Grange, and if William should die before his parents, remainder to their son Peter for life if he should reside in The Grange; and Henry and Eleanor were seised by virtue of this demise, and William died before them; and then they died, and Peter entered and was seised, and continuously thereafter resided in The Grange; and the plaintiff, claiming by colour etc., entered upon him; and the defendant re-entered. To this plea the plaintiff demurred, and the case was argued in banc three terms later. The arguments about the form of the plea are here omitted.

Plowd. 21.

... *Pollard* Sjt. briefly recited the case [and argued that] the remainder seems to be void, for various reasons. One reason is because the limitation of the remainder is here appointed during the particular estate, and every remainder ought always to be appointed and limited to take effect after the particular estate has ended and not during the particular estate; for if it is limited and appointed to take effect during the particular estate it shall be

---

10   Apparently the same as 'Matthew' Colthurst (d. 1559), M.P. for Bath 1545, a professional auditor: S.T. Bindoff (ed.), *The House of Commons 1509–1558* (1982), vol. I, p. 679.

11   This strange name seems more correctly to be 'Bewshin'. In a grant of 1547 The Grange is said to have been leased to Henry Bewshyn: *Calendar of Patent Rolls of Edward VI*, vol. I, p. 194. As Henry 'Bewchyn' he bought the abbey cloisters after the dissolution: *Victoria County History of Somerset*, vol. II, p. 78.

utterly void, because it is repugnant to the first estate. For instance, if a lease is made for life, remainder for life, and if the first tenant for life should die then it shall remain over to a stranger in fee: this remainder is void, because it is appointed to take effect immediately after the first estate for life has determined, and when the first estate for life has determined the remainder for life begins, and from thence it shall continue; and if it shall continue from thence, it follows that the remainder in fee cannot take effect immediately after the first life has ended, for if the remainder in fee were to begin to take effect then it would avoid the first remainder for life, which cannot be avoided since it was appointed first; and therefore, since the remainder in fee is limited to take effect during the precedent estate, which precedent estate the remainder ought to avoid (or it will [itself] be void), it seems to me that it shall be void for repugnancy. Likewise if a lease is made to two, remainder over in fee after the death of the first of them: this remainder is void, because the survivor of them shall hold over after the death of the other, and since the survivor of them shall have the land immediately after the death of the other it cannot immediately remain over to another in fee, for if it did it would drown (*mergera*) the first estate, which continues, and therefore the remainder shall rather be void for repugnancy than that it shall drown the first estate, which was appointed and limited before the remainder; and so the remainder shall be void. Likewise in the principal case. It is given to the husband and wife for their lives, remainder to the eldest son for life, on condition that if he died while the husband and wife were alive it should remain to the defendant for life: which is tantamount to saying that the defendant should then immediately have the land, and that cannot be, because the first estate continued at that time and if the remainder were good it would drown the first estate which the husband and wife have—and that it shall not do, and for that reason the remainder shall be void on account of the repugnancy and contrariety between it and the first estate. The remainder is also void for another reason: namely, because it is limited to commence upon a condition; and no remainder can do that, for conditions always work in privity, so that none but privies shall take advantage of them. For no one shall enter for breach of condition except the feoffor, donor or lessor, or their heirs. And just as none but privies shall avoid an estate already made, for breach of condition, in the same way none but privies shall take a new estate by performance of a condition. Therefore if a lease is made for life, reserving rent, on condition that if the rent is behind it shall remain to a stranger in fee after the first estate has ended, this remainder is void in that it depends upon a condition and none but the privies shall take advantage of it; and this stranger to whom the remainder is appointed is not a privy, but a stranger, ergo he shall not take advantage by the remainder, and thus the remainder is void . . . If, however, an estate is made for life upon condition that if the tenant for life dies it shall remain over, this remainder is good because it commences upon the determination of the estate, which is certain and not uncertain, and therefore is not a condition. But this here, which is uncertain,[12] may be termed a condition—and there is no condition unless it is uncertain and may be either performed or broken—and here it is uncertain, and therefore a condition, and therefore the remainder is void. So the remainder here is void for the two reasons set out before. Moreover, my lords, it is to be considered, noted and known that in every common weal it is necessary and requisite that things are conveyed with certainty; for certainty begets repose, and uncertainty contention; and our law, foreseeing the causes of such contention, has prevented them. And for that reason our law has ordained certain ceremonies to be used in the alteration and transmutation of things from one person to another—and especially in the case of freeholds, which are of greater price and esteem in our law than other things—in order to know a certain time when the things will pass. Therefore in every feoffment the law has ordained that livery and seisin shall be made, and in every grant of a reversion or rent that attornment shall be made; and these are certain points containing times when and to whom estates shall pass. For the same reason the law has ordained and appointed that every remainder shall have three things besides those mentioned before, as certain guides and rules to know and discern when remainders are good, namely: [1] a precedent estate made at the same time when the remainder begins, [2] that the particular estate should continue when the remainder vests, and [3] that the remainder should be out of the donor at the time of the livery. And if any of the said three things is lacking, the remainder is void . . . The cases prove that in our case the remainder did not pass out of the lessor at the time of the livery, inasmuch as the condition precedes the remainder; and also that the remainder commences upon a condition; and also that the remainder is appointed to commence after the commencement of the particular estate, which is contrary to the first principles (*groundes*) of the law: therefore, for this and the other reasons, the remainder shall be void. So, for

---

12   I.e. the death of William in the lifetime of Henry and Eleanor.

the insufficiency of the matter of the bar, and of the form also, the plaintiff shall recover.

Coke Sjt.[13] to the contrary . . . The cause why the remainder shall not be good is alleged in two main points: [1] because the fee does not pass presently out of the lessor, and [2] because the remainder may not pass upon condition. It seems to me that the remainder does pass out of the lessor presently, as in the case in Littleton: if someone makes a lease for five years, upon condition that if he pays him £20 within the first two years he shall have the fee, the fee passes out of the lessor presently.[14] Likewise where a lease is made for life, remainder to the right heirs of John Style, who is living, the remainder is out of the lessor presently even though it cannot vest at once. So shall it be here. And, sir, a remainder may well commence upon condition. For instance, if a lease is made for life upon condition that if John Style marries my daughter during the life estate it shall remain to him: this is a good remainder, and yet it commences upon condition, for there is here an estate upon which the remainder may be based. And just as I could have given it to him immediately, so may I give it to him by a mean distance of time, and upon condition: for whatever I may give without condition I may give upon condition . . .[15]

HALES J. thought that for the insufficiency of pleading only the plaintiff ought to recover . . . As to the matter in law, it seems to me that the remainder is good. For God has committed all earthly things to the ordering and disposition of men, so that when someone lawfully has any such things he may order, convey or give them away where, when and how he will, according to his intention, so long as his intention is not contrary to law, contrary to reason, or repugnant. And here when the lessor appoints the remainder to the defendant (as above), his intention may be thereby perceived; and reason wills that his intention should be performed: namely, that the defendant should have it in the manner and form which he has appointed. This limitation of the remainder is not against the law, nor against any principle thereof, as I will prove later, and it is not repugnant in itself: ergo, the remainder is good . . . If a feoffment were made upon condition that the feoffee and his heirs should not take any profits from the land, that condition would be void and the feoffment simple.

---

13 I.e. William Coke.
14 Littleton *Tenures*, s. 350, where it is said to be a fee simple conditional: but livery of seisin must be made to the lessee at the time of the lease. (Co. Litt. 216b–218a marshals authorities for and against this proposition.)
15 Arguments by Morgan, Brooke, Saunders and Harris Sjts. are here omitted.

Likewise here, if there had been any such contrariety or repugnancy, I would confess that the remainder was void. But there is nothing of the kind here; and, since the lessor's intention appears to be that the defendant shall have the remainder, reason wills that he should have it. And neither his intention nor the limitation is against the law or repugnant, and therefore the remainder is good. However, on account of the defect alleged above in the pleading, the plaintiff ought to recover.

HYNDE J. It seems to me that the plaintiff shall be barred. . . The remainder is good. As to what has been said to the contrary—namely, that the remainder here was to commence upon condition—sir, that is not so, for the remainder here is limited to the defendant if William should die while the husband and wife were living, and that is not a condition but a limitation when the remainder shall commence. For no words amount to a condition unless they restrain the thing given—such as a condition that he shall not perform a certain act, and the like— but these words here limit the time when the remainder shall commence, and do not restrain the gift, and therefore cannot be called a condition but only a limitation . . . And I do not see any cause or reason why I may not make a remainder commence and vest in the midst of a particular estate, just as I may at the beginning or end of the particular estate; for there is no repugnancy even though it shall begin to vest at any time during the particular estate, for when the fee simple is in me I may condition with it as I please, so long as it is not against the law . . .

At another day, BROWNE J. argued to the same purpose . . . that the remainder was good upon condition; and if it was not good upon condition, he said it would be good for the defendant as a grant of the reversion, and so the plaintiff should be barred.

MOUNTAGUE C.J. to the same purpose . . . The remainder seems good. First, it seems to me that it is not here a condition upon which the remainder depends but a limitation, and an appointment of the time when the remainder should vest; and I am of my brother Hinde's opinion on this point. Assume, however, that it is a condition, or call it a limitation, or give it whatever other term you please, and still it seems to me that the remainder is good. For everyone who is the lawful owner of land may give it to whatever person, in whatever manner and at whatever time he pleases, so long as his gift is not contrary to law or repugnant . . . When I was at the bar, I was of counsel with Mr. Melton in the following case: a fine was levied *sur grant et render*, whereby the conusee granted and rendered the tenements to the conusor in tail upon condition that the conusor and his heirs of his body should bear the conusee's standard when he went into battle, and if the conusor or his heirs failed in doing this the land was to remain to a stranger. And I moved the case to the court then, and it was greatly wondered that the fine had been received upon condition. But Mr. [Justice] Fitzherbert then held the remainder good, and they did not wonder at it or hold it any great question but that it might commence upon condition.[16] Likewise a remainder may be to marry my daughter, or upon any other lawful condition. But if the condition is to kill someone, or such like, or is an impossible condition, the remainder shall not be good ... Likewise if a gift is made in tail upon condition that if the donee alienates it shall remain to someone else, this is repugnant; for when he has alienated to a stranger, then it is contrary to the alienation for it to remain over. With respect to remainders, however, we have a learning in our law: that the remainder must have a precedent estate. Therefore if a lease for life is made to a monk, remainder in fee, this remainder shall be void because the monk had no capacity to take the estate for life, and therefore the estate preceding the remainder is void, and by consequence the remainder is void.[17] We also have another learning concerning remainders: that even if there is a precedent estate the remainder shall be void if the thing was not previously in existence. For instance, if I grant a rent out of my land, remainder in fee, this remainder is void because the rent was not in existence before. As to the argument that the remainder did not pass out of the lessor presently by the livery: sir, I deny that utterly; for it passed out of the lessor even though it did not vest in the defendant until William's death, and it was in abeyance until the performance of the condition, on account of the possibility that it might be performed. Similarly, if I give land to a man who has a wife, and to another woman who has a husband, and to the heirs of their two bodies, a fee tail passes out of the donor presently because of the possibility that they may afterwards marry each other—for if the man donee's wife and the woman donee's husband die, the donees may well marry each other—and in the mean time the inheritance, namely the entail, shall be in abeyance. Likewise here, the remainder passed presently out of the lessor, upon a possibility to be performed afterwards, and was in abeyance until William's death.

---

16 Reported in Y.B. Mich. 27 Hen. VIII, fo. 24, pl. 2: '... *Mountague*. Is this a good remainder? FITZHERBERT. I have never until now seen a fine levied with a condition; but it is clear that if a fine is taken with a condition it is good ... And it seems that the remainder is good, and is in the remainderman before the condition is broken, and that he takes it at the time of the livery ...'

17 See *Faryngton v Darell* (1431), at p. 73, above, per Godered.

And so I do not see any reason why the remainder should not be good ... and therefore the plaintiff shall be barred.

The record shows that the plea was held sufficient, and judgment entered for the defendant in Easter term 1551.

BALDWYN v SMYTH (1595)[18]

Record: CP 40/1533, m. 1676d; 1 Co. Rep. 63. William Baldwyn brought replevin against John Smyth for taking 28 sheep in a meadow at Bocking, Essex, on 9 January 1594. The defendant avowed the taking as bailiff of John Kent, for damage feasant in his freehold. The plaintiff pleaded that John Archer was seised of the place in question, and on 8 January 1594 licensed the plaintiff to put in his beasts to pasture. The defendant replied that it was Kent's freehold, and issue was joined on this. In Easter term 1595 the jury at bar found a special verdict: Francis Archer was seised, and had issue Robert Archer, who had issue John Archer (his right heir apparent); in 1578 Francis devised the land by will to Robert for life, remainder 'to the right and next heir of the same Robert Archer and to the heirs of his body lawfully begotten for ever'; Robert entered, and in 1584 enfeoffed John Kent, the father of the aforesaid John Kent, in fee simple; then, during Robert's lifetime, John Archer entered, and John Kent re-entered; in 1585 John Kent the elder devised the land by will to his son John, who entered; then Robert Archer died, and John Archer entered upon John Kent the younger, and on 8 January 1594 gave the licence to the plaintiff to put in his beasts, which he did on 9 January. If the court considered the freehold to belong to John Kent, the jury found for the defendant with 12d. damages and 2d. costs; otherwise they found for the plaintiff with 12d. damages and 2d. costs. The question was argued in banc in Michaelmas term 1595.

1 Co. Rep. 66.[19]

... It was agreed by ANDERSON C.J., WALMSLEY J., and the whole court:

(1) That Robert had only an estate for life, because Robert had an express estate for life devised to him, and the remainder is limited to the next heir male in the singular number; and the right heir male of Robert cannot enter for the forfeiture in Robert's lifetime, for he cannot be heir as long as Robert lives.

(2) That the remainder to the right heir male of Robert is good, even though he cannot have a right heir during his lifetime, but it is

---

18 Also known as *Archer's Case*.
19 Also reported in Cro. Eliz. 453; 2 And. 37. Coke's report is wrongly dated Mich. 1597, the date when he entered the case in his notebook: BL MS. Harley 6686, fo. 236v.

sufficient that the remainder vests in the instant that the particular estate determines . . .

(3) This was the principal point of the case. It was agreed by the whole court[20] that by the feoffment of the tenant for life the remainder was destroyed; for every contingent remainder ought to vest either during the particular estate or at least in the instant that it determines: for if the particular estate is ended or determined (in fact or in law) before the contingency occurs, the remainder is void. And in this case, since by Robert's feoffment his estate for life was determined, by a condition in law annexed to it, and cannot be revived afterwards by any possibility, for this reason the contingent remainder is destroyed . . . And it was said it was agreed by Popham C.J. and various justices in the argument of the case between *Dillon* and *Freine*,[1] and denied by none . . .

The record shows that judgment was entered in Trinity term 1596 for the defendant to have return irreplevisable, and to recover 12d. damages and £19 costs.

PUREFOY d. BROUGHTON v ROGERS (1671)

Record: KB 27/1927, m. 428. George Purefoy brought ejectment against Dr. George Rogers and five other defendants in respect of six messuages in the parish of St Olave, Hart Street, London, which had been leased to him by Sampson-Shelton Broughton. The defendant pleaded Not guilty, and on 7 June 1671 at the Guildhall, London, before Hale C.J., the jury found a special verdict: Sampson Shelton was seised of the tenements, and in 1648 died without issue, leaving them by will to his wife Isabel for life, 'and if it shall please God to bless her with a son, if she cause it to be called by my Christian name and surname, namely Sampson Shelton, then I give my inheritances of my lands and houses unto him after his mother's life; and if he die before he come to the age of twenty and one years, then I give my inheritances of lands after my wife's life to my heirs for ever'; his widow Isabel on 1 October 1649 married Richard Broughton; and on 21 October 1649 John Shelton, as brother and heir to Sampson, sold the tenements in fee for £250 to Richard and Isabel Broughton, and conveyed them by fine the following term; then, on 8 January 1650, Isabel had a son (by Richard) whom she caused to be christened Sampson-Shelton; and in 1657 Richard and Isabel sold the tenements to William Weston, and conveyed them by fine. The defendants derived their title from Weston.[2] Sampson-Shelton

---

20 Cf. 2 And.: '. . . Some would have it that the feoffment alone will defeat this kind of limitation in remainder; and several judges were of that opinion, but not all . . .'

1 (1594); see p. 150, below.

2 By purchase from Weston's sister and heir, Elizabeth Feilding.

Broughton entered after the death of Isabel and Richard, and in 1670 made the lease to Purefoy, who was ejected by the defendants. The jury awarded 12d. damages in case the court held the defendants to be guilty.

1 Wms Saund. 380 (untr.).[3]

. . . And on this special verdict two points were moved: (1) whether the conveyance, namely the bargain and sale and fine of the said John Shelton, the heir of the devisor, to Broughton and his wife in fee, before the birth of the said Sampson-Shelton Broughton (the lessor of the plaintiff), had so destroyed the contingency that the estate should never vest in the said Sampson-Shelton Broughton (the plaintiff's lessor); (2), admitting that the contingency was not destroyed, then whether the will of the devisor was well observed in baptising the lessor of the plaintiff by the Christian name of Sampson-Shelton, so that the estate should vest in him according to the will, or not.

And *Saunders*, for the plaintiff, argued as to the first point that by the conveyance of John Shelton to Broughton and his wife, before the birth of the lessor of the plaintiff, the contingent remainder was not destroyed. And first he submitted that John Shelton (the heir of the devisor) had no reversion or estate in him, but it was in abeyance, because by the will an estate for life was given to the wife, and the remainder in fee to her son on the said contingency; but if such son should die within the age of 21 years, then the tenements were devised to the right heirs of the devisor, so that there was a fee simple devised on a contingency: wherefore, before it could be known whether the contingency would happen or not, the reversion was in abeyance and not in the heir, and then his conveyance did not give any estate to Broughton and his wife, but they were only tenants for life of the wife as they were before.

But HALE C.J. interrupted him, and said it was clear that the reversion was in the heir of the devisor by descent, and was not in abeyance.

Wherefore *Saunders* passed over and said that, notwithstanding this, he conceived that the contingent remainder was not destroyed. And he took it for a ground that where a remainder *in esse* is not devested or turned to a right, there a contingent remainder will not be destroyed; but in this case, if the contingent remainder had been *in esse*, it would not have been devested by the acceptance of the reversion by Broughton and his wife, being tenant for life, from John Shelton, although it was by fine . . . But he said that in

---

3 Also reported in 3 Keb. 11; 2 Lev. 39; 1 Eq. Cas. Abr. 189.

all cases where the particular estate is determined by alienation, there the contingent remainder is destroyed, as appears in ... *Archer's Case*.[4] But here the particular estate was not aliened, but only the reversion granted to it: which, as he conceived, did not prevent the arising of the contingent remainder ...[5] And so he prayed judgment for the plaintiff.

HALE C. J. said to *Saunders* that he had taken his foundation too large; for he said that in all cases where the particular estate is merged in the reversion, there the contingent remainder is gone, though there is no devesting of any estate. And therefore he said that if there be tenant for life, remainder in tail in contingency, remainder over in tail *in esse*, if tenant for life and he in remainder in tail *in esse* levy a fine of their estates, this is no discontinuance or devesting of any estate, because each of them gives such estate as he has—according to the rule in *Bredon's Case*[6]—and yet the mesne contingent remainder is thereby destroyed.

Holt junior, of Gray's Inn, argued for the defendants that here the contingent [remainder] is destroyed by the conveyance of the reversion to the particular estate before the contingency happened ...

HALE C.J. By the bargain and sale and fine of John Shelton to Broughton and his wife, the estate for life in the wife was merged for the time—although the wife after coverture might waive the estate granted by the bargain and sale and fine, and claim her first estate for life—but, the particular estate being once merged, the contingent remainder is wholly destroyed, though the particular estate should be revived again. For he said that if the contingent remainder cannot take effect immediately on the first determination of the particular estate, whether it be determined by merger or surrender or in any other way whatsoever, it will never vest afterwards, though the particular estate should come *in esse* again. Wherefore he said that here the contingent remainder was destroyed, and the plaintiff has no title ...

TWISDEN J. doubted whether the devisor intended that the son which his wife should have by the devisor himself should have the tenements devised.

But the chief justice answered that it was clear that the son of his wife by any other husband should have the tenements, because he

4 (1595); see p. 84, above.
5 The second point—whether the plaintiff's lessor was within the terms of the will by being christened Sampson-Shelton, though he had the surname Broughton— is here omitted, being solely a question of construction.
6 (1597) 1 Co. Rep. 76.

has enjoined such son to be called by his surname, which had been superfluous if he had meant only a son of his own body ... But on the first point of the case, that the contingent remainder was destroyed by the conveyance of the inheritance to Broughton and his wife (being the tenant for life), whereby the particular estate for life was merged before the birth of the son, the court gave judgment for the defendant *nisi* etc.

Winnington, for the plaintiff, said that he would not speak to the case unless the estate limited to the son would enure by way of executory devise.

To which the chief justice answered, that clearly it was not an executory devise; for where a contingency is limited to depend on an estate of freehold which is capable of supporting a remainder, it shall never be construed to be an executory devise, but a contingent remainder only, and not otherwise.[7]

Wherefore the defendants had their judgment, for it was not moved afterwards.

The judgment shows that judgment was entered for the defendants in Easter term 1672, with £15 costs.

SMITH d. DORMER v PARKHURST (1740)

In 1662 John Dormer made the following settlement upon the marriage of his eldest son: to John, the eldest son, in tail male, remainder to the use of his second son Robert for 99 years, if he should so long live, and after his death or other sooner determination of the term to the use of trustees to preserve the contingent uses from destruction during the lifetime of Robert, and after the end or sooner determination of the term to the use of the first and other sons of Robert (successively) in tail male, remainder to Fleetwood (the third brother), remainder to Peter (the fourth), remainder to Euseby (the fifth), for life, remainder to the trustees to preserve contingent uses, remainder to the first and other sons of each brother (successively) in tail male.

The estate, in Quainton, Buckinghamshire, passed from Sir William Dormer in 1726 to his uncle, Mr. Justice Dormer, who died later the same year. The judge (as tenant for life) levied a fine and suffered a recovery, in which his son Fleetwood (who also died in 1726) was vouched as remainderman in tail. After the judge's death (on 18 September), his daughters went into

---

7   Cf. LI MS. Misc. 500, fo. 596: '... HALE C.J. said it is a remainder, for if the devise is good according to the limitation at common law at the beginning we shall not have recourse to an executory devise. HALE also said that if there was a remainder to such son as should be named William, it would not be good, because it is a possibility upon a possibility; but if it was to his son if he was baptised William it would be good, because it is a condition precedent'.

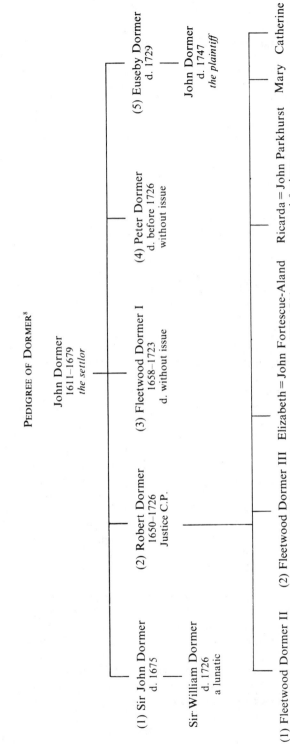

PEDIGREE OF DORMER[8]

John Dormer
1611–1679
the settlor

(2) Robert Dormer
1650–1726
Justice C.P.

(3) Fleetwood Dormer I
1658–1723
d. without issue

(4) Peter Dormer
d. before 1726
without issue

(5) Euseby Dormer
d. 1729

John Dormer
d. 1747
the plaintiff

(1) Sir John Dormer
d. 1675

Sir William Dormer
d. 1726
a lunatic

(1) Fleetwood Dormer II
d. 1695 unmarried

(2) Fleetwood Dormer III
1696–1726
d. without issue

Elizabeth = John Fortescue-Aland
1670–1746
Justice C.P.
co-defendants

Ricarda = John Parkhurst
co-defendants

Mary   Catherine

8   From G. Lipscomb, *History of the County of Buckingham*, vol. I, p. 415; and the reports.

possession as heirs general. The person then next entitled under the 1662 settlement was Euseby, the judge's uncle. Shortly after Euseby's death, his son John brought an ejectment; but this failed for technical reasons. In 1735 he made another entry and brought a new ejectment, which was tried at bar in the King's Bench in 1738. The jury found the facts specially, and the court gave judgment for the plaintiff. The defendants appealed to the House of Lords.

(a) 6 Brown P.C. 351.

... The defendants therefore brought a writ of error in parliament, contending (*Dudley Ryder, John Strange*) that the estate—being limited to the trustees after the death of Mr. Justice Dormer, during his life—was a void limitation, because it could never take effect in possession; and that it could not be made good by rejecting the words 'after his death', because the sense would not be complete without them ... That if the limitation to the trustees should not be void, but the words 'after the death of Robert Dormer' might be rejected, and the limitation to the trustees take effect in the disjunctive (viz. 'or other sooner determination of the term'), yet it was conceived that the trustees by force of those words took no vested remainder, but their estate remained in contingency; for no remainder can be said to be vested unless it be so limited as to come into the possession of the remainderman upon every determination which may happen of the particular estate; but the words 'other sooner determination of the term' cannot extend to a determination of the term by effluxion of time, because the estate 'after the end of the term' (which in a legal sense always signifies the end by effluxion of time) is by express words limited to the first son of Robert Dormer: so that the words 'other sooner determination' can extend only to a determination of the term by surrender or forfeiture, which might or might not happen. It was admitted that when a remainder is limited to take effect in possession upon an event which of necessity must happen, such remainder will vest; but if it be limited to take effect in possession upon an event which may never happen, then it does not vest. Now, it was not an event which must necessarily happen that Mr. Justice Dormer's term should end by surrender or forfeiture, because it might determine by effluxion of time or death. So that the present case was no more than this: viz., a limitation to Mr. Justice Dormer for 99 years, if he so long live, and if his estate shall determine by surrender or forfeiture ...˙ then to the trustees during his life, and which was plainly no more than a contingent remainder; the consequence of which must be, that on the death of Sir William Dormer the freehold vested in Fleetwood, the son of Mr. Justice Dormer, and consequently was well conveyed by the fine to the tenants to the *praecipe*, and the recovery was well suffered. That this construction of the limitation to the trustees was most agreeable to, and best answered the intention of the parties to the settlement: the end and design of appointing trustees to preserve contingent remainders (in this and all other marriage settlements) being only to give them a right to enter upon any conveyance made by the particular tenant for life or years to destroy the contingent remainders *before they arise*; but not to prevent the particular tenant and his son, who has a vested remainder in tail, from suffering a common recovery...

On the other side it was argued (*Francis Chute, Thomas Bootle*) that the title of the lessor of the plaintiff to the premises in question was clearly found: it appearing by the special verdict that the several intermediate remaindermen between him and John Dormer, who made the settlement, were all dead without issue. That the estate limited to the trustees to preserve the contingent remainders was a vested remainder, to take effect in possession during the life of Robert Dormer upon the determination of the particular estate limited to him for 99 years...

After hearing counsel on this writ of error, it was proposed to ask the judges their opinions on the two following questions, viz. (1) Whether the remainder limited to the first son of Euseby Dormer was good in its original creation, or not? (2) If good, whether it was well barred by the fine levied by Mr. Justice Dormer and his son Fleetwood Dormer, and the recovery suffered by the said Fleetwood Dormer?

The judges having taken time to consider, the lord chief justice of the Court of Common Pleas acquainted the House 'that the judges had considered the said questions, and though they all agreed in opinion, yet as this cause was elaborately spoken to by the counsel at the bar it was apprehended their lordships might expect the judges should give their reasons as well as their opinions'. And accordingly the lord chief justice delivered the reasons of the judges at large...

(b) Atk. 138.

[WILLES C.J.C.P.]... Whether the estate to the trustees was a vested or contingent estate appeared to us the great difficulty in the case. The doctrine of contingent remainders is very nice and intricate, and if we were to cite all the cases in the books I fear we should rather puzzle than explain the difficulty. The definition of a contingent remainder laid down by counsel for the plaintiff, that a remainder was contingent when it was uncertain whether it would take effect or not, is by no means the legal notion of a contingent remainder. If an estate is limited to A. for life, remainder to B. and the heirs of his body, everyone will allow that this is a vested remainder: and yet it must be allowed that it is uncertain whether B. may not die without heirs of his body before the death of A., and consequently the remainder may never take effect in possession. We have considered this point a good deal, and are of opinion that all contingent remainders may be reduced to these two heads: First, where a remainder is limited to a person not in being and who may possibly never exist. And secondly, where a remainder depends upon a contingency collateral to the continuance of the particular estate. I will give an example of each. If an estate is limited to A. for life, the remainder to his first son (before he has any child), this is a contingent remainder of the first kind, for it is uncertain whether he will have any son. If an estate is limited to A. for life, and after the death of J.S. to B. in fee ... this is a contingent remainder of the second kind, for it is uncertain what time J.S. shall die ... For as the law, for many good reasons, will not permit the freehold to be in abeyance, it expects the contingent remainder to take place when the particular estate determines; and it cannot immediately vest in those cases when it is uncertain whether the contingency will happen.

The present case comes under neither of these heads: the trustees are in being and capable of taking; the estate does not depend upon any contingency collateral to the continuance of the particular estate. We, therefore, are of opinion that (subject to the term of 99 years) a good estate vested in the trustees during the life of Robert Dormer ...

If the estate limited here to the trustees is contingent, so are the limitations to trustees in all settlements, and consequently all the settlements for these 200 years (ever since the Statute of Uses) may be questioned. But can we conceive, my lords, that everyone has been mistaken for these 200 years, and that this new light is just now arisen to us? Surely it is a much less evil to make a construction, even contrary to the common rules of law (though I think this is not so), than to overthrow (I may say) a hundred thousand settlements: for it is a maxim in law, as well as reason, *communis error facit jus* ...

Upon the whole we are of opinion that the fine and recovery were no bar to the remainders.

The House of Lords accordingly ordered that the judgment be affirmed, and the record remitted, and that the plaintiffs in error should pay £10 costs: 6

Brown P.C. 356. John Dormer also sued successfully in Chancery for an account of the rents and profits from 1729 (when Euseby died): *Dormer v Mr. Justice Fortescue* (1742–44) 2 Atk. 282, 3 Atk. 124, Ridg. *temp.* Hard. 176.

4 Uses, wills and trusts

DE ST EDMUNDS v ANON. (1371)

Y.B. Trin. 45 Edw. III, fo. 22, pl. 25.

T. de St Edmunds, knight, brought a writ of wardship against one J. and claimed the wardship of the body and the lands of John son and heir of L. de W.; and he claimed the manor of C. which was held of him for homage. And J. put forward to the court a deed by which that same L. in his lifetime had enfeoffed himself and others of that manor in fee simple; and he asked judgment whether the action lay.

Cavendish said that he did not admit the deed; but he said that the livery was made upon condition that [J. and the others] would enfeoff the infant when he came of age, and so by collusion to oust us from our wardship etc.

Belknap said that [T.] should not be received to this averment contrary to the deed which was in fee simple. But the opinion of the court was that he would be received, because if the case were so the infant when he came of age could enter.

Belknap was willing to take issue that the feoffment was not made upon condition as [T.] had alleged, ready.

And the others said the opposite, that it was by collusion.

Belknap then asked in accordance with the statute[1] for process against the witnesses to the deed; and he had it.

MESSYNDEN v PIERSON (*c.* 1420)

Bill in Chancery: C1/5/11; printed in Selden Soc. vol. 10, p. 114 (in French).

To the most reverend and most gracious father in God, the bishop of Durham,[2] chancellor of England:

---

1 Statute of Marlborough, 52 Hen. III, c. 6; see p. 9, above.
2 Thomas Langley, lord chancellor 1417–24.

Humbly beseecheth your continual orator, Thomas Messynden the younger, that, whereas Thomas Messynden his father enfeoffed Richard Pierson, parson of Hatcliffe church, John West, parson of Bradley church, John Barneby the younger of Barton, and John See of Little Coates, in certain lands and tenements in the vill of Healing, in the county of Lincoln, to the value of £10 a year, on condition that the said feoffees should enfeoff the said supppliant in the aforesaid lands and tenements when he reached the age of 18 years; and now the said suppliant is aged 18 years and more, and has often requested the said feoffees to enfeoff him in the said lands and tenements according to his father's wish (*volunte*) and condition, and they utterly refuse and say that they will hold the said lands and tenements to their own use: may it please your most gracious lordship to grant certain writs to send for the said feoffees upon certain pains by you to be limited, to answer before you in the Chancery, and to declare why they will not enfeoff the said suppliant according to the aforesaid wish and condition; for God and as a work of charity, considering (most gracious lord) that the said suppliant can have no recovery at common law.

CARDINAL BEAUFORT'S CASE (1453)

31 Hen. VI, Statham Abr., Subpena, pl. [1].[3]

If I enfeoff a man in order to perform my last will, and he enfeoffs someone else, I may not have a *subpoena* against the second feoffee because he is a stranger. But, by the opinion of YELVERTON [J.K.B.] and KYRKBY M.R.,[4] I shall have a *subpoena* against my feoffee and recover damages for the value of the land. And on the same occasion KYRKBY said that if my feoffee in trust enfeoffs someone else of the same land upon trust, and dies, I shall in this case have a *subpoena* against the second feoffee; but it is otherwise where he enfeoffs him in good faith, for there I am remediless. And so it was adjudged in the case of the cardinal of Winchester,[5] in a *subpoena* in the Chancery.

---

3 Inaccurately abridged in Fitz. Abr., *Subpena*, pl. 19.
4 Misprinted in Fitz. Abr. as 'Wylby clerkez des rolles'.
5 Henry Beaufort, bishop of Winchester 1404–47.

ANON. (1464)

Y.B. Pas. 4 Edw. IV, fo. 8, pl. 9.

In a writ of trespass '... [to show] why with force and arms he broke the plaintiff's close and cut the trees and trod down and consumed the grass', *Catesby* [pleaded in bar]: you ought not to have an action, for we say that long before the supposed trespass one J. B. was seised of certain land (and he showed what it was), whereof the place where the trespass is supposed was part, in his [demesne] as of fee; and, being seised of the same in fee, he enfeoffed the plaintiff in fee to the use of the defendant upon trust (*confidence*); and later the defendant, by the plaintiff's sufferance and at his will, occupied the land, and cut the trees on the same land, and spoiled the grass; which is the same trespass for which the plaintiff has conceived this action.

Jenney. That is no plea, for the sufferance of the plaintiff is not a certain fact, nor is the occupation by the defendant at the plaintiff's will. Such sufferance and will cannot be tried, for a man's intention is uncertain; and one must plead facts which are or can be known to the jury if issue is taken upon them. That is not so of this sufferance or will of the plaintiff by which the defendant occupied, and therefore in such a case in order to make a good issue on traversable facts one must plead the plaintiff's lease to the defendant to hold at will, which is traversable and may be tried.

Catesby. Why should he not have these facts, when it follows from reason that the defendant enfeoffed the plaintiff to the defendant's use, and thus that the plaintiff is rightfully in this land only to the defendant's use? The defendant made the feoffment to the plaintiff upon trust and confidence, and the plaintiff suffered the defendant to occupy the land, and so in reason the defendant occupied at his will. This proves that the defendant shall now take advantage of pleading this feoffment in trust to justify the occupation of the land for that cause.

MOYLE. These would be good facts in the Chancery, for there the defendant shall aver the intention and purpose of such a feoffment; for in the Chancery, by conscience, one shall have a remedy according to the intention of such a feoffment. But here, by the course of the common law in the Common Pleas or King's Bench, it is otherwise; for the feoffee shall have the land, and the feoffor shall not plead a justification against his own feoffment— whether it was on trust or otherwise.

Catesby. The law of the Chancery is the common law of the land; and there the defendant shall have advantage of such facts and [shall set out the] feoffment. Why, then, should it not be the same here?

MOYLE. It cannot be, here in this court, as I have told you: for the common law of the land in this case differs from the law of the Chancery on this point.

Catesby moved on; and, as to the trees, he pleaded the feoffment of the land to the plaintiff on trust (as before), and that the defendant occupied by the sufferance and will of the plaintiff. Sir, we have no other facts with respect to that. As to the grass, however, we say that the plaintiff was seised in fee, and leased the land to the defendant to hold at will, as a result of which the defendant entered and did the trespass in the way supposed, and it is for this that his action is brought here.

Jenney. As to the plea with respect to cutting the trees, [no law compels us to answer] the plea pleaded in the manner [and form aforesaid] etc.[6] And as to the spoiling of the grass, the plaintiff traverses the lease; and the other side *contra*.

NOTES (?1465)

Y.B. Mich. 5 Edw. IV.

(a) Fo. 7v, pl. 16.

If J. enfeoffs A. to [J's] use and A. enfeoffs R., even though [A.] sells to [R.], if A. gives notice to R. of the intent of the first feoffment, [R.] is bound by writ of *subpoena* to carry out [J.'s] will. [Again] if a tenant in borough English enfeoffs one to the use of himself and his heirs, the youngest son will have the *subpoena* and not the heir general. Again if a man makes a feoffment upon trust [for himself] of land which descended to him through his mother, and dies without issue, the heir on his mother's side will have the *subpoena*. [Again] if the tenant of a special estate tail makes a feoffment to his own use, without declaring his will, and dies, the reversioner will have the *subpoena*. But if there is a tenant in tail with remainder over in fee, and the tenant in tail makes a feoffment in fee to his own use without declaring his will and dies, the remainderman will have the *subpoena*—but query this. [Again] if a husband and wife are seised in right of the wife, and the husband makes a feoffment without declaring his will, the wife will never have the *subpoena*.

(b) Fo. 7v, pl. 18.

There are lord and tenant and the tenant enfeoffs one [to his own

6 This denotes a demurrer.

use] without expressing his will, and commits felony and is convicted: query who will have the *subpoena*, because the lord will not.

(c) Fo. 8, pl. 20.

If a man enfeoffs another [to his own use] without specifying his intention, and he later makes his will, the last will shall be observed. But if the feoffment is made with some certain intention, that shall be observed without any variation: unless the intention was that [the land] should be [held] to the use of the feoffor and his heirs, [in which case] he can change and make a new will, because no third party has acquired an interest. It is otherwise if [the feoffment] is made with the intention that [the feoffor] should take an estate tail: then he cannot make any change, because it is not like an estate general [in himself].

ANON. (1467)
Y.B. Trin. 7 Edw. IV, fo. 14, pl. 8.[7]

There was a case in the Chancery, as follows: a man was enfeoffed to the use of a woman, who took a husband, and they sold this land to a stranger for a certain sum of money, and the wife received the money; and the husband and wife asked the person who was enfeoffed to the wife's use to make an estate of this land to the stranger, and he enfeoffed the stranger; and afterwards the husband died, and the woman brought a *subpoena* against the person who was enfeoffed to her use; and he showed all these facts, and she demurred in judgment. And the case was stated in the Exchequer Chamber before the chancellor and the justices of both benches.

Starkey, for the plaintiff. This plea is not sufficient, for what the wife did was void. If she had been seised of the land, and the husband and wife had made a feoffment, she would have had a *cui in vita* after the husband's death because the feoffment made by the wife during the marriage is void. Likewise here, in conscience, this sale by the husband and wife was entirely the husband's act and not the wife's.

The whole court agreed.

And THE CHANCELLOR[8] said that the wife could not consent during the marriage. If something was done out of dread or coercion, it could not be called consent; and whatever a married

7 Also reported, in the Exchequer Chamber, in Selden Soc. vol. 64, p. 12.
8 Robert Stillington, bishop of Bath and Wells, appointed on 20 June.

woman does may be said to be done for dread of her husband.[9] And they should take no notice of the fact that the wife received the [purchase] money, because she could not have had the benefit of it, but only the husband.

THE CHANCELLOR said to *Starkey*: what are you asking for?

Starkey. We pray that the defendant be committed to prison until he satisfies us for the same land.

THE CHANCELLOR. You could have a *subpoena* against the vendee, who is in possession of the land, and recover the land against him.

YELVERTON [J.K.B.] The *subpoena* lies against him if he was aware of the deceit and wrong done to the wife, but not otherwise.[10]

THE CHANCELLOR. He knew the woman had a husband.

Starkey. We pray that the defendant be committed to prison; and as to the *subpoena* against the other person, we will be advised. . . .

For the judgment in this case, see fn. 12, p. 100, below. The variant Y.B. says it was agreed by Danby C.J., Choke and Yelverton JJ., in the Exchequer Chamber, that the widow should have a *subpoena*.

ANON. (1478)

Y.B. Mich. 18 Edw. IV, fo. 11, pl. 4.

In the Chancery there was a case as follows: a woman made a feoffment on trust when she was single, and then she took a husband, and during the marriage she made her will that her feoffees should make an estate to her husband, unto him and his heirs for ever; and she died; and after her death her husband sued a *subpoena*. The case is, whether or not this will was good.

Tremayle. It seems the will was good, and that the feoffees shall be compelled to make an estate according to the will; for, just as a wife may appoint executors with her husband's agreement, so by her husband's agreement she may make her will that the feoffees should make an estate to the husband: and conscience requires well enough that this be done.

Vavasour. There is a great difference between your case and this case. There are various cases where a wife, with her husband's

---

9 Cf. Exchequer Chamber report: 'ubi non est libertas, ibi non est consensus'.

10 Cf. Exchequer Chamber report: '. . . It was also said by them that if I enfeoff a man to my use, and then he enfeoffs someone else in return for a certain sum [of money], if this stranger knows that he was enfeoffed to my use, I shall clearly (*bien*) have a *subpoena* against the stranger'.

agreement, may appoint executors. For instance, if a bond is made to the wife when she is single, she may appoint executors during the marriage by her husband's agreement, and in this case the executors shall have the action of debt on the bond, because the husband may in no way have an action on it after the wife's death, for his interest is determined by the death. She may also make a testament, with her husband's agreement, for her clothing—which in our law is called *paraphernalia*—and this shall be good even though they are the husband's goods. In the present case, however, the law is otherwise; for the law will not allow anything done by her during the marriage to be good. If she makes a feoffment of her land during the marriage, it is void: and this well proves that nothing done by her during the marriage concerning any inheritance is good. For the writ of *cui in vita* says, 'whom in her lifetime she could not gainsay', and this proves well that her act and will is void during the marriage.

Jay to the same effect. If this will were good, a wife's inheritance would not be safe from her husband's alienation during the marriage; for the feoffment made before the marriage was made with the intention that the husband's alienation should be of no effect. Moreover, if the will were to be effective, it would prejudice the heir.

Sulyard conceded this.

THE CHANCELLOR.[11] The will cannot be good, for she may not gain or lose the land during the marriage without her husband; and since she may not do it at common law, and since any act done by her is absolutely void, the law of conscience likewise says that her will shall be void and of no effect.

Tremayle. A fine levied by a husband and wife is good.

Vavasour. The reason is because the wife shall be examined openly in court by the justices, and her purpose is proved by matter of record.

But at this time the opinion of them all, except *Tremayle*, was that the will was void. . . .[12]

11 Thomas Rotherham, bishop of Lincoln.
12 The reporter notes that Vavasour cited the case of 1467 (see p. 98, above), and said that the *subpoena* was maintainable and that the woman in that case had judgment.

STATUTE CONCERNING FEOFFMENTS BY CESTUY QUE USE (1484)

1 Ric. III, c. 1;
Statutes of the Realm, vol. II, p. 477 (untr.).

Because, by secret and unknown feoffments, great uncertainty, trouble, costs and grievous vexations do daily grow among the king's subjects, inasmuch as no one who buys lands, tenements or other hereditaments, nor women who have jointures or dowers in any lands, tenements or other hereditaments, nor men's last wills to be performed, nor leases for term of life or of years, nor annuities granted to any person or persons for their services for term of their lives or otherwise, are in perfect surety nor without great trouble and doubt of the same: for the remedy thereof it is ordained, established and enacted, by the advice of the lords spiritual and temporal and the commons in this present parliament assembled, and by authority of the same, that every estate, feoffment, gift, release, grant, lease and confirmation of lands, tenements, rents, services, or other hereditaments, made or had (or hereafter to be made or had) by any person or persons being of full age, of sound mind, at large and not in duress, to any person or persons, and all recoveries and executions had or made, shall be good and effectual to him to whom it is so made, had or given, and to all others to his use, against the seller, feoffor, donor or grantor thereof, and against the sellers, feoffors, donors or grantors and his and their heirs, claiming the same only as heir or heirs to the same sellers, feoffors, donors or grantors, and every of them, and against all others having or claiming any title or interest in the same only to the use of the same seller, feoffor, donor or grantor, or sellers, donors or grantors and his or their said heirs, at the time of the bargain, sale, covenant, gift or grant made; saving to every person or persons such right, title, action and interest by reason of any gift in tail made thereof, as they ought to have had if this act had not been made.

STATUTE CONCERNING WARDSHIP OF THE HEIR OF CESTUY QUE USE (1490)

4 Hen. VII, c. 17;[13]
Statutes of the Realm, vol. II, p. 540 (untr.).

Where, by a statute made at Marlborough[14] it was ordained that,

---

13 Though cited as of 4 Hen. VII, this chapter was passed at the prorogued session which began on 25 January 1490, in the year 5 Hen. VII.
14 52 Hen. III, c. 6; see p. 8, above.

when tenants made feoffments in fraud to make the lords of the fee to lose their wards, the lords should have writs to recover their wards against such feoffees, as in the said statute (among other things) appears more plainly at large; since the making of which statute many imaginations have been had and yet been used, as well by feoffments, fines and recoveries as otherwise, to put lords from their wards of lands holden of them by knight's service: it is therefore ordained, established and enacted by authority of the said present parliament, that the said statute of Marlborough be observed and kept in all manner of things after the form and effect thereof.

And over that it is ordained and enacted by the said authority that if any person or persons of what estate, degree or condition he or they be of, be or hereafter shall be seised in demesne or in reversion of estate of inheritance, being tenant immediate to the lord of any castles, manors, lands and tenements or other hereditaments holden by knight's service, in his or their demesne as of fee, to the use of any other person or persons and of his heirs only; [and] he to whose use he or they be so seised dieth, his heir being within age, [and] no will by him declared or made in his life touching the premises or any of them: the lord of whom such castles, manors, lands, tenements and hereditaments been holden immediately shall have a writ of right of ward, as well for the body as for the land, as the lord should have had if the same ancestor had been in possession of that estate so being in use at the time of his death, and no such estate to his use [had been] made or had . . .

The statute further provides that if the heir of cestuy que use is of full age he shall pay relief; and that when cestuy que use in ward comes of age he shall have the like action of waste against the lord as if his ancestor had died seised. The act was to take effect in respect of persons dying after Easter 1490.

GREGORY ADGORE'S READING ON USES
(*c.* 1490)

Reading on 1 Ric. III, c. 1, in the Inner Temple:
CUL MS. Hh. 3. 10, fo. 22v; UCO MS. 162, fo. 107;
LI MS. Maynard 3, fo. 197. There is a fourth text in
KU MS. D 127.

. . . If a husband and wife make a feoffment, it shall be presumed to the use of the husband. If an abbot makes a feoffment, it shall be presumed to the use of the feoffee; and the law is the same if the feoffment is with the conventual seal. If several persons make a feoffment, it shall be presumed to the use of them all; but if one of them was the owner,[15] then it shall be to his use according to the facts. If my feoffees make a feoffment over, these second feoffees shall be to my use; but it is otherwise if the feoffment is made by express words to the use of the first feoffees, in which case I am put to my remedy in the Chancery. Matter to prove a use is sometimes in writing: as where the *habendum* says, 'to such and such a use', then is the use sufficiently proved. The law is the same if the *habendum* says, 'for £100 which he has paid': this is sufficient proof. So likewise concerning an estate for life, with remainder over in fee, it seems the use is changed. Sometimes the use shall be changed and proved by words: as where the owner says upon the livery that the feoffees shall be seised to his use and to [the use of] his heirs of his body begotten, or his heirs male, or his heirs female. So it is if he declares upon the livery that they shall find a chaplain to sing for him. If a use is to someone for life, and after his decease to another in fee, it seems that this cannot be changed because of the prejudice to the third person; but where the lease is only to himself, as for finding a chaplain and such like, it seems that he may change it well enough. Moreover, if a man has feoffees and they make a feoffment, and the owner declares (*monstra*) the use, it is now changed and caused to be in the other feoffees. Also, where my feoffees make an estate, and I declare the use and make the estate, the livery is void—as where I enter upon my termor, or upon the king's possession, and make a feoffment—and yet it seems that the use is changed by such an estate. Also, the use may be changed upon matter of fact, that is, matter of substance, but not bare words— unless it is upon the livery, and then it may be, as above. Also, if a man discusses a marriage, and says that his son shall have such land (and says what) after his decease, or at once, the use is changed when the marriage is performed; but not before the marriage occurs, for before then he has an election, and so it is uncertain . . .

THOMAS AUDLEY'S READING ON USES (1526)

Reading on 4 Hen. VII, c. 17, in the Inner Temple:
BL MS. Hargrave 87, fo. 438; CUL MS. Ee. 5. 19, fo. 7.

. . . The words of this statute[16] are, 'If any person etc. be seised in

---

15 In this reading the English word 'owner' is used repeatedly for the cestuy que use.
16 See p. 102, above.

demesne or in reversion of estate of inheritance ... to the use of any other etc. ...': now, since by these words the lords cannot have wardship of their tenants' heirs by reason of this statute except in cases where their tenants had an estate in use at the time of their death, I will show what a use is, how it is made, and on what things a use may depend.

First, a use is a property or ownership of land or something else, real or personal, depending solely on confidence and trust between those who are in actual possession and are accounted owners by the common law of such lands and things whereon the use depends, and those who have a use in the same thing whereon the use depends. By reason of a use, those to whom the use of such lands or things belongs shall take the profits of such lands and things whereon the use depends, through the confidence and sufferance of them in whom the possession exists at common law. And this is directly contrary to the learning of the common law; for if a man makes a feoffment, proviso that the feoffee shall not take the profits, but the feoffor, this proviso is void: for the common law adjudges the feoffee to be the true owner. Therefore it is agreed in 7 Edw. IV[17] that the feoffee in trust shall have an action of trespass against cestuy que use, and there is no remedy to defend the plea by the common law.

Next, although these uses were at first contrived for a good purpose, namely for power to make wills of land[18] in this realm, whereas inheritances in old times were ruled and governed by the common law (which for the most part consists of ordinary and certain rules): nevertheless to a great extent they have been pursued by collusion for the evil purpose of destroying the good laws of the realm, which now by reason of these trusts and confidences is turned into a law called 'conscience', which is always uncertain and depends for the greater part on the whim (*arbitrement*) of the judge in conscience. And by reason of this no man can know his title to any land with certainty; for now land passes by words and bare proofs in the Chancery, whereas by the common law it could only pass by solemn livery on the land or something equivalent, or by matter of record or in writing. Also, the trial of title to land in this realm was never by proofs but by verdict, whereas now it is contrary.

17 Probably a slip for 4 Edw. IV; see p. 96, above.
18 The text is obscure in both MSS., and appears to read: 's. pur powar de terre en cest royalme ... s. darrein soll' bon'. The word 'soll'' has been read as 'vol[unte]', since a later passage says the original purpose of uses was 'pur faire darreyn voluntes bon de terre'.

By reason of uses and confidences men who had rights of action were defrauded of their lands, until provision was made by various statutes . . . By reason of these uses, lords were defrauded of lands alienated in mortmain, until the statute of 15 Ric. II.[19] And by reason of uses lords lost their heriots, wards and reliefs until this statute and the statute of 19 Hen. VII.[20] At the present day by reason of uses a man shall not be tenant by the curtesy, and the lord shall not have his escheat, and a widow shall not be endowed; nor can any land be made secure. Thus, so great have been (and still are) the mischiefs by reason of these uses that it follows that these uses were contrived to a great extent to defraud the good laws of this land. I think the main reason why uses were contrived [was] to make good last wills of land, because land was not devisable by the common law. Therefore at the beginning of the common law there were no uses, but only confidence between person and person, which was there from the beginning. However, no notice was taken of uses, for cestuy que use could not have an action, and an action did not lie against him, until various statutes were made for that purpose. . . And by the statute of 1 Ric. III[1] it is provided that every feoffment, gift, and so on, made by cestuy que use, should be good: and by this statute . . . a possession passes by reason of a use.

Again, these uses may depend on every kind of possession purely real, such as land, rent, common, and the like; and on a chattel real such as a wardship and a lease for years; and on a chattel purely personal, such as plate, a horse, and other goods. But a man may not give his goods to uses in order to defraud creditors, which is void by the statute of 3 Hen. VII.[2]

Audley concludes this part of the reading by explaining the methods of creating uses. There are, he says, two ways: (1) upon an alteration of possession, such as a recovery, fine, feoffment or release; (2) by bargain, covenant, gift or will. There is then a detailed exposition of the law relating to wills, and Audley argues that if a will is void it is 'no will by him declared' for the purpose of the statute of 1490.

RE LORD DACRE OF THE SOUTH (1535)

Record summarised in J.M.W. Bean, *The Decline of English Feudalism* (1968), pp. 275–283. Thomas Fiennes, Lord Dacre of the South, died on 9 September 1533. Most of his lands were vested in feoffees to uses, and by his

---

19 15 Ric. II, c. 5.
20 19 Hen. VII, c. 15.
 1 See p. 101, above.
 2 3 Hen. VII, c. 4.

last will he left several manors to his younger sons in tail male and the bulk of his lands to be retained by the feoffees until the heir came of age and then conveyed to the heir. Inquisitions *post mortem* were held in Kent and Sussex, and the jurors found that the will had been made by fraud and collusion between Lord Dacre and his counsel to defraud the king of the wardship of the body and lands of the heir. The Kent inquisition was traversed in Chancery by the feoffees in February 1535, and the case was argued in the presence of the judges in Easter term following.

(a) Y.B. Pas. 27 Hen. VIII, fo. 7, pl. 22;
LC MS. Acc. LL 52960, 27 Hen. VIII, fo. 21.

In the Chancery, before the chancellor[3] and all the justices of England, *Oneley* apprentice recited that it was found by virtue of an office before the escheator of Kent that certain persons were seised to the use of the Lord Dacre and his heirs, and while they were seised the said lord (by covin and collusion with Polsted[4] and others, with the intention of defrauding our lord the king of the wardship and marriage of his son) declared his will—the terms of which were found by the jury and entered verbatim—which provided inter alia that the feoffees should pay a woman, [one of his kinswomen, £5][5] for her marriage, and another woman £100; and he recited in his will that his goods were not sufficient to pay his debts and funeral expenses, and so he willed his feoffees to take the profits for that purpose in tail, with remainder in tail, remainder in fee; and he devised the manor of B. to his youngest son in tail. And it was found that the land was held of the king, and that [Lord Dacre's] son and heir was 18 years old; and [the inquisition] was returned. The aforesaid feoffees came into the Chancery and complained that by virtue of this office they had been wrongfully expelled from the possession of the same land, and (while denying by protestation that [the testator] made his will by covin and collusion) said that they demurred in law. It seems to me that this office is not sufficient. First, I do not think any will can be declared by collusion; for the law presumes when a man is on the point of death that he will not commit any deceit or covin against another. His will is made under such necessity, because he has no time [left to carry out his wishes himself]; and the law construes every will favourably and according to the testator's intention: . . . as, for the payment of his debts and marriage of his daughters, which the

3   Sir Thomas Audley.
4   Thomas Polsted (d. 1533), of the Inner Temple, who practised as an attorney in Surrey and Sussex and was also counsel to the earl of Arundel and the borough of Guildford.
5   MS. Reads 'for her costs' in print, misreading 'cosin' as 'costes'.

testator cannot do when he is dead. Therefore, because of the necessity of it, it cannot be thought to have been done by collusion. If, then, a will cannot be made by collusion, this finding by the jurors is irrelevant; for, notwithstanding that the jurors find a thing which in law cannot be, that shall be determined by the judges, and their finding is void ... Then again, the statute of 4 Hen. VII[6] provides that lords should have the wardship of the heir of cestuy que use where no will is declared; and this implies in itself (*en luy*)[7] that if cestuy que use declares any will the heir shall not be in ward ... Likewise here.

Whorwood to the contrary ...[8]

Yorke to the contrary. It seems to me that uses were at common law; for a use is nothing other than a trust which the feoffor puts in the feoffees upon the feoffment. If we were to say that there were no uses at common law, it would follow that there was no trust at common law; and that cannot be, for a trust or confidence is something very necessary between man and man, and at least no law prohibits or restrains a man from putting his confidence in another. That there were uses at common law is proved by statutes ... and moreover it has been held for many years that uses were at common law, by the common opinion of the whole realm. So it seems to me that it should no longer be disputed, for it cannot be said that all the statutes of uses hitherto made are utterly void ...[9]

Pollard apprentice to the contrary. First, with respect to the point that a will cannot be declared by collusion because of the presumption which was mentioned: it would be an amazing presumption, for the law to presume something plainly against the truth [and] which appears from an office to be otherwise. For it is evident (*appiert*) that the Lord Dacre declared his will by collusion, which is clean contrary to the presumption. Next, it seems that there are no such things as uses (*nest ascun use*). For if there should be any use it must necessarily have some foundation, either by common law or by statute. And it seems that there were no uses at common law, for it would be inconsistent for me to enfeoff you with my land (and thus part with it) and nevertheless to have it, contrary to my feoffment and gift. There is no mention of any uses in our old year books (*auncient ans et livres*), and if there had been

6 See p. 101, above.
7 Misprinted as 'en un lieu'.
8 His argument is substantially repeated by Richard Pollard, below.
9 He then argues that uses are testamentary, since they may pass by word and therefore do not have to be conveyed in the same way as land; and that the statute of 1490 does not apply, because Lord Dacre had declared a will.

uses at common law it would have been mentioned in our old law books. Also, it seems to me that if a man made a feoffment in fee before the statute *Quia emptores terrarum*,[10] the law created a tenure between the feoffor and the feoffee, and that tenure was a consideration whereby the feoffee was seised to his own use; and therefore before that statute there were no uses, because of the aforesaid consideration. And if uses did not exist before that statute, it follows that uses had their beginning after the statute was passed, and so the use was not created by the law. For I think nothing can be maintained to be law except such things as have continued since time immemorial: that is, before the time of King Richard I . . . Therefore, since these uses had their beginning after that statute, they are not at common law. Neither are they by statute, for no statute has been passed by which uses are made. Thus there are no such things as uses. But admit that there are: it [nevertheless] seems that they are not testamentary. For the use shall follow the nature of the land, and is like a rent issuing out of the land; and a rent shall be of the same nature as the land. For a use of land in gavelkind shall be partible in the same way as the land (that is, as between daughters in respect of land at common law); and in borough English the use shall descend to the youngest son:[11] and this proves that a use shall follow the nature of the land from which it issues. It follows that it may not be devised, and therefore descends to the heir of the Lord Dacre, and therefore the king shall have the wardship. [It has been argued that the king shall not have the wardship here because the statute of 1490 says 'no will by him declared', whereas][12] here a will has been declared. But, sir, the aforesaid statute shall be taken and understood to mean, 'where a good and lawful will has been declared', and not a collusive will made to defraud the lord of his right. It appears from the office that this will was made for that purpose and therefore in law it is no will for the purpose of ousting the king from his wardship.[13] Moreover, it seems to me that collusion by declaring a will to oust the lord of his wardship shall be remedied by the equity of the Statute of Marlborough . . .

Mountague to the contrary. First, it seems to me that it cannot be said that this will was made by collusion; for the making of a testament is the last act a man performs, and when a man sees that he is on the point of dying it is hardly likely that he would do

---

10   (1290); see p. 9, above.
11   *Note* (1465); see p. 97, above.
12   The text is garbled in MS. and in print.
13   Cf. Audley's argument in 1526; see p. 105, above.

anything which would prejudice or wrong his neighbour,[14] but rather that he wishes to make his testament and last will solely [for necessity, because he cannot][15] do and perform it himself, and for that reason he puts his trust in others and declares his will to be carried out by others ... But even if it is the law that a will may be made by collusion, nevertheless there cannot be said to be collusion in this will. The Lord Dacre willed that his feoffees should be seised to the use of one A., his son, in tail, the remainder over in fee; and that cannot be called collusion, for collusion cannot be averred upon an estate tail, any more than a use can be upon an estate tail. And it was recently adjudged by advice of all the justices that a tenant in tail cannot be seised to another's use.[16] Also, he has given the manor to his youngest son, and declared that certain moneys must be raised for the marriage of one of his kinswomen and for the payment of his debts, which things prove that the will was not made by collusion to defraud the lord of his wardship. Moreover, it seems that uses were at common law. For the common law is nothing but common reason, and common reason wills that a man may put his trust in another; and a use is a trust between the feoffor and the feoffee, which trust is by common reason (as I have said), and common reason is common law: and therefore it follows that uses are by the common law. And to prove that uses were at common law, there is a writ in the register called *causa matrimonii praelocuti*, which lies where a woman enfeoffs a man with a view to marrying him, and later he will not marry her, and she demands the land back: this writ is based entirely on a trust which the woman put in the feoffee, and it clearly proves that a trust (and, by consequence, a use) was at common law. Also, as has been said, it is proved by many statutes that uses were at common law ... And the length of time for which the law has been so held, and continuance thereof, makes it law even if there was no reason to prove it: in the civil law it is said that *communis error facit jus*, and it would be a great mischief to change the law now, for many inheritances in the realm depend today on uses, so that there would be much confusion if this were done. [Moreover],[17] it seems that a use is devisable. For the statute of 1 Ric. III[18] says that all

---

14   MS. Reads 'lord' in print.
15   MS. Reads 'in order that others may do what he cannot' in print.
16   *Anon.* (1532) in Brooke Abr., *Feffements al uses*, pl. 40.
17   'Ouster' in MS., misread in print as '*Oneley*', though it is clearly a continuation of Mountague's argument.
18   See p. 101, above.

feoffments, gifts and grants made or to be made by cestuy que use shall be good, and a devise is in effect like a gift or grant. If a man devises devisable land in tail, and the tenant in tail enters after the devisor's death and enfeoffs a stranger, and dies, his issue shall have formedon and shall count on a 'gift': for a devise is a gift, and even though it is not within the words it is taken to be within the equity of the statute, because it is in equal mischief.

(b) Trin. 1535: Spelman, *Reports*, p. 228, pl. 4.

Remember that the following matter came into question in Chancery before SIR THOMAS AUDLEY, knight (previously a serjeant at law), and THOMAS CROMWELL, the king's secretary. An office was found *virtute officii* before the escheator after the death of the Lord Dacre of the South, and it was thereby found that A. and B. were seised in fee of the manors of F. and G. to the use of the said lord, and that he made his last will in respect of these and all his other lands that his youngest son should have the manor of F. in tail, remainder to Thomas the said lord's kinsman and heir (namely, son of the lord's son William), to have unto him and his heirs male of his body, remainder to someone in tail, remainder in fee to one R.; and that the said Thomas was under age, and that the said manor of F. was held of the crown in chief; and that another son should have the manor of G. in tail, remainder over in the same way; and that, with respect to the rest of his lands, he willed that his executors should take the profits in order to pay his debts and funeral expenses, and to pay for the marriage of various kinswomen of the said lord, and then remainder to Thomas as above; and that the said lord at the time of his death had goods and chattels to the value of 500 marks; and that the will was made by collusion to defraud the said king of the wardship of the said Thomas and of the lands. Thereupon the said feoffees came and demurred in law upon the office. And it was argued for a long time by the apprentices and serjeants, the justices of both benches being present by the said chancellor's command.

Afterwards, in the Exchequer Chamber, by appointment of the aforesaid chancellor and secretary, all the justices and the chief baron were assembled in order to give their opinions privately in this case. (ENGLEFIELD J. was not there, however, because he was on the king's business in Wales.) The points were these:

1   Were there uses upon feoffments at common law, before any statute was made? Many of the justices were of opinion that this word 'use' was in old times called 'trust' or 'confidence', and is now

called 'use' by various statutes of Richard II, Richard III and Henry VII, and incorporated into the law. For cestuy que use may have an action of waste against his guardian, and vouch in formedon, and have aid.

2   Can cestuy que use make a will of his lands? As to this question, the said chancellor, the said secretary, LYSTER C.B., BALDWIN C.J.C.P. and LUKE J.K.B. were of the opinion that such a will was ineffective and void. For no land is devisable by will, except by custom, since it is against the nature of land to pass in such a way. Another argument put forward was that the land was in the feoffee for all purposes, and therefore it would be against reason for cestuy que use (who in effect has nothing) to make a will and thereby give another's land to whom he pleases.

But SPELMAN J.K.B., SHELLEY and FITZHERBERT JJ.C.P., and FITZJAMES C.J.K.B., were of the contrary opinion. For such a will is a declaration of trust: namely, a showing to the feoffee of his intention as to how the feoffee should act. The feoffee is obliged in conscience to perform the trust; but the devisee has no remedy at law to compel the feoffee to perform the will. And by his will the devisor does not give any of the land, but only his use, and so the feoffee's estate is not impaired in any respect: but because the use is changed out of cestuy que use into the person to whom he has given it by his will, the devisee may enter and make a feoffment under the statute of Richard III.[19]

PORT J.K.B. was of the same opinion, but he spoke so softly (*cy base*) that the said chancellor and secretary understood him to be of the other opinion; and therefore they thought the majority of justices were of the same opinion as themselves.

Therefore all the justices were commanded to appear before the king; and the king commanded them to assemble in order to agree in their opinions. And those who were of opinion that the will was void would have the king's best thanks.

Then the justices reassembled before the said chancellor and secretary, and debated this question. And FITZJAMES C.J., FITZHERBERT and SPELMAN JJ., perceiving the opinion of the chancellor, secretary and other justices, who were men of great reason (and also the greater part in number[20]), conformed with their opinion. However, SHELLEY J. was not there because he was ill, and ENGLEFIELD J. was in Wales.

19   1 Ric. III, c. 1; see p. 101, above.
20   In the absence of Shelley J. Spelman does not say whether Port J. attended this meeting.

THE STATUTE OF USES (1536)

27 Hen. VIII, c. 10;
Statutes of the Realm, vol. III, p. 539 (untr.).

Where by the common laws of this realm lands, tenements and hereditaments be not devisable by testament, nor ought to be transferred from one to another but by solemn livery and seisin, matter of record [or] writing sufficient, made bona fide without covin or fraud; yet nevertheless divers and sundry imaginations, subtle inventions and practices have been used whereby the hereditaments of this realm have been conveyed from one to another by fraudulent feoffments, fines, recoveries and other assurances craftily made to secret uses, intents and trusts, and also by wills and testaments sometimes made by nude parols and words, sometimes by signs and tokens, and sometimes by writing, and for the most part made by such persons as be visited with sickness in their extreme agonies and pains, or at such time as they have scantly had any good memory or remembrance, at which times they being provoked by greedy and covetous persons lying in wait about them do many times dispose indiscreetly and unadvisedly their lands and inheritances; by reason whereof, and by occasion of which fraudulent feoffments, fines, recoveries and other like assurances to uses, confidences and trusts, divers and many heirs have been unjustly at sundry times disherited, the lords have lost their wards, marriages, reliefs, heriots, escheats, aids *pur faire fitz chivaler et pur file marier*, and scantly any person can be certainly assured of any lands by them purchased nor know surely against whom they shall use their actions or executions for their rights, titles and duties; and also men married have lost their tenancies by the curtesy, women their dowers, manifest perjuries by trial of such secret wills and uses have been committed; the king's highness hath lost the profits and advantages of the lands of persons attainted, and of the lands craftily put in feoffments to the uses of aliens born, and also the profits of waste for a year and a day of lands of felons attainted, and the lords their escheats thereof; and many other inconveniences have happened and daily do increase among the king's subjects, to their great trouble and inquietness, and to the utter subversion of the ancient common laws of this realm; and for the extirping and extinguishment of all such subtle practised feoffments, fines, recoveries, abuses and errors heretofore used and accustomed in this realm, to the subversion of the good and ancient laws of the same, and to the intent that the king's highness or any other his subjects of this realm shall not in any wise hereafter by any means or inventions be deceived, damaged or hurt by reason of such trusts, uses or confidences: it may please the king's royal majesty that it may be enacted by his highness, by the assent of the lords spiritual and temporal and the commons in this present parliament assembled, and by the authority of the same, in manner and form following, that is to say:

1 That where any person or persons stand or be seised, or at any time hereafter shall happen to be seised, of and in any honours, castles, manors, lands, tenements, rents, services, reversions, remainders or other hereditaments, to the use, confidence or trust of any other person or persons, or of any body politic, by reason of any bargain, sale, feoffment, fine, recovery, covenant, contract, agreement, will, or otherwise, by any manner means whatsoever it be; that in every such case, all and every such person and persons and bodies politic that have or hereafter shall have any such use, confidence or trust in fee simple, fee tail, for term of life or for years, or otherwise, or any use, confidence or trust in remainder or reverter, shall from henceforth stand and be seised, deemed and adjudged in lawful seisin, estate and possession of and in the same honours, castles, manors, lands, tenements, rents, services, reversions, remainders and hereditaments, with their appurtenances, to all intents, constructions, and purposes in the law, of and in such like estates as they had or shall have in use, trust or confidence of or in the same; and that the estate, title, right and possession that was in such person or persons that were, or hereafter shall be, seised of any lands, tenements or hereditaments to the use, confidence or trust of any such person or persons or of any body politic be from henceforth clearly deemed and adjudged to be in him or them that have, or hereafter shall have, such use, confidence or trust, after such quality, manner, form and condition as they had before, in or to the use, confidence or trust that was in them . . .[1]

[Concerning jointures:]

4[2] And be it further enacted by the authority aforesaid, that whereas divers persons have purchased, or have estate made and conveyed of and in divers lands, tenements and hereditaments unto them and to their wives, and to the heirs of the husband, or to the husband and to the wife and to the heirs of their two bodies begotten, or to the heirs of one of their bodies begotten, or to the husband and to the wife for term of their lives or for term of life of

---

1 Section 2 contains a similar provision where several feoffees were seised to the use of any of themselves; and s. 3 enacts that where there was a use for payment of rent, the person entitled to the rent should be deemed to be seised of the rent.
2 Section 6 in *Statutes at Large*.

the said wife; or where any such estate or purchase of any lands, tenements or hereditaments hath been or hereafter shall be made to any husband and to his wife in manner and form expressed, or to any other person or persons and to their heirs and assigns to the use and behoof of the said husband and wife or to the use of the wife as is before rehearsed, for the jointure of the wife: that then in every such case, every woman married having such jointure made or hereafter to be made shall not claim nor have title to have any dower of the residue of the lands, tenements or hereditaments that at any time were her said husband's, by whom she hath any such jointure, nor shall demand nor claim her dower of and against them that have the lands and inheritances of her said husband; but if she have no such jointure, then she shall be admitted and enabled to pursue, have and demand her dower by writ of dower after the due course and order of the common laws of this realm, this act or any law or provision made to the contrary thereof notwithstanding . . .[3]

[Preservation of status quo:]

9[4]　And forasmuch as great ambiguities and doubts may arise of the validity and invalidity of wills heretofore made of any lands, tenements and hereditaments, to the great trouble of the king's subjects, the king's most royal majesty (minding the tranquillity and rest of his loving subjects) of his most excellent and accustomed goodness is pleased and contented that it be enacted by the authority of this present parliament that all manner true and just wills and testaments heretofore made by any person or persons deceased, or that shall decease before the first day of May that shall be in the year of our Lord God 1536, of any lands, tenements or other hereditaments, shall be taken and accepted good and effectual in the law, after such fashion, manner and form as they were commonly taken and used at any time within 40 years next afore the making of this act; anything contained in this act or in the preamble thereof, or any opinion of the common law to the contrary thereof,[5] notwithstanding . . .

3　There follow three provisos: that dower should not be barred if the jointure was lawfully recovered against the widow without collusion; that the act should not extend to widows whose husbands were dead before it was passed; and that a widow could refuse a jointure assured after marriage and demand dower instead.

4　Section II in *Statutes at Large*.

5　This presumably refers to *Lord Dacre's Case*; see p. 105, above. The act recognises that the decision had changed the received opinion, and prevents it from having retrospective effect.

THE STATUTE OF ENROLMENTS (1536)

27 Hen. VIII, c. 16;
Statutes of the Realm, vol. III, p. 549 (untr.).

Be it enacted by the authority of this present parliament that from the last day of July which shall be in the year of our Lord God 1536 no manors, lands, tenements or other hereditaments shall pass, alter or change from one to another whereby any estate of inheritance or freehold shall be made or take effect in any person or persons, or any use thereof to be made by reason only of any bargain and sale thereof, except the same bargain and sale be made by writing indented, sealed, and enrolled in one of the king's courts of record at Westminster; or else within the same county or counties where the same manors, lands or tenements so bargained and sold lie or be, before the *custos rotulorum* and two justices of the peace and the clerk of the peace of the same county or counties, or two of them at the least, whereof the clerk of the peace to be one; and the same enrolment to be had and made within six months next after the date of the same writings indented ... Provided always that [neither] this act, nor anything therein contained, extend to any manner lands, tenements or hereditaments lying or being within any city, borough or town corporate within this realm, wherein the mayors, recorders, chamberlains, bailiffs or other officer or officers have authority or have lawfully used to enrol any evidences, deeds or other writings within their precinct or limits, anything in this act contained to the contrary notwithstanding.

THE STATUTE OF WILLS (1540)

32 Hen. VIII, c. 1;
Statutes of the Realm, vol. III, p. 744 (untr.).

Where the king's most royal majesty in all the time of his most gracious and noble reign hath ever been a merciful, loving, benevolent and most gracious sovereign lord unto all and singular his loving and obedient subjects, and by many times past hath not only shewed and imparted to them generally by his many, often and beneficial pardons heretofore by authority of his parliament granted, but also by divers other ways and means many great and ample grants and benignities, in such wise as all his said subjects been most bounden to the uttermost of all their powers and graces by them received of God to render and give unto his majesty their most humble reverence and obedient thanks and services, with their daily and continual prayer to Almighty God for the continual preservation of his most royal estate in most kingly honour and prosperity; yet always his majesty, being replete and endowed by God with grace, goodness and liberality, most tenderly considering that his said obedient and loving subjects cannot use or exercise themselves according to their estates, degrees, faculties and qualities, or to bear themselves in such wise as that they may conveniently keep and maintain their hospitalities and families, nor the good education and bringing up of their lawful generations, which in this realm (laud be to God) is in all parts very great and abundant, but that in manner of necessity, as by daily experience is manifested and known, they shall not be able of their proper goods, chattels and other movable substances to discharge their debts and after their degrees set forth and advance their children and posterities: wherefore our said sovereign lord, most virtuously considering the mortality that is to every person at God's will and pleasure most common and uncertain, of his most blessed disposition and liberality, being willing to relieve and help his said subjects in their said necessities and debility, is contented and pleased that it be ordained and enacted by authority of this present parliament, in manner and form as hereafter followeth, that is to say:

1   That all and every person and persons having, or which hereafter shall have, any manors, lands, tenements or hereditaments, holden in socage or of the nature of socage tenure, and not having any manors, lands, tenements or hereditaments holden of the king our sovereign lord by knight's service, by socage tenure in chief, or of the nature of socage tenure in chief, nor of any other person or persons by knight's service, from the twentieth day of July in the year of our Lord God 1540 shall have full and free liberty, power and authority to give, dispose and devise, as well by his last will and testament in writing or otherwise by act or acts lawfully executed in his life, all his said manors, lands, tenements or hereditaments, or any of them, at his free will and pleasure; any law, statute or other thing heretofore had, made or used to the contrary notwithstanding.

2   And that all and every person and persons having manors, lands, tenements or hereditaments holden of the king our sovereign lord, his heirs or successors, in socage, or of the nature of socage tenure, in chief, and having other manors, lands, tenements or hereditaments holden of any other person or persons in socage, or of the nature of socage tenure, and not having any manors, lands, tenements or hereditaments holden of the king our sovereign lord by knight's service, nor of any other lord or person by like service, from the twentieth day of July in the said year of our Lord God

1540 shall have full and free liberty, power and authority to give, will, dispose and devise, as well by his last will or testament in writing or otherwise by any act or acts lawfully executed in his life, all his said manors, lands, tenements and hereditaments, or any of them, at his free will and pleasure; any law, statute, custom or other thing heretofore had, made or used to the contrary notwithstanding.

3   Saving always and reserving to the king our sovereign lord, his heirs and successors, all his right, title and interest of primer seisin and reliefs, and also all other rights and duties for tenures in socage, or of the nature of socage tenure, in chief, as heretofore hath been used and accustomed; the same manors, lands, tenements or hereditaments to be taken, had and sued out of and from the hands of his highness, his heirs and successors, by the person or persons to whom any such manors, lands, tenements or hereditaments shall be disposed, willed or devised, in such like manner and form as hath been used by any heir or heirs before the making of this act; and saving and reserving also fines for alienations of such manors, lands, tenements or hereditaments holden of the king our sovereign lord in socage, or of the nature of socage tenure, in chief, whereof there shall be any alteration of freehold or inheritance made by will or otherwise as is aforesaid.

4   And it is further enacted by the authority aforesaid that all and singular person or persons having any manors, lands, tenements or hereditaments of estate of inheritance[6] holden of the king's highness in chief by knight's service, or of the nature of knight's service in chief, from the said twentieth day of July [1540] shall have full power and authority by his last will by writing or otherwise by any act or acts lawfully executed in his life to give, dispose, will or assign two parts of the same manors, lands, tenements or hereditaments in three parts to be divided, or else as much of the said manors, lands, tenements or hereditaments as shall extend or amount to the yearly value of two parts of the same in three parts to be divided, in certainty and by special divisions, as it may be known in severalty, to and for the advancement of his wife, preferment of his children, and payment of his debts, or otherwise, at his will and pleasure; any law, statute, custom or other thing to the contrary thereof notwithstanding.

5   Saving and reserving to the king our sovereign lord the custody, wardship and primer seisin or any of them, as the case shall require, of as much of the same manors, lands, tenements or

---

6   By 34 & 35 Hen. VIII, c. 5, s. 3, this is defined to mean estates in fee simple only, so that an entail could not be barred by will.

hereditaments as shall amount and extend to the full and clear yearly value of the third part thereof, without any diminution, dower, fraud, covin, charge or abridgment of any of the same third part or of the full profits thereof.[7]

6   Saving also and reserving to the king our said sovereign lord all fines for alienations of all such manors, lands, tenements and hereditaments holden of the king by knight's service in chief, whereof there shall be any alteration of freehold or inheritance made by will or otherwise as is abovesaid.

[Sections 7–9 provide that a person holding some land in chief by knight service and other land by knight service may devise two-thirds, with a similar saving to the king. Sections 10–11 provide that a person holding land of mesne lords by knight service, and holding other land in socage, may devise two-thirds of the land held by knight service and all the land held in socage, reserving to the lord the wardship of the land held by knight service. Sections 13–16 deal with procedural matters, and s. 14 with joint tenancies and dower.]

EXPLANATION OF THE STATUTE OF WILLS (1542)

34 & 35 Hen. VIII, c. 5;
Statutes of the Realm, vol. III, p. 901 (untr.).

Where in the last parliament[8] ... it was ... enacted how and in what manner lands, tenements and other hereditaments might be by will or testament in writing or otherwise by any act or acts lawfully executed in the life of every person given, disposed, willed or devised, for the advancement of the wife, preferment of the children, [or] payment of debts of every such person, or otherwise at his will and pleasure, as in the same act more plainly is declared; since the making of which statute divers doubts, questions and ambiguities have arisen, been moved and grown by diversity of opinions taken in and upon the exposition of the letter of the same statute: for a plain declaration and explanation whereof, and to the intent and purpose that the king's obedient and loving subjects shall and may take the commodity and advantage of the king's said gracious and liberal disposition, the lords spiritual and temporal and the commons in this present parliament assembled most

---

7   This is explained by 34 & 35 Hen. VIII, c. 5, s. 9, as extending to lands which descend to the heir of the devisor in fee tail as well as in fee simple.
8   Statute of Wills (1540); see p. 115, above.

humbly beseech the king's majesty that the meaning of the letter of the same statute concerning such matters hereafter rehearsed may be by the authority of this present parliament enacted, taken, expounded, judged, declared and explained in manner and form following . . .

[Sections 3–10 define more closely the estates and interests to which the 1540 statute applied, and provide also that a devise of all lands held in knight service should be good as to two-thirds, and if the division was not made in writing by the devisor it would be made by commission from the Court of Wards, or (in the case of mesne lords) from the Chancery. Sections 11–13 deal with procedural matters.]

14 And it is further declared and enacted by the authority aforesaid that wills or testaments made of any manors, lands, tenements or other hereditaments by any woman covert, or person within the age of 21 years, or by any person *de non sane memory*, shall not be taken to be good or effectual in the law.

15 And be it further enacted by the authority aforesaid that if any person or persons having estate of inheritance of or in manors, lands, tenements or hereditaments holden of the king by knight's service in chief, or otherwise of the king by knight's service, or of any other person or persons by knight's service, hath given at any time since the twentieth day of the said month of July [1540] or hereafter shall give, will, devise or assign by will or other act executed in his life his manors, lands, tenements or hereditaments, or any of them, by fraud or covin, to any other person or persons for term of years, life or lives, with one remainder over in fee, or with divers remainders over for term of years, life or in tail, with a remainder over in fee simple to any person or persons, or to his or their right heirs; or at any time since the said twentieth day of July [1540] hath conveyed or made, or hereafter shall convey or make, by fraud or covin, contrary to the true intent of this act, any estates, conditions, mesnalties, tenures or conveyances to the intent to defraud or deceive the king of his prerogative, primer seisin, livery, relief, wardship, marriages or rights, or any other lord of their wardships, reliefs, heriots or other profits which should or ought to accrue, grow or come unto them, or any of them, by or after the death of his or their tenant, by force [of] and according to the former statute and of this present act and declaration; and the same estates and other conveyances being found by office to be so made or contrived by covin, fraud or deceit, as is abovesaid, contrary to the true intent and meaning of the said former act and of this act: that then the king shall have as well the wardship of the

body and custody of the lands, tenements and hereditaments, as livery, primer seisin, relief, and other profits which should or ought to appertain to the king, according to the true intent and meaning of the said former act and of this present act, as though no such estates or conveyances by covin had ever been had or made, until the said office be lawfully undone by traverse or otherwise.

16   And that the other lord and lords of whom any such manors, lands, tenements, or hereditaments shall be holden by knight's service as is aforesaid shall have their remedy in such cases for his or their wardships of bodies and lands by writ of right of ward; and shall distrain and make avowry or cognisance by themselves or their bailiffs for their reliefs, heriots and other profits which should have been to them due by or after the death of their tenant, as if no such estate or conveyance had been had or made . . .

ANON. (1538/39)

Brooke Abr., *Feffements al uses*, pl. 50.

If A. covenants with B. that when A. shall be enfeoffed by B. of three acres in Dale, then the said A. and his heirs and all others seised of the said A.'s land in Sale shall be seised thereof to the use of the said B. and his heirs; and A. makes a feoffment of his land in Sale; and then B. enfeoffs A. of the said three acres in Dale: there A.'s feoffees shall be seised to B.'s use, even if they had no notice of the use, for the land is and was bound with the aforesaid use into whose hands soever it should come. It is not like the case where a feoffee in use sells the land to someone who has no notice of the first use, for in the above case the use had no existence until the feoffment was made of the three acres, and then the use began.

TYRREL'S CASE (1557)

Dyer 155 ('in the Court of Wards').[9]

Jane Tyrrel, widow, for the sum of £400 paid by G. Tyrrel her son and heir apparent, by indenture enrolled in Chancery in 4 Edw. VI, bargained, sold, gave, granted, covenanted and concluded to the said G. Tyrrel all her manors, lands, tenements, etc., to have and to hold the same to the said G. Tyrrel and his heirs for ever, to the use of the said Jane during her life without impeachment of waste, and immediately after her decease to the use of the said G. Tyrrel and

9   Also reported in 1 And. 37, pl. 96; Benl. 61, pl. 108.

the heirs of his body lawfully begotten, and in default of such issue to the use of the heirs of the said Jane for ever. Query well whether the limitation of those uses upon the *habendum* is not void and impertinent, because a use cannot be springing, drawn or reserved out of a use, as appears prima facie. And here there ought to be first a use transferred to the vendee before any freehold or inheritance in the land can be vested in him by the enrolment. And this case has been doubted in the Common Pleas before now, so query what the law is.

But all the judges of the Common Pleas, and SAUNDERS C.B., thought that the limitation of uses above was void: for, suppose the Statute of Enrolments[10] had never been made, but only the Statute of Uses,[11] then the above case could not be; because a use cannot be engendered of a use.[12]

BARTIE v HERENDEN (1560)

(a) BL MS. Lansdowne 1067, fo. 27;
MS. Add. 35941, fo. 31v; LI MS. Maynard 77, fo. 31;
MS. Maynard 86, fo. 110; HLS MS. 2079, fo. 124;
French text in 93 L.Q.R. 36.

Note that the course of the Chancery (*cursus cancellariae*) by reason of equity is used contrary to the common law in that a use may be averred upon a fine, feoffment or recovery, against a use expressed in the same feoffment or set out in the indenture which expressly leads the use to the other. And this was recently in experience there in a suit between the duchess of Suffolk[13] and Herenden of Gray's Inn.[14] For when the duchess went across the sea in the time of Queen Mary, she levied a fine to Herenden in respect of various manors and hereditaments, and an indenture was made between them reciting a consideration of a large sum of money paid by Herenden to the said duchess, and several other considerations, and also reciting that the use should be to Heren-

10 See p. 115, above.
11 See p. 112, above.
12 Cf. Anderson: '. . . for the bargain for money in itself implies a use, and the limitation of the other use is absolutely contrary. . .'
13 Katharine Bartie (1519–80), baroness Willoughby d'Eresby, dowager duchess of Suffolk, now the wife of Mr. Richard Bartie (the actual plaintiff). She had escaped from house arrest in 1555 and fled to the Continent to escape religious persecution, having in 1554 conveyed her property to Herenden (in the manner indicated in the report) to avoid its forfeiture: 93 L.Q.R. 34; Dyer 176; *House of Commons Journals*, vol. I, p. 41.
14 Walter Herenden, admitted in 1541.

den and his heirs, with various covenants in the same indenture that the tenements should be free from incumbrances and that the duchess and her heirs would make further assurance, and the like. And, notwithstanding all these facts, when the duchess returned from [Poland] she exhibited a bill in Chancery,[15] averring that this whole conveyance was upon trust and confidence to her use, and [to the use] that Herenden and his heirs would re-enfeoff her etc. And she was received to make this averment of this secret use, against the consideration and the express use; and upon proof thereof she had a decree against Herenden to re-enfeoff her. (By the report of Serjeant Barham.[16])

There was a like case between the earl of Pembroke, heir to the marquess of Northampton, complainant, and R. King and Geoffrey Skot, defendants, in Chancery. But the first case was stronger: that a use in secrecy and confidence should be averrable against a bargain, consideration, express use, indenture and fine.

(b) Decree of Sir Nicholas Bacon L.K.:
C33/22, fo. 62 (untr.).

A decree is upon the deliberate and advised hearing and debating of the matter between the said parties, in the presence of their learned counsel, this present term of St Hilary [1560], that is to say the twelfth day of February in the second year of the reign of our sovereign lady Elizabeth by the grace of God queen of England, France and Ireland, defender of the faith etc., made for the plaintiff in these words following:

Forasmuch as it did manifestly appear to the lord keeper and to this court, and was well and substantially proved in this court, as well by sundry depositions of sundry persons of good credit as also by divers notes of accounts, letters and other notes in writing as well of the proper hand of the said defendant as of others, and by divers other good and substantial matters proved and shewed to this court, that the said lands and tenements in the counties of Norfolk, Lincoln and Warwick, conveyed to the said Walter Herenden and his heirs, and the said lease . . . by the said complainant and Lady Katharine his wife were made upon special, faithful and secret trust and confidence and to have been employed to the use and behoof of the said complainant and Lady Katharine and

---

15 A *subpoena* was granted in Trinity term 1559; C33/19, fo. 187.
16 Nicholas Barham, serjeant at law 1567–77, who was admitted to Gray's Inn in 1540, and as a fellow Kentishman must have known Herenden well. This recollection by him was reported in 1572, not in 1560.

other the intents and meanings aforesaid, and not meant to be to the profit or benefit of the said defendant: it is therefore ordered, adjudged and decreed by the said lord keeper and the said Court of Chancery that the said lease so made upon trust and confidence as is before declared shall be and is now absolutely surrendered, made void and cancelled ... and ... that the said complainant and Lady Katharine his wife, their heirs and assigns, shall quietly have, occupy and enjoy the said manors ... and all other the premises with their appurtenances in the counties of Norfolk, Lincoln and Warwick, conveyed and assured to the said Walter Herenden and his heirs as is aforesaid, without any let, interruption or disturbance ... [and that Herenden and his wife should make such assurance to the plaintiff and his wife as the plaintiff's counsel should advise.] And this decree, being signed with the hand of the said lord keeper, is delivered to Thomas Powle, attorney for the said plaintiff, to be enrolled.

Powle.

Herenden died soon after this decree, and Richard Bartie sued his heir by bill in Parliament: *House of Commons Journals*, vol. I, p. 63 (21 January 1563).

ANON. (1563)

Moo. K.B. 45, pl. 138; BL MS. Add. 24845, fo. 61v.

A fine was levied by a husband and wife, and the conusee rendered the same lands back to the husband and wife and the heirs of the wife; and an indenture was made whereby it was recited that the render should be to the use of the husband and wife and the heirs of the husband. The question was, whether the limitation of the use by the indenture would hold?

DYER C.J. It seems to me that it is good enough, for the indenture should rule the use even though there is an implied use in the render to their own use.

BROWNE J. The possession is transferred to the [cestuy que] use by the statute, and therefore a use cannot be expressed upon a use. For instance, a feoffment to John Style to his own use, and that he should be seised to the use of R. H.: this is void with respect to R. H., because the use and possession were already in John Style. Likewise, if a man bargains and sells his lands for money, and limits a use thereon, it is void. But here the render must of necessity be to the heirs of one of them, and no use is implied by it.

WESTON J. to the same effect. For there is no use implied on a fine, any more than on a feoffment.

Therefore they[17] held the limitation over perfectly good.

DYER C.J. If the render were made in tail, the conusee would be seised of the reversion to his own use.

This was conceded by *Bendlowes*, and other serjeants.

NOTE (1573)

Harpur's reports, CUL MS. L1. 3. 8, fo. 186v; LI MS.
Maynard 87, fo. 183; abridged in LI MS. Misc. 791,
fo. 10v; YLS MS. G. R29.2, fo. 150.

WRAY J. said it was clear that if a lease for years is made to two persons to the use of one of them, or to one person to the use of a stranger, this use is not executed by the statute.[18] He said he had heard that it has been the opinion of the Middle Temple that it should be executed; but all the judges of the law in England are of opinion that it is not executed. Therefore, even though a lease is [devised][19] to the plaintiff and another, to the sole use of the plaintiff, nevertheless by the law the other has power to have and to enclose a moiety. This was in the Chancery, as he said. (Query whether he may not have an action on the case.)

WYTHAM v WATERHOWSE (1596)

Record: C 33/90, fo. 852 (main entry). Arthur Johnson assigned a term of years to Robert and John Waterhowse to the use of their sister, Ann, whom Arthur married; Arthur made Ann his executrix and died, and she afterwards married Robert Wytham; and the brothers permitted Robert and Ann to take the profits during Ann's life, and on her death took out letters of administration of her goods and claimed the term to their own use as her administrators. Wytham claimed the term as his by virtue of his marriage to Ann. The defendants brought a suit in the Council of the North, where (with the advice of the justices of assize for Yorkshire) it was held that both in law and in equity the administrators ought to have the term, and was so decreed. Wytham now sought to reopen the question in Chancery, claiming the use in equity. Sir John Puckering L.K. consulted Popham C.J.K.B. who conferred with the judges 'of the same house' (probably meaning Serjeants' Inn, Fleet Street).

---

17   Reads 'he' in MS.
18   Statute of Uses (1536); see p. 112, above.
19   Reads 'dev'' (*devant*, before) in MSS.

HLS MS. Acc. 704776, fo. 84v.[20]

A man possessed of a term granted it to two brothers to the use of their sister, whom he afterwards married; and they suffered the husband to take the profits; and he died; and the woman afterwards took the profits; and the woman died; and the assignees to use took out administration of their sister's goods. And Wytham sued in Chancery for the said term; and it was there decreed by all the justices of England that neither in law nor in equity did the use thereof belong to the husband.

The decree, dismissing the suit, was made on 10 February 1596: C33/90, fo. 875v; C33/92, fo. 532v (a second bill dismissed, in so far as it again reopened the same question).

WILDEGOSE v WAYLAND (1596)

CUL MS. Gg. 3. 25, fo. 92v; Gouldsb. 147, pl. 67
(untr.).

This question arose in Chancery: if A. is seised upon trust and confidence to the use of B. and his heirs, and A. sells the land to someone who has notice of the trust, to whose use shall the vendee be seised? It was also moved: if before the sale someone comes to the vendee and says to him, 'Beware how you buy such land, for A. has nothing therein except on trust to the use of B.'; and someone else comes to the vendee and says to him that it is not as he has been informed, for A. is seised of this land absolutely; and so the vendee buys the land; is this first caveat given to him as above a sufficient notice of the trust, or not?

[EGERTON] L.K. said it was not, for flying reports are more often fables than true; and if it were sufficient notice, then any man's inheritance might easily be slandered . . .

HENRY SHERFIELD'S READING ON WILLS
(1623)

Reading on 32 Hen. VIII, c. 1, in Lincoln's Inn:
BL MS. Hargrave 402, fo. 34v (untr.).

. . . Now [the use] is become a usurper, and hath encroached so much upon the right of estates—the ancient darling of the common law—that now estates in land wrought by the common law are but

---

20 Also reported in Cro. Eliz. 466. In the margin of the MS. and the index, and in 1 Rolle Abr. 346, line 4, the use is referred to as a 'trust'.

as shadows, and the use the body and substance. The use was wont to follow and attend the estate, but now the estate is passed and repassed as the use doth pass: it draws the estate to it, and not it to the estate. And now, because the use is somewhat clogged, that it cannot dance up and down at all times so lightly as it could before it was clogged with the estate,[1] there is now a bastardly use started up by the true name which the use had at first—which is 'trust and confidence'. For now a man may pass his lands by fine or feoffment, etc., to the use of John Style in fee, and yet upon trust and confidence for the feoffee or any other: which is now an use upon a use, like the project of making salt upon salt[2] all nought. And this upstart hath as great a place in the Court of Chancery as ever uses had; and it will be no doubt as perilous to the common laws. And I did then, and still do, think that it were most happy to this state if uses and trusts of that kind were extirpated totally...

SAMBACH v DASTON (1635)

Chancery: record summarised in 74 L.Q.R. 554–57. A gift was made upon marriage to a husband (Price) and his wife Margery and the heirs of their bodies, remainder to the husband's right heirs. In 1627, after the marriage, the entail was barred and Price conveyed the land to Daston and Willis to the use of them and their heirs, to the use of Price and the heirs of his body, and in default of such issue to Margery in tail, remainder to an adopted child, with further remainders over. Mr. Price died without issue, and his widow Margery married Sambach. Willis died, and Mr. and Mrs. Sambach sued the surviving trustee (Daston) to compel him to convey the land to them in tail, with remainders over. Daston pleaded that he did not claim the estate to his own use, but only as trustee to carry out the first husband's intentions: if the conveyance was made, Sambach and his wife would bar the entail and cut off the remainder to the adopted child. The case was argued before Lord Coventry L.K. in 1635.

(a) Nelson 30 (untr.).

... counsel [for Sambach] insisted that the limitation in [the last] deed, namely to Daston the trustee and his heirs..., was inserted only through the ignorance of the writer;[3] for, if those words had been omitted (as they ought), then the plaintiff Margery would

---

1 By virtue of the Statute of Uses (1536); see p. 112, above.
2 See the patent of 1582 mentioned in 16 L.Q.R. 47. A patent for salt manufacturers was held void in 1626: *House of Commons Journals*, vol. I, pp. 842, 856, 864.
3 I.e. the scrivener or conveyancer.

have an estate tail, as was intended by the said Price her first husband; otherwise she had but an estate for life, which she had before by the settlement of her father.[4]

But the defendant's counsel insisted that the clause was inserted by Price on purpose to bar his widow from doing any act to prejudice those in remainder.

And, for that Price was likely to have no issue by Margery, and did afterwards die without issue, it was decreed that she should have the lands for life, remainder to her issue if she should have any; and that if the plaintiff [Sambach][5] should have any issue by her which should die, then he to be tenant by the curtesy and hold the same during his life. And a conveyance was directed to be drawn for that purpose, and to bar Margery to prejudice the estates in remainder.

(b) Tothill 188, pl. 168 (untr.).

Sambach *contra* Dalston, because one use cannot be raised out of another, yet ordered, and the defendant ordered to pass according to the intent.

LORD NOTTINGHAM ON TRUSTS (c. 1674)

From *Prolegomena of Chancery and Equity* (D.E.C.
Yale, ed., 1965), pp. 236–238, 244–248 (untr.).

Chapter XII. Of trusts in general: *quid sint.*

1   That which now is a trust is conceived by some to be only an use at second hand; and for this they urge the definition of an use in *Chudleigh's Case*,[6] an use is a trust or confidence, not issuing out of the land, but as a thing collateral annexed in privity to the estate and person: namely, that cestuy que use shall take the profits and the terre-tenant shall make estates according to his direction. Bacon's [*Learned*] *Reading*, 7: 'Usus est dominium fiduciarium'.[7]

2   Yet doubtless that which is now a trust is and always was a thing quite different from an use: otherwise there could be no such

---

4   She was a tenant in tail after possibility of issue extinct, which was tantamount to being a tenant for life.
5   Misprinted throughout Nelson as 'Lambeth'.
6   (1594); see p. 150, below.
7   *The Learned Reading of Sir Francis Bacon upon the Statute of Uses* (1642), p. 7: '... *Usus est dominium fiduciarium*: use is an owner's life in trust ... And for a trust, which is the way to an use, it is exceeding well defined by a Civilian of great understanding: *Fides est obligatio conscientiae unius ad intentionem alterius*'.

thing as a trust now, for the statute 27 Hen. VIII[8] doth in express words declare that where any person is seised to the use, trust or confidence of another, possession shall go according etc.

3   And therefore if a trust at this day did not differ from such trusts or confidences as are mentioned in the statute of 27 Hen. VIII, it would follow that all trusts now would be executed as uses, and so there could be no such thing left as a bare trust.

4   The difference is conceived to be this. The statute of 27 Hen. VIII is intended only of such trusts and confidences by virtue of which the cestuy que trust had power to dispose of land by 1 Ric. III,[9] which indeed is all one with an use: for the mischief after 1 Ric. III was that he who had a conveyance from cestuy que use was not sure of his title, because there might be a secret conveyance from the feoffees to others, and therefore 27 Hen. VIII did execute the use etc. But where the trust was of such a nature that cestuy que trust could not dispose of the land by 1 Ric. III, there was no such mischief; and therefore no such trust was executed.

5   The first kind of trust ever was and still is a mere use only. 'Tis now turned to an estate in law, which before the statute was merely an equity. The latter kind of trust remains still as it was at common law, namely an equitable interest in the land which enables no man to use or enjoy the possession or profits of the land without the help of a court of conscience by way of *subpoena*.

6   And therefore some have said that if, before the statute of 27 Hen. VIII, a man had enfeoffed A. and B. to the use of them, C. and D. and their heirs in trust that the feoffor should receive the profits, this trust built on an use would not have been executed by the statute, no more than it is at this day; for such a trustee could not have disposed of the land within 1 Ric. III, because 1 Ric. III makes good the conveyance of cestuy que use against all persons claiming only to his use, which reaches not the cases of them who claim to their own use but in trust for another.

7   So again, if feoffment be made to the use of A. for life, and after his death that B. shall take the profits, this is an use in B.; but if it be said that feoffees shall take the profits and deliver them over to B., this is not [an] use in B., but a trust, for B. cannot take the profits unless by the hands of the feoffees. 36 Hen. VIII, Brooke Abr., *Feffements al uses*, pl. 52.

8   Such kinds of trusts in the civil law are called *fideicommissa*, because they depend on the good faith of heirs, whence they take their name. These trusts continued a long time among the Romans

8   Statute of Uses (1536); see p. 112, above.
9   See p. 101, above.

without any way to compel the performance of them . . . But at last Divus Augustus, lest an opportunity be given for human perfidy, brought them under the control of law . . .[10]

Chapter XIV. Wherein uses at common law and trusts at this day may be said to agree, and where not.

1 At common law, if feoffee to uses make feoffment over without consideration, whether with or without notice, the feoffee is seised to the first uses: for he who comes [in] in the *per* without consideration is either presumed to have notice or bound without it, for the old use cannot be changed without consideration . . . But he who comes in in the *post*, as lord by escheat, disseisor, etc., is never subject to the former uses. And this is the standing rule for trusts at this day, as appears by common experience.

2 At common law, if feoffee to uses make feoffment over with consideration, if second feoffee hath notice of the first uses, he must be subject to them though he was a purchaser . . . And this is also the standing rule for trusts at this day, as appears by common experience and the printed cases[11] . . .

3 At common law the king cannot be seised to an use, because he is a body politic and is not compellable by *subpoena*, and comes in in the *post*. So likewise in case of a trust . . .

4 At common law [an] use shall be of the same nature with land, and shall descend as the land should . . . So of trust . . .

5 At common law, if fine, recovery or feoffment were made without consideration, an use did result back again to the donor by implication of law . . . So also at this day a trust results in such cases . . .

6 It is said in *Chudleigh's Case*[12] that [an] use is neither chattel nor hereditament, and so no assets to the heir or the executor. And so it seems of a trust too. In the case of *Bennet v Box*,[13] a man who had purchased land to him and his heirs in the name of John Style,

---

10 He returns to this in ch. XIV, ss. 15–17, and continues the comparison (at p. 252): 'At last these trusts or *fideicommissa* grew to be so many, they were fain to have a special chancellor or praetor to dispatch these causes, who was distinguished from other praetors by the name of *praetor fideicommissarius* . . . But at last the Romans, finding the inconvenience of them, made a law much like our statute of 27 Hen. VIII . . . by which they made cestuy que use to be heir in substance . . .' This passage is based on Bacon's *Learned Reading*, pp. 15–16.

11 Lane 60; 2 Rolle Rep. 105, 116.

12 See p. 150, below.

13 (1662) 1 Ch. Cas. 12; 2 Freem. 184.

his trustee, did afterwards become bound in an obligation, and died, and then John Style died. The heir of the purchaser exhibits bill against the heir of trustee for conveyance. The creditor brings debt against the heir of the purchaser on the obligation, who pleads Nothing by descent. Then comes the creditor into Chancery, and exhibits bill against the heirs of the obligor and trustee, and prays that when the estate in trust shall be declared to be executed it may likewise be decreed to be assets. But on reference to all the judges of England it was resolved by them, and so decreed by CLARENDON C., it shall not be assets.

7   The reasons on which the judges went were these: (i) at common law an use was not assets in equity; (ii) a statute made 19 Hen. VII, c. 15, to subject lands in use to the execution of a judgment—therefore without statute it could not be; (iii) when a trustee executes an estate to the heir, he is not in by course of descent, therefore equity cannot make him liable . . .; (iv) otherwise a mischief would ensue, for the heir would be in a worse condition where assets descend in equity than when he has assets at law, for assets at law may be aliened before the writ brought, [but] assets in equity cannot be aliened.

8   Yet the practisers in Chancery are much dissatisfied with this resolution; for they think it but reasonable that equity should advance the payment of debts and suppress fraud, else a man may borrow money to buy land and by taking the conveyance in trust no assets shall descend to his heir. And why should not the descent of a trust in fee to the heir be assets in equity, as well as the trust of a term be assets to the executors (which is everyday experience)? . . .[14]

9   There are many mischiefs at common law introduced by uses and many of the same mischiefs are still remaining by trusts: (i) inheritances passed without livery—so they do still by secret declaration of trust; (ii) uses were devisable by parol, *idque in extremis*—so trusts at this day may be [devised] by parol; (iii) heirs were disherited by secret uses—so they are now by secret trusts; (iv) estates by curtesy and dower were defeated by uses—so it seems they are by trusts . . .

10   Yet there are some cases in which uses at common law and trusts at this day seem to be very different. As for example, whether tenant in tail can stand seised to an use is a point much controverted in our books . . . And at length 14 Jac., B.R., in *Cowper and Franklin's Case*, 1 Inst.,[15] it was settled that he cannot . . . But however

---

14   The decision was reversed in effect by the Statute of Frauds (1677), s. 10, which Lord Nottingham is believed to have drafted.
15   (1616) Co. Litt. 19: 1 Rolle Rep. 332, 384; Cro. Jac. 400; 3 Buls. 184; Godb. 269.

the authorities have not prevailed in cases of an use, yet the law is otherwise in cases of a trust, for tenant in tail may stand seised to a trust: and so it was ruled by ROLLE C.J., Pas. 1650, [in] *Furse and Wike's Case.*[16] . . .

THE STATUTE OF FRAUDS (1677)

29 Car. II, c. 3:
Statutes of the Realm, vol. V, p. 840 (untr.)

. . . 5 And be it further enacted by the authority aforesaid, that from and after the said four and twentieth day of June [1677] all devises and bequests of any lands or tenements, devisable either by force of the Statute of Wills,[17] or by this statute,[18] or by force of the custom of Kent, or the custom of any borough or any other particular custom, shall be in writing and signed by the party so devising the same, or by some other person in his presence and by his express directions; and shall be attested and subscribed in the presence of the said devisor by three or four credible witnesses; or else they shall be utterly void and of none effect.

6 And moreover no devise in writing of lands, tenements or hereditaments, nor any clause thereof, shall at any time after the said four and twentieth day of June be revocable otherwise than by some other will or codicil in writing, or other writing declaring the same, or by burning, cancelling, tearing or obliterating the same by the testator himself or in his presence and by his directions and consent...

7 And be it further enacted by the authority aforesaid, that from and after the said four and twentieth day of June all declarations of trusts or confidences of any lands, tenements or hereditaments shall be manifested and proved by some writing signed by the party who is by law enabled to declare such trust, or by his last will in writing, or else they shall be utterly void and of none effect.

8 Provided always that where any conveyance shall be made of any lands or tenements by which a trust or confidence shall or may arise or result by the implication or construction of law, then and in every such case such trust or confidence shall be of the like force and effect as the same would have been if this statute had not been

16 Sub nom. *Furse v Weekes* (1650) 2 Rolle Abr. 90.
17 See p. 115, above.
18 Section 12 provided that any estate *pur auter vie* should be devisable by will in writing.

made, anything herein before contained to the contrary notwithstanding . . .

SYMPSON v TURNER (1700)

Record: C33/294, fo. 466 (main entry). Under a marriage settlement made in
March 1668, John Roberts conveyed property in Canterbury to Sir William
Turner upon the following trusts: to his sons in tail, remainder to his wife
Elizabeth in tail special (i.e. to her and her heirs by Roberts), remainder to
Elizabeth in tail general, remainder to his daughters Elizabeth and Margaret
in fee simple, remainder to his right heirs. The settlor died in 1677 without
male issue, so that his widow became entitled as tenant in tail special by
virtue of the first remainder. She suffered a recovery to bar the trusts, and
devised the land for payment of her debts, dying a widow in 1692. The
daughters (Elizabeth Sympson and Margaret Epps), together with the
settlor's grandson and co-heir (John Sympson, infant son of Elizabeth
Sympson), brought this suit in Chancery against the heirs in gavelkind of the
trustee, and the wife's creditors, on the grounds that the recovery by the
widow was void and operated as a forfeiture of her estate under the statute
of 11 Hen. VII, c. 20.[19]

(a) 1 Eq. Cas. Abr. 220.

The question was, whether this was such a jointure made on the
wife as to make the recovery a forfeiture within the statute 11 Hen.
VII?

For the defendants it was objected that a court of equity ought
not to give any assistance, because the statute makes the recovery a
forfeiture of her estate and gives a remedy by way of entry; and in
this case she has only a trust and no estate to forfeit . . .

On the other side, it was said that this was to aid a forfeiture; but
as the statute makes the suffering a recovery a forfeiture, and gives
an entry to the person that has the next estate, so in another place it
makes all recoveries suffered by a jointress void: and upon that
clause it is proper to come into equity to have an execution of the
trust. And this case is within the words of the statute, for the
statute says 'any estate limited to the wife or to her use'; and this
statute was before the statute of 27 Hen. VIII,[20] of uses, at which
time a use was the same thing that a trust now is . . .

---

19   This provided that if a woman had an estate in lands 'of the inheritance or
     purchase of the husband', and after the husband's death suffered a common
     recovery, the recovery should be void and the person to whom the land would
     belong on the wife's death could enter.
20   Statute of Uses (1536); see p. 112, above.

And of the same opinion was my Lord Keeper,[1] and decreed accordingly.

(b) Continued in 1 Eq. Cas. Abr. 383.

By the 27 Hen. VIII, c. 10, it is provided that the use and possession shall be always united ... but, notwithstanding this statute, there are three ways of creating an use or a trust which still remains as at common law, and is a creature of the court of equity and subject only to their control and direction:

First, where a man seised in fee raises a term for years, and limits it in trust for A., etc., for this the statute cannot execute, the termor not being seised.

Secondly, where lands are limited to the use of A. in trust to permit B. to receive the rents and profits, for the statute can only execute the first use.

Thirdly, where lands are limited to trustees to receive and pay over the rents and profits to such and such persons, for here the lands must remain in them to answer these purposes.

And these points were agreed to ... *per curiam.*

On 9 July 1700, Sir Nathan Wright L.K. held that the trust limited to Elizabeth Roberts was within the statute of 11 Hen. VII and that the recovery was void; and decreed that the Turners should execute conveyances of the trust estate, make full discovery of the relevant documents, and account for the profits: C33/294, fo. 467.

1   Sir Nathan Wright.

5 Executory interests under the Statute of Uses

ANON. (1552)

Brooke Abr., *Feffements al uses*, pl. 30.

Note: if a man made a feoffment in fee before the Statute of Uses made in 27 Hen. VIII,[1] or does so after the statute, to the use of W. and his heirs until A. pays £40 to the said W., and then to the use of the said A. and his heirs; then the Statute of Uses executes the estate in W., and then A. pays the £40 to W.: in this case (according to many) A. is seised in fee, if he enters. But some think that A. is seised in fee by [reason of] the payment unless the feoffees enter. (Query this.) Therefore it seems safest for A. to enter in the name of the feoffees and in his own name, and then either way the entry will be good and shall cause A. to be seised in fee. Thus observe that at the present day a man may make a feoffment to use, and the use shall change from one person to another by an act *ex post facto*, by condition (*circumstance*), just as before the statute of 27 Hen. VIII concerning uses.

HADDON'S CASE (1576)

CUL MS. Ll. 3. 8, fo. 263 (Q.B.).

It was held by GAWDY and JEFFREY JJ. that a suspended use was not executed by the statute of 27 Hen. VIII; and also that if it was

1 See p. 112, above.

perfectly executed in another the possession could not be drawn out of someone who had it by way of escheat, attainder or otherwise . . . And GAWDY J. said that a use which depended on a contingency was outside the statute of 27 Hen. VIII for the purpose of being executed; and, as he thought, it was extinguished by the same statute: for the statute was made to avoid those mischiefs which were used at common law by reason of subtle practices, and if the freehold should be in abeyance it would be inconvenient, for one would not know against whom to bring his action and therefore all disseisin would be upheld, and that would be a law to uphold wrong and not right, which would be contrary to all laws . . .

SOUTHCOTE J. and WRAY C.J. to the contrary.[2]

BRENT'S CASE (1575)

C.P.: case reconstructed from the reports. The lessee of Elizabeth Brent brought ejectment for lands in Somerset, and upon a demurrer to the evidence the facts appeared to be that, in the time of Edward VI, Richard[3] Brent had made a feoffment to the use of himself and his first wife Dorothy for their lives, and if he should survive Dorothy to the use of himself and such wife as he should afterwards marry, for their lives, to provide her jointure, remainder over in fee; and later, with Richard's consent, the feoffees and the remainderman in fee joined in a feoffment to other uses, and Richard also levied a fine to those uses; and Richard did survive Dorothy, and subsequently married Elizabeth; and after Richard's death Elizabeth, in the name of the first feoffees, entered to raise the uses limited to Richard's future wife, and made the lease to the plaintiff; and the plaintiff was ejected by someone claiming under the later feoffment.[4]

2 Cited by Coke in *Perrot's Case* (1594) Moo. K.B. 368, at 372: '. . . Haddon devised to someone for life, and likewise afterwards to every person who should be his heir, for life only; and this was adjudged an estate in possession to the first, and a remainder for life to the next heir, and not to the others'.

3 'Robert' in 2 Leon. But he seems to be the Richard Brent who died in 1571 (C142/156/14). See *Calendar of Patent Rolls of Elizabeth I*, vol. III, no. 548 (licence to alienate for Richard and Dorothy Brent and Thomas Broughton, 1564); and fn. 4, below.

4 Cf. *Brent v Gilbert* (1572) BL MS. Add. 24845, fo. 111v; CUL MS. Gg. 3. 3, fo. 7; MS. Gg. 5. 2, fo. 176. This earlier case, in the Queen's Bench, arose from a marriage settlement between Richard Brent and Thomas Broughton which contained a similar remainder to Richard and such wife as he should marry. The court held that the use to the future wife 'could be in suspense for the time being well enough and that 'there is no necessity for a use to vest presently'. It was also said in this case that such a use could not be barred by fine, because a fine could only bar estates which were *in esse* at the time.

(a) 2 Leon. 14, pl. 25, emended and augmented with
passages from YLS MS. G. R29.2, fo. 174; CUL MS.
L1. 3. 14, fo. 229.

... MOUNSON J. conceived that the entry by the second wife was
lawful, irrespective of the assent or command of the feoffees. A use
may be limited to someone who is *in esse* or *in posse*; and the second
wife here was *in esse* when the use was limited, and also *in posse*: for
there was a possibility that the first wife might die and also that the
feoffor might marry this woman ... A use is nothing other than a
trust and confidence, and it was no inheritance by the course of the
common law; for no mention is made of uses in our old books,
when the common law greatly flourished, as in the time of Edward
I and Edward III. [I think uses began after Edward III's time, when
the controversy was between the families of Lancaster and York,
for fear that they should lose their land by attainder in that
troublesome season: though they erred, for their feoffees might
also have forfeited it].[5] ... Also uses were not subject to the
grounds of the law ... [and] were at first invalid, but afterwards by
continuance *communis error facit jus*, so that they were taken and
esteemed to be inheritances. And they cannot be more suitably
compared to anything than to copyholds, which at first were only
tenures at will and were unknown to the common law, but now are
of the same reputation in law as inheritances. And they are not
guided by the rules of the common law, but by the intention of the
parties: which in this case at the bar appears to have been that she
who should be the second wife of [Richard] Brent, the feoffor,
should have the lands as above. Therefore this use shall arise, and
the statute of 27 Hen. VIII shall draw the possession after it.[6] When
the feoffor and the feoffees joined in a fine of the land in which the
future use is wrapped, I conceive that the use (being in abeyance

5   The MS. also mentions Brooke Abr., *Feffements al uses*, pl. 9, where Brooke
comments on a case of 1370 (where the feoffees of Sir Bartholomew Burghersh
sued the king by petition), 'and so observe that there were feoffees in trust in
those days'. But Mounson J. dismisses the comment as 'only a slight collection'.
For a clearer case from this period, see p. 44, above.
6   The rest of this speech is printed in 2 Leon. after that of Dyer C.J.

and consideration of the law[7]) could not be touched by the fine . . . [And so it seems to me that there is no need for an entry by the feoffees, but the use is in the second wife; and that the action here is maintainable.]

MANWOOD J. As to the beginning of uses, they have been as long as mankind has been guided by reason; [for so long have trusts been]. Although uses are not mentioned in our old books, that is no argument that uses have only existed in recent times: uses were uncommon, therefore not at all, is a *non sequitur* . . . I have seen various old deeds of uses; and in olden times you will not find anyone purchasing to himself alone, but had two or three joint feoffees with him . . . The reason why uses are not mentioned in our old books is because men were of better consciences then than they are now, and so the feoffees did not give occasion to their feoffors to bring *subpoenas* to compel them to perform the trusts reposed in them . . . [As to the objection that this now goes as a possession and not as a use, it nevertheless retains its old property. Therefore the second wife is capable of the use; for it falls in even though it did not when it was limited. And uses may arise in other ways than possessions, and also may determine in other ways. For example, a feoffment made to J. S. to the use of C. until C. pays £100, and then to C.: this is a void remainder in possession, and yet good in use.[8] For a remainder may depend on a contingency and be good, provided it does not cut down any estate of the particular tenant. Land ought to be in some person, but this is not so of the use. A fee simple of land may not be defeated, but it is otherwise of a use. For land was made by God in perpetuity, whereas uses, commons, rents and so forth were made by men and may therefore be dissolved by men] . . . [Therefore, uses] are not directed by the rules of the common law but by the will of the owner of the lands: for the use is in his hands as clay is in the hands of the potter, which he in whose hands it is may put into whatever form he pleases. And even though the possession is now executed to the use,[9] the property and

---

7 Cf. MS. ('this future use was in abeyance and in the preservation of the law'); Dyer 340 ('this possibility of a future use to the second wife is reserved and preserved in the custody of the law, and if anything is left in the feoffees it is but a power and authority to make an entry, which is not an interest in right in the land, and then it follows in consequence that nothing passed by their feoffment to the new feoffees').

8 See *Anon.* (1552), p. 134, above.

9 By the Statute of Uses (1536).

quality (as abstracted from the possession) shall nevertheless not be drowned in the possession; and so, forasmuch as uses were [before the statute] by permission of law guided at the wills of the parties, so also shall be the possessions [after the statute]. Therefore, since a use (as abstracted from the possession) might well have been limited to a wife to be, even though at the time of such limitation there was no such wife in being, in the same manner shall it be now, when the possession is executed to the use. And so in this case the second wife shall be capable of this use, according to the will and direction of the owner . . .[10] [But when this remainder was limited in use and was not ascertained (*conus*)—for Richard Brent might not have survived his first wife, or might not have remarried, so that the use could not shine out of the clouds, whereas the use of Richard Brent and Dorothy was ascertained and therefore executed by the statute—this other use could not be executed, and therefore the trustees are put in trust with it. It follows that by their feoffment their estate (which was the root of the uses) was gone, and therefore the use (which was the branch) must perish: for every branch must draw its sap from the root. If, however, the branches have their sap and their fruit, it is immaterial if the root decays.] If the uses had been *in esse*, so that the persons to whom they were limited were known, then the statute would execute the possession to such uses. As to my brother Mounson's objection that the law shall keep and preserve the use, and that it shall arise at its due time notwithstanding anything done by the feoffees: that cannot be; for the statute of 27 Hen. VIII does not say [that any such uses in abeyance shall be executed; for the words 'have or hereafter shall have in use'[11] mean these cloudy uses only if it can be said, 'this is the person who has this use', and then the use may be executed. It might be asked what estate the feoffees have by the statute before such contingent uses are executed; to which the answer is that they have a fee simple determinable, such as a lord has when he enters upon his villein who purchases in tail. And I think that the law does not preserve this use in its keeping, because *de minimis non curat lex* . . .]

HARPUR J. [Uses began as trusts that the feoffees should take the

---

10   The following part of this speech is placed last in 2 Leon., where it is somewhat garbled. The sense is reconstructed by heavy interpolation from the MS.

11   See p. 113, above.

profits, and this taking came in time to be called 'use'; for the profit was the principal thing. In the civil law it is called *usufructus terrae*. And I take it that usufructs and uses began on account of the danger, in time of war, that land would be forfeited; and this seemed to begin in King John's time, when there were the barons' wars, and continued during the reign of Henry III.[12]] But they did not come into common practice before the time of King Henry VI, when the great contention took place between the two great houses of York and Lancaster, at which time uses were in great estimation for the preservation of inheritances. Afterwards, uses by deceit (*practice*) became mischievous and prejudicial to the public justice of the realm and to many particular persons . . . As to the making of the statute of 27 Hen. VIII, the truth is that the king was displeased by the loss of wardships and other injuries done to him, and therefore he complained to the judges of the realm about the defect of the law in that case; and they thereupon shewed the king the causes of those injuries and losses to the king, and further shewed the king that if the possession might be joined to the use all would go well, and all the injuries, wrong and loss which came to the king by reason of such uses, wills and secret feoffments would be avoided; and so the king commanded his counsel to frame a bill for that purpose, and present it to the House of Commons in the twenty-fourth year of his reign; but it was then rejected. And the king at that time would have been content if only the fourth part of the land should descend. From that time the king stayed further proceeding in the said cause until 27 Hen. VIII, at which time the statute took effect. And their cure then was to pen the statute so precisely that nothing should be left in the feoffees, but that the whole estate should be executed by the statute. Thus the said statute utterly took everything out of the feoffees . . .[13]

DYER C.J. [I think uses were in the time of Edward I, after abbeys were restrained from purchasing lands 'by craft or engine',[14] for despite this they purchased in the name of their friends and they took the profits: which craftiness is revealed in the statute of 15

---

12 Cf. 2 Leon.: '. . . Uses began around 18 Edw. II, after which time there was such a general liking of them that they were anew used'.

13 The remainder of this argument is omitted in 2 Leon., but is in the MSS.: (1) the statute had taken everything out of the feoffees; (2) Elizabeth's right could not be extinguished, since it was not *in esse* at the time of the feoffment; and (3) the use was executed in Richard and Dorothy, and they were not parties to the feoffment. Therefore Elizabeth should succeed.

14 Statute of Mortmain, *De viris religiosis*, 7 Edw. I.

Ric. II, c. 5,[15] where this word 'use' is the first I have found in our law books ... And in the civil law there has always been such a division of the land and the use, and the terre-tenants are called *proprietarii* and the cestuys que use *usufructuarii*. It must be granted that the purpose of the statute of 27 Hen. VIII was to devest all the interest out of the feoffees, in order to avoid the mischiefs of uses; but their purpose was not to devest it until the use was *in esse* in some person. For the words are 'that they shall have the possession etc. in the same manner etc. as they had the use'.[16] Thus, as to the wife's right, the estate to be revived and given to her is in the feoffees, and they have an inheritance in them and it may pass from them, whilst at the time of the feoffment the second wife had nothing—and, as it seems to me, she never shall have, because she was not *in esse* at the time of the first wife's death, when her remainder ought to have commenced, for on Dorothy's death the whole freehold vested in [Richard] Brent, and Elizabeth comes too late. And the limitation to her was void at the outset, for by the statute of 27 Hen. VIII the use shall go as far as the possession goes; and because the second wife was not capable at the time, she shall not have the use. And even if such conveyances were good before the statute, nevertheless since the statute it is not so, for the statute has made uses to resemble the cases of possession: and if this remainder had been in possession, it has been agreed by everyone that it could not have been ... Likewise here, since it cannot take effect in possession, it cannot take effect at all ... But even admitting that she ought to take, there are now impediments: for it appears that the feoffees, and also [Richard] Brent, agreed to abrogate it; and at common law the feoffees have power to preserve or destroy the use, and here all the persons having an interest joined in the feoffment and no one may gainsay it ... Therefore when Elizabeth entered she was a disseisor, and therefore the *ejectione firmae* does not lie.

(b) Dyer 340.

... And the opinion of MANWOOD J. and DYER C.J. was that, although the future use was in abeyance and *in nubibus*, and in no person certain or known, nevertheless when the contingency happened (and the use also) it was necessary for the feoffees to enter in

---

15 This statute (1391) refers to evasions of the Statute of Mortmain by means of feoffments 'to the use of religious people' whereby such people took the profits. It required such feoffees either to amortise the land (i.e. convey it to the religious house), with the king's licence, or to alienate it to some other use.

16 Statute of Uses (1536); see p. 113, above (here paraphrased).

order to raise this last and dead use; for they were the persons put in trust by the feoffor who created the trust, and the feoffment and estate which the feoffees accepted was the very root and foundation of all the said uses, which are as branches and fruit of the body or trunk of the tree... At common law the feoffees had sufficient power to alter, change or dissolve the use and trust by their alienation or limitation, and there was no remedy for the land but only a *subpoena* in conscience to make recompense or receive punishment for the breach of trust; and this is so even if the alienation is made to persons who have notice of the trust, so long as it is upon consideration and the use is expressed contrary to the first use. (Query this.) But here the case is not stated to be that the new feoffees had any notice of the former uses, and when the new feoffment was made to the new uses by the will and assent of the feoffor himself, and also of his feoffees, no wrong was done in any way to the second wife, who was not at that time in being or an ascertained person. And although by the words of the statute the freehold of the land, and the fee simple also which the feoffees receive, are deemed to be already vested in the cestuys que use, yet there still remains some spark of right and title (*scintilla juris et tituli*) as some medium between both estates...

The matter was adjourned into the Exchequer Chamber, and there in the next Michaelmas term [1575] it was argued by *Jeffrey* and *Barham*. But afterwards the parties settled between themselves, and judgment was given by default.[17]

ANON. (1580)

LI MS. Misc. 488, fo. 72v (Q.B.).

A man made a feoffment in fee to the use of himself for life, remainder to the use of his last will in fee. Afterwards, he and his feoffees levied a fine of the aforesaid land to a stranger. And after that he declared his will thereof to John Style and his heirs in fee, and died.

The question, moved by *Cowper* of the Inner Temple, was whether the conusee[18] should have the land, or the devisee.

---

17 In *Dillon v Freine* (1595) Poph. 70, at 76, Anderson C.J. said: '... And for *Brent's Case*, I have always taken the better opinion to be that the wife cannot take in that case, because of the mean disturbance; [and this] notwithstanding the judgment which is entered thereupon, which was by assent of the parties and given only upon a default made after an adjournment upon the demurrer (for he said he had viewed the roll thereof on purpose)...'

18 I.e. the person to whom it was granted by the fine.

It seemed to WRAY C.J. that the devisee [should have it], for after the feoffment to the aforesaid use the fee was in abeyance until he had made his testament; and therefore it could not be granted by fine; and so the devise afterwards is good.

SOUTHCOTE J. It seems that the fee was in the feoffor before his last will was declared, [even] after the aforesaid feoffment; for it is clear that if he had not declared his will his heirs would now have it (assuming no fine had been levied). Thus the law accounts the fee to be in his power to pass or not; and this levying of the fine is a controlling of his intent, that he will not have the fee pass to the use of his last will but to the use of the fine.

Then *Cowper* moved: if the fee is accounted in abeyance in this case, and if it passes by the devise, shall the use be in the devisee without regress made by the feoffees for this purpose (namely, to the use of the will)?

It seemed to WRAY C.J. that it should, and that it vested presently in the devisee by virtue of the first livery. Similarly, if a man makes a feoffment in fee to the use of himself and his heirs, on condition that if R. S. paid £10 the feoffees should be seised to his use in fee, here by the performance of the condition by R. the use is in him without a re-entry by the feoffees for that purpose.[19]

AYLOFFE J. On this matter—when the feoffees shall make regress or entry in order to raise a use—I have always taken this distinction: where the use is not utterly discontinued or interrupted, but remains as it was at the time of the feoffment, the use vests without entry by the feoffees for that purpose (as in the said latter case of R. S.); and also if a man makes a feoffment to the use of himself for life, remainder to his eldest son of his body, remainder to the eldest son of the eldest son, and so on in perpetuity (*sempeternity*), if any of the particular tenants die the use shall be in the others at once, without any entry by the feoffees; but it is contrary where the use is interrupted, for there it shall not be in the tenants without an entry.

Cowper said that 4 Edw. VI[20] is to the effect that it shall be in the tenants without a re-entry made by the feoffees.

WRAY C.J. I do not think the book is so: nor is any other book. (But as to the principal case he said:) it is good to be advised, for by such a joinder of the tenant and the feoffees—if the law should be as my brother Southcote says— the estates of perpetuities which are now commonly made for the continuance of land in the blood, by such means and fines, shall be prevented; and therefore it is good to be considered.

19   See *Anon.* (1552), p. 134, above.
20   Ibid., the correct date of which is 6 Edw. VI.

WOLFE v SHELLEY (1581)

Record: KB 27/1269, m. 58; 1 Co. Rep. 88. Nicholas Wolfe brought trespass against Henry Shelley for breaking his close and house at Barham Wick in Angmering, Sussex, on 7 November 1578. The defendant pleaded Not guilty, and on 11 May 1579 the jury at bar found a special verdict: King Henry VIII granted the tenement by letters patent in 1540 to one Anne Cobham for life, remainder to Edward Shelley and Jane his wife and the heirs of their bodies, remainder to the right heirs of Edward Shelley in fee simple; and Anne entered and was seised, and died; and after her death Edward and Jane entered and were seised as of fee tail, and they had issue Henry (the first son) and Richard; then Jane died; then Henry, the eldest son, married Anne, had issue Mary, and died, leaving Anne pregnant with the defendant; then Edward Shelley on 25 September 1554 covenanted to suffer a recovery to the use of himself for life, remainder to three friends (presumably trustees) for 24 years, remainder 'to the only use, profit and behoof of the heirs male of the body of the said Edward Shelley lawfully begotten, and of the heirs male of the body of the said heirs male lawfully begotten'; remainder to the heirs male of the body of his father John Shelley, and the heirs male of the body of such heirs male, remainder to the right heirs of Edward Shelley in fee simple; and the recovery was suffered accordingly in the octave of Michaelmas 1554; on the same octave (9 October 1554), between 5 a.m. and 6 a.m., Edward Shelley died, and on 19 October the sheriff delivered seisin to the recoverors; then on 4 December 1554 the defendant was born, his sister Mary being then alive; and then on 9 October 1578 (after the expiry of the term of years) Richard Shelley entered and leased the tenement to the plaintiff, who entered and was in possession when the defendant entered on 7 November. The case was argued in banc in 1581.

PEDIGREE OF SHELLEY

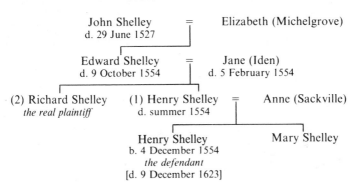

(a) 1 Co. Rep. 93.[1]

... This case was divided into four principal questions:

1   If tenant in tail suffers a common recovery, with a voucher over, and dies before execution, may execution be sued against the issue in tail?

2   If tenant in tail makes a lease for years, and afterwards suffers a common recovery, is the reversion (by the judgment of the law) presently in the recoveror before any execution sued?

3   If tenant in tail has issue two sons, and the elder died in his father's lifetime, his wife being *privement enseinte* with a son, and then tenant in tail suffers a recovery to the use of himself for life, and after his death to the use of A. and C. for 24 years, and then to the use of the heirs male of his body lawfully begotten and of the heirs male of such heirs male, and immediately after judgment a *habere facias seisinam* is awarded, and before execution (namely, between five and six in the morning of the same day on which the recovery was suffered) the tenant in tail dies, and after his death but before the birth of the elder son's son the recovery is executed, and by force thereof Richard the uncle enters, and then the elder son's son is born, is his entry upon the uncle lawful or not?

4   The last point: may the uncle in this case take as a purchaser, forasmuch as the elder son had a daughter who was heir general and right heir of Edward Shelley at the time of the execution of the recovery?

This case was argued by *Anderson* Q. Sjt., and *Gawdy* and *Fenner* Sjts., for the plaintiff; and by *Popham* S.-G., *Cowper* and *Coke*, for the defendant ...[2]

As to the third point, which was the great doubt of the case, [the plaintiff's counsel] argued that the said Richard (the uncle) was in by purchase, and in consequence the defendant's entry upon him was unlawful. And this in effect was their principal argument: that which vests originally in the heir, and was not in the ancestor, vests in the heir by purchase; but this use vested originally in Richard

---

1   This report was first published by Coke in manuscript in 1582, with a dedication to Lord Buckhurst: [1972A] C.L.J. 71. It was first printed in 1600, and was also reported in Moo. K.B. 136 (probably an abridgment from Coke); Dyer 373.
2   Argument on all but the third point is here omitted.

Shelley, and never was vested in Edward Shelley, and therefore the use vested in Richard Shelley by purchase ... And they said that, since the words 'heirs male of the body of Edward Shelley' might be words of purchase, the law in this case will construe and take them as words of purchase, for otherwise the following words ('and the heirs male of their bodies') would be void: and such construction is always to be made of a deed that all the words, being agreeable to reason and conformable to law, may if possible take effect according to the intent of the parties ... So they concluded this point: first, that no use could arise until execution sued; no execution was sued in Edward Shelley's lifetime; and therefore it first vested in Richard as a purchaser, before the elder son's son was born ...

And on behalf of the defendant it was argued to the contrary ... because the use vested in Richard Shelley, though not directly by descent (so as to have his age, or toll an entry, and so forth), yet in the nature of and degree of a descent, by reason of an original act begun in the ancestor's lifetime. And their argument in substance was to this effect: where the heir takes anything which might have vested in the ancestor, the heir should be in by descent ... It was also asked: out of what fountain should this use arise? And who was the mother who conceived this use? And the indenture answers: the recovery. For the indenture says that the recovery shall be to the uses specified. Then it was said, if the recovery is the mother that conceived this use, and the fountain from whence it arose, forasmuch as this recovery was had in the lifetime of Edward Shelley (although the use slept and was like an embryo in its mother's womb until execution sued), yet when the execution was had it shall have respect to the recovery and raise the use, which was previously asleep; and once this use was awakened, or raised, it took its life and essence from the recovery, which was in Edward's lifetime ... But the indentures direct that the heirs male of the body of Edward Shelley shall take it by limitation of estate, and not by name of purchase; for when execution was had, the indentures immediately guided the use to Richard by reason that he was at that time heir male of the body of Edward Shelley, and this Richard is not heir male after the birth of the elder son's son. Further it was said, even admitting that all the matter above would not serve for the defendant—which the defendant's counsel held strongly it would—yet it is to be considered in this case that the estate vests in Richard by way of limitation of use, and not by any conveyance by the common law in possession. Therefore suppose

our case had been before the making of the statute of 27 Hen. VIII
... which of them would have had the *subpoena*? And the defendant's counsel conceived that the elder son's son would have had
the *subpoena*, even though the use first attached in the uncle; for if
the intention of Edward Shelley can appear to the court that the
elder son's son should have this use, then that is the rule by which
the use is to be guided and directed. For at common law it was the
parties' intentions that directed uses, they being determinable and
to be adjudged only by the chancellor (who is a judge of equity) in
the Chancery (which is a court of conscience): and, as Bracton says
(fo. 18),[3] 'Nothing is so consonant with natural equity as that the
will of the owner (*dominus*) should be observed in transferring
something to another' ... Now, the intention of Edward Shelley is
to be proved by various circumstances appearing in the record[4] ...
And as to what has been objected, that since the limitation was to
the heirs male of the body of Edward Shelley and the heirs male
lawfully begotten of the heirs male, the heirs male of the body of
Edward Shelley should be purchasers, for otherwise the subsequent
words would be void, the defendant's counsel answered that it is a
rule of law, when the ancestor takes an estate of freehold by any
gift or conveyance, and an estate is limited in the same gift or
conveyance either mediately or immediately to his heirs (in fee or in
tail), that always in such cases 'the heirs' are words of limitation of
the estate and not words of purchase. That appears in the *Provost
of Beverley's Case*, 40 Edw. III[5] ... and in various other books.
Thus, since Edward Shelley in this case took an estate of freehold,
and an estate is then limited to his heirs male of his body, the heirs
male of his body must of necessity take by descent and cannot be
purchasers. (It is otherwise where an estate for years is limited to
the ancestor, remainder to another for life, remainder to the right
heirs of the lessee for years: there his heirs are purchasers. Or if the

3   *Bracton*, vol. II, p. 67.
4   I.e. Edward would not have used such a settlement if he had intended to benefit
     Richard; nor would he have inserted the lease for 24 years (since Richard was
     then 18). The true purpose of the recovery was evidently to bar Mary's interest
     and keep the land in the Shelley family; and so it was only intended to go to
     Richard if Anne gave birth to a girl.
5   *Sutton's Case* (1366); see p. 65, above.

remainder is limited to the 'heir', in the singular number, after a lease for life: there the heir takes an estate for life by purchase.[6]) And if it were to be admitted that, having regard to the subsequent words, the right heirs male should have by purchase to them and the heirs male of their bodies, then a violence would be offered both to the words and to the meaning of the party: for if the heir male of the body of Edward Shelley took as purchaser, then all the other issue male of the body of Edward Shelley would be excluded from taking anything by the limitation; and it would be against the express limitation of the party, for the limitation is to the use of the heirs male of the body of Edward Shelley and of the heirs male of their bodies begotten, and for default of such issue to various other persons in remainder; and so if Richard Shelley (the heir male of the body of Edward Shelley at the time of his death) took by purchase, then only the heirs male of the body of Richard Shelley would be inheritable, and no other sons of Edward Shelley or their male heirs, and consequently if Richard died without male issue the land would remain over to strangers . . . So in our case the heirs male of the body of Edward Shelley are named only to give Edward Shelley an estate tail, and not to make any other purchaser than Edward Shelley. Therefore the uncle in our case cannot claim the land as a mere purchaser, but if he takes it in any sort he shall take it in the nature and course of a descent . . . and therefore the [son of the] elder son shall enter upon him . . .

After the said case had been argued openly and at large on three several days by the counsel on each side in the Queen's Bench, the queen heard of it—for such was the rareness and difficulty of the case, being so important that it was generally known—and of her gracious disposition, to prevent long, tedious and chargeable suits between parties so near in blood, which would be the undoing of both (being gentlemen of a good and ancient family), she directed her gracious letters to Sir Thomas Bromley, knight, lord chancellor of England, who was of great and profound knowledge and judgment in the law, thereby requiring him to assemble all the justices of England before him to give their resolutions and judgments therein, after conferring among themselves upon the said questions.

And thereupon the lord chancellor, in Easter term [1581], called before him at his house (called York House) Sir Christopher

6 See *Baldwyn v Smyth* (sub nom. *Archer's Case*) (1594); see p. 84, above.

WRAY, knight, lord chief justice of England, and his fellow justices of the Queen's Bench, SIR JAMES DYER, knight, lord chief justice of the Court of Common Pleas, and all his fellow justices of the same court, and SIR ROGER MANWOOD, knight, lord chief baron of the Exchequer, and the barons of the Exchequer; before whom the aforesaid questions were moved and briefly argued by *Fenner* Sjt. on behalf of the plaintiff, and [*Coke*] on behalf of the defendant. And at that time the lord chancellor was of opinion for the defendant, and openly declared his opinion before all the justices that upon the third question the law was for the defendant, and therefore the defendant's entry upon the uncle was lawful. But the said questions were not resolved at that time, because the said justices desired time to consider the questions. Eight or nine days later in the same term, all the said justices and barons met together in Serjeants' Inn, Fleet Street, for the resolution of the said case. And there the case was again shortly argued by them; after which arguments the justices at that time conferred among themselves, and took further time to consider the said questions in the next vacation, until the beginning of Trinity term then next following. And accordingly at the beginning of Trinity term, after great study and consideration of the said record of the special verdict, all the said justices and barons met again in Serjeants' Inn, in Fleet Street, at which time, upon conference among themselves, all the justices of England, the lord chief baron and the barons of the Exchequer, except one of the puisne justices of the Common Pleas,[7] agreed that the defendant's entry upon the said Richard (the uncle) was lawful.

And four or five days after their last meeting, one of the defendant's counsel came to the bar in the Queen's Bench, and moved the justices to know their resolutions in the said case, for their resolution was not known to the defendant or his counsel. And SIR CHRISTOPHER WRAY, knight, lord chief justice, answered that they were resolved; and thereupon asked the plaintiff's counsel (being then at the bar) if they could say any more on behalf of the plaintiff, who answered that they had said as much as they could; and likewise asked the defendant's counsel if they had any new matter to say for the defendant, who said they had not. Then

7 Named in the MS. as Mead J.

the said chief justice gave judgment that the plaintiff should take nothing by his bill. And because the counsel on both sides were desirous to know upon which of the said points their resolution did depend, the said chief justice openly declared ... that all the justices of England and barons of the Exchequer (except one of the justices of the Common Pleas) were agreed as to the third point: that the uncle was in in course and nature of a descent ...

The record shows that judgment was entered for the defendant in Trinity term 1581.

(b) 1 And. 69, pl. 143.

... The last and main point was whether this new use should be in nature like an estate created in possession in the father, and should make an estate tail or fee in use in the father, which descended to the next heir male of his body, or not. And it was argued not, for during the father's lifetime there was no use created, but only an intention to raise the use by the recovery, which the father could not do in his lifetime because the recovery was not executed in his lifetime, and by consequence there was nothing in the father which commenced by the indenture and recovery and which might descend. Another reason alleged was that it should be a remainder in Richard because it is limited to the heirs male of the body of Edward and the heirs male of their bodies, and by these words Edward's intention appears to have been that he would not have these words 'heirs male of the body of Edward' to be words of inheritance, but words of purchase ...

Notwithstanding which, judgment was given for the said Henry, and it was agreed that he ought to have the land. But the reason was not published by the court.[8]

Note that Mr. Coke, the Attorney General, has now made a report in print of this case, with arguments and the agreements of the chancellor and other judges; but none of that was spoken in court or shown there.

---

8 Cf. Dyer: '... The following term it was resolved by the opinions of the justices of both benches, and the chief baron, that the posthumous son should have the land, as the nearest and eldest heir male; and that seems also to have been the intent and will of the creator of this special tail. And the uncle could not have it as purchaser, because he is not the heir of the body of his father, for the eldest son's daughter is heir general: therefore he is not heir male of the body of the father in order to purchase unless he was both heir and male, which he was not; but he took by the limitation of the said entail by descent until the son was born ...'

DILLON v FREINE (1594)⁹

Record: KB 27/1308, m. 65; 1 Co. Rep. 113. William Dillon brought a bill
of trespass against John Freine for breaking his close in Tawstock, Devon,
on 16 November 1587. The defendant pleaded Not guilty, and on 7 July
1589 at Exeter assizes (Anderson C.J.C.P., Gent B.) the jury found a special
verdict: Sir Richard Chudleigh had four sons, Christopher, Thomas, Oliver
and Nicholas; and on 26 April 1557 he enfeoffed various persons to the use
of himself and his heirs begotten on the body of Mary (then wife of Thomas
Carew), and likewise (for default of such issue) with respect to five other
married women in succession, and in default of such issue to the use of his
last will for ten years following his death, and then to the use of the feoffees
and their heirs during the life of Christopher the first son, and after his death
to the use of the first issue male of the body of Christopher and the heirs of
the body of such issue, and for default of such issue to the second issue male
of the body of Christopher and the heirs male of the body of such issue, and
so on to the tenth issue, and for default of issue male of Christopher to the
use of Thomas the second son in tail, and likewise successively to the other
sons, and for default of all such issue to the use of the right heirs of Sir

PEDIGREE OF CHUDLEIGH¹⁰

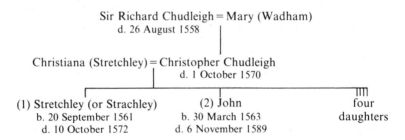

Sir Richard Chudleigh = Mary (Wadham)
d. 26 August 1558

Christiana (Stretchley) = Christopher Chudleigh
d. 1 October 1570

(1) Stretchley (or Strachley)   (2) John   four
b. 20 September 1561   b. 30 March 1563   daughters
d. 10 October 1572   d. 6 November 1589

Richard in fee simple; then on 17 November 1558 Sir Richard died without
issue by any of the women named, and in 1559 the feoffees enfeoffed
Christopher in fee simple (he having notice of the uses in the deed of 1557);
and in 1561 Christopher had issue Strachley, his eldest son, and in 1563

---

9   Also known as *Chudleigh's Case*.
10   From the record; and J. L. Vivian, *The Visitations of the County of Devon*
     (1895), p. 189. There is no mention in any of the pedigrees of Thomas, Oliver
     and Nicholas, younger brothers of Christopher, so perhaps they died young.

John, his second son; on 1 July 1564 Christopher bargained and sold the land for £220 to Sir John Chichester in fee simple, and enfeoffed him with warranty, and in 1565 Sir John enfeoffed Philip Chichester, who in 1573 granted a copyhold estate for life to John Freine; Strachley died without issue in 1570, and on 11 March 1586 John Chudleigh (his brother and heir) entered and enfeoffed William Dillon,[11] who entered; and John Freine re-entered. If Freine's re-entry was unlawful, the jurors found for the plaintiff with 4d. damages and 20s. costs. The question was argued in the Queen's Bench in 1591,[12] and was later referred to all the judges of England in the Exchequer Chamber, before whom it was argued in 1594.

(a) 1 Co. Rep. 120.[13]

... The question in this case is no other than whether these contingent uses [to Christopher's sons] were destroyed and over-turned before their existence, by the said feoffment [of 1559], so that they shall never rise out of the feoffees' estate after the birth of the issue. And this case was argued many times at the bar in the Queen's Bench, on both sides; and because the case was difficult and of great consequence and importance, it was thought necessary that all the justices of England should upon solemn argument show their opinions in this case openly in the Exchequer Chamber. Afterwards, in Hilary term [1594], the case was argued in the Exchequer Chamber before all the justices of England, by *Hugh Wyat* on behalf of the plaintiff, and by *Coke*, the queen's solicitor-general, on behalf of the defendant; and afterwards in Easter term following by *Robert Atkinson* on behalf of the plaintiff, and by *Francis Bacon* on behalf of the defendant, but I did not hear their arguments...[14]

And because only WALMSLEY J.C.P. and PERYAM C.B. argued that judgment should be given for the plaintiff, and all the other judges and barons concluded against the plaintiff, I will begin with

11 William Dillon, later knighted, married Elizabeth, daughter and co-heir of Philip Chichester, in 1579: J. L. Vivian, *The Visitations of the County of Devon* (1895), p. 285.

12 Another case arising out of the 1557 settlement was commenced in the Queen's Bench in 1585: CUL MS. Hh. 2. 1, fo. 83. This was an action of ejectment by George Chudleigh, on the demise of John Chudleigh, against William Dyer, who had been granted the manor of Lanreath, Cornwall, by Christopher Chudleigh. The MS. reports the arguments of Egerton, Tanfield and Coke, but no judgment.

13 Also reported in 1 And. 309; Poph. 70.

14 Bacon's argument is printed verbatim in *Letters and Life of Francis Bacon* (J. Spedding, ed.), vol. VII, pp. 617–636. The others may be found at length in Coke. They covered much the same ground as in *Brent's Case* p. 135, above.

the effect of their two arguments. Before the statute of 1 Ric. III,[15] the feoffees had not only the whole estate in the land, but also the whole power to give and dispose of it, for cestuy que use was a trespasser if he entered upon the land against their will ... And PERYAM C.B. and WALMSLEY J. said that the statute of 27 Hen. VIII[16] was not made to extinguish or eradicate any uses, but had advanced uses and had now established safety and assurance for cestuy que use against his feoffees; for before the statute the feoffees were the owners of the land, and now the statute has made cestuy que use the owner of the land. Before the statute the possession governed and ruled the use; but now since the statute the use governs and rules the possession: for by the said act of 27 Hen. VIII the possession is a subject and follower of the use ... And it would be against the meaning and the letter of the law also to say that any estate or right (or *scintilla juris*) should remain in the feoffees after the statute of 27 Hen. VIII, for it appears by the preamble that the makers of the act intended to uproot and eradicate the whole estate of the feoffees ... so that by a judgment given by the whole parliament the estate shall be out of the feoffees. And PERYAM C.B. said that *scintilla juris*, which is mentioned in 17 Eliz.,[17] is like Sir Thomas More's *Utopia*.[18] And they said that since this statute no trust or confidence was reposed in the feoffees, for now (as WALMSLEY J. said) the feoffees may not do or permit anything in prejudice of cestuy que use. Before the statute the office of the feoffee was to execute the estate according to the use; but now the statute has taken away all the office of the feoffees, and now the act executes the possession to the use, and takes away all the trust and power from the feoffees ... And WALMSLEY J. said that, as a fountain gives to everyone who comes in his turn his just measure of water, so the first seisin and estate in fee given by the feoffment to the feoffees is sufficient to yield to all persons to whom any present or future use is limited a competent measure of estate in their time ...

PERYAM C.B. conceived that these future uses before their births

---

15 See p. 101, above.
16 Statute of Uses (1536); see p. 112, above.
17 *Brent's Case* (1575); see p. 141, above.
18 I.e. a figment of the imagination.

are not preserved in the bowels and belly of the earth, but are in the clouds (*in nubibus*) and in the preservation of the law. For he fully agreed with WALMSLEY J. that by virtue of the act the whole estate shall be out of the feoffees; and therefore of necessity it must be in some person, or in abeyance and in consideration of the law; and it would be absurd to say that the feoffees should have a lesser estate than they took by the first livery; and so, since nothing remains in the feoffees, and this future use cannot be executed until the person who is to take it comes into being, it must of necessity be meanwhile in the preservation of the law ... And he and WALMS-LEY J. also agreed in their argument that the uses in this case should follow the rules of estates at common law; and therefore if the tenant for life in this case died before the birth of the son, the remainder in use would be void, for it would be void by the rule of the common law (if it had been made in possession) if the remainder did not vest during the particular estate, or at least when the particular estate determined; and there is no difference between uses and estates in possession as to this purpose. So they concluded that judgment ought to be given for the plaintiff.

On the other side it was argued by EWENS B., OWEN J.C.P., BEAUMONT J.C.P., FENNER J.Q.B., GAWDY J.Q.B., CLARKE B., CLENCH J.Q.B., ANDERSON C.J.C.P. and POPHAM C.J.Q.B. tò the contrary. And it was agreed by them all that the feoffment made by the said feoffees, who had an estate for life by limitation of the use, devested all the estates and the future uses also. And it is immaterial that [Christopher] Chudleigh, their feoffee, had notice of the first use, because all the old estates were devested by the said feoffment; and this new estate cannot be subject to the old uses which arose from the old estate which was devested by the feoffment ...

And it was held by EWENS B., OWEN, BEAUMONT and FENNER JJ., CLARKE B., CLENCH J., ANDERSON C.J. and POPHAM C.J. that at common law both future uses and uses in contingency are devested and discontinued by a disseisin, or by such a feoffment as in the case at bar: as also are uses *in esse*, until the first estate out of which the uses arise is recontinued. And the statute of 27 Hen. VIII does not transfer possession to any use except uses *in esse* only, and not to any uses in future or in contingency until they come into being ... and since at common law there can be no use *in esse* if there is no seisin out of which the use shall arise, therefore no use can be executed by the statute of 27 Hen. VIII unless there is seisin in some person subject to the use at the time when it is executed . . .

CLARKE B. said that some have supposed these future uses to be preserved in the bowels of the earth, and that the land should be charged with them into whose hands soever it should come; and some have supposed them to be preserved in the clouds, and in the custody of the law. But he said, in our case, if they are below the earth they should be perpetually buried and should never come up again, and if they are up in the clouds they should stay up there for ever and never come down. For he said that the sons of Christopher Chudleigh in our case were not born in due time, and (as this case is) they should never take the future uses . . .

So all the justices and barons of the Exchequer, except PERYAM C.B., WALMSLEY and GAWDY JJ., concluded that, since the statute of 27 Hen. VIII extends only to uses *in esse* and to persons *in esse*, and not to any uses which depend only in possibility, for that reason the contingent uses in the case at the bar remain (so long as they depend in possibility only) at common law, and by consequence they may be destroyed or discontinued before they come into being by all such means as uses might have been discontinued or destroyed by at common law.

And all the justices and barons of the Exchequer did agree with the chief baron and WALMSLEY J. in this point: that these remainders limited in use in the case at the bar should follow the rule and reason of estates executed in possession by the common law; and therefore they all unanimously agreed that if the estate for life in the case at the bar had been determined by the death of the feoffees before the birth of the eldest son, the remainders *in futuro* would have been void and would never have taken effect, even if the sons were born afterwards; for a remainder in use ought to vest during the particular estate, or at least in the instant when it ends, just like an estate in possession . . . [19]

The record shows that Freine's re-entry was held good, and judgment was entered for the defendant in Hilary term 1595.

---

19 Popham C.J.'s remarks about perpetuities are given, at more length than in 1 Co. Rep., at p. 156, below.

(b) 1 And. 338.

... There are many of these cases in our books, with which several [speakers] furnished their arguments and spent much time, but which are left to those who take pleasure in those sorts of arguments. Neither these cases, nor any other reasons or previous dicta by anyone to maintain that this statute is to be taken by the equity, are sufficient to prove the law to be so. And so it was said that this matter of equity is of no avail, the case in question being as it is. Against this it has been said that, if the law was as the greater part of the judges held it, divers houses of noble persons and others of great living would be destroyed, which by this means of giving power and prerogative to the uses would be continued, and their heirs and lands preserved in dangerous times of civil dissension; and to destroy these uses is unfitting, and tends to destroy Nebuchadnezzar's tree, whereon rest the fowls of the air, and in the shade whereof lie the beasts of the earth.[20] Whereupon those who argue thus draw the conclusion that it would be inconvenient to have another course than is contended for by them, for it would be mischievous, since the poor and common sort of people lie down beneath this tree and rest upon the branches. To the contrary of this it was said by the other side that the destruction of nobility or their houses was not good in general terms, but if it pleased God to have a noble house uprooted or ended, or a realm, or an empire, it is not for anyone to imagine that this by itself is simply bad; for there is no doubting that such an imagination is vain and offensive to God, being against his judgment and his power, whereby he may remove great and small alike and take away whatever he has given or permitted them to have. And this may well be perceived through the tree mentioned before. The story where that is remembered was, in brief, that the said Nebuchadnezzar was a king of great power and ruled many realms and people, and his greatness reached to the heavens and his dominion to the ends of the earth; and this tree cut down to the ground (before remembered) indicated that the said king for his iniquity lost all his realms and dominions—one excepted—by the sentence of God, and this punishment came to him for iniquity done by him, and so it befell him by the sentence of God; and when that king was dead, his son also offended God, and therefore his

20 *Daniel*, 4.10 et seq.

realm and kingdom was also taken from him. And similar examples have happened in kingdoms, great houses, and people of all sorts, great and small, for their sins and offences committed by them; and therefore no assurance may be devised or made by man to prevent the ordinance and sentence of the Almighty, and therefore it is vain for man to compass or imagine it . . .

(c) CUL MS. Hh. 2. 1, fo. 105.

. . . POPHAM C.J. argued notably as to the mischiefs [arising from the Statute of Uses], and pursued it with various notable reasons. For he said that uses were and are at this day more perilous and mischievous to the common weal than ever they were before the passing of the said statute; and whereas it has been said that various men have erected their houses and families in name and blood by such conveyances, thinking to perpetuate (*eternise*) them and their posterity by such perpetuities, in truth after two or three descents it had been and would be the utter subversion of such families who have so provided for their posterity, and the utter decay thereof in time to come [because the issue could not dispose of the land to pay their debts or meet other needs] . . . which is utterly contrary to the providence of God, *qui dedit terram filiis hominum*[1] to be disposed by them for their better profit and advancement and not to continue it always in the same sex or blood, which in the end will take away all commerce and dealing between men. Also by these means he cannot provide for his second or younger children, nor for advancement of his daughters in marriage, but is as a man locked up and *quasi* tied to a post, and can do nothing other than is limited and appointed for him to do. For no one in the world can be prescient of his necessities and occasions, and therefore such is the imperfection of human policy and prudence that God in his providence turns that to our destruction in which we have supposed and have put our greatest confidence and assurance. Secondly, this manner of conveyance breaks asunder the law of nature and rends in sunder the very entrails of nature, so that when the disobedient and sensual son

---

1   I.e. 'who gave the earth to the sons of men'.

considers to himself that his father cannot dispose of his land at his good pleasure but must leave the heritage to him willy-nilly, by this way of thinking (*imagination*) in his unripe and immature years, being seduced by those vices and passions which for the greater part infest youth, he becomes undutiful in demeanour against his parents, in manner and conversation dissolute, and in the end subject and made as prey to all brokers and usurers and wrongfully subverted and ruined to the overthrow of the family and impregnable grief to his parents and friends. Moreover, these kinds of assurances and conveyances of future uses impair all natural love, which God by the rules of nature has engrafted between kinsmen of one blood, name and progeny; and those who have limitations of such uses or provisos that they should not alienate their remainders over to others have been so watchful of the remainders upon them, and in all points prepared and ready to take every advantage as should be incredible had not experience made it apparent and manifest. And POPHAM said that lately, within 24 hours before his argument, he had had good intelligence of this. For someone had acknowledged a fine before him, and another came to him praying to have a copy of the conusance . . . to the intent that (being a kinsman of the conusor) he might take advantage thereof [as next in line in remainder]; so watchful are they to take advantage, one against the other, in such respects. Thirdly, he said he would remember a notable, hard and lamentable event which occurred, in which he and Plowden were retained as counsel: a man of great estate who had such a perpetuity made of his inheritance by his ancestors—which inheritance was of the annual value of £1,000 and more—had a wife who eloped and was living in adultery, and the question was what means the husband might use to disinherit the bastard;[2] for it was limited that if he alienated or sold, or went about to alienate, his estate should cease and be in another. In this case Plowden thought he could not alienate without endangering his estate, and it seemed to [Popham] that he could. But since that time Plowden was so moved with the event that he would never afterwards put his hand to subscribe to encourage men to take such assurances . . .

---

2 The child born in adultery would be presumed legitimate, since his mother was married.

CORBETT v CORBETT (1600)

Record: CP 40/1021, m. 1049; 1 Co. Rep. 77. Arthur Corbett[3] brought trespass against Roland Corbett for breaking his close at Stockerston, Leicestershire, on 20 June 1598. The defendant pleaded that Christopher Corbett (father of both parties) was seised of the land, and on 12 April 1588 covenanted in consideration of paternal love and affection and the advancement of his sons that he and his heirs should stand seised to the use of himself for life, and after his death to the use of Roland and his heirs male of his body, and for default of such issue to the use of Arthur and his heirs male of his body, with various further remainders; and, by the operation of the Statute of Uses, Christopher was thereby seised as tenant for life; and on Christopher's death Roland entered as tenant in tail, and Arthur entered upon his possession, and Roland re-entered. To this plea Arthur replied that there was a further covenant or condition in the deed of 1588, not mentioned in the plea: that whenever Roland or his heirs should devise, attempt or put in motion any fine, recovery or other conveyance whereby any estate entailed to them would be barred, then immediately after the act leading towards such a conveyance (and before the conveyance was executed) the estate of the person performing that act should cease as if he were naturally dead, and the land should then pass to the person next entitled; and he said that Christopher died on 31 May 1588, and that in Hilary term 1594 Roland (having then no issue) suffered a common recovery to the use of himself in fee simple, whereupon Arthur on 30 June 1594 entered in his remainder by force of the proviso. To this replication Roland demurred, and the court took advisement until Easter term 1600.

(a) 1 Co. Rep. 84.[4]

. . . In this case various matters were moved at the bar which were not unanimously agreed by the justices at the bench; and various matters were moved by the justices in their arguments concerning perpetuities in general: but I will only make a summary report of the principal reasons and causes of their judgment, in which all the justices of the Common Pleas were unanimously resolved.

1 It was resolved by the lord ANDERSON C.J., WALMSLEY, GLANVILL and KINGSMILL JJ. that this proviso to cease an estate limited to someone and his heirs male of his body, as if the tenant in tail were dead, was repugnant, impossible and against law: for

---

3 Note that the real disputants were the Mildmays, and the facts entered on the record were fictitious; see pp. 162, 163, 164, fn. 8, below.
4 Also reported in 2 And. 134; Moo. K.B. 601.

the death of a tenant in tail is not a cesser of the estate tail ... and if the estate tail should cease as if he was dead his issue inheritable to the estate tail would have it by descent in his father's lifetime, or the remainderman or reversioner would have it in the lifetime of the tenant in tail, which is impossible: for death, either civil (such as entering religion) or natural (that is, dissolution of the soul from the body), is requisite to every descent, remainder or reversion upon the determination of an estate tail ...

ANDERSON C.J. cited two adjudged cases in point, one in the case of a will and the other in the case of a use.

The case of the will was in an action of waste between John Germyn and Arthur Arscott in the Common Pleas, Hil. 37 Eliz. rot. 1758 ...

[Record: CP 40/1543, m. 1758. Germyn counted against Arscott for waste in lands in St Giles on the Heath, Devon, which Arscott held for years under an assignment which Thomas Carie made to him for 99 years on 14 March 1583; and on 26 March Thomas Carie made his will, leaving the reversion to his son Peter Carie and the heirs male of his body, and for default of such issue to Henry Carie in tail male, with similar successive remainders to Fulfard, Richard, Andrew, Gregory and Mary Carie; and Thomas died, and Peter entered, and in 1585 levied a fine in which the present plaintiff was querent[5] and Peter, Fulfard, Richard, Andrew, Gregory and Mary (with her husband) were deforciants. The defendant confessed the lease to himself by Thomas Carie, and Thomas's will, but set out a clause against discontinuance (not mentioned in the count): that if any of the sons or their issue should attempt to sell or discontinue, then immediately after the attempt (and before the sale or alienation was executed) the estate of the person making the attempt should cease and determine as if the person were naturally dead. (For the clause in full, see 1 Co. Rep. 85.) The plaintiff demurred, and in Michaelmas term 1595 the plea was held bad and judgment entered for the plaintiff. The case is reported in 1 And. 186; 2 And. 7; 4 Leon. 83; Moo. K.B. 495; and in Coke's notebook, BL MS. Harley 6686, ff. 128v–133.]

And upon solemn argument it was adjudged by all the justices of the Common Pleas that the action of waste was maintainable, and that the said proviso of restraint was void, for two principal reasons: (1) because it was against law, and (2) because it was repugnant and self-contradictory. [It was] against law for two reasons: (i) be the said proviso a condition or a limitation, the whole estate ought to be defeated by it, and it cannot determine the estate in part and continue it for the residue, and an estate in land cannot cease for a time and then revive and revest; (ii) when a man

---

5 I.e. the grantee, who brought the collusive action.

gives land to someone and his heirs male, with remainders over, he cannot by the rules of law determine this estate in tail as to one person and dispose the same estate to another person ... And it was resolved that said proviso was repugnant for two reasons: (i) because when he had devised the land to someone and the heirs male of his body, which is an estate of inheritance, and by express limitation determinable on death without issue male, such a proviso to cease as if he was dead is repugnant, for the death of the tenant in tail is no determination of the estate, but only death without issue; (ii) it was repugnant because the first part of the proviso was, 'if he should attempt or go about to discontinue, bar etc.' and shall accomplish and effect the same, and then his estate should cease from the time of the attempt and before such alienation: in which it was agreed that there was a manifest repugnancy, for by the first part the estate should not cease until an attempt and an accomplishment, and by the later part it should cease after attempt and before accomplishment. And these were the reasons for their judgment in the case of *Germyn v Arscott*, which being in the case of a will—which receives a more benign interpretation according to the testator's intention—is stronger, as the lord ANDERSON said, than the case at the bar.

The other case which the lord ANDERSON cited was adjudged Hil. 37 Eliz. between Cholmeley, plaintiff, and Humble, defendant, in the Common Pleas ...

[Record: CP 40/1516, m. 2018. Richard Cholmeley the younger (an infant) brought trespass against Richard Humble, vintner of London, for trespass to his close at Thornton on the Hill, Yorkshire, on 10 March 1592. The defendant pleaded in bar that the land was called 'Thornton's Tenement' and was part of the manor of Thornton, whereof Sir Richard Cholmeley was seised in fee; and on 31 October 1579, in consideration of the preferment of his younger sons, and the continuance of the manors in his name and blood, and the preservation of his house, and the love of his posterity, Sir Richard granted the manor to various feoffees, to make an estate to the use of Sir Richard for life, and afterwards to the use of his son Francis for life, and afterwards to the use of the first son of Francis and the heirs male of his body (and so on successively to the tenth son), with similar remainders to another son Henry and his sons, and then successively to the four sons of Roger Cholmeley deceased, and so forth; and if Sir Richard should die without executing this estate, it was agreed that Sir Richard and his heirs would stand seised to these uses; and Sir Richard did not execute the estate, and so by the operation of the Statute of Uses he was seised for life; then he died, and Francis entered, and died without male issue; and Henry entered in his remainder, and had issue Richard (the plaintiff); and in 1591 a fine was levied between the defendant as querent and Henry and the other remaindermen as deforciants, as a result of which the defendant was seised in fee; and the plaintiff entered, and the defendant re-entered. The plaintiff confessed the facts in the bar, but set out a proviso against attempting to alienate, very similar to that in the previous case. The plaintiff demurred, and in Hilary term 1595 the replication was held insufficient and judgment given for the defendant. The case is reported in 1 And. 346; Cro. Eliz. 379; Moo. K.B. 592; and in Coke's notebook, BL MS. Harley 6686, ff. 228v–230.]

It was adjudged against the plaintiff. And the principal reason of the judgment, as the lord ANDERSON said, was that the said proviso to cease an estate tail as if tenant in tail were dead was utterly against law, impossible, and repugnant ... for he cannot by proviso or condition determine the estate in the land to which it is annexed in part. For when the statute of 27 Hen. VIII has transferred the use into possession and estate of the land, he cannot make a fraction in that estate in case of a limitation of a use, which he cannot make in a gift in tail by livery in possession; for the statute has not transferred the possession to the use, but has transferred and incorporated the use in the estate of the land ...

WALMSLEY J. said that when an estate is given to someone it may be defeated wholly by a condition or limitation; but the same estate, or any part of it, cannot be determined as to one person and given in part or in whole to another, for that is repugnant to the rules of law. For instance, if a man makes a lease for life on condition that if he does not pay £20 someone else shall have the land, this future limitation is void ... And WALMSLEY said that if a man makes a feoffment in fee of land to the use of A. and his heirs every Monday, and to the use of B. and his heirs every Tuesday, and to the use of C. and his heirs every Wednesday, these limitations are void; for we do not find such fractions of estates in law ... If one could limit estates in land to cease during the minorities of heirs, and other persons to have the land during that time, then all wardships might be defeated and great inconveniences would ensue; and therefore, he said, this way of ceasing estates and of carrying one and the same estate (or any part thereof) from one to another without determination, namely from one living person to another living person, is impossible and against law and reason ...

And for these reasons it was resolved by the whole court, *nullo contradicente*, that judgment should be given against the plaintiff ...

The record shows that judgment was given accordingly in Hilary term 1600, and that a writ of error was brought in the Queen's Bench on 12 April 1600. The dispute continued as *Mildmay's Case*, below.

(b) W. Burton, *The Description of Leicester Shire* (1622), p. 271 (untr.).

Stockerston ... This place is memorable for that great case of perpetuities between Corbet and Corbet ... set down at large in the lord Coke's first part of *Reports*, wherein it appeareth that the action was here laid for the trial of the title. The truth is, never any Corbet was lord of this manor, neither was that a true case as between those two Corbets,[6] but a feigned case in names caused by Sir Anthony Mildmay of Apethorpe in the county of Northampton, knight, whose lands being perpetuated in the same manner, and having only one daughter (now married to Francis Vane of Kent) to whom he intended to pass all his inheritance, was desirous to be ascertained of the law in this case, otherwise, loth to hazard a forfeiture, therefore caused this action thus to be brought as is above shewed.

But SIR EDMUND ANDERSON, then chief justice of the Common Pleas, at first not being made privy to the business, but after understanding the circumstances *a latere*, was in such a chafe at the first hearing of it, being then upon the bench at Westminster, that in a fury he flung out the Hall, saying he came not thither to argue any counterfeit cases. I was then standing by, being a reporter in the same court.[7] But after, being better qualified, he argued the case and gave judgment against perpetuities.

---

6   They seem nevertheless to have been real people, settled at Wanlip: J. Nichols, *History of Leicestershire*, vol. III, pt. 2, p. 1100.

7   William Burton was then a student below the bar, having been admitted to the Inner Temple in 1592–93. He was called in 1603.

MILDMAY v MILDMAY (1602)

Record: CP 40/1661, m. 829. Anthony Mildmay brought trespass against Humphrey Mildmay for breaking his close at Newton, Northamptonshire, on 26 June 1600. The facts mentioned in the defendant's plea in bar were substantially the same as those admitted by demurrer in *Corbet's Case*, except that it was Sir Walter Mildmay (d. 1589), chancellor of the Exchequer, who in 1588 covenanted to stand seised to the use of himself for life, remainder to Anthony (the plaintiff), remainder to Humphrey (the defendant), and so forth, with the same proviso against attempting to bar the entail; and it was Anthony who, in 1600, suffered the recovery. To this plea the plaintiff demurred.

Moo. K.B. 632, pl. 868.

... It was argued by the justices at the bench, namely WARBURTON, WALMSLEY and KINGSMILL JJ., and ANDERSON C.J., who were equally divided.

WARBURTON J. argued that there are now many uses which are not executed by the statute of 27 Hen. VIII: such as tortious uses, fraudulent uses, uses upon uses, troublesome uses (to stand seised to the use of someone on Tuesday and someone else on Wednesday), and likewise uses of perpetual freeholds. But contingent uses are serviceable to the common weal, and are usual in the recent books. And the proviso in the principal case is not repugnant, nor does it contain any facts not issuable or triable.... and he held 'going about' [to do any act to bar the estate] was issuable, for he may go about by some overt act which a jury may take notice of, such as purchasing a writ in the Chancery, or sealing indentures; though speaking with his counsel is not 'going about'... As to the repugnancy, he said that the words 'as if he were naturally dead and not otherwise' were but abundance and surplusage, and not repugnancy; and the sentence shall be construed as lawfully as may be, and that is that the estate shall cease during his lifetime and afterwards arise again in his issue—which is not repugnant or unfitting... As to *Corbet's Case*, that was a feigned case and is not to tie the conscience of any judge. And as to the case of *Germyn v Arscott*, that concerned a possession and not a use. And *Cholmeley v Humble* differed from the case in question.

WALMSLEY J. agreed with WARBURTON J. ... that the condition was not repugnant, and said that he delivered a doubtful opinion on that point in *Corbet's Case*, but now upon better advice and deliberation he resolved that it was not repugnant, but that the estate tail might cease throughout the lifetime of Anthony (the offender) and afterwards be revived in his issue. And he said that the proviso went on to say that the use should be to such person to whom it would descend or remain if he were dead, which leads a future contingent use to the issue in tail, which may be interposed well enough . . .

KINGSMILL J. and ANDERSON C.J. to the contrary, and they insisted wholly upon the reasons and precedent of *Corbet's Case* . . .

The record shows that the action was not continued beyond Easter term 1602.

HETHERSAL v MILDMAY (1605)

This was a third case between the Mildmays, the facts being substantially the same as in the previous two cases.

6 Co. Rep. 40.

This term, on a special verdict in an action for a trespass done at Newton, Northamptonshire, the case between James Hethersal (lessee of Humphrey Mildmay, esquire), plaintiff, and Sir Anthony Mildmay, knight, defendant—which was *mutatis mutandis* all one with *Corbet's Case* reported by me in the first part of my *Reports*— was argued at the bar, as it had been in various terms past.[8] And it was also argued by the judges, and adjudged against the plaintiff according to the judgment given in *Corbet's Case*.[9] And in this case some points were resolved upon great consideration which were not moved in *Corbet's Case*:

1   That all these perpetuities were against the reason and policy of the common law; for at common law all inheritances were fee simple . . . but the true policy and rule of the common law in this

---

8   Cf. HLS. MS. 2069, fo. 49: '*Coke* A.-G. came to the bar to argue *Corbet's Case* (which had been adjudged) by the name of *Mildmay's Case*; for it seems that the former case was only to know the opinions of the judges, but now the true case comes along unmasked (*sans vizard*) . . .'

9   See p. 158, above.

point was in effect overthrown by the statute *De donis conditionalibus*,[10] which established a general perpetuity by act of parliament for all who had or would make it . . . until about 12 Edw. IV, when the judges (upon consultation among themselves) resolved that an estate tail might be docked and barred by a common recovery . . .

2   It was resolved that it was impossible and repugnant that an estate tail should cease as if the tenant in tail was dead, whether or not he had issue; for an estate tail cannot cease as long as it continues . . .

3   It was resolved that if a man makes a gift in tail, upon condition that he shall not suffer a common recovery, this condition is repugnant to the estate tail and against law. For there are various incidents to an estate tail: (i) to be unpunishable for waste; (ii) that his wife shall be endowed; (iii) the husband of a woman tenant in tail, after issue, shall be tenant by the curtesy; (iv) that tenant in tail may suffer a common recovery and thereby bar the estate tail, and the reversion or remainder also. And these inseparable incidents, which the law annexes to an estate tail, cannot be prohibited by condition. Therefore if a man makes a gift in tail on condition that the donee shall not commit waste, or that his wife shall not be endowed, or that the husband of a woman tenant in tail shall not be tenant by the curtesy, or that tenant in tail shall not suffer a common recovery, these conditions are repugnant and against law . . .

4   . . . It was resolved that the words 'attempt etc. or go about etc.' are uncertain and void in law; and God forbid that men's inheritances and estates should depend upon such uncertainty . . .

5   Lastly, the intent of the statute of 27 Hen. VIII, as appears by the preamble, was to restore the old common law and to root out and extinguish all subtle inventions, schemings and practices of uses, which had introduced many mischiefs and inconveniences mentioned in the preamble. And that was very good and necessary for the common weal; for the common law has certain rules to direct the estates and inheritances of lands, and therefore it is better without any comparison to have estates and inheritances directed by the certain rules of the common law—which has been an old, true and faithful servant to this common weal—than by the uncertain scheming and conjecture of any of these new inventors of uses, without any approved ground of law or reason.

---

10   (1285): see p. 48, above.

Note, reader: this judgment agrees with the former judgments, both in *Corbet's Case*, and in *Cholmeley v Humble* and *Germyn v Arscott* there cited, and with the judgment in *Dillon v Freine*. And in this case it was observed that in the said proviso, found at large by the special verdict, there are more than a thousand words; whereas in our [year] books, when tenant in tail was restrained from alienation, there were not 12 words: such was the sincere faith and simplicity of that age, which put all the grounds of faith in a few lines.

So this case has now been adjudged in both courts.

PELLS v BROWNE (1620)

Record: KB 27/1489, m. 44. Edward Pells brought replevin against William Browne for taking three cows in Pickmere Close, Rendham, Suffolk, on 4 October 1619. The defendant justified the taking for damage feasant in his freehold, and the plaintiff traversed the freehold. On 8 March 1620 at Bury St Edmund's assizes (Mountague C.J., Dodderidge J.) the jury found a special verdict: William Browne, the defendant's father, was seised of the land in fee, and had two sons, William (the defendant) who was the eldest, and Thomas; in 1587 he devised the land to Thomas and his heirs for ever, subject to various charges, and if Thomas should die without issue while William was living, then William should have the land unto him and his heirs for ever, subject to the same charges; and on the father's death Thomas entered and was seised, and had a daughter Cicely, who died without issue in Thomas's lifetime; then in 1609 Thomas suffered a common recovery with single voucher by Cyprian Sallowes and Edward Pells to the use of Thomas in fee simple, so that by virtue of the Statute of Uses Thomas was seised; and in 1619 Thomas (dying without issue) devised the land to Edward Pells and Margaret his wife in fee simple; Pells entered and was seised, and put in his animals, and William Browne on 4 October 1619 entered and took them as damage feasant. The jurors said they did not know whether the place was the defendant's freehold at that time, but if it was they assessed the damages as 1d. with 12d. costs, and if not *vice versa*. The case was argued in banc in 1620.

(a) Cro. Jac. 590 (untr.).[11]

... This case was twice argued at the bar, and afterwards at the

---

11 Also reported in Palm. 131; 2 Rolle Rep. 196, 216.

bench. And the matter was divided into three points: (1) whether Thomas had an estate in fee or in fee tail only; (2) admitting he had a fee, whether this limitation of the fee to William be good (to limit a fee upon a fee); (3) if Thomas hath a fee, and William only a possibility to have a fee, whether this recovery shall bar William, or that it be such an estate as cannot be extirpated by recovery or otherwise.

As to the first, all the justices resolved that it is not an estate tail in Thomas, but an estate in fee; for it is devised to him and his heirs for ever ... and the clause 'if he died without issue' is not absolute and indefinite, whenever he died without issue, but it is with a contingency ('if he died without issue, living William'): for he might survive William, or have issue alive at the time of his death, living William ...

Secondly, they all agreed that this is a good limitation of the fee to William by way of that contingency, not by way of immediate remainder; for they all agreed it cannot be by remainder: as, if one deviseth land to one and his heirs, and if he die without heir that it shall remain to another, it is void and repugnant to the estate, for one fee cannot be in remainder after another; for the law doth not expect the determination of a fee by his dying without heirs, and therefore cannot appoint a remainder to begin upon determination thereof .. but by way of contingency, and by way of executory devise to another, to determine the one estate and limit it to another upon an act to be performed, or in failure of performance thereof etc., for the one may be and hath always been allowed ...

To the third point, DODDERIDGE J. held that this recovery should bar William; for he had but a possibility to have a fee, and *quasi* a contingent estate, which is destroyed by this recovery before it came *in esse*: for otherwise it would be a mischievous kind of perpetuity which could not by any means be destroyed[12] ... But all the other justices were herein against him, that this recovery shall not bind; for he who suffered the recovery had a fee, and William Browne had but a possibility, if he survived Thomas, and (Thomas dying without issue in his life) no recovery in value shall extend thereto unless he had been party by way of vouchee ... And if such recovery should be allowed, then if a man should devise that his heir should make such a payment to his younger sons, or to his executors, otherwise the land should be to them, if the heir by recovery might avoid it it would be very mischievous and might frustrate all devises. And there is no such mischief that it should

12   For a fuller version of this part of the speech, see (b), below.

maintain perpetuities, for it is but in a particular case, and upon a mere contingency which paradventure never may happen, and may be avoided by joining him in the recovery who hath such a contingency. And on the other part it would be far more and a greater mischief, that all executory devises should by such means be destroyed . . .

And it was adjudged for the defendant.

(b) HLS MS. 2075, fo. 22v.

. . . DODDERIDGE J. held a different opinion from all the other three (namely, MOUNTAGUE C.J., HOUGHTON and CHAMBERLAINE JJ.), that this possibility should be barred. And his reason was on account of the mischief of perpetuity. For if such a gap should be opened, then a new kind of perpetuity would be established: and perpetuities are most perilous and pernicious in a common weal; for although it is a laudable thing for someone who has risen from little or nothing, or who has an estate descended to him from his ancestors, to desire the continuance thereof in his name and family so long as he leaves it subject to the providence of God, neverthe-less·when a man will endeavour to make it so firm and stable that neither the law of the realm nor the providence of God can alter it, this is an unlawful thing. And such attempts have never succeeded well, for it may be said to them (as it was to the fool in the Gospel): 'Thou fool, this night shall be taken from thee all that thou hast'[13] . . . And those who act in that way are described by David in the psalms as being 'such as join land to land and call their houses after their own names'.[14] And if such perpetuities should be suffered, this in a short time will take away all commerce and contract from the realm, for no one would be able to buy or sell any land upon any cause, be it never so important, being restrained by a condition of perpetuity. In this case, then, if this possibility were not barred by this assurance, this would be a means to make a new perpetuity, even though the common perpetuities have been overthrown. And note that there is no sufficient assurance of land except by feoffment and the like for fee simple, and in the case of a fee tail by common recovery, which was invented for this purpose

13   *Luke*, 12.20.
14   *Psalms*, 49.11.

to dock the estate tail and all remainders and other estates dependent thereon by force of the presumed recompense...

So note the difference of opinion as to this point, and study it well, for it is of good consequence. And HOUGHTON J. said to Mr. Hedley, the reporter,[15] that although judgment was given for the avowant, nevertheless this point should be set down specifically according to the reasons delivered. Also the court took further time to advise thereof...

The record shows that in Michaelmas term 1620 judgment was entered for the defendant, to have return irreplevisable, and to recover 1d. damages and £15 costs.

HOWARD v DUKE OF NORFOLK (1682–85)

Record: C33/257, fo. 722v (main entry). Henry (d. 1652), earl of Arundel, father of both the parties, conveyed the barony of Greystock on 21 March 1647 to four feoffees to the use of himself for life, remainder to trustees to raise a portion of £8,000 for his daughter Katharine, remainder to his countess for life, remainder to trustees for 200 years upon the trusts set out in another deed of the same date, remainder to his second son Henry (the first defendant) in tail male, with successive remainders to his other younger sons in tail male. The trust deed declared that the term of 200 years should attend the inheritance so long as the earl's eldest son, Thomas (Lord Maltravers), or any of his issue male, were living; but if he should die without issue male, so that the earldom of Arundel descended to his brother Henry, then Henry was to have no further benefit of the term, but the benefit was to redound to Charles (the plaintiff) and the other younger sons successively in tail male.

In 1675 the sole surviving trustee of the 200-year term assigned it, at the defendant's request, to one Richard Maryott,[16] who assigned it to Henry. Thomas (who was insane) succeeded his father in 1652, but died without issue in 1677. The earldom of Arundel (together with the revived dukedom of Norfolk) thereupon descended to Henry. Charles brought a bill in Chancery against Henry, and also against his son Henry (Lord Mowbray) and Richard Maryott, seeking execution of the trust of the 200-year term

---

15 Thomas Hetley or Headley (d. 1637) was appointed an official reporter in the King's Bench in 1617, and was still described as a reporter in 1623, but his reports have not been identified: Selden Soc. vol. 22, pp. xix–xxiii; *Legal History Studies* (1972), p. 17. (The volume printed as 'Hetley' contains Common Pleas reports by someone else.)

16 Maryott was later accused of occasioning the suit by his breaches of trust, and made personally liable for some of the profits: C33/263, ff. 700, 702 (June 1685).

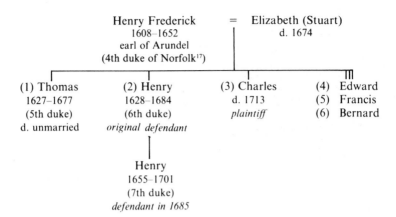

PEDIGREE OF HOWARD

Henry Frederick = Elizabeth (Stuart)
1608–1652 d. 1674
earl of Arundel
(4th duke of Norfolk[17])

(1) Thomas	(2) Henry	(3) Charles	(4) Edward
1627–1677	1628–1684	d. 1713	(5) Francis
(5th duke)	(6th duke)	*plaintiff*	(6) Bernard
d. unmarried	*original defendant*		

Henry
1655–1701
(7th duke)
defendant in 1685

and an account of the profits since Thomas's death in 1677. It was agreed that the term had merged with the inheritance. The question was whether the duke was bound by the 1647 limitation of the trust in favour of the plaintiff,[18] or whether it was void for perpetuity. The case was argued in November 1681, and in January 1682 Mountague C.B., North C.J.C.P. and Pemberton C.J.K.B. gave their opinions in Chancery that the trust was void.

(a) 3 Ch. Cas. 1, 20 (untr.).

... NORTH C.J. .... The only point is this: whether this contingent trust of a term limited to Charles upon the dying of Thomas without issue male, whereby the honour did descend to Henry, be good in point of creation and limitation... My lord, I take the rules of this court in cases of trusts of terms to be the same with rules of law in devises of terms. For I conceive the rules of law to prevent perpetuities are the polity of the kingdom, and ought to take place in this court as well as any other court. So I take it, then, that the trust of a term is as much a chattel and under the

17 I.e, 4th of the title created in 1514. The title had been forfeited in 1572 by the attainder of the 3rd duke for high treason, but Thomas was restored to it in 1660.
18 It was generally agreed that the remainders to Edward, Francis and Bernard were void 'as tending to a perpetuity': C33/257, fo. 723.

consideration of this court as the term itself; and therefore I cannot see why the trust of a term upon a voluntary settlement should be carried further in a court of equity than the devise of a term in the courts of common law...

PEMBERTON C.J.... There is no great question but it might have been made good and effectual by the limitation of two terms: for if one term had been limited to determine upon the death of Thomas without issue, and that to be for the now duke of Norfolk, and another term then to commence and go over to Charles, that would certainly have been good and carried the estate to Charles upon that contingency. But as this case now is, I do think that this way that is now taken is not a good nor a right way... I must look upon this indeed as a new case of novel invention; for in truth I think it is *primae impressionis*, and none of the former cases have been exactly the same ... and if there should be such a limitation admitted ... we know not what inventions may grow upon this. For I know men's brains are fruitful in inventions, as we may see in Matthew Mannings case.[19] It was not foreseen or thought when that judgment was given what would be the consequence when once there was an allowance of the limitation of a term after the death of a person. Presently it was discerned there was the same reason for after 20 men's lives as after one, and so then it was held and agreed that so long as the limitation exceeded not lives in being at the creation of the estate it should extend so far. That came to grow upon them then; and now if this be admitted no man can foresee what an ill effect such an ill allowance might have there, might such estates come in as would incumber estates and mightily entangle lands...

(b) Selden Soc. vol. 79, p. 905[20] (untr.).

[LORD NOTTINGHAM C.] I am in a very great straight by the advice which hath been given me. For as on one side I may safely concur with the three chief justices, since, if I should err in so doing, I should err very excusably (because I should *errare cum patribus*), so on the other side, where the decree must be mine and I alone am to answer for it, I dare not (notwithstanding the reverence I have for

19 See p. 192, below.
20 Lord Nottingham's own report, also printed in 2 Swa. 454. Differently reported in 3 Ch. Cas. 26.

their advice) pronounce a decree in any case where I cannot concur with it myself.

The main inquiry is whether the limitation to Charles be void. Wherein these things are plain: (1) The term in question, though it were attendant on the inheritance at first, yet after the contingency happened it is severed and become a term in gross. (2) The trust of a term in gross can be limited no otherwise in equity than the estate may be limited in law. (3) The legal estate of a term for years, whether it be a long or a short term, cannot be limited to anyone in tail with a remainder over, for this tends directly to a perpetuity . . . Nevertheless, if a term be limited to one for life with 20 several remainders for lives to other persons successively, who are all alive and in being, so that all the candles are lighted together, this is good enough, though it be a possibility upon a possibility; as was ruled 13 Car. II in *Alford's Case*.[1] Nay, if a remainder be limited to a person not in being, as 'to A. for life, remainder to B. for life, the remainder to the first issue male which B. shall have for life', though this be a contingent upon a contingent, yet (it being only a contingency for life) this is also good: as was ruled 14 Car. I, *Cotton v Heath*;[2] for to limit a possibility upon a possibility, or a contingency upon a contingency, is neither unnatural nor absurd. But the rule which is laid down to the contrary by Popham C.J. in the rector of Chedington's case, Coke lib. I,[3] looks like a reason of art, but hath nothing at all of true reason in it. And I have known that rule denied at law, and my lord Coke himself denied that rule when he was chief justice . . .

But the matter chiefly insisted on is that the limitation to Charles is against the rules of law and tends directly to a perpetuity. If this be so, there needs no other reasons or arguments to destroy it, for the law hath so long laboured to defeat perpetuities that now it is become a sufficient reason of itself against any settlement to say it tends to a perpetuity. Let us therefore examine what a perpetuity is, and how far that is here introduced, or any other rule of law broken. A perpetuity is a settlement of an estate or interest in tail

---

1   (1661) 2 Freem. 163; 1 Ch. Cas. 4.
2   (1638) 1 Rolle Abr. 612, line 33; 1 Eq. Rep. 191.
3   *Lloyd d. Roberts v Wilkinson* (1598) 1 Co. Rep. 153, 156.

with such remainders over that no act or alienation of the present tenant in tail can ever bar those remainders, but they must continue perpetually and be as a cloud hanging over the present possession. Such perpetuities fight against God by affecting a stability which human providence can never attain to, and are utterly against the reason and policy of the common law. But yet future interests, or springing uses or trusts, or executory remainders, which are to emerge and arise upon contingencies, are quite out of the rule and reason of perpetuities, and out of the danger of them too, though they are not dockable by recovery nor capable of being barred, especially if the contingency be not remote nor of long expectation, but such as will wear out in a short time . . . therefore I utterly deny that rule which hath been laid down by my Lord Chief Justice North, viz. that where no present remainder can be limited there can be no remainder upon contingency . . .

Suppose it had been said, 'if Thomas die without issue, living Henry, not only the trust to Henry but the very lease itself for 200 years should cease, and in such case a new term should be created for another 200 years to vest in the same trustees for the benefit of Charles in tail': no man can doubt but this new lease would have been good. And my Lord Chief Justice Pemberton confesses that this way the intentions of the earl of Arundel might have taken effect. Then I would be glad to hear a tolerable reason why may not a new springing trust be limited upon the same lease, as well as a new springing lease upon the same trusts. Surely to deny this were to make a distinction without a difference? Nay, I will be bold to say that a new springing lease is the harder case of the two, for it hath a direct tendency to a perpetuity, if such a practice be allowed, and is much more inconvenient than a new springing trust upon the same lease can be . . .

No reason at all is given why this may not be, but that the law hath so mean a consideration of a term of years (which is but a chattel interest) it will never suffer such contingent limitations to be built upon it. Now, as this is no reason in any other part of the world, so 'tis a reason that by this time begins to be quite exploded out of Westminster Hall, and most certainly can never take place in Chancery. There was a time when this reason did so far prevail that all the judges of England, being assembled in Chancery for the assistance of the Lord Chancellor Rich, declared the law to be that if a lease be devised to A. for life, and if A. die living B., B. to have the residue of the term, the remainder is void; for in the consideration of the law the life of a man was a greater estate than any lease for years; therefore A. had the whole term. So it was ruled, 6 Edw. VI[4] . . . And the same opinion held current in other cases, until 10 Eliz., Dyer 277. But this being a reason against sense and nature, it was impossible for the world to be long governed by it [and so the judges reversed this opinion].[5] So now, at last, notwithstanding the exility of a term and the meanness of a chattel interest, there may be a devise of it for life with executory remainders. But 'tis true the judges did very wisely refuse afterwards to enlarge this rule to executory devises in tail with remainders over, for that were directly a perpetuity. Yet why they should refuse to admit of a devise without such contingent limitations or trusts, which do not lead to a perpetuity nor are attended with any inconveniences, is hard to understand; nor is any reason given but *Child and Baylies* case[6] . . .

It hath been urged at the bar: where will you stop if you do not stop at *Child and Baylie's* case? I answer, I will stop everywhere where any inconvenience appears; nowhere before. It is not yet resolved what are the utmost bounds of limiting a contingent fee upon a fee; and it is not necessary to declare what are the utmost bounds to the springing trust of a term, for whensoever the bounds of reason and convenience are exceeded the law will quickly be known.

I have done with the legal reasons of this case. The equitable reasons are much stronger. (1) It was prudent to take care that when the honour descended upon Henry, a little better support should be provided for Charles, the next brother. (2) This prudent care was the effect of a deliberate consultation of the whole family, after advising with learned counsel[7] upon it. (3) Though it were uncertain whether Thomas would die living Henry, yet it was nearly certain that whenever Thomas did die he would die without issue; for it so

---

4 *Anon.* (1552) Dyer 74; see p. 186, fn. 18, below. Rich was lord chancellor from 1547 to 1551.

5 *Weltden v Elkington*, p. 188, below; *Manning's case*, p. 192, below; *Lampet's case*, p. 193, below.

6 See p. 195, below. Lord Nottingham proceeded to criticise, and also to distinguish that case.

7 Lord Nottingham emphasised that the conveyance in question had been drawn by Sir Orlando Bridgman: Selden Soc. vol. 79, p. 905.

much concerned the honour of the family not to have it propagated by him[8] that care was taken so to keep him that he might never marry till he were recovered. 4 It is a very hard thing for a son to tell his father that the provision made for his next brother is void, and it is yet harder to tell him so in Chancery, especially where the reasons for making the conveyance void are not gross and apparent but depend upon such a nicety and subtlety of law as will justify different opinions . . .

The case was subsequently reargued, but Lord Nottingham C. maintained his opinion and on 17 June 1682 decreed that the plaintiff should enjoy the barony for the residue of the 200 years, that the duke should make a conveyance to him accordingly, and that he should account for the profits since 1677.

(c) 1 Vern. 163.

Lord Nottingham died on 18 December 1682, and two days later North C.J. was appointed lord keeper. The duke then brought a bill of review, asking North L.K. to reverse his predecessor's decision. The case was reargued on 1 May 1683.

. . . The LORD KEEPER [NORTH] declared he saw no reason to change his former opinion. He said the late lord chancellor declared upon a hearing of this cause that the trust of a term was to be governed by the same rules as the limitation or devise of a term at law was, and therefore thought he was unreasonably pressed by the defendant's counsel,[9] who insisted on the equity of the case and would make a difference between the limitation of the trust of a term and a devise of a term or limitation of a term itself. A perpetuity is a thing odious in law and destructive to the commonwealth: it would put a stop to commerce and prevent the circulation of the riches of the kingdom, and therefore is not to be countenanced in equity. If in equity you should come nearer to a perpetuity than the rules of common law would admit, all men being desirous to continue their estates in their families would settle their estates by way of trust; which might indeed make well for the jurisdiction of the court, but would be destructive to the commonwealth. And the intention of a man is not always to be

---

8   This refers to his insanity.
9   North L.K. had urged them to relieve his embarrassment by trying the question in an action at common law.

pursued in equity . . . It was an hard case, but the rules of law must be observed.

North L.K. reversed the decree on 15 May 1683, and the duke was restored to possession. Charles Howard then appealed to the House of Lords, and on 19 June 1685, after a two-day hearing, the House of Lords reversed North's decree and affirmed the decree of Lord Nottingham: record printed in 3 Ch. Cas. 53. On 23 June the Court of Chancery decreed, by consent, that the final process be revived[10] and that the plaintiff might proceed with his suit for a conveyance and an account: C33/263, ff. 700, 702. After a dispute about whether a particular tenement was part of the barony, Lord Jeffreys C. in 1687 ordered that a conveyance be made in the words of the 1647 deed of settlement, leaving any further questions to be tried at law: C33/267, ff. 307, 998 (referred to Master Legard, 4 July 1687).

10 The duke had refused to obey the original writ of execution, and so on 14 October 1682 the court had ordered a writ of assistance to the sheriff of Cumberland: C33/257, fo. 936v; C33/259, ff. 5, 20, 21, 43, 429. This had been revoked by North L.K.'s decree in 1683.

6 The term of years

(1) Specific recovery of the term: *quare ejecit* and ejectment

ANON. (before 1317)

Y.B. 4 Edw. II, Selden Soc. vol. 42, p. 181.

Note that, according to SIR HERVEY DE STANTON, in a *quare ejecit infra terminum* where the term is past the plaintiff will recover only in damages; and if the term is not finished, he will recover his term for the time remaining. And to this BRABAZON, ROUBERY and HERTILPOLE agreed. I asked the same of *Miggele* and *Walyngford*, and they said he would have his term [for the time remaining] and his damages etc.

HERTFORD v PERCY (1312)

Y.B. 6 Edw. II, Selden Soc. vol. 34, p. 223.

Adam de Hertford lays before you this[1]: that Henry de Percy wrongfully deforces him of six messuages and six bovates of land etc. in Buckden which Reyner de Knol leased to him for a term which is not yet past, and wrongfully for this reason, that whereas Reyner leased the tenements to him [on such a day] for a term of seven years next following; and under that lease Adam was in seisin

---

1 This report, unusually by this date, opens with an abridged version of the plaintiff's count.

177

from the aforesaid day until [another day] when this same Reyner sold the aforesaid tenements [to the aforesaid Henry], by reason of which sale this same Henry ejected him wrongfully to his damage [of £100].

Scrop. You hear how he bases his action on a lease for a term, which term—if the lease was made as he says, which we do not admit—is past. And [by this action] he seeks to recover the term. [We ask] judgment whether he should be answered.

Denum. Will you then acknowledge the lease?

Scrop. I need not do that since you suppose that the term is past. Even if there was a lease, which we do not admit, [we ask] judgment whether we should be charged, since you have your recovery by writ of covenant against Reyner or his heir.

Denum. Our writ was purchased during the term. And since you can not deny the lease or the ejectment etc. [we ask] judgment. And even if I can recover against Reyner by writ of covenant, that does not oust me from this recovery: perhaps it is my election to choose.

STANTON to *Scrop.* Answer to the ejectment.

Scrop. [We are] ready to aver that he never had anything by lease [of the aforesaid Reyner].

Denum. That is no answer unless you answer to the ejectment.

STANTON [to *Denum*]. How could you be ejected if you never had anything?

Denum. Since we base our action on the ejectment, he must answer to that.

STANTON. He answers you enough. And the averment was received that he had nothing by lease [of the aforesaid Reyner].

NOTE (1454)

Y.B. Mich. 33 Hen. VI, fo. 42, pl. 19.

Note that according to *Choke*, if a lease is made to me for a term of years, and the lessor alienates to a stranger during the term . . . if I am put out from my possession of my term by the said alienee, I can have a general writ of trespass *quare vi et armis* against him, as has been adjudged, as well as the *quare ejecit infra terminum* etc. But in the writ of trespass I shall recover only damages etc., whereas in the *quare ejecit* etc. I shall recover my term, if any is left, and for such of it as is past I shall recover in damages, or if it is all past I shall recover wholly in damages. (Query [whether this is so] in writ of covenant and in *ejectione firmae* . . .)

NOTE (*c.* 1495)

Port's notebook, HEHL MS. HM 46980, fo. 164.

Query whether, in *ejectione firmae*, he shall recover his term? For some have said that he shall recover everything in damages. But in *quare ejecit infra terminum* it is clear that he shall recover his term, if the term be not ended. And if the lessor puts out the lessee from his term he can have *quare ejecit infra terminum* or *ejectione firmae*, at his pleasure. If, however, [the lessor] makes a feoffment over, [the lessee] shall have only *quare ejecit* against the feoffee and not *ejectione firmae*. So it is if the lessor is disseised and he releases to the disseisor: [the lessee] shall have *quare ejecit*; and that is adjudged.

OLD NATURA BREVIUM

Translated from the edition of *c.* 1516, fo. xlix.

Note that an *ejectione firmae* is only an action of trespass in its nature, and the plaintiff shall not recover his term which is to come, any more than in trespass a man shall recover damages for a trespass not yet done but to be done.

A. FITZHERBERT, LA NOVEL NATURA BREVIUM (1534)

Translated from the 1635 ed., fo. 220.

The writ *de ejectione firmae* lies where a man leases land for a term of years and then the lessor ejects him, or a stranger ejects him, from his term: now the lessee shall have this writ *de ejectione firmae*. And the form of the writ is:

The king to the sheriff etc. If A. shall make etc. then put etc. B. that he be before our justices etc. to show why with force and arms he entered the manor of J., which T. demised to the aforesaid A. for a term which has not yet expired, and took and carried away the goods and chattels of the same A. to the value etc. found in the same manor, and ejected him the said A. from the aforesaid farm, and offered other outrages against him, to the grave damage etc. . . .

And in this writ he shall recover his term, if the term has not expired, and also his damages. And the process is attachment and distress, and process of outlawry.

And in the year 14 Hen. VII, in *ejectione firmae* brought against a stranger, the plaintiff had judgment to recover his term; and thereupon the defendant sued a writ of error, and the judgment was affirmed and execution awarded to the plaintiff.[2]

And in the year 17 Hen. VIII a similar judgment was given in the Common Bench, that he should recover his term and his damages.[3]

ANON. (*c.* 1602)

CUL MS. Gg. 2. 31, fo. 460v, pl. 185 (untr.).[4]

My Lord Keeper [EGERTON] calls this *ejectione firmae* whereby titles are tried 'pick-purse actions', because he cannot come to know the plaintiff's title; but, having held a possession of long time, shall be turned out upon a quirk in law, against which the defendant hath no defence. And though titles also are tried by actions of trespass *quare clausum fregit*, upon Not guilty pleaded, yet there is no loss of possession in that action as in the other.[5]

PROCEDURE IN THE QUEEN'S BENCH (1703)

Lilly, *Entries* (3rd ed.), p. 203.[6]

2 *Gernes v Smyth* (1500) CP 40/948, m. 303 (with note of writ of error dated 11 October 1499); Rastell, *Collection of Entrees*, fo. 252v (taken from Lucas's MS.); KB 27/956, m. 21 (*scire facias* for damages). No entry of the King's Bench judgment has been found.

3 *Soole v Edgare* (1525) CP 40/1044, m. 505 (verdict, but no judgment entered); Stubbe's entries, BL MS. Add. 24078, fo. 18. Yorke also reports a decision to the same effect as in Fitzherbert: BL MS. Hargrave 388, fo. 210v. There was further confirmation in 1530: Pollard's reports, Selden Soc. vol. 94, p. 181, fn. 8.

4 Differently reported in Hertfordshire Record Office, Verulam MS. XII. A. 50, fo. 68.

5 Cf. Verulam MS., which reports a second objection: that in ejectment the plaintiff could not be made to disclose his title in pleading, as he could in trespass *quare clausum fregit*. See also Egerton's *Memorials for Judicature* (HEHL MS. EL 2623, untr.): '... The general practice of the action of *ejectione firmae*, as of late time it hath been used, is another of the greatest causes of uncertainty of judicature, and of multiplicity and infiniteness of suits. There is no example to be found of it, in such sort as of late years it is commonly practised, before anno 14 Hen. VII, and very rare many years after that time; and always misliked by many of the reverend and learned judges, as Sir Anthony Fitzherbert, Sir James Dyer, etc. It hath been a great decay of the true knowledge and learning of the law in real actions, and hath almost utterly overthrown all actions real that be possessory: as, assizes of novel disseisin, and writs or entry, etc'.

6 English translation from the Latin record, here slightly reworded. The same forms, together with a copy of the complete record in an ejectment action, will be found in the appendix to W. Blackstone, *Commentaries on the Laws of England* (1765), vol. III.

(a) Declaration.

Hilary term in the first year of the reign of Queen Anne.

Middlesex. Lawrence Legawe, late of London, gentleman, was attached to answer Thomas Leake, gentleman, in a plea why with force and arms he entered into 3 messuages, 30 acres of land, 20 acres of meadow and 10 acres of pasture with the appurtenances in Hadley, which the Honourable Vere Booth, spinster, demised to the same Thomas for a term which is not yet past, and ejected him from his farm aforesaid, and committed other outrages on him, to the great damage of the said Thomas and against the peace of the now lady the queen etc. And thereupon the said Thomas Leake, by John Lilly his attorney, complains that, whereas the said Vere Booth on the twentieth day of November [1702] in the first year of the reign of the lady Anne now queen of England etc. demised to the same Thomas the tenements aforesaid with the appurtenances, to have and to hold the tenements aforesaid with the appurtenances unto the same Thomas and his assigns from the seventeenth day of the same month of November then last past unto the end and term of five years from then next ensuing and fully to be completed and ended, by virtue of which demise the same Thomas entered into the tenements aforesaid with the appurtenances and was thereof possessed: the said Lawrence (the said Thomas being so possessed thereof) afterwards, namely on the same twentieth day of November in the first year abovesaid, with force and arms etc., entered into the tenements aforesaid with the appurtenances, which the said Vere Booth demised to the same Thomas in form aforesaid for the term aforesaid, which is not yet past, and ejected him the said Thomas from his farm aforesaid, and other outrages etc., to the great damage etc., and against the peace etc.; whereby he says that he is the worse, and has damage to the amount of £40. And thereof he produces suit etc.

(b) Letter to defendant from casual ejector.[7]

To Sir William Buck, Bart.

I am informed that you are in possession or claim title to the premises in this declaration of ejectment mentioned, or to some part thereof; and, being sued in this action as a casual ejector, and having no claim or title to the

---

7 This letter was delivered with a copy of the declaration. In the 18th century, both documents were obtainable from law stationers as standard forms, with blanks, printed on the same sheet of paper. This document effectively initiated the suit, since the usual mesne process was unnecessary.

same, do advise you to appear the first day of the next Hilary term in Her Majesty's Court of Queen's Bench at Westminster, by some attorney of that court, and then and there by rule of the same court to cause yourself to be made defendant in my stead; otherwise I shall suffer a judgment to be entered against me, and you will be turned out of possession.

Your loving friend,

[Date.]   Lawrence Legawe.

(c) Rule *nisi* to enter judgment.

Unless the tenant in possession shall appear and plead to issue within one week next after the end of this term, let judgment be entered for the plaintiff against the now defendant Legawe. On the motion of Mr. Brodrick.

By the court.

(d) The consent rule.[8]

It is ordered by the consent of the parties that William Buck, baronet, be made a defendant in the place of the now defendant Legawe, and shall appear without delay at the suit of the plaintiff, and shall receive a declaration in a plea of trespass and ejectment for the tenements in question, and shall without delay plead thereto Not guilty; and on the trial of the issue aforesaid shall confess the lease, entry and actual ejectment from the tenements in question, and shall insist on the title only, otherwise judgment to be entered for the plaintiff against the now defendant Legawe by default; and if on the trial of the issue aforesaid the same William shall not confess the lease, entry and ejectment, whereby the plaintiff shall not be able to prosecute his writ against the said William, then no costs or charges shall upon such non prosecution be adjudged, but that the said William shall pay to the said plaintiff the costs and charges thereon to be taxed; and it is further ordered that if on trial of the issue a verdict shall be given for the defendant William, or if it shall happen that the plaintiff shall not further prosecute his writ aforesaid against the said William for any other cause than for not confessing the lease, entry and actual ejectment aforesaid, that then the lessor of the plaintiff aforesaid shall pay to the said William the costs and charges by the court here to be taxed.

John Powell[9]   H. for the plaintiff.
    for costs £12.   L. for the defendant.

---

8   Printed in Lilly, *Entries* before (a), with the name of Henry Plumer (here altered
     to William Buck) as the real defendant.
9   Signature of judge in chambers.

(2) Protection against the lessor's lord

ANON. (1306)

Mich. 34 Edw. I, Fitz. Abr., *Garde*, pl. 129; abridged
in *Covenant*, pl. 31.

Note that if the tenant leases his land for a term of years, and dies, leaving his heir under age, the lord shall oust the termee[10] and have it in ward; and the termee shall have a writ of covenant against the heir at his full age for this term: adjudged by the justices . . .

This doctrine is repeated, without further dispute, throughout the year books (see 4 Co. Rep., at p. 82) and at inns of court readings (see Selden Soc. vol. 93, pp. 144, 176) until the first decade of the 16th century.

ANON. (*c.* 1514)

(a) GI MS. 25, fo. 172 (K.B.).[11]

It was argued whether the lord shall oust the tenant for term of years made by the heir's father.[12]

CONINGSBY J. It seems not, for just as one may make a feoffment for life, and the lord shall not oust [the life-tenant], for the same reason he shall not oust the tenant for years. If one charges the land with a rentcharge for years, the lord shall hold charged. (This was conceded by all the justices.) . . . Here he is lord, and he claims from the day of the tenant's dying and not before, for the writ says, 'he died in his homage': therefore the lease precedes his title to the wardship, and so he shall not oust [the lessee].

BRUDENELL J. to the same effect. Here priority and posteriority

---

10 I.e. lessee, or termor.
11 After 1509 (when Coningsby became a judge), and before 1520 (when Brude-nell became C.J.C.P.); probably before 1516, since a reading of 1516 follows in the MS. Cf. the date of (b), below.
12 I.e. A. is freehold tenant of B. and leases for years to C. A. dies, leaving an infant heir D. Does B. have the land (as D.'s guardian), or does C. have it as A.'s lessee?

is not to be argued, because that is always as between two lords. But here the lease is a thing which is vested, and it may not afterwards be devested ... Also it seems that here is a lord, mesne and tenant: for a tenant for years shall do fealty, as is agreed in 5 Hen. VII, and thus there is a mesne and a tenant; and therefore the lord shall not have anything from the mesne except the [body of the] heir and all things that are reserved ...

FYNEUX C.J. to the same effect ...

(b) Spelman, *Reports*, p. 142.[13]

It was adjudged that the lord shall not have the wardship of the land during a term of years: that is, he shall not oust the termor who had a lease for years from the infant's ancestor.

But before the same judgment it was common learning that the lord could oust the termor, and at the full age [of the lessor's heir] the termor could have his term again.

Then the other justices, after the death of the lord FYNEUX [C.J.K.B.][14] (who was of opinion that the lord could not oust the termor), were of another opinion. And FITZHERBERT [J.C.P.] said that this was the old learning, and that there were many judgments on this contrary to the said chief justice's opinion.

A. FITZHERBERT, LA NOVEL NATURA BREVIUM (1534)

Translated from the 1635 ed., fo. 142.

... The guardian [may] oust the termor who holds for a term of years by the lease of his tenant. And the Statute of Marlborough[15] in a way proves that he may do so. And there are several old books to prove this, by the judgments given there. And it seems reasonable that it should be so, by reason of the earlier title which the lord

---

13   This is dated 5 Hen. VIII (1513–14), and is probably a reference to the foregoing case. The remainder is an addition made between 1525 and 1538. Cf. the addendum in Spelman, *Reports*, p. 144: 'Remember that it was adjudged in 15 Hen. VIII that the lord shall not oust the termor ...'. '15' here may be a miscopying of '5'.

14   Sir John Fyneux (d. 1525).

15   52 Hen. III (1267), c. 6; see p. 9, above.

has, when he reserves such services upon his feoffment, to have the ward if [his tenant] dies leaving an heir under age . . .[16]

ANON. (1544)

Brooke Abr., *Leases*, pl. 58.

36 Hen. VIII . . . Note, by all the justices, that the guardian of an heir in chivalry shall not oust the termor of the heir's ancestor: which is contrary to Fitzherbert's opinion in the new *Natura Brevium*. And the law is the same of the lord by escheat.

This opinion was followed in *Sir Andrew Corbet's Case* (1599) 4 Co. Rep. 81, and does not seem to have been disputed again.

(3) Estates in terms of years

ANON. (1541)

Brooke Abr., *Chattelles*, pl. 23.

If the lessee for years devises his term by testament to someone for term of life, remainder over to another, and dies; and the devisee enters and does not alienate the term, but dies: the remainderman shall have it. But if the first devisee had alienated in his lifetime, there the remainderman would have been without remedy for it.

In *Foster v Foster* (1572) LI MS. Maynard 77, p. 80, Dyer C.J.C.P. affirmed that in such a case an alienation by the first devisee defeated the remainder: '. . . as was agreed upon a like sale made by the wife of one Brooke, which wife's vendees are to this day enjoying the term after the vendor's death by force of that assignment; and there is no remedy for the devisee in remainder, not even in the Chancery—as was held in the time of the Lord Wriothesley [L.C. 1544–47]'.

ANON. (1548)

Brooke Abr., *Devise*, pl. 13.

. . . The occupation [of a chattel] may remain, but if the thing itself

16 Cf. fo. 198: '. . . If a man leases land for term of years and then dies without heir, and the lord enters by escheat and ousts the termor, it is doubted whether he shall have *quare ejecit infra terminum* against the lord by escheat. But it seems reasonable that he should have it. Likewise if a villein leases land for term of years, and then the villein's lord enters and ousts the termor, there it seems that the lessee shall have this writ . . .'

is devised to the use the remainder is void: for a gift or devise of a chattel for an hour is a gift for ever, and the donee or devisee may sell and dispose of it, and the remainder dependent thereon is void . . . And in 2 Edw. VI, where a man devised that W. O. should have the occupation of his term during his life, and if he should die within the term that it should remain to John Style, this is good: for the first had only the occupation, and the other afterwards has the property.

This decision was confirmed at Serjeants' Inn in 1553 by Portman J.Q.B. and Hales J.C.P.: Dalison's reports, BL MS. Harley 5141, fo. 6v.

ANON. (1550)

BL MS. Hargrave 4, fo. 116v (C.P.).

John Style, having a lease for years, by his testament devised a moiety thereof to his wife during her life for the support of his children if she kept herself single and unmarried, but if not then remainder to Thomas his son and his heirs male, and for failure of such issue remainder to B. the eldest son of the said John.

Coke[17] moved at the bar whether the wife should have the whole moiety of the term unto herself and her executors, or whether it remains to Thomas and his heirs.

MOUNTAGUE C.J.[18] and MOLYNEUX J. were of the opinion that this remainder to Thomas and his heirs male is good, even though it is only a chattel.

HALES J. was of the contrary opinion, that a chattel cannot be entailed, for it is against the nature of a chattel to be entailed.[19]

ANON. (1559)

Gell's reports, MS. at Hopton Hall, fo. 100 (C.P.).

A man possessed of a term of years granted it to someone for life,

---

17   I.e. William Coke Sjt., appointed J.C.P. the following year.
18   Cf. *Anon.* (1552) Dyer 74, where he sided with Hales J. in holding that a 'remainder' in a lease could be destroyed by sale, adding that 'the case was ruled by the opinion of all the justices in the time of Lord Rich, when he was chancellor' (i.e. 1547–51). But in the present case the destructibility of the remainder was not in issue. The dispute was presumably between Thomas and his mother's executors.
19   For this rule, see p. 194, below.

and the remainder of the years remaining after the grantee's death to John Style. And it was moved whether this remainder was good.

WESTON J. said that the remainder is good if the first grantee does not grant it over during his lifetime.

BROWNE J. I am of the same view, as advised at this time, but I am doubtful. If it had been by devise, however, the remainder would clearly have been good if the tenant for life did not grant it over.[20] And if I grant you my term [of years] for life, on condition that if you should die within the term then the residue should remain to John Style, this is a good remainder. I take it that if I grant you my term, and grant that if you die within the term the residue should remain to John Style, this also is a good remainder, because the *si contingat*[1] is a condition and limitation of how the term shall pass. This case was agreed here within recent times: someone was possessed of a term, and granted by indenture that if he should die during the term the reversion of the term should remain to his daughter; and it was [held] a good remainder in the daughter of the residue of the years after his death.

ANON. (1572)

BL MS. Add. 24845, fo. 91 (C.P.).

Barham prayed the opinion of the court in this case: one Staunford, being possessed of a term of 40 years, devised it to his wife if she should so long live, and if she should die within the term then the residue of the years which remained then unspent to R. his son; and he died; and then the wife remarried, and the husband and wife (being possessed of the term) granted the entire term to a stranger, with the intention that the remainders should not be defeated but that the first will should be performed; and the grantee regranted to the husband and wife 'the only occupation and receipt of the rents and profits of the said lands' for the entire term, if the wife should so long live, and if she should die within the term then he granted 'the only occupation and receipt of the rents and profits of the said lands' for the residue of the 40 years which then remained unspent to the said R. Did this grant of 'the only occupation and receipt of the rents and profits' amount to a lease of the land? For, if so, the remainders can now be defeated, just as they could upon the devise.

---

20 For this distinction, see also *Anon.* (1568) Dyer 277, where Walsh, Weston and Harpur JJ. 'agreed that the remainder of a term devised to someone for term of life is good by devise, though not by estate executed in the lifetime'.

1 I.e. the condition, 'if it chances [that you die]'.

DYER C.J.   In 37 Hen. VI[2] a man devised the use and occupation of a grail, and the book says that he had only the use and not the property of the grail. And I have known someone who was learned to devise by his will the use and occupation of his plate to his son and the heirs male of his body; and there the son had no property, but only the use of the thing. And if a man grants the vesture of his land, the soil itself does not pass, but the grass and such like.

MANWOOD J. was of the contrary opinion, and said that there is a difference between the occupation of land and of goods; for the occupation of land is of all the profit of the land, but the occupation of goods is not so.[3]

WELTDEN v ELKINGTON (1578)

Record: CP 40/1344, m. 1226; Plowd. 516; Benl. 308. William Weltden brought trespass against Thomas Elkington for breaking his close and house and depasturing his grass at Minchinhampton, Gloucestershire, on 21 October 1568. The defendant pleaded Not guilty, and in Easter term 1577 the jury at bar found the following special verdict: on 16 March 1543 Lord Windsor leased the land for 60 years to Thomas Davis; Davis entered into possession, and in 1545 by will bequeathed the residue of the term to his wife Jane for life, remainder to his younger son Francis and his assigns; Jane, who was also his executrix, proved the will and entered into possession, and in 1552 married Richard Herbert; then in 1557 Jane and Richard Herbert attempted to destroy the remainder by assigning the whole unexpired portion of the term to two persons, who reassigned to Jane and Richard to have and to hold for the residue of the 60 years; meanwhile, Francis had died intestate, and in 1565 administration of his goods and chattels was granted to Mary Weltden, the plaintiff's wife; in 1567 Herbert assigned the term to three persons, who in 1568 assigned it to John Scudamore and George Vaughan; later in 1568 Jane Herbert died, whereupon Mary

2   *Glover and Brown v Forden* (1459) Y.B. Trin. 37 Hen. VI, fo. 30, pl. 11; CP 40/794, m. 291; Dyer 359. In an action of trespass by the churchwardens of Walberton, Sussex, for a service book (an ordinal), the defendant pleaded that the custody and occupation had been devised to one of the executors for life, remainder to the defendant for life, and that the first devisee for life had given it to the churchwardens, and that after that devisee's death the defendant had seized the book by command of the other executor (and claiming the remainder). Issue was joined on the gift to the churchwardens.

3   In the following year, Manwood J. held that by a devise of 'the profits and occupation' the land itself passed: 'for what is a term other than the profits and revenues of [the land]? It is not like a devise of the occupation of the hangings, plate or other purely personal chattels, which is no more in effect than a custody or use in the thing, without profit, and therefore can be severed from the thing itself . . .'. The other justices did not share his doubts: *Anon.* (1573) LI MS. Maynard 77, p. 187.

Weltden's husband entered (to claim Francis's interest in remainder); and the trespass complained of was an entry by the defendant as servant of Scudamore and Vaughan. The main question was whether Jane had effectively destroyed the remainder in 1557, in which case Elkington's entry was lawful; or whether the remainder had escaped destruction, so that it passed to Francis Davis's representatives. Argument on other points is here omitted. The case was argued by the serjeants in Hilary term 1578, and by the judges in Easter term.

(a) Hil. 1578: Plowd. 520.

... *Popham,* [for the defendant] ... [The wife] has the whole term and the entire interest in herself, for the words of the testament are ... tantamount to saying that she should have the term during her life, and in that case he cannot limit or appoint any remainder over; for a lifetime in judgment of law is greater than a period of years. And if someone who has a term of years grants it to another during his life, this is as much as if he had granted it during all the years; for the limitation for life is as great as a limitation for all the years, and in judgment of law comprehends all the years ... And from this it follows that the plaintiff, who claims through a remainder which was void, shall be barred ...

Against this argued [*Baber* and *Anderson*], the serjeants of counsel with the plaintiffs, and all the justices. For when the testator devised that his wife Jane should have and occupy the tenements for as many years as she should happen to live, he thereby expressed his intention to be that she should have the tenements during her life ... And since the testator's intention is evident from these words, it is the office of the court—as *Anderson* and MANWOOD J. said (and as MOUNSON J. also said to me afterwards)—so to marshal the words and construe them that the intention shall take place and the thing take effect, and not be confounded ...

And, as to what has been said, that what the wife was to have by the devise was only an occupation and no part of the term or interest, and therefore the wife's occupation shall not be an execution of the term because it is something else: MANWOOD J. and the lord DYER C.J. said that it is not so, for the interest limited to the wife and that limited to the son are of one and the same thing, and not distinct things. For they said that what is limited to each of them is the land itself; for the devise that Jane should have and occupy the land is a gift of the land itself to Jane, and she has *jus possessionis* (as DYER C.J. termed it), though not *totius proprietatis* ...

MANWOOD J. said it was not strange in our law to see two people having a separate interest in one same term, and two properties therein. For, he said, if a lessee for years grants over his term by deed indented to another, rendering rent, and for default of payment that he shall enter and retain until the grantee has paid him the rent, there if he enters for default of payment and retains he has a property—and it is uncertain, for upon payment of the arrears by the other it shall be determined—and the grantee also has another property, for his interest is not wholly gone, but he has a property of a kind and may have the whole upon payment of the arrears ... And he said that in chattels merely personal, such as sheep leased for a time to compost land, or a chain pledged (as the case was in 5 Hen. VII[4]), the owner has a property; and he to whom the sheep are leased, or to whom the chain is pledged, has another. A fortiori, there can be two properties in a lease, which is a chattel real and has a long certain continuance ...

(b) Pas. 1578; Dyer 358.

... And in Easter term [1578] the case was argued at the bench.

MEAD J. (appointed last term),[5] who had been of counsel with the defendant at the bar, having changed his opinion, argued against his client—and MOUNSON J. also, on the first day—that the alienation by the husband and wife should not prejudice the remainder.

And on the morrow MANWOOD J. and DYER C.J. argued to the same purpose. For the entire and absolute right in the term is not devised to the wife for any time, but there is a separation of the right of possession from the right of property. Yet the wife had an interest by possibility in the whole term, if she survived the [remainder of the] 60 years ... And if the testator had devised and bequeathed first his entire term to his son Francis, provided that (*ita quod*) the wife should have the occupation and use of the land during her life, that would have been good and the wife could not have aliened the entire term.[6] Note the words of the will—'I will that Jane my wife shall have etc. and after her decease I give and bequeath the residue of the years etc. to Francis my son etc.'— which clearly prove his intention and purpose that the wife should be restrained from power to alien the entire term.

---

4   *Lord Dudley v Lord Powles* (1489) Y.B. Mich. 5 Hen. VII, fo. 1, pl. 1.
5   Actually in November 1577, which suggests this report may relate in part to Hilary term 1578. Dyer gives the date as 19 Eliz. (1577), but this is clearly incorrect.
6   In 1573 Manwood J. had recommended this device as safer than a devise to the wife for life, remainder to the son: LI MS. Maynard 77, 187.

The record shows that judgment was entered for £8 damages and £66 costs (increased by the court from £2).

AMNER d. FULSHURST v LUDDINGTON (1583)

Record: KB 27/1287, m. 495 (proceedings in error, setting out Common Pleas record of 1581). Thomas Amner brought ejectment against Nicholas Luddington for ejecting him on 13 October 1580 from a messuage in St Swithin's, London,[7] which had been leased to him for seven years by Alice Fulshurst. The defendant pleaded Not guilty, and on 13 June 1581 at the Guildhall, London (before Dyer C.J.C.P.), the jury found a special verdict: one Hugh Weldon was seised, and on 20 August 1532 leased to Thomas Perpoynte, his executors and assigns for 99 years; Perpoynte entered into possession, and in 1544 by will left the messuage to his wife Mary for life, 'and after her decease I will it go among my children unpreferred'; Mary, who was also his executrix, entered into possession, and later married Sir Thomas Fulshurst; then in 1556 one William Beswick brought an action of debt against Sir Thomas, and obtained judgment by default to recover the debt of £140 and damages, and in 1557 sued a writ of *fieri facias* against Sir Thomas upon this recovery; and the sheriffs of London returned to this writ that Sir Thomas (who was of Crewe, Cheshire) had no goods or chattels in London, except that he was possessed in right of his wife of the said messuage for the unexpired term of 74 years, which they valued at £142 and sold for that sum to one Richard Reynoldes, and paid the sum to Beswick; and Richard Reynoldes on 1 January 1559 granted all his interest to Luddington, who entered and was possessed; then Sir Thomas sued several writs of error, and finally in 1578 the judgment in the action of debt was reversed. The jurors further found that Mary died on 4 August 1569, and at that time Alice Fulshurst was the only child of Thomas Perpoynte left unpreferred; therefore, after the judgment of reversal (in 1578), Alice entered upon Luddington and on 13 October 1580 made the lease to Amner for seven years; and Amner entered, and was ejected by Luddington.

HLS MS. 2071, fo. 83v.[8]

... This Hilary term, 25 Eliz., it was adjudged that the remainder-man should have it by the limitation, and not the wife's executors.[9]

ANDERSON C.J., MEAD and WYNDHAM JJ. held there was no difference whether the term was devised or the occupation of the term, for life with remainder over; but that in both cases the remainderman should have it after the death of him to whom it was

---

7 According to the special verdict, it was in St Nicholas's Lane.
8 Also reported in 1 And. 60.
9 This is a slip: the action was not brought by the wife's executors, but by the lessee of the remainderwoman Alice.

devised for life, even if the devisee grants, aliens or otherwise disposes of it during his lifetime.[10]

PERYAM J. was of the contrary opinion, and held there was a difference whether the term was devised or the occupation thereof: that is, whether by the death of the devisee of the term the remainderman should have nothing, or whether the occupation is devised for life with remainder over.

Nevertheless judgment was given as [stated] above.

Gawdy Sjt. said that the party against whom judgment was given had brought a writ of error, and prayed that the court would allow it.

ANDERSON C.J. said he has spoken with some of the justices of the Queen's Bench, and they are of the above opinion.

And *Gawdy* said, if it may appear that those of the Queen's Bench are of the same opinion then his client will be satisfied. . . .

The record shows that the Common Pleas gave judgment in Hilary term 1583 for the plaintiff to recover 6s. 8d. damages and £13 costs; and that a writ of error was brought on 24 January, and a technical error assigned in Michaelmas term; but no more is entered after Easter term 1584. The arguments in the Queen's Bench are reported in 2 Leon. 92, 3 Leon. 89, where it is said that the Common Pleas judgment was affirmed; and in Godb. 26, which ends obscurely.

CLARKE v MANNING (1608)

Record: CP 40/1767, m. 1829. William Clarke brought debt on a bond against Matthew Manning, as administrator of Edmund Manning. The defendant pleaded Fully administered, and on 9 May 1607 at the Guildhall, London, a doubt arose at the trial before Coke C.J.C.P. and a special verdict was found: Edmund Manning (d. 1588) had a lease for 50 years of a mill at Clifton, Oxfordshire, and left it to his wife and executrix Mary for life, remainder to his brother Matthew on condition that he should not sublet or sell the same but leave it to Matthew's son John, and that Mary was to have the use and occupation during her lifetime, and was to pay £7 a year to Matthew; and Mary paid this £7 a year until she died intestate in 1604, when Matthew entered. The question was, whether the lease of the mill had passed to Matthew and could be accounted assets.

8 Co. Rep. 94.[11]

. . . The case was argued at the bar, and on various separate days at the bench.

---

10 Cf. 1 And.: '. . . the common argument about remainders was not material . . .'.
11 Dated Hil. 7 Jac. (1610), whereas the record shows that judgment was given in Michaelmas term 1608. Perhaps Hil. 5 Jac. is intended.

And it seemed prima facie to WALMSLEY J. that the devise to Matthew Manning after the wife's death was void; for the wife— having had it devised to her during her life—had the entire term, and the devisor cannot devise over the possibility . . . and although there have been recent opinions in the case that the remainder was good, yet the old opinion (which seemed more right to him) was that the remainder was void.

But COKE C.J., WARBURTON, DANIEL and FOSTER JJ. to the contrary, that the devise to Matthew Manning was good. And five points were resolved:

1   That Matthew Manning did not take it by way of remainder, but by way of executory devise; and one can devise an estate by his last will in such a way that he could not by any grant or conveyance in his life . . .

2   The case is stronger because this devise is only of a chattel, for which no *praecipe* lies, and which may vest and revest at the devisor's pleasure without prejudicing anyone . . .

3   There is no difference when one devises his term for life with remainder over and when one devises the land, or his lease or farm, or the use or occupation or profits of his land; for in a will the intent and meaning of the devisor is to be observed, and the law will construe the words so as to satisfy his intent and put them in such order and course that his will shall take effect. And the devisor's intention expressed in the will is always the best expositor, director and disposer of his words: and when a man devises his lease to one for life, this is as much as to say that he shall have so many of the years as he shall live for, and that if he should die within the term another should have it for the residue of the years; and although it is uncertain how may years he will live at the beginning, nevertheless when he dies it is made certain how many years he has lived and for how many years the other shall have it, and so by act subsequent all is made certain.

4   That after the executor has assented to the first devise, it does not lie in the power of the first devisee to bar him who has the future devise, for he cannot transfer more to another than he himself has.

5   In many cases a man by his will can create an interest which he could not create in his life by grant or conveyance at common law . . .

LAMPET d. LAMPET v STARKEY (1612)

Common Pleas: record summarised in 10 Co. Rep. 46. Richard Lampet brought ejectment against Margery Starkey for ejecting him from a house and land in Cow Honeybourne, Gloucestershire, which had been leased to him for four years by William and Elizabeth Lampet. The defendant pleaded Not guilty, and the jury found a special verdict: on 14 May 1593 Lord Lumley and others leased it to John Morrice the younger for 5,000 years; Morrice entered into possession, and in 1596 devised the term to John Morrice his father for life, remainder to his sister Elizabeth in tail; the elder John Morrice entered into possession, and in 1603 Elizabeth (and her husband William Lampet) purported to release her executory interest to him; on 1 October 1604 John Morrice, the elder, leased for ten years to Starkey, the defendant, and in 1609 he died; Elizabeth and William Lampet, claiming the residue of the 1593 lease in remainder under the devise, entered and made the lease to the plaintiff.

10 Co. Rep. 47.[12]

... This case of a devise of a lease for years to one for life, and after his death to another during the residue of the term, hath produced *septem quaestiones vexatae et spinosae*:[13]

1   When a man, being possessed of land for years, devises the use or profits of the land (or the land itself) to someone for life, and afterwards to another during the residue of the term, is the devise of a chattel after the death of the first devisee good? And it has been adjudged, as appears in *Manning's Case* in the eighth part of my reports,[14] that such an executory devise is good. And so it was held by all the court in the argument of this case.

2   The second question hath been, whether an executory devise after the death be good, when the term itself (and not the use or occupation) was devised to the first for life and afterwards to others. And it is adjudged that in such case also the executory devise was good, as in the said case of Manning appears. And so it was resolved in the argument of this case by all the justices ...

As to the cases which have been urged by the serjeants on the other side ... It would be inconvenient for such manner of perpetuity to be made of a chattel, when no perpetuity can be established of an inheritance, either by act executed by the common law, nor by limitation of a use, nor by devises in last wills. And if it were to be allowed, it would be the cause of contentions, suits, and other inconveniences. And it was observed that these leases for so many hundreds and thousands of years (which were in truth made to

---

12   Also reported in 2 Brownl. 172, which gives the arguments of Sjts. Dodderidge and Nichols for the plaintiff, and of Sjts. Harris and Shirley for the defendant. Coke characteristically mixes all the arguments into a composite essay.

13   I.e. seven vexed and thorny questions.

14   (1608); see p. 192, above.

deceive and defeat the king or other lords of their wards and other lawful duties[15]) are many times unfortunate, and subject to be lost by outlawry or other forfeitures; and if the owner thereof dies intestate the ordinary shall grant administration, and thereby women will lose their dower, men their tenancies by the curtesy, and many other inconveniences in subversion of the common law will from thence ensue. Therefore it would be of all other things most dangerous to make a perpetuity out of them.

CHILD d. HEATH v BAYLIE (1623)

King's Bench: record reconstructed from the reports, which give incorrect references to the plea roll. John Child brought ejectment against Baylie and others for ejecting him from land in Alvechurch, Worcestershire, which had been leased to him by Thomas Heath. The defendant pleaded Not guilty, and the jury found a special verdict: Nicholas Heath, bishop of Worcester, in 1553 leased the land for 76 years to William Heath; on 10 April 1568 William sublet to Walter Blunt and John Middlemore from the day of his death until 1 May 1629 (which was 25 days before the end of the main lease), provided his wife Dorothy should so long live and not remarry;[16] and shortly afterwards[17] William devised the residue of the term after Dorothy's death to his son William, and his assigns, provided that if William died without issue living at the time of his death his next son Thomas should have the lease, and that if Thomas died without issue his daughters should have it; and Dorothy, who was also her husband's executrix, entered and assented to the legacy and granted all her interest in the term to William; William later assigned the whole term to Dorothy, who assigned it to one Cocke (or Comb, or Cooper), under whom the defendants claimed; then Dorothy died, and William died without issue living; and Thomas entered as devisee in remainder, and made the lease to the plaintiff, who was ejected by the defendants.

(a) Turnour's reports, HLS MS. 106, fo. 13.[18]

... *Bridgman* argued that judgment ought to be given for the plaintiff. First, he held clearly that here is a good remainder to Thomas Heath by way of executory devise, according to *Lampet's Case*[19] and *Manning's Case*.[20] Secondly, he held that this grant by William Heath to Dorothy was good, for there was an actual

---

15 As a result of the establishment of Fyneux C.J.'s view: see p. 184, above.
16 Presumably in trust for Dorothy.
17 His will was proved in 1569: P.C.C. 3 Lyon.
18 Also reported in Cro. Jac. 459; Palm. 48; 2 Rolle Rep. 129; 1 Rolle Abr. 612.
19 (1612); see p. 193, above.
20 (1608); see p. 192, above.

reversion in him of twenty-five days, which was to take effect in him for a greater or lesser time according to [the date of] Dorothy's death . . . Thirdly, he held that, the remainder being good, it could not be prevented by any grant made by him who had the particular estate: according to *Lampet's Case.*

George Croke to the contrary. And he held, first, that the remainder to Thomas was void. If Thomas was to have any possibility in the remainder it was by virtue of the proviso, which comes after the devise made to William; and the proviso cannot do this, because it is repugnant to the premises: for, having devised the entire term and interest to William Heath and his assigns, he cannot afterwards make an abridgment thereof by a proviso . . . And he said that the cases of *Lampet* and *Manning*, put above, are not like our case, because in them the remainders did not rest on a proviso (as in the case at bar), but were good by way of executory devises: which cannot be here. Secondly, even if we admit the proviso to be good, yet the limitation of the remainder in the case at the bar shall not be good, since it is dependent on an estate tail, which by presumption is perpetual . . . Thirdly, even if we admit that a possibility may be good, nevertheless a possibility upon a possibility shall never be allowed: as 1 Rep. 156.[1] And here there is a possibility upon a possibility: for William has only a possibility if Dorothy dies before the year 1629, and Thomas has only a possibility if Dorothy dies before this time and William also dies without issue.

After this, in Michaelmas term 17 Jac. [1619], this case was argued again, by *Davenport* and *Thomas Crewe*;[2] but I omit their arguments because they were upon the same reasons and authorities as were before used by Bridgman and Croke.

MOUNTAGUE C.J., DODDERIDGE and HOUGHTON JJ. (CROKE J. being absent on account of illness) were of opinion that the judgment should be for the defendant:

1   They resolved that the remainder limited to Thomas Heath was void: (1) because it depended on a possibility upon a possibility . . . (2) William's estate, being limited unto him and his heirs male of his body, might have continuance for ever, ergo *remota possibilitas*, and a remainder limited upon a remote possibility shall not be good . . . (3) The remainderman shall never be respected by

---

1   *Lloyd d. Roberts v Wilkinson* (1598), usually known as *The Rector of Chedington's Case.*
2   They are briefly reported in Palm., at 49.

an equitable construction when the law will not respect the issue . . .

2 It was resolved that William Heath, by reason of the reversion that he had reserved to himself for the space of 25 days, had such an interest that he might devise; for it is not a mere possibility, but clothed with an interest which may be devised.

3 It was resolved that the instrument made by Dorothy to her son shall be rather [construed as] an instrument of assent to the legacy than an assignment of the reversion as executrix . . .

And judgment was given for the defendant; and a writ of error brought in the Exchequer Chamber, where the judgment was affirmed by all the justices of the Common Pleas and barons of the Exchequer, save for TANFIELD C.B.[3]

(b) Exchequer Chamber: Cro. Jac. 460 (untr.).[4]

. . . Note: upon this judgment a writ of error was brought in the Exchequer Chamber, and the error assigned in point of law, that the remainder of this term limited to Thomas Heath after the death of William without issue then living was good, and the alienation of William shall not bind him in remainder . . . [But] after divers arguments, all the judges of the Common Pleas (namely, HOBART C.J., WINCH, HUTTON and JONES JJ.) and all the barons except TANFIELD C.B.[5] agreed with the first judgment. For they said that the first grant or devise of a term made to one for life, remainder to another, hath been much controverted—whether such a remainder might be good, and whether all may not be destroyed by the alienation of the first party—and if it were now first disputed it would be hard to maintain: but being so often adjudged they would not now dispute it. But, for the case in question, where there was a devise to one and his assigns, and if he died without issue then

3 His dissent is noted briefly in HLS MS. 106, fo. 136: '. . . TANFIELD C.B. put this case. John Style has a son aged ten years, and devises his term to him, proviso that if he should die without issue before he reached the age of 24 years it should remain over: this is a good remainder, for the contingency is common and usual. And he showed a record, Hil. 9 Jac. rot. 895, between *Rothericke* and *Chappell*: Carew devised the occupation and profits of his term to his wife, and that if she died within the term W. should have the profits and occupation thereof so long as he lived and had issue of his body, proviso that if he died without issue and unmarried it would remain to two daughters; the wife died; and W. died without issue, unmarried; and it was adjudged a good remainder, and the court held that the words 'occupation etc.' made no difference.

4 Also reported in Wm Jones 15; Palm. 333.

5 Jones adds Denham B., but Palm. expressly lists him with the majority.

living that it would remain to another, it is a void devise . . . for the mischief which would otherwise ensue if there should be such a perpetuity of a term . . . And in Hilary term 20 Jac. [1623] it was affirmed.[6]

6　Cf. Palm., at 335: '. . . the remainder over to Thomas in this case is void, because it tends to create a perpetuity of a chattel, which could by no means be docked, and which in its proportion would be as equal in mischief to the common weal as a perpetuity in an estate tail. And even though such a judgment has been given in the King's Bench as allows the remainder to be good, nevertheless time has discovered the inconvenience which such limitations have introduced in the republic . . .'

7 Copyhold

NICHOLAS SON OF NORMAN v HEMFRID, SERJEANT OF THE CASTELLAN OF BERGUES (1214)

Curia Regis Rolls, VII, p. 60.

Northamptonshire. An assize comes to declare whether Hemfrid the serjeant of the castellan of Bergues and Herbert the reeve, Walter son of William and Richard [Walter's] brother unjustly and without judgment disseised Nicholas son of Norman of his free tenement in Ashby within [the limitation period of] the assize.

And Hemfrid was not found, and the others come and freely concede [that] the assize [be taken].

The jurors say that indeed the same Nicholas and his father Norman held that tenement for servile customs by fork and flail; and they could not marry a daughter without [paying] ransom. But the same Norman so persuaded [the lord] that the works and customs were commuted into money for as long as pleased him. And [Nicholas] has held that land on these terms for 20 years.

And so it is adjudged that they did not disseise him, and that Nicholas is to be amerced.

ANGER SON OF HUGH v GILBERT SON OF HARALD (1218)

Rolls of the Justices in Eyre for Lincolnshire, 1218–19, and Worcestershire, 1221, Selden Soc. vol. 53, pl. 174.

[Lincolnshire]. An assize comes to declare whether Gilbert son of Harald unjustly and without judgment disseised Anger son of Hugh of his free tenement in Conisholme within [the limitation period of] the assize.

And Gilbert comes and concedes [that] the assize [be taken].

The jurors say that [Gilbert] did not disseise him of his free tenement because the land is [part of] Gilbert's villeinage and the same Anger holds it in villeinage.

Judgment: Anger is to be amerced for a false claim.

ALDWIN SON OF ROBERT v BISHOP OF WINCHESTER (1203)

Curia Regis Rolls, II, p. 146.

Berkshire. An assize of mort d'ancestor for a half virgate in Waltham St Lawrence between the claimant Aldwin son of Robert and the bishop of Winchester, tenant, remains [not taken] because that Aldwin had in the same way brought a writ before justices at Reading and that assize had remained [not taken] because the bishop said the land was his villeinage, and again the same Aldwin in the same way brought a writ against the bishop before justices at Winchester when Aldwin was amerced; and Aldwin acknowledges this. So he is put in jail.

ANON. (1453–54)[1]

Statham Abr. *Subpena*, pl. [2].

A man who is tenant at will by copyhold shall have a *subpoena* against his lord if he puts him out: by the opinion of KYRKBY [M.R.] and POLE [J.K.B.], in a *subpoena* in the Chancery.

T. LITTLETON, THE NEW TENURES (1481)[2]

Sections 73–77 (as numbered in later eds.).

Tenant by copy of court roll is where there is a custom which has been used time out of mind in a manor, that certain tenants within the manor are accustomed to have lands and tenements to hold unto them and their heirs in fee simple, or in fee tail, or for life, and so forth, at the will of the lord according to the custom of the manor. Such a tenant may not alien his land by deed, for the lord could then enter as in a thing forfeited to him; but, if he wishes to alien his land to another, he must according to custom surrender

---

1 Also in Fitz. Abr., *Subpena*, pl. 21 (probably from Statham Abr.).
2 Written *c*. 1465–75.

the tenement in some court into the lord's hands to the use of the person who is to have the estate ... And such tenants are called tenants by copy of court roll because they have no other evidence concerning their tenements save the copies of the court rolls. Such tenants shall neither implead nor be impleaded for their tenements by the king's writ; but if they wish to implead others for their tenements they shall have a plaint made in the lord's court ... in the nature of the king's writ of assize of mort d'ancestor, of an assize of novel disseisin, or formedon in the descender at common law, or in the nature of any other writ ... And although some such tenants have an inheritance according to the custom of the manor, yet they have but an estate at the will of the lord according to the course of the common law. For, as it is said, if the lord puts them out they have no other remedy but to sue to their lords by petition; for if they had another remedy they would not be called tenants at the will of the lord according to the custom of the manor. But the lord will not break a custom which is reasonable in such case.

[BRYAN, however, said his opinion had always been and ever would be that if such a customary tenant, having paid his services, is ejected by the lord he shall have an action of trespass against him: Hilary 21 Edw. IV.[3] And so was the opinion of DANBY, Michaelmas 7 Edw. IV:[4] for he said that a tenant by the custom had the like claim of inheritance to have his land as he who has a freehold at common law.][5]

ANON. (1467)

Y.B. Mich. 7 Edw. IV, fo. 19, pl. 16 (C.P.).

... If the lord enters and puts out his tenant at will according to the custom of the manor, has he any remedy against the lord?

DANBY [C.J.]. It seems he has, for if the lord puts him out he does him wrong ...

LITTLETON [J.]. I once saw a *subpoena* brought by such a tenant against his lord, and it was held by all the justices that he should

---

3   Y.B. Hil. 21 Edw. IV, fo. 80, pl. 27: '... *Brigges*. If the lord puts him out he has no remedy: which proves that he is only a tenant at will. BRYAN [C.J.] That was never my opinion, and I believe it never will be; for then all the copyhold in England would be defeated. Therefore I think that, if the tenant pays his customs and services, whenever the lord puts him out of possession he shall have an action of trespass against him'.

4   Y.B. Mich. 7 Edw. IV, fo. 19, pl. 16 (printed above).

5   Passage added in 1530 ed.

not recover anything thereby; for it was held that the lord's entry was permissible, since he is a tenant at will.

ANON. (1529)

Pollard's reports, BL MS. Hargrave 388, fo. 51.

In the Common Bench it was said by FITZHERBERT J. that if the lord puts out the termor by copy of court roll, within the term, he shall have a good writ of trespass against the lord. (Query, however.)

ANON. (1544)

LC MS. Acc. LL 52960, 36 Hen. VIII, fo. 22v (C.P.).

Note that it was said by SHELLEY J. that the lord by copy of court roll can put out his tenant at will, and the tenant shall have no remedy against him: for he cannot have any action against him. And if all the books are looked at, including Littleton, Bracton and the *Natura Brevium*, and other old records, and they are well noted and construed, I doubt not that the better opinion is that the lord may oust him. I have seen tenants sue in such cases for a remedy, and they could have none. If it were to be proved by reason it would be hard to prove that [such] tenants should have a remedy.

BROWNE J. to the contrary. In the present king's time this matter was appointed to be argued, but on account of the mischief which would have ensued if it had been adjudged as your opinion is, a command was sent by the king's council that it should not be argued.

BALDWIN C.J. agreed with this, and was against SHELLEY J. in it. (But query what the law is.)[6]

ANON. (1573)

BL MS. Harley 5143, fo. 175.[7]

... It was held in the Queen's Bench that if [a copyholder] is ejected he may maintain [*de*] *ejectione firmae* at common law.

6   In 1553 Hales J.C.P. and Portman J.Q.B. held at Serjeants' Inn that the lord could not oust the copyholder: C. M. Gray, *Copyhold, Equity and the Common Law* (1963), pp. 62–63. There does not seem to have been much dispute after this.
7   French text in *Gray*, p. 202, fn. 22. Cf. p. 207, below (perhaps the same case).

But the better opinion of the justices of the Common Bench was contrary, because he cannot be put in possession of a copyhold by *habere facias seisinam* . . .

ANON. (1584)

HLS MS. 2079, fo. 86v.

It was agreed by WRAY C.J.Q.B. and ANDERSON C.J.C.P. in the county of Suffolk, at the assizes in their circuit,[8] that there shall be no tenant by the curtesy of a copyhold except where such an estate has been used within the manor where the land lies; for, just as a copyholder's estate is by custom, so also no estate shall be allowed in copyhold lands except those which have been used by custom within the manor where the land lies.

DELL v HYGDEN (1595)

Record: KB 27/1330, m. 547d. Thomas Dell brought a bill of ejectment against Walter Hygden as lessee of land in Flamstead, Hertfordshire, from Richard Fanche. Hygden pleaded Not guilty, and on 5 August 1594 at Hertford assizes (Clarke B., Drewe Sjt.) the jury found a special verdict: the land was held of the manor of Flamstead by copy of court roll at the will of the lord according to the custom of the manor, by which it was grantable in fee simple, fee tail, for life or for years; in 1532 King Henry VIII was seised of the manor and, by his steward, granted the land to Jane, widow of Thomas Fanche, for life, remainder to Henry, son of Thomas, and the heirs male of his body, remainder to his brother Richard and the heirs male of his body; Jane entered, and died; Henry entered, and had issue Isabel, now the defendant's wife; and at a manorial court on 24 April 1581 Henry surrendered the land to the use of the defendant, against whom a common recovery was suffered by a plaint in the nature of entry *sur disseisin* in the *post*, in which Henry was vouched and Henry's vouchee defaulted; and the recoveror immediately surrendered to the use of Henry in fee simple; Henry was readmitted, and in 1584 surrendered to the use of himself for life, remainder to Walter and Isabel Hygden in fee simple, and they were all admitted accordingly; then Henry died, and the Hygdens entered; then Richard Fanche entered upon them, as remainderman under the 1532 settlement, and made the lease to Dell, who was ejected the next day. The jury also found that there had been no common recovery in the manorial court of Flamstead before 1581. They left it to the court to decide whether Hygden's re-entry was lawful: if not, they assessed the damages as 10s., with 12d. costs. The court took advisement until 22 January 1595.

---

8   The two chief justices rode this (the Norfolk) circuit together from 1581 to 1585.

HLS MS. 110, fo. 126; BL MS. Add. 25198, fo. 48.[9]

... *Foster* argued that this recovery was void, because according to the custom copyholds are transferred by conveyance—by surrendering into the lord's hands—[whereas] here this recovery is based on a warranty, which is at common law and is not warranted by the custom (it being expressly found by the verdict that there was no such recovery there before). And he cited 23 Hen. VIII, Brooke [Abr.], *Recoverie in value*, 27,[10] that a plaint of land held by copyhold and recovery by warranty is not good, because he may not warrant... and if the recovery were good, an inconvenience would follow, for then the lord would have a tenant without his privity, and also the tenant could create an estate without paying any fine. So the title of the party who claims under this recovery is not good.

Tanfield said that if a copyhold is given for life, remainder in tail, remainder over, the admittance of the tenant for life is an admittance of all the remaindermen. Therefore, it being here found that the tenant for life was admitted, and died, and that the remainderman died without issue [male], the entry by the other remainderman and his lease are good ... And he did not doubt but that an estate tail may be of copyhold perfectly well, because Littleton says[11] that a writ in the nature of formedon may be sued in the manor court for copyhold land ... As to the recovery, if a lessee for life or years had surrendered to the use of another at common law, this surrender was never good. And even if the statute now saves it, yet a warranty cannot be annexed to such a use. A fortiori in this case, the warranty shall not be good, because he who made it was only tenant at will: and therefore the recovery is void, since it is made by reason of the warranty. There cannot be any discontinuance, because the tenant in tail was not tenant at the time.[12] So the entry of the tenant in tail in remainder was good; and it follows that his lease is good, and the recovery of no effect against him.

9   Also reported in Cro. Eliz. 372; Moore K.B. 358; 1 Rolle Abr. 506, line 16. The French text of the report here is in *Gray*, pp. 228–233.
10   '... such a recovery with voucher is used to dock the tail in ancient demesne upon a writ of right and voucher over, and this is for freehold there: query, however, concerning such a recovery upon a plaint there for land of base tenure, for that cannot be warranted...'
11   See p. 201, above.
12   Cf. the fuller explanation in BL MS. Add. 25200, fo. 37 (*Gray*, p. 234): 'the tenant in tail surrendered to the use, whereby his estate was drowned, and no warranty could be annexed ... and the person to whose use the surrender was made took his estate from the lord, not from the tenant in tail, and therefore he could not have a warranty from the tenant in tail whereby he could vouch him'.

Gray to the contrary. He said that an estate tail could not be created of copyhold by any custom, for that estate is founded solely on the statute *De donis conditionalibus*; and it is clear that copyhold lands were not within that statute, any more than they were within the statutes concerning uses, aid prayer, and wills . . . Now, if the land was not within the statute, the custom cannot create an estate in this customary land by warrant of the statute, because he is tenant in fee simple upon condition (as before, at common law), and therefore after issue born he has power of alienating as absolute tenant in fee simple . . . As to the recovery with voucher, it is good; or at least it is only voidable . . .

All the justices agreed as one that admittance of the particular lessee for life, where there are various remainders over, is an admittance of all the remainder[men] also.

POPHAM C.J. When the tenant for life comes to be admitted he shows the copy in court to the steward, in which copy all the remainders are comprised, and the steward makes an entry on his roll that he was thereupon admitted. But the remaindermen shall pay their fines, or else it is a forfeiture of the copyhold for their refusal. And it is no more a prejudice to the lord to have his fine from the remainderman without admitting him than it is to have it from the heir of the tenant in fee after his father's death (whereby he is tenant before admittance).

CLENCH J. Custom cannot create an estate tail in copyhold, unless the custom also proves that the estate had been recovered by formedon in the descender or remainder after a discontinuance committed: and then it is an estate tail by reason of the custom of recovery, not by reason of the gift, for the gift alone (without the custom to recover) makes an estate in fee simple conditional at common law. And here it is not found by verdict that the custom was to recover after a discontinuance, and so it is no estate tail.

GAWDY J. There can be an estate tail in a copyhold, according to 15 Hen. VIII, Brooke [Abr.], *Tenant per copie*, 24;[13] and formedon in the descender lies for it at common law. And it shall

13 'Note that it was stated as law that a tail may be of copyhold, and that formedon in the descender may lie for it by protestation in the nature of a formedon in the descender at common law, and it is good, by all the justices; for although formedon in the descender was only given by statute, the writ nevertheless now lies at common law, and it shall be presumed to have been a custom there from time immemorial; and the demandant shall recover, by advice of all the justices. A similar matter occurred in Essex in Michaelmas 26 Hen. VIII, and Fitzherbert J. afterwards affirmed it in the Duchy Chamber of Lancaster. And Littleton agrees, in his chapter on tenants by copy of court roll'. The Littleton passage is printed at p. 200, above.

be presumed that this has been a custom since time immemorial, even though the writ of formedon is given by the Statute of Westminster.[14] Therefore, since the custom has been found that the land held by copy was demisable in tail, this is a good tail according to the custom. When a copyholder surrenders to the use [of another] he cannot annex any warranty to this conveyance, because he is reputed by the common law to be in the same degree as a tenant at will; and it is a good counterplea to a voucher to say that he who made the feoffment had but an estate at will. In consequence, therefore, the voucher is idle, and no recompense shall be gained from it; and so it follows that the recovery cannot be a discontinuance... If it had been found by the verdict that the custom was to have recoveries upon vouching, this would have been a bar of the estate tail; but here it is expressly found to the contrary.

FENNER J. This estate tail is made by the equity of the Statute of Westminster II, and not by the custom, because there was no estate tail at common law. And various demises in tail by copy, and the possession continuing accordingly, is sufficient evidence to prove [the custom of] entail without any recovery in formedon. But, whether it be an estate by the common law or by the custom, *secundum aequum et bonum* and in good conscience this recovery is a bar of it, for there is no right which cannot be given away if the parties join. And it is the common course and conveyance to bind estates tail by recoveries...

POPHAM C.J. An estate tail of copyhold is outside the custom, for no custom can warrant it, because there was no such estate at common law. But if this estate can be recovered after a discontinuance, and if the writ on the statute gives a remedy to recontinue it, then the equity of the statute (and not the custom) gives the estate... A warranty by a copyholder is good. And hereupon he took this distinction: if a copyholder for life surrenders into the lord's hands to the use of someone in fee, with warranty, and the lord admits him to whose use the surrender was made according to the form of the surrender, this warranty can never be good, because the estate was already extinguished in the lord and after admittance the other is in in the *per* through the lord ... but if a copyholder in fee or in tail surrenders to the use of someone else, with warranty, this is a good warranty if the lord makes admittance accordingly, because the other is in in the *per* through the surrenderor... And he said that he knew, of his own knowledge, that such a con-

---

14 Statute of Westminster II, c. 1; p. 50, above. But see S. F. C. Milsom, 'Formedon before De Donis' (1956) 72 L.Q.R. 391.

veyance to dock the estate tail by a recovery in respect of copyhold land had been allowed by [WRAY] C.J. his predecessor here, and by Plowden 30 years since ... In many cases copyhold is reputed in equal degree with land at common law, and is not to be compared with a tenancy at will. For the same reason, the common law working upon the custom will dock estates tail and bar them for ever. And just as the custom does not give the estate tail, neither is it founded on the custom, but on the equity of the statute working upon the custom: and this equity gives the means (by formedon) to recontinue it when it is discontinued. For the same reason, the common law working upon the custom shall bind the estate by recovery and the supposed recompense; and so the recovery is a good bar. And this is the better exposition, for otherwise much confusion (*garboyles*) will follow by reason that many of these conveyances have already been made, if they were now overturned.

The case was further adjourned to Easter term 1595, but no judgment was entered.

E. COKE, COMPLETE COPYHOLDER (1635)

Supplement, s. 20 (untr.).

In *ejectione firmae*, the case was that the plaintiff was lessee for years of a copyhold, and the custom of the manor was that a copyholder might let the land for three years. It was the opinion of ANDERSON C.J. that the lessee of a copyholder cannot maintain the *ejectione firmae*; but if he might he ought to show his lessor's estate, or his licence, or a special custom to warrant it.[15]

A copyholder made a lease for years by indenture, warranted by the custom. It was adjudged that the lessee should maintain an *ejectione firmae*, although it was strongly objected that (if it were so) then the plaintiff should have an *habere facias seisinam*, and so copyholds should be ordered by the laws of the land[16] ...

Note, it was resolved by the justices that the lessee of a copyholder for a year may maintain an *ejectione firmae*, for

15 *Wells v Partridge* (1596) Cro. Eliz. 469.
16 *Anon.* (1572) cited in *Heydon's Case* (1583) 1 Leon. 4, Moore K.B. 128; perhaps the case (dated 1573), p. 202, above. Cf. *Anon.* (1572) BL MS. Add. 35940, fo. 650: 'Another question was moved: shall a copyholder who makes a lease for years by custom have an *ejectione firmae* at common law? The doubt arises because the lessee is a customary tenant, just as the copyholder himself, and should sue in the lord's court and not at common law. But it seems that a lessee for years by the lord's licence by indenture shall sue at common law by *ejectione firmae*'.

inasmuch as his term is warranted by law (by force of the general custom of the realm) it is but reason that, if he be ejected, he should have an *ejectione firmae*: for it is a speedy course for a copyholder to gain the possession of the land against a stranger, being no more than what right requires to be yielded him for the recovery of his estate.[17]

17   *Melwich v Luter* (1588) 4 Co. Rep. 26 (K.B.). See also *Goodwin v Longhurst* (1596) Cro. Eliz. 535 (Exch.). The Common Pleas in 1594 refused to accept this view: *Gray*, pp. 202–203, fn. 25.

8 Debt

(1) Suit and wager of law

VEIL v BASSINGBOURN (1226)

Curia Regis Rolls, XII, pl. 1609;
Bracton's Note Book, pl. 1693.

Cambridgeshire. William le Veil claims against Warin of Bass-
ingbourn that he render 12 marks which he owes him of the debt
[incurred by] his father Wimer, whose heir [Warin] is.

As to which the same William says that the same Wimer took
from him cloths to the value of 50 marks; and thereof he produces
suit which attests this.

And Warin comes and denies against him and against his suit
that he owes anything, and he asks that William's suit be heard.

And [the suit] is heard, and they acknowledge that they know
nothing at all about the matter. And [William] has neither tally nor
charter.

And so it is adjudged that Warin [is to go] quit; and William is to
be amerced.

ANON. (*c.* 1294)

Y.B. 21 & 22 Edw. I, Rolls Series, p. 457.

Note: if someone demands a debt against executors by a tally or by
suit, that in this case, because executors cannot do law for a
deceased person, the plaintiff must prove his tally; or, if he has suit,
the suit should be examined. And this is true whether or not he is a

merchant, for otherwise it would follow that he would lose his debt.

In the following century, it was settled that debt would not lie against executors unless there was a deed: *Anon.* (1367) Y.B. Trin. 41 Edw. III, fo. 13, pl. 3. For the means of escape from this rule, see pp. 218, fn. 10, 446–457, below.

ANON. (between 1292 and 1297)

Y.B. 2 & 3 Edw. II, Selden Soc. vol. 19, p. 195.

One A. brought a writ of debt against B. and said that wrongfully he detained from him ten marks etc.

Howard. What have you [in proof] of the debt?

Spigurnel. Good suit.

Howard. Have you anything else to bind us to the debt?

Spigurnel. No.

Howard. Sir, they demand a debt of ten marks and show the court nothing that binds us: neither writing nor tally nor anything else that [supports them] save only their own bare word. We ask judgment whether he need be answered.

Spigurnel. We have tendered suit, and to this you do not answer. We ask judgment against you as undefended.

BEREFORD. Answer to their suit.

Howard. They have nothing but their suit: we ask that it be examined.

Spigurnel. There is no need for that, for suit serves no purpose but to attest what the party has said and entitle him to an answer.

BEREFORD. In this case the defendant can choose any of three courses: to put himself upon the countryside; to be at his law; to put himself upon your suit that you have tendered, which is tantamount to the countryside. And here he has [chosen] the examination of the suit that you have tendered. And so [since you refuse it] the court adjudges that you take nothing by your writ but be amerced, and that B. go quit etc.

DUNMAN v WELDON (1329)

Y.B. Eyre of Northamptonshire,
Selden Soc. vol. 97, p. 476.

William Dunman brought debt for grain worth 100s. against Robert of Weldon, parson of Isham, and counted that on 7 August 1318 he bought from the defendant five quarters each of barley, rye and beans, worth 100s., for 100s., and that the defendant had refused to make delivery.

... *Elmdon* denied and said that he did not sell any grain to the plaintiff, nor does he withhold any: ready to do his law against the plaintiff and his suit.

Bacon. This contract lies in the knowledge of the country, and so you should not be received to wage law.

SCROP. If you were to be received to wage your law in this case, it would have to be upon the receipt of the money, for the receipt is the cause of the indebtedness (*duité*). Therefore take heed, at your peril, whether you wish that as your answer.

Elmdon. He sold the plaintiff no grain, nor did he receive any money from him by reason of such a sale, nor does he withhold any grain: ready to do his law.

SCROP. Do you want the averment?

Elmdon did not dare to abide by wager of law, and put forward the averment that he sold the plaintiff no grain and received no money by reason of such a sale: ready to aver. (*Et alii econtra*).

SCROP to *Elmdon.* You waged your law upon the withholding (*la detenue*), and the law cannot be received on that point: for if you traverse the withholding, the court will take the sale of the grain and the receipt of the money as conceded; and once the sale and the receipt of money have been confessed, you can only excuse the withholding by an affirmation of payment: and then the plaintiff would properly be able to wage his law against the payment. So wager of law is not receivable in this case, against the withholding.

The record shows that the defendant denied the sale, the receipt of the price, and the withholding, and put himself on the country. The jury found that the plaintiff bought two quarters of wheat and rye and four quarters of barley and assessed the damages at 100s. Judgment was given accordingly, even though the plaintiff had not mentioned wheat in his count, and even though the jurors had said nothing about the payment of the price or the withholding of the grain.

ANON. (1330)

Y.B. Eyre of Northamptonshire,
Selden Soc. vol. 98, p. 744.

Two women waged their law jointly in a plea of debt, and came to do their law. Both of them swore jointly, and then one of them went from the bar to look for the people who were due to swear with her, because only two were standing ready to make their oath with the women. As soon as the woman had left the bar, the plaintiff caused her to be demanded,[1] and she did not answer. But meanwhile the justices took the oaths of the two men, and immediately after that was done the woman came back with enough men to finish the law. The plaintiff refused the oath of the others, and demanded judgment of the women as having failed in their law; for he said that someone who is to do law must be always ready, just as one who has waged battle.

But, even though the party demurred in judgment on this point until another day, the court said that it would receive the law.

ANON. v WARREN (1343)

Y.B. 17 & 18 Edw. III, Rolls Series, p. 73 (C.P.).

Debt brought against master John Warren, canon of St Peter's church, York, for a certain sum owed, [and the plaintiff counts] as to part on a bond, part on a contract.

Richemund. As to the bond, we cannot deny it. As to the rest, what have you [in proof] of the debt?

Moubray. Good suit.

Richemund. Let his suit be examined at our peril.

Moubray. Do you mean that for your answer?

Richemund. Yes, because in this case of contract you rely upon suit by way of proving your action.

Moubray. Suit is tendered only as part of the form of the count; so [we ask] judgment etc.

SHARDELOW. One has heard of suit being examined in such a case; and this opinion was later disapproved. Yes, even that justice who examined the suit by way of issue saw that he had made a mistake, and condemned his own opinion.

Gaynesford. In a plea of land the tender of suit is [indeed] only a matter of form. But in a plea which is founded upon contracts, which require attestation, the suit is a matter of attestation to this extent: that without suit, if the point is challenged, the party is not entitled to an answer.

SHARDELOW. That is certainly not so, and therefore [answer].

Richemund. [The defendant] owes him not a penny; ready etc.

Moubray. To that you shall not get, because you have [staked your whole case] upon the tender of another issue.

Richemund. You said that the first was not a [good] issue; and so your own [argument] gives me the advantage.

---

1 I.e. solemnly called by the crier.

And notwithstanding KELSHALL adjudged that the plaintiff should recover the whole debt and damages taxed by the court etc.

ANON. (1356)

Y.B. Mich. 30 Edw. III, fo. 18 (C.P.).

Where a man brought a writ of debt against another, and demanded 24 marks as owed to him for wools and other things sold to [the defendant] by such a one his servant—and he named the servant—*Claymond* made denial and said that [the defendant] owed nothing in the manner that [the plaintiff] counted; ready to do his law.

THORPE. Are you ready to do the law now?

Claymond. Yes, sir.

Skipwith. You see that we have counted that he is our debtor by reason of a contract made by another, a thing which naturally lies within the knowledge of the country, and so we ask judgment whether the law lies.

Claymond. And we [ask] judgment, since you have put forward no writing in proof of the debt, or alleged anything other than the supposal of a bare contract, in which case the law is receivable; and since you have refused the law, we pray that you be barred.

Skipwith. Why does the law lie in this case any more than in a writ of account when one counts that [the defendant] was his receiver by another's hand?

GREENE. In this writ you have counted that you yourself sold him the wools, by such a one your servant; and so you have supposed that the contract was made by yourself; and there is no distinction between your selling by your own hand or by your servant's hand, since the contract is yours.

Skipwith. I counted that my servant sold them.

GREENE. If we record that, you would have no action against the defendant; instead your action would be against your servant who made the sale, by way of account; and so we take it that you counted as the law requires you to count, and we so recorded; for otherwise the [defendant] would have another answer, and I am sure he would not [just] have tendered his law if you had counted in that way.

And because [the plaintiff] had refused the law when it was acceptable, WILLOUGHBY adjudged that he should take nothing by his writ etc.

A LECTURE ON WAGER OF LAW (15th century)

Reading on Magna Carta, c. 28:
CUL MS. Ii. 5. 43, fo. 40v.

Note that in a case where a man ought to wage his law there must be eleven lawful men to do his law, and he must be the twelfth (and that is sufficient). It is a good question, however, in the case where a writ of debt is brought against two, and they wish to wage their law, whether it is sufficient for them to bring ten men, or whether [they need] eleven. Some hold that [ten are not] sufficient, because when the writ is brought against the two of them it is brought against them only in effect as against one, and if they wish to wage their law they ought to wage only as one man; and then if they have only ten men, and the two of them are but one in effect, they are only eleven, and the law cannot be taken by eleven; and so they must have eleven men with them.

And note that a man may wage his law in a writ of debt in some cases, but in some not. For instance, in the cases where a writ of debt is brought upon a recovery, or a recognisance, or is based on a specialty (such as a bond), the defendants may not wage their law. Nor may they in a writ brought for arrears of an account before appointed auditors, because it lies in the knowledge of the country. But they may in a writ of debt brought on a simple contract, because it does not lie in the knowledge of the country. And note that if a servant brings a writ of debt against his master for his salary in arrear, the master may not wage his law that he owes him nothing, because it lies in the knowledge of the country.

And note that a man may wage his law in a writ of account in some cases, and in some not. For instance, in a writ of account brought against a man supposing that he was his receiver by his own hands, he may wage his law. But if the plaintiff supposes by his writ that the defendant was his receiver by another's hands, then he may not wage his law, because someone else has knowledge and therefore it lies in the knowledge of the country. And in the case where he supposes that he was his bailiff of some manor, he may never wage his law, because it lies in the knowledge of the country whether he was his bailiff or not.

And in the case where a writ of detinue is brought against a man, and the plaintiff supposes that he bailed to the defendant certain chattels to be rebailed to him, or the plaintiff supposes that certain chattels were bailed to him by a stranger to rebail to the plaintiff, he may in either case wage his law generally that he detains nothing from him; and the reason is because the bailment is not traversable in a writ of detinue, but he must answer to the detaining generally. And so note a distinction between this case and the case of account.

A man may wage his law in a writ of trespass in a court baron, but not at the common law.

SLOUFORT'S CASE (1425)

Y.B. Pas. 3 Hen. VI, fo. 42, pl. 13; collated with
BL MS. Harley 452, fo. 63; MS. Harley 5155, fo. 34v;
Bod. Lib. MS. Rawl. D. 363, fo. 108v. (C.P.).

A writ of debt was brought in London against W. Sloufort.[2]

Rolf, for the plaintiff, counted that on a certain day and in a certain year the plaintiff covenanted[3] with this same defendant, in a certain ward, to be his scalder[4] for two years next following, that is to say, that the plaintiff would scald his pigs and all the other beasts and birds which the defendant should bring him, and that the plaintiff would find wood, fuel, vessels and all other necessaries thereunto belonging, taking 100s. a year; and he showed that he had done the scalding, and that his salary was in arrear to the amount of the sum in demand.

Cottesmore. Sir, you plainly see that he has declared in effect on a covenant, of which he shows nothing.[5]

Rolf. That [plea] is to the action.

MARTIN. This is only a simple contract, of which he need not show anything.

And that was the opinion of the whole court.

So *Cottesmore* moved on, and said: he owes him nothing, and is ready to do his law.

Rolf. Sir, you plainly see that we have declared in effect on a retainer, which is as strong as if we had declared that we were his servant, and in that case he would not have had his law. Therefore, in default of an answer, we pray our debt and our damages.

COKAYNE. It seems to me that he should have his law; and I say that there is a distinction between this case and the case of a common servant. For a common servant shall be required by law

---

2 'Slouflot' in Bod. Lib. MS.
3 Reads 'was retained' in Bod. Lib. MS.
4 One who scalded swine or poultry in order to remove hairs or feathers.
5 I.e. no deed. Cf. pp. 283, 284, 286, below.

to serve against his will, and what he is to have for his service is defined by the statute, and therefore his action to demand his salary is provided by the statute; in which case debt does not lie. But in the case at bar the law is otherwise; for the plaintiff was not the kind of servant the statute speaks of, because he could not[6] be compelled to serve in such a service as he was [in] against his will; and therefore the action is brought and based solely on a simple contract, for which by law he shall have his law.

Rolf. Suppose I make a covenant with someone to be my ploughman, and to find everything needed in that occupation, such as the plough itself, carts, and all the other things necessary for it, taking ten marks a year; in a writ of debt against me for this salary, shall I have my law? I say no, because it is brought for a retainer's salary. [Likewise here.][7]

COKAYNE. I say that in your case he shall have it; and I say that it is all one case, for his service was not a common service. For [in the case of common service] the master should [provide] all the necessary things, not the servant; and since the servant has taken upon himself to find something during the term he has thereby changed his service [from common service].[8]

MARTIN. In this very term it was adjudged in such a case against William Pole, where a writ of debt was brought against someone for the arrears of a salary, and the plaintiff declared that he was retained with him for three years to be of his counsel, taking £10 a year, and the defendant tendered his law that he owed him nothing; and Pole demurred against him, that law did not lie; and it was debated here and adjudged that, because Pole refused the law, he was barred.[9] (So he said to *Rolf*: it were good for you to take heed.)

It was adjourned.

---

6 Omitted in MS.

7 MS. only.

8 Omitted in MS.

9 Reported in Y.B. Hil. 3 Hen. VI, fo. 33, pl. 26; Bod. Lib. MS. Rawl. D. 363, fo. 100v: '. . . *Strangeways*. He owes him nothing and is ready to do his law. *Pole*. For default of answer we demand judgment and pray our debt and damages; for if a servant brings a writ of debt for his salary, the defendant shall not have his law, and no more shall he here. MARTIN. I say that there is all the difference between the two cases. (Query.) It was adjourned, and the next term it was awarded that he take nothing by his writ'. It might seem strange for Pole (a serjeant at law) to liken himself to a common servant, but his argument apparently was that (like a servant, but by a different authority) he was compellable to be of counsel for anyone: that is how the case is noted in Y.B. Mich. 21 Hen. VI, fo. 4, pl. 6.

ANON. (1460)

Y.B. Mich. 39 Hen. VI, fo. 18, pl. 24 (C.P.).

[In] debt the plaintiff counted that the defendant, on such a day in such a year, retained him for the sum now demanded to go to Rome to purchase a [papal] bull, and he specified what bull. And the defendant waged his law that [he owed] nothing. And the plaintiff demurred [to this wager, asking] whether the law could be received on this special matter; and the demurrer was entered [on the plea roll].

PRYSOT [C.J.]. He will have his law well enough, because this retainer is at common law; and it is not like the retainer of agricultural labourers which is given by statute, in which case they are compelled to serve according to the statute; and because they are compelled by the statute to serve against their will, for that reason their masters can not wage their law against them. But if a man retains a priest or a gentleman or a yeoman, butler, cook, and such like, which are necessary occupations, and they bring action of debt for their salary, their masters will be received to their law, because servants of that kind can not be compelled to serve in the said occupations according to the statute; and so, etc. And as to what is said [in a passage missing from this report] about its lying in notice [of the countryside], so does an arbitration lie [in notice], upon which [the defendant] can have his law; and so etc.

And such was the opinion of all the justices, so it was adjudged that the plaintiff was barred. But there was a question among the justices whether a man could wage his law in a writ of debt brought against him for his commons, namely his board or the like.

MOYLE and DANBY held that he could.

PRYSOT and NEDEHAM, the contrary: which note.

MOYLE said in the same case: if I come to an innkeeper to lodge with him and he refuses to provide lodging for me, I shall have upon my case an action of trespass against him. And similarly if I come to a victualler to buy victuals and he refuses to sell, I shall have trespass upon my case against him; and yet in such cases if he wishes to bring action of debt against me for what is owed in this way, I shall have my law.

PRYSOT. It is true that in those cases the defendant may wage his law; but the victualler or the innkeeper is not bound to sell you his victuals if he does not want to, nor the innkeeper to provide lodging for you if he does not want to; but it lies in their election; which note; query about this.

DANBY said that an innkeeper is not bound to give fodder to his guest's horse until he is paid cash in hand, because the law does not force him to trust his guest for the payment, etc.

ST GERMAN'S DOCTOR AND STUDENT (1531)

Selden Soc. vol. 91, p. 232 (Dialogue II, ch. 24)
(untr.).

Student . . . Though there lie no action in the king's court against executors upon a simple contract,[10] yet if they be sued in that case for the debt in the spiritual court a prohibition lieth. And in like wise if a man wage his law untruly in an action of debt upon a contract in the king's court, yet he shall not be sued for that perjury in the spiritual court: and yet no remedy lieth for that perjury in the king's court. For the prohibition lieth not only where a man is sued in the spiritual court of such things as the party may have his remedy in the king's court, but also where the spiritual court holdeth plea in such case where by the king's prerogative and by the ancient custom of the realm ought none to hold.[11]

ANON. (1563)

Dalison 49, pl. 11; BL MS. Add. 24845, fo. 66v
(C.P.).[12]

A man brought an action of debt on a contract, and counted that the defendant bought 20 sheep from him for £11. The defendant

---

10 This overlooks (or rejects) the use of *assumpsit* for this purpose; see p. 446, below. An earlier means of avoidance was suggested in Gray's Inn, *c*. 1500: 'If a man is indebted [to me] in £20 by a simple contract, and dies, I have no remedy by the common law against the executors; but I may have *quominus* in the Exchequer, supposing that I am indebted to the king and that their testator owed me so much, whereby I am the less able to pay the king: [this was] practised by *Dudley*, and is common usage' (Bod. Lib. MS. Rawlinson C. 705. fo. 55v; Selden Soc. vol. 94, p. 63, fn. 4).

11 Cf. Sjt. Yorke's reports, BL MS. Hargrave 388, fo. 213; MS. Lansdowne 1072, fo. 33; MS. Hargrave 3, fo. 22v: 'Note that *praemunire* and prohibition are always based in effect where the matter comprised touches the king's crown and dignity. Therefore if an executor is sued in the spiritual court upon a contract of debt made by the testator, where the action does not lie at common law against executors, a prohibition lies even though he shall have no action against him at common law. And the reason is because the same kind of action and matter lie at common law. The law is the same upon *laesio fidei*, where he deposes for paying a certain sum of money: if he is sued in the spiritual court for the money a prohibition lies, but not if he is sued for the breach of faith'.

12 Also reported in Moo. K.B. 49, pl. 148.

said that he bought the sheep from him for £8, without this that he bought them for £11.

Harpur thought that the defendant ought to do his law, and not traverse the contract.

Carus. The law would be to the effect that he does not owe £11 'or any part thereof', and so we cannot do it.

DYER C.J. It seems to me that he can confess the action as to £8, and do his law as to the rest.

Carus. We will do that, if he wishes.

BROWNE J. It seems to me that the plaintiff could then afterwards have an action of debt on the true contract for £8. I think he can traverse the contract perfectly well, for although our books say that the defendant cannot traverse the contract because he may do his law, that is to be understood where they agree on the contract; but if they differ I think he may traverse, and shall not be bound to risk submitting it to ignorant people. Therefore, if they differ on the day or place, and the day and place are part of the contract, this is traversable; but the day and place is not generally material, for a man may well use an action in this county for a contract in another county. Therefore I conclude that in the case at bar the plea is good.

WESTON and WALSH JJ. thought he should do [his] law.

And WALSH J. said that if a man buys two horses for £8, and then the seller brings an action of debt for £10, the buyer can do his law.

Then the plaintiff asked *Harpur* what was [to be] done, and he said the defendant could do his law or else plead another plea.

ANON. (1587)
Goulds. 57, pl. 14 (C.P.) (untr.).

Upon a wager of law, it was said by ANDERSON C.J. that if I am bound to you to pay you a certain sum of money, and a stranger deliver you a horse by my assent for the same debt, this is no satisfaction. So if I be indebted upon a simple contract, and a stranger make an obligation for this debt, the debtor cannot wage his law; for this debt doth not determine the contract.

No one denied this.

MILLINGTON v BURGES (1587)
Goulds. 65, pl. 5 (C.P.) (untr.).

Dorothy Millington brought debt against J. Burges for £9, and declared that he had bought certain woad. And the truth of the case was, this woad was sold to him upon condition that if she did not prove it to be good and sufficient then he should pay nothing for it. And all this was disclosed by the defendant upon his wager of law.

WYNDHAM J. If the case be so, then you may wage your law.

And it was said that she must have detinue for the woad.

ANON. (1587)
BL MS. Lansdowne 1076, fo. 122v.

Note that in the Star Chamber it was ruled (*overrulé*) by the lords of the Council that if in an action at common law a man wages his law, even though he makes a false oath, he shall not be impeached for it by bill in the Star Chamber.[13] And the reason was that it is as strong as a trial.

And the Chancellor [HATTON] asked the judges whether he was discharged by the wager of law; and they said he was.

MANWOOD C.B. That is the plaintiff's foolishness, because he could have sued him in an action on the case upon *assumpsit*, in which he should not wage his law.

ANON. (1588)
4 Leon. 81, pl. 172 (C.P.) (untr.).

A poor man was ready at the bar to wage his law, and upon examination it was found that the defendant was indebted to the plaintiff in £10 to be paid at the feast of Christmas, and that upo.. communication between them it was agreed that the defendant should pay to the plaintiff at the said feast £5 in satisfaction of all the debt due to the plaintiff, and as to the other £5 that he should be acquitted of it.

Upon this matter the justices were clear of opinion that the defendant ought not to be admitted to wage his law; for, notwithstanding that bare communication, the whole debt remained due [and] not extinguished by that communication. For £5 cannot be a satisfaction for £10. But contrary of a collateral thing in recompense of it, etc. And satisfaction and agreement to pay £5 before

---

13 Nor anywhere else; see p. 218, above.

the said feast of Christmas [is]¹⁴ satisfaction of the whole £10. Upon such matter shewed the court was of opinion that the defendant might be admitted to wage his law.

BLOCK'S CASE (1597)
LI MS. Misc. 491, p. 252 (C.P.).

Block waged his law in debt for £10, and (being now examined) he confessed that he owed 13s. 4d. to the plaintiff and said he had satisfied him for the remainder, and prayed that he might do his law for everything but the 13s. 4d.

But BEAUMONT and WALMSLEY JJ., being alone in the court, said he could not do his law save for the whole sum in respect of which he had waged it. (All the clerks agreed to this.)

But it was moved that there were several contracts, and so he could wage his law for [all but] 13s. 4d., this being a contract by itself.

Brownlowe, chief prothonotary, said there was no difference, since he had waged his law for the whole sum and so could not apportion it.

So he pleaded to the country.

HAGGER'S CASE (1598)
CUL MS. Ll. 3. 10, fo. 60v (C.P.).

Oliver Hagger sued a writ of debt. The defendant was ready at the bar to wage his law, but made some scruple because he did not know whether his wife had bought anything or not.

The court, however, resolved that if the wife bought something and the husband did not agree to it afterwards, that is not the husband's contract—unless (as WALMSLEY J. said) she had a general authority beforehand—and the husband may safely wage his law.

So the plaintiff was non-suited.¹⁵

---

14 Conjectural correction of 'in'. The passage seems to mean that part payment *before* the day would be satisfaction and that the defendant could wage his law if that was the agreement. For that distinction, cf. *Pynnell v Cole* (1602), p. 259, below.

15 Presumably by his own consent, to avoid judgment, see Powell, *The Attourney's Academie* (1623), p. 223, below.

BARNAM v BARRET (1602)

BL MS. Lansdowne 1074, fo. 410; LI MS. Maynard
87(2), fo. 304v; HLS MS. Acc. 704774, p. 99
(C.P.) (untr.).

Barnam and Cartwright brought an action of debt against Barret
and Buckley for £500. Buckley was outlawed. Barret appeared and
pleaded *Nil debet per legem*. And because the sum was so great, the
court refused to take his law then and willed him to bring some of
his neighbours, because the plaintiff was there to prove the debt.
And at two other days he came again with his neighbours, and the
plaintiff came also and was non-suit.[16]

ANDERSON C.J. I have known divers times that three friends
coming together and only one buying, and the others neither
agreeing nor saying anything, yet the shopkeeper puts them all
down as debtors in his book; whereas indeed they ought to take the
hand of the debtor to their book.

T. POWELL, THE ATTOURNEY'S ACADEMIE (1623)

Pp. 130–133 (untr.).

If any man be sued upon a simple contract . . . the defendant may
wage his law: that is, he may depose that he oweth the plaintiff
nothing, and so avoid his suit. Wager of law is to be done in this
wise, viz. that he plead *Nil debet per legem*, and so he is to get day
over until the next term to do his law, or else he may do his law
presently, at his own election . . .

When the defendant cometh in to do his law, he is to bring in
some of his neighbours or acquaintance to depose with him in
manner following, viz. every of them must make oath that he
believeth that the oath which the defendant taketh and deposeth is
true—he, the defendant, deposing before them that he oweth no
such debt to the plaintiff as the plaintiff declareth, nor any part
thereof. And the defendant should bring with him 12 such neighbours or acquaintance, compurgators with him, who should all
depose in like manner as aforesaid. But there is an officer here for
the ease of the subject, who will furnish the defendant in this case
of wager of law with 12 such compurgators as occasion shall
require; for with a less number you cannot wage your law.

When the defendant hath his said full number of 12, then his
attorney is to get the prothonotary to take his wager of law. Then

---

16 Cf. *Hagger's Case*, p. 221, above.

will the crier of the court cause the defendant to stand up at the bar, and the justices will examine him whether he oweth or detaineth the money (or goods or chattels) contained in the declaration, or any part or parcel of the same: whereunto the defendant is to answer Yea or No. And if the defendant deposeth that he doth not owe or detain from him the plaintiff the same, nor any part or parcel thereof, and the plaintiff will stand to his action, then is the defendant quit thereof for ever, and the plaintiff loseth his action. But if the plaintiff will not abide his oath, intending to charge him otherwise afterwards, the plaintiff may be non-suit,[17] pay the defendant his costs, and be at liberty to begin anew again at another time, and to lay his action so (in some cases) that no wager of law shall lie therein.

CRISTY v SPARKS (1680)

Sir Francis North's reports,
BL MS. Add. 32521, p. 54 (C.P.) (untr.).[18]

The defendant, being sued in debt upon account and for rent, waged his law for part—viz. that which was upon the account—and as to the rest pleaded to the country; and the first day of the term came to make his law; and, having [been] sworn, answered some questions, whereupon I was not satisfied with his answers, as that the plaintiff (being an attorney at law) was overpaid by some execution money he had received upon some suits, and, being asked whether he would discharge him of those sums, he said, 'No'; whether those sums were ever brought into the account, and he said, 'No'; and that there never was any account; but he stuck to the main that he owed him nothing. But when he was asked for his compurgators, his attorney called upon the criers and said the prothonotaries told him (the sum being under £20) there needed no special compurgators, but the criers were taken in that case and had a fee for it; but when the criers were asked they refused to swear, the man being wholly a stranger to them. We did not blame their tenderness. The defendant did after send into the hall and into the streets for others, but none could be persuaded or hired (as one of the criers said). I was glad to see there was so great tenderness of swearing, which proceeded from the disuse in that case. Thereupon the court recorded the failure of the law, and stayed giving

---

17 For examples, see pp. 221, 222 above.
18 A transcription from North C.J.'s autograph report book. This was brought to our notice by Mr D. E. C. Yale.

judgment till the plaintiff came to town (who appeared by attorney), it seeming reasonable to us that he (being misinformed) relied upon the criers who failed him. I observed hence that the making of law was no such unreasonable thing, for [1] if the defendant did not answer the questions proposed reasonably the compurgators ought not to purge him of the debt. (2) The court may be as strict as they please in examining the compurgators as to their credit and ability, so that they may take care the law shall not be allowed against reason. (3) The consequence of wager of law when generally known was very good, for it made men very careful to take such evidence of their debt whereupon a wager of law should not be allowed. (4) I remember Lord Chief Justice Hale said it would be a very good reformation to give wager of law in *assumpsit*, in restitution of the common law.[19] Upon which I used to observe that *assumpsits* were brought in upon pretence that wager of law was the occasion of perjury, and men lost their debts; but the true reason was to give the King's Bench a jurisdiction;[20] and now that jurisdiction is settled, to restore wager of law would shew plainly that it was the profitable jurisdiction that occasioned the changing debt into *assumpsit*, and not the policy of the law.

W. STYLE, PRACTICAL REGISTER (1694)

P. 572 (untr.).

The manner of waging of law is this. He that is to do it must do it *duodena manu*, viz. he must bring six compurgators with him who are to swear that they believe that he swears true; and stand at the end of the bar towards the right hand of the chief justice. And the secondary asks him whether he will wage his law. If he answers that he will, the judges admonish him to be well advised, and tell him the danger of taking a false oath. And if, notwithstanding, he persist, then the secondary speaks words to this effect following unto him; and he that wageth his law doth repeat every sentence distinctly after him:

Hear ye this, ye justices, that I W.S. do not owe to B.B. the sum of [naming

---

19 See p. 444, below.
20 See pp. 406–445, below. Cf. also *Edgcomb v Dee* (1670) Vaugh. 89, at 101, per Vaughan C.J.C.P.: '... that illegal resolution of *Slade's Case* [p. 420, below], grounded upon reasons not fit for a declamation, much less for a decision of law ... And that which is so commonly now received, that every contract executory implies a promise, is a false gloss, thereby to turn actions of debt into actions on the case; for contracts of debt are reciprocal grants'.

the sum in the declaration] nor any penny thereof in manner and form as B.B. hath declared against me. So help me God.

And then kisseth the book. But before he takes the oath the plaintiff is called by the crier thrice, and if he do not appear he becomes nonsuited, and then the defendant goes quit without taking his oath; but if he appear, and [the defendant] swears that he owes the plaintiff nothing, and the compurgators do give in their verdict that they believe he swears true, then the plaintiff is barred for ever ...

The reason why wager of law is suffered is because the contract upon which the action is brought being a private contract and not to be proved, it may be intended that the discharge may be in private and not be proved otherwise than by the oath of the party, whom the law will not presume to take a false oath. (Hilary term 1649, Upper Bench, 31 January. And his oath shall rather be accepted to discharge himself than to suffer him to be charged upon the bare assertion of the plaintiff.) This wager of law was most practised in those times that craft, subtlety and knavery had not got firm footing in this nation; but it being abused by the iniquity of the people, the law was forced to find out another way to do justice to the nation, and that was by turning of actions of debt into actions upon the case by ways of *indebitatus assumpsit*, which hath now ousted the defendant of his *ley gager*. See *Slade's Case* in the Lord Coke's reports.[1]

(2) Debt in cases where there is no deed

ANON. (1292)

Y.B. 20 & 21 Edw. I, Rolls Series, p. 139.

[Count:] 'This sheweth you John, who is here, that B., who is there, wrongfully detains from him chattels worth £10; and wrongfully because on a certain day this same John leased to the aforesaid B. all the land which he had in C. (namely one carucate), rendering therefor 20 quarters of wheat annually at certain terms, according to the covenant between them; and continually from then to the present, namely for two years, B. has so held the land; and John has often gone to him at the said terms and asked him to

---

1 4 Co. Rep. 92; see p. 420, below.

render unto him the aforesaid chattels, and he would not render them and still will not, wrongfully and against the covenant, to his damages of 20s.'

Huntingdon. Will you [avow] the count?

Tilton. Yes, just as you have heard it.

Huntingdon. Sir, he brings a writ of debt against us, and demands from [us] chattels worth £10 by reason that he leased to [us] his land in return for 20 quarters of wheat a year: therefore a writ of annuity lies in this case, and not a writ of debt. So we demand judgment of the writ.

Tilton. What you say would be absolutely right if we had leased to him a freehold for a certain annual sum; but we leased him the land to hold of us for 20 quarters at our will, and the freehold is ours: therefore a writ of annuity does not lie.

Huntingdon. The writ is nevertheless invalid, for this reason: since you demand from us chattels worth £10 by writ of debt, and rely in your count on a covenant made between you and us, you thus suppose that the chattels were bailed to us at a certain price— in other words, that the chattels or the fixed price were to be rendered on demand to the bailiff. But you never did bail chattels to us at a certain price. So we demand judgment of the writ; for a writ of covenant lies better in this case than a writ of debt.

Tilton. One shall have a writ of debt in several cases where a writ of covenant lies; and since it is in our election to take one or the other, we pray judgment whether our writ is not perfectly good.

ANON. (1293)

Y.B. 21 & 22 Edw. I, Rolls Series, p. 111 (C.P.).

A. brought a writ of debt against B. and demanded £7. 10s. by reason that, whereas on a certain day in a certain year he delivered to B. a piece of land in C. for the term of 14 years, [on condition] that B. should cause a house worth £14 to be built on the piece of land, and that if he did not do so he would pay A. the difference in value within two years next following: the house [which he built] was only worth £6. 10s., and so he went to B. and demanded the £7. 10s. within the two years and afterwards, and he would not pay.

Est. We think he ought not to be answered as to this writ, by reason that A. counted on a condition that if he did not cause a house worth £14 to be built etc., in which case a writ of covenant lies, because he has broken a covenant. So I demand judgment whether he ought to be answered in this writ.

HERTFORD. If I lease to you a piece of land for a term of years, in return for 10s. a year rent, and you do not pay, do you think I shall not have recovery by a writ of debt? For I shall. Likewise here.

Est. The writing says that the house was to be surveyed; but we say that it was not viewed or appraised by good men, as the writing requires, and this we will aver.

BEREFORD. It may be that B. would not have the house viewed and appraised by good men, so that he could delay A. for ever from having his debt. So answer his demand.

Lutlington. We say that he should have warranted us [a piece of land] 40 feet long and 20 feet wide, whereas one Thomas de C. ejected us from half of it. So we demand judgment whether he should be answered with respect to the full amount, since he did not cause us to have the whole piece.

Ashby. We leased to him all that we had, and therefore no wrong has been done to him. Ready etc.

FRANSSEYS' CASE (*c.* 1294)

Y.B. 21 & 22 Edw. I, Rolls Series, p. 599 (printed as
from the eyre of Middlesex, but perhaps C.P.).

Master Adam de Fransseys and the others named in the writ, as executors of Gilbert de Fransseys, demanded by a writ of debt against one Michael 200 marks and £10 by reason that, whereas it was covenanted between the aforesaid Michael and Gilbert that Michael would give Gilbert 200 marks and £10 for the marriage of one his sons to Michael's daughter; and if it should happen that William (Michael's eldest son) married Gilbert's daughter, the £10 would be deducted (*recoupés*): Gilbert delivered his son Richard to Michael, together with the manor of Porruho, to be managed for the infant's benefit, and Gilbert often went to Michael and asked him to cause his son to marry his daughter in accordance with the covenant, but Michael would not consent to it, and so Gilbert often demanded the 200 marks and £10 in his lifetime, and we as executors have since often demanded these sums, but Michael would not pay and still will not, to the damage etc. . . .

Louther. The writing mentions his covenant, and so a writ of covenant properly lies for it in this case. We demand judgment whether he ought to be answered as to this writ of debt.

METINGHAM. If a covenant is made between Robert of Hertford[2] and me that he will enfeoff me with a carucate of land and put me in

---

2 The name of one of the judges.

seisin at Easter, in return for 30 marks, and I pay him 30 marks and come Easter he does nothing for me: in this case I may choose whether to demand the money by writ of debt or to demand by writ of covenant that he should keep the covenant with me concerning the land. Likewise here. So make further answer.

Louther then confessed the 'contract', but alleged that on Gilbert's death Richard was still unmarried and under age, and was seized in ward by the king, and that Michael had to pay £300 to the king for the wardship. He prayed aid of the king. Warwick, for the executors, said that Gilbert had caused Richard to be affianced to Michael's daughter when both were of marriageable age, and then delivered Richard to Michael, so that if the marriage was not solemnised before Gilbert's death it was by his own laches and not Gilbert's fault. The rest of the argument turned on the points thus raised.

ANON. (1313–14)

Y.B. Eyre of Kent, vol. II, Selden Soc. vol. 27, p. 36.

One A. brought his writ of debt etc.

Howard. He owes him nothing, ready etc.

Spigurnel. You should not be answered on that, because you make the one denial, 'owes nothing', and it can mean either of two things: either that he never owed him anything, or that he was at one time bound to him but has paid him; and we ask judgment whether you should get to this averment with a double meaning.

Herle. We were at one time bound, but have paid in full, ready etc.

Spigurnel. Since you have acknowledged that you owe[d] the money, and put forward no acquittance attesting the payment, judgment etc.

Howard. There is no need in this case to have an acquittance: [that is needed] only against a writing; and we demand judgment.

Spigurnel. Acknowledgement made in court is of higher nature than is a writing because acknowledgement in court confirms [the debt]; and so we demand judgment.

ANON. (1338)

Y.B. 11 & 12 Edw. III, Rolls Series, p. 587 (C.P.).

A writ of debt was brought against someone, and the plaintiff counted that by a covenant between himself and the defendant he had been made the defendant's attorney for ten years, taking 20s. each year, and they were in arrear.

Pole. This count begins with a covenant and ends with a duty. We demand judgment of such a count, as unwarranted.

(He was driven from this objection.)

Pole. He has nothing proving the covenant.

SHARESHULL. If one were to count simply of a grant of a debt, he would not be received without specialty. But here you have his service in return for his hire, of which knowledge may be had; and you have *quid pro quo*.

So *Pole* waged his law that he owed him nothing; and the other counterpleaded it.

The court to *Gaynesford.* Will you accept the law at your peril?

So he accepted the law.

ANON. (1344)

Y.B. 18 Edw. III, Rolls Series, p. 23 (C.P.).

Debt. The plaintiff counted that one A. ([and he specified] the day, year and place) bought from him ten great beasts for ten marks to be paid on a specified day; [and this was] in the presence of W. against whom this writ is brought, who undertook that if A. did not pay on the day specified, [W.] would pay and become principal debtor for the payment; and on the day A. did not pay and has not the means to pay; and so [the plaintiff] has often come to W. and asked him [to pay]; and he has not paid and still will not.

SHARESHULL to the plaintiff. Do you not put forward a specialty [attesting] the covenant?

Pole. We shall have something to say about that.

ANON. (1369)

Y.B. Pas. 43 Edw. III, fo. 11, pl. 1
LI MS. Hale 189, fo. 265v. (C.P.).

One W. sued a writ *de plegio acquietando* against one R., and counted that [R.] had not acquitted the plaintiff against one J. for £20: and wrongfully for this reason that whereas R. was indebted to J. in the aforesaid £20 to be paid on a certain day in London, and the said W. at the said R.'s request had become surety to pay the said £20 on that same day in default of payment [by R.], by reason of which suretyship and because R. did not pay the money on the day the said J. thereupon caused action to be brought against the said W. in London by plaint, and the said W. sent to the said R. to acquit him and the said R. would not acquit him, so that the said W. was arrested at the same J.'s suit and paid the £20 in default of [R.'s] acquittance; and often since the said W. has come to the said R. and asked if he would pay him the said £20, but he would not pay but withholds it wrongfully etc.

Fencotes. You see that he has not [counted] that the said W. was bound to J. in the £20 as surety for R., and so even though he was surety without deed, the law would not have charged him without an obligation, and so etc.

Belknap. We say that W. became surety in London and was arrested in London, and the custom of London is that if one becomes surety for another, even though it is without deed, he [the creditor] will have recovery against him; and so action [against the principal debtor] accrues to him.

Fencotes. He has not counted upon such a custom, and so the count is bad.

FYNCHEDEN. In many cases one counts a general count and has the action and maintains it by special matter; as in the case of the writ of mesne, he counts a general count and has the action, and then later he shows the particular matter in which he is aggrieved; so as to that the writ is good.

Fencotes. Although he helps himself by [reference to] the custom of London, this action is at common law; and by the common law W. would not have been liable [to J.] without deed, so that even if he pleads wrongly, it is not right that R. should be bound.

FYNCHEDEN. He does not plead wrongly, when the custom binds him to pay without deed ... It must be right that he has action against you without deed when by judgment he has paid for you without deed; and so answer.

Fencotes. He has shown no contractual cause in his count by which R. was bound to pay the £20 to J.

FYNCHEDEN. There is no need when he shows cause to maintain his action against R.; and so answer.

Fencotes. As to £10, R. paid J. and J. made an acquittance to R. and W.; and if W. had wished to come and ask for the acquittance, R. was ready to deliver the same acquittance to W. and would have acquitted him, without this that W. was impleaded and paid in default of acquittance from R., ready etc. And as to the other £10, [R.] was never indebted to J. and W. never became surety for R.; ready etc.

And the others said the opposite.

ANON. (1372)

Y.B. Hil. 46 Edw. III, fo. 6, pl. 16 (C.P.).

Debt was brought in which the plaintiff counted that wrongfully the defendant withholds and does not yield up to him 40s. due upon a certain contract etc. And the defendant says that he does not admit that the contract was made for as much as [the plaintiff] has alleged, but only for 4s. which he has been always ready to pay, and still is; and as to the 40s. he owes him nothing in the manner he has alleged, [and on this] he is ready to make his law. And the [plaintiff] demands judgment on the ground that [the defendant] has in a way acknowledged the contract [and so] cannot get to his law as to the balance without showing an acquittance, etc.

FYNCHEDEN. He cannot plead otherwise to save his position, because if the case is that the contract was made for 40s. and he paid all but 4s., and if he had alleged the payment of all but the 4s., then on his own acknowledgement that there was such a contract, which would be as effective as an obligation, he would have suffered judgment for want of an acquittance; and so he has pleaded as best he can in this case.

ANON. (1402)

Y.B. Pas. 3 Hen. IV, fo. 17, pl. 14 (C.P.).

Debt was brought and [the plaintiff] claimed £20 on a contract.

Rede. As to £10 [the plaintiff] has a bond which was made in respect of the same contract, so [we ask] judgment whether he should have his action [against us].

Colepeper. You see clearly that we have counted on a contract, and to this he makes no answer at all; and so we ask for our debt and damages. And no law puts us to answer to what he has alleged, because it could well be that he owes us £10 on a bond and also this [debt now claimed] for different causes; and if indeed it is for the same cause, he can safely [in conscience] wage his law.

Rede. Since you do not deny that the bond is in respect of the same contract, and by the making of the bond we are discharged from the contract, and we are prepared to aver [that the bond was made in respect of the same contract], we therefore demand judgment and ask that you should be barred.

Colepeper. Suppose that the bond was burnt or lost, still we should have action on the contract.

MARKHAM denied this, and said that that would be adjudged

your own foolishness, inasmuch as you would not look after it better.

Colepeper said that the bond was made for another cause, and not in respect of the same contract; and he was driven to specify for what cause.

Rede tendered the opposite [proposition], namely that the bond was made for the same cause, ready [etc.]

And issue was joined on that.

BAKER v ANON. (1410)

Y.B. Trin. 11 Hen. IV, fo. 79, pl. 21 (C.P.).

Ralph Baker brought a writ of debt for the arrears found due in an account before duly appointed auditors at Staines.

Norton. You should not have your action on this writ, because we say that a long time after this account the defendant, on such a day at Kenn in the county of Devon, made a bond in respect of this same indebtedness to the plaintiff; and [we ask] judgment whether [he should have his] action [against us].

Skrene. And since we have brought an action as above, and the plea that he pleads is not sufficient to bar us, we demand judgment and ask for our debt and damages.

And so the case went to judgment.

HANKFORD. He was in a strong enough position before, without any bond. And if you bring debt on a bond, it is no plea to say that he has another bond for the same indebtedness; nor is it here. And the indebtedness on the account is in no way extinguished by the bond.

Norton. No sir; but if I am a debtor by simple contract, and then make a bond for the same inebtedness, I will [be able to] drive him to bring his action on the bond, because I must not be charged twice over. And here for the same reason he will be driven to bring his action on the bond.

HILL. In a case where [the defendant] can wage his law on the original contract, he has the plea as you say. But where he can not get to his law, as in a writ of debt [for the rent due] on a lease for a term of years, it is no plea to say that [the plaintiff] has a bond for the same indebtedness; nor is it here.

THIRNING. When he was found in arrears before duly appointed auditors, he was debtor as it were of record against which he could not wage his law. And this was sufficient assurance from the beginning, and when afterwards he made a bond that was his foolishness. And the defendant has expressly acknowledged the account, and so the plea is not at all sufficient.

HANKFORD adjudged that the plaintiff should recover his debt and his damages taxed by the court etc.

ANON. (1410)

Y.B. Trin. 11 Hen. IV, fo. 91, pl. 48 (C.P.).

A writ of debt was brought against executors, [and] the plaintiff counted that their testator was found in arrears before duly appointed auditors in the amount contained in the writ.

Norton. Sir, you see clearly that he has brought a writ of debt against us as executors, and counted that our testator was found in arrears before duly appointed auditors; and this matter is not enough to maintain action against executors, so we demand judgment etc.

Skrene. Since in this case your testator was found in arrears before duly appointed auditors, who are judges of record by commission, [so that] in his lifetime he could not have his law against us, we demand judgment and ask for our debt and our damages.

COLEPEPER. There is the same matter in law pleaded to judgment before us [in another case] which is still pending.

Horton [Norton?]. If we had not the clearest [matter of fact] we would want to demur. [But] we say that our testator did not account before duly appointed auditors, ready etc.

And issue was joined on that.

ANON. (1421)

Y.B. Pas. 9 Hen. V, fo. 2, pl. 6 (C.P.).

John of T. of Northampton brought a writ of debt against one R. and counted through *Cottesmore* upon a lease for a term of years.

Hals.[3] To this we say that we paid you the same debt and the same amount in another county; ready.

Strangeways. That is not an issue without saying 'and so he owes him nothing', for otherwise he does not answer to our writ.

And nevertheless it was adjudged a good plea, because it was alleged that the payment was in another county; for if he concluded

---

3 Name from BL MS. Harley 5145; omitted in print.

'and he owes him nothing', this would be tried where the writ was brought; and that would be a mischief, and so etc.

SOMER v SAPURTON (1428)

Y.B. Mich. 7 Hen. VI, fo. 5, pl. 9;
Selden Soc. vol. 51, p. 38, pl. 13.

Henry Somer, chancellor of the Exchequer, and five others brought a bill of debt in the Exchequer for £310 against Roger Sapurton, warden of the Fleet Prison, complaining that, whereas they had recovered £300 damages and £10 costs against one John Shenyfelde in the Court of Exchequer for forgery, and Shenyfelde had been committed to the Fleet, the defendant had allowed Shenyfelde to go at large: and therefore (since Shenyfelde had still not paid) an action accrued to the plaintiffs to demand the £310 from the defendant. After a preliminary dispute about pleading, the defendant pleaded that Shenyfelde's committal had been to secure the fine to the king for contempt, and that there was no record of any committal until he paid the damages. The plaintiffs replied that it was apparent from the record as a whole that the committal was for both purposes; and to this the defendant demurred. The case was adjourned into the Exchequer Chamber, and argued in Michaelmas term 1428. One of the questions was whether debt was the appropriate action against the warden.

... *Rolf.* It seems to me that the plaintiff should recover; for the law is that the justices will not take a fine for the king until satisfaction has been given to the party. I can therefore prove by a syllogism that the warden should be charged: for even if the plaintiff said nothing [about satisfaction] and the defendant is imprisoned for the fine, he shall not come out until the party receives satisfaction, and the fine shall not be received until he has given satisfaction; ergo, he shall not come out until he has paid the fine, and shall not pay the fine until he has given satisfaction, and consequently he shall not come out until he has given satisfaction. It follows that, since he came out before then through the fault of the warden, and the warden let him go at large, this was against the law and a grievance to the party, and in reason the party should have an action against him. And it seems that it should be an action of debt. For the statute 1 Ric. II[4] provides that if the warden allows a prisoner, who is in the Fleet by judgment at the suit of a party, to go by mainprise, baston or bail, the party in these cases should have his recovery by writ of debt against the warden. It therefore follows that at common law, if the warden allowed him to go at

4   1 Ric. II, c. 12; *Statutes of the Realm*, vol. II, p. 4.

large, the party would have recovery by writ of debt; for otherwise
he would have been without remedy by this statute . . .

Chaunterell. It seems to me that this writ is not warranted by the
common law or by statute; for in all your books you will never find
a writ of debt brought in such a case, but a writ on his case—and
that is the writ mentioned and expressly set out in the register. The
statute mentions neither, for the statute only provides a certain
remedy where the party had no remedy at common law, and
nothing is said of this case in the statute: therefore this case is at
common law, as it was before the statute was made . . .

Paston. There are many cases about which doubts have never
arisen; and it does not follow that, because a writ of trespass lies, a
writ of debt does not. That is a bad argument: for a man may have
a writ of account and a writ of debt for the same thing. (But he did
not say how.) . . .

Newton. It seems to me that this action is not maintainable at
common law, for in the register there is a writ founded on the case.
And if a writ of debt had been maintainable, it would have been
[put in the register] instead of a writ of trespass, for it is the better
remedy for recovering my whole debt in certain than putting my
recovery in the mouths of 12 men, who perhaps will not award half
the debt; and therefore it cannot be supposed that anyone would
have wanted to bring a writ of trespass if he could have had the
other. And a writ of trespass has been brought in such cases, as the
reports (*termes*)[5] mention. As to Mr. [Serjeant] Rolf's argument
that he shall not pay a fine until he has given satisfaction, that is
not *rigore juris* but by the king's kindness (*facetia*) . . .

Vampage, apprentice. I fully concede what you have said about
a man having account and debt for one thing, because both sound
in an indebtedness (*duyté*). But it would be unfitting to have
trespass and debt for one same thing, because they are contrary: for
one begins by contract and consent of the parties, and the demand
is an indebtedness, and the basis of the action is an indebtedness;
and the other begins by a wrong, and without the consent of the
parties, and the demand is to have a wrong punished, which is
prima facie uncertain. Therefore, since it is granted by all our
masters that trespass lies for this at common law, it would be
unfitting to have debt for it. There was never any contract between
the parties, either in fact or in law, and so at common law an action
[of debt] is not maintainable. Nor is it maintainable by the statute,
for it does not fall within the terms of the statute, and he has not
based his bill on the statute . . .

5 Books of 'terms', or year books.

The Y.B. does not report the judges' views on the question of the form of action. No judgment was entered.

ANON. (1458)

Y.B. Mich. 37 Hen. VI, fo. 8, pl. 18; corrected from
Bod. Lib. MS. Lat. misc. C.55, fo. 126v (C.P.).

In a writ of debt the plaintiff counted that on such a day, in such a year, at such a place, an agreement (*accorde*) was made between the plaintiff and the defendant that the plaintiff would marry the defendant's daughter Alice, and that in return for this marriage the defendant would give the plaintiff 100 marks; and he then showed that he had married the said Alice, and that the espousals were solemnly celebrated between them according to the form required by Holy Church (setting out when and where); and after this the plaintiff came to the defendant and asked him for the 100 marks, but he would not pay him and still will not do so: and so an action has accrued to the plaintiff.

PRYSOT. It seems that this writ and count are not sufficient to maintain this action, for this action is [not][6] based on a contract,[7] such as sale. For instance, if a man buys a cow or a horse from me for 20s., I shall have a good action of debt against him by reason of the sale; and yet it is possible that the buyer had no *quid pro quo*, for it may be that I have no horse, but I shall nevertheless have a good action of debt because it is no plea for him to say that I had no horse at the time of the sale, and so *caveat emptor*. If, however, I do have a horse, he may take it out of my possession by virtue of the sale. But in some cases I shall have a good action of debt against a man because of a sale, and I have the thing sold, and yet he shall not take it by reason of the sale. For instance, if I sell a man the manor of Dale (whereof I am seised) for £100, I shall have a good action of debt against him on the contract; and yet the property of the manor is not in the purchaser by this contract, and he may not enter into the manor by virtue of this sale without livery and seisin. Moreover, I shall have a good action of debt even if I have no manor; but that is because of the contract. Thus a contract is a sufficient matter to maintain the action [of debt]. A man may also have an action of debt on a retainer. For instance, if I am retained with a man to be of his counsel, and am to have 40s. a

---

6   Omitted in MS.
7   MS. Reads 'covenant' in print.

year, I shall have a good action of debt on this retainer;[8] but in this case I must declare in my count that I was with him and counselled him, or at least that I would have counselled him had he asked me. Similarly, if a servant is retained by me, he shall have a good action of debt against me once he has performed his service; but he must declare that he was in my service throughout the time [agreed]. And although that is not a pure contract,[9] nevertheless it is a retainer and [the master] has *quid pro quo*, [though] he does not have it until [the servant] has performed his service. In the case at bar, however, he has not declared on a pure contract or on a retainer, but only that an agreement was made; and on that it seems this action is not maintainable.

DANVERS. It seems that this action is good and maintainable on the facts set out; for although it is not a pure contract it is much the same in effect. For the agreement was that he would marry his daughter, [and for that he would have 100 marks, and he has said that in fact he did marry her,][10] in which case the defendant has *quid pro quo*. For the defendant was charged with his daughter's marriage, and by the espousals he is discharged; and thus the plaintiff has done the thing for which the sum was to be paid. Similarly, if I say to a man that he will have 40s. if he carries 20 quarters of wheat from Master Prysot to G., he shall have a good action of debt against me for the 40s. if in these circumstances he carries the 20 quarters; and yet the thing is not done to me, but is done by my command. Likewise here, he has shown that he performed the espousals, and therefore a good action has accrued to him. It would have been otherwise if he had not performed the espousals.

ASHTON. I think the contrary, and that on these facts he shall not have an action by our law, but only by the spiritual law: for marriage, and the contract of marriage, are spiritual and belong to the spiritual court. Now, if the principal thing is spiritual, the accessory must be of the same condition. For instance, if a man by his testament leaves me certain goods, I shall not recover them by our law but by the law of Holy Church, because the testament (which is the principal) is spiritual and belongs to the court christian, and therefore so does the action in respect of incidental things. [Likewise in respect of all personal things,][11] if they are not changed by contract. For instance, if someone sells me his tithes, I

8   MS. Reads 'contract' in print.
9   Reads 'mere contract' in print, 'merement un contract' in MS.
10   MS. Omitted by haplography in print.
11   MS. Omitted by haplography in print.

shall have a good action of debt on this contract, for *per venditio-nem res spirituales sunt temporales*.[12] But if they are not changed by contract they shall be demanded in court christian. It is otherwise of things real, such as lands or tenements, for there I shall have an action to recover them by our law even where the principal belongs to the court christian. For instance, if someone devises to me certain lands and tenements, I shall have an *ex gravi querela* and recover them. Also the writ *causa matrimonii praelocuti*. Thus there is a distinction between things personal and things real.[13] Here, however, this thing is in the personalty, and the principal thing (the matrimony) belongs to the court christian: for if he will not marry her you cannot compel him by our law, but only by the law of Holy Church. And by the same argument that cognisance of the principal belongs to the court christian, so shall [cognisance of] the accessory.[14]

DANBY. It seems to me that he may not have an action on these facts, for it is not a contract or a retainer,[15] but merely a covenant, on which an action cannot be maintained without specialty. For the writ says *concordatum est*, and that is not a contract or a retainer but merely a covenant. In the case which Danvers put, about carrying wheat, he must declare on a retainer for £100.[16] Suppose the present matter had been written in an indenture, thus: 'This indenture witnesseth that the aforesaid J. shall marry A., daughter of the aforesaid S., and that the aforesaid S. shall give him 100 marks', would he then have had an action of debt on this deed? (He implied that he would not, because there is no word of grant.) If he had said, 'in return for which marriage he has granted to give him 100 marks', then perhaps he would have had an action of debt on this deed, by reason of the word 'granted'. Here, however, there are no words to give him an action of debt. And if he could not have had an action of debt had it been in writing, a fortiori he cannot when it is not written down. Thus it seems the action does not lie.

MOYLE. I think the contrary. As to the argument that this sounds in covenant, that is irrelevant once the thing has been performed. For instance, if I retain a carpenter to build me a house, and he is to have 40s. for doing it, he shall have a good action of

12 'By sale spiritual things are [made] temporal'.
13 In the printed edition the distinction is between things spiritual and temporal, probably because the preceding haplography had obscured the true distinction.
14 Reads 'action' in print.
15 MS. Reads 'accord' in print.
16 Sentence completely garbled in print.

debt against me if he builds the house; and yet this sounds purely in covenant [before he does so], for if he will not build the house I shall not[17] have an action against him without specialty, because it sounds in covenant; but when he has done the thing this action accrues to him to demand what is owing. For once the thing is done it suffices for him to maintain his action. Similarly, if I say to a surgeon that I will give him 100s. if he will go to one J., who is sick, and give him medicines and cure him,[18] and the said surgeon gives the said J. medicines and cures him, he shall have a good action of debt against me for the [100]s. Yet the thing is done to a stranger and not to the defendant himself, and so he has no *quid pro quo*; but he has much the same in effect. Likewise here, when he promised to give him 100 marks to marry his daughter, which he has done, it seems the action is maintainable.

PRYSOT. That is a good case to prove the case at bar, and so is the case which Danvers put concerning the carrying of wheat. But we must now see whether there is any distinction between them.

It was adjourned.

ANON. (1459)

Y.B. Mich. 38 Hen. VI, fo. 5, pl. 14. (C.P.).

In debt the plaintiff counted that on such a day in such a year the defendant appointed auditors—and he specified their names— before whom [the plaintiff] was to account for the period during which he was receiver of [the defendant's] money by the hands of such an one and such an other; and before those auditors a balance was found due to the plaintiff in the amount now demanded.

Choke. It appears that [he was accountable] as receiver, and he does not say [receiver] for the purpose of trading; and in that case if a balance was due to the plaintiff that was his foolishness, and no action accrues to him. But if he had said he was [the defendant's] bailiff, then if a balance was due to the plaintiff he would have a good action of debt for that: but not when he is merely receiver of money to account.

Laken. That is to our action, so let him demur if he wants.

MOYLE. If a balance is found due to the bailiff, by reason that he is bailiff of his master's manor to have [the master's] goods at his disposal and to collect rents and make payments and to [perform] various other duties which he is bound by his office to do, in that

17 MS. Omitted in print.
18 Reads 'recure' in MS., 'face luy safe et sound' in print.

case [the bailiff] can not know whether expenses and payments do or do not exceed his receipts until he has accounted. And the law is the same for one who is [the master's] receiver for the purpose of trading, who is sometimes in profit and sometimes in loss, because he is only a labourer for his master to incur costs and expenses for the purpose of trading; and in that case if a balance is found due to the receiver, it is right that he has action [of debt for the balance so found]. But [it is otherwise] of the receiver of a certain sum for which he is to render account, because then he is not bound to do any labour or go to any expenses or costs, and if he wishes to pay out more than the amount of his receipt that will be adjudged his own foolishness; and so etc. But it seems to me that in an action of account the count is not good if [the plaintiff] does not declare that [the defendant] was his receiver for the purpose of trading.

PRYSOT clearly denied this, [saying] that the count is good enough [if it says] that he was his receiver of his money to render account without saying that it was for the purposes of trading; and to this the others agreed.

And he [presumably MOYLE] said: Sir, in some cases if a balance is found due to the receiver he will have a good action even though he was not [receiver] for the purpose of trading, as if a man has a receiver who is perhaps to receive £100 a year; but [this] receiver has to go to each county in which the land is, to receive the money at each manor; and perhaps he can not collect any money, or perhaps he receives £10 and his expenses and costs come to £20; is it not right that he should have action for the £10 which is the balance due to him (as if to say that it is right) just as in the other cases [of the bailiff, or the receiver for the purpose of trading]? But perhaps where he is not his receiver otherwise than to receive one certain sum, and not his receiver retained in his service, if a balance is found due to him it would be a strong thing to maintain action for that balance, [and then indeed] it can be said that it was his foolishness to pay out more than the sum [received]; and note this.

Choke then asked the justices to record the roll as it stood, and that it should not be amended; and this was agreed. And then he said that these facts appear [on the record], and pleaded 'He owes nothing, ready to make his law [here and] now'. And he asked that [the plaintiff] might be examined according to the statute,[19] and this was not allowed him; and then he held to his law to be made [here and] now.

Laken. No law [obliges us to accept this]. And because he has

19   5 Hen. IV, c. 8.

counted that the account was before duly appointed auditors, in which case if the balance was found against the plaintiff he would not be received to his law, it follows that [the defendant] equally can not use it against him.

NEDEHAM [spoke] in the same sense, and said that the account before auditors is governed by the statute of Westminster II[20] so it is not right that he should be received to his law.

DANVERS. At common law before the statute of Westminster II, even if the account was before auditors [the accountant] was still received to his law; and the reason why he can not [now] make his law is because of the statute of Westminster II; and that statute was not for the benefit of the accountant but only of the master, so that etc. But it seems to me that there is another reason why he can not be received to his law, [namely] because he is compelled to render his account; and when the law drives him to render account, and the balance is found due to him, it is not right that [the master] should be received to his law any more than for the salary of a servant who is compellable by the Statute of Labourers: [there] the master will not be received to his law because he can force the servant to serve him against his will; and so [here] he can force him to account by writ of account.

Choke then did not dare demur, but said 'He owes nothing, ready to go to the country'. (And note this, because all who were in the *pekenes* were surprised at this.)

PRYSOT said to [*Choke*]: 'O thou of little faith, wherefore didst thou doubt?',[1] as if to say that he would without doubt have been received to his law. (Note this.)

ANON. (1477)

Y.B. Hil. 16 Edw. IV, fo. 10, pl. 3 (C.P.).

In debt the plaintiff counted that he sold the defendant certain cloths, and that on a certain day, in a certain year and at a certain place the defendant retained him for a certain time (which he set out certainly) to shape and cut out various gowns and hoods, and therefore an action accrued to the plaintiff [to demand his salary].

Catesby repeated the count, and on behalf of the defendant waged his law concerning the cloths; and as to the remainder he demanded judgment of the count, because this is a retainer and sounds in covenant. I do not think an action of debt lies on a

20 C. 11.
1 *Matthew*, 14.31.

retainer, apart from the action for labourers which is given by the statute.

But this objection was not allowed, because it is a natural contract; for it clearly appears that the defendant had *quid pro quo*. And in this and similar cases the defendant may wage his law: but not against a common labourer, because he is compellable by the statute to do service and therefore his service is compulsory by matter of record.

So the defendant moved on, and said that the retainer was on condition that he would be paid if he happened to make the garments well and sufficiently, otherwise not. And we say that he did not make them well and sufficiently; which matter [we are ready to aver].

BRYAN [C.J.]. Be very wary about pleading that; for if I am retained with you for a certain period to serve you well and loyally, and I serve for the whole term, and then I bring an action of debt for my salary, shall you aver that I did not serve you well and loyally throughout the period? I say no. Likewise here. (Note that.)

It was adjourned.

QUESTION FROM THE MASTER OF THE ROLLS (1477)

Y.B. Trin. 17 Edw. IV, fo. 4, pl. 4.

The Master of the Rolls[2] asked the justices of the Common Bench [the following question]: if a man promises a certain sum of money to another to marry his daughter or his servant, and [the other] marries her accordingly, will he have an action of debt at common law for that money or not?

Townshend.[3] It seems to me no action [lies] in our law, because it is only a bare promise, and *ex nudo pacto nulla oritur actio*; as if I promise you £20 to rebuild your hall, here no action lies because there is no *quid pro quo*; and it is not the same as where I promise you six shillings a week to have such a one at board, because then there is *quid pro quo*, and the law takes it that he is someone by whose service I gain advantage. Moreover in the case at bar the thing that is [undertaken] to be done is spiritual, which can not be sold nor can the party be compelled to do it; and so it is not right that the other should be charged.

2 Dr. John Moreton.
3 At this date still a bencher of Lincoln's Inn. The question was presumably asked in Chancery.

Rogers and *Sulyard* to the contrary: and as to what is said, that this is only a bare promise, that is not so; for he has *quid pro quo* inasmuch as his daughter or friend is taken to be advanced by the marriage; for if I promise a schoolmaster so much money to teach my son, which he does, he will have action of debt; and so it is where I promise a physician or surgeon a certain sum to cure a certain poor man; or if I promise a labourer so much money to repair a certain road which is the highway, good action lies on this; and so here.

And then CHOKE and LITTLETON agreed with the Master of the Rolls that in the principal case no action lies at common law, because the marriage on which the promise was based is a spiritual thing that can not in any way be sold.

CORE v MAY (1536)

Record: KB 27/1097, m. 33; printed in Selden Soc. vol. 94, p. 327. John Core, a grocer of London, brought debt in the Common Pleas against Thomas May of Wadhurst, Sussex, administrator of the goods and chattels of George Woddy, painter-stainer of London, for £20, and counted on a bill sealed by the deceased in London on 5 September 1533. The bill was set out (at the defendant's request) in English, as follows:

Be it known to all men by these presents that I, George Woddy of London, painter-stainer, have received of John Core, grocer of the same city, the sum of £20 sterling, [of] the which £20 sterling I the forenamed George to bear the adventure of exchange to Rouen and there to bestow the said £20 in French prunes for the behoof and use of the forenamed John, and to see them safely shipped as I do mine own wares; this done, the forenamed John to bear all manner [of] adventure and charges from the quay of Rouen in France to his own house in the city of London. In witness and truth of the same I the forenamed George Woddy have written this bill with mine own hand, and set to my seal, the fifth day of September 1533.

The plaintiff counted that the deceased never invested the £20 in prunes, and so an action accrued to him to demand the £20. The administrator pleaded Fully administered, and at the Guildhall before Norwich C.J.C.P. the jury found for the plaintiff by default. Judgment was given for the plaintiff to recover the £20 debt, with 6s. 8d. damages and £3 costs. On 23 April 1535 May purchased a writ of error, and on 6 November assigned as error that 'it evidently appears from the bill that by the law of the land a writ of account could have been conceived and maintained' against the deceased. This was argued in the King's Bench in 1536 and in Hilary term 1537.

Dyer 20.[4]

... *Baker*, A.-G., thought that the judgment should be reversed; for no action of debt lay for this against the [deceased].[5] The bailment was with the intention of having an increase and profit from the money, and not of having the money back; and for the money no action of debt lies, but an action of account: for the money was delivered with the intention that it should be employed and invested in prunes, and not to be preserved whole for the bailor's use ... It resembles the case in 41 Edw. III[6] ... and there it is said that debt lies in this case, but it seems that that is not law ...

Mountague to the contrary. For I have learned it as law that if a man delivers money to be handed over [to a third party], and the bailee does not perform the condition, he is a debtor for the money or accountable at the bailor's pleasure. The case of 41 Edw. III well proves that. For when a man has received [my] money, and has not employed and invested it according to the trust and condition, he is a guardian of the same money to my use, as my debtor if I will: for it is more prejudicial to me if I elect for my action of debt, since I shall only recover the bare sum which was bailed, whereas if I bring account I shall recover the increase and profits of the same sum besides the sum itself. And when a man has two actions given by the law, he may elect whichever he wishes ...

Afterwards, in Hilary term [1537], it was argued again.

Luke J. argued that this judgment was erroneous. First, it is clear that an action of account would be well maintainable, because the £20 was bailed in order to buy prunes. If a man bails money to someone to trade with, and he does not lay out the money, [the bailor] shall have account against him and shall have an account of the increase and profit which he has (or might have) gained by using the money: for in these cases he is a receiver and accountable. And no action of debt lies without a contract ...

Spelman and Port JJ., and Fitzjames C.J., to the contrary, and that the first judgment should be affirmed ... In the common opinion of the books it is in the bailor's election whether to have an action of debt or account in such a case ... If I bail £10 to you to give away in alms on my behalf, you are accountable to me, for the property stays in me at all times until the alms are given, and I may countermand the performance; and if you keep the £10 in your hands afterwards, I shall have a good action of debt against you for it.[7]

---

4 Also reported by Spelman, Selden Soc. vol. 93, p. 132, pl. 2.
5 Reads 'testator'. The same error is made in the King's Bench record.
6 See p. 291, below.
7 This seems to refer to the unprinted case, *Duchess of Norfolk v Aleyn* (1497) CP 40/942, m. 333; John Port's MS. notebook.

FITZJAMES C.J. thought in the case here that the property in the £20 was in the bailee, because he had liberty by [the terms of] the bailment to exchange the £20; and yet he did not have it to such an extent that the property does not revest in the bailor if the trust is not observed . . . Besides, if I bail £20 to someone to keep to my use, and the £20 is not contained in a bag, coffer or box, an action of detinue does not lie, because the £20 could not be identified or known to be mine; but debt or account lies there, at my pleasure. Similarly, if I bail certain plate to someone to look after for me, and he exchanges the plate, I shall have an action on the case or detinue at my election: 18 Edw. IV.[8] Likewise, said FITZJAMES C.J., this case was argued and ruled in the time of Henry VII,[9] when Frowyk was chief justice: a man bought 20 quarters of barley, to be delivered at a certain place on a certain day; the vendor did not perform his contract, and so the vendee was driven to buy barley for his business as a brewer at a much greater price;[10] and upon these facts the vendee was permitted to bring an action on the case, and it was adjudged maintainable.[11] And he might well have had an action of debt for the barley: but not detinue, for the property in the barley could not be known, since one quarter cannot be distinguished from another . . .

So it seemed that the judgment was good, and affirmable, and so it was adjudged. (Note that.) And May had an injunction in the Chancery for this matter, and there judgment was given for Core. . .

The record shows that the judgment was affirmed by the King's Bench in Hilary term 1537, and a further 43s. 4d. awarded for costs. For the remains of the damaged bill in Chancery, see Selden Soc. vol. 94, p. 328.

BRETTON v BARNET (1599)

Owen 86 (C.P.) (untr.).[12]

A man delivers money to John Style, to be redelivered to him when he should be required, which John Style refused, and therefore an action of debt was brought; and the defendant demurred, for that an action of debt would not lie, but an account, as in 41 Edw. III.[13]

8   See p. 526, below.
9   *Orwell v Mortoft* (1505); see p. 406, below.
10   This was not alleged in *Orwell v Mortoft*, but in *Pykeryng v Thurgoode* (1532); see p. 411, below.
11   No judgment was entered in *Orwell v Mortoft*. Again, Fitzjames C.J. seems to have been thinking of *Pykeryng v Thurgoode*.
12   Also reported, Noy 72.
13   See p. 290, below.

WALMSLEY J. An action of debt will lie very well. And he drew a distinction between goods and money. For if a horse be delivered to be redelivered, there the property is not altered, and therefore a detinue lies for they are goods known. But if money be delivered it cannot be known, and therefore the property is altered, and therefore a debt will lie. And if portugals, or other money that may be known, be delivered to be redelivered, a detinue lies.

OWEN and GLANVILL JJ.[14] agreed to this . . . And judgment was given for the plaintiff.

LADY CHANDOS v SYMPSON (1602)

Record: KB 27/1367, m. 587. In 1598 James Sympson sued Frances Bridges, Lady Chandos, in the Common Pleas for a debt of £256. He counted on 24 separate contracts, the second count being that on 3 July 1593 she retained the plaintiff in London to embroider a black silk gown with black velvet for her daughter's maid, taking 40s. for his work and stipend. (The other counts are not relevant.) The plaintiff alleged that he had done the work but had never been paid. Judgment was given against Lady Chandos in 1600 for default of an answer. On 29 January 1601 she brought a writ of error in the King's Bench, and on 14 May assigned three errors: (1) that the action of debt was here founded on a naked pact containing no consideration to maintain the action; (2) that the declaration was uncertain; (3) that judgment should have been given for the defendant.

(a) Hil. 1602: BL MS. Add. 25203, fo. 453v; LI MS.
Misc. 492, fo. 395; YLS MS. G. R29.14, fo. 274v.

. . . *Tanfield* assigned for error that this declaration was insufficient. First, because no action of debt lies on these facts, since the defendant had no *quid pro quo*: but the plaintiff should have brought an action on the case, since the benefit which moved this contract redounded to a stranger and not to the plaintiff [in error] herself. For this he cited 44 Edw. III, 21,[15] where the case was that someone lent 100s. to another, to be repaid at a certain day, and at the day the money was not paid, and therefore another person came to the debtee and asked him to give the debtor more time and said that, if he did not pay, then he promised to pay: this is no contract to charge the person who made the promise, by action of debt, but only by action on the case. And to the same effect he cited

---

14   Glanvill J. cited two Common Pleas cases where money was paid to the defendant to perform a service, which was not performed, and debt lay: Noy 72.
15   Y.B. Trin. 44 Edw. III, fo. 21, pl. 23.

Nelson's case,[16] which was in the Common Bench, where John Style retained [William Nelson][17] to be attorney for John Doe, taking therefor his usual fees, and upon this retainer the attorney brought an action of debt against John Style for his fees, and it was adjudged that the action of debt did not lie. By the same argument, it does not lie in the case at bar, since the defendant was not to have any benefit from the contract, but all the benefit of it was to the stranger. Also the declaration is uncertain, since it is not alleged for whom the gown was to be embroidered, but only 'for her daughter's maid' without further certainty; and she might have several daughters, or her daughter might perhaps have had several maids; and so the count is completely uncertain in this respect.

As to the first matter it was agreed by GAWDY and FENNER JJ. that an action of debt well lies. For this they cited 37 Hen. VI, [fo.] 8.[18] If I say to another person that he will have £40 if he carries someone else's wheat, or if I say to a surgeon that he shall have 100s. if he cures a sick man, or if I say to someone that he shall have such and such a sum if he will marry such and such a woman, in these cases an action of debt lies for the money even though all the benefit of the contract is to a stranger.

As to the second matter, however, GAWDY J. thought the maid's name should have been put into the declaration; but FENNER J. thought it was good in that point also.[19] So, on this point, it was adjourned until the next term.

(b) Easter term 1602: BL MS. Add. 25203, fo. 478;
LI MS. Misc. 492, fo. 396; YLS MS. G. R29.14, fo. 282.[20]

The case between Lady Chandos and Sympson was moved again many times this term, in the absence of POPHAM C.J.

It was moved by *Tanfield* and *Stevens* that an action of debt does not lie against the lady on the retainer to embroider a gown for a stranger. For this *Tanfield* cited *Nelson's* case (cited by him last term); and also the *Lady Gresham's* case, where someone retained a miller for Lady Gresham to grind her corn, taking a certain sum each week for his labour, for which the miller brought an action of

---

16 (1585–6), according to Cro. Eliz. 880.
17 Chief prothonotary 1583–90: Selden Soc. vol. 94, p. *376*. Identified in YLS MS. G. R29.15, fo. 26.
18 See p. 236, above.
19 Cf. YLS MS. G. R29.15, fo. 26: 'FENNER J. doubted, and said that if I say to you, who are a draper, "Deliver to my son's man such cloth as he shall come for, and I will pay you for it", here is enough certainty imported'.
20 Also reported, sub nom. *Shandois v Simpson*, Cro. Eliz. 880.

debt against the person who retained him, and it was adjudged that the action did not lie.

On the other side, *George Croke* said that this case was not to be compared with any of the cases cited, for in them the person who retained the attorney or the miller did it only as a servant of the person for whom they were retained, and the attorney's fees and the miller's salary were not to be paid by the retainor but by the person for whom they were to be retained; and therefore no action of debt lies against him, but against his master. (If, however, at the time of the retainer he made any collateral promise for the payment of the money, he is chargeable with it by an action on the case.) But in our case there is a contract made solely in the name of the lady; for the plaintiff cannot demand anything against the maid for whom the gown was embroidered, it being expressly agreed that the lady would pay. Moreover, although the plaintiff embroidered the gown for a stranger, he did so not as servant to the stranger but as servant to Lady Chandos, who is the defendant, and therefore he must demand his salary from her.

The court granted this . . .

There was further discussion of the uncertainty of the declaration. Finally, Lady Chandos's counsel said that the judgment had been entered through her attorney's negligence in failing to plead, and they offered to try the issue in a new action on payment of £10 costs. The case was thereupon adjourned again. Later in the term the court held the declaration sufficiently certain, and affirmed the judgment. The record adds that in Michaelmas term the plaintiff acknowledged that the debt had been paid.

MILTON'S CASE (1668)[1]

Hardres 485, pl. 1 (Exch.) (untr.).

In an action [of debt][2] for £100 upon a bill of exchange accepted, the plaintiff declared that by the custom of England if a merchant send a bill of exchange to another merchant to pay money to another person, and the bill be accepted, that he who accepts the bill does thereby become chargeable with the sum therein contained; and that a certain merchant drew a bill of exchange upon the defendant, payable to the plaintiff, which bill the defendant accepted, whereby an action accrued. And, upon *Nil debet* pleaded, a verdict passed for the plaintiff.

---

1   Name from 1 Mod. 286, where it seems to be the case cited by Raynsford C.J. and Offley as an *indebitatus assumpsit*.
2   This is suggested by the plea *Nil debet*; but cf. fn. 1, above.

And now it was moved in arrest of judgment by *Offley*: (1) that the declaration is naught; (2) that an action of debt lies not. For the first, he said the declaration was naught because the plaintiff declared that 'by the custom of England etc.', which he said was naught because the custom of England is the law of England and what the judges are bound to take notice of[3] ... Secondly, an action of debt lies not in this case, because there is no privity betwixt the plaintiff and defendant, nor any contract in deed or in law, and where these fail debt lieth not ...

Stevens, for the plaintiff. As to the first exception, it has been made a doubt formerly, but is now settled to be good ... And for the second, it is a rule in law that where the common law or any particular custom creates a duty, debt lies for it; as in case of a tailor, who by the common law may have an action of debt or a *quantum meruit* for making up a suit of clothes ...

[HALE] C.B. This is a case of weight and concern for the future, and deserves consideration. Declarations upon bills of exchange have often varied: sometimes declarations have been upon a custom amongst merchants only, without laying an express promise; afterwards they came to declare upon an *assumpsit*. And after all, if an action of debt will lie, it will be a short cut and pare off a long recital. For, if debt lies, a man may declare upon a bill of exchange accepted in debt, or in *indebitatus assumpsit*, for so much money. But, for the plaintiff's inserting the custom of the realm into his declaration here, I hold that to be mere superfluity and redundancy, which does not vitiate the declaration ... But the great question here is whether or no a debt or duty be hereby raised. For if it be no more than a collateral engagement, order or promise, debt lies not: as in the case that has been cited, of goods delivered by A. to B. at the request of C., which C. promiseth to pay for if the other does not; for in that case a debt or duty does not arise betwixt A. and C., but a collateral obligation only. In our case the acceptance of a bill amounts clearly to a promise to pay the money; but it may be a question whether it amounts to a debt or not ... And it were worthwhile to enquire what the course has been amongst merchants, or to direct an issue for trial of the custom amongst merchants in this case. For, although we must take notice in general of the law of merchants, yet all their customs we cannot know but by information. And although the verdict here finds it in effect, and so might seem to inform us, yet it does not appear that the custom was in issue; so that we can have no certain information of the custom by this verdict.

3 I.e. it should not have been pleaded as a fact.

It was adjourned. Precedents were ordered to be searched. And afterwards, in Hilary term [1669], 20 Car. II, it was moved again, and precedents shown that by the opinion of Chief Justice [   ]⁴ debt lay not. And all the clerks in Guildhall certified that they had no precedent in London of debt in such case.

Afterwards, in Hilary term [1670], 20 & 21 Car. II, the court declared their opinions that an action of debt would not lie upon a bill of exchange accepted, against the acceptor; but that a special action upon the case⁵ must be brought against him: for that the acceptance does not create a duty ... and he that drew the bill continues debtor, notwithstanding the acceptance which makes the acceptor liable to pay it. And this course of accepting bills being a general custom amongst all traders both within and without the realm, and having everywhere that effect, as to make the acceptor subject to pay the contents, the court must take notice of that custom. But the custom does not extend so far as to create a debt, [but] only makes the acceptor chargeable (*onerabilis*) to pay the money ... Wherefore, and because no precedent could be produced that an action of debt had been brought upon an accepted bill of exchange, judgment was arrested.

(3) Debt on a bond or specialty

LOVEDAY v ORMESBY (1310)

Y.B. 3 Edw. II, Selden Soc. vol. 20, p. 191 (C.P.).

William Loveday brought his writ of debt and counted that one Sibilla granted that she was bound to this same William in £200.

Herle. What have you [in proof] of the debt?

Loveday. As to £140, see here your own deed. As to the rest, good suit.

Toudeby. He has counted that Sibilla granted that she was bound in the whole sum; and that grant lies in specialty. And in support of his action he puts forward a deed as to £140 and tenders suit as to the rest. Judgment of the count.

Loveday. You are bound to us in the amount, and we have a deed for only the £140; so we cannot count otherwise.

---

4   Blank.
5   See p. 459, below.

Friskeney. Every grant and every demand based upon grant must be by specialty. But upon other [kinds of] contract such as bailment or loan one can demand by suit. So since you demand this debt by reason of grant and show specialty for part only, [we ask] judgment.

STANTON. They would have done better to count on two [separate] contracts or on one grant and one contract.

And the plaintiff was non-suited.

ABBOT OF GRACE DIEU v ANON. (1306)

Y.B. 33–35 Edw. I, Rolls Series, p. 331 (C.P.).

The abbot of Grace Dieu brought a writ [of debt] for 24 marks against one R., and counted upon a contract made between his predecessor and the said R., and put forward R.'s deed which attested [the debt].

Roston. As to four marks he can claim nothing, because his predecessor was fully paid those [four marks]; and see here [the predecessor's deed of] acquittance. And as to the remainder he can claim nothing, because we handed over to the aforesaid A. his predecessor eight bovates of land and a quarry from which he took stone to enclose his park of T. in satisfaction of the said 20 marks, of which land [the abbot] himself is still seised; and we ask judgment if he can claim anything.

Hedon. What have you [to show] what you have said?

Roston. Ready [to aver it].

Hedon. As to the acquittance, we cannot deny it. As to the remainder, we ask judgment since we have your deed, which you have admitted and which binds you for this debt; and to unbind you from this debt you have neither acquittance nor anything else but words...

Roston. We put forward against you something as good as an acquittance, because the countryside can have notice of it; and we plead our true facts, to which the court should have regard.

STANTON. Although you plead your true facts, he intends to plead as the law allows him. And since you were bound to him by deed, why did you hand over your land to him without deed? You have acknowledged the deed, and have nothing which unbinds you. And so [the court] adjudges that he recover the 20 marks and his damages of 100s. taxed by the court. And as to the four marks [the plaintiff] is to take nothing but to be amerced.

GLASTON v ABBOT OF CROWLAND (1330)

Eyre of Northamptonshire, Selden Soc. vol. 98, p. 665.

John of Glaston brought debt against the abbot of Crowland, Lincolnshire, and counted that on 24 January 1314 the abbot's predecessor had bound himself by deed in 50 marks payable to the plaintiff on 24 June 1314, that the predecessor did not pay, and the present abbot refused to pay. The abbot confessed his predecessor's deed, but said that the predecessor had paid, whereupon his deed was returned to him in lieu of an acquittance; and the predecessor had put the deed in a chest at Crowland abbey, where it remained until the plaintiff with force and arms broke the chest and took it. The abbot said he was now suing in trespass in the Common Pleas for this taking. (That case is reported in Y.B. Mich. 3 Edw. III, fo. 30, pl. 1, and refers to this action of debt.) The plaintiff demurred to the plea because the abbot had no deed proving payment.

(a) First argument, Hil. 1330.

... Hillary. Sir, as you see, we have put forward his predecessor's deed and he has acknowledged it, and he does not show any acquittance which discharges him from the same debt. Therefore we pray our debt and our damages.

Shareshull. We have explained that your will (*gré*) was done, and it is not right that you should be paid twice when there is only one debt.

Hillary. If things are as you say, then when a verdict is given against the plaintiff in your writ of trespass you will recover damages in respect of what you have lost.[6] However, the mere fact that you are bringing a writ of trespass does not prove that things are as you have said; and so there is no mischief in law if you are charged in this action.

Shareshull. If the plaintiff recovers this debt against us now, he may perhaps die before he comes to answer [in our writ of trespass], or part with all his property, so that we should never recover anything by our writ. So we think the law does compel him to answer what we have said.

Hillary. If you had said that we made you an acquittance and you lost it, that would not have discharged you. Nor does this.

Aldborough. When I accuse you of having taken it from me by force, that is quite different from my saying that I have lost it; for losing it is my own act, which cannot discharge me.

---

6 In the trespass action, however, Stonore C.J. expressed doubt whether the abbot could allege that he had already paid the debt, because this rested on specialty: Y.B. Mich. 3 Edw. III, fo. 30, pl. 1.

CAMBRIDGE. In a plea of land, if you had right to demand certain land against me, and then released to me all your right, and then came and took the same release out of my possession with force, and then used your action against me, and I pleaded the plea which he is now pleading against you, the law would compel you to answer.

Hillary said that was not so.

Aldborough. If certain covenants are drawn up between you and me, whereby I am to make a bond to you for a certain debt in consideration (*par encheson*) of the performance of the same covenants, and I have my bond sealed in my hand and you will not perform the covenants, but take the bond against my will and then bring action on it, I shall plead the facts and drive you to answer them, even though I do not have an acquittance. Likewise here.

Shareshull. It is a lesser mischief for him to answer our case than that he should recover; for if he answers our case and his answer is found true, that is a sufficient answer for him in the writ of trespass. Thus we shall not be charged on our side, nor he on the other, which is fair (*equité*).

Hillary as above; and so to judgment after Easter.

(b) The adjourned argument, Pas. 1330.[7]

... *Aldborough* [after stating the facts]: and we demand judgment whether he may have an action upon this writing while the writ of trespass is pending, since it is possible that it will be found that this writing was delivered to our predecessor in form aforesaid.

Bacon. [Then] anyone could be delayed in his writ of debt by the defendant thus purchasing a writ of trespass. Moreover, the recovery which we shall have against you will give you good cause to recover damages in your writ of trespass.

SCROP. We cannot, in this writ of debt, enquire whether he came with force and arms and took away this writing. Since you have confessed the delivery by your predecessor, and the plaintiff now has it in his hands, it ought not to be an issue in this writ whether [the plaintiff] returned the writing to your predecessor.

Aldborough. If a covenant is made between us that you will pay me £10 and I will enfeoff you, and I make a sealed charter and retain it in my hands until you have paid me, but you take away this charter by force, I believe I can prevent you from taking advantage of that charter on the grounds that you took it out of my possession.

---

7 Selden Soc. vol. 98, p. 666. Cf. a different report, ibid., p. 678.

SCROP. I do not believe so. Even if it were so, the cases are not alike; for you have confessed that your predecessor delivered this writing to the plaintiff, whereas in your put case you did not deliver the charter. Nevertheless, a man once made a charter and a letter of attorney, and sealed them and retained them in his keeping until he should be paid, and the person in whose favour the charter was made took the charter and the letter of attorney with force and arms and caused himself to be put in seisin; and the person who made the charter petitioned parliament for a remedy. Another did so to establish that a child was not his son, because he was overseas for three years before the child was born and for two years afterwards. And neither of them could have any remedy, except that next time the one should keep a better eye on his seal and the other on his wife when he was away.

It was awarded that the plaintiff should recover his [50 marks] against the abbot, and his damages taxed by the court at ten marks, and that the abbot should be in mercy. And the bond was destroyed.[8]

The record shows that judgment was given on 25 April 1330, and that on 21 June the plaintiff acknowledged that he had been paid.

ANON. (1378)
Y.B. Trin. 2 Ric. II, p. 33, pl. 8 (C.P.).

A man brought a writ of debt against another, and in proof of the debt he put forward a sealed tally; and the sum was marked on the tally by notches, in the usual way. The defendant said he owed him nothing in the way he had counted, and was ready [to make the averment].[9]

Burgh [for the plaintiff]. The tally is sealed by you, and so we do not think you shall have the averment without answering the tally. So we demand judgment, and pray our debt and our damages.

BELKNAP. If the tally had been written, with words of indebtedness (*parole de duité*) and the sum also written on the tally (rather than marked with notches), then perhaps he would have been driven to answer it as if it were a bond. But it is not so: the subject matter (*chose*) and the sum are marked with notches. Therefore we

---

8 Another report (at p. 679) puts the judgment in the mouth of Redenhall J.: 'Because you have confessed the bond, and because the trespass which you allege cannot be tried on this writ, the court awards that he should recover his debt'.

9 The averment (*et hoc paratus est verificare*) tendered an issue of fact which, if accepted by the other party, resulted in a jury being summoned.

must do as it has been done in former times. So, do you want the averment?

Hanmer. Even if the sum was written on the tally, he could still have removed the writing by hand, by washing it with water, or with fire, or in some other way. So, as it seems to me, you should oust him from the averment.

BELKNAP. You could say that of a bond: a man could erase the deed and rewrite it, as in your example.

Then *Burgh* accepted the averment; *et alii econtra*.

DONNE v CORNWALL (1486)

Y.B. Pas. 1 Hen VII, fo. 14v, pl. 2 (C.P.).

One John Donne brought an action of debt on a bond for £10 against E. Cornwall[10] and his wife. It was pleaded for the defendants that the wife had paid the said £10, and the plaintiff had delivered the bond back to her in lieu of an acquittance, and after this redelivery the plaintiff with force and arms, at such a place, took the bond from her; and they demanded judgment *Si action*. And the plaintiff, through *Vavasour*, demurred to the plea.

Vavasour . . . The bond took effect at the beginning, and when it was delivered in lieu of an acquittance it was still a deed. And this delivery is not a discharge of the obligation, but [only a putting of the bond into] the defendant's hands, for the deed is not dissolved when the bond comes into the plaintiff's possession [again] . . . So it seems to me that this bond remained at all times a deed; and in that case, if its force is not lost, this matter in fact is no plea against this specialty. For in no case may a man avoid a bond without specialty of as high a nature as the deed is . . . So it seems to me that the plaintiff should recover.

Callow thought the contrary . . . It seems to me that the bond lost its force by the delivery in lieu of an acquittance . . . and this delivery is better than any other acquittance, since the obligor can cancel it . . .

Tremayle . . . It seems that the plaintiff should be barred [to prevent] circuity of action: for by this taking out of his possession [the defendant] may have an action of trespass, and perhaps also the other shall have an action of debt on this bond, which is a circuity of action and shall not be allowed . . .

HUSSEY [C.J.K.B.][11] . . . There is a distinction between a deed

10 Reads 'Downe' and 'Cornwales' in BL MS. Hargrave 105, fo. 91.
11 His presence suggests that this debate was in the Exchequer Chamber, as was the continuation below.

which is good and effectual at the outset (which cannot be avoided by matter in fact) and a deed which is not good at the outset but voidable (which may well be avoided by matter in fact, as in the cases of infancy and so forth)... In some cases, nevertheless, an obligee can by his own act make a deed bad where it was once good: for instance, where the obligee changes part of the sum in a bond by erasure, or by writing in more, the other shall say *Non est factum* (*nient son fait*) in an action brought upon it. But to my mind there is no case in the world in which a man shall avoid a simple deed (in the absence of any condition), when it was once good and effectual, with bare matter in fact.

Kebell... The plaintiff should be barred, because this delivery of the bond in lieu of an acquittance was a sufficient discharge. It is at the obligee's election, when the obligor comes to him to pay his money, whether he will give him an acquittance or return the bond in lieu of an acquittance; and, if the obligor refuses [the latter], he shall be charged with the damages in debt, when these facts are disclosed, because he refused this sufficient discharge. And if that is the law—as I have always understood it to be—then, when the bond is delivered in lieu of an acquittance, the property is now in the obligor; and it follows that it would be against reason for the other to recover against him on this bond, for it is his own chattel. Moreover, it is repugnant [to good sense] that I should be once discharged of a bond, and afterwards charged again, the property continuing in me. As to whether a deed may be avoided by bare matter in fact: yes it can, sir, in various cases. For instance, if I am bound to a single woman, and then I marry her; or if I am bound to a villein, and then purchase the manor to which he is a villein regardant. If three men are bound to me, and I break off one of their seals, or if one of the obligees enters religion,[12] I shall plead these facts against this specialty. And in all the above cases I shall plead these bare matters in fact to avoid the bond. Thus the plaintiff should be barred.

... [On another day] BRYAN [C.J.C.P.]... I do not see in any case in the world how a man can avoid a specialty by bare matter in fact concerning the deed itself, if the deed was good at the outset. There is a distinction between this case and the cases previously put [concerning deeds] which are voidable, because they were never good. I fully concede Kebell's cases, for there the deeds are voidable by matter in law and by extrinsic matter which does not concern the same deed itself, and there it is by operation of law.

12 I.e. is professed as a monk.

Also, the party would suffer a mischief if that should be the law in our case, for a man could unfairly defeat another in a foreign county by his false plea ...

They were adjourned in the Exchequer Chamber to another day, at which *Vavasour* argued that this redelivery cannot be in lieu of an acquittance, for there are no words of acquittance ... And afterwards the case was argued in the Common Bench.

BRYAN repeated his own distinction, as above, and said that where a specialty is avoided by matter in law (as in Kebell's case of a bond made to a villein and subsequent purchase of the manor) this is a discharge by the act of the law; and if the party could not avoid it by answer, as above, he would be without remedy. But here it is a discharge only by the act of the party, and not by the act of the law; and the party suffers no mischief, for if the plaintiff recovers in this writ of debt, [the defendant] shall recover back the same amount in damages in a writ of trespass for the taking.

For this reason, the court awarded that the plaintiff should recover his debt and his damages.

WABERLEY v COCKEREL (1541)

Dyer 51.

In the King's Bench the case was as follows. One Edmund Cockerel and one Henry Huttoft were jointly bound in a single bill to one John Waberley of London; and Huttoft died; and Waberley brought an action of debt in London against the other one alone, and declared on this bill. The defendant pleaded that he ought not to be charged for the said bill, because, as to part of the money, Huttoft paid the plaintiff at such a ward in London, and the residue he himself paid to the plaintiff at the same place at another time, and the plaintiff received it in full satisfaction and delivered the said obligatory bill to the said defendant in the name of an acquittance of that debt, by reason of which the said bill wholly lost its force and effect; and afterwards the plaintiff took the said bill from him with force and arms; and so the defendant says the said bill is not his deed, and of this he puts himself upon the country. To this plea the plaintiff demurred in law.

Now it was argued by *Staundford* and *Bromley* Sjts., for the plaintiff, that the plea was bad ... because he has not shown an acquittance of the payment; for the maxim in law is that a single bill cannot be avoided and answered by bare matter, but it must be by matter of as high a nature as the bond is, namely writing.[13] Thus it was adjudged in 4 Hen. VI[14] that an [arbitration] award was not a bar in debt on a bond . . . Even if it is the truth that the plaintiff was paid his money, it is nevertheless better to suffer a mischief to one man than an inconvenience to many, which would subvert the law. For if matter in writing could be so easily defeated and avoided by such a surmise, by naked breath, a matter in writing would be of no greater authority than a matter of fact. Besides, this bill cannot be an acquittance, because it is not made in the name of the obligee, nor are there any words of acquittance; and it cannot be the obligee's deed because a deed which was once good can never have two deliveries, for the second delivery is utterly void for the purpose of making it the party's deed.

ANON. (1557)

BL MS. Harley 1624, fo. 57 (C.P.).

An action of debt is brought on a bond. The defendant says that the bond is endorsed with a condition that if before a certain day he repaired all the banks of a river in a certain place then the bond would be void; and he says that, immediately after the date of the said bond, a great quantity of rain fell by the providence of God so that the place remained flooded throughout the time and so he was unable to repair it.

Browne asked whether this was a good plea.

THE COURT. Yes.

Browne. What if it were not so flooded but that he might have repaired it at great expense?

BROOKE C.J. Then it would be necessary to make an issue of that.

Browne. If it was flooded, was it not his own foolishness to bind himself to such an inconvenience?

STAUNDFORD J. There is a distinction between a man binding himself to an impossibility, and binding himself to do something possible which afterwards becomes impossible. If a man is bound to an impossibility, the condition is void and the bond single. But if the condition is possible on the day when the bond is made, and afterwards becomes impossible by act of God, the bond is dis-

---

13   I.e. a deed.
14   Y.B. Pas. 4 Hen. VI, fo. 17, pl. 3, where the action of debt was not brought on a bond, but on a finding by auditors in an action of account (which was a matter of record).

charged: as in the common case where I am bound to enfeoff you of my manor of Dale before a certain day, and you die [before the day], I am discharged of the bond. (Note that.)

PYNNELL v COLE (1602)

(a) Record: CP 40/1684, m. 501.

Wiltshire. James Cole, late of West Harnham in the county aforesaid, husbandman, otherwise called James Cole of West Harnham in the said county of Wiltshire, husbandman, was summoned to answer Thomas Pynnell in a plea that he render to him £16 which he owes him and unjustly withholds etc. And thereupon the same Thomas, by John Puxton his attorney, says that, whereas the aforesaid James on the fourteenth day of December [1596] in the thirty eighth year of the reign of the present lady the queen, at Wilton, by a certain obligatory writing of his granted himself to be bound to the same Thomas in the aforesaid £16, to be paid to the same Thomas when he should be thereto requested: nevertheless the aforesaid James, though often requested, has not yet rendered the aforesaid £16 to the same Thomas but has until now refused and still refuses to do so. And he says he is thereby the worse, and has damage to the extent of £10. And thereof he produces suit etc. And he proffers here in court the aforesaid writing, which witnesses the aforesaid debt in form aforesaid; the date whereof is the day and year mentioned above etc.

And the aforesaid James, by Robert Holmes his attorney, comes and denies the force and wrong when etc. And he prays oyer of the aforesaid writing; and it is read to him etc. He also prays oyer of the endorsement of the same writing; and it is read to him in these words:[15]

The condition of this obligation is such, that if the within-bounden William Mathewe,[16] his executors, administrators or assigns, or any of them, do well and truly content and pay or cause to be contented and paid unto the within-named Thomas Pynnell, his executors, administrators or assigns, the sum of £8. 10s. of current English money in manner and form following— that is to say, 50s. of current English money in and upon the one and twentieth day of December which shall be in the year of our lord God 1600; and 50s. of like good money in and upon the four and twentieth day of June then next following; and 50s. of like good money in and upon the one and

---

15 The condition is in English.
16 Cole must have been bound jointly with Mathewe as a surety.

twentieth day of December which shall be in the year of our lord God 1600; and 20s. of current English money in and upon the four and twentieth day of June then next and immediately ensuing; the said several payments to be had and made at or in the south porch of the parish church of St Thomas within the city of New Sarum [i.e. Salisbury] in the county of Wiltshire— that then this obligation to be void and of none effect, or else it to stand, remain and be in his full force, strength, effect and virtue.

Which having been read and heard, the same James says that the aforesaid Thomas ought not to have his aforesaid action against him, because he says that after the making of the aforesaid writing and before the aforesaid 21 December first mentioned above in the aforesaid condition, namely on 1 October [1600] in the forty-second year of the reign of the present lady the queen, at Wilton aforesaid, at the special instance and request of the aforesaid Thomas, he paid the said Thomas £5. 0s. 10d. of lawful money of England; and the same James further says that after the making of the aforesaid writing and before the aforesaid 21 December first mentioned above in the aforesaid condition, namely on the same 1 October [1600] in the abovementioned forty-second year of the reign of the present lady the queen, at Wilton aforesaid, at the instance of the aforesaid Thomas and by his appointment, he similarly paid 16d. of similar lawful money of England to a certain John Blathatt, which sums amount in all to £5. 2s. 2d.: which £5. 2s. 2d. (paid and satisfied in form aforesaid) the aforesaid Thomas Pynnell then and there accepted in full satisfaction of the aforesaid £8. 10s. mentioned above in the aforesaid condition, and in satisfaction of all other sums of money then owed to the said Thomas by the same James. And this he is ready to aver. And so he prays judgment whether the aforesaid Thomas ought to have his aforesaid action against him etc.

And the aforesaid Thomas says that the aforesaid James's plea, pleaded above in bar, is insufficient in law to bar him the said Thomas from having his aforesaid action against the said James; and that he has no need and is not bound by the law of the land to answer that plea, pleaded in manner and form aforesaid. And this he is ready to aver. And so, for want of a sufficient plea by the aforesaid James in this behalf, the same Thomas prays judgment and that his debt, together with his damages by reason of the withholding of that debt, may be awarded to him etc.

And the aforesaid James, inasmuch as he has above alleged sufficient matter in law to bar the said Thomas from having his aforesaid action against the same James, which he is ready to aver, which matter the aforesaid Thomas does not deny or in any way answer, but utterly refuses to admit the averment, prays judgment as before; and prays that the aforesaid Thomas be barred from having his aforesaid action against him etc.

And because the justices here wish to be advised of and upon the foregoing before they give judgment therein, a day is given to the aforesaid parties here until the octaves of Michaelmas for hearing their judgment therein, since the same justices here are not yet thereof etc. At which day both the aforesaid Thomas and the aforesaid James come here by their aforesaid attorneys. And thereupon, the foregoing having been seen and fully understood by the justices here, it seems to the same justices here that the plea of the aforesaid James, pleaded above in bar, is insufficient in law to bar the aforesaid Thomas from having his aforesaid action against the said James (as the aforesaid Thomas has above alleged). Therefore it is decided that the aforesaid Thomas do recover against the said James his aforesaid debt, and his damages by reason of the withholding of that debt, which are awarded to the same Thomas with his consent by the court here as 95s.; and that the aforesaid James be in mercy etc.

(b) 5 Co. Rep. 117.

Coke simplifies the pleadings by stating that the £8. 10s. was all due on 11 November 1600, and that the defendant paid £5. 2s. 2d. to the plaintiff on 1 October.

... And it was resolved by the whole court[17] that payment of a lesser sum at the day, in satisfaction of a greater, cannot be satisfaction for the whole because it appears to the judges that by no possibility can a lesser sum be satisfaction to the plaintiff for a greater sum. But the gift of a horse,[18] sparrowhawk or robe, and so forth, in satisfaction is good: for it shall be presumed that a horse, sparrowhawk or robe will be more beneficial to the plaintiff than

17 In Coke's contemporary autograph note of this case, he says it was resolved 'by Sir Edmund Anderson and all except Walmsley'. The text is otherwise as printed.
18 This had been a common example for over a century. See, e.g., *Anon.* (1484) Y.B. Mich. 2 Ric. III, fo. 22v, pl. 52 (held a good plea that the defendant paid a horse in full satisfaction of 100s., and the plaintiff agreed to it); *Vavasour v Polend* (1494) Y.B. Hil. 9 Hen. VII, fo. 20v, pl. 16, per Vavasour J. ('If I am bound to you on condition that I pay you £10 on a certain day, and I now give you a horse for the said £10 and you receive it, I shall be excused and discharged'); *Anon.* (1495) Y.B. Hil. 10 Hen. VII, fo. 14, pl. 11, per Bryan C.J. ('If I am bound in £20 to pay £10, and I pay a horse, or enfeoff the obligee with an acre of land, the condition is well performed; for there is satisfaction for the money'); *Anon.* (1496) Y.B. Pas. 11 Hen. VII, fo. 21, pl. 6, per Jay Sjt. ('You will not deny that if the condition of a bond is that I should pay 20s., it is a good plea to say that I paid you a horse in the name of the 20s. and you received it').

the money, in respect of some circumstances, or else the plaintiff would not have accepted it in satisfaction. But when one entire sum is due, by no presumption can acceptance of part be satisfaction to the plaintiff. In the case at the bar, however, it was resolved that the payment and acceptance of part before the day, in satisfaction of the whole, shall be a good satisfaction in respect of the circumstance of time; for perhaps part of it before the day will be more beneficial to him than the whole sum at the day, and the value of the satisfaction is immaterial. Likewise, if I am bound in £20 to pay you £10 at Westminster, and you request me to pay you £5 at the day at York, and you accept this in full satisfaction of the whole £10,[19] this is a good satisfaction for the whole; for the expense of paying it at York is a sufficient satisfaction.

But in this case the plaintiff had judgment, on account of the insufficient pleading. For he did not plead that he had paid the £5. 2s. 2d. in full satisfaction—as by law he ought—but pleaded the payment of part generally, and that the plaintiff accepted it in full satisfaction. But the method of tender and payment shall always be directed by the person who makes the tender or payment, not by the person who accepts them. And for this reason judgment was given for the plaintiff.

(c) BL MS. Lansdowne 1074, fo. 417; LI MS.
Maynard 87, fo. 327v (untr.).

. . . *Harris*, for the defendant: that a payment of a lesser sum before the day of payment in discharge of all shall be good in respect of the benefit that may redound to the plaintiff thereby.

ANDERSON C.J. If a man be bound to pay me £10 in London, and I am bound to pay another man £5 in Newcastle, and I say to my debtor before the day of payment, 'Go pay my creditor £5 in Newcastle', and I am content with this in satisfaction of my bond: is not this good satisfaction, in consideration of the journey?

And the court insisted much how long the day of satisfaction was before the day of payment in the condition.

Adjourned, and demurrer.

Judgment for the plaintiff, because the defendant doth not plead that it was [paid][20] in full satisfaction etc.; and also he doth not aver any extraordinary good that it did the plaintiff, nor any necessity that the plaintiff had to use it before the day.

---

19   Reads '20' in 1st ed.
20   Reads 'accepted' in MS.

(d) LI MS. Maynard 66, fo. 56.

... and by the opinion of WALMSLEY and KINGSMILL JJ. it is no plea.

But WARBURTON J. doubted, since it was paid and accepted before the day. He said, however, that if it had been on the day it would not have been good because £5 cannot be satisfaction for £8 ...

ANDERSON C.J. held strongly that it was a good plea, for the same reason as [WARBURTON J.], namely that it was paid before the day; because perhaps it was more beneficial to him to have £5 when it was paid than £8 on the day ...

This was conceded by KINGSMILL J.

All were agreed that if someone is bound to pay at a certain place or a certain day, and he pays at another place or day, this is nevertheless good by reason of the other's acceptance; and it may be pleaded in bar, because all is paid according to the condition. But in the principal case all is not paid.

WALMSLEY J. If an obligee says to the obligor that, whereas he ought to pay him so much money on such a day, he will forbear him until a certain day thereafter, he may not plead this matter in bar in debt on the bond, but must have an action on the case or a remedy in conscience for it.

9 Detinue

MORTIMER v MORTIMER (1292)

Y.B. 20 & 21 Edw. I, Rolls Series, p. 189.

Roger Mortimer brought his writ of detinue for a charter against lady Maud Mortimer, who came by her attorney and said: sir, on the day and the year on which they say that the charter was bailed to lady Maud, her husband Roger Mortimer was alive, so that she could not at that time bind herself. [We ask] judgment whether she is required to answer; and if you so adjudge, she will answer willingly.

Huntingdon. Sir, our plaint is of the wrongful detinue of a charter which the lady herself is now detaining. [We ask] judgment whether she should not answer for her own wrong.

Louther. The cause of your action is indeed the bailment, and at that time she could not bind herself. [We ask] judgment whether she should answer for something for which she could not bind herself.

Spigurnel. If you had delivered 30 marks to the lady while she was married, to keep and to return when you requested them, would she now be bound to answer? I think not; and so here.

Howard. That is not like this case. In a writ of debt you would say 'she owes' and here you say 'which she wrongfully detains'. [We ask] judgment, etc. And besides, our action arises from the wrongful detinue and not from the bailment. [Again we ask] judgment etc.

Louther [argued] as before.

Howard. If I had bailed 20s. or a charter to a [married] woman, I should then have an action jointly against husband and wife during the husband's lifetime. And for the same reason I should after the death of the husband have a good action against the woman alone upon the bailment made to the woman. And in the same way I should have a good action against the woman alone after the husband's death upon a bailment made to husband and wife; and so here, for a thing bailed to the woman alone in her husband's lifetime.

ANON. (*c.* 1310)

Y.B. 2 & 3 Edw. II, Selden Soc. vol. 19, p. 195 (C.P.).

One A. complained against one B. that wrongfully he detains and does not deliver up chattels to the value of 30s., namely ten sheep, price so much, one cow, price etc., which he bailed [to B.] to pasture on such a day and to keep from Michaelmas until such a day; on which day he came and demanded them and could not have them etc., but etc.

Herle denied wrong and force and said that never did he bail ten sheep and one cow as he has counted against us: ready to do against him, etc., by our law etc.

Ingham. To your law you should not be received, for a man should not get to his law about a contract or covenant about which the country can have knowledge; but the parties should go to the country ...

Herle. Suit [relied upon] in court does not put a man to any answer other than to be at his law unless [he] is willing. And since A. puts forward no writing which attests the contract, but only suit, [we ask] judgment whether we should not be received to our law.

Bereford. Now God forbid that he should get to his law about a matter of which the country can have knowledge, for then with a dozen or half-a-dozen rogues he might swear an honest man out of his goods. And if we were to award wager of law in this case, other people ... might take it as a precedent to award law in every case in which the party has only suit. So will you say anything else?

Herle. No.

So this court awards that A. recover what he demands and B. is to be amerced.

BOWDON v PELLETER (1315)

Y.B. 8 Edw. II, Selden Soc. vol. 41, p. 136.

William of Bowdon, clerk, brought his writ of detinue of chattels against one [Emma, the widow of David le Pelleter], complaining that she wrongfully detains from him etc. [chattels which he bailed to her on such a day], namely rings, silver [clasps] and other jewels.

Miggele. Sir, we tell you that this same William bailed to us to keep [and to return at his request] a chest locked with his own key, and he himself took away the key. We did not know that jewels and other things were in it as he says. And we tell you that thieves came by night and broke into [Emma's] room and took the chest out into the fields and there broke it open; and they took our own goods and chattels with his, ready etc.

Russel. That he bailed to you the aforesaid jewels to redeliver at his request, without their being enclosed [in a chest or under lock], ready etc.

And the others said the opposite.

LONDON v GARTON (1321)

Y.B. Eyre of London, II, Selden Soc. vol. 86, p. 140
(second report).

One Henry of London brought his writ of detinue for a horse against one [William of Garton] and the writ was: Command [William] to deliver up to [Henry] one horse which he wrongfully detains. And the count was: he wrongfully detains from him one horse which a certain [John of Canterbury], [Henry's] man, bailed to him on such a day to redeliver to this same Henry, his master, on demand etc. And he has since often demanded it of him, etc.

Bacon. Whereas you have counted that we received a horse by delivery from your man etc., we are ready to deny against you and your suit by our law that we received any [horse].

Fastolf. We have counted that somebody other than ourself delivered the horse to you; and this is another's contract, so that we can not be party to receiving or you to doing the law . . .

Bacon. The receipt [of the horse] is our own doing, and concerning our own act we can do our law.

Scrop. He has counted that you received his horse and detained it and still detain it; so answer.

Bacon. Ready to deny by our law that we received any [horse] or detained any [horse].

Scrop. As to the detinue, you cannot be at your law in this case any more than in a replevin action.

HERLE. This bailment is not so private that the country cannot have knowledge of it.

Claver. In a writ of account charging [the defendant] as receiver [of my money] if I count that he received my money by another's hand, he can in no way be at his law, but if by my own hand he will be received to his law. So here.

HERLE. Are you willing to aver?

Bacon. If the court so adjudges.

HERLE. The tender of his law is one issue; and if you give one issue the court will not adjudge that you should give another. So say whether you will aver it.

And so to the country that he received no [horse] etc.

ANON. (1339)

Y.B. 12 & 13 Edw. III, Rolls Series, p. 245 (C.P.).

Detinue of chattels to the value of £100 [brought] against an abbot by a man and his wife [based upon] a bailment made by the woman's father when she was under age, to be returned to his daughter when she was of full age at her request; and he counted that he bailed pots, towels, cloths and £20 sealed up in a bag.

Pole. They demand money, which by nature sounds in debt or account. [We ask] judgment of the count.

Stouford. We do not count of a loan, which sounds in debt, or of the receipt of money to trade with, which would give account, but of money delivered into [the abbot's] keeping under seal etc.; and [the coins] could not be changed. And if your house were burnt down, that would be an answer.

SHARDELOW [SHARESHULL?]. Answer over.

Pole. We do not detain as he has counted, ready to deny by our law.

Stouford. We have counted upon a bailment made by a third hand, so do you mean that for your answer?

Pole. But the detinue alleged is by our own hand, and the receipt etc.

WAGWORTH v HALYDAY (1355)

Y.B. Trin. 29 Edw. III, fo. 38 (C.P.).

In detinue of chattels against Alice Halyday [brought] by Peter de Wagworth for a belt and a purse etc., [Wagworth] said that he bailed the things to one G. Halyday to redeliver [on request], and he said that after G.'s death they came into the keeping of Alice.

WILLOUGHBY. How did they come into her keeping?

Wychyngham. It does not matter how.

WILLOUGHBY. Nevertheless it would be better for you if you said how; and it is a mere formality and in no way against you, because the manner is not traversable.

Wychyngham. Then we tell you that they came into her keeping as executor.

Fyncheden. And since you are to recover the principal from us and damages also as from an executor, and we are not named as executor, [we ask] judgment of the writ. And sir, if this writ were upheld the following mischief would ensue: in case there were other executors who had released [the claim], that could not now be pleaded; for we could not allege that there were others if we are not named as executor.

Wychyngham. You have not denied that the goods came into your keeping, and it does not matter whether as executor or otherwise since that is not traversable; and even if I had not said [it was as executor] my count would not have been less good. Once my chattels have come into your keeping, that [is what] charges you in itself and gives me this action against you, and not that you are executor. And so [we ask] judgment and pray our damages.

WILLOUGHBY to *Fyncheden.* Say something else.

Fyncheden. Show what you have [in proof] of the bailment.

Gour. The bailment may be averred; and we tell you further that the goods came into her possession. And so everything that we say and allege can well be averred, and so etc.

Fyncheden. He has alleged the bailment to our testator and is to charge us as executor, and so etc. And in a writ of debt against an executor, you have to show specialty.

WILLOUGHBY. Say something else, because he does not bring this action against you as against an executor. He has shown in his count how [the goods] came into your keeping as executor only to make a privity between you and the bailee; and so answer.

Fyncheden. The chattels that he demands did not come into our keeping, nor do we detain them in the manner he alleges, ready etc.

Gour. She has not denied the substance of our action, namely the bailment made to G. And if [the goods] came into her keeping at some time after G.'s death, but perhaps in a manner other than as we have counted, perhaps for example not as executor, she has traversed the manner [but not] the substance directly. And so we do not think the law makes us answer this averment.

GREENE. The issue is wide enough, because she has traversed that the goods ever came into her keeping or that she detains them; and that is enough on this writ because she has traversed altogether. And although she says 'in the manner you allege', those words mean 'as you allege by [your] writ'; and such a mention makes any issue taken go to traverse of the writ.

Gour. The chattels came into her keeping, ready etc.

Fyncheden. You say that we detain, and we have traversed that, and you do not maintain it; [and so we ask] judgment. And although we have said further that the goods never came into our keeping, your replication always goes to your writ, namely that we are detaining the goods.

And then issue was joined on the one point and the other, namely that the goods came into her keeping and that she is detaining them, ready etc.

And the others said the opposite.

SOMERVILLE v ANON. (1410)

Y.B. Hil. 11 Hen. IV, fo. 50, pl. 27 (C.P.).

John Somerville brought a writ of detinue for a box with charters [writings obligatory?] contained in it, and counted on a bailment made in London, on condition that the defendant would re-deliver in the same city on demand.

Horton. A long time after he bailed it to us, we re-delivered the same box to him at a certain place in the county of Leicester; and this we wish to aver, and we demand judgment.

Tildesley. Tantamount to 'he does not detain' which is to traverse our action: ready to aver it.

COLEPEPER. In your writ of detinue the bailment is not traversable, but he answers to the detinue which is the cause of action; and when he has traversed the cause of action, that will be tried where the writ was brought; and in a writ of debt one can not plead that he paid in another county, but the issue shall be that he owes nothing; and so in this case it shall be that he does not detain.

HANKFORD. That is no wonder in a writ of debt, because the defendant suffers no mischief since he can have his law if in conscience the truth is such. But here he can not have his law, and if indeed the bailment was in London to re-deliver there, the London people can not know about the re-delivery later in the county of Leicester. And at one time it was the usual thing in debt on account for the defendant to plead that he owed nothing, ready to aver by the countryside: and because the issue was too general, jurors would sometimes find against the defendant when the case was that the defendant was indebted to the plaintiff [whether] on the arrears of an account or upon some other contract; and so it has become usual for [the defendant] to traverse the account in particular and for issue to be taken upon that; and it therefore seems that the plea should be as the defendant pleaded.

THIRNING [C.J.]. There would be a great mischief for the other party if the bailment was made in London and the defendant is still detaining the charter and yet by such an allegation can get to a Leicestershire jury. And the detinue is the cause of action and the detinue is laid in London, and so he must answer the plaintiff's action, whether or not he detains as the plaintiff says.

Tildesley. We wish to aver that the bailment was made in London, and that he is there and now detaining our charters; and so we demand judgment and ask for the writings and our damages.

Horton. And we wish to aver the re-delivery a long time after [the bailment] at A. in the county of Leicester; and as to your wish to aver that we are now detaining, no law makes us answer that, and we demand judgment and ask that [your claim] be barred.

HILL. That he is still detaining [your] charters is not to the point, because you have counted of a bailment as above, and that bailment the defendant has fully acknowledged, and answers by a later re-delivery; and so he has discharged himself of the bailment and the detinue alleged by your writ; and if the fact is that you [again] bailed him the box after that re-delivery, you have gone wrong on your count and declaration, and so [etc.].

THIRNING to *Horton.* Will you demur?

Horton. Yes sir.

And the plea was adjourned etc.

ANON. (1431)

Y.B. Pas. 9 Hen. VI, fo. 9, pl. 24 (C.P.).

In a writ of detinue of charter, *Chaunterell* pleaded in bar a redelivery in another county etc.

Rolf. That is no plea, and so we ask delivery [of the charter].

Chaunterell. If we do not have this plea we are at great mischief, because those of the county in which the writ is brought can not know whether he detains or not.

Rolf. This plea is no more than an argument; as if one brings a writ of debt on a lease for a term of years in the county in which the lease was made, and the defendant pleads that [the rent] has been levied by distress in the county in which the land lies, that is no plea, but he must conclude 'and so he owes him nothing'.

COTTESMORE. This has been held a good plea, and so consider whether you will demur [on it].

PASTON. I can not see how this can be a good plea according to reason etc., and so etc.

Chaunterell said that he would imparl.

PASTON to *Chaunterell*. If you wish [it to go to] demurrer, Rolf will want to imparl.

Rolf. No indeed, because I will demur to this plea at all risks if he wishes to plead in that way; and you may so record at all risks.

MARTIN. This is a good plea, for the reason already given.

PASTON. So one can aver payment upon a simple contract!

MARTIN. No one can not, because in such a case one can wage his law.

PASTON. Then this is a good plea in debt for the arrears of an account. (Query about detinue for an obligation.)

PRIOR OF BERMONDSEY v HARDING (1482)

Y.B. Pas. 22 Edw. IV, fo. 2, pl. 8 (C.P.).

The prior of Bermondsey brought a writ of detinue against John Harding, and the plaintiff counted that the defendant detained from him a gold chain weighing four ounces and certain silver bullion amounting to the value of £10.

Starkey, for the defendant, said as to the bullion that he wished to wage his law by advice of the court; and he showed that the plaintiff had delivered to the defendant certain bullion in contentment of a certain sum of money which he owed him. Thus it seems to me that we may do our law that we do not detain them.

THE COURT. You may well do so.

So he was given a day to wage his law as to the bullion.

Starkey. As to the chain, we wish also to wage our law if the court will [so] advise; and he showed that the chain which was delivered to him weighed only two ounces, and he showed it in court, whereas the plaintiff mentions a chain of four ounces. Thus it seems to me that we may in conscience wage our law that we do not detain any such chain as he has counted.

BRYAN [C.J.] It seems to me that you may well do your law with good conscience. I conceive there is a difference between when a man counts to the value of a sum, and when he counts of a certain thing by a specific name. Thus there is a difference between alleging that he detains from me a horse worth £20 and alleging that he detains a white or a brown horse; or between counting of certain pieces of cloth worth £3 and counting of six yards amounting to the value of 40s. If I count a horse worth £20, even if it is only worth

20d. he cannot in conscience wage his law, for he cannot value the horse; and in this case if he says that he does not detain such a horse, ready to go to the country, then even if it is not worth 20d. the jury are bound on pain of attaint to find that he does detain the horse, and they shall state its value. But if he counts of a white or a black horse, worth so much, and it is a brown horse which I have, I can wage my law perfectly well to the effect that I do not detain it; and if it was being enquired into [by jury], they would be bound so to find, for it is true in fact that I do not detain any horse of that colour. And there he can have a better action.[1] Likewise in this case, if he had counted that he detained a chain worth £10, then even if in fact it was only worth 100s. he could not wage his law. But since he has said it is a chain weighing four ounces ... and you say that it is only two ounces, you may wage your law ...

And all the justices agreed; so he had a day to do his law.

ANON. (1526)

Y.B. Mich. 18 Hen. VIII, fo. 3, pl. 15;
LC MS. Acc. LL 52960, 18 Hen. VIII, fo. 3.

In detinue the plaintiff counted upon a bailment of certain goods by another hand, and the defendant tendered his law, and it was agreed by the court that he should have his law because the defendant cannot answer [just] to the bailment but must answer to the detinue. The same reason [leads to the same result] in debt on a contract made by another's hand; but it is otherwise in account [based] upon receipt through another's hand, because the receipt [itself] is traversable.

ANON. (1535)

Y.B. Pas. 27 Hen. VIII, fo. 13, pl. 35;
LC MS. Acc. LL 52960, 27 Hen. VIII, fo. 28v (C.P.).

Note that FITZHERBERT [J.] drew a distinction between where a man comes into possession of goods by bailment and where by finding. For where a man comes into possession by bailment he is chargeable by force of the bailment, and if he bails them over or they are taken out of his possession he is still chargeable to his bailor by force of the bailment. It is otherwise, however, where a man comes to the goods by finding, for there he is not chargeable

---

1 I.e. detinue for a brown horse.

except by reason of the possession, and if he is lawfully out of possession before the person entitled brings his action, he is not chargeable. (SHELLEY [J.] agreed with this.) Therefore it is a good plea in a writ of detinue, if the plaintiff counts on a bailment, for the defendant to say that he found the goods and delivered them to John Style before the action was brought, without this, that the plaintiff bailed [him] the goods.

SHELLEY. It is not, for it is only the general issue, namely that he owes him nothing.[2]

FITZHERBERT. It is clearly good, because of the unpredictability (*aweroust*)[3] of the jurors (*laies gentz*). (Query this; but they both agreed that in many cases the bailment is traversable in a writ of detinue.)

SHELLEY. So is the trover traversable in some cases. (Query this, for FITZHERBERT denied it.)

ANON. (1550)

BL MS. Hargrave 4, fo. 110v, pl. 18 (C.P.).

In a writ of detinue the plaintiff counted that he had delivered to the defendant a casket with various things in it, to be kept safely to his use, and to be returned to him on request; and he showed that the defendant had converted it to his own use, and the plaintiff had often requested its return.

Morgan. An action of detinue does not lie in this case, but an action on the case for misusing the goods.

MOUNTAGUE C.J. and HALES J. The writ lies well enough.

Morgan. I will demur on it.

HALES J. And you will have the writ ruled against you.

ANON. (1572)

BL MS. Add. 35941, fo. 35v; LI MS. Maynard 87, fo. 145v; CUL MS. Ll. 3. 8, fo. 160 (C.P.).

DYER C.J. was of the opinion that if a man finds something and then loses it, he is not chargeable in detinue. But if he bails it to a stranger to look after, or if he sells it, then it is reasonable that he should be chargeable in detinue to the first owner.

---

2 Presumably a slip for *Non detinet*.
3 Or 'bewilderment': *aweroust* means 'doubt'.

FRY'S CASE (1584)

CUL MS. L1. 3. 14, fo. 258 (C.P.).

Fry brought detinue against another for a horse, and counted of a finding. The defendant waged his law, and when he was ready to do it the facts were disclosed to the court: which were, that a felon had stolen the horse from the plaintiff and sold it in market overt to the defendant.

Thereupon ANDERSON C.J. said: be well circumspect, for by the law and statutes of the land[4] if toll is not paid and the horse ridden for an hour in the market and the marks entered in the book, or if any of these fail, the property is not altered.

But the defendant said that all these circumstances had been performed; and so he had his law.

ANON. (1595)

CUL MS. Ii. 5. 12, fo. 63 (C.P.).

In detinue on a bailment of goods, if they are taken or stolen from the defendant's possession he may not wage his law. And if a man puts his horses to livery, and the innkeeper afterwards attaches the horses by the custom of London for their sustenance,[5] he may not in detinue for them wage his law.

SOUTHCOTE v BENNET (1601)

(a) 4 Co. Rep. 83 (Q.B.).[6]

Southcote brought detinue against Bennet for certain goods, and declared that he bailed them to the defendant to keep safely. The defendant confessed the bailment, and pleaded in bar that after the bailment one John Style feloniously stole them out of his possession. The plaintiff replied that the said John Style was the defendant's servant, retained in his service, and demanded judgment. And upon this the defendant demurred in law.

Judgment was given for the plaintiff. And the reason and cause of the judgment was because the plaintiff bailed the goods to be

---

4 An Act against the Buying of Stolen Horses (1555), 2 & 3 Phil. & Mar., c. 7.
5 The custom was that if a horse left in an inn ate more than he was worth, he could be appraised and sold by the innkeeper to pay for the fodder: *Moss v Townsend* (1612) 1 Buls. 207.
6 Also reported in Cro. Eliz. 815, pl. 4.

kept safely, and the defendant had taken that upon himself by the acceptance of such delivery, and therefore he must keep them at his peril, even though in such a case he was to have nothing for their safekeeping. Likewise if A. bails goods to B. generally, to be kept by him, and B. accepts them without having anything in return for it, and the goods are stolen from him, he shall nevertheless be charged in detinue; for to be kept, and to be kept safely, are the same thing. But if A. accepts goods from B. to keep as he would keep his own goods, and the goods are stolen, there he shall not answer for them. Or, if goods are gaged or pledged to him for certain money, and the goods are stolen, he shall not answer for them, for he did not there undertake to keep them save as he keeps his own, for he has property in them and not merely custody, and therefore he shall not be charged, as is adjudged in 29 [Lib.] Ass., pl. 28.[7] But if before the stealing the party who pledged them tenders the money, and the other refuses, then there is fault in him and consequently the stealing after such a tender shall not excuse him, as is there held. Likewise, if A. bails to B. a locked coffer to keep, and he takes away the key himself, in this case if the goods are stolen B. shall not be charged, for A. did not trust B. with them and B. did not undertake to keep them: as is adjudged in 8 Edw. II, *Detinue* 59.[8] Thus the doubts which were conceived upon various discordant opinions in our books ... are well reconciled. But in account it is a good plea before the auditors for a factor to say that he was robbed ... for if a factor (even though he has wages and a salary) does all that he can do by his industry, he shall be discharged; and he takes nothing upon himself, but his duty is as a servant to trade as well as he can, and a servant is bound to perform the command of his master. But a ferryman, a common innkeeper or carrier, who take hire, must keep the goods in their keeping safely, and shall not be discharged if they are stolen by thieves: see 22 [Lib] Ass., pl. 41; Brooke [Abr.], *Action sur le case*, 78.[9]

And the court held the replication idle and vain, for it did not say by whom the defendant was robbed. See 33 Hen. VI, 1: if traitors break a prison, this does not discharge the jailer, but it is

7 *Anon.* (1355): 'There was a suit in the Exchequer by the king's debtor for a cup which was bailed by him to the defendant, and the defendant said that the plaintiff bailed him the cup in gage for certain moneys and he put it amongst his other goods, and they were stolen from him. The plaintiff was compelled to answer, and said that he tendered the moneys before the stealing and the defendant refused them ...'

8 Fitz. Abr., *Detinue*, pl. 59 (1315); same case as on p. 265, above.

9 *Humber Ferry Case* (1348), p. 358, below, which is not exactly in point.

otherwise of the king's enemies from another realm.[10] For in the one case he may have his remedy and recompense, and in the other he may not.

Note, reader: it is a good policy for whoever takes any goods to keep to take them in a special manner, namely to keep them as he keeps his own goods, or to keep them as well as he can at the plaintiff's risk, or on terms that if they chance to be stolen or purloined he shall not answer for them. For he who accepts them must take them in this or a similar way, or else he may be charged by his general acceptance. Likewise if goods are delivered to someone to be delivered over, it is a good policy to provide for himself in such a special manner, for fear of being charged by his general acceptance, which implies that he undertakes to do it.

> (b) BL MS. Add. 25203, fo. 306; LI MS. Misc. 492,
> fo. 205v; HLS MS. 2076, fo. 109; YLS MS.
> G. R29.14, fo. 145.[11]

... *Dodderidge* moved that the plaintiff ought to be barred. Yet he agreed that in detinue for goods bailed to the defendant it is not a good plea that they were stolen by thieves, as it is taken in 8 Edw. II, *Detinue* 59.[12] But those books draw a distinction between a general and a special bailment. For if a man bails his goods generally, and the bailee is robbed, he is discharged as against the bailor; but where a man undertakes to look after goods at his peril, he shall be charged even though his goods are stolen from him by thieves. And in our case it was a general bailment, in which case the law does not compel the bailee to be more careful and diligent in the custody of these goods than he is of his own goods; and so the theft of his goods discharges him. And it is in no way material that the person who stole them was his servant; for there is no doubt that a man may be robbed by his own servant just as he may by a stranger... So it seems that the plea in bar is good and the replication invalid.

Pine to the contrary. The bailment here is strong to charge the defendant, for the plaintiff bailed the goods to him to keep safely, and therefore he must keep them at his peril. It is not as if he had

---

10 Y.B. Mich. 33 Hen. VI, fo. 1, pl. 3; debt against the marshal of the Marshalsea. (Jailers were held liable for the debts of imprisoned debtors who escaped from their custody, by the equity of the statute 1 Ric. II, c. 12, concerning the warden of the Fleet.)

11 This report begins with the same opening statement as Coke's, which suggests that Coke may have had a contemporary copy of it.

12 See pp. 265, 275, above.

accepted the goods to look after in the same way as his own, in which case if he had been robbed of them and of his own goods he ought to have been discharged as against the bailor. And it is not all one case where the defendant is robbed by a stranger and where by his own servant, for when he is robbed by his servant the law imputes default to him, because he ought to oversee his servants . . .

GAWDY J. agreed. This is not a special bailment, whereby the defendant accepts the goods to look after in the same way as his own goods, but it is a bailment which charges him to keep them at his peril. And it seems that it is no plea to say in a writ of detinue that the defendant was robbed of a certain person's goods, for even if a man takes goods feloniously there is nevertheless no doubt that the person from whom they were taken may have a writ of trespass and recover his damages. Also the defendant in our case, although he had no property in the goods, could have an appeal. Thus he has a remedy over to have his goods back or damages for them, if he will pursue his remedy specially . . . Next we must see whether the replication is good. For if it is not, then even if the bar is utterly insufficient he shall not have judgment, because the demurrer is joined upon the replication and the plaintiff's pleading ought to be perfect and sound in every point . . . but he held the replication to be good; and so the plaintiff should have judgment.

CLENCH J. agreed.

So they, in the absence of the others, gave judgment for the plaintiff *nisi* ('unless anything should be said to the contrary on Friday next').

For a discussion and revision of the law of bailment as stated in this case, see *Coggs v Barnard* (1703), p. 370, below.

10 Covenant

WILLIAM SON OF BENEDICT v KERSEBROC (1225)

(a) *Curia Regis Rolls*, XII, pl. 495.

Essex. William son of Benedict of London claims against Joan widow of Henry de Kersebroc that she keep the covenant made between them about the wardship of the land and of the heir of the said Henry in Cheshunt and in Darcies.

As to which the same William says that she granted him the marriage of that heir and all the land which she held in the same vills, saving to the same Joan her dower, so that the same William should have the principal capital messuage, namely that of Cheshunt, and she should have the second messuage, if it was worth so much [as the third part due to her in dower]; and if it was not [worth so much] he would make it up to her. And that this is so, he produces suit etc.

And Joan comes and denies against him and against his suit that she ever made that covenant; and she offers to deny it in whatever way the court shall adjudge.

And so let her make her denial with her own hand the twelfth, and let her come with her law five weeks after Michaelmas . . .

(b) Ibid., pl. 1865.

Joan de Kersebroc waged law against William son of Benedict of London in a plea of covenant, the record of which is in the octave of Trinity in the year last past. And on this day she has done her law, and so [the entry ends there].

ESTHANNEY v DRAYTON (1248)

Roll and Writ File of the Berkshire Eyre of 1248,
Selden Soc. vol. 90, pl. 272.

[Berkshire.] Thomas de Drayton was summoned to answer Maud widow of Peter de Esthanney on a plea that he keep the covenant made between them about one virgate of arable land with the appurtenances in East Hanney as she can rightfully show etc.

And the aforesaid Thomas comes and denies force and wrong [and will deny it] when [and where he should]; and he says that he never made any covenant with her, nor was any covenant made between them about that land. And the aforesaid Maud shows nothing [to prove] the aforesaid covenant which is supposed to have been made between them but only her own bare word.

And so it is adjudged that the aforesaid Thomas is to go without day and that the aforesaid Maud is to take nothing by that writ, but is to be amerced for a false claim . . .

SYFREWAST v SYFREWAST (1248)

Roll and Writ File of the Berkshire Eyre of 1248,
Selden Soc. vol. 90, pl. 450.

Richard de Syfrewast was summoned to answer Roger de Syfrewast on a plea that he keep the covenant made between them about the manor of Herriard with the appurtenances.

And on this the same Roger says that whereas it was agreed between them that the same Richard, with Roger bearing his rightful share of the cost, was to do all he could to get hold of the inheritance due to Richard in Herriard, so that neither the said Richard nor his heirs should leave anything undone in getting hold of the aforesaid inheritance [or cease] to sue for their right in the aforesaid inheritance, thereby preventing Roger and his heirs from having half of the aforesaid inheritance [under a wider agreement between Roger and Richard]: the same Richard in breach of that covenant refuses to sue at Roger's cost to get his right in the aforesaid inheritance; and [Roger] says that in consequence he is the worse off and has damage to the value etc.; and he proffers a certain document [in the form of] a chirograph made between them which attests more fully the aforesaid covenant.

1 This action had been begun in the Common Bench: p. lxviii and pl. a210. It concerned land in Hampshire and was part of a wider dispute.

And Richard comes and denies force and wrong . . .; and he fully acknowledges the aforesaid agreement and whatever is contained in the aforesaid document; but he says that he will willingly sue together with Roger at Roger's cost to get hold of the aforesaid inheritance; and he says that he has never in any way acted in breach of the aforesaid covenant; and this he offers to deny against [Roger] and [against] his suit in whatever way the court shall adjudge.

And so it is adjudged that the aforesaid Richard is to wage his law with himself as the twelfth hand, and he is to come with his law [on such a day].

Afterwards the aforesaid Roger comes and lets [Richard] off [doing his] law; and so it is adjudged that the aforesaid Richard is [to go] without day, and that Roger is to be amerced.

CADIGAN v SAY (1256)

Roll of the Shropshire Eyre of 1256,
Selden Soc. vol. 96, pl. 119.

[Shropshire.] Robert de Say was summoned to answer Richard Cadigan's son Ellis on a plea that he keep a covenant made between this Ellis and the aforesaid Robert's father Hugh de Say, whose heir [Robert] is, about one messuage and half a virgate of arable with the appurtenances in Moreton.

And on this Ellis complains that, whereas Robert's father Hugh, whose heir [Robert] is, demised to him the aforesaid land and messuage for a term of ten years, so that [Ellis] was in seisin for three years in Hugh the father's lifetime, immediately upon [Hugh's] death Robert ejected him from that land, so that seven years of his term are in arrears to him; and thereby he is the worse off and has damage to the value of 100s.; and thereof he produced suit etc.

And the aforesaid Robert comes and denies force and wrong . . . And he asks to be shown, if [Ellis] has any, the writing or charter or any other document by which [Robert's] father Hugh demised to [Ellis] the aforesaid land for the aforesaid term of ten years.

And the aforesaid Ellis says he has nothing from the aforesaid Hugh showing the aforesaid term, neither charter nor any other document, but only his own bare word; and he offers the lord king one mark for an inquiry to be made by the country.

And the aforesaid Robert, since [Ellis] shows neither charter nor any other document for the aforesaid term nor anything but his own bare word, asks judgment whether he can put [Robert] to his law or to an inquest of the countryside for something [supposed to have been] done by his father.

There follows a long space in the roll, but no judgment. At pl. 297 there is another action against Robert de Say in respect of a lease by his father; but the plaintiff in that case produced an indenture, and Robert confessed the covenant, so judgment was given that the plaintiff should recover his seisin of the property and damages.

STATUTE OF WALES (1284), c. 10

Statutes of the Realm, vol. I, p. 65.

... There is provided a writ of covenant, by which sometimes movables are claimed sometimes immovables, on the basis of a covenant made between the parties which departs from the law ... When the plaintiff's count with the reason for his claim has been heard, the defendant answers: and through assertion by one party and denial by the other the case may go to a jury and be decided by jury of the countryside. And it is to be known that sometimes a free tenement is claimed by writ of covenant, as in the case when one grants land to another for a certain fixed farm, adding in the written covenant a condition that if he is not satisfied in respect of the farm it shall be lawful for him to enter and hold the land granted; and if the grantee does not make satisfaction for the farm, and the grantor lacks the power to enter the land granted according to the tenor of his writing because of his adversary's strength, in this case he should recover the tenement together with his damages by writ of covenant. And sometimes when it is agreed between the parties that the one should enfeoff the other of a tenement and should make seisin to him on a fixed day, and then afterwards he transfers that tenement to a third party and enfeoffs him, since that feoffment cannot be annulled on the basis of the earlier unperformed contract, the only redress the wronged party can obtain by writ of covenant is for his damage to be made good in money. And so in [one] case he has his action to claim the tenement by writ of covenant and in [another] case to recover money or damages [without] the tenement. And because covenants bind in an infinite variety of ways, it is difficult to mention each in particular: but according to the nature of each covenant, by the assertion of one party and the denial of the other the case will come either to a jury on the facts of the business, or to an acknowledgement of the writings put forward in court so that judgment will follow from that acknowledgement, or, [if] the writings are denied, then it will come to an inquiry into the making of the writing by the witnesses (if any) named in the writing together with [a jury of] the countryside; and if no witnesses were named or if [those named] are dead, then [inquiry must be] by a jury of the countryside only.

CORBET v SCURYE (1292)

Shropshire Eyre 1292, before John de Berwick.

(a) Record: JUST 1/740, m. 42d.

Thomas, son of Peter Corbet, complains against Richard Scurye and Richard son of Richard Pryde that, whereas the same Thomas on the Wednesday [23 January 1292] next after the feast of SS Fabian and Sebastian in the twentieth year of the king's reign, in the vill of Shrewsbury, delivered to the aforesaid Richard and Richard a horse (price 30 marks) on condition that if the aforesaid horse should be maimed or should die in their custody the aforesaid Richard Scurye and Richard Pryde ought to pay 30 marks to the aforesaid Thomas on the feast of the Purification of the Blessed Mary [2 February] next following; and the aforesaid horse did die in their custody, and for that reason the aforesaid Thomas afterwards often asked for the aforesaid 30 marks from them according to the form of the aforesaid covenant: [nevertheless] the aforesaid Richard Scurye and Richard Pryde have at all times thereafter withheld the aforesaid 30 marks and refused to yield them to him, whereby he says he is the worse and has damage to the amount of £40. And of this he produces suit.

And Richard and Richard come; and they are agreed. And Richard Scurye gives one mark for leave to make accord, and the accord is as follows: that the aforesaid Richard Scurye only acknowledges that he owes the aforesaid Thomas 20 marks for the aforesaid horse . . . And in return for this etc. the aforesaid Thomas waives his damages etc.

(b) First report: Y.B. 20 & 21 Edw. I, Rolls Series, p. 223, from CUL MS. Dd. 7. 14.

One Thomas Corbet brought a bill of covenant against B., complaining that, whereas it was covenanted between them (at a jousting which took place in the suburbs of Shrewsbury) that Thomas would bail his horse worth £20 to the aforesaid B. on the terms that if the horse was maimed or killed in the field and could not be restored in as good condition as when it was received, B. would pay him £20 at the Christmas next following: Thomas did bail the horse to him, and it was maimed, and as a result it died in his keeping; and Thomas came at Christmas and demanded the £20 according to the aforesaid covenant, but nothing [was paid], wrongfully etc.

Louther. What [proof] have you of the covenant?

Spigurnel. Good suit.

Louther. Have you anything else?

Spigurnel. No.

Louther. We pray judgment whether we need answer his suit, in the absence of writing.

(c) Second report: LI MS. Hale 188, fo. 15v; French
text only in Y.B. 20 & 21 Edw. I, Rolls Series, p. 487.

Thomas Corbet by plaint demanded £20 against Richard Scurryn and Richard FitzPride, and said that on a certain day he bailed to them a horse worth £20, to be paid at a certain day, and this same Thomas went to them to ask them to give back this beast and they would not.[2]

Louther. Sir, it is enacted by statute[3] that no one should be compelled to answer for a debt which amounts to 40s. or more without a writ; and by this plaint he demands £20 without writ; and so we demand judgment whether he need be answered in the absence of a writ.

Spigurnel. That exception would be effective if we were in the county, hundred[4] or court baron; but here we are directly before justices *ad omnia placita*, whom the king has specifically empowered to do this and to hear all manner of plaints by whomever wishes to plead, even if the debt amounts to a thousand pounds.

Louther. What you say would be right if this bailment had been made since the summoning of the eyre; but you yourself have complained that two years have passed since you bailed them this horse.[5]

It was awarded that he should make further answer.

So *Louther* asked what he had [in proof] of the debt.

Spigurnel. Good suit.

[This seems to be the point where the first report begins. If so, the objection taken in that report must have been overruled, because no mention of it is

---

2 The facts are more garbled in this report. The reporter treated the case as debt rather than covenant, and inserted it under the heading 'Debt' in a topical collection.

3 Statute of Gloucester (1278), c. 8.

4 'H', which is extended as 'heyr' in the printed Y.B.

5 This assertion does not tally with the record, where the transaction was alleged to have occurred in the January before the eyre came (in Michaelmas 1292).

made here. In this report Lowther moved on to a jurisdictional point concerning the law of arms. This too was overruled, because it applied only where both parties were participants in the joust.]

Louther. Sir, the bailment was made in form aforesaid, but because no one can know at once whether horses are [seriously][6] wounded or not, the law of arms says that they shall remain for 40 days in the keeping of those to whom they were bailed, under a certain price, until it is known whether they have been impaired or not; and we say that within three weeks we gave him back the horse in as good a condition as it was when bailed to us, if not better, and he refused it; ready etc.

Spigurnel. It was impaired by the maiming; ready etc.

The record shows that the parties settled, on terms that Scurye would pay 20 marks.

ANON. (1304)

Y.B. 32 & 33 Edw. I, Rolls Series, p. 199.

One Roger brought his writ of covenant against William, and said that, whereas he had leased to him 40 acres of land in T. for the term of two years, on condition that [William] would execute a writing [to the effect] that he would not hold the land over the two years: he has nevertheless held the land for eight years over the term, wrongfully and contrary to the covenant, to his damage of ten shillings.

Hedon. He has counted that he ought to have executed a writing, which presupposes that the covenant has not been made; and [yet] the writ says, 'to keep the covenant made between them': [so we pray] judgment of the variance.

Est. Our count says that you have held the land contrary to the covenant, and the writing would only have provided evidence of the covenant. Therefore, since you have held the land over the term—which is the main point of our action—you cannot assign variance.

Hedon. What have you [to show] the covenant?

Est. [We are] ready [to aver it].

Hedon. Covenant naturally depends on specialty (*covenaunt chiet naturelment en especialté*), and you show nothing of that [covenant]: [so we pray] judgment.

Tilton. When we complain that you should have made a writing

6   Text unclear.

and did not, and that you held the land over the term, this lies in the knowledge of the countryside; and we offer to aver these things, and you refuse the averment; [so we pray] judgment.

Hedon's objection did not prevail, for he went on to plead freehold title.

ANON. (1312)

Y.B. Pas. 5 Edw. II, CUL MS. Hh. 2. 4, fo. 118v (C.P.).[7]

A tenant in dower leased her estate, the lessee committed waste, and so the heir brought a writ of waste against the woman as tenant in dower and recovered the place where the waste had occurred. Then the woman tenant in dower brought a writ of covenant against the lessee, and she was received notwithstanding that she had no specialty to evidence the covenant: by the decision of the court.

ANON. (1321)

Eyre of London 1321, II, Selden Soc. vol. 86, p. 286 (first version).

A man brought a writ of covenant against [a defendant] and said that on a certain day in London a covenant was made between them that [the defendant] should take delivery from [the plaintiff] of a certain [quantity of] hay in Waltham for carriage from there to London for six shillings; and [the plaintiff] paid three shillings cash down; and then [the defendant] took delivery of the hay at Waltham for carriage [to London], and did not carry it but still detains it wrongfully.

Gregory. He counts that we took delivery at Waltham etc., which is outside your jurisdiction. [We ask] judgment whether you will hear the case.

Fastolf. The covenant was made in this town.

Gregory. If we were to deny that we took delivery at Waltham, you would not be able to [try the question].

HERLE. He is not complaining that you did not take delivery; and if you choose to deny [that you took it], we shall do what we have to do. So perhaps that will not be your answer.

---

7   Also reported in 4 Edw. II, Selden Soc. vol. 42, pp. 171, 192; and perhaps in Y.B. 32 & 33 Edw. I, Rolls Series, p. 296. One of Bereford C.J.'s reasons was that the deed would be in the lessee's possession; the other, that waste was a wrong.

Gregory. What have you [to show] the covenant?

Falstolf. [We are] ready [to aver it].

Gregory. Every covenant depends upon specialty, and you show none. [We ask] judgment.

Fastolf. You do not have to have specialty for a cartload of hay.[8]

HERLE. And for a cartload of hay we shall not undo the law. Covenant is nothing other than the assent of the parties, which lies in specialty.[9]

And it was adjudged that [the plaintiff] should take nothing by his writ.

The law which could not be undone for a cartload of hay may have been set aside for an untreated arrow wound, in *Warner v Leach* (1330) (Bedfordshire Eyre, unreported); see Kiralfy, *Source Book*, p. 18.

WELSHE v HOPER (1533)

Record: KB 27/1088, m. 26.

Hugh Welshe sued Hugh Hoper in the Guildhall Court of Hereford, and on 9 December 1532 counted as follows: that on 29 September 1530, at the request of Jenkin Wever of Presteigne, the defendant at Hereford covenanted with the plaintiff that he would pay him five marks on behalf of Wever, in two instalments (on named days), but he had not done so and therefore had broken his covenant. Hoper pleaded that he made no such covenant as the plaintiff alleged, and put himself on the country. On 10 December the 12 jurors returned by the serjeants-at-mace found that Hoper did make the covenant, and awarded five marks damages and three shillings costs. Judgment was given accordingly the same day. On 15 February 1533 Hoper purchased a writ of error, and in Michaelmas term assigned five errors (see Selden Soc. vol. 94, p. 324), only one of which is set out below.

... Hugh Hoper says that there is manifest error in the record and process and also in the giving of the aforesaid judgment, in that ... whereas, according to the law and custom of the realm of England, no plaint or action for breach of covenant is maintainable without specialty or writing, the aforesaid Hugh Welshe declared against the selfsame Hugh Hoper in and upon the aforesaid plaint of breach of covenant by bare words, without any specialty or writing bearing witness to the covenant ...

As to the aforesaid matter assigned above as error by the

---

8 Cf. variant III, per Asshele: 'Sir, a man cannot make a writing for every little covenant like this.'

9 Cf. variant II: 'which cannot be sued without specialty'.

aforesaid Hugh Hoper, that by the law and custom of the realm of England no plaint or action is maintainable without specialty or writing ... the same Hugh Welshe says that the record aforesaid is diminished[10] in that between the words 'before midday of the same seventh day of December' and the words 'at this court'[11] are wanting the words 'and that in the same city there is (and from time immemorial has been) a custom, amongst others, that all covenants in the same city ought to be (and have from time immemorial been) pleaded by plaintiffs orally, without any written specialty'. ...

In Michaelmas term 1534 the court rejected all the errors assigned by Hoper and affirmed the judgment. It seems from Spelman, *Reports*, p. 120, that the argument in the King's Bench turned mainly on other procedural points. Cf. *Wetenhale v Arden* (1346) in Kiralfy, *Source Book*, p. 181; Y.B. 20 Edw. III, part II, Rolls Series, p. 148; where the King's Bench held that by the 'common law' no one need answer an action of covenant without specialty, and that this rule could not be displaced by usage in eyre (in that case the eyre of Cheshire at Macclesfield) if the first eyre in the county had been held within the time of legal memory.

EDEN v BLAKE (1605)

6 Co. Rep. 43 (C.P.).[12]

Eden brought a writ of covenant against Blake, as assignee of Price,[13] and the breach was in not repairing a house. The defendant pleaded an accord between himself and the plaintiff, and execution thereof, in satisfaction and discharge of the aforesaid failure to repair; and thereupon the plaintiff demurred ...

It was objected that this action of covenant was based on a deed, which cannot be discharged except by matter of as high a nature: not by any accord or matter in pais. For nothing is so consistent with natural equity as that everything should be dissolved by the same bond with which it is tied. And it appears from all our books that neither an arbitration nor an accord with satisfaction is a plea

10 The defendant in error could allege 'diminution' if the record as set out omitted anything material.
11 This refers to the caption of the court held at Hereford on 7 December 1532, when Welshe entered his plaint and prayed the initial process against Hoper.
12 Coke's autograph report is in BL MS. Harley 6686, fo. 660. It is also reported in Noy 110, which gives the further reason that the breach assigned was only in not repairing between two certain dates, and so the accord was 'only a bar *pro tempore*, and not for a perpetual bar of the said covenant'.
13 I.e. Price had assigned his lease to Blake. It had been decided in *Spencer v Clark* (1583) 5 Co. Rep. 16, that covenant lay against the assignee of a lease.

when the action is based on a deed ... Secondly, when the action is in the realty, or mixed with the realty, accord with satisfaction is no plea ...

But it was resolved by the whole court that the defendant's plea was good in the case at the bar. For there is a distinction. When an indebtedness (*dutie*) accrues by the deed in certainty at the time when the writing is made, as by a covenant, bill or bond to pay a sum of money, this certain indebtedness takes its essence and operation originally and solely through the writing, and therefore it must be avoided by matter of as high a nature, even if the indebtedness is purely in the personalty: but when no certain indebtedness accrues through the deed, but a subsequent wrong or default together with the deed gives an action to recover damages (which are solely in the personalty) for such wrong or default, an accord with satisfaction is a good plea. As in the case at the bar, the covenant does not at the time when it is made give the plaintiff any cause of action; but the wrong or default afterwards in not repairing the house, together with the deed, give an action to recover damages for default in repairing: and since the end of the action is only to have amends and damages in the personalty for this wrong, for this reason amends and satisfaction given to the plaintiff is a good plea. For the action is not founded purely on the deed, but on the deed and also the subsequent wrong, and the wrong is the cause of action for which damages are to be recovered ...

11 Account

PERTON v TUMBY (1317)

Y.B. 10 Edw. II, Selden Soc. vol. 54, p. 109 (C.P.).

[Walter of Perton] brought a writ of account against John of Tumby and demanded an account of money which [Tumby] received at Boston on such a day from [Perton], by the hand of certain named persons [acting] on [Perton's] instructions, [for Tumby] to trade with and make profit for [Perton's] benefit; for which reason [Perton] demanded an account and [Tumby] wrongfully refused etc.

Toudeby. Sir, that on that day in that year and at that place we received any money from him by reason of his instructions, we are ready to deny against him etc.—and he meant to [wage his client's] law.

Scrop. That is a final answer to the whole [action]; and so we ask that his client or the attorney should avow it.

Toudeby. In such a plea I do not at all think that one need be avowed. And on the other hand I regard a receipt by my instructions and by my own hand as all one.

Scrop. Be avowed.

And because [*Toudeby*] saw well that he would not be [received] to the law, because the receipt was alleged [to have been made] through another's hand, *Toudeby* abandoned this answer and put himself upon the country that he received not a penny etc. . . .

ANON. (1318)

Y.B. Hil. 11 Edw. II, Selden Soc. vol. 61, p. 264 (C.P.).

One Geoffrey brought a writ of account against one B. and counted that he wrongfully did not render him an account of the time when he was his receiver etc. in that, whereas this same Geoffrey had sold so many things to X. and so many to Y., B. had received the [purchase] moneys etc.

Cambridge. Judgment whether he ought to be received to such a count; for he has counted that we wrongfully did not render [an account] etc. and has not said anything to bind us to account. You have not said that we received [the money] for our common profit, to trade or to spend, or that [we were his] common receiver; and so we demand judgment.

Ingham. We have pursued [the words of] our writ, which says no more than 'receiver of moneys'.

Cambridge. Your action is reserved against the person to whom you sold, and if you were to recover against him and against us you would have [the money] twice.

BEREFORD [C.J.]. You say nothing to bind him etc.

MUTFORD. Because you have brought your writ of account and demanded an account of what he received by the hands of X. and Y., and you have not said that he was your common receiver—whereof the country could have knowledge—[the court] awards that you take nothing [by your writ etc.].

ANON. (1367)

Y.B. Pas. 41 Edw. III, fo. 10, pl. 5 (C.P.).

In a writ of account the defendant traversed the receipt, and it was found that the plaintiff delivered £10 to the defendant upon condition that if the defendant made a conveyance (*assurance*) to him of certain land he should have the £10, and if he did not make the conveyance on a certain day he should hand it back to the plaintiff; and he said that the defendant did not make a conveyance to him of the land between those days,

Belknap. It is found that he was our receiver, and so we pray the account.

Cavendish. It is found that he was not your receiver *pur accompt rendre*, but that you handed him certain money to be handed back again upon a certain condition, and for that you shall have a writ of debt and not a writ of account. [We pray] judgment of the writ.

Belknap. We cannot have a writ of debt, for there is no contract on which we could count, such as a loan or the like; and so we cannot have another action than this here.

Cavendish. If I hand certain money to you to hand to one John, he shall have a writ of account, because the property is in him as soon as you receive the money by my hand; and he cannot have an action by writ of debt. But here at the time of the bailment the property was in the person to whom the bailment was made, so that [the bailor] can have a writ of debt and not a writ of account.

WYCHYNGHAM. When something is given upon condition, one cannot know whose property it is until the condition has been performed or broken; but here the condition is not performed, and so the property is adjudged to have been in him all the time down to the present.

Cavendish. Surely not, for at the time of the bailment the property was in the person who received the money, and when the condition was broken an action accrued to the bailor to demand the money by a writ of debt.

THORPE [C.J.] If he can have an action of debt and also an action of account, he can choose which of them he will have. So, although he can have a writ of debt, that does not oust him from the action of account.

And so he was adjudged to account.

ANON. (1367)

Y.B. Mich. 41 Edw. III, fo. 31, pl. 37 (C.P.).

In a writ of account against someone in respect of the time when he was receiver of the plaintiff's money, *Cavendish*, for the defendant, said that the plaintiff handed the money to him to carry to one John, and we delivered it to him; and we pray judgment whether you ought to have an account in respect of this.

Belknap. Sir, you plainly see that he has confessed the receipt; and what he now says would be a plea to discharge him upon the accounting.[1] So we pray the account.

Cavendish. It has always been the law that if money is handed to someone to carry to someone else, and he does not carry the money to this same person, a writ of account lies against him; but if he carries the money, and hands it to him, he is discharged of the account.

Belknap. What you say is true in so far as he is discharged upon the accounting; but not otherwise.

FYNCHEDEN. If he receives the money to hand over to someone else, then he does not receive it accountably (*de accompt rendre*). So you can say that he received it accountably, without this that he handed it to John as he says.

---

1 I.e. before the auditors.

Later they were at issue in that way.

HASTYNGES v BEVERLEY (1379)

(a) Record: CP 40/474, m. 274.

Yorkshire. Thomas of Beverley was summoned to answer Ralph of Hastynges, knight, concerning a plea that he render to him his reasonable account of the time when he was receiver of the moneys of the selfsame Ralph. And thereupon the same Ralph, by William Cruer his attorney, says that, whereas the aforesaid Thomas was receiver of the moneys of the selfsame Ralph from Michaelmas [29 September 1375] in the forty-ninth year of the reign of Edward [III] late king of England, grandfather of the present lord king, until Martinmas [11 November 1375] then next following, and during the same time received ten marks of the money of the selfsame Ralph by the hand of John Gervays of Beverley, at Beverley, for trading and making a profit therewith for the selfsame Ralph, and so that he should render a reasonable account thereof to the same Ralph when he should be requested: the aforesaid Thomas, though often requested, has not yet rendered his reasonable account of the aforesaid money to the said Ralph but has until now refused to render it and still refuses to do so. Whereby he says he is the worse and has damage to the value of £20. And thereof he produces suit etc.

And the said Thomas, by Richard of Beverley his attorney, comes and denies the force and wrong when etc. And he says that on the day and in the year aforesaid, at Beverley, he received ten marks from the commonalty of the vill of Beverley by the hand of the aforesaid John Gervays, to be delivered to the said Ralph on behalf of the aforesaid commonalty, which ten marks the same Thomas (after he received the same ten marks) has always been ready to pay to the said Ralph; and he often offered and is still ready to render to the said Ralph the same ten marks, and now proffers them here in court; without this, that he received any other money by the hand of the aforesaid John Gervays so that he should render an account thereof to the aforesaid Ralph, as the aforesaid Ralph has above counted against him. This he is ready to aver, and so he prays judgment . . .

The plaintiff demurs to this plea, and the defendant joins in demurrer.

(b) Report: Y.B. Pas. 2 Ric. II, p. 121, pl. 4.

. . . *Holt.* Since you have confessed the receipt of our money by the hand of [John Gervays],[2] as we have counted, and you are accountable to us for the profits thereof, we demand judgment and pray the account and our damages for withholding our money in your hand.

BELKNAP [C.J.] It is settled law (*ley positif*) that one shall not have damages in an action of account. As to the rest, he has recited by his answer that he was only a messenger, and he is not accountable for that by law, nor for any profit from it, when he has all along proffered the money and now does so in court—even though by the law the plaintiff cannot have another action to get his money back except by writ of account—for the receipt was not for the purpose of trading but as a messenger to hand the money to the plaintiff; for if the receipt had been for profiting and trading the lord would have stood to lose as well as to gain. And suppose my bailiff of my manor receives rent from my tenants of the manor, and retains the money in his hands for two or three years, I shall not have any action except by writ of account, and in that action I shall not recover anything but the very sum which he received; and he shall not account for any profit arising therefrom in the meantime, for he had no authority to invest the money speculatively (*il navoit my nulle garraunti de mettre lez deners en nul profit a gainer ne a perdre*). So, do you want the money or not?

PERCY. Suppose I was receiver of your money for profiting and trading, and I retained the money in my hands without putting it in trade, so that I neither gain nor lose anything, shall I not be compelled to account for the profits therefrom?

BELKNAP. Yes, certainly, for upon the accounting you will be charged that you could have put the money in trade to profit him, and if you cannot excuse yourself of that by oath or otherwise you shall be charged in respect of reasonable profits.

SKIPWITH agreed with that, because he received the money in that case upon condition that he would put the money in trade if he would, or if it could be done. But that is not so in this case, for on the facts shown he had no authority to let the money out of his hands. (So he told *Holt* that it would be as well if he took the money.)

Holt. Sir, we wish to think it over.

BELKNAP. If I am a debtor to Percy in £100, and I bail the money to John Holt to pay the money to him, and John Holt does not pay him the money, he shall have an action of account and no other action; but by this action he will recover only the same amount of money, even if Holt retains it in his hands for ten years.

2 Reads 'Ralph Bernard' in the report.

This was agreed all round.

BELKNAP. Take the money, for you will have nothing else from us. And it will be entered in the record that you have received it and [that] you will not be amerced since the defendant came on the first day and the plaintiff had a good action.

And it was so entered.[3]

ANON. (1418)

Y.B. Hil. 5 Hen. V, fo. 4, pl. 10 (C.P.).

A writ of account was brought by one A. against one H., and A. supposed by his writ that H. was his receiver of £20 accountably (*pur accompt rendre*).

To this the defendant said, by *Strangeways*, that the plaintiff bailed to him £20 by the hands of one E. to take to a Lombard in London and make an exchange, and to receive the letters of exchange and send them to the said A.; by virtue whereof he made the exchange, and received the letters and sent them to the said A., without this that [he was] his receiver in another way. We will aver these facts, and we demand judgment *Si action*.

Hals. For anything that he has said we demand judgment, and pray the account; for his plea goes in discharge of the account.[4]

HILL [J.] His plea now is quite sufficient, for this plea is tantamount to saying that he was never your receiver accountably; for he says that when the bailment occurred it was in order to exchange and not to render an account. If, however, he had said that he was [your] receiver accountably and that afterwards [you] had commanded him to make an exchange, that would not have been a plea to excuse him from accounting, though it would have been a good plea in discharge of the account.

Hals, seeing this to be the opinion of the court, said that he was his receiver accountably, without this that he made exchange in the manner alleged by him. This we will aver; and we pray the account. account.

---

3 This is confirmed by the record: 'because it seems to the court here that the aforesaid Thomas ought not in this case to account, it is decided that the aforesaid Ralph should have the aforesaid ten marks and that the aforesaid Thomas should go thereof without day etc.; and nothing concerning amercement of the aforesaid Thomas because he came on the first day of the plea etc. And be it known that the aforesaid ten marks are delivered here in court to the aforesaid William Cruer, the aforesaid Ralph's attorney'. This unusual form of judgment resulted from the defendant's having paid the money into court.
4 I.e. before the auditors.

Strangeways. He made the exchange in the way we have supposed.

ANON. (1557)

BL MS. Harley 1624, fo. 66v (C.P.).

In an action of account it is not a plea in bar of the action to say that he repaid the money by the plaintiff's command, for he [would then] confess the receipt for which he is accountable. But it is a good plea in discharge of the account.[5]

If, however, he says that he received the money to give to X., this is a good plea, because he did not receive it accountably (*pur accompt render*): per DYER J.

TOTTENHAM v BEDINGFIELD (1572)

Dalison 99, pl. 30; BL MS. Add. 24845, fo. 90v;
abridged in Owen 83 and 3 Leo. 24, pl. 50 (C.P.).

Account was brought in Suffolk by Tottenham against Edmund Bedingfield, esquire, who pleaded 'Never his bailiff *pur accompt rendre*'.

Gawdy prayed the opinion of the court whether the action would lie on the facts, for otherwise he would not trouble the jury. The case was that the plaintiff had a lease for years of a parsonage, and the defendant (having no lease nor claiming any title) took and carried away the tithes when they were set forth. Can the lessee have account against such a trespasser, or not?

MANWOOD J., who was made a justice the previous day, was of opinion that he could not. Account lies where there is privity; but wrongs are always without privity. Nevertheless, I quite agree that if someone receives my rents I may have account against him, and I create a privity by my consent afterwards in bringing the action; for although he has received the rent, he has done me no wrong, since it is not my money until it is paid to me: and therefore in the same case I may resort to my tenant and compel him to pay it to me, even though he has paid it to someone else. Thus, because the receipt of the rent is no wrong to me, I may create a privity by my consent and have account. It is otherwise if someone disseises me of land, for that is absolutely a wrong. And in our case, when the tithes are once set forth by the parishioners, the law says that they

5   I.e. before the auditors, if the account is taken.

are immediately in the parson's possession, and therefore when the defendant takes them he is a wrongdoer, and no action of account lies against him. So it was lately adjudged in the case of one Monoux of London, where someone entered by colour of a devise and occupied for a period of 20 years, and then it was adjudged for some reason that the will was void, and thereupon the person who had the right brought account; and it was adjudged that the action did not lie. Likewise here.

HARPUR J. An action of account lies against a proctor; and here the plaintiff can charge the defendant as a proctor, and it is no plea for him to say that he was not his proctor. Neither is it a plea for someone who occupies as guardian in socage to say that he was not the plaintiff's next friend.

DYER C.J. There are only three actions of account: (1) against a man as bailiff; (2) as receiver; (3) as guardian in socage. And if someone brings account against another as a receiver, he ought to charge him with the receipt of the money. And I think that if a man thinks he is an owner it is contrary to the nature of an accountant, and therefore he is not chargeable in account; but he may say that he was 'Never his bailiff *pur accompt rendre*'. For, as my brother Manwood has said, an accountant must come in by privity. But if someone claims as [against] a bailiff, even if he was not a bailiff he is still chargeable in account, just as if he were claimed to be a guardian in socage. An abator or disseisor, however, cannot be charged by account, because they pretend to be owners. And in our case the defendant pretended to be owner, and therefore no action of account lies; but the lessee may have trespass against him by the common law, for the possession of the tithes was in the lessee as soon as they were set forth and before seizure, because they are transitory. And by the statute of 32 Hen. VIII[6] he may have *de ejectione firmae*.

And in this case it was agreed that if a disseisor assigned a stranger to receive his rents, the disseisee could not have account against that receiver.

6   An Act for the true Payment of Tithes, 32 Hen. VIII, c. 7; confirmed by 2 & 3 Edw. VI, c. 13.

12 Trespass

(1) Force and arms and the king's peace

ANON. (1304)

Y.B. 32 & 33 Edw. I, Rolls Series, p. 259.

R. brought his writ against J. and others etc., and said that they came wrongfully with force and arms and cut and carried away the wood of this same R.

The defendants pleaded Not guilty.

The inquest came and said that they cut his wood, but not with force and arms.

BEREFORD therefore adjudged that [R.] should recover his damages etc., and that the defendants should be taken [and imprisoned] notwithstanding that they did not come with force and arms etc.

ANON. (1310)

Y.B. 3 Edw. II, Selden Soc. vol. 20, p. 104.

A man brought his writ of trespass for a battery etc. in the reign of the former king. During that reign the parties pleaded to the country that [the defendant] was Not guilty. Before the inquest was taken, that king died.[1] After his death the resummons was sued etc., and it was this term found that the defendant was guilty, to the

---

1 King Edward I died in 1307.

plaintiff's damage of 40 marks; and the trespasser was adjudged to prison. And so note that one was adjudged to prison for a trespass done during the reign of another king, because [the parties] had pleaded during such reign; for otherwise he would not have had the punishment.

PETSTEDE v MARREYS (1310)

Y.B. 3 & 4 Edw. II, Selden Soc. vol. 22, pp. 29, 208.

[Adam de Petstede and Joan] his wife brought a writ of trespass in the King's Bench against one [William de Marreys and others], and counted that whereas a third part of the beasts in the park of [Glynde] were assigned to this same [Joan] in dower by the assignment of this same [William], the defendants came with force and arms [on such a day and entered the park and hunted in it and took deer] and took and carried away the third part [of those deer] which belonged to the aforesaid [Joan's] dower.

Claver. They have counted supposing that we came with force etc. and took etc. the third part of the beasts and supposing [also] that the park is ours; and since the law will not allow that a [plaintiff] should recover damages on the basis that [the defendant] came with force and arms to [the defendant's] own park, [we ask] judgment whether we need answer to such a count.

Willoughby. The cause for which we should recover damages is not the coming with force and arms in itself, but the taking and carrying away of our beasts. Although we have made mention of a coming [with force and arms] these are but [formal] words etc. It is not force and arms that give cause [of action] for damages, but the wrong, etc; and so the writ is good enough.

Hertilpole. Whereas they say that we came [with force and arms] and are supposed to have taken the third part of the beasts, the other two parts [being ours], they are asserting a claim to recover [damages] for a chattel held in common and not severed. [We ask] judgment whether they should be answered on such a writ.

Willoughby. The third part [was] assigned to us, and we were seised of taking every kind of profit belonging to the third part. So we ask judgment whether this writ does not lie against him.

Hertilpole. If you were disturbed and ousted, bring the assize [of novel disseisin] and not a writ of trespass.

BRABAZON. [The plaintiff] is seised of the third part of the profit [in respect of every part and of the whole]; and he cannot be helped by any writ other than this. And then [BRABAZON] adjudged the writ good.

And then [the defendants] pleaded Not guilty. And so, etc.

TAUMBES v SKEGNESS (1312)

CP 40/192, m. 138; printed in Y.B. 5 Edw. II, Selden
Soc. vol. 31, p. 215.

Lincolnshire. Brother Walter of Skegness, master of Nun Cotham priory, is to be amerced for several defaults.

The same Walter was attached to answer Hervey de Taumbes and Agnes his wife on a plea why, whereas the same Agnes had in good faith handed to the said master at Nun Cotham a certain written agreement for inspection, the aforesaid brother Walter with force and arms took and carried away that writing and did her other grave wrongs to the serious damage of the aforesaid Hervey and Agnes and against the [king's] peace.

And as to this the same Hervey and Agnes by ... their attorney complain that whereas the aforesaid Agnes on the Friday next after the feast of the Apostles Philip and James at Nun Cotham handed over the aforesaid written agreement for inspection the aforesaid brother Walter with force and arms, namely with swords and bows and arrows, took and carried away the writing against the [king's] peace, by which they are the worse off and have suffered damage to the value of £10; and thereof they produce suit.

And brother Walter by ... his attorney comes and denies force and wrong [and will deny it] when [and where he should]. And he says that he should not answer to this writ, because he says that whereas it is said in the writ that the aforesaid Agnes in good faith handed the aforesaid writing to the aforesaid master for inspection, and afterwards in the same writ it is alleged that this brother Walter took and carried away that writing with force and arms against the [king's] peace, these two assertions are mutually repugnant; and he asks judgment of the writ etc.[2]

And Hervey and Agnes can not deny this. And so the aforesaid brother Walter [is to go] without day; and the aforesaid Hervey and Agnes are to take nothing by their writ, but are to be amerced for a false claim.

---

2 The Y.B. report is mostly concerned with an objection that the prioress of Nun Cotham should have been joined. The concluding sentence makes the defendant waive this and take the repugnancy point.

ANON (1313)[3]

Y.B. 7 Edw. II, Selden Soc. vol. 39, p. 14 (C.P.).

One A. brought his writ of trespass against B. and counted of an agreement made between them according to law merchant by which [B.] was to sell [A.] four sacks of good wool at the price of £10 a sack; and there went this same B. and treacherously put in with the wool a quantity of hemp to the weight of four stone. And the writ said 'other grave wrongs against [the king's] peace'.

Hedon. [We ask] judgment of the writ, because he has counted of an agreement made [between them], and he has counted 'against the [king's] peace'; so we ask judgment.

Friskeney. The writ says 'other grave wrongs against the [king's] peace'.

BEREFORD. Nothing can be against the [king's] peace unless it is done with force [etc.]; and [breach of the king's peace] carries imprisonment, and you have shown nothing that was done by force. So think again...

RATTLESDENE v GRUNESTONE (1317)

CP 40/218, m. 179; printed in Y.B. 10 Edw. II,
Selden Soc. vol. 54, p. 141.

Suffolk. Richard de Grunestone and his wife Mary were attached to answer Simon de Rattlesdene on a plea why, whereas the same Simon had lately bought from the aforesaid Richard at Orford a certain tun of wine for 6 marks 6s. 8d. and had left that tun in the same place until he should require delivery, the aforesaid Richard and Mary with force and arms drew off a great part of the wine from the aforesaid tun, and instead of the wine so drawn off they filled the tun up with salt water so that all the wine became rotten and was altogether destroyed to the grave damage of this Simon and against the [king's] peace.

And as to this the same Simon by his attorney complains that whereas the same Simon had bought from the aforesaid Richard at Orford the aforesaid tun, and had left it in the same place until etc., the aforesaid Richard and Mary on the Thursday [1 July 1316] in

3 Cf. Y.B. 30 & 31 Edw. I, Rolls Series, p. 487, at p. 491 per Est: 'In a writ of trespass which says "beat him and did him other grave wrongs", I can not through the phrase "other grave wrongs" count of things more serious in themselves or different in kind from the substantive wrong specified in the writ, because the "other grave wrongs" refers to similar things ancillary to the substantive wrong previously specified'.

the octave of St John the Baptist in the ninth year of the present king's reign with force and arms, namely with swords and bows and arrows, drew off a great part of the wine from the aforesaid tun and instead of the wine so drawn off they filled the tun with salt water so that all the aforesaid wine was destroyed etc., to the grave damage etc., and against [the king's] peace etc. whereby he says that he is the worse off and has suffered damage to the value of £10; and therefore he produces suit etc.[4]

And Richard and Mary come by . . their attorney and they deny force and wrong [and will deny it] when [and where they should] etc. And well do they deny that on the day and in the year aforesaid they ever drew off the aforesaid wine with force and arms or instead of the wine put in salt water or did him any other wrong as the aforesaid Simon complains. And of this [they] put themselves upon the countryside, and so does Simon. And so the sheriff is told to cause to come [a jury on such a day].

TOTESHALLE v ORFEVRE (1321)

Eyre of London, Selden Soc. vol. 86, p. 149.

John de Toteshalle complains by bill that, whereas he delivered a sealed coffer in which there was £40 to a certain John Orfevre of London to look after, the aforesaid John Orfevre and John de Bretham with force and arms took the aforesaid coffer and broke it open, and took the money and carried it away etc. And because a man could not be understood to take a thing that was in his own keeping by force and arms against the peace, and because a bill of detinue of chattels would have served him appropriately in this case, he was not answered.[5]

And note[6] that there is a difference between putting something in deposit and in custody. In deposit is where I hire some place in your house from such a time until such a time, and put a hutch or coffer there at my own risk: and if you come and break open this coffer I shall have a writ of trespass against you for breaking open my coffer with force and arms, notwithstanding that it is [in] your own house. But if I lease or deliver to you a coffer full of money or

---

4 The Y.B. reports two objections advanced by the defendants before they took the issue recorded in the roll, one being this: '[We ask] judgment of the count, for you have said that we were seised and that we came with force and arms, and this does not make sense . . .'
5 I.e. the bill abated.
6 This note follows in only two of five manuscripts.

something else, to keep until a certain day, and I bring a writ of trespass [alleging] that you came with force and arms and broke open this coffer, you shall abate the writ: for you cannot come with force and arms to break open what is in your own keeping, because if the coffer was plundered or lost through your fault (or in any other manner) you would have to answer why you detained it beyond the time. In that case I shall not have recovery from you unless by a writ of covenant or detinue of chattels.

HOUTON v PASTON (1321)

Eyre of London, Selden Soc. vol. 86, p. 282.

John of Houton complained of John of Paston that on 13 August 1313 he, together with others who did not appear, at Cheap in London, beat and wounded him so that 14 splinters were removed from his head, and falsely imprisoned him in Newgate for eight days. The defendant pleaded Not guilty.

A man complains by bill of battery by three persons. One came, and the other two made default. The one who appeared pleaded Not guilty.

The inquest came and was charged concerning this same person who had pleaded, and HERLE [J.] told them they ought not to inquire in respect of the others. Then the inquest came [back] and said that he had struck him.

HERLE asked them whether it was with force and arms.[7]

HERVEY [DE STANTON J.]. They have told us that he struck him, and so it was with force and arms.

HERLE. No sir. If he struck him by misadventure, or in some other manner without intending it (*saunz son gree*), that would not be with force and arms; for there can be no force without the will to use force.

Then the inquest found that he struck him with force and arms, to his damages of 100s.

[HERVEY. He says he was wounded, and that 14 splinters were taken out of his head, and lost a whole half year's earnings (*purchace*), and was in danger of death. Think again, therefore, as to the damages.

The inquest. There were others who did more than he did, and you have only charged us concerning him.][8]

---

7   Another text puts the question in terms of the *contra pacem*.
8   From different text.

HERLE. Good people, assess the damages for the whole trespass, even though this party only did him part of the harm and the others did another part.

[*The inquest.*] Sir, you did not charge us concerning the others.

HERLE. [You are not asked to find] whether they are guilty or not[9]; but you should know that the trespass is all one in itself, and if he recovers damages now against this same party he shall never after recover damages for the same trespass against anyone else. If, however, the others are later attainted at his suit for the same trespass, they shall make contribution to the damages now recovered.

Therefore the inquest assessed the damages as 20 marks.

KNOSTON v BASSYNGBURN (1329)

Eyre of Northamptonshire, I,
Selden Soc. vol. 97, p. 363.

A bill was brought against someone, saying that the defendant took a certain horse worth 12s. in the king's highway and still detains the same horse, against the peace etc.

And the words 'in the king's highway' were taken out, because taking a horse in the king's highway is remedied by statute,[10] and this bill is wholly at common law, not mentioning the statute.

And because the bill is a bill of trespass against the peace, in which detaining (*le detinet*) is not a cause of action, they took out the *detinet* clause on the ground that it was not the correct form ...[11]

COLAN v WEST (1367)

Record: KB 27/428, m. 56.

John West, carter, was attached to answer Christine Colan in a plea why ...[12] on the Tuesday next after the quindene of Easter in the fortieth year of the reign of the present king, with force and

9 'Ceo est verdict a dire le quel il sunt coupable ou noun': the meaning is unclear. The other text says, 'You are not charged as to the trespass which he committed, but as to the damages for all the trespass committed by him and the others ...'

10 Statute of Marlborough, c. 15.

11 The record shows that the bill was amended to a complaint in common form of taking and leading away the horse: *cepit et abduxit* instead of *cepit et adhuc detinet*.

12 Note of writ omitted here.

arms, namely with swords etc., he so improvidently drove a certain cart at London in the parish of St Vedast, in the ward of Farringdon Within, that a certain piece of timber fell upon the aforesaid Christine and knocked her to the ground, and the same John drove the cart over her when she was thus lying on the ground, so that her face is extremely deformed and her head so badly crushed that she has lost her sight, hearing and sense of smell, against the peace of the lord king; whereby she says she is the worse and has damage to the extent of £100. And thereof she produces suit etc.

The city of London came and claimed the right to hear the case, which was conceded. The case does not appear in the city plea rolls.

ANON. (1374)

Y.B. Mich. 48 Edw. III, fo. 25, pl. 8.

One Henry T. brought his writ of trespass against a woman, and supposed by his writ that she had burnt his house in G. with force and arms; upon this the woman had earlier pleaded Not guilty. And now the inquest came and was charged on the point; and the inquest said that the house was burnt by the woman's fault through bad care.

WYCHYNGHAM to the inquest. Did the woman come with force and arms to do this wrong as the plaintiff has supposed, or did it happen by her negligence and not by force?

The inquest. Sir, the house was burnt by the woman's negligence, and not by force and arms [or] by her malice, because the woman had the house as the plaintiff's tenant from year to year at a rent of 11s. a year.

Belknap. [So] you find that the woman had no right in the house except at the plaintiff's will, to put her out whenever he chose.

And then the inquest was about to say what *Belknap* had told them, for which WYCHYNGHAM reproached him.

And the *the inquest* said definitely that she was in for a term of one year at a rent of 11s.

WYCHYNGHAM. In case the action is held good, tell us how much the damages should be.

The inquest. Sir, to his damages of 100s.

And then the inquest was bidden farewell.

Belknap. Sir, the inquest at one point said that she had the house only as tenant at will, and so this action is available to us and no other, because we can not have a writ of waste against tenant at will; nor is the writ of waste available to us in this case because it is found that she had only a term of one year [whereas] the writ [of waste] speaks of a term of years [in the plural].

WYCHYNGHAM. It is expressly found that she had a term of one year, etc.; and that seems to be right, because it is found that the rent reserved was to be paid by the year, which must be understood as entitling her to hold throughout the entire year, because no rent could have been reserved upon a tenancy at will; so we wish to consider until the next court day etc.

For an unsuccessful attempt to bring an action on the case against a tenant in similar circumstances, see *Countess of Shrewsbury v Crompton* (1600), p. 565 below.

ANON. (1390)
Y.B. Hil. 13 Ric. II, p. 103, pl. 2.

In trespass brought against a husband and wife, *Woderove* counted of a horse killed with force and arms in a certain place.

Gascoigne. We make protestation that we do not confess that [we] came with force and arms, but we say that the same wife had the horse as a loan from the plaintiff to ride to a certain place, and we demand judgment whether he can maintain this action against us.

And this was held a good plea.

So *Woderove*, for the plaintiff, said: it is perfectly true that the wife had the horse as a loan to ride to a certain town; and we say that she rode to another town, as a result of which the horse was weakened to the point of death; and then she brought the same horse back to the place mentioned, where the husband and wife killed it. And we demand judgment.

Gascoigne. Now we demand judgment of his writ, which says 'with force and arms', for by his own confession he ought to have had a writ on his case. (Note that.)

So *Woderove* said: we will imparl.

NOTE OF AN INNER TEMPLE DISCUSSION
(*c.* 1491)
BL MS. Hargrave 87, fo. 51v.

If I lose my money at dice through the procurement of another, without compulsion, there is no remedy because it was foolish of me and was an unnecessary thing. But if it was by compulsion, an action *vi et armis* [may be] joined with trespass on the case. If, however, a tailor destroys my gown by bad workmanship, there [I shall have] trespass on the case and not *vi et armis*. (The reason is apparent.) And there it is a necessary thing, like food and drink, whereas playing with dice is not. That distinction has been [approved], by opinion of the justices. And there was a similar case in a writ in Sheffield's register,[13] supposing that the defendant *vi et armis* compelled the plaintiff to kiss someone's toe, *in opprobrium etc.* It is to be remembered that the writ was *vi et armis* mixed with matter on the case, [and so] it is like playing dice by compulsion. But without compulsion there is no remedy in either case.

ANON. (1592)

BL MS. Lansdowne 1073, fo. 131 (C.P.).

In trespass the words *vi et armis* were omitted in the declaration and the verdict. And, according to WALMSLEY J., this is a matter of substance, and is the only difference between an action on the case and this action: ergo, it shall not be amended.

BRIGGES v SHREEVE (1596)

Record: KB 27/1334, m. 359; cited, 2 Buls. 215. William Shreeve brought a writ of trespass in the Common Pleas against Richard Brigges for a battery at Tunstead, Norfolk, on 1 January 1594. Judgment by default was entered for £6 13s. 4d. damages as assessed upon a writ of inquiry, and £60 damages awarded by the court on view of the wound. The defendant brought a writ of error in the King's Bench, and assigned as error that the count (in the imparlance roll) was 'whereas (*cum*) the selfsame Richard on the first day of January . . . *vi et armis* assaulted the selfsame William etc.', and so made but a recitation of the trespass mentioned in the writ.

Cro. Eliz. 507, pl. 32 (untr.).[14]

. . . *Clerke.* The first declaration is so [i.e. with the *cum* clause], but thereto the defendant imparled, and after entered this second declaration against him and in that *cum* is omitted, and judgment is given thereupon for the plaintiff.

Sed non allocatur, for the first declaration is the principal, and

---

13 The text is corrupt at this point, and it is possible that this is a case put by Sheffield. The reference is to Robert Sheffield (d. 1518), bencher of the Inner Temple.

14 Sub nom. *Briggs v Sheriff.*

thereupon the judgment is given, and the second ought to accord with the first, *et non è converso*. Wherefore it was reversed.

The margin of the roll is marked 'judgment reversed', though no formal entry of reversal was made. The judgment was followed in *Sherland v Heaton* (1614) 2 Buls. 214.

SPENCER'S CASE (1613)

CUL MS. Ii. 5. 26, fo. 43v (K.B.).

A man brought an action on the case for coursing a bull with dogs, whereby it died; and the writ said 'coursed with force and arms with certain dogs' (*cum quibusdam canis vi et armis fugavit*).

And by the opinion of CROKE J. it was good nevertheless, for this may be with force and arms.

And it was said at the bar by someone who was not of counsel with the [parties][15] that this is purely of the nature of an action on the case. (Query.)

REYNOLDES v CLARKE (1615)

Record: CP 40/1963, m. 1185d.

Norfolk. John Clarke, late of Shipdham in the aforesaid county, husbandman, was attached to answer Nathan Reynoldes concerning a plea why with force and arms he so improvidently steered a certain wagon ... Whereupon the same Nathan, by John Cooke his attorney, complains that the aforesaid John, on 20 September [1613] in the eleventh year of the reign of the present lord king as king of England, with force and arms etc. at Hingham, so improvidently steered a certain wagon of his that by the improvident steering the aforesaid wagon overturned and threw to the ground a certain mare of the said Nathan's which was tethered to and drawing Nathan's wagon, loaded with various goods and chattels, and broke one of the leg-bones of the aforesaid mare, so that by the throwing of the aforesaid mare to the ground and the breaking of its aforesaid leg-bone the aforesaid mare (worth £10) died; and other outrages etc.; to the grave damage etc.; and against the peace etc.: whereby he says he is the worse, and has damage to the amount of 20 marks. And thereof he produces suit etc.

And the aforesaid John, by Robert Halman his attorney, comes and denies the force and wrong when etc. and prays leave to imparl

15   Reads 'plaintiff' in MS.

therein here until the octaves of St Hilary. And he has it etc. The same day is given to the said Nathan, here etc.

No more is entered.

HIDE v CYSSELL (1620)

Record: KB 27/1482, m. 157. Humfrey Hide brought trespass against Edmund Cyssell (*alias* Sisson), alleging that on 21 August 1608 in London he assaulted Elizabeth, the plaintiff's wife, and beat and ill-treated her, and took and carried away the said Elizabeth together with a gown, a petticoat, a smock and a head-dress (*gallerum*), valued at £20, of the plaintiff's goods and chattels, and detained and kept her for five years without the plaintiff's leave, whereby (*per quod*) the plaintiff wholly lost the comfort and company (*solamen et consortium*), and also the advice and help in domestic affairs, which the plaintiff could and should have had and enjoyed with his wife during that time. Cyssell pleaded Not guilty, and on 12 May 1619 at the Guildhall, before Mountague C.J., the jury found for the plaintiff with £300 damages. Judgment was given accordingly. The following February a transcript of the record was transmitted to the statutory Exchequer Chamber by virtue of a writ of error.

(a) Cro. Jac. 538, pl. 6 (untr.).[16]

. . . The first error assigned was because the action was [brought] by the husband solely, for the battery of his wife, which ought not to be: for the tort and damages are properly done to the wife; and therefore the husband sole, without the wife, could not maintain this action . . .

But all the justices and barons held that, true it is the husband, for the battery of his wife, ought to join his wife with him in the action, if this had been brought for that cause; but here the action is not brought for the battery of his wife, but for the loss and damage of the husband for want of her company and aid . . .[17]

Wherefore the judgment was affirmed.

(b) HLS MS. 1080, fo. 182v.[18]

. . . The error assigned was that the words *per quod solamen etc.* refer solely to the last clause (namely the detaining for five years), and for the assault no action lies by the husband alone without his

16 Sub nom. *Hyde v Scyssor*, and dated Trin. 17 Jac. I.
17 The same reasoning is found in the slightly earlier King's Bench case of *Guy v Livesey* (1618) Cro. Jac. 501; 2 Rolle Rep. 51. Reference was made in the case to *Cholmley's Case* (1585), where a husband successfully brought an action for the battery of his wife 'whereby his business remained undone'.
18 Sub nom. *Scisson v Hyde*, and dated Trin. 19 Jac. I.

wife, unless he has alleged a special cause; and since the damages are given entirely [i.e. for both matters] it is erroneous.

But the opinion of the court was that the *per quod* has reference to everything, since all was contained in one sentence and all was alleged to have been done at one time. If, however, the assault had been on one day and the taking on another, it would have been erroneous.

Another objection was that the declaration said *cepit et abduxit*, where it should have been *rapuit et abduxit*.

To this the court said that it was good enough, being in the declaration; though it seems it would have been otherwise had it been in the writ.

And the judgment was affirmed.

The record shows that the Exchequer Chamber affirmed the judgment on 11 November 1620. The decision was cited and followed in the Exchequer Chamber in the very similar case of *Younge v Priddie* (1627) KB 27/1553, m. 777; Cro. Car. 89. The record of the latter case shows that the London jury awarded a husband £200 damages in trespass for taking his wife with various chattels, and detaining her for half a year, whereby the husband lost *solamen et consortium necnon concilium et auxilium in rebus domesticis*.

THE NEWE LITTLETON (*c.* 1644)

Lord Littleton's Regal digest, HLS MS. 2106
from the title *Adultery* (untr.).

If a man come into another man's house or upon his land, and there commit adultery with his wife, he may have an action of trespass for coming there and by reason of the general words *et alia enormia ei intulit* may give in evidence the adultery for increasing of damages. And hereof there have been divers cases allowed by the judges,[19] and very great sums given by the jurors thereupon for damages, the foulness of the fact requiring it. And this extends to the abuse of a man's child, and the action to be brought in the father's name.[20] And I take it to be so for a servant, especially if

19 Littleton's own marginal note reads: 'Cole's case (the first [deleted]). Moore's case of the county of Salop, wherein I was of counsel, and £400 damages given, about the end of the reign of King James; and many more'.

20 Littleton's own marginal note reads: 'Such an one tried at Norwich, at the summer assizes 16° Caroli [1640] before me, being then chief justice of the Court of Common Pleas, for an abuse to a daughter by one that pretended to be a suitor and under that show had access and got her with child'. See also *Norton v Jason* (1653) Style 398; printed at p. 353, below; *Sippora v Basset* (1664) 1 Sid. 225; *Russell v Corne* (1704) 2 Ld Raym. 1031, 1032, per Holt C.J.

there be loss of service—as it can hardly be otherwise. And by a special custom in London if information be given unto any constable there that any within his jurisdiction is with any woman in adultery, he may call the beadle and others of the same parish and go unto the house, and if they find the man in adultery to take and conduct him unto the compter[1] and there leave him in prison until he shall pay so much or be there delivered by the due course of the law; and this is held to be a good custom . . .[2]

(2) Justifications and other pleas in bar

GYSE v BAUDEWYNE (1310)

Y.B. 3 & 4 Edw. II, Selden Soc. vol. 22, p. 4 (K.B.).

John de Gyse brought a writ for the abduction of his wife against [Thomas Baudewyne] and others; [and the writ demanded] why on the eve of the feast of the Conversion of St Paul with force and arms etc. they carried away and abducted Isabel his wife together with [his] goods and chattels to [such a] value etc.

Laufare denied the coming with force and arms and anything against the [king's] peace etc., and the abduction and anything against the statute[3] provided for such a case, and the damages; and he said: you can not have action by this writ because this Isabel whom you call your wife is our wife, and was so years and days before you obtained your writ and on the day of which you have counted. Ready etc. And we ask judgment whether you can have such an action.

Claver.[4] That Isabel was our wife and that we were seised of her as of our wife on the day of which [you] have counted, [we are] ready etc. And besides you yourself have sued a divorce, so supposing that she is not rightly your wife, which suit is still pending. [We ask] judgment whether you can say that she is your wife.

Westcote. Whereas you say that we sued a divorce and therefore that she is not our wife, you argue badly. And we ask judgment, since you acknowledge that we sued a divorce and that the suit is still pending and therefore that she is still our wife, whether you

1 A London prison: cf. pp. 413, 414, below.
2 *Gylys v Watterkyn* (1485) Y.B. Mich. 1 Hen. VII, fo. 6, pl. 3; CP 40/893, m. 244 (pleaded as a justification in false imprisonment; no judgment).
3 Statute of Westminster II, c.34.
4 Before this speech, a speech for the plaintiff may be missing.

ought to be answered as to something contrary to your own admission.

Claver. What we said about the divorce is not the substance of our answer: rather do we say that she was our wife on the day of which you have counted, and years and days before then was she our wife. Ready [are we to aver] that on such a day in such a year and in such a place she was espoused to us; and she lived with us as our wife until John de Gyse abducted her with force, so that we came to such a place and there found her clothed in the same clothing that we had given her, and she followed us [thence]. And we ask judgment, as before.

BRABAZON [C.J.]. So you did not abduct his wife.

Passelewe. That she was our wife espoused to us on such a day in such a year and in such a place, [we are] ready etc.

BRABAZON. If she was your wife, she was not his. And so you can say that you did not abduct [his wife].

Passelewe. Statute[5] gives action to the husband only because of the chattels taken away with his wife. So we say that she is our espoused wife, and so etc.; [and we ask that inquiry on this be made by the jury of] the place where the espousals were made.

BRABAZON. It is not for this court to inquire into the making of the espousals, nor will we send to the bishop to inquire whether she was your wife. Rather must you answer whether you abducted his wife or not.

Passelewe. That [we did] not, [we are] ready etc.

And the others said the opposite.

And note that [on this issue] it is not proper to have a writ to get a jury from the neighbourhood where [the defendant said] the espousals had taken place. And [this is] hard [on him].

ANON. (1348)

Y.B. 22 Lib. Ass., pl. 56.

In a bill of trespass for beating, wounding, maiming and imprisoning [the plaintiff]:

Fyncheden. As to the maiming and the wounding, Not guilty. And as to the battery and the imprisonment, we tell you that at the time the plaintiff was in a mad fit and doing great harm; and for this reason the defendant and [the plaintiff's] other relations took him and tied him up and put him in a house and chastised him and beat him with a rod, without this that we imprisoned or beat him in

5 Statute of Westminster II, c.34.

any other manner; and we do not think that for such imprisonment and battery he can assign wrong in our person.

Richemund. You did it of your own wrong, and without such cause; ready etc.

And the others said the opposite.

Note that in a bill of false imprisonment, the defendant justified the imprisonment on the ground that the plaintiff came with other wrongdoers in the township of C. with swords and bucklers etc. and beat and wounded J. de F. so that his life was despaired of, and the hue and cry was therefore raised so that [the defendant] as steward of the same township took and arrested the plaintiff until it should be known whether the same [J. de F.] would live or die; and we do not think that for this you can assign wrong in our person. And the plaintiff tendered the averment that [the defendant did it] of his own wrong [and without such cause]. And the others said the opposite.

Again in trespass for beating and wounding, the defendant justified what he had done on the ground that one W. de M. attacked the defendant with a drawn knife in his hand and tried to stab the defendant, and [the defendant] seized the handle of the knife in his hand, and the plaintiff came to that W.'s aid and seized the blade of the knife from the defendant's hand and so cut his own hand with the same blade, without this that [the defendant] beat and wounded him, ready etc.[6]

Scrop. You beat and wounded us as we allege, ready.

And others said the opposite.

ANON. (1353).

Y.B. 27 Lib. Ass., pl. 64.

Note that in the King's Bench one A. brought a bill of trespass against a [defendant] for having taken his horse of such a price at S. and led it from there to P. and there killed it wrongfully and against the [king's] peace etc.

The defendant. We tell you that we took the horse damage feasant in our several pasture at S. and led it to [P.] which was the common pound of the same township of S. and put it within the said pound etc.; and the horse was unbroken, and three times it almost jumped over the enclosure of the said pound, although [that enclosure] was as high as it had ever been as far back as anyone can remember; and so we took [the horse] and tied it with a halter to a

---

6 This second reminiscence added to the principal report seems to be from an earlier time.

post in the same pound, and later it struggled so much that it strangled itself. And we ask judgment whether for that you can assign wrong in our person.

And *the plaintiff* said: since you have acknowledged the killing of our horse, as above, we ask judgment and pray our damages.

And *the defendant*: we ask judgment of the bill since you have acknowledged that the property was in us at the time of the killing etc. which is the reverse of your bill; because by the wrongful taking the property was at that moment divested from you and vested in us, and it follows that we could not kill our own horse against the peace and so etc.

SHARESHULL [C.J.] was about to abate the bill on this ground. But the plaintiff had another bill in court, by which nothing was alleged except that the defendant had killed his horse against the peace.

And *the defendant* sought to justify what had happened on the grounds given above.

And so it was adjudged that the plaintiff should recover his damages.

ANON. (1367)

Y.B. Mich. 41 Edw. III, fo. 29, pl. 30 (C.P.).

One John brought a writ of trespass against a man and his wife and counted that they wrongfully took his horse.

Belknap. We say that William, the [defendant] husband, as he was on his way to Canterbury bailed six dishes to the plaintiff to be redelivered on his return; and he did not redeliver them, so that we sued a plaint against him in the court of W. of T.; and the bailiff came and attached the [plaintiff's] horse, and we came in aid of [the bailiff]; judgment whether [you can assign] wrong [in us].

And on behalf of his wife *the husband* said that she [too] came in aid of the bailiff.

Kirkton. [That is] tantamount to Not guilty.

FYNCHEDEN. It would be badly pleaded to plead Not guilty in such a case.

Belknap. At least for the wife he ought to plead Not guilty, because whatever she did it was together with her husband, and that can not be adjudged her own doing but the doing of the husband; because a wife can not conspire with her husband.

FYNCHEDEN. The wife could lead the horse away from where it was, and then she would be party to the taking.

And so *Kirkton* said that they took [the horse] of their own wrong without any such cause, ready.

And the others said the opposite.

ANON. (1481)

(a) Y.B. Pas. 21 Edw. IV, fo. 28, pl. 23 (C.P.).

Trespass for breaking a close, turning over land, and treading down grass in H. The defendant pleads in bar that the place in question is an acre of land called a 'furrer',[7] and that the custom of that land from time immemorial was for everyone who has land on the said furrer (i.e. headland), when ploughing his land, to turn his plough upon the said headland; and that the defendant had half an acre of land abutting on the said land, and in ploughing the said acre he turned his plough on the said land, and while turning the point of his coulter scraped a small piece of his land, and also one of his oxen took a mouthful of grass: and that is the same trespass.

And now, this term, *Townshend* recited the plea and thought it should not be good; for the custom which he has alleged is not alleged to be throughout the region (*pais*) or throughout a vill, but only in one close, and so it is not a custom. The plea is therefore not good.

LITTLETON. It seems to me that he must show that the land was not sown. And even if he alleges this custom, it is to no avail, for if a prescription is unreasonable (*encounter reason*) it is void. That was ruled here, when a custom was alleged that no one should put his beasts in the common before the lord put in his beasts, and this custom was adjudged to be nought, for it is unreasonable: for if the lord would never put his beasts in the tenants would lose the profit of their soil.[8] (It would be otherwise if a day was specified.) Likewise in the case at bar, it would be unreasonable to prescribe to turn upon his land when it has been sown, for by the turning the crops (*lembleer*) would be destroyed.

BRYAN [C.J.] If I have an acre of land near your land, [I cannot occupy my land unless I turn upon your land],[9] and *vice versa*. So it makes no difference whether it is sown or not, for each has the same advantage against the other: and it is a custom used throughout the realm of England to do this.

---

7 This word is not in the English dictionaries, but it corresponds to Latin *foreria* and Anglo-Norman *forere*, a headland.

8 Y.B. Trin. 2 Hen. IV, fo. 24, pl. 20.

9 Words omitted by haplography in the 1680 ed.

Later they demurred in judgment.

(b) Y.B. Pas. 22 Edw. IV, fo. 8, pl. 24.

A writ of trespass was brought, and the plaintiff counted by *Townshend* according to his writ, '[that] he turned over his soil in four acres of land, and damaged and consumed his grass etc., to the value etc.'

Sulyard, for the defendant, said Not guilty as to all the trespass supposed in all the lands except half an acre, parcel thereof; ready. As to this half acre, the plaintiff ought not to have his action; for we say that the custom in the county of Middlesex (where this action is sued) is that when anyone goes ploughing in the same county it should be lawful for him to turn his plough round on the next adjoining land, if it be not sown with other grain; and he set out the custom.

CATESBY [J.] You do not make out a good justification, for you say 'it should be lawful', and yet even if it is lawful it is no good if it has not been used. Therefore you must set out also that it has been used since time immemorial in the same county.

This was the opinion of the whole court ... And so *Sulyard* said that they were accustomed in the county of Middlesex that whenever anyone went ploughing in the same county it should be lawful for him to turn his plough round on the next adjoining land, if it was not sown with other grain.

CATESBY. As to that [last] point, the custom is that he may turn his plough whether or not the land is sown. That is the custom in my county[10] and also in yours,[11] and in all the counties in England. So you need not say 'if it was not sown'.

So he set out the custom as above, and said that this half acre was the next land adjoining the plaintiff's land, and he went ploughing there, and by virtue thereof he turned his plough round on the said half acre. And as to the turning over of the soil, we say that on account of the rashness (*reclessure*)[12] of the horses and other beasts in the plough [we] could not well control them, and against [our] will [we] turned over the quantity of one foot, which is the same turning over of the soil. As to damaging the grass growing there, we say that one of [our] oxen going in the plough, against our will took one mouthful only at the same place where the turning over occurred, and that was in turning our plough; which was the same damaging. And we demand judgment.

10 Catesby lived in Northamptonshire.
11 Sulyard lived in Suffolk.
12 Exact meaning is uncertain: perhaps an attempt to turn 'recklessness' into French.

Townshend. Since he has confessed a trespass, we demand judgment; for it should not be lawful for anyone to take a mouthful of grass in someone else's soil.

CATESBY. I say that he can indeed justify as he has done here, if the custom is as he has alleged. For if a man comes with a drover of oxen along the highway, where trees, wheat and other grain is growing, I say that if any of the beasts take part of this grain against the will of the person who drives them, he may well justify; for the law will presume that a man cannot govern them as he wishes all the time. But if he allows or continues them, it is otherwise.

BRYAN [C.J.] to *Townshend.* They do in my county[13] as Sulyard has said, and in every county that I know of, except yours (i.e. Norfolk), where you gag your horses so that they cannot do it.

The justification was held good, if the custom was as he supposes; and it was adjourned.

CUNY v BRUGEWODE (1506)

Record: CP 40/978, m. 449. Robert Cuny, esquire, and William Draycote, clerk, brought trespass against Thomas Brugewode and three others for breaking their close at Caverswall, Staffordshire, and taking 42 cartloads of wheat, oats, rye and barley standing in sheaves. The defendants pleaded (as to part) that the place in question was a barn and four acres in a great field in the parish of Caverswall, and the grain was separated out as tithes, and the prior of St Thomas's as parson imparsonee leased the barn and the tithes to the plaintiffs for three years; and since the grain was lying out in the field, in danger of destruction by cattle belonging to the men of the vill, the defendants entered and collected the sheaves and put them in carts and took them to the barn, to the plaintiff's use, in order to save them. The plaintiffs demurred.

Y.B. Trin. 21 Hen. VII, fo. 27, pl. 5.[14]

... *Brudenell.* The plea is not good, for when the [tithe] corn was separated from the nine parts and left on the land where it grew, it was in a place apart and convenient for storage, in which case it is not lawful for anyone to enter and take it. Similarly, if a man takes my horse for fear of it being stolen, it is not justifiable. And if a woman loses her way, so that she does not know where she is, a man shall nevertheless not take her to his house, unless she is in

13 Bryan C.J. lived in Buckinghamshire.
14 Briefly reported in Keil. 88, pl. 4.

danger of being lost through the night or drowned with water.[15] Likewise here ... and so the bar is not good.

Palmes. We have alleged that they were in danger of being lost, and if we had not taken them they would certainly have been lost; and that is a sufficient and reasonable cause for us to justify the taking. Similarly, if I see my neighbour's chimney burning, I shall justify entering his house to save the things inside, and taking the goods which I find there to save them ...

KINGSMILL. Where someone's goods are taken against his will, it must be justified either as a thing necessary for the common weal or by reason of a condition in law ... But we are outside those cases here, for this is not a case concerning the common weal or a condition. Even though the corn was in danger of being lost, it was nevertheless not in such danger but that the party might have his remedy. If I have beasts which are damage feasant [on someone else's land], I shall not justify entering to drive them out, but must first tender amends. Here, therefore, when the defendant took the plaintiff's corn so that it should not be destroyed, it is nevertheless not justifiable; for if it had been destroyed the plaintiff could have had his remedy against him who destroyed it. And although he took it to the plaintiff's barn, it is possible that the plaintiff would have kept this barn for something else, and so no advantage to the plaintiff can be presumed from it; and so the bar seems not good.

REDE [C.J.]. Although the defendant's intention here was good, nevertheless the intention cannot be construed. In felony, however, it shall be: as where a man shoots arrows at the butts, and kills a man, it is not a felony [because] he did not have the intention of killing him ... But to return to the case here, when he took the corn, even though it was a good deed with respect to the damage which a stranger's beasts might do to it, yet it is not a good deed or any kind of justification against the party whose property the corn was, because if it had been destroyed he could have had his advantage (by action) against the person who destroyed it ... and it is not like the case where things are put in danger of being lost in water, or by fire, and such like, for then there is destruction without remedy against any person for this destruction. Thus the plea is not good.

FISHER [J.] was of the same opinion...

The record shows that the court held the plea insufficient in Hilary term 1507, but judgment was not entered until the issue of fact had been tried. The jury found for the plaintiffs, and judgment was then given accordingly.

15 Perhaps the meaning is 'drenched with rain'.

ANON. (1560)

Moo. K.B. 19, pl. 67 (C.P.).

In a writ of trespass, the defendant justified by reason that one John Style was seised of an acre of land and leased it to him for ten years, and then one A. entered in the said land thus leased and cut down certain trees growing there and made them into timber, and then carried [the timber] off into the land where the trespass is supposed, and then gave the timber to the plaintiff; and so the defendant entered into the said land and took back his timber, as well he might. And the writ was 'wherefore he broke his close and took his timber'.

Bendlowes. It seems to me that the plea is not good for two reasons. The first is that, when he took the trees and made timber from them, the notice of them was lost, and thus the property in them was altered ...

And as to the first point, all the justices thought the plea good, for although by the cutting of the trees the notice is taken away the property still remains. In all cases where a thing is taken wrongfully and altered in form, if what remains is still the principal part of the substance, then the notice is not lost. Thus, if a man takes my cloak and makes a doublet from it, I can nevertheless take it back. Likewise, if a man takes from me a piece of cloth, and then he sews on to it a piece of gold, still I can take it back. And if a man takes certain trees and makes boards from them, yet the owner may take them back, *quia major pars substantiae remanet.* If, however, the trees are fixed on the ground, or if a house is built from the timber, it is otherwise; for now the house is the principal substance.[16]

ANON. (1607)

ECO MS. 93, fo. 99v (K.B.).

In trespass for battery, the defendant justified because he was vicar of 'Colbichurch'[17] in Kent, and because the plaintiff was in the said church fooling around (*pueriliter ludens*) irreverently the defendant struck him moderately with a walking stick which he had in his hand. The plaintiff demurred upon this plea, and it was adjudged in his favour without any argument.

---

16 Cf. *Anon.* (1596) Sheppard Abr., I, 273: 'If the nature of the goods delivered is altered, as if leather was delivered and made into shoes, or parchment or paper was made into writings, [detinue] will not lie for it, but some other [action], per Fenner J'. See further pp. 526, 532–533, below.

17 Unidentified; perhaps a slip for Ivychurch.

Croke said that Monkester,[18] the schoolmaster of St Paul's, because someone came into the school and expostulated with him in some matter, said to his pupils, *tollite*,[19] whereupon they gave him three or four good 'lamskins'; and he brought his action of battery.

Man.[20] That went against Monkester.

(*George Croke* for the defendant.)

HAWE v PLANNER (1666)

Record: KB 27/1875, m. 925. Henry Hawe brought a bill of trespass against John Planner, yeoman, for a battery on 4 September 1664 at Wokingham, Berkshire. The plea and demurrer summarised in the report were entered on 21 May 1665.

(a) 1 Saund. 13, pl. 3.[1]

... The defendant, as to the force and arms and the wounding, pleads Not guilty; and, as to the residue, he says that before and at the time when the trespass is supposed to have been committed, he was one of the churchwardens of Wokingham aforesaid, and the plaintiff, being an inhabitant of the said parish, before the said time when etc., namely on 21 August [1664], being a Sunday, was in church at the time of the celebration of divine service therein; and that at the time when prayers were made in the church by the congregation of the people there, the plaintiff irreverently had his hat upon his head; whereupon the defendant requested the plaintiff to be uncovered, which the plaintiff refused to do; wherefore the defendant took the plaintiff's hat from his head, and then and there delivered it to him; which said taking is the same assaulting, beating and ill-treating whereof the plaintiff complains. And traverses that he is guilty of assaulting, beating and ill-treating on the said 4 September or at any other time than the said 21 August, or otherwise or in any other manner. And thereupon the plaintiff demurs.

And it was objected that the defendant had traversed the day, where it was not material; for he might have justified on the same day the plaintiff complains of, without any traverse. Also, that the defendant had not justified any battery, because the taking off of the plaintiff's hat was no battery; and so the plea bad.

---

18 Richard Mulcaster or Muncaster (d. 1611), high master of St Paul's 1596–1608.
19 Take him away.
20 William Man, secondary of the King's Bench and filazer for Kent.
 1 Also reported in 2 Keb. 124; 1 Lev. 196.

But the court, taking this to be a great misdemeanour in the plaintiff, gave judgment against him, without any regard to the objections.

Saunders of counsel with the plaintiff.

(b) 1 Sid. 301, pl. 7.

... the whole court, except TWISDEN J., held that this was a good plea, and that a churchwarden could justify the appeasing of any disturbance in the church.

TWISDEN J. said that so could anyone else; but this is only a charge of irreverence. And whether it is so or not is some doubt upon the words of the Canon: namely, what hat the Canon means.[2] If, however, it is an irreverence, that ought to be presented by the defendant in the spiritual court, and there the plaintiff shall be punished; but he may not lay hands upon him, because that tends to the disturbance of the peace. Even if it is punishable under the Canon, it is not justifiable by our law to lay hands upon someone to take off (*diveller*) his hat from his head.

But judgment was, that the plaintiff take nothing by his bill.[3]

No judgment is entered on the roll, but there is a marginal note, 'Judgment for the defendant'.

(3) Questions of fault

BRAINTON v PINN (1290)

Select Cases in the Court of King's Bench, I,
Selden Soc. vol. 55, pl. 181.

Devon. Herbert of Pinn and his son John are to be amerced for several defaults.

The same Herbert and John were attached to answer Walter de Brainton on a plea why they burned that Walter's houses at Holewey, and his goods and chattels in them, to the value of £200, and [did him] other great wrongs to that Walter's grave damage and against the [king's] peace etc.

2 Constitutions and Canons Ecclesiastical (1603), no. 18: 'In the time of divine service, and of every part thereof, all due reverence is to be used ... No man shall cover his head in the church or chapel in the time of divine service, except he have some infirmity, in which case let him wear a night-cap or coif ...' Twisden J. may have recalled that judges wore their coifs in church, even when they were not infirm.

3 1 Lev. 196: '... for although the churchwardens may present this in the ecclesiastical court, yet they are not bound in the meantime to permit such irreverence and indecency in the church'.

And as to this [Walter] complains that, whereas the said Herbert and John on the Thursday next after the Assumption of the Blessed Mary in the sixteenth year of the present king's reign were lodged in Walter's house at his manor of Kenn, by their ill sense and carelessness and failure to look after a lighted candle they burned his aforesaid houses with all his goods, namely the crops stored in his granges and granaries, meats, fish, woollen and linen cloths, silver spoons, gold rings, charters, writings, household utensils and other goods to the value of £200, whereby he is harmed and has suffered damage to the value of £200, and thereof he produces suit, etc.

And Herbert and John, by their attorney, come and say that they were lodged in that Walter's houses by his good will, so that if there was any damage to Walter's houses and goods by fire or in any other way, that was by accident and not by any ill care or wickedness of theirs. And of this they put themselves upon the countryside etc.; and Walter [does] likewise. So a jury is to come three weeks after Easter wherever [the king shall then be] unless before then the justices [have taken a verdict in the neighbourhood].

Afterwards, three weeks after Easter in the twenty-first year of the present king's reign, the parties came and also the jurors, who say upon their oath that the aforesaid Herbert and his son John together with one Thomas de la Weye, the parson of Upton church and that Herbert's steward, were staying in the aforesaid Walter of Brainton's manor on the aforesaid day and year, and while Herbert lay asleep in his bed in a certain grange of the aforesaid manor the aforesaid Thomas did not let the aforesaid Herbert's son John put out a certain candle fixed to a post of the same grange, so that the aforesaid John went to bed with the candle burning and at once fell asleep, and the aforesaid Thomas went out, and before he came back the aforesaid candle fell and at once set light to the grange, and this at night-time so that part of Herbert's bed was burnt before he woke up, and also the whole of Walter's aforesaid manor together with his other goods was burnt by the aforesaid fire.

The entry ends with this special verdict, but a marginal note shows that the jurors assessed the damages, if any were found to be due, at £100.

ANON. (1368)

Y.B. 42 Lib. Ass., pl. 9 (Essex Assizes).

Item, a man sued a bill against another for the burning of his house with force and arms. [The other] pleaded Not guilty, and it was found by verdict of the inquest that the fire started suddenly in the defendant's house without his knowing, and burned his goods and also the plaintiff's house. And upon this verdict it was adjudged that the plaintiff should take nothing by his [bill], but should be amerced.

JANKYN'S CASE (1378)

Y.B. Mich. 2 Ric. II, p. 69, pl. 7 (C.P.).

Thomas Jankyn brought a writ of trespass for breaking his house and taking and carrying away his stones and tiles in Rochester with force and arms.

Clopton. As to the coming with force and arms and carrying away the tiles and stones, Not guilty. And as to the breaking of his house, we tell you that we have a house in Rochester adjoining his, and this house was ruinous and in need of repair; and so we hired masons and carpenters to repair our house, and as we were dismantling our house in order to repair and rebuild it a small quantity of stones and timber fell onto the plaintiff's house, without our wishing it and against our will, without any malice on our part. And we demand judgment whether you can assign any wrong in our person in respect of any such breaking.

Burgh. We are complaining about our house being broken, which fact he neither denies or admits nor justifies for any reason, and so he has not answered us at all. So we demand judgment and pray our damages.

PERCY to *Clopton.* You have not alleged on behalf of the defendant that you tendered him any amends at home, between neighbours, by reason that it was done against your will.

Clopton. Indeed, sir, speaking off the record, we did offer him fourpence at his home; and, as I am informed, he did not even have one pennyworth of damage. [Therefore], even if the party is found guilty (*attaynt*) of this act by the law, he shall not be amerced or fined in this case.

KIRKTON denied that.

BRIDELYNGTON v MIDDILTON (1388)

(a) Record: CP 40/512, m. 124.

Yorkshire. William, the son of Richard de Middilton of Beverley, draper, was attached to answer Gregory de Bridelyngton in a plea why with force and arms he assaulted the selfsame Gregory at Beverley and beat, wounded and ill-treated him, and inflicted other outrages upon him, to the grave damage of the selfsame Gregory and against the king's peace etc. Whereupon the same Gregory, by John of Wilton his attorney, complains that the aforesaid William, on the Monday [22 August 1384] next after the feast of the Assumption of the Blessed Virgin Mary in the eighth year of the reign of the present lord king, with force and arms, namely, with swords, bows and arrows, at Beverley, assaulted the selfsame Gregory and beat, wounded and ill-treated him, and other outrages etc. against the king's peace etc. Whereby he says he is the worse and has damage to the value of £20. And thereof he produces suit.

And the aforesaid William, by Thomas de Lynton his attorney, comes and denies the force and injury when etc. And as to the coming with force and arms and whatever is against the king's peace, he says that he is Not guilty, and thereof he puts himself on the country; and the aforesaid Gregory likewise. And as to the beating and wounding of the aforesaid Gregory he says that at the time in question he and the aforesaid Gregory were under the ages of nine and ten and were playing together at Beverley in a certain place called the Feegang, and there by their common consent they wrestled together playfully (*ludendo . . . simul luctaverunt*), and the harm (if any) which the aforesaid Gregory then sustained was done while they were thus playing, unintentionally (*sine voluntate*) and without any malice on the part of the selfsame William. And this he is ready to aver. Wherefore he does not think any wrong can be attributed to his person therein etc.

And the aforesaid Gregory says that the aforesaid William wilfully and of his own malice committed the trespass against him, as he has above complained against him. And this he prays may be enquired into by the country; and the aforesaid William likewise. Therefore the sheriff is commanded to cause 12 men to come here in three weeks from Easter . . .

(b) *Report: Y.B. Hil. 12 Ric. II, p. 125, pl. 16.*

A man brought a writ of trespass against another, and counted that on a certain day he beat, wounded and ill-treated him.

Rikhill. We say that on the same day that he has counted, the plaintiff and the defendant by their common accord played and sported together (*entrejeuerent et entreluderent ensemble*), so that the injury which he had (if any) was done in play, without this that he did him any other injury. And we demand judgment whether you ought to have such an action against us in respect of such play.

John Hill. It is quite true that on the same day they played together, and we say that when the plaintiff had played enough he went away and did not want to play, and then when he had gone away the defendant came to him and assaulted, beat and wounded him, of his own wrong. And we demand judgment and pray our damages.

Robert Hill. We say that throughout that day and at all times they played together by their common accord and consent, and he received the injury in play, without this that we beat him in any other way; ready etc.

And the other side to the contrary.

ANON. (1439)

Y.B. Mich. 18 Hen. VI, fo. 21, pl. 6.

In an action on the Statute of Westminster I, c. 20, for trespassing in the plaintiff's park and killing a deer, Sjt. Markham first sought to challenge the plaintiff's title to the park. After discussion, Paston J. indicated that such a plea would not be good.

... *Markham.* In that case, protesting that you have no park there either by prescription or by grant, we say by way of plea that adjoining the fence of the close which you call a park there is a highway leading from a certain vill to another, and the defendant came along the road leading a brace of greyhounds on his leash; and a doe skipped over the fence into the said road, and the dogs in their excitement (*corage*) broke the leash and killed the doe, without this that we are guilty of breaking your park or hunting in any other manner.

PASTON. That is no plea, for you have not confessed any breaking or hunting in the park. To what purpose is it, then, to say in effect that there was no other manner of hunting?

Markham. Sir, it is the common pleading if you bring a writ of trespass against me for breaking your close in a vill, for me to say that I have a close in another vill in the same county which I broke, as well I might, without this that I am guilty in any other manner. Likewise here.

PASTON. Suppose a writ is brought against you for battery in one place, and you justify in another place in the same county by reason of an assault committed against you by the plaintiff, without this that you are guilty in any other manner; and in this case you are found guilty in the place where you justified ... you would [be liable to] render damages upon this verdict. Similarly, if you were found guilty in a third place, of which you have not spoken. But even if it is found that you deliberately (*de vostre bon gré*) let slip your greyhounds in the highway, or somewhere else outside the park, you shall not render damages.

Fortescue. Truly. Nor is it a plea in his own case of breaking a close, in the way he has said. But it is good enough in battery, as Mr. Paston has well said; and in a writ for carrying away goods.

NEWTON [C.J.] and AYSCOUGH. If you had said that the doe re-entered the park, and the dogs followed it, without this etc. (as before), perhaps the plea would have been good.[4]

Then he said as before, and that the doe re-entered the park, and the dogs followed it, and that he did all he could to call them back, without this that he was guilty in another manner; and, as to the taking and carrying away of his doe, Not guilty.

Fortescue. We have complained of a buck, and he has justified in respect of a doe.

NEWTON. He has said enough, for he says 'without this that he is guilty in another manner', which covers everything.

Fortescue. In that case, we say as to the taking and carrying away that he is guilty; ready. And as to the breaking of the park and the hunting we say that you entered our park of your own wrong, and let slip your dogs to run, of your own free will, and you hunted as before; ready.

And the other side to the contrary.

A similar problem occurred in *Hampden v Doyly* (1443) CP 40/730, m. 337, where in an action for breaking a park and killing deer the defendant pleaded: 'that on the same day he went hunting in the same vill of Pyrton on his own soil and freehold, having with him two greyhounds on the leash, and before him in the distance the aforesaid three deer leaped out of the aforesaid park into his said soil; and therefore the same Thomas Doyly released his aforesaid greyhounds to chase the same deer; and the same deer for their safety speedily ran away from them towards the aforesaid park for cover; and when the same Thomas perceived the deer to be approaching the said park, he assiduously blew his horn to call back his greyhounds so that they should not enter the park: nevertheless, having seen the aforesaid deer enter the park, [the dogs] in their excitement and eagerness (*ex eorum coragio et appetitu*), and against the will of him the said Thomas Doyly, followed the deer into the said park and took them ...' To this plea the plaintiffs demurred, and the court took advisement until Hilary term 1444. No judgment is entered.

4 A reader on the statute a few years later, evidently referring to this opinion, stated definitely that 'an action does not lie against him, for it would be against all reason if he were to be punished, since there was no fault in him' (CUL MS. Ee. 5. 22, fo. 141v).

ANON. (1456)[5]

Y.B. Mich. 35 Hen. VI, fo. 11v, pl. 18 (C.P.).

A writ of trespass was brought against an infant under age, supposing that he had assaulted the plaintiff and beat him ... and the plaintiff declared, through *Wangford.*

And *Billing* came and made defence, and said: sir, you plainly see that the child is but four years old, and this well proves that he has no discretion to commit a trespass, and does not know any malice.

MOYLE [J.] said to *Wangford.* Can you find it in your conscience to declare against this infant of such tender age? I believe he does not know any malice, for he is not a person of much power, as you may see for yourself. (And, with this, MOYLE lifted up the infant with his hand and put him in the place; and said to *Wangford:*) here is the same person, so be advised.

Wangford. I do only as I am instructed. Here is the plaintiff, and the trespass appears openly upon him; for by the same trespass one of his eyes was put out.

Billing. If an infant is indicted for felony, and is thereupon arraigned and pleads Not guilty, and is found guilty, the justices may nevertheless dismiss him at their discretion if it appears to them that because of his nonage he knows nothing of felony or of the penalty for it. And if that is so, a fortiori here.

MOYLE. I fully concede the case of felony, and the reason is because there is no remedy in felony but to plead Not guilty, because felony may not be justified; and therefore the justices at their discretion may dismiss him if it appears that he is of such an age that he has no discretion. But it is otherwise in trespass, for in a writ of trespass the party may justify the trespass and is not compelled to plead Not guilty; and therefore the justices do not have the like power.

Billing. Then we pray you will record a guardian [*ad litem*] for him, because he cannot make an attorney.

MOYLE. We will, sir, gladly.

---

5   Statham Abr., *Transgressio*, third case from the end, notes a similar discussion the same year in a criminal case at Newgate, probably arising from the same incident. A child under five was charged with putting out someone's eye with an arrow. The justices were asked whether an action would lie, and they held it would not, because 'the law for punishing trespass' was intended as a deterrent, and children of similar age would not be deterred by an award of damages: 'But they said that a child under the age of seven years was in the same case as an ox or a dog who damages someone, in which case no punishment lies against them; but perhaps an action lies against their master (query)'.

So Copley[6] made a record for his guardian.

Billing. By your leave, we will imparl until the morrow of All Souls.

The court granted him this.

HULLE v ORYNGE (1466)
THE CASE OF THORNS

Record: CP 40/815, m. 340; Kiralfy, *Source Book*, p. 128. Henry Hulle brought a writ of trespass against Richard Orynge for breaking his close at Topsham, Devon, cutting and taking trees and underwood valued at £5, and trampling on grass valued at 5 marks. As to the trees, Orynge pleaded Not guilty; and this was found against him at Exeter assizes. As to the breaking of the close and trampling on the grass, Orynge pleaded a plea which compelled the plaintiff to assign the trespass in five acres of meadow and six acres of land. As to the meadow, the defendant pleaded Not guilty; and this also was found against him at the assizes. As to the six acres of land, Orynge pleaded that he was seised of another acre of land in Topsham, adjoining the plaintiff's six acres, and that a thorn hedge was growing on his land; that he cut the thorns in the hedge, and they fell against his will onto the plaintiff's land; and that he immediately went onto the plaintiff's land and took the thorns and threw them back onto his own land. To this plea the plaintiff demurred. There are two surviving reports of the discussion in banc.

(a) Bod. Lib. MS. Lat. misc. C. 55, fo. 6.[7]

Trespass for breaking a close and trampling on his grass by walking.

Jenney. You ought not to have an action, because the plaintiff was seised of the land whereof the place where the alleged trespass occurred was part, and the defendant was seised of a close adjoining the plaintiff's land, and between the plaintiff's land and the defendant's land there is a hedge on the defendant's land in which various thorns were growing; and the defendant cut the thorns, and they fell on the plaintiff's land (part of which is the place in question), against the defendant's will and without his fault, and so the selfsame defendant at the time in question entered the land whereof the place in question is part and threw them back.

Fairfax. That is no plea, for there is a distinction between felony and trespass. In felony the intent and will of a man shall be construed,[8] and in accordance therewith he shall be acquitted or

6 William Copley, the third prothonotary.
7 This manuscript belonged to Robert Constable (d. 1500), who was admitted to Lincoln's Inn in 1477.
8 Pehaps meaning 'inferred from his actions', or else merely 'taken into account'. Cf. p. 317, above.

attainted. In trespass, however, one should not have regard to the intent or will but only to the matter in fact. For instance, if a man shoots at the butts—which is a lawful game—and by misfortune or misadventure he wounds someone standing near the butts, he shall be punished by writ of trespass even though it was against his will. If, on the other hand, he killed the man, he would be acquitted of felony. However, if I drive my cattle along the highway, or else keep them in my several, and they escape against my will into your land, and I enter at once and take them back, this entry is lawful: for there the cattle trespassed by reason of their animal (*bestial*) nature, and there is no fault in my entering at once to take them back.

Catesby. If the case of my driving beasts along the highway is the law—as I think it is, for it is the usual pleading—it follows that the plea in bar is a good bar: for the defendant can look after his cattle just as well as he can look after his thorns, to ensure that they do no damage in another's land. Suppose a man takes my goods and puts them on another person's soil: it is quite permissible for me to enter and take them back. (Query this case, which was conceded by all the serjeants except *Bryan*.)

LITTLETON. It seems to me that the plea is not good, and that the cattle case is not law: for a man is bound to keep his cattle and also his fire [from doing harm], and if he does not he shall be punished.

CHOKE to the same effect. If he wants to make a good plea out of this, he should show what he did to prevent the thorns from falling, so that we can judge whether or not he did enough to excuse himself. Similarly, if you wish to justify imprisoning someone because he was suspected of felony, you must set out the [grounds of] suspicion in your plea, so that we can judge whether or not he was suspicious. As to the cattle case, it seems to me that it is not law: for if their [entry][9] was against the law, as it was, then the entry to drive them out was against the law.

DANBY [C.J.] to the same effect. Even though it was lawful for him to cut his thorns, it was not lawful to allow them to fall into another person's soil, for he was to cut them in such a way that they did not damage others. Similarly, if I put willow trees in my soil in a watercourse which runs to your mill, and they later grow so large that they stop up the water, I say that you shall have an assize of nuisance: and yet there was no wrong done at the outset. The law is the same if I cut down my trees, and they fall into the water which runs to your mill so that the water does not run as freely as it did, you shall have an assize. Moreover, the cutting was his own act and

9 Conjectural: the text says 'possession'.

it is not right that he should take advantage of it. If two people take my horse to the use of one of them, and then he to whose use it was taken sells the same horse to the other in market overt, I may still take my horse [back], because the buyer was privy to the wrong: and yet if it were sold to a stranger I could not take it back. I say also that if my apples fall onto someone else's land I may not enter to get them back. Moreover, if someone builds a house on his land so that my land is overshadowed, and my grass or grain will not grow as it did before, I may knock down the eaves (*esynges*) which overhang my land, so long as I do not go onto his soil. The law is the same concerning tree branches which overhang my soil. And I shall have an assize of nuisance for what I cannot break or cut [off], or else I can forgo the aforesaid breaking and cutting [altogether] and punish the whole in an assize of nuisance. (Query this.)

Neele. If I give you all the fish in my pond, you may [not] break the pond and make the water run out of it in order to catch the fish; but you must catch them with engines (*gynes*) and in other ways which cause me the least damage.[10] Likewise here, if the plea is to be good it must be shown that he entered in the least damaging way he could.

Jenney. That shall be presumed unless the contrary is shown.

Later the plaintiff released part of his damages, and had judgment to recover; and the defendant put in a writ of error.

The record shows that judgment on the demurrer was given for the plaintiff, but that the plaintiff released all the damages in respect of that part of the trespass. The outcome of the writ of error is not known, but presumably it was withdrawn because of this compromise.

(b) Printed text: Y.B. Mich. 6 Edw. IV, fo. 7, pl. 18.

... *Catesby.* Sir, it has been argued that if a man does something whereby injury and damage are done to another person against his will, even though the thing is lawful, nevertheless if he could by some means have avoided this damage he shall be punished for it. But I, sir, think the contrary. In my view if a man does something lawful whereby damage befalls another, against his will, he shall not be punished. Let me put the case that I am driving my cattle along the highway, and you have an acre of land lying alongside the way, and my cattle enter your land and depasture your grass, and I

---

10 *St Quintin v Gyrton* (1378) Fitz. Abr., *Barre*, pl. 237; Y.B. Mich. 2 Ric. II, p. 38, pl. 2. In trespass to land, the defendant pleaded a grant of fish by the plaintiff and said that he entered and drained the pond because there was no other way of getting the fish. The plea was held bad, because the defendant could have caught them in a less damaging way, e.g. with nets.

immediately come and drive them out of your land, in this case you shall not have an action against me because the driving was lawful and their entry in your land was against my will. Neither shall the plaintiff have an action here, for the cutting was lawful and the falling onto your land was against my will, and consequently the taking back was good and permissible in law. Suppose, sir, that I lop my trees and the boughs fall on a man and kill him: in that case I shall not be attainted of felony, because my cutting was permissible in law and their falling on the man was against my will. No more [is the defendant liable] here.

Fairfax. I think the contrary. I say that there is a distinction between doing something from which felony will follow and doing something from which trespass will follow. In the case which Catesby has put it was not felony because felony is by malice aforethought, and when it was against his will it was not *animo felonico*. But if someone is lopping his trees[11] and the boughs fall on a man and injure him, in this case he shall have an action of trespass. Also, sir, if a man is shooting at the butts and his bow swerves in his hand and [the arrow] kills a man, against his will, this (as has been said) is not felony. If, however, he injures a man by his archery, the man shall have a good action of trespass against him: and yet the archery was lawful, and the injury which the other suffered was against his will. Likewise here.

Pigot to the same effect ...

Yonge. I think the contrary. In cases where a man has *damnum absque injuria* he shall not have an action; for if there is no wrong it is not right that he should recover damages. So it was here when he went into the plaintiff's close to take the thorns which had fallen in: this entry was not wrongful, because when he cut them and they fell into the plaintiff's close against his will the property in them remained his all the time, and consequently it was lawful for him to take them away from the plaintiff's close. Thus, although the plaintiff was damaged, he suffered no wrong.

Bryan. I think the contrary. To my mind, when someone does something he is bound to do it in such a way that no prejudice or damage is done to others by his action. For example, if I build a house, and when the timber is being hoisted a piece of it falls onto my neighbour's house and breaks it, he shall have a good action: and yet the building of the house was lawful, and the timber fell against my will.[12] Also, if a man assaults me, and I cannot get away from him without him beating me, and in my own defence I raise

11   Reads 'herbes', which must be a misprint for 'arbres'.
12   Cf. *Jankyn's Case* (1378), p. 322, above.

my staff to strike him, and there is someone behind me who is hurt when I raise my staff, he shall in this case have an action against me: and yet raising my staff to defend myself was lawful, and I hurt him against my will. Likewise here.

LITTLETON to the same effect. If a man suffers damage it is right that he should be compensated. In my view, the case which Catesby put is not law; for if your cattle come onto my land and eat my grass, then even if you come at once and drive them out you must make amends for what your cattle have done, however great or small it may be ... Sir, if it were the law that he could enter and take the thorns, he might by the same argument cut large trees, and come in with horses and carts to take them out: and that would be unreasonable, because the plaintiff might perhaps have corn or other crops growing. Neither is it reasonable here, for the law is the same in great things as in small; and he shall have amends according to the magnitude of the trespass.

CHOKE. I am of the same view; for where the principal thing was unlawful, then anything which depended on it was unlawful. When the defendant cut the thorns and they fell onto my land, this falling was unlawful, and consequently his coming to take them out was unlawful. As to the point that they fell against his will, that is no plea; but he must say that he could not have acted in any other way, or that he did all he could to keep them out, or else he shall answer for the damage. Sir, if the thorns (or a large tree) fell onto the plaintiff's land through the blowing of the wind, he could in that case have gone in to take them, because the falling was not his act but was caused by the wind.

The printed text does not mention Danby C.J.

WEAVER v WARD (1616)

Record: CP 40/1973, m. 2136; abstracted in Kiralfy, *Source Book*, p. 132. Thomas Weaver brought trespass against George Ward, and counted that on 18 October 1614 in the parish of St Mary-le-Bow, London, with force and arms (namely with swords, clubs and knives), the defendant beat, wounded and ill-treated the plaintiff so that his life was despaired of, against the king's peace. The defendant pleaded in bar that both parties were members of a band of 105 trained soldiers under the command of Captain Henry Andrews, having been trained and prepared in martial exercises under the direction of the Privy Council for the king's service in England whenever they should be called up; that the plaintiff and defendant were then and there armed with muskets charged with gunpowder, and by command of the said captain were skirmishing and discharging their muskets against a similar band under the command of

Captain Hugh Hammersley; and that in these circumstances the defendant accidentally and by misfortune and against his will, in discharging his musket, injured and wounded the plaintiff; which wounding is the same trespass of which the plaintiff complains; without this that the defendant is guilty of the trespass and assault in any other way. To this plea the plaintiff demurred.

(a) HLS MS. 112, p. 319.

... *Hutton* Sjt. argued that such a thing as this, which happened accidentally in doing something for the public good, and upon a lawful command, was excusable: as in 21 Hen. VII, fo. 27, making bulwarks in another's soil; 13 Hen. VIII, fo. 16, pulling down a burning house to save a city; 8 Edw. IV, fo. [18], drying nets by fishermen on another's land; 5 Hen. VII, arresting night-walkers justifiable by anyone; 11 Hen. VII, fo. 23, if any damage befalls anyone in wrestling or jousting, where this is by the king's licence and authority, even if death ensues it is not felony.[13] See Keil. 108.

Harries Sjt. to the contrary. The plea in bar is bad, since he does not say that he could not by any means avoid it; and therefore the plea is short and defective in this respect: 6 Edw. IV, fo. 7[14]. . . And he cited the case of fish in Fitz. [Abr.], *Barre*, 237.[15] And he said there was a great difference between a felony and a trespass. For a felony may be excused, even though he could have avoided and eschewed it by some means: for instance, if a man strikes another by misfortune, *se invito*, he is still punishable in trespass, though if he kills him by misfortune he shall be excused and shall thereupon have his pardon of grace under the Statute of Gloucester, c. 9. This difference between felony and trespass is taken by Rede [J.] in 21 Hen. VII, fo. 28.[16] Also he said that if the defendant's plea were good he should not traverse that he was guilty in any other way . . .

Afterwards, upon putting the case again, the truth was [disclosed], and so it was pleaded that the plaintiff and defendant were both of one company under the command of one captain, and, being fellows, this happened accidentally in discharging a musket by the defendant, the plaintiff being the nearest man to him in the ranks.

Afterwards, in Hilary term 14 Jac. I [1617], HOBART C.J. and WINCH J. were of opinion that the justification was bad; but WARBURTON J. to the contrary. Afterwards the plaintiff had a day given him by mediation of the court, and so no judgment was entered.

13 For these and similar cases, see Selden Soc. vol. 94, pp. *34–35, 312–313.*
14 *The Case of Thorns*; see p. 327, above.
15 *St Quintin v Gyrton* (1378); see p. 329, fn. 10, above.
16 See p. 317, above.

The record does contain a judgment that the plea was bad, but the parties probably compromised upon the writ of inquiry into the damages.

(b) Hobart 134 (untr.).[17]

... And upon demurrer by the plaintiff, judgment was given for him. For though it were agreed that if men tilt or tourney in the presence of the king, or if two masters of defence[18] playing [for] their prizes kill one another, that this shall be no felony—or if a lunatic kill a man, or the like—because felony must be done *animo felonico*; yet in trespass, which tends only to give damages according to hurt or loss, it is not so. And therefore if a lunatic hurt a man he shall be answerable in trespass. And therefore no man shall be excused of a trespass (for this is in the nature of an excuse, and not of a justification *prout ei bene licuit*) except it may be adjudged utterly without his fault. As, if a man by force take my hand and strike you. Or if here the defendant had said that the plaintiff ran across his piece when it was discharging, or had set forth the case with the circumstances so as it had appeared to the court that it had been inevitable[19] and that the defendant had committed no negligence to give occasion to the hurt.

ANGELL v SATTERTON (1663)

Record: KB 27/1850, m. 623. William Angell brought an action of trespass in the King's Bench against Christopher Satterton, *alias* Shatterden, for an assault and battery in the parish of St Mary-le-Bow, London,[20] on 10 June 1662. The defendant pleaded Not guilty, and at the Guildhall (before Foster C.J.) on 29 January 1663 the jury found for the plaintiff with £10 damages.

1 Sid. 108, pl. 22.

In an action of trespass the plaintiff declared generally that the defendant maimed him. And upon issue he gave in evidence[1] 'that the defendant discharged a great gun in a ship without giving notice according to the custom, in the narrow seas and ports, and so the plaintiff (being then uncorking the said gun on the outside of the said ship) by the said discharge lost one of his eyes and one of

---

17 Report by the presiding chief justice, Sir Henry Hobart.
18 I.e. prize-fighters.
19 Cf. the brief report in Moo. K.B. 864, pl. 1192: '... It was adjudged that the justification was not good, but that he ought to have said further that he could not otherwise have avoided the fact. Also, when he justifies the whole fact, there is no need of a traverse'.
20 From the evidence it appears that this was a fictitious venue.
1 The rest of the sentence is in English, as if a quotation.

his legs'. And upon the evidence this appeared to have been done without the defendant's knowledge and against his will, and therefore the jury gave the plaintiff but £10 damages. Therefore he, by his counsel, moved the court to increase the damages upon the view of the mayhem (as they might). And a day was given to the plaintiff to produce his witnesses; but because they were to the aforesaid purpose the court would not increase the damages ...

The record confirms that judgment was given in Hilary term 1663 for £10 damages, with £8. 10s. costs.

BURFORD (AND WIFE) v DADWEL (1669)

1 Sid. 433, pl. 26 (K.B.).

Trespass for assaulting and ill-treating the wife, and striking the mare on which she was riding, so that she was thrown to the ground and another horse trod on her, as a result of which she lost the use of three of her fingers. Upon Not guilty, and a verdict for the plaintiff with £8 damages, it was moved that the damages should be increased upon a view of the woman and after hearing the surgeons.

But the court would not hear this [motion], because it was doubted whether this would be increased on the view, since there is no maiming or wounding here done directly by the party, but it is rather by accident (namely, the coming of the other horse: and how it came, or whether the woman could have avoided it, are matters of evidence). Therefore they refused to increase the damages.

DICKINSON v WATSON (1682)

Record: KB 27/2018, m. 576; abstracted in Kiralfy, *Source Book*, p. 134. Robert Dickinson brought a plaint of trespass in the sheriffs' court of York against John Watson, and complained that on 1 May 1681 at York the defendant assaulted, beat, wounded and ill-treated him with force and arms (namely with pistols, swords, sticks and knives), so that his life was despaired of, and did then and there shoot hail-shot into the plaintiff's left eye with a pistol, whereby the sight of that eye was lost. The defendant pleaded in bar that he was at the time of the trespass an officer appointed to collect the hearth tax under various acts of parliament, and therefore kept various firearms, both in order to safeguard the moneys he collected for the king's use and in order to defend his own person from the assaults and dangers which were often incident to his office; that at the time in question he was armed with the pistol mentioned in the declaration, loaded with hail-shot, and, intending to discharge it in such a way that no damage should befall any of the king's subjects (no one being in sight), he discharged the pistol; and the plaintiff accidentally wandered into the way as it was discharging; and if any harm thereby befell the plaintiff it was inevitable, and against the defendant's will. The plaintiff demurred, and the sheriff's court held the plea insufficient. Judgment was entered for £30. On 6 February 1682 Watson brought a writ of error in the King's Bench, and assigned as error that the declaration was insufficient and that judgment should have been given for him.

T. Jones 204.

... The court held [the plea] to be insufficient, for in trespass the defendant shall not be excused without unavoidable necessity, which is not shown here. Besides, the defendant did not traverse 'without this that he was guilty in any other way' as was done in the case of *Weaver v Ward*, Hob. 134;[2] and yet judgment there given for the plaintiff.

GIBBON v PEPPER (1695)

(a) Record: KB 27/2105, m. 64.

Middlesex ...[3] Thomas Gibbon complains of Thomas Pepper, in the custody of the marshal of the Marshalsea of the lord king and lady queen, being before the said king and queen themselves, for that the same Thomas Pepper on the first day of May [1694] in the sixth year of the reign of the Lord William and Lady Mary now king and queen of England etc., at the parish of St Martin in the Fields in the aforesaid county of Middlesex, with force and arms etc., made assault upon him the said Thomas Gibbon and then and there beat, wounded and ill-treated him so that his life was despaired of, and inflicted other outrages upon the same Thomas Gibbon, against the peace of the said present lord king and lady queen, and to the damage of him the said Thomas Gibbon of £40. And thereof he produces suit etc.

And the aforesaid Thomas Pepper, by Peter Courtney his attorney, comes and denies the force and wrong when etc. And, as to the coming with force and arms or whatever is against the peace of the said present lord king and lady queen, and the whole of the aforesaid trespass except the aforesaid assault, battery, wounding and ill-treatment, he says that he is not guilty thereof. And of this

2 See p. 331, above.
3 Memorandum that the bill was preferred on Tuesday [22 October 1695] next after three weeks from Michaelmas, through Whitelocke Bulstrode, the plaintiff's attorney.

he puts himself upon the country; and the aforesaid Thomas Gibbon thereupon does likewise. As to the aforesaid assault, battery, wounding and ill-treatment above supposed to have been committed, the same Thomas Pepper says that the aforesaid Thomas Gibbon ought not to have or maintain his aforesaid action against him for that, because he says that before the aforesaid time when the aforesaid assault, battery, wounding and ill-treatment are above supposed to have been committed, and also at the same time when etc., the same Thomas Pepper was (and he still is) the servant of a certain John Willis (the same John then being innkeeper of a certain common inn called the Angel Inn in the parish of St Clement Danes in the aforesaid county of Middlesex), and—the same Thomas Pepper being thus the servant of the selfsame John as aforesaid—the same Thomas Pepper at the aforesaid time when etc. in the service of the aforesaid John and by his command rode a certain horse of him the said John in, through and over a certain street called Drury Lane (being a royal highway for all persons wishing to ride) in the parish of St Giles in the Fields in the aforesaid county of Middlesex, in order to water the aforesaid horse; and, while the same Thomas was so riding as aforesaid, the aforesaid horse was then and there frightened (*terrificatus*) so that the aforesaid horse then and there violently ran away with the same Thomas Pepper, and the same Thomas Pepper could not then and there govern the aforesaid horse; whereupon the same Thomas Pepper then and there in a loud voice gave notice to the passers by in the aforesaid street to take care of themselves; but nevertheless, the aforesaid Thomas Gibbon at that time remaining there in the aforesaid street, the aforesaid horse ran upon the same Thomas Gibbon against the will of the selfsame Thomas Pepper and then and there threw down the same Thomas Gibbon to the ground: and these are the same assault, battery, wounding and ill-treatment whereof the same Thomas Gibbon now complains above. And the same Thomas Pepper is ready to aver this. And so the same Thomas Pepper prays judgment whether the aforesaid Thomas Gibbon ought to have or maintain his aforesaid action against him upon that etc.

The plaintiff demurred to the plea, and there is a continuance for advisement until a date left blank. There is no judgment on the roll.

(b) Report: 1 Ld Raym 38 (untr.).

... And Sjt. *Darnall*, for the defendant, argued that if the defendant in his justification shows that the accident was inevitable, and that the negligence of the defendant did not cause it, judgment shall be given for him. To prove which he cited *Weaver v Ward*[4]...

Northey, for the plaintiff, said that in all these cases the defendant confessed a battery which he afterwards justified; but in this case he justified a battery which is no battery.[5]

Of which opinion was the whole court. For if I ride upon a horse, and John Style whips the horse so that he runs away with me and runs over any other person, he who whipped the horse is guilty of the battery, and not me. But if I, by spurring, was the cause of such accident, then I am guilty. In the same manner, if A. takes the hand of B. and with it strikes C., A. is the trespasser and not B. And, *per curiam*, the defendant might have given this justification in evidence upon the general issue pleaded.

And therefore judgment was given for the plaintiff.[6]

4　See p. 331, above.
5　4 Mod. 405 adds: '... He should have pleaded the general issue, for if the horse ran away against his will he would have been found not guilty, because in such case it cannot be said with any colour of reason to be a battery in the rider'.
6　Cf. 2 Salk. 638: '... The plaintiff demurred and had judgment; not but if the defendant had pleaded Not guilty this matter might have acquitted him upon evidence. But the reason of their judgment was because the defendant justified a trespass and does not confess it'.

13 Trespass on the case

BERNARDESTON v HEIGHLYNGE (1344)

Record: CP 40/330, m. 304 (Pas. 1342); proceedings in error, KB 27/338 m. 41d (Mich. 1344); abstracted in Y.B. 16 Edw. III, Rolls Series, I, p. 259, fn. 3 (apparently from the former); Selden Soc. vol. 32, p. 309 (from the latter); Kiralfy, *The Action on the Case* (1949), p. 209. Thomas de Bernardeston brought an action on the case in the Common Pleas in 1340[1] against John de Heighlynge (of Healing, Lincolnshire) and declared that, whereas the defendant ought by reason of his tenements in Great Coates, Lincolnshire, (as all the other tenants of those tenements have been so accustomed since time immemorial) to repair and mend four perches of sea-wall in the same vill with stakes, hurdles and timber, to guard against the tide of the River Humber: the defendant, though often requested, had not done the repairs, and as a result 200 acres of the plaintiff's meadow were flooded by the tide from 1336 until 1341, and the plaintiff had lost the profit from the meadow. The defendant traversed the custom to repair the wall, and the jury found specially that the tenants ought to repair, and that as far back as memory stretched before 1336 there had been only two defects, which were repaired by the then tenants; and in the defendant's time there had only been the defects now complained of.

(a) In the Common Pleas: Y.B. 18 Edw. III,
Rolls Series, p. 235, pl. 6.

Trespass in the form of *de wallia reparanda*, in which they were at issue that the defendant and the tenants of the land had not always repaired. It was found by the inquest that the tenants of the land ought to do it, but the defendant had never done so; and it was

---

1 The original writ was copied as an addition to a manuscript register (under 'Trespass'), with the date Mich. 14 [Edw. III], in CUL MS. Add. 3506, fo. 46v.

further found that the walls decayed within memory only twice, and then they were repaired by the tenants of the land.

Thorpe. It is found that by right the tenants of the land ought to do this, and even though he has not done it, this is because they did not fall down in his time until now; and so the issue is found for the plaintiff. [So we pray] judgment.

Pole. It is found that within memory it was never done by the tenants of the land except twice, which being found specially does not prove that they ought to do it of right; and therefore the court cannot have regard to this general finding that they ought to do it of right, since the special fact which is received as part of the verdict does not prove it.

Thorpe. The issue is found for the plaintiff, that the tenants of the land ought to do it; and that what they say about it only having been done twice within the time of memory is to be understood as meaning since the time they can remember.

WILLOUGHBY. What you say is true, and since it is found that they ought to do it of right the court awards that the plaintiff recover his damages, assessed at 20s., and that the other be amerced.

(Query how he shall be made to repair the walls.)

The next day *Thorpe* came back and prayed that the judgment might be amended, since it had not been awarded that the defendants should repair the walls.

WILLOUGHBY awarded that they should repair the walls, and that they should be distrained to do it; and he caused the roll to be amended.

The record shows that judgment was entered in these terms. The defendant thereupon brought a writ of error to remove the record *coram rege* in Chancery. The defendant in error (Bernardeston) rejoined specially to each of the assigned errors as shown below.

(b) Pleadings in error, *coram rege.*

[1] [H:] The aforesaid justices erred in that they held plea upon the aforesaid writ after Thomas had shown [in his count] that all was in the right, in which case he should have had a writ of *reparari facias.*[2]

[B:] As to that, the justices did not err, because the aforesaid writ which he then brought was a certain formed writ conceived upon his case (*breve formatum in suo casu conceptum*) and not wholly

---

2 This was in the form *praecipe quod reparari faciat wallias.* For early precedents, see Selden Soc. vol. 87, p. 70.

for the trespass done to him, but upon the right and the trespass, and his explanation in his count agrees with his writ and was not challenged by John at the time when it could have been . . .[3]

[2] [H:] The aforesaid justices admitted an issue in the aforesaid plea which was all in the right, whereas the matter of the writ required an issue upon the wrong (*injuria*), and there was no answer to the wrong; and in admitting such an issue they erred.

[B:] As to that, the justices did not err, because the aforesaid writ was conceived upon the right (namely, that he ought to repair the walls) and also upon the trespass (namely, that John did not repair the walls, so that by his default the walls decayed and Thomas's land was flooded); and in this case the issue can be in the right or in the personalty at the will of the parties . . .

[3] [H:] The aforesaid justices erred in that they gave judgment for the said Thomas, where the issue in the aforesaid plea passed against him the said Thomas, since it was found that the aforesaid John never repaired the aforesaid walls and the issue in the plea was that the aforesaid John (and the tenants of the land and those whose estate they have in the same) have always repaired etc.

[B:] As to that, the aforesaid justices did not err, because it is found by verdict (as appears by the record) that the tenants of the land always repaired the walls until the aforesaid John's time, and so the issue was expressly found in Thomas's favour.

[4] [H:] The aforesaid justices gave judgment that the aforesaid John ought to repair the walls aforesaid, which is in the right and not warranted by the aforesaid writ of trespass, especially after he the said Thomas recovered his damages.

[B:] As to that, the justices did not err, because the aforesaid writ was a formed writ conceived upon his case, upon the trespass and also upon the right, by reason whereof the aforesaid John ought to be chargeable both to repair the walls and to render damages, and especially since this tends to the common profit . . .

No judgment is entered upon the proceedings in error, which were discontinued in Trinity term 1345 after a writ of protection was produced for Bernardestone, who was about to join the earl of Oxford's expedition in Brittany.

THE OCULIST'S CASE (1329)

LI MS. Hale 137(1), fo. 150 (eyre of Nottingham).

A man complained by bill that, whereas [the defendant] had

---

3 I.e., if there was any variance between the writ and the count, it had been cured by pleading over in bar.

undertaken to heal his eye with herbs and other medicines, he caused his eye to fail[4] so that he lost it, to his damages.

Launde. Sir, you plainly see how he supposes that he had submitted himself to his medicines and his care; and after that he can assign no trespass in his person, inasmuch as he submitted himself to his care: but this action, if he has any, sounds naturally in breach of covenant (*en covenant enfreint*). We demand judgment whether he ought to be answered in respect of such a bill.

W. DENUM. I saw a Newcastle man arraigned before my fellow justice and me for the death of a man. I asked the reason for the indictment, and it was said that he had slain a man under his care, who died within four days afterwards. And because I saw that he was a man of that profession (*mestrie*), and that he had not done the thing feloniously but against his will, I ordered him to be discharged. And suppose a farrier, who is man of skill (*home de mestier*), injures your horse with a nail, whereby you lose your horse: you shall never have recovery against him.[5] No more shall you here.

Afterwards the plaintiff did not wish to pursue his bill any more.

THE FARRIER'S CASE (1372)

Y.B. Trin. 46 Edw. III, fo. 19, pl. 19;
LI MS. Hale 181, fo. 58; MS. Hale 187, fo. 217v;
UCO MS. 150, fo. 163.

Trespass was brought against a farrier for injuring a horse with a nail; and the writ said 'to show why, at a certain place, he drove a nail into the quick of the horse's hoof, whereby the plaintiff lost the profit from his horse for a long time'.

Percy. He has brought a writ of trespass against us, and does not say 'with force and arms'. We pray judgment of the writ.

FYNCHEDEN [C.J.] He has brought his writ according to his case. (So he thought the writ good.)

Percy. The writ should be 'with force and arms', or should say that he drove the nail maliciously; and since there is neither the one nor the other, we pray judgment. Also, he has not supposed in his count that he bailed the horse to us for shoeing, and so it should be presumed otherwise: namely, that if any trespass was done it was against the peace. So we pray judgment.

Then the writ was held good. And the defendant took issue that

---

4 Translation uncertain: 'fist son oylle que se creva'.
5 Cf. the following case.

he shod the horse, without this that he injured it with a nail; ready
etc.

PROCESS IN ACTIONS ON THE CASE (1504)

19 Hen. VII, c. 9;
Statutes of the Realm, vol. II, p. 653 (untr.).

Forasmuch as before this time there hath been great delays in
actions of the case that hath been sued as well before the king in his
Bench as in his Court of Common Bench, because of which delays
many persons have been put from their remedy: be it therefore
ordained, enacted and established by the king our sovereign lord,
by the advice and assent of the lords spiritual and temporal and the
commons in this present parliament assembled, and by authority of
the same, that like process be had hereafter in actions upon the
case, as well sued and hanging as to be sued, in any of the said
courts,[6] as in actions of trespass or debt.[7]

A. FITZHERBERT, LA NOVEL NATURA BREVIUM (1534)

Translated from the 1635 ed., ff. 92–95.

There is another form of writ of trespass—upon the case—which is
to be sued in the Common Bench or King's Bench; and in this writ
he shall not say *vi et armis* etc., but at the end of the writ he shall
say *contra pacem* etc. . . . . A man shall have an action of trespass on
the case against his neighbour who has lands between him and the
sea, and who ought to build certain banks and clean certain ditches
and sewers between him and the sea, and he does not make [the
banks] or clean [the ditches] as he ought, whereby the man's lands
are flooded, he shall have a writ of trespass on his case for this not
making or not cleaning.[8]

And if a man is committed to gaol for debt, or arrears of

---

6 The statute was held not to extend to other courts: *Rogers v Marcal* (1665) 1 Sid.
248, 259.

7 I.e. three writs of *capias* and then outlawry. This process had been available at
common law in actions of trespass *vi et armis*, and was extended to account in
1285 (Statute of Westminster II, c. 11), and to debt, detinue and replevin in 1351
(25 Edw. III, stat. 5, c. 17). In 1531 it was further extended to covenant, annuity,
and actions on the 1381 statute of forcible entry: 23 Hen. VIII, c. 14.

8 See *Bernardeston v Heighlynge* (1344), p. 338, above; *Abbot of Stratford's Case*
(1406) Y.B. Hil. 7 Hen. IV, fo. 8, pl. 10.

account, and the gaoler of his malice aforethought puts on him so many irons, or puts him in stocks and withholds food from him, whereby he or his flesh is so much spent (*exust*) that he becomes decrepit or has some other infirmity, he shall have a writ on his case against the gaoler.

And if a man distrains some prior or other prelate, when he is riding on a journey, by his horse which he is riding, for or upon any contract, debt or trespass committed by him or by his predecessor, when he could have distrained or attached other chattels belonging to the same prior or prelate, he shall have a writ on his case as follows[9]. . .

And if a man promises and undertakes to make someone else certain carts for carrying, or some other thing, and takes part of the money for doing this in advance, and then does not do it according to his undertaking or promise, the other shall have a writ of trespass on his case.[10] And the writ shall be as follows:

If W. [shall make you secure concerning the prosecution of his claim] then put [by gage and safe pledges to be before our justices etc.] J. to show why, whereas the same J. had undertaken at S., for a certain sum of money (one part of which he received in advance), to make and build three carriages (*currus*)[11] for conveying the victuals and equipment of the selfsame W. to parts beyond the sea, within a certain period of time agreed between them, the same J. has not bothered to make and build the aforesaid carriages within the aforesaid period of time, as a result of which the same W. has wholly lost various goods and chattels of his to the value of 100 marks, which he should have conveyed in the aforesaid carriages, for want of the aforesaid carriages, to the grave damage of the selfsame W., as he says. And have [you there the names of the pledges and this writ].

And if a man is harboured or lodged in some inn, and some of his goods are taken from thence by a stranger, he shall have an action of trespass on his case against the innkeeper.[12] And the writ shall be as follows:

The king to the sheriff etc. If A. shall make etc. then put etc. B. that he be etc. [to show] why, whereas according to the law and custom of our realm of England innkeepers who keep common inns to accommodate men travelling in those parts where such inns are, and lodging in the same, are bound day and night to keep intact the goods of such travellers which are deposited within those inns so that no damage in any wise befalls such guests through the fault of the selfsame innkeepers or their servants: certain wrongdoers took and led away a certain horse belonging to the selfsame A., worth 40s.,

---

9 *Registrum Brevium* (1531), fo. 100v.
10 See further pp. 378–405, below.
11 Meaning obscure. Perhaps some kind of barge is intended.
12 See further pp. 552–557, below.

which was found stabled in the same B.'s inn at S., through the fault of the selfsame B., and other outrages etc., to the grave damage etc. And have etc. Witness etc.

And if a man sells a horse to another, and warrants him to be sound and good, and the horse is impotent or diseased so that it cannot work, he shall have a writ of trespass on his case against him. Likewise if a man bargains and sells someone certain pipes of wine, and warrants them to be good, and they are sour (*corrupts*), he shall have a writ of trespass on his case against him. But note that he must warrant it to be good, or the horse to be sound, or else he shall not have an action: for if he sells the wine or the horse without such a warranty, the other must buy it from him at his own risk, and his eyes and his taste should be his judges in that case.[13]

But if a smith injures my horse with a nail, I shall have a writ of trespass on my case without any warranty made by the smith to do it properly[14]. . .

And if a man plays at dice with others, and he has false dice with which he plays and wins money from the others by these false dice, he who loses his money may have an action on his case for this false deceit.[15] And the form of the writ is this:

The king to the sheriff etc. If A. shall make etc. then put etc. T. of D. etc. that he be etc. to show why, whereas the same T. of D., scheming deceitfully to defraud the selfsame A. and to extort various sums of money from the same A., enticed and procured the same A. to play at dice with the selfsame T. in a certain game called 'the dozen', for various sums of money, at Burton on Trent; and whereas the same A. played dice there with the selfsame T. in the aforesaid game: the aforesaid T. delivered to the same A. certain dice with true figures (*veraciter titulatos*) to play with, and when the aforesaid dice happened to come into the hands of the selfsame T. the same T. falsely and fraudulently cast certain other dice which were falsely and deceitfully numbered and which he knew would turn up the number 12 and no other number at every throw, whereby the same A. lost great sums of money to the same T. at that game, and the same T. falsely and deceitfully took and carried away those sums under colour of having won, to the damage of the selfsame A. of 100s., as he says. And have there the names of the pledges and this writ. Witness etc.

This writ was sued in 5 Edw. IV . . . And even if the defendant does not entice the plaintiff to play, nevertheless if the defendant plays with such false dice and thereby wins the plaintiff's money, it seems

---

13 See further pp. 506–523, below.
14 See *The Farrier's Case* (1372), p. 341, above; p. 384, below; *Registrum Brevium* (1531), fo. 106.
15 Cf. p. 621, below.

that the plaintiff shall maintain his action well enough, because the cause of action is not the enticing but the casting of the false dice whereby he wins the money.[16]

JAMES HALES' READING ON COSTS (1537)

Reading on 23 Hen. VIII, c. 15, in Gray's Inn:
BL MS. Hargrave 92, fo. 37v.

The statute goes on to say, 'or any action, bill or plaint upon the case', and so it is necessary to see where an action on the case lies: where it lies for nonfeasance (and where not); where it lies for defamation (and where not); where it lies on a bargain (and where not); and where an action on the case lies by reason of purchasing a protection or *supersedeas* (and where not).

[1 Nonfeasance]

First, where an action on the case lies for nonfeasance, and where not. If a man comes to me and says that if I will give him £10 he will make me a good, sufficient barn of a certain length and width, by a certain day, whereupon I give him £10 to do this, and he does not do it before the day, I shall have an action on my case against him. The law is the same if he says to me that if I will give him £10 he will plough and sow 40 acres of land for me before a certain day, and thereupon I give him 40s. and tell him that he will have the rest when he has done it, and he does not plough and sow the said land, I shall have an action on the case against him. But if a man promises me to make me a house before a certain day, or to plough my land, and does not do it, I shall not have an action on my case against him.[17] The law is the same if he promises to do it for £20 which he already owed me, and does not, I shall not have an action

---

16 The precedent was followed in *Davies v Sparks* (1586) Co. Entr. 8, where Sparks was alleged to have enticed Davies to play 'tick-tack' and had used dice which always showed 12, 11 or 10 at every throw. A similar action (arising from a game called 'five or nine') was upheld in *Harris v Bowden* (1588) Cro. Eliz. 90, after a dispute about the correct Latin for 'dice'. In 1633 a similar action was brought for using false dice in a game called 'passage', and the declaration in this form was again upheld: *Hartwell v Oake* (1633) 1 Rolle Abr. 100, line 39. Another adaptation of the formula, for cheating in a card-game with *quadam falsa carta vocata* 'a bum card', was upheld in *Baxter v Woodward* (1606) YLS MS. G. R29.19, fo. 119; Moo. K.B. 776, pl. 1075. And in *Marston v Keysar* (temp. Jac. I or Car. I) it was held that the action lay for cheating in a game called 'hide under hat' or 'cross and pile': entry in CUL MS. Add. 7577, fo. 94v. All these cases were in the King's Bench.

17 I.e. in the absence of prepayment.

on my case. If, however, I lease land to a man for a term of six years, yielding 20s. a year to me, and the lessee promises upon the same lease to build a house upon the same land within the term, and does not do so, I shall have an action on my case against him for not building the house. The law is the same if a man undertakes to look after my sheep until a certain day, whereupon I deliver them to him, and he leads them to another place, and afterwards they are drowned through his fault, I shall have an action on the case against him. But if I desire a man to look after my sheep until a certain day, and he promises to do so, and then they are drowned, I shall not have an action on the case.[18] If, on the other hand, a man requests me to be bound for him to a stranger in a bond for £20, and he promises to save me harmless, whereupon I bind myself for him, and I am afterwards impleaded for it, I shall have an action on the case. The law is the same if I request a man to be bound for me to another in £20, and if he will do so I promise him that I and two sufficient men with me will be bound to him in £20 within eight days then next following, whereupon he binds himself, and I and two others with me are not bound to him, he shall have an action on the case. But if I promise someone that, whereas he is bound to such and such a person in £20, I will save him harmless, and I do not do so, he shall nevertheless not have an action on the case. The law is the same if I promise a man that I will [become] bound to him in £20 before a certain day, and I do not do so, he shall not have an action on the case against me. But if I am bound to a man in a single bond for £20, and he comes to me and says that if I will pay him the said £20 he will deliver the bond (wherein I am bound to him) to me within three days thereafter, whereupon I pay him the said £20, and he will not deliver the bond, I shall have an action on my case against him.[19] It is otherwise, however, if I am bound to a man in a conditional bond for payment of a lesser sum before a certain day, and he says to me that if I will pay him the said sum in the condition he will deliver the bond to me within ten days then next following, and he does not do so, I shall nevertheless not have an action on the case against him for this.

If I am riding along the road and my horse loses one of its shoes, and I go to a smith (there being no other smith in the same vill[20]) and offer him twopence to put a shoe on him, and he has shoes ready but will not do it out of malice, I shall have an action on the

---

18   The distinction seems to be that in the second case the sheep are not handed over to the promisor. Cf. p. 398, below.

19   Because I (the debtor) remain liable to an action of debt: pp. 251–258, above.

20   This qualification is added in an interlineation.

case. It is otherwise if I go to someone who has a common inn, and request him to lodge me, and tender him money to do so, and he refuses, I shall nevertheless not have an action.[1]

If I sell a man ten haycocks which are on my land, and later he does not carry them from my land, whereby my land is impaired, I shall have an action on the case. If, however, I have a right of common in a large field, where various men have land, and after the corn is cut one of those who has land in the same field will not carry away his corn, but allows it to lie there, I shall not have an action on the case.

If a man ought by prescription to clean out a ditch, and does not do so, as a result of which my meadow is flooded, I shall have an action. The law is the same where a man ought by prescription to repair a bridge, over which I have my way from my house towards a certain vill, and he does not repair it, so that I cannot pass over the bridge, I shall have my action.[2]

But if my feoffee to my use will not enfeoff me I shall not have an action on my case.[3] The law is the same if a bond is made to another to my use, and he will not sue. The law is the same if a bond is made to two, and one of them will not sue. The law is the same if I am seised of land in fee, and someone has adjoining land, by reason of which he ought to fence between himself and me, and will not do it, I shall not have an action on my case against him. But if I have land for a term of years, and another has land adjoining it, by reason of which he ought to fence between himself and me, and does not do so, I shall have an action on the case against him. The law is the same if a person who ought to pay tolls in a market buys a horse in a fair or market and does not pay the toll, an action on the case lies against him for this for not paying the toll. The law is the same if I have cause to bring a writ of right for land in ancient demesne, and the lord out of malice which he bears towards me will not hold a court, I shall have an action on my case against him. If my beasts are impounded in the gildable,

---

1 This was a moot point at the time. In Y.B. Pas. 5 Edw. IV, fo. 2, pl. 20, is the clear statement: '... And it was said by all the justices that if a common innkeeper will not lodge me, I shall not have an action against him, but shall complain to the ruler of the vill and he shall give direction therein'. Prysot C.J. was of the same opinion in Y.B. Mich. 39 Hen. VI, fo. 18, pl. 24. But Moyle J. in that case held that 'if I come to an innkeeper to lodge with him, and he will not lodge me, I shall have on my case an action of trespass against him'. This latter opinion is also found in Y.B. Pas. 14 Hen. VII, fo. 22, pl. 4, per Heigham Sjt.; Dyer 158, *per curiam* (1558); and it eventually prevailed.
2 See p. 402, below.
3 See Selden Soc. vol. 94, pp. *197–198*.

and I go to the sheriff and show this to him and offer him that I will enter a plaint before him against the person who took them, and also to find him pledges of prosecution and of making return, and I show him where the beasts are, and he refuses to replevy them to me, I shall have an action on my case against him. The law is the same if I deliver to the sheriff a sealed writ of *capias* to take the body of John Style, and I show him the said John Style and request him to arrest the said John Style, and he will not, and later returns the writ, I shall have an action on the case against him.

[2   Defamation]

Next [we must consider] where an action on the case is maintainable upon defamation, and where not. If a man out of malice or ill will calls me a villein, in front of various men, I shall nevertheless not have an action on the case for this. But if he calls me the villein of a particular person, regardant to his manor of Dale, so that the said man claims me as his villein, whereas I am free, an action on the case lies.[4] So it is if he calls me a thief, and does not say what goods I have stolen.[5] So it is if he calls me a murderer, and does not say what person I have murdered. So it is if he says I use false weights and measures, and does not say which. So it is if he says I am a traitor.[6] In these cases it behoves me to allege in my writ how and in what way I am damaged by reason of being so called. Nevertheless it is not traversable whether I am thereby damaged or not, but it is necessary to answer as to what he has called me.[7] If, however, a man calls me a heretic, I shall not have an action on the case against him, even though I have alleged that I am damaged thereby and have shown how and in what way.[8] The law is the same if he calls me an adulterer, or a knave, poller, or shaver.[9] The law is the same if he calls me a deer-stealer, I shall not have an action on the case. But if he says what deer I have stolen, and it is not so, ɪ shall have an action on the case. And if I say to a man that he has

---

4   In *Wyberd v Richardson* (1522) KB 27/1042, m. 63, the defendant pleaded that the plaintiff called him a whoremaster, and so he called him a churl, without claiming him to be a villein: issue was joined on the claiming.

5   See further pp. 633, 634, below.

6   See p. 635, below.

7   See pp. 626, 633, below.

8   Because the matter is spiritual: see p. 626, below.

9   A poller or shaver (literally a haircutter or barber) was, in Tudor slang, an extortioner or swindler. In *Gascon v Snape* (1519) KB 27/1033, m. 29, a plaintiff recovered £6 damages for the words 'poller and extortioner'. But in *Kene v Smyth* (1526) CP 40/1052, m. 409, another action for 'poller', the court took advisement and no judgement was entered.

robbed me of so much, which is not true, and no one hears, he shall not have an action, even if he alleges that he was thereby damaged. But if [I say] to someone that if [I meet] him [I] will arrest him for the same felony, and for that reason he does not dare to go about his business, an action lies perfectly well. If a man calls me a fool, a madman, a lunatic, a niggard, or a glutton, I shall nevertheless not have an action on the case for that. The law is the same if he calls me a vagabond, or a beggar, or an apostate. But if a man says of a miller that he is accustomed to take excessive tolls, he shall have an action on the case for that. The law is the same if a man calls a vintner a brewer of wine.

[3 Deceit on a bargain]

Next [we must consider] where an action on the case lies on a bargain, and where not.[10] If I sell a man a horse for £10, and upon the bargain I warrant him that the horse is safe and sound, whereas it then has bolts,[11] from which it dies, I shall have an action on my case against him even though the horse was there at the time of the bargain. It is otherwise, however, if the warranty is made after the contract. The law is the same if I sell a man a horse for £10, and warrant him that it has two eyes, and in fact it only has one, he shall not have an action if the horse was there at the time of the bargain. The law is the same if I sell someone 20 ewes, which are present, and warrant that they are wethers, the vendee shall not have an action on the case. If, however, I sell someone a hundred lambs and warrant that they are bred in a particular country, whereas they were not bred there, he shall have an action on the case. The law is the same if I warrant that they are only two years' old, and they are four years' old. But if I sell a man a cloth, which he has looked at, and warrant him that it is scarlet, where it is crimson, he shall not have an action on the case. If, on the other hand, I sell a man a cloth and warrant that it is well and substantially made, and it is stopped and thicked with flocks,[12] the vendee shall have an action on the case. But if I sell a man wheat, and warrant that it will grow if he sows it, and it is sown but does not grow, he shall nevertheless not have an action on the case. The law is the same if I sell a man a horse and warrant that it will bear him 40 miles a day, and it will not do so, an action on the case does not lie.[13] The law is the same if I know my horse is diseased, and I

10 See further pp. 506–523, below.
11 Meaning obscure, but presumably a hidden defect.
12 Cf. 33 Hen. VIII, c. 18, s. 3 (stopped with flocks).
13 See pp. 513, 518, below.

sell it to a man, he shall not have an action unless I warranted the horse. The law is the same of lambs. But if I sell a man wine which is stale, without warranting it, but knowing that it is stale, an action on the case lies. The law is the same if someone sells me unwholesome beef or mutton, without a warranty, I shall nevertheless have an action.[14] If I take a man's horse in pledge, and sell it to someone else for 40s. to be paid at Easter then next following, and then (before the said feast and before the money is paid) the owner takes the horse from the vendee, he shall have an action on the case against [me]. (But if the sale was in market overt, it would be otherwise.) The law is the same if I go to a man and show him a sample of wheat or barley, and offer to sell him 20 quarters, and warrant him that, if he will buy it, all 20 quarters shall be as good as the sample, and they are not as good, the vendee shall have an action on the case.

If I command my servant to sell a certain horse at a certain market, and I know that it is infected with malanders,[15] by virtue of which my servant sells the same horse and warrants that it is safe and sound, the vendee shall nevertheless not have an action on the case either against me or my servant. But if I deliver various things to my servant to sell at a certain market, and I know they are unwholesome, and my servant sells them and warrants them good and wholesome, the vendee shall have an action against me (but not against my servant).[16]

[4 Abuse of procedure]

Next [we turn to the question] where an action on the case lies by reason of purchasing a protection or *supersedeas*, and where not. If the defendant in an action of debt, after the parties have joined issue and two triers have been sworn to try the array,[17] casts a protection *quia profecturus* with such and such a person in France on a voyage royal, and it is allowed, and then the defendant stays all the time in England and does not go with the said captain, an action on the case lies for the plaintiff against this defendant who cast the protection.[18] But it is otherwise if he goes across the sea with the said captain and returns within the year. The law is the same if the tenant in a *praecipe quod reddat* makes default after

---

14 See pp. 510, 515, 516, below.
15 A dry scabby infection behind a horse's knee.
16 See pp. 511–512, below.
17 I.e. because the array of potential jurors has been challenged: see Selden Soc. vol. 94, pp. *105–106*.
18 See p. 514, below.

default, and someone else comes and prays to be received, and sets out that he is the reversioner, and the demandant counterpleads the receipt, and they are at issue on this, and at the day of *nisi prius* a protection is cast for the prayee, and allowed, the demandant shall nevertheless not have an action on the case against the prayee. But if the tenant in the *praecipe quod reddat* prays aid, and when the summons *ad auxiliandum* is returned a protection *quia profecturus* is cast for the prayee, so that the matter is adjourned *sine die*, and he does not go but stays here, the demandant shall have an action on the case against the prayee. But if the tenant in a *praecipe quod reddat* prays in aid, and at the return of the summons *ad auxilian-dum* it is not returned, and a protection *quia profecturus* is put forward for the prayee, so that the matter is adjourned *sine die*, and still the prayee does not go in accordance with the protection but stays in England, an action on the case does not lie against him.

If a man is sued in London in debt, and the defendant purchases a *supersedeas* out of the King's Bench, reciting that he is a servant to an officer of the said court, whereas he is not so, and by reason thereof they stay proceedings in London, the plaintiff shall have an action on the case against the defendant.[19] If a husband and wife are sued in London in an action of debt, and a *supersedeas* is put forward for them because the husband is a minister of the Chancery, and on that account they are discharged from the said suit in London, whereas the husband is not a minister of the Chancery, he shall nevertheless not have an action on the case. The law is the same if someone is sued in London, and the defendant purchases a *supersedeas* because he is sued in the King's Bench, whereas he is not being sued there, and by reason thereof they stay proceedings in London, the plaintiff shall nevertheless not have an action on the case. The law is the same if a defendant who is sued in the Common Pleas purchases a *supersedeas* out of the Chancery because he is one of the ministers there, whereas he is not so, and by reason thereof the justices stay, the plaintiff shall nevertheless not have an action on the case.

COX v GRAY (1610)

CUL MS. Gg. 5. 5, fo. 299.[20]

... Trespass is *nomen collectivum*, and in the Register and by

---

19   See pp. 513–515, below.

20   *The Case of the Marshalsea*; also reported in 10 Co. Rep. 68; 1 Buls. 207.

Fitzherbert (in his *New Natura Brevium*[1]) it is divided into two sorts, namely trespass *vi et armis* and trespass *super casum.* Trespass is the genus, trespass *super casum* and trespass *vi et armis* are species... In a writ of error between Bull and Lamaire in the King's Bench, Hil. 1 Jac. rot. 363, it was assigned as error that the *venire facias* was 'in a plea of trespass' where the action was trespass on the case, and so the words 'on the case' were left out in the *venire facias*; and this was adjuged by all the justices to be no error, and the judgment was affirmed, because every action of trespass on the case is trespass...

BOULTER v BEST (1632)

(a) Record: KB 27/1589, m. 276 (the bill printed
here is entered as a 'plea of trespass').

Berkshire. Anthony Boulter complains of William Best, being in the custody of the marshal of the lord king's Marshalsea before the king himself, that, whereas the aforesaid William knowingly kept (*scienter retinuit*) at Wallingford in the county aforesaid a certain mastiff dog which was accustomed to bite pigs, on 10 June [1630] in the sixth year of the reign of the lord Charles now king of England, the same mastiff dog at Wallingford aforesaid in the county aforesaid so seriously bit, injured and wounded a sow belonging to the selfsame Anthony which was great with pigs and worth 40s. that the sow became (*detinuit*, for *devenit*)[2] ill and afterwards died, to the damage of the selfsame Anthony of £5. And thereof he produces suit etc.

Best pleaded Not guilty, and a jury was summoned. No more is entered, though the report says that a jury found for the plaintiff.

(b) Beare's reports, CUL MS. Ii. 5, 23, fo. 49v;
HLS MS. 1166, fo. 106; HLS MS. Acc. 704782, fo. 98v;
LI MS. Coxe 93, unfol.

... *Tisdale* moved in arrest of judgment, because the plaintiff entered his plaint 'in a plea of trespass' and declared in an action on the case.

But it was held by the court to be good, because trespass is the genus of this action.

Secondly, he said that it is no offence for a dog to bite hogs, for it

---

1   For his treatment of case, see p. 342, above.
2   This slip was also pointed out in arrest of judgment.

is lawful for everyone to hunt and bite hogs which come into his land and trespass.

But the court denied this, and said that it is not lawful to hunt and bite hogs which come into someone's land; [for] although he may chase them out gently without [committing] a trespass, if he makes his dog bite them he is a trespasser . . .

And judgment was given for the plaintiff accordingly.

JASON v NORTON (1653)

Style 398 (untr.).[3]

In an action upon the case for entering into the plaintiff's house, and making an assault upon his daughter, and getting a bastard child upon her, the jury found a special verdict, upon which the case was this: Norton sojourned in the house of Jason, and during his sojourning there he got his daughter with child; four years after, Jason brought an action upon the case against Norton for assaulting his daughter, and getting her with child, *per quod servicium amisit*. The question here was whether, because no action was brought by the daughter for the wrong done to her within four years, and thereby she was barred by the Statute of Limitations to bring her action,[4] Jason the father might now bring his action upon the case for the damage done to him by the loss of his daughter's service, or should be also barred by the statute.

Powys argued that he was not barred, though the daughter was . . . and said that, though the trespass and the assault was done to the daughter, yet here is a *per quod servicium amisit* declared of, which doth belong to Jason, the father.

ROLLE C.J. This action is an action brought for the damage done to the master; and though the servant will release the battery, yet the master may have an action for the damage caused to him by the battery; and although the daughter cannot have an action, her father may—although not for entering into his house, because it was with his leave, nor for assaulting his daughter and getting her with child, because this is a wrong particularly done to her, yet for the loss of her service caused by this he may have an action. But it is a pretty case, and fit to be argued. Therefore bring us books, and we will advise upon it.

3 Sub nom. *Norton v Jason*. The reference there given to the plea roll is incorrect.
4 21 Jac. I, c. 16, s. 3, laid down a limitation period of four years for assault, battery, wounding and imprisonment; and of six years for other forms of trespass and case (except slander, for which it was two years).

At another day the case was again spoken unto by *Baldwin* of the Inner Temple on the defendant's part. And he made the question to be whether this be an action of trespass *vi et armis* or an action upon the case which is here brought; and he argued that it is a trespass *vi et armis* and not an action upon the case... And although the action conclude with a *per quod servicium amisit*, yet it sounds more in trespass than to be an action upon the case, and then he is barred by the Statute of Limitations...

ROLLE C.J.... The cause of action is *per quod servicium amisit*, and for this he hath brought it within the time limited by the statute, for it is an action upon the case. Although the *causa causans*[5] is the *vi et armis*, which is but inducement to the action, [yet][6] the *causa causata* viz. the loss of the service is the ground of the action...

REYNOLDS v CLARKE (1725)

Record: KB 122/103, m. 474 (Trin. 1722). William Reynolds complained that Edward Clarke, on various dates between 1 June and 20 October 1721, with force and arms, broke and entered the plaintiff's house and back yard in Abingdon, Berkshire, and cast filth (*fetidates et sordida*) there, and put up a spout from which rainwater overflowed into the plaintiff's stable and brewhouse and rotted and spoiled the timbers and foundations thereof. The defendant pleaded Not guilty as to everything except the entry and erection of the spout; and, as to that, he set out a title[7] to use the yard in common with the plaintiff, and that the rainwater had always been accustomed to run from his messuage into the yard, and that in order to make necessary use of his messuage he entered the yard and put up the spout, to convey the water into the yard, as well he might. The plaintiff demurred.

Sir Nathaniel Gundry's notebook,
LI MS. Misc. 31, p. 85 (untr.).[8]

... When this case was first argued, PRATT C.J. (who was then chief justice) seemed to have great doubt whether trespass did not lie, for he said that where a person hath the use of a thing and uses it in a

---

5 See *Earl of Rutland v Spencer* (1610), sub nom. *The Earl of Shrewsbury's Case*, 9 Co. Rep. 46, at fo. 50v.

6 Reads 'and', which does not make sense.

7 John Fountain conveyed a house and yard to the plaintiff in 1708, reserving the use of the yard for the tenants and occupiers of two adjoining messuages; in 1710 he devised both messuages to his wife for life, remainder to Daniel Yate; the wife died; Yate in 1713 devised both messuages to his wife; and Yate's wife in 1716 conveyed them to the defendant.

8 Also reported in 2 Ld Raym. 1399; 1 Strange 634; 8 Mod. 272; Fort. 212.

different manner than what the use warrants, in his opinion he seemed a trespasser.[9] If a man hath a watercourse within his own ground, and diverts it to the prejudice of another, an action of the case lies; but if he diverts it in such manner that he overflows the ground of his neighbour, an action of trespass will lie.

Afterwards, in Trinity term [1725], 11 Geo. Regis, this case was argued a second time.

And RAYMOND C.J. said that actions must be confined to their proper bounds,[10] and the distinction made by Fazakerley[11]. . . is very right . . . and was clearly of opinion that the present action of trespass could not be maintained, but that it ought to have been an action upon the case.

POWYS J. of the same opinion.

FORTESCUE J. This action in its nature is an action upon the case for a nuisance, and trespass is improper. The Civilians call action upon the case *actio injuriarum*, which is very proper. To maintain trespass there ought to be an immediate act working a wrong.[12] Everyone hath a right to the highway, and if John Style throws a log upon one in the highway and hurts him, this is an immediate wrong for which an action of trespass lies; but if John Style should lay the log in the highway, and one comes and stumbles over it, in this case an action upon the case lies . . .

REYNOLDS J. Acts injurious in themselves are proper for actions of trespass; but acts at first lawful and which become only injurious in their consequences must be punished by actions upon the case. The act of the defendant in the present case was not the wrong, but the consequence only was the wrong; and as soon as the conse-

---

9 Cf. Edward Leeds' notebook, LI MS. Hill 91, fo. 83: '[PRATT] C.J. If the defendant should break up the stones or pavement of this yard, he would be a trespasser; and though the entry into the yard be lawful, yet the putting a spout in his house to the detriment of his neighbour seems to me a trespass'.

10 Cf. 1 Strange: 'We must keep up the boundaries of actions, otherwise we shall introduce the utmost confusion'.

11 Counsel for the defendant. His argument is given earlier in the MS.: 'Actions upon the case and actions of trespass must not be confounded. The known distinction is that when an act is done which is an immediate wrong to the party, there trespass lies; but where an act is done which does not immediately work a wrong to the party, but only a remote or consequential wrong, then an action upon the case lies. It will not be denied but that trespass will not lie for a nonfeasance; and what the defendant in this case is charged with is no more, for the only wrong is his negligence in not managing his spout so as to be no prejudice to the plaintiff'.

12 Cf. 1 Strange: 'FORTESCUE J. . . . The difference between trespass and case is that in trespass the plaintiff complains of an immediate wrong, and in case of a wrong that is the consequence of another act'.

quence happened then the plaintiff had a right to have an action upon the case, but not an action of trespass . . .

A marginal note in the record shows that judgment for the defendant was signed on 16 November 1725.

EXTRACT FROM A BOOK ON PLEADING (*c.* 1730)

HLS MS. 1074, vol. II, p. 185 (untr.).

[Actions on the case] are founded on some fraud or deceit in contract or some secret injury to a man's right or property,[13] and are said to rise from a nonfeasance, malefeasance or misfeasance.

Nonfeasance is when a man does not perform something which he ought to perform, either by his own express undertaking (called an *assumpsit* express) or by the implication or requiring of law (called an *assumpsit* implied), by the not doing of which the plaintiff receives damage.

Misfeasance is the doing something (which a man hath expressly undertaken to do or which the law by implication requireth him to do) otherwise than he undertook, by the misdoing whereof the plaintiff receives damage.

Malefeasance is when a man does purposely of his own head, fancy or humour something without any express *assumpsit*, implication or requiring by law, by which ill-doing the plaintiff likewise receives damage.

Although in some cases an injury happens to a man in his property by the neglect of another, yet if by law such person was not obliged to be more careful no action will lie. As, if a man finds butter and by his negligent keeping it putrefies, yet no action will

---

13 Cf. J. Mallory, *Modern Entries* (1734), vol. I, p. 229: 'Actions on the case are to be brought for a satisfaction in damages for injuries done to a man either with respect to his own person or the persons of those in whom he has an interest, and for injuries done to his property or to the property wherewith he is entrusted by law for the benefit of others . . . Actions upon the case for injuries relating to a man's property may be thus considered: that, as a man is capable of acquiring property, so he hath by law a right to have it preserved to him. And the law with regard to the preservation of property hath these three following rules relating thereto: first, that no man is to deprive another of his property, or wilfully to do a damage thereto, nor disturb another in the enjoyment thereof. Secondly, every man by the rules of law is bound to take due care and preserve his own property so as the neglect thereof may not tend to injure his neighbour. Thirdly, every man is so to use and enjoy his property that he does not, in the manner of his use and enjoyment thereof, do a damage to the property of his neighbour'. Cf. pp. 560–561, below.

lie.[14] Or, if a man finds garments and by negligent keeping they are moth-eaten, no action lies. So, if a man finds goods and loses them again, or if he finds a horse and gives him no sustenance, no action lies: for in these cases the law has laid no duty on the finder; for it would be too rigorous to oblige him to be charitable in behalf of a careless owner.

But if a man makes gain and advantage of the thing he finds, as if he rides an horse; or if he abuses them, as by putting paper into water, or if he kills sheep etc.: he shall answer for them . . .

The difference between trespass and case is, that in trespass [the] plaintiff complains of an immediate wrong and in case of a wrong that is the consequence of another act. The distinction is, if the act in the first instance is unlawful trespass will lie; but if the act is prima facie lawful and the prejudice to another is not immediate but consequential, it must be an action on the case[15]. . .

14 See *Walgrave v Ogden* (1591), p. 569, below.
15 See *Reynolds v Clarke* (1725), p. 354, above.

14 Assumpsit for misfeasance

BUKTON v TOUNESENDE (1348)
THE HUMBER FERRY CASE

(a) Record: KB 27/354, m. 85.

Yorkshire. It is found by the jury upon which John de Bukton of
Cave, plaintiff, and Nicholas atte Tounesende of Hessle, ferryman,
put themselves that the same Nicholas on the Monday next after
Martinmas in the twentieth year of the king's reign [13 November
1346] at Hessle received a certain mare from John to carry safely
across the River Humber in Nicholas's boat, and the same Nicholas so loaded the boat against John's will that he lost the aforesaid
mare through Nicholas's fault, in the way that the same John
complains by his bill, to John's damage of 40s.; but that the same
John did not lose any goods or chattels there, as he complains by
the same bill. Therefore it is decided that the same John should
recover against the said Nicholas his aforesaid damages; and that
the same Nicholas should be taken etc.; and that the same John
should be in mercy for his false claim with respect to the aforesaid
chattels...

(a) Report: 22 Lib. Ass., pl. 41; corrected from
LI MS. Hale 116.

John de [Bukton] complains by bill that [Nicholas atte Toune-
sende] on a certain day and year at B.[1] upon Humber had
undertaken to carry his mare in his boat across the River Humber

---

1 According to the record, this should be Hessle; but BL MS. Harley 811, fo. 38
  extends it as 'Brokst'—perhaps Brough (which is where Ermine Street met the
  Humber).

safe and sound, and yet the said [Nicholas] overloaded his boat with other horses, as a result of which overloading his mare perished, wrongfully and to his damage.

Richemund. We pray judgment of the bill, which supposes no wrong in us, but proves that he should have had an action by way of covenant rather than[2] by way of trespass.

BAKEWELL. It seems that you did him a trespass when you overloaded his boat so that his mare perished. So answer.

Richemund. Not guilty.

[The plaintiff's counsel.] Ready to aver our bill.

WALDON v MARESCHAL (1369)

Y.B. Mich. 43 Edw. III, fo. 33, pl. 38; collated with LI MS. Hale 187, fo. 104v.

William of Waldon[3] brought a writ against one John Mareschal,[4] and alleged in his writ that the aforesaid John undertook[5] to cure the aforesaid William's horse of an illness, and afterwards the aforesaid John so negligently applied his treatment that the horse died.

Kirkton challenged the writ because it said *contra pacem*, and in his count he has counted of negligent treatment as a result of which the horse perished, and therefore it cannot be said to have been against the peace.

The justices were of the opinion that the writ was bad. But then the writ was read, and there was no *contra pacem* in it; and so the writ was held good.

Kirkton. Since he has confessed that the defendant undertook to cure his horse of an illness, he should in that case have had an action of covenant. So we pray judgment of the writ.

Belknap. We cannot have that without a deed. This action is brought because you performed the treatment so negligently that the horse died, and therefore it is right to maintain this special writ according to the case, rather than to abate it, for we can have no other writ.

Kirkton. You could have had a writ of trespass, alleging in general terms that he killed your horse.

---

2 Some MSS. say 'and not'. The printed edition of 1679 says 'or', which gives quite the wrong sense.
3 Reads 'Walton' in MS.
4 A marshal was a horse-leech, or veterinary surgeon.
5 Reads 'manucepit' in print, 'manucepisset' in MS.

Belknap. We could not have had a general writ, because the horse was not slain by force but died for want of being cured. Moreover his plea is to the action, not to the writ; and if you want to plead to the action, we will imparl.

Then the writ was held good.

It was said by THORPE [C.J.] that he had seen a leech[6] indicted, where he had undertaken to cure a man of an illness and killed him by default of his cure.

Kirkton. John performed the treatment as well as he knew how, without this that he undertook to cure the horse of the illness. [And he could not be received to plead to this issue, but was driven to say that he performed the treatment as well as he knew how, without this that the horse died by default of his cure];[7] ready etc.

The other side to the contrary.

STRATTON v SWANLOND (1374)

Although the defendant is named in the Y.B. as Morton or Merton, Professor Kiralfy has conjecturally identified the case from the record: KB 27/453, m. 100d; abstracted in *Source Book*, p. 185. Robert of Stratton and Agnes his wife sued John Swanlond, a surgeon, in an action on the case. They declared that the defendant had agreed to heal a wound in Agnes's hand, but had so negligently treated her that the wound became septic and she was maimed. The defendant pleaded an agreement in Billingsgate Ward, London, to conduct an operation on her almost severed hand, which he performed; and denied that he had guaranteed to heal her, or had maimed her through his negligence. The plaintiffs replied that the defendant had guaranteed his cure, in Tower Ward, and that he did maim her through his negligence. No outcome is recorded.

Y.B. Hil. 48 Edw. III, fo. 6, pl. 11;
corrected from LI MS. Hale 181, fo. 105v;
Statham Abr., *Action sur le case*.[8]

A woman brought a writ of trespass against John Morton, a surgeon, and the writ alleged that, whereas her right hand had been wounded by one Thomas Blenchden, the person against whom the

---

6 Reads 'un myre' in MS., 'un M.' in print.
7 Omitted in 1679 ed.
8 There is some confusion over the names. Hasty becomes Gascoigne in the printed edition, Honington becomes Percy in Statham, and Cavendish becomes Fyncheden in Statham. Statham also turns Tower Ward into 'Strond crosse' (i.e. Charing Cross). Blenchden is simply B. in the printed edition, and is not mentioned in the record. The texts are nevertheless the same.

writ is brought undertook to heal her injured hand; and by the negligence of this same John and his cure her hand was made so much worse that she is now maimed, to her injury and damage. (Observe that there was no mention in this writ of the place where he undertook, as above, though in her count she declared that he undertook in the ward of Tower Street, in London, in the parish of Barking. And the writ did not say *vi et armis*, or *contra pacem regis*.)

Hasty. He did not undertake to heal her wound, as she has supposed; and this he is ready to deny by his law.

Honington. This is an action of trespass for something which lies in the knowledge of the countryside, in which case wager of law is not grantable. So, for want of an answer, we demand judgment and pray our damages.

CAVENDISH. This writ does not suppose force and arms, or *contra pacem*, and so it seems wager of law is quite acceptable. Do you therefore wish to accept the law, or not?

Honington. We will not accept wager of law, come what may.

CAVENDISH. Then we will record that you have refused law, as above. And I must tell you that you are in a difficult position (*en fort case*) (meaning, that wager of law was acceptable).

And that was the opinion of the whole court. But because the defendant saw that he would be adjourned until another term, he waived the tender of law and said that he did not undertake to heal her hand, as above; ready.

And the other side to the contrary.

Hasty. Sir, you now see plainly that the writ does not mention the place where he undertook to heal her, and so the writ is defective in matter; for the court cannot know from what venue to summon the country.

Percy. Because there is no place specified in the writ, we demand judgment of the writ.

Honington. Since we have assigned in our count the place where he undertook to heal us, so that what is not contained in the writ is contained in the count, we must in that regard permit the country to come from the place where we have assigned the undertaking. So we pray judgment whether our writ is not perfectly good.

CAVENDISH. Now is the time to challenge the writ because he has not assigned where the thing was undertaken, because it is necessary to summon the country from that place. But if you had demurred in law according to your first issue, and wager of law had been [allowed], it would not have been necessary to assign a place in the writ. Also, this action of covenant is of necessity maintainable without specialty, because a man cannot always have a clerk to make a specialty in respect of such a small matter.

Honington. The writ asserts that she was maimed by him, and so it is to be supposed that she is suing in the nature of trespass, in which it is needful for the place to be mentioned.

CAVENDISH. She was not maimed by the surgeon, but by the other person who struck her; and so, even if she now recovers damages against the defendant, she will afterwards have an appeal against the person who maimed her.

Honington. If I deliver my horse to a smith for shoeing, and he injures it with a nail, I shall have a writ of trespass against him. Or, if my horse is injured with a nail, and I deliver it to a horse-leech[9] to heal, and by his negligent cure my horse is maimed, I shall have a writ on the facts. Likewise in the present case.

CAVENDISH. That is true, because the horse cannot have an action: namely, an appeal of mayhem against the person who struck him. In this case, however, the woman may have an appeal of mayhem against the person who struck her. And if a farrier undertakes to heal my horse, and by his negligence or failure to cure it within a reasonable time the horse is made worse, it is right that he should be held guilty. But if he does all he can, or puts all his diligence into the cure, it is not right that he should be held guilty, even though the horse is not healed. There is a great difference between the two cases.

Later, because the place where the cure was undertaken was missing from the writ, the writ was abated by judgment, and the plaintiff was amerced.

SKYRNE v BUTOLF (1388)

(a) The count: CP 40/509, m. 230.

London. Thomas Butolf, leech, was attached to answer Robert de Skyrne concerning a plea ... And thereupon the same Robert, by William Woderhawe his attorney, complains that, whereas the same Thomas on the Monday [29 April 1387] next before the feast of the Invention of the Holy Cross in the tenth year of the reign of the present lord king, in return for a certain sum of money (namely 56s. 8d.) paid to him beforehand in London in the parish of St Magnus in Bridge Ward, had undertaken competently to cure the aforesaid Robert of a certain infirmity from which he suffered

---

9 I.e. 'marshal'; see p. 359; above.

(namely, ringworms), the aforesaid Thomas so negligently and improvidently applied his cure in the parish of St Mary-le-Strand without the bar of the New Temple, London, in the county of Middlesex, where the same Robert then dwelt, that is to say, that he applied medicines contrary to the aforesaid disease, that the aforesaid Robert remained uncured in default of the selfsame Thomas, so that the same Robert in order to recover his health was compelled to seek a cure elsewhere; whereby he says that he is the worse and has damage to the value of 100s. And thereof he produces suit etc.

(b) Report: Y.B. Pas. 11 Ric. II, p. 223, pl. 12.

Robert Skyrne, clerk, brought his writ of trespass on his case against a leech (*mire*),[10] and counted by *Penrose* that on a certain day in a certain year in London, in a certain place in the parish etc., a covenant was made between the plaintiff and the leech concerning a certain disease of worms which the plaintiff had, and the leech took from him a certain sum of money which the plaintiff paid him in hand to cure him of the said disease, which sum he took, and he was to come daily to the Strand to apply his medicines; and he came to the Strand and applied his medicines to the plaintiff's disease, and they were contrary to his disease, as a result of which he was made worse than he was before and was on point of being lost had he not sought another leech to cure him; wrongfully and to the plaintiff's damage. (And the writ was according to his case, and was brought in London.)

Therefore *Sydenham* said: sir, you see clearly that the plaintiff has brought this writ in London and has counted that the leech was to come to the Strand, and that he came there to the place where the plaintiff supposes the wrong to have been done, which is in the county of Middlesex. So we pray judgment of this writ brought in London.

Penrose. Sir, I have counted on my case, and how the covenant was made in London, and the defendant took our money beforehand; and so we pray judgment whether our writ is not sufficiently good.

Rikhill. It seems that the writ should abate, for the plaintiff alleges by his count that the wrong was done in the Strand, and that is the cause of his action. Suppose they were at issue on the cure: I say that the jury could not come from London, for Londoners could not know anything about this, but there must be

10 Cf. p. 360, above.

a jury from the country where the wrong is supposed. When, therefore, the plaintiff himself has supposed that the wrong was done in the Strand, which is in the county of Middlesex, I say that this writ is clearly abated.

Markham. The writ is perfectly good in either county.

Wadham. Sir, it seems to me also that the writ is abated; for it is not the covenant in this case which gives the right of action but the wrong which he has supposed, and that is in another county. Suppose in a case under the Statute of Labourers a man makes a covenant with me in one county and I retain him in another county, and afterwards he departs from my service and I bring a writ where he made the covenant, my writ is abated; for if he wishes to take issue that he did not depart etc., or that he was not retained etc., a jury could not come from the county where the covenant was made, but only from the county where the departure or retainer occurred. Likewise in this case, if they were at issue on the cure, the jury must come from the country where the wrong is alleged; for this is a writ of trespass and not of covenant. If, however, it were a writ of covenant, it would be another matter.

So THIRNING said: the writ is perfectly good, brought in either county; for if the defendant wishes to take issue on the covenant it is well brought, and if he wishes to take issue on the cure or the medicines it is not improper to cause a jury to come from the other county. Causing a jury to come from another county has often been seen in such a case. [So it may be done] in the case here . . .

Then the writ was adjudged perfectly good.

So *Rikhill* said: sir, we make protestation that we do not admit that the defendant came to the Strand at any time or applied any medicine to the plaintiff there, in the way he has counted; but we say that this same Robert Skyrne came to us in London, in the same parish and ward as he has counted, and told us that he had a certain disease of worms in his head, and asked us if we would cure him of the same disease; and at that time we told him that, with God's grace, we would cure him; and we say that there in the same parish and ward we gave him medicines and applied them to his disease, as a result of which he was cured and healed of his disease, and so the covenant was performed. Therefore no law compels us to answer the matter which he has alleged, and we demand judgment whether he can maintain this action against us.

Penrose. And we make protestation that we do not confess anything that he has alleged; but since he does not deny that he came to us in the Strand and there applied his medicines, which were contrary to our disease, as a result of which we were made worse and on point of being lost, to which he answers nothing, we pray judgment and our damages.

Then *Penrose* asked leave to imparl.

The next day *Rikhill* recited the case, as above, and asked judgment.

CHARLTON [C.J.] to *Rikhill*: be well advised, for when you had cured and healed the plaintiff [in London], why did you afterwards commit the wrong against him in the Strand? (This was not answered.[11]).

THIRNING explained that what had been said concerning a covenant in a certain parish in London referred only to the formation (*commencement*) of the covenant; but he has said expressly that you came to the Strand and there so negligently applied the medicines which were contrary to his disease that he was made worse and on point of being lost, and thus he alleges that all the wrong was done in the Strand. Do you think, then, that it is an answer for you to say that he was healed and cured in London, without answering him? (Implying that it was not.)

So *Rikhill* imparled.

Then, on another day, he made protestation that he did not admit that the defendant came to the Strand, but said that the plaintiff came to him in London in the same parish and ward as he had counted and there the defendant made a covenant with him and undertook to cure him (as above); and that he applied good medicines to him, whereby he was healed and cured there; and so this action cannot be maintained without the preceding covenant: therefore, since he was healed and cured there, we demand judgment whether he can [have this action]. Moreover, he said, 'without this that there was any other covenant'. (See this plea above, in effect.)

Penrose. Sir, we make protestation that we do not confess anything that the defendant has said; but since we have alleged that he came to the Strand where we were dwelling and there negligently applied his medicines to us, which were contrary to our disease, as a result of which we were made worse and not mended—which was his act and wrong, to which he has answered nothing—we demand judgment and pray our damages.

And so to judgment.[12]

Afterwards, in Trinity term, *Penrose* and *Rikhill* by consent of both parties, came to the bar and took issue that the defendant did

11 The printed Y.B. says 'Quod non est ratio', but 'ratio' is a misreading of 'responsum', abbreviated to 'r'.

12 A special demurrer was entered; see (c), below.

not heal the plaintiff in London, as he had counted, and they were received. (Note this, that even though the plea was thus pleaded to judgment and entered, at any time before judgment is given the parties may by consent take issue on the plea at will.[13])

(c) The pleading as entered: CP 40/509, m. 230.

And the aforesaid Thomas comes in his own person and denies the force and injury when etc. And, protesting that he never applied any cure to the aforesaid Robert to cure him of any disease in the parish of St Mary-le-Strand in the aforesaid county of Middlesex, he says that he lives in London in the parish and ward aforesaid where the aforesaid covenant was made, and that on the aforesaid Monday when he alleges that the aforesaid covenant was made the aforesaid Robert came to him the selfsame Thomas there, begging the same Thomas to cure him the said Robert of the aforesaid disease; and he says that he there completely cured the aforesaid Robert of the aforesaid disease according to the form of the covenant between them made therein; and with respect to what the same Robert has above alleged, that he the same Thomas applied his cure to the selfsame Robert in the aforesaid parish of St Mary-le-Strand in the aforesaid county of Middlesex, so negligently and improvidently with medicines contrary to the disease, he has no need by the law of the land to answer. And so he prays judgment whether the aforesaid Robert ought to maintain his aforesaid action against him in that behalf.

And the aforesaid Robert, while not admitting anything alleged above by the selfsame Thomas, nor that the aforesaid answer can by the law of the land be adjudged true, says that the aforesaid Thomas applied his cure to him the said Robert in the aforesaid parish of St Mary-le-Strand in the aforesaid county of Middlesex, so negligently and improvidently with medicines contrary to the aforesaid disease, that the same Robert remained uncured by default of him the said Thomas, in the way he has declared above; which he is ready to aver if etc., and the aforesaid Thomas refuses to admit this averment; and by the law of the land he has no need to answer the aforesaid averment put forward above by the selfsame Thomas; and he prays judgment and that damages be awarded to him in this behalf.

And the aforesaid Thomas says that, since he offers to verify that he completely cured the aforesaid Robert of the aforesaid disease, at London in the parish and ward aforesaid (where the aforesaid

---

13 I.e. by waiving the demurrer.

covenant was made between them), according to the form of the covenant made between them therein, and the same Robert utterly refuses to admit this averment, he also prays judgment as before, and that the aforesaid Robert be barred from his aforesaid action.

Thereupon a day is given to the aforesaid parties until the octaves of the Holy Trinity for hearing their judgment therein etc ... On which day the aforesaid parties come in their own persons. And thereupon, waiving the plea aforesaid whereon the aforesaid parties have pleaded to judgment, by consent of each party, the aforesaid Thomas says that he completely cured the aforesaid Robert of the aforesaid disease in London in the parish and ward aforesaid, according to the form of the aforesaid covenant, as he has alleged before; and this he is ready to aver; and so he prays judgment.

And the aforesaid Robert says that he the aforesaid Thomas did not completely cure him the said Robert of the aforesaid disease in the way that the same Thomas has alleged above. And he asks that this may be enquired into by the country; and the aforesaid Thomas likewise ...

A jury is summoned for Michaelmas term, but nothing more is recorded.

MARSHAL'S CASE (1441)

Y.B. Hil. 19 Hen. VI, fo. 49, pl. 5;
BL MS. Harley 4557, fo. 212 (C.P.).

A writ of trespass on the case against one R. Marshal, on the grounds that the defendant undertook at London to cure his horse of a certain disease, and that he so negligently and carelessly applied medicines that the horse died.

Portington. To that we say that we undertook at Oxford, in Oxfordshire, to cure the horse of the disease whereof you speak, and that we sufficiently did so, without this that we undertook at London to cure your horse. Ready etc.

Markham. That is no plea, for I allege by my writ that he has killed my horse through his negligence, and so that is the effect of my grievance and of my action, and that is what must be traversed, not the undertaking. Similarly, in the case where a carpenter undertakes to build me a good and sufficient house, and never does it, I shall not in this case have an action against him: which proves that the misfeasance is the cause of action, and it is that to my mind which must be traversed.

NEWTON [C.J.] It seems that the plea is good, for it may be that he undertook at Oxford to cure your horse, as is said, and did, and that afterwards at London your horse had the disease again and he applied his medicines of his good will (*de son bon gré*)[14] and then your horse died. Now, for what he did of his own free will you shall not have an action. Ergo, in our case there is no need to traverse it . . . [Suppose] my horse is sick, and I go to a marshal[15] for advice, and he says that one of his horses had such a disease and he applied certain medicines to his horse, and will do the like for my horse; and he does so, and then the horse dies; shall I have an action? I say I shall not. It follows, therefore, that the plaintiff shall not have an action in our case, unless he took it upon himself: and that is what must be traversed, and he has done so.

PASTON to *Markham*. You have not set out that he is a common marshal for curing such a horse, in which case even if he kills your horse by his medicines you will not have an action against him without an undertaking. That proves that the traverse should be taken on the undertaking.

Fortescue. Markham has said that if a carpenter undertakes to build me a house, and does not do so, I shall not have an action, and that this proves that the undertaking in his view is not the cause of action, and therefore the traverse should not be taken upon it. To that I say that in some cases where one undertakes to do something and does not do it, I shall have a good action for his nonfeasance and the traverse shall come on the undertaking, which proves that the undertaking is the cause of action: from whence it follows that the traverse should be taken on the undertaking. For example, suppose I have a ruinous house, and a carpenter undertakes well and sufficiently to mend the said house before a certain day, and does not do so, as a result of which the whole house falls down, I shall have an action against him, and the traverse may well be taken on the undertaking. Likewise here, even though the horse died through his negligence, nevertheless when he has undertaken the cure of the same horse and has not performed it, the action shall be taken on that, just as it shall where the house falls down through his negligence. So it seems that the plea is perfectly good.

AYSCOUGH. It seems that the undertaking is the cause (*effect*) which gives rise to the action, in the same way as if there had been a warranty in the case. Suppose I sell you a hundred sarplers of wool, with a warranty that they are good and merchantable, and then you find the sarplers full of moths: this warranty is as much the

14 I.e. gratuitously, or out of kindness.
15 Cf. pp. 359, 362, above.

cause of your action as the unwholesomeness of the wool, and the traverse may well be taken on this warranty. Likewise in this case, the undertaking is the cause of action; and so the issue may well be taken on it. Similarly, in an action on the Statute of Labourers, the retainer may be traversed just as well as the departure may.

Markham. The writ says that he 'negligently and carelessly applied his medicines', and so it seems that he killed it by these contrary medicines, and therefore the killing of the horse is the cause of his action, and ought (in my view) to be traversed.

NEWTON. The wording 'negligently applied' is void. If I have a disease in my hand, and he applies a medicine to my heel, and by this neglect my hand is maimed, I shall nevertheless not have an action unless he undertook to cure me.

Markham. Then, by your leave, we will imparl.

BARTILMEWE v SHRAGGER (1498)

This entry was copied into the precedent book of John Lucas (d. 1525), an officer of the King's Bench, and from thence into the *Collection of Entrees* compiled by William Rastell (d. 1565), where it is on fo. 2v: see Selden Soc. vol. 94, p. *365*.

KB 27/949, m. 4.

Norwich. Richard Shragger, late of Norwich, barber, was attached to answer Henry Bartilmewe in a plea why . . .[16] Whereupon the same Henry, by William Leg his attorney, complains that, whereas the aforesaid Richard had undertaken at Norwich on 6 December [1497] in the thirteenth year of the reign of King Henry the seventh after the conquest to shave the beard of the selfsame Henry well and in a workmanlike manner with a clean and wholesome razor: the aforesaid Richard then and there so negligently shaved the beard of the selfsame Henry with a certain unclean and unwholesome razor in an unworkmanlike manner that the face of the selfsame Henry became diseased and scabby; to the damage of the same Henry 40s. And thereof he produces suit etc.

The barber pleaded Not guilty, and process to summon a jury was continued until Michaelmas term 1500 because the sheriffs did not execute the writs. No more is recorded.

---

16   Recital of writ is omitted, because it is repeated in the count.

POWTNEY v WALTON (1597)

YLS MS. G. R29.9, fo. 239v; abridged in
HLS MS. 2069, fo. 277; 1 Rolle Abr. 10, line 1.

Powtney brought an action on the case against Thomas Walton, a farrier, and declared that he was possessed of a horse which was gravelled in his feet, and that the defendant took upon himself to cure the said horse, and that the defendant so improvidently and negligently treated the horse that it died at Westminster, to the damage of the plaintiff.

Exception was taken to this declaration, since it was not shown how much the defendant was to have for the cure, and so there is no consideration for the *assumpsit*.

But FENNER and CLENCH JJ. (the rest being absent) ruled the declaration good, notwithstanding this; for the defendant's negligence is the cause of action, and not the *assumpsit*.

COGGS v BARNARD (1703)

(a) The plaintiff's bill: KB 122/5, m. 435.

John Coggs complains of William Barnard, being in the custody of the marshal of the lady queen's marshalsea before the queen herself, for that, whereas the said William on the tenth day of November [1701] in the thirteenth year of the reign of the lord William III, late king of England, at the parish of St Clement Danes in the aforesaid county of Middlesex, undertook to take up safely and securely various casks of brandy belonging to him the said John, then being in a certain cellar situated in a certain place called Brook's Market in the parish of St Andrew Holborn in the aforesaid county, and undertook to lay the same down safely and securely in a certain other cellar situated in a certain other place called Water Street in the parish of St Clement Danes in the aforesaid county: he the said William, his servants and agents, afterwards, namely on the same day in the same year, in the aforesaid parish of St Clement Danes, so negligently and improvidently managed the said casks of brandy in laying them down in the cellar last mentioned that for want of the good care of the said William, his servants and agents, one of the same casks of brandy was then and there staved and a great quantity (namely 150 gallons) of brandy in the said cask was by that means spilled on the ground and lost . . .

The plaintiff also alleged that another cask was similarly staved on 13

November, but with the slight variation that the *assumpsit* was to put the casks in a cart to carry them. This second count may have been a pleading device, putting the facts differently. In Michaelmas term 1702 the defendant imparled, and in Hilary term 1703 he pleaded Not guilty. On 10 February 1703, at the Guildhall, London, before Holt C.J., the jury found for the plaintiff with £10 damages and 20s. costs.

(b) Report: 2 Ld Raym. 909 (untr.).[17]

... there was a motion in arrest of judgment for that it was not alleged in the declaration that the defendant was a common porter, nor averred that he had anything for his pains. And the case being thought to be a case of great consequence, it was this day argued seriatim by the whole court.

GOULD J. I think this is a good declaration. The objection that has been made is because there is not any consideration laid. But I think it is good either way, and that any man that undertakes to carry goods is liable to an action, be he a common carrier or whatever he is, if through his neglect they are lost or come to any damage: and if a *praemium* be laid to be given, then it is without question so. The reason of the action is the particular trust reposed in the defendant, to which he has concurred by his assumption, and in the executing which he has miscarried by his neglect. But if a man undertakes to build a house, without anything to be had for his pains, an action will not lie for non-performance, because it is *nudum pactum*. So is the 3 Hen. VI, fo. 36[18]. ... *Southcote's Case* is a hard case indeed, to oblige all men that take goods to keep to a special acceptance that they will keep them as safe as they would do their own, which is a thing no man living that is not a lawyer could think of: and indeed it appears by the report of that case in Cro. Eliz. 815 that it was adjudged by two judges only ... But when a man undertakes specially to do such a thing, it is not hard to charge him for his neglect, because he had the goods committed to his custody upon those terms.[19]

POWYS J. agreed upon the neglect.

POWELL J. The doubt is because it is not mentioned in the declaration that the defendant had anything for his pains, nor that he was a common porter (which of itself imports a hire and that he is to be paid for his pains): so that the question is, whether an action will lie against a man for doing the office of a friend, when

---

17 Sub nom. *Coggs v Bernard*; also reported in Comyns 133; Holt 13, 131, 428; 1 Salk. 26; 3 Salk. 11; BL MS. Hargrave 66, ff. 85–106.

18 See p. 380, below.

19 See p. 274, above.

there is not any particular neglect shown. And I hold, an action will lie, as this case is . . . But it is objected that here is no consideration to ground the action upon. But, as to this, the difference is between being obliged to do the thing and answering for things which he has taken into his custody upon such an undertaking. An action indeed will not lie for not doing the thing, for want of a sufficient consideration; but yet if the bailee will take the goods into his custody he shall be answerable for them, for the taking the goods into his custody is his own act. And this action is founded upon the warranty upon which I have been contented to trust you with the goods, which without such a warranty I would not have done. And a man may warrant a thing without any consideration. And therefore when I have reposed a trust in you, upon your undertaking, if I suffer when I have so relied upon you I shall have my action . . . *Southcote's Case* is a strong authority, and the reason of it comes home to this, because the general bailment is there taken to be an undertaking to deliver the goods at all events, and so the judgment is founded upon the undertaking. But I cannot think that a general bailment is an undertaking to keep the goods safely at all events. That is hard . . .

HOLT C.J. . . . I have had a great consideration of this case, and because some of the books make the action lie upon the reward and some upon the promise, at first I made a great question whether this declaration was good. But, upon consideration, as this declaration is I think the action will well lie. In order to show the grounds upon which a man shall be charged with goods put into his custody, I must show the several sorts of bailments.

And there are six sorts of bailments. The first sort of bailment is a bare naked bailment of goods, delivered by one man to another to keep for the use of the bailor; and this I call a *depositum*, and it is that sort of bailment which is mentioned in *Southcote's Case*. The second sort is when goods or chattels that are useful are lent to a friend gratis, to be used by him; and this is called *commodatum*, because the thing is to be restored *in specie*. The third sort is when goods are left with the bailee to be used by him for hire; this is called *locatio et conductio*, and the lender is called *locator* and the borrower *conductor*. The fourth sort is when goods or chattels are delivered to another as a pawn, to be a security to him for money borrowed of him by the bailor; and this is called in Latin *vadium*, and in English a pawn or a pledge. The fifth sort is when goods or chattels are delivered to be carried, or something is to be done about them for a reward to be paid by the person who delivers them to the bailee, who is to do the thing about them. The sixth sort is when there is a delivery of goods or chattels to somebody who is to carry them, or do something about them, gratis, without any reward for such his work or carriage: which is this present case. I mention these things, not so much that they are all of them so necessary in order to maintain the proposition which is to be proved, as to clear the reason of the obligation which is upon persons in cases of trust.

As to the first sort, where a man takes goods in his custody to keep for the use of the bailor, I shall consider for what things such a bailee is answerable. He is not answerable if they are stolen without any fault in him; neither will a common neglect make him chargeable; but he must be guilty of some gross neglect. There is I confess a great authority against me,[20] where it is held that a general delivery will charge the bailee to answer for the goods if they are stolen, unless the goods are specially accepted to keep them only as you will keep your own. But my Lord Coke has improved the case in his report of it, for he will have it that there is no difference between a special acceptance to keep safely and an acceptance generally to keep. But there is no reason or justice in such a case of a general bailment, and where the bailee is not to have any reward, but keeps the goods merely for the use of the bailor, to charge him without some default in him. For if he keeps the goods in such a case with an ordinary care, he has performed the trust reposed in him. But according to this doctrine the bailee must answer for the wrongs of other people, which he is not nor cannot be sufficiently armed against. If the law be so, there must be some just and honest reason for it, or else some universal settled rule of law upon which it is grounded; and therefore it is incumbent upon them that advance this doctrine to show an undisturbed rule and practice of the law according to this position. But to show that the tenor of the law was always otherwise, I shall give a history of the authorities in the books in this matter, and by them show that there never was any such resolution given before *Southcote's Case* . . .[1]

As to the second sort of bailment, namely *commodatum* or lending gratis, the borrower is bound to the strictest care and diligence to keep the goods so as to restore them back again to the lender, because the bailee has a benefit by the use of them, so as if the bailee be guilty of the least neglect he will be answerable. As, if a man should lend another a horse to go westward, or for a month, if the bailee go northward or keep the horse above a month, if any

---

20 *Southcote's Case* (1601); see p. 274, above.

1 Holt C.J. then cites several Y.B. cases, the practice at the Guildhall since the 1600s, *Bracton*, fo. 99, and Justinian's *Institutes* 3.15.

accident happen to the horse in the northern journey or after the expiration of the month the bailee will be chargeable, because he has made use of the horse contrary to the trust he was lent to him under; and it may be if the horse had been used no otherwise than he was lent that accident would not have befallen him. This is mentioned in *Bracton* ... I cite this author, though I confess he is an old one, because his opinion is reasonable and very much to my present purpose, and there is no authority in the law to the contrary. But if the bailee put this horse in his stable, and he were stolen from thence, the bailee shall not be answerable for him. But if he or his servant leave the house or stable doors open, and the thieves take the opportunity of that and steal the horse, he will be chargeable; because the neglect gave the thieves the occasion to steal the horse. *Bracton* says the bailee must use the utmost care, but yet he shall not be chargeable where there is such a force as he cannot resist.

As to the third sort of bailment, namely *locatio* or lending for hire, in this case the bailee is also bound to take the utmost care and to return the goods when the time of the hiring is expired. And here again I must recur to my old author[2]... From whence it appears that if goods are let out for a reward, the hirer is bound to the utmost diligence, such as the most diligent father of a family uses; and if he uses that he shall be discharged. But every man, how diligent soever he be, being liable to the accident of robbers, though a diligent man is not so liable as a careless man, the bailee shall not be answerable in this case if the goods are stolen.

As to the fourth sort of bailment, namely *vadium* or a pawn, in this I shall consider two things: first, what property the pawnee has in the pawn or pledge, and secondly for what neglects he shall make satisfaction. As to the first, he has a special property, for the pawn is a securing to the pawnee that he shall be repaid his debt, and to compel the pawnor to pay him. But if the pawn be such as it will be the worse for using, the pawnee cannot use it (as clothes, etc.); but if it be such as will be never the worse, as if jewels for the purpose were pawned to a lady she might use them. But then she must do it at her peril, for whereas if she keeps them locked up in her cabinet, if her cabinet should be broken open and the jewels taken from thence, she would be excused, if she wears them abroad and is there robbed of them she will be answerable. And the reason is, because the pawn is in the nature of a deposit, and as such is not liable to be used ... But if the pawn be of such a nature as the pawnee is at any charge about the thing pawned to maintain it, as a horse, cow, etc., then the pawnee may use the horse in a reasonable manner, or milk the cow, in recompense for the meat. As to the second point, *Bracton*, fo. 99b, gives you the answer ... In effect, if a creditor takes a pawn he is bound to restore it upon the payment of the debt; but yet it is sufficient, if the pawnee use true diligence, and he will be indemnified in so doing, and notwithstanding the loss yet he shall resort to the pawnor for his debt ...

As to the fifth sort of bailment, namely a delivery to carry or otherwise manage for a reward to be paid to the bailee, those cases are of two sorts: either a delivery to one that exercises a public employment, or a delivery to a private person. First, if it be to a person of the first sort, and he is to have a reward, he is bound to answer for the goods at all events. And this is the case of the common carrier, common hoyman, master of a ship, etc., which case of a master of a ship was first adjudged in the case of *Mors v Slew*.[3] The law charges this person thus entrusted to carry goods against all events but acts of God, and of the enemies of the king: for though the force be never so great, as if an irresistible multitude of people should rob him, nevertheless he is chargeable. And this is a politic establishment, contrived by the policy of the law, for the safety of all persons, the necessity of whose affairs oblige them to trust these sorts of persons, that they may be safe in their ways of dealing; for else these carriers might have an opportunity of undoing all persons that had any dealings with them, by combining with thieves, and yet doing it in such a clandestine manner as would not be possible to be discovered. And this is the reason the law is founded upon in that point. The second sort are bailiffs, factors and such like. And though a bailiff is to have a reward for his management, yet he is only to do the best he can; and if he be robbed, etc., it is a good account ...

As to the sixth sort of bailment, it is to be taken that the bailee is

---

3 (1671) 1 Vent. 190, 238; 2 Lev. 69; 2 Keb. 866; 3 Keb. 72, 112, 135; 1 Mod. 85; T. Raym. 220. This was an action against the master of a ship for the loss of three trunks of silk stockings and silk which had been laden on the ship for carriage to Cadiz in return for freight. The jury found a special verdict that there were a sufficient number of men on board to look after the goods, but the goods had been seized by 11 men pretending to be in the king's service pressing seamen. The court (of King's Bench) was reluctant to hold the master liable when he was not at fault, but in the end did so. The plaintiff had set out a custom of the realm that masters should keep goods safely; and it also appeared that this master was to receive a reward, because the plaintiff was to pay freight to the shipowner, who was to pay wages to the master. (For the custom of the realm in relation to carriers, see further pp. 561–563, below.)

to have no reward for his pains, but yet that by his ill-management the goods are spoiled. Secondly, it is to be understood that there was a neglect in the management. But thirdly, if it had appeared that the mischief happened by any person that met the cart in the way, the bailee had not been chargeable. As, if a drunken man had come by in the streets and had pierced the cask of brandy: in this case the defendant had not been answerable for it, because he was to have nothing for his pains. Then, the bailee having undertaken to manage the goods, and having managed them ill, and so by his neglect a damage has happened to the bailor, which is the case in question: what will you call this? In *Bracton*, fo. 100, it is called *mandatum*. It is an obligation which arises *ex mandato*. It is what we call in English an acting by commission. And if a man acts by commission for another gratis, and in the executing his commission behaves himself negligently, he is answerable ... I do not find this word in any other author of our law besides in this place in *Bracton*, which is a full authority if it be not thought too old. But it is supported by good reason and authority.

The reasons are, first, because in such a case a neglect is a deceit to the bailor. For when he entrusts the bailee upon his undertaking to be careful, he has put a fraud upon the plaintiff by being negligent: his pretence of care being the persuasion that induced the plaintiff to trust him. And a breach of a trust undertaken voluntarily will be a good ground for an action ... But secondly it is objected that there is no consideration to ground this promise upon, and therefore the undertaking is but *nudum pactum*. But to this I answer that the owner's trusting him with the goods is a sufficient consideration to oblige him to a careful management. Indeed, if the agreement had been executory, to carry these brandies from the one place to the other such a day, the defendant had not been bound to carry them. But this is a different case, for *assumpsit* does not only signify a future agreement, but in such a case as this it signifies an actual entry upon the thing, and taking the trust upon himself. And if a man will do that, and miscarries in the performance of his trust, an action will lie against him for that, though nobody could have compelled him to do the thing... [I]n the 11 Hen. IV, fo. 33, this difference is clearly put; and that is the only case concerning this matter which has not been cited by my brothers. There the action was brought against a carpenter for that he had undertaken to build the plaintiff a house within such a time, and had not done it, and it was adjudged the action would not lie. But there the question was put to the court: what if he had built the house unskilfully? And it is agreed in that case an action would have lain . . .[4]

I have said thus much in this case, because it is of great consequence that the law should be settled in this point. But I do not know whether I may have settled it, or may not rather have unsettled it. But however that happen, I have stirred these points which wiser heads in time may settle.

And judgment was given for the plaintiff.

The record shows that judgment was signed on 23 June 1703 for £32, the plaintiff's costs being increased by £21.

4   See p. 379, below.

15 Assumpsit for nonfeasance

WATTON v BRINTH (1400)

Y.B. Mich. 2 Hen. IV, fo. 3v, pl. 9;
BL MS. Harley 5144, fo. 3; MS. Harley 5145, fo. 16v;
MS. Hargrave 1, fo. 3v; LI MS. Hale 189, fo. 88 (C.P.).

One Laurence of Watton brought a writ formed on his special case[1]
against Thomas Brinth,[2] and the writ was: 'in a plea that he
show why, whereas the same Thomas had undertaken to rebuild
certain of the selfsame Laurence's houses at Grimsby within a
certain time, nevertheless the aforesaid Thomas had not built the
aforesaid Laurence's houses within the aforesaid time, to the
damage of the selfsame Laurence of £10, as he says'. And he
counted accordingly,

Tyrwhit. Sir, you plainly see how he has counted in respect of a
covenant, and he has shown nothing [in proof] of it; [so we
demand] judgment.

Gascoigne. And, since you have in no way answered us, we
[demand] judgment and pray our damages.

Tyrwhit. This is purely a covenant.

BRENCHELEY. So it is. If perhaps he had counted, or if it had
been mentioned in the writ, that the work had been started and
then by negligence not done, it would have been otherwise.

---

1 Several MSS. have the marginal note: 'Trespass in the nature of covenant'.
2 Reads 'Brynch' in MS. Harley 5144, 'Brygesley' in MS. Harley 5145, and
  'Brigesley' in MS. Hargrave. Perhaps the name was Brencheley, like the judge,
  though he came from Kent.

HANKFORD. He could have a writ on the Statute of Labourers.[3] This carpenter is a workman, and so you could have a good action against him on the statute.[4] For you are well aware that a man may not have an action of covenant against his servant, for acting against his covenant, if he has no deed thereof.

RIKHILL. Since you have counted on a covenant, and you have shown nothing [in proof] of it, take nothing by your writ but be in the mercy etc.

ANON. (1409)

Y.B. Mich. 11 Hen. IV, fo. 33, pl. 60; BL MS. Harley 5144, fo. 123; MS. Harley 5145, fo. 104; MS. Harley 5158, fo. 54v; MS Hargrave 1, fo. 154v; MS. Add. 26747, fo. 304v; CUL MS. Gg. 5. 8(3), fo. 24v; MS. Hh. 2. 12, fo. 175v (C.P.).

A writ[5] was brought against a carpenter on these facts: whereas the defendant had undertaken to make the plaintiff a new house within a certain time, he had not made the house, to the plaintiff's injury.

Tildesley. Sir, you plainly see how this matter sounds in the [nature][6] of covenant, of which covenant he shows nothing; so we demand judgment whether [he ought to have an] action without specialty.

Norton. And we pray judgment. Sir, if he had made my house badly, and had ruined my timber, I should have had an action on my case perfectly well without a deed.

---

3 The 'statute' (an ordinance of 1349) rendered servants liable to imprisonment if they departed from their service without reasonable cause, or licence. An action for damages was held to lie upon the equity of this provision: see Y.B. Mich. 11 Hen. IV, fo. 24, pl. 46, per Hankford J. ('I had no action at common law if my servant left me, and the reason was that between my servant and me the contract sounds in manner of a covenant in itself, and no action was given upon that at common law without specialty; and the statute was ordained by reason of that mischief, and an action was given upon it . . .'). In a case of 1371 (LI MS. Hale 146, fo. 104) a defendant sought to plead that the covenant to serve was made on condition, and the plaintiff argued that such terms could not be alleged without specialty: but the court held that since this 'action of covenant' lay without a deed, the servant could likewise rely on special terms without a deed. The analogy with covenant led also to the conclusion that the action lay for purely executory breaches of covenant, without actual service, and issue could be joined on the covenant to serve (Y.B. Mich. 41 Edw. III, fo. 20, pl. 4; Mich. 47 Edw. III, fo. 14, pl. 15). The writ was, nevertheless, of the trespass family.
4 Cf. the next case, and p. 380, fn. 7.
5 'An action on his case' (MS. Hargrave); 'a writ of covenant' (MS. Harley 5158, MS. Add. 26747). In MS. Hh. 2. 12, 'a writ of covenant' has been altered (*c.* 1500) to 'a writ of trespass'.
6 So in most MSS.; but it reads 'maner' in print, and 'mater' in both CUL MSS.

THIRNING [C.J.] I quite agree, in the case you have put, because there he must answer for the wrong he has done in making the house negligently. But when a man makes a covenant, and will not do anything under this covenant, how shall you have an action against him without specialty?

HILL. He could have had an action on the Statute of Labourers in this case, alleging that the defendant was retained in his service to make a house;[7] but the present action is too weak.

So HANKFORD[8] [gave judgment]: since it seems to the court that this action is taken at common law for something which is a covenant in itself, of which nothing is shown, the court hereby awards that you shall take nothing by your writ, but be in the mercy etc.

WATKINS' (or WYKES') CASE (1425)

Y.B. Hil. 3 Hen. VI, fo. 36, pl. 33;
CUL MS. Gg. 5. 8(10), fo. 34; Bod. Lib. MS. Rawl. D. 363, fo. 35;
BL MS. Harley 452, fo. 57 (C.P.).

A writ of trespass was brought by one William B. against Watkins[9] of London, mill-maker; and he counted, by *Strangeways*, on his case: namely, that on a certain day in a certain year at London, in a certain ward, he took upon himself to make a mill for this same plaintiff, and he set out what mill it should be, and that it should be all ready and erected between that day and Christmas next following; but the mill was not erected within that period, to the wrong and damage of the plaintiff of ten marks.

Rolf. [We demand] judgment of the writ, for it is supposed by

7 Cf. the previous case. The courts had been unwilling, however, to extend the scope of the remedy beyond servants. It did not apply to apprentices (Y.B. Mich. 39 Edw. III, fo. 22), to craftsmen retained to do piecework (Y.B. Mich. 47 Edw. III, fo. 22, pl. 53), or to professional persons such as a parochial chaplain (Y.B. Trin. 50 Edw. III, fo. 13, pl. 3). On the same folio as this action on the case (Y.B. Mich. 11 Hen. IV, fo. 33, pl. 62) is an action on the statute against a carpenter, in which it was held necessary to count 'on [the] special case' and not generally, because a carpenter was not bound to perform all kinds of service. Masons and carpenters became compellable to serve under the statute 34 Edw. III (1360), c. 9, which nevertheless made it permissible for employers to covenant for their work 'in gross' (i.e. for piecework). This distinction may explain the appearance of *assumpsit* actions against carpenters retained for particular jobs of work.

8 So in most MSS.; but it reads 'Hill' in print and in MS. Gg. 5. 8.

9 Reads 'R. Wykes' in MSS. MS. Harley 452 begins: 'A writ of trespass was brought against Richard Wikes by W.B. and named the defendant "of London, mill-maker" . . .'

the writ that the defendant ought to have made a mill, and he has
not declared with certainty how much he was to have for making it.

Strangeways. Since he has said nothing, we demand judgment
and pray our damages.

BABINGTON [C.J.] If I bring a writ of deceit against someone on
the ground that he was my attorney, and that through his negligence and fault I lost my land, in this case I must declare how he
was retained with me for his wages, or else the writ abates.
Likewise here.

MARTIN. I cannot see in law how such a writ lies upon such
facts, for by the writ he has not supposed any wrong to have been
done, but only that he promised him to do something which has
not been done: in which case a good writ of covenant would have
lain if he had had specialty. If, however, he had made a mill which
was not good, and had badly spoiled (*tout confoundu*) the timber, a
good writ of trespass would lie. Take the case where a farrier
covenants with me to shoe my horse, and by his negligence he
misdrives a nail into my horse, a good writ of trespass on the case
(*sur le matter monstré*) lies: for though in the setting out of the
facts a covenant is supposed, I say that, since he has done badly the
thing that was covenanted, the covenant is thereby changed and
made into a wrong, for which a good writ of trespass lies. But in the
case at bar this is not so, for there no wrong is supposed by the writ
in the sense of anything having been done (*per le fesance dun chose*),
but only the not doing (*le noun fesaunce*) of a thing, and that
sounds solely in covenant.

BABINGTON. I think the contrary. Suppose someone covenants
with me to roof my hall in[10] a certain house, within a certain period,
and he does not roof it on time, so that for want of roofing the
timber of my house is rotted through by the rain, I say that in this
case I shall have a good writ of trespass *sur le matter monstré*
against the person who made the covenant with me: and in that
case I shall recover damages because I am damaged by the
nonfeasance of the [roof. Likewise here, the plaintiff is damaged by
the nonfeasance of the][11] mill.

COKAYNE to the same effect. As to the first point which was
moved, that he should have declared that he made the covenant
with him in return for a certain sum: sir, it seems to me that he has
already said as much, for it shall be presumed that he would not
have made the mill for nothing. Therefore, by this plea, that much

10 MSS. Reads 'or' in print.
11 Omitted in print by haplography, destroying the sense.

is implied (*encludé*),[12] just as if he had said it expressly in pleading. As to the other point, the writ lies perfectly well *sur le matter monstré*. Suppose someone covenants to clean out (*mounder*)[13] certain ditches which are near[14] my land, and he does not do it, so that through his default the water which should have run in the ditches floods my land and destroys my corn: I say that I shall have a good writ of trespass for this nonfeasance. Likewise here.

Rolf. With respect to your first point, it seems to me that he ought to have mentioned expressly in the writ what he was to have had; and I say that there is all the difference between someone who is hired (*allowé*) by another to do something and a common labourer. For it is made certain by the statute[15] what a labourer is to have, and in that case even if nothing is said in the covenant about what he is to have the servant shall have a good action of debt against [his master] for his salary, according to the statute. But if I covenant with someone to go with me or to do a certain thing, and I do not say for certain what he is to have for doing it, in that case I say that the covenant is void as against both parties: for if he does not perform the covenant I shall never have an action against him, and if he does perform it he shall not have an action [of debt] against me to recover anything for his efforts, unless it was stated in certain what he was to have. Therefore it seems to me that if this action is to be maintained upon this matter, the principal thing which causes the action should be declared openly in the writ: and that is the covenant, which is not good unless it is stated with certainty what he is to have.

Strangeways. I think the contrary. As to what my Master Martin has moved—that the writ ought not to lie because no wrong is supposed in the writ—sir, it seems to me that the writ shall lie. Suppose someone covenants with me to be my cook (*kue*),[16] and then I command him to go with my cart, and he refuses to do so, I say that I shall have a writ of trespass against him for this refusal, though it is not doing something (*le noun fesaunce dun chose*). Likewise here.

MARTIN. I fully concede it there, because that refusal is a departure from your service, for which a good action lies.[17] But

---

12   MSS. Reads 'conclude' in print.
13   MSS. Reads 'mend (*amender*)' in print.
14   MSS. Reads 'on' in print, which also makes sense.
15   Statute of Labourers (1349); see p. 329, fn. 3, above.
16   MSS. Reads 'servant' in print, which may be the correct sense.
17   On the Statute of Labourers.

truly it seems to me that, if this action should be maintained upon the present facts, then a man would have an action of trespass for every broken covenant in the world.

BABINGTON. All our discussion is in vain, for they have not yet demurred. (Therefore he said to *Strangeways* and *Rolf*:) plead and say what you will, or else demur, and then it can be debated and disputed in the fullness of time.

So *Rolf* moved on, and said that long after the time when he is supposed to have made the covenant (namely, on such a day) the defendant came to the plaintiff (in such a ward) and told him that the mill was quite ready to be erected, and asked him when he would like him to come and put it up; and the plaintiff said he did not want to have the mill,[18] and completely discharged him with respect to the mill. And we demand judgment whether the action is maintainable.

Strangeways. He did not discharge him; ready etc. (And the other side *econtra*.)

(Query Martin's opinion.)

ANON. (1435)

Y.B. 14 Hen. VI, fo. 18v, pl. 58;
BL MS. Harley 4557, fo. 112v (C.P.).

One R. sued a writ of trespass on his case, and counted that the plaintiff had bargained [to buy] certain land for a certain sum from the defendant (setting out the details), and that the defendant covenanted that he would cause strangers to make a release to him within a certain time, and they did not do so, and so the action accrued to him.

Ellerker. This action sounds in the nature of covenant, in which case he should have had a writ of covenant and not this action. Judgment of the writ.

Newton. Since the trespass has been confessed by you, and you have not shown any other facts, we demand judgment.

Ellerker. It seems that the writ should abate, for various cases of a similar kind have been held as law before the present time. For instance, in the case where I make a covenant with a carpenter to make me a house within a certain time, and he does not make me

---

18 This clause is omitted by a haplography in the 1679 ed.

my house, I shall have no action except a writ of covenant. The law is the same if someone undertakes to shoe my horse, and does not do it: I shall have no other action but a writ of covenant if he has done nothing, and if specialty is lacking the action fails. Likewise here: he has undertaken to cause strangers to release, which is a covenant, and it is set out that they did not release, which is nothing but a broken covenant. So it seems the writ should abate.

Newton thought the contrary and that the writ was good. I quite agree that the case of the carpenter, which Ellerker has put, is law; but if the carpenter covenants to make me a good, strong house of a particular form, and makes me a weak, bad house of another form, I shall have a good action of trespass on my case. Also, if a farrier covenants with me to shoe my horse well and competently, and in shoeing it he injures it with a nail, I shall have a good action on my case. Again, if a leech undertakes to cure me of my illnesses and gives me medicine but does not cure me, I shall have a good action on my case. Also, if a man covenants with me to plough my land at a seasonable time, and he ploughs it at an unseasonable time, I shall have an action on my case. And the reason in all these cases is that he has taken upon himself a matter in fact beyond that which sounds in covenant. So it is in the case at bar: he has undertaken that strangers will make a release to the plaintiff, which is an undertaking, and since it was not done the plaintiff is wronged, as in the cases set out above.

PASTON thought the same. As to the assertion that if a carpenter covenants with me to make me a house and does not do so I shall not have an action on my case: sir, I say that if an hostler or farrier covenants with me to shoe my horse and does not do it, so that when I go on my way my horse is unshod and is lost for want of shoes, I shall have an action on my case. And if you, who are a serjeant at law, undertake to plead my plea, and do nothing—or do something otherwise than as I have told you—so that I suffer loss, I shall have an action on my case. It seems the same to me in the case at the bar, and that the writ is good.

JUYN thought the same. As Paston has said, if a farrier does not shoe my horse I shall have an action, as well as if he had shod it and injured it with a nail; for [the latter wrong] is wholly dependent on the covenant, and since [the negligent performance] is only accessory to and dependent on the covenant, then as well as having an action for what is only accessory I shall also have an action for the principal.

PASTON. That is very well said.

SOMERTON v COLLES (1433)

(a) The writ:[19] Y.B. Pas. 11 Hen. VI, fo. 25, pl. 1.

The king to the sheriff [of Oxfordshire], greeting. Distrain John Colles of North Aston by all his lands [to be before us on etc. to show] why, whereas William Somerton had retained the said John Colles at North Aston, for a certain amount (*pro quodam certo*) to be paid to the same John Colles by the said William in a manner agreed between them, to be of his counsel in buying the manor of North Aston from John Boteler for the said William and his heirs, or at least in obtaining a lease for a term of years; and the aforesaid John Colles there undertook, in return for the said certain amount agreed between them as aforesaid, to purchase the aforesaid manor for the same William and his heirs, or at least for a term of years, from the said John Boteler: the aforesaid John Colles, by collusion between him and John Blount at North Aston aforesaid, scheming wickedly to defraud the selfsame William in that behalf, maliciously revealed all his counsel in that behalf to the said John Blount, and there falsely and fraudulently became of counsel with the same John Blount, and purchased the aforesaid manor for the said John Blount to have for a term of years from the said John Boteler, contrary to his aforesaid promise and undertaking, to the damage of the selfsame William etc.

(b) Y.B. Trin. 11 Hen. VI, fo. 55, pl. 26.[20]

... *Godered.* Judgment of the writ, for the writ says that the defendant was retained 'for a certain amount', without saying what—such as, a horse, or 40s.

COTTESMORE. Whatever it is, that is not the substance of the

---

19 Not the original writ, but a *distringas* following the wording of the original. The record has not yet been found, but in the rolls for Easter term 1433 there are two cases of related types. In *Frome v Byle* (CP 40/689, m. 310d) the plaintiff alleged that he had retained the defendant (an attorney) to sue a writ of formedon, and had handed to him various title-deeds, and that the defendant had craftily revealed his counsel and delivered the documents to the other side. No *assumpsit* is alleged. The case was never tried, because Byle went to serve in Ireland and had letters of protection. In *Cornewayle v Herbray* (ibid., m. 405) the plaintiff counted that the defendants had sold him the manor of Stepp- ingley, Bedfordshire, for the agreed sum of £40, and had delivered seisin, and had undertaken (*assumpsissent*) to make such assurance (i.e. written instrument of conveyance) as counsel should advise; and counsel advised a release and quitclaim enrolled in Chancery, which the defendants refused to execute. This case ends with an imparlance.

20 Though printed as a later term, this seems to precede the other Y.B. passages.

matter ... And [in any case] he has declared by his count that he was retained with him for 40s.

Godered. Judgment of the writ, for it contains in itself double matter for one same cause: one is that he retained the defendant as his counsel to buy the manor and that he disclosed his counsel and became of counsel with Blount (as above), which is a good matter without more; and the other is that the defendant undertook to purchase the said manor for the plaintiff and his heirs, which is a sufficient matter to maintain his action, since he became of counsel with Blount and caused him to have the same manor. Therefore if we traverse the retainer—namely, that we were not retained with him—he will conclude upon us[1] since we have not denied that we undertook that he should have the manor and then became of counsel with Blount concerning the same manor. And if we traverse that we undertook that he should have the manor in the way the writ supposes, then he will conclude upon the retainer.

COTTESMORE. The matter is not double.[2] The fact that he retained him to be of his counsel is a fact put in by him to introduce the cause of his grievance; for he cannot otherwise show any grievance. When, therefore, the defendant undertook to carry out the aforesaid retainer, and did the contrary, these facts are the whole grievance: and so to join all these facts together, namely that he undertook to do everything for which he was retained, is a sufficiently single matter and one issue can answer the whole— namely, that he was not retained with him in the manner in which he has declared. So, when this issue answers the whole, it is sufficiently single.

PASTON to the same effect. Is it not all one if I retain someone to be my butler, and he undertakes to be my butler? That is not double matter, and no more is it here.

Godered thought the contrary. For if I bring a writ of trespass against someone, and suppose that he was retained with me to make a house well and suitably, and also that he undertook to make the house well and suitably, and that by his want of skill the house was not well made, that is double matter: one matter is the

---

1 I.e. demur for want of defence.
2 Cf. Y.B. Hil. 11 Hen. VI, fo. 18, pl. 10, per Cottesmore J.: 'The matter of the writ is single enough, for if I retain you to serve me, and you undertake to serve me, this is not double matter, because you do not undertake to do anything more than you were retained to do, and so *unum et idem* ...' Cf. Martin J., ibid.: 'If I come to someone and say that I retain him to serve me, this is to no purpose without further speech or agreement by the other party. Therefore when the other undertakes to serve me, these words on his side make the covenant between us ...'

retainer to make the house well and suitably, for which I may have an action without more; but I shall also have an action supposing that he undertook to make me a house well and suitably and that the house has been lost through his default.

PASTON. It would be hard to maintain an action on his case supposing that he warranted him to buy the manor for him and his heirs, for that is clearly a covenant; and he ought to have an action of covenant for that, if he wants to have an action for that alone, and show specialty. It seems to me, however, that the matter here is sufficiently single, for he did nothing but undertake to do what he was retained to do . . .

(c) Y.B. Hil. 11 Hen. VI, fo. 18, pl. 10.

. . . PASTON. There is a great difference between where someone is retained and warrants to do what he is retained for, and where he warrants to do more than he was retained for. If I retain someone to serve me, or to make me a house, and he warrants to do the same thing, it is all in effect the same thing, since he does not undertake to do more than he was retained to do. So here, when he retained the defendant as his counsel to have the manor, if he did his best for the plaintiff to cause him to have it, even though he did not get it, he shall be excused. But if he warrants me that I shall have the manor, then even if he does his best this will not excuse him, because he has warranted to do more than he was retained for . . .

MARTIN . . . Even if a man retains another to do something, and he undertakes to do [more], it shall not be double. For instance, if I sell you a tun of wine, and I warrant the wine to be wholesome and not sour, you shall have one action upon this matter and shall allege that I, knowing the wine to be sour, [sold it to you warranting it as wholesome].[3] In the same way you shall have an action supposing that someone sold you a horse and warranted to you that the horse was sound in all its limbs, knowing the horse had such and such a disease. Likewise here, for the cause of action is not the retainer, or the warranty which the other made to do it, but the cause is that the other has disclosed his counsel and become of counsel with someone else.

BABINGTON [C.J.] to the same effect. If I retain a man to purchase a manor for me and he does not do it, I shall not have any action against him unless I have a deed—in which case I may have a writ of covenant—because he has not done what he was retained

3 See pp. 506–523, below.

for. But if he becomes of counsel with another in this matter, I shall have an action on my case, because he has deceived me; for he is bound to keep my counsel [secret] while he is retained with me. If, however, a man shows his title-deeds to a lawyer, and he afterwards becomes of counsel with another and discloses his counsel concerning the said title-deeds, the client shall not have an action against him on these facts, since he was not retained with him. And even if he made a warranty to him to purchase the manor, he shall nevertheless not have an action on these facts—unless it is an action of covenant, and then he must have a deed. Thus, even if he was retained with him to purchase the manor, and warranted him to do it, this is nevertheless only a covenant; and if he does not do it he cannot have an action of trespass on his case, for it is but a covenant broken, and for that he ought to have an action of covenant. If, however, he discloses his counsel and becomes of counsel with another to purchase the manor for him, this is now a deceit for which he shall have an action on his case. Thus the retainer to purchase the manor, and the warranty to do it, are merely an introduction to the cause of his action.

COTTESMORE to the same effect. And I say that matter which lies wholly in covenant may by matter *ex post facto* be converted into deceit. For even if I warrant to you that I will purchase a manor for you, and you repudiate (*defaites*) this, I shall not have any action against you on this bare word, without a deed thereof. In the same way, if I warrant to pay you £20, without a deed, you shall not have an action, for the warranty sounds in covenant. But although the retainer by one party and the warranty by the other sound wholly in covenant, nevertheless when he becomes of counsel with someone else this is a deceit and shall change what was previously only a covenant between the parties; and for this deceit he shall have an action on his case . . .

(d) Y.B. Pas. 11 Hen. VI, fo. 24, pl. 1.

. . . *Godered.* Again we pray judgment of the writ, for the conclusion of the writ is that he has disclosed his counsel, which is one trespass; and that he became of counsel with someone else, which is another trespass; and that he has not caused the plaintiff to have the manor for a term of years, which is another trespass. Thus the writ contains a triple trespass.

MARTIN. A man may have one writ for several trespasses, such as beating, wounding and ill-treating him and breaking his house. So answer.

Godered. You ought not to have the action,[4] for we say that we have done our best [in treating with] John Boteler to cause the aforesaid William Somerton to have the manor, without this that we took upon ourselves to cause him to have the manor in the way he has alleged; ready etc.

Newton. Since you have not denied that he was retained with us and has disclosed his counsel and become of counsel with someone else, we pray judgment and our damages.

Godered. In the same way if we had traversed the retainer in the manner supposed he could reply that he has supposed that the defendant undertook to buy the said manor and has disclosed his counsel; and so it is double matter.

MARTIN. To say that he was not retained in the manner supposed is a good issue and answers the whole of his action . . . But by your plea you do not traverse the retainer, which is the principal cause of his action . . .

Godered. By protestation we never undertook to buy the manor or to cause him to have this manor on lease, and we never disclosed our counsel, and we never became of counsel with someone else; and for a plea we say that we have well and lawfully done our best for the said plaintiff, and that we went to the said John Boteler and spoke to him about selling the said manor to the aforesaid plaintiff or leasing it to him for a term of years, and he said that the plaintiff should never have the said manor by his feoffment, or for a term of years; without this that we became of counsel with someone else and caused him to have the manor at farm in the way alleged; ready etc.

Newton. We will imparl.

After further argument on another day, the plea was amended so as to conclude, 'without this that he disclosed his counsel and without this that he became of counsel with the other in the manner supposed', and issue was joined on this traverse.

ANON. (1440)

Mich. 19 Hen. VI, HLS MS. 156, unfol. (C.P.).

In a writ of trespass on his case the plaintiff counted that he made a bargain with the defendant that before a certain day the defendant would enfeoff the plaintiff of certain lands whereof the defendant

---

4 Having failed in his various motions to abate the writ, Godered now begins to plead tentatively in bar of the action.

was then seised, and that the day was passed and he had not enfeoffed him, to his injury and damage.

Markham. This bargain sounds in covenant rather than trespass. So show what you have of the covenant.

Fortescue showed nothing.

AYSCOUGH. It seems this bargain is purely a covenant. If I bargain with a carpenter to make me a house before a certain day, and he does not do it, I shall not have a writ of trespass for such nonfeasance, but an action of covenant—if I have specialty, otherwise I am without remedy. But if a carpenter makes me a house, and does it badly, I shall for such misfeasance have a writ of trespass on my case. In the present case, however, nothing has been done.

Browne, the second clerk.[5] If a man pays a sum of money to have a house made for him, and it is not done, he shall have an action of trespass on his case because the defendant has *quid pro quo* and the plaintiff is damaged. (This was privately denied to him.)

SHEPTON v DOGGE (no. 1) (1442)

Record: CP 40/725, m. 49d (Pas. 1442).

London. William Shepton, by Hugh Brent his attorney, offered himself on the fourth day[6] against Joan, who was the wife of William Dogge of London, widow, in a plea why, whereas the same William [Shepton] had bargained with the said Joan in London to buy from her two messuages, 28 acres of arable land and one acre of meadow with the appurtenances in Hoxton in the county of Middlesex, for a certain sum of money paid in advance to the same Joan; and the same Joan had there undertaken to make a feoffment thereof to the said William and his heirs within a certain period now elapsed: the aforesaid Joan, craftily scheming to defraud him the said William in that behalf, sold the aforesaid messuages, land and meadow with the appurtenances within the aforesaid period to John Melburne, and within the same period falsely and deceitfully made a feoffment thereof to the same John and his heirs; to the damage of the selfsame William £40 etc.

The defendant did not appear, and so a *sicut prius capias* was issued and then two writs of *sicut pluries*. No continuance is recorded beyond Michaelmas 1442. In his second action (opposite) Shepton becomes 'Shipton'.

---

5 Thomas Browne, second prothonotary of the Common Pleas.
6 This formula was used for entries of process prior to the defendant's appearance.

SHIPTON v DOGGE (no. 2) (1442)
DOIGE'S CASE[7]

Record: KB 27/717, m. 111; abstracted in Kiralfy, *Source Book*, p. 192. In Trinity term 1442 (on 20 June) Shipton commenced another action in similar form, but in the King's Bench. The bill is entered as 'a plea of falsity and deceit' and adds the details that Mrs. Dogge had undertaken to convey the land in fee simple within a fortnight of the sale, which was on 12 February 1439, and that she had been paid £110. The words 'in that behalf' were also replaced, so that she was alleged to have craftily schemed to defraud the plaintiff of the messuages, land and meadow. The damage was laid as £200. Mrs. Dogge entered a special demurrer, on the express ground that the facts alleged amounted to a covenant, and so the plaintiff should have brought an action of covenant rather than deceit. The court took advisement until Hilary term 1443. Meanwhile the matter was adjourned into the Exchequer Chamber for consultation with the other judges, and the Y.B. reports the argument there in Trinity term 1442.

Y.B. Trin. 20 Hen. VI, fo. 34, pl. 4;
Selden Soc. vol. 51, p. 97.

... AYSCOUGH [J.C.P.] If a carpenter undertakes to make me a house, and does not do it, I shall not have a writ of trespass but only an action of covenant (if I have a specialty). But if he makes the house, and does so badly, I shall have an action of trespass on my case: for my cause of action derives from this misfeasance.[8] Likewise in our case, if the defendant had retained the land in her hands without making a feoffment to another person, then the plaintiff would only have had a writ of covenant. And I think it is just the same when the defendant makes a feoffment to a stranger as when she retains the land in her hands; and therefore the action does not lie. Also, the bill says 'he had bargained to buy', and those words do not prove that he bought: consequently it cannot be taken as deceit, when the bargain did not reach the stage of an accord.

PASTON [J.C.P.] Yes, sir: the bargain proves an accord, namely when the money was paid.

BABTHORPE [B.] Suppose the defendant had charged the land after making the bargain, and then enfeoffed the plaintiff: he would not have had a writ of deceit. (AYSCOUGH agreed with this.) And the

7 The case has become well known by this spelling, which is given in the printed Y.B. In the King's Bench record the name is 'Dog', which must be an abbreviation for Dogge. The latter spelling is also found in a record of 1447 (CP 40/744, m. 359) where she sues as widow of William Dogge, citizen of London; and in her will, proved in 1457 (P.C.C., 11 Stokton).

8 MSS. Reads 'malfeasance' in print.

law is the same, in my view, whether the defendant charged the land or whether she enfeoffed another of all the land.

Wangford. The defendant has done something badly, and the action of deceit is founded on that. For when she enfeoffed a stranger she thereby disabled herself from making the feoffment to the plaintiff, even if she bought the land back later and enfeoffed him: for if there was a warranty to her heirs and assigns on her first possession, and she had enfeoffed the plaintiff according to the bargain, the plaintiff could have vouched as an assign, but as a result of the feoffment and taking back of an estate before the feoffment to the plaintiff he is in by another estate, and so the plaintiff's ability to vouch as an assign is lost, and the action is founded on the loss of this ability. Also, if I retain a man for a certain sum to purchase a manor for me, and then he purchases the same manor for himself, I shall have an action of deceit on this.[9] It is the same, therefore, in our case.

Stokes to the same effect. Suppose I retain a man who is learned in the law to be of counsel with me in the Guildhall of London on such a day, and on the day he does not come, so that my cause is lost; he is liable to me in an action of deceit, and yet he did nothing. But because he did not do what he had undertaken to do, whereby I am damaged, that is the cause of my action. Likewise here; because she has not enfeoffed me, but has enfeoffed someone else whereby I am damaged, she shall be charged by an action of deceit.

PASTON. Suppose a man bargains to enfeoff me, as our case is, and afterwards he enfeoffs another, and then re-enters and enfeoffs me, and the other ousts me: an action of covenant would not be available, because he has enfeoffed me according to his covenant; and yet there remains the deceit, on which an action shall be founded. This clearly proves that it is not always true that whenever there is a covenant an action of deceit will not lie.

BABTHORPE. Suppose the defendant had enfeoffed a stranger, and taken back an estate in tail, and then enfeoffed the plaintiff: would that not have been a great deceit? (Implying that it would have been.) And yet it sounds in covenant.

AYSCOUGH. The feoffment made by such fraud is something done wrongly, as in the above case of misfeasance. But in our case no feoffment is made to the plaintiff, either properly or wrongly, and therefore the plaintiff suffers no wrong except the broken covenant.

NEWTON [C.J.C.P.] The defendant has disabled herself from

---

9 See *Somerton v Colles* (1433), p. 385, above.

keeping the covenant with the plaintiff, because she has enfeoffed another, and also the day has passed by which the feoffment should have been made. To what purpose, then, would he have a writ of covenant when the defendant could not keep the covenant with him, even if there was a specialty? (Implying that it would be pointless.) Now, when the plaintiff has made a firm bargain with the defendant, the defendant may at once demand her money by a writ of debt; and in conscience and in right the plaintiff ought to have the land, even though the property may not pass to him by law without livery of seisin. It would be amazing law, then, if there should be a perfect[10] bargain under which one party would be bound by an action of debt but would be without remedy against the other. Therefore the action of deceit clearly lies.

FORTESCUE [C.J.K.B.] If I lease land to a man for a term of years by deed indented, and then during the term I oust him, and 20 years (say) after the term has ended he brings an action of covenant against me, this action clearly lies: and yet he cannot recover the term. But he will recover everything in damages. As to the argument that he had disabled himself, and the action of deceit is based on that, I will put a case to you where the party has disabled himself and yet no action will lie but covenant. Suppose I make a lease to Paston for a term of years, and then I lease the same land to Godered, who occupies: I have disabled myself from causing Paston to have the lease, and yet he shall only have a writ of covenant against me.

PASTON. Even if a man can have a writ of covenant, that does not prove that he shall not have a writ of deceit; for it may be that all the covenants have been performed, and yet he was deceived. For instance, suppose a carpenter undertakes to make me a house of a certain length, width and height, and he does this, but the joinery is faulty or he defaults in some similar way which is not covered by any covenant: an action of covenant is not here available, because he has kept all the covenants, and yet I shall have an action of trespass on my case inasmuch as he has done something wrong. Likewise here, even though I could have had a writ of covenant, nevertheless I shall have an action of deceit inasmuch as she has disabled herself.

NEWTON. If I hand a certain sum of money to Paston to hand over to Fortescue, and Paston does not hand it over, he is liable to me in an action of account, and also by an action of debt; and it is at my pleasure which I will choose. But once I have had the benefit

10 Reading 'par fait' as 'parfait'.

of one of the said actions the other is extinguished.[11] Likewise in our case, although there are two actions (namely, covenant and deceit), the party can have deceit if he wishes.

FRAY [C.B.] If the defendant in our case had ousted her feoffee and then enfeoffed the plaintiff, all the covenants would have been fulfilled. Suppose the feoffee afterwards ousted the plaintiff: would he not then have an action of deceit, since he could not have a writ of covenant? I say he would.

AYSCOUGH. No, sir; he will not[12] have an action of deceit in your case, for it was his foolishness to take such an estate (which was defeasible) where he could have waived that estate and relied on his writ of covenant, which remained available until this estate was taken.

PASTON. It is not true that in every bargain there is a covenant. For if I buy a horse from you, without a warranty that he is sound, here is no covenant; and yet there is a bargain, and if the horse has an internal illness I shall have a writ of trespass on my case against you for selling him to me, knowing that he was ill. There was such a case in the Common Bench, where the plaintiff bargained to have 14 bales of grain from the defendant, and the defendant, knowing the said grain to be contaminated[13] with sand, sold it to him; and the action was clearly maintainable. (But see this record, for there was a warranty that the grain should be merchantable.) So it is right that the plaintiff should have a writ of deceit on such a bargain, just as he should have a writ of covenant if he had a specialty.

WESTBURY [J.K.B.] If, after such a bargain as in our case, and before the feoffment, the defendant made a statute merchant[14] and then made the feoffment, the party would have a writ of deceit. Likewise here.

FORTESCUE. If the case put by Newton be law, then there is no question concerning the law in our case: for if each party to a bargain should be bound by an action, it must follow that this action of deceit is maintainable.

PASTON. Let us go on, then, to the present case.

FORTESCUE. Willingly. I quite agree that if I buy a horse from you, the property in the horse is at once mine and therefore you shall have a writ of debt for the money and I shall have detinue for the horse upon this bargain. But that is not so in our case, for even

---

11   Reads 'extinct' in print, 'expiré' in MSS.
12   Omitted in print.
13   Reads 'eveigné' in all texts.
14   A form of secured loan which made the land liable to execution.

if the plaintiff has a right to this land in conscience, nevertheless the land will not pass without livery.

PASTON. In your case the contract is good without any specialty. And a good contract must bind both parties. What reason is there, then, why one should have an action of debt and the other should not have an action? (As if to say, there is no reason, since in right he should have the land.)

It was adjourned.

The record shows that in Hilary term 1443 judgment was given for the plaintiff to recover £20 damages, as assessed upon a writ of enquiry. It will be noted that the damages fell far short of the purchase price and the £200 claimed by the count.

Later the same year the Common Pleas gave judgment in a similar case: *Dynot v Cryspyng* (1443) CP 40/730, m. 126 (whereas the defendant had undertaken to convey to the plaintiff a marsh in West Mersea, Essex, which the plaintiff had bought for £20, of which 20s. was paid, the defendant had fraudulently sold and conveyed it to a third party; the defendant pleaded a parol discharge before the date set for performance, but the jury found for the plaintiff with £10 damages and judgment was entered accordingly; the defendant brought a writ of error). Six years later, however, another Common Pleas case resulted in an undetermined demurrer to the declaration: *Tyrell v Hill* (1449–51) CP 40/753, m. 137 (whereas the plaintiff had bargained to buy land at Little Waltham, Essex, for five marks, and the defendant had undertaken to deliver possession within three weeks, the defendant had fraudulently sold and delivered seisin to a third party, so that the plaintiff could not have the land according to the form of the bargain). But in *Cook v Iwyns* (1475) CP 40/856, m. 334, the plaintiff in another such case recovered the £4 purchase money.

TAILBOYS v SHERMAN (1443)

(a) HLS MS. 169, unfol. (C.P.).[15]

In a writ of trespass the plaintiff counted that there was a bargain between the plaintiff and the defendant for five tuns of wine to be brought, and that he was to carry the five tuns to the plaintiff at a certain place before a certain day, and he did not carry them thither, to the damage [of the plaintiff] etc.

Bingham. [We pray] judgment of the writ, for it well appears by his action that he ought to have a writ of covenant and not a writ of trespass. For a man shall never have a writ of trespass without

---

15 Anonymous, but probably the same case as the following. This report is dated Pas. 21 Hen. VI.

supposing a wrong [done] by the defendant; and he has not supposed any wrong done by him, and so it seems to me that the writ should abate.

AYSCOUGH. If my arm is broken, and I make a covenant with someone else to put plasters (*salves*) to it, and he does not do so, whereby my arm is lost, I shall have an action of trespass on my case.

DANVERS. If [I] covenant with someone to build a house by a certain day, and he does not build any part of the house before the day, I shall never have an action of trespass, but a writ of covenant. But if he cuts up my timber, and does not build, or builds part of the house and not the whole, or builds badly, I shall have a writ of trespass on my case.

And the opinion was that the plea was to the action, and not to the writ. Therefore the defendant prayed leave to imparl.

(b) Y.B. Trin. 21 Hen. VI, fo. 55v, pl. 12; collated
with BL MS. Harley 4557, fo. 327v.

William Tailboys brought a writ of trespass on his case against William Sherman and counted that he had bargained with him at Lincoln for two pipes of wine for ten marks, and the defendant was to deliver the two pipes of wine to the plaintiff at Goltho before Christmas last; and said that in fact he did not deliver to him the two pipes of wine before the said feast at the place aforesaid, and so an action is given to him.

Bingham. It seems that this writ does not lie on the case, and that the plaintiff should be put to his writ of debt.

Danby. As soon as the bargain was made, the property was in the plaintiff, and so he ought rather to have a writ of detinue than a writ of debt. If someone sells me a horse, I shall not[16] have a writ of debt against him, but a writ of detinue.

PASTON. What difference is there between 'bargained' and 'sold' (or 'bought')? I do not think there is any.

Bingham. He cannot have this action which he has conceived upon the facts as shown, for the facts sound in covenant; and so he should have a writ of covenant. Where the plaintiff ought upon the bargain to deliver the wine to Goltho by a certain date, that is a covenant; and although it is not performed the plaintiff shall not have an action of trespass on his case. For if a carpenter makes a bargain or covenant with me to make a good and sufficient house

---

16 MS. Omitted in printed edition, which reverses the sentence and says 'but not a writ of detinue'.

of a certain length by a certain day, and he makes no house for me, I shall not have a writ of trespass on my case against him, but a writ of covenant (if the covenant is in writing). But if he makes the house contrary to my covenant, even if the covenant is not in writing I shall have a writ of trespass on my case against him. The law is the same if a smith makes a covenant with me to shoe my horse, and he shoes it and injures it with a nail, I shall have an action on my case for trespass; but if he does nothing to the horse I cannot have an action against him. Likewise, it seems, here.

AYSCOUGH. If a surgeon makes a covenant with me for a certain sum to cure my head or my arm, and he does not come and give me any medicine, so that my head [gets worse] or my arm is lost (*perish*), I shall have a writ of trespass on my case against him.

Bingham. If he gives you contrary medicines, so that your arm is lost, you shall have a writ of trespass on your case against him.

AYSCOUGH. So I may even if he gives me no medicine.

PASTON. If I come riding along the road, and I pass through a town where a smith lives, and he has sufficient stuff to shoe my horse, and my horse has lost his shoes, and I request the smith at a reasonable hour to shoe him, and offer him enough for his labour, and he refuses, so that by his default my horse is afterwards lost for want of shoes, I say that in this case I shall have an action of trespass on my case.

Later the parties settled, and nothing further was done in this case.

ANON. (1449)

Trin. 27 Hen. VI, Statham Abr.,
Actions sur le cas, pl. [25] (C.P.).

Someone brought an action on the case because he had delivered to the defendant nine sacks of hay to look after, and the defendant (in return for six shillings, which the plaintiff paid) took upon himself to keep them safely, and for want of good keeping they were taken and carried away.

Danby. This action does not lie, for it plainly appears that he could have a writ of detinue. Also, he does not set out in his count by whom the sacks were carried away.

PORTINGTON. If he says they were carried away by persons unknown it is sufficient. But it seems the action does not lie, for the former reason.

PRYSOT [C.J.] The action clearly lies, in my view. (But he did not say why.)

Then *Danby* answered the action.

(And I[17] believe the reason why the action lay was because the defendant had taken six shillings to look after the sacks, which six shillings could not be recovered back by a writ of detinue.) (Query.)

ANON. (1487)

Y.B. Hil. 2 Hen. VII, fo. 11, pl. 9;
BL MS. Hargrave 105, fo. 109v (C.P.).

The case was this: a man had a hundred sheep to look after, and negligently through his fault he allowed them to drown.[18]

Rede. It seems that the action does not lie. An action on the case does not lie for nonfeasance, because for that the party shall have a writ of covenant. If a man has cloth to look after, and it is wasted or moth-eaten or rotten, no action on the case lies, but an action of detinue.

Wode. It seems to me that the action lies perfectly well. Suppose a man undertakes to carry glasses or pots, and he breaks them through negligence, I shall have an action on my case.

Kebell said that nonfeasance shall not cause an action on the case. If, before the Statute of Labourers, a retained servant would not perform a service for his master, no action lay for this nonfeasance.[19]

It was touched upon in argument that if some act were done by the party, then an action would lie perfectly well. For example, if I bail a chest with a bond, and the bailee breaks it open; or if I bail a horse to ride ten leagues, and the bailee rides twenty leagues, an action on the case lies. Or if, perhaps, the party had driven the sheep into the water, for that act an action on the case would lie.

TOWNSHEND. When the party has taken upon himself to look after the sheep, and afterwards allowed them to perish through his fault, since he has undertaken and executed[20] his bargain, and has

---

17 This note may be by Statham himself, if the abridgment is truly his work. He was already a member of Lincoln's Inn in 1449.

18 No *assumpsit* is mentioned, and it is possible that case would lie against a bailee for negligence even in the absence of an undertaking: see p. 563, below. The printed *Registrum Brevium* (1531) has specimens of similar actions against bailees of sheep both with and without an undertaking (ff. 107, 110v). It seems from the remarks of Townshend J. that an undertaking may have been alleged here.

19 See p. 379, fn. 3, above.

20 Townshend J. appears to use this word in two senses. Here he obviously means 'begun to perform'.

them in his keeping, and afterwards does not attend to them, an action lies. Here there is his act: namely, his agreement together with an undertaking. And when that is afterwards broken on his side, that will cause the action. Suppose a horse is bailed to a man to look after, and afterwards he does not feed it, so that it dies, an action on the case lies. Or, if a carrier takes my goods to carry, and afterwards loses or breaks them, an action on the case lies perfectly well to make him answer as to why he has not executed his bargain, [when he] has taken upon himself to do that thing. If, however, a covenant is made with me to look after my horse, or to carry my goods, and he does not do it,[1] an action of covenant lies and no other action, for in these cases he never executed his promise.

JOHNSON v BAKER (1493)

(a) The record: CP 40/914, m. 104.

Oxfordshire. John Baker, late of Henley-on-Thames in the aforesaid county, innholder, was summoned to answer Edward Johnson in a plea . . . And thereupon the same Edward, by Thomas Aylove his attorney, says that, whereas the aforesaid John on 10 December in the fifth year of the present king [1489], for a certain sum of money, namely 21s. 8d. previously paid to the said John, had undertaken at Henley aforesaid safely and surely to carry 65 quarters of malt in a certain barge of his by the River Thames as far as the city of London, and there to deliver them to the said Edward: the same John so negligently and improvidently steered the barge that the barge and malt aforesaid were completely sunk through the fault of the selfsame John at Burnham in the county of Buckingham, to the damage of the selfsame Edward of £14.

And the aforesaid Edward, by William Denne his attorney, comes and denies the force and injury whenever etc. And he says that he did not take upon himself to carry the aforesaid malt in the manner and form in which the aforesaid Edward, by his writ and count aforesaid, has above supposed. And thereof he puts himself on the country; and the aforesaid Edward likewise.

In July 1492 at Oxford assizes (Hody C.B., Tremayle J.) the jury found for

---

1   I.e. does not assume the custody.

the plaintiff, with £4 damages and 40s. costs. The plaintiff prayed judgment in Michaelmas term, and the court took advisement until Hilary term 1493.

(b) Caryll's report, BL MS. Harley 1624, fo. 28;
LI MS. Maynard 86, fo. 37v.

Rede ... Sir, I think you will not give judgment, for an action on the case does not lie on the facts, because these facts sound entirely in covenant. An action on the case lies only where a thing is done badly, by an actual act. For instance, if a carpenter undertakes to build me a house, and he builds the house badly, an action on the case lies; but for not building the house a writ of covenant lies, if there is writing, and if not there is no remedy. Likewise here: the defendant undertook to carry the corn to a vill in a different county, and did not do so, and for this nonfeasance the plaintiff may have a writ of covenant, but not an action on the case. Even if the corn was destroyed in transit through the defendant's negligence, still no actual act is assigned [to have been done by] him, and consequently there can be no action on the case.

BRYAN [C.J.] If a common farrier misdrives a nail in shoeing my horse, so that it is lamed, does not an action on my case lie?

Rede. Yes, sir, because there he has actually done something.

BRYAN. So did the defendant when, through his bad management, the ship perished. If someone undertakes to carry certain wine for me from one place to another, and afterwards carries it badly [so that it is damaged] through his fault in carrying it, an action on the case lies without doubt. Therefore this point is not worth arguing in this case.[2]

This was agreed.

Rede then moved on to argue that there was a jeofail, because the plaintiff had alleged an undertaking in Oxfordshire and a perishing in Buckinghamshire, and the defendant had traversed the undertaking, whereas he should have traversed the perishing in Buckinghamshire; and also that the action should have been brought in Buckinghamshire. (Cf. p. 363, above.) The court overruled this objection, saying that the plaintiff could elect to sue in either county. But no judgment was given. It is recorded in the margin of the plea roll that the case was not continued beyond Hilary term 1493, so perhaps the parties settled.

---

2 Cf. abridged report in BL MS. Harley 1691, fo. 76v, which ends: 'And it was adjudged that the action lay, for this point is not to be argued in this case, for inasmuch as the corn perished through his negligence it was a great misfeasance'.

A DICTUM IN GRAY'S INN (1499)

Trin. 14 Hen. VII, Fitz. Abr., *Action sur le case*,
pl. 45; also inserted in Y.B. Mich. 21 Hen. VII, fo. 41,
pl. 66, from Fitzherbert.

In Gray's Inn.[3] Note, if a man makes a covenant to build me a house by a certain date, and does nothing about it, I shall have an action on my case for this nonfeasance as well as if he had built badly, because I am damaged by it: per FYNEUX.[4] And he said that it had been so adjudged, and he held it to be law. It is likewise if a man bargains with me that I shall have his land unto me and my heirs for £20, and that he will make an estate to me if I pay him the £20, and he does not make an estate to me according to the covenant, I shall have an action on my case and need not sue out a *subpoena*.

A GRAY'S INN MOOT (1516)

At the reading of Peter Dillon on the Statute of
Ireland *De coheredibus*: LI MS. Misc. 486(2), fo. 7v.

A man covenants to build a house, and does not: he [to whom the covenant is made] shall have an action on the case.[5]

Harlakenden and *Hales* to the contrary: for a man shall not have an action on the case for not doing something, albeit he shall for misfeasance. Thus, if he had built the house in a way which was not in accordance with the covenants, [the other] should have an action on the case; but not for nonfeasance.

Tingleden. It seems that he shall [not][6] have an action on the case. But he said he would not take that maxim too generally, since if the nonfeasance caused injury to something else he should have an action on the case. Thus, if a man has a house without a roof, and he covenants with a man by parol to tile his house by a certain day, and the man does not do it, he shall have an action on the case, because some other thing (namely, the timber) is injured by this nonfeasance. Likewise, if a man covenants by parol to look after my sheep, and then they drown, I shall have an action on my case.[7]

---

3 In margin of 1514 ed., but omitted from later editions.
4 Sir John Fyneux (C.J.K.B. 1495–1525) was a former bencher of Gray's Inn and regularly attended the readings there. This dictum may have been at the summer reading of 1499.
5 Presumably a proposition put forward by the reader. It is not obvious how it arose from his text.
6 Conjectural correction. The MS. is a corrupt copy.
7 See p. 398, above.

Likewise, if a man is bound by the tenure of his land to repair a sea-wall and does not do it, so that my land is flooded, I shall have an action on the case.[8] Likewise, if a man is bound to keep a ditch or bridge clean, and does not do so, I shall have an action on the case; for as a result of this nonfeasance the common way is impaired. But where the nonfeasance is no injury except to my person,[9] I shall not have an action on the case. And that is the case here: therefore [the action does not lie].

Dillon to the contrary. For every law is grounded on reason, and reason wills that if a man has an injury he should have an action. Now, he has injury by this nonfeasance; and so if he should not have the action on the case he will be without remedy. So he thought that he should have an action on the case.

William Martin agreed.

NOTE (*c.* 1530)

Yorke's reports, BL MS. Hargrave 3, fo. 23; MS.
Hargrave 388, fo. 214v; MS. Lansdowne 1072, fo. 34;
Gonville & Caius Coll. MS. 601, fo. 63v.

Note that if a man detains my goods, and by the detention my goods are moth-eaten or in some other way perished, in this case if I bring a writ of detinue I shall recover the thing and damages for the detention: and so I shall have no remedy for the perishing of the goods. Therefore the policy is to bring an action on my case, and recover everything I have lost through the detention, which I cannot recover in a writ of detinue; for in detinue I shall only recover the thing as it is, and damages only for the detaining, but there I shall have an action on the case for the miskeeping of the thing, and not for the detention. Note this opinion (*conceite*).

ANON. (*c.* 1530)

Yorke's reports, BL MS. Hargrave 388, fo. 215; MS.
Hargrave 3, fo. 23; MS. Lansdowne 1072, fo. 34;
Gonville & Caius Coll. MS. 601, fo. 63v.

The case was that a man delivered a bond to one John Style[10] to

8 See p. 338, below.
9 It is not clear whether Tingleden means this literally, or whether he is referring to economic loss or inconvenience. Actions on the case had long been available for physical injury to the person, and such injury might result from nonfeasance (e.g., by a surgeon).
10 Not a real name.

keep safely, and he took it upon himself to do so, and then the seal was broken off (*devast, devest*) while it was in John Style's keeping, and thereupon the obligee[11] brought an action on his case against John Style. The question was: shall he have an action on the case, or a writ of detinue?

It was held by all, except ENGLEFIELD J.,[12] that he should have an action on the case if he wished. As to the maxim (*ground*) put forward, that where he can have an original writ at common law he shall not have an action on the case, this is not so: for he may have either, though not upon the same point for which he may have the action at common law (such as detinue). For if he brings an action on the case and declares on the detaining of the deed, this is invalid, for he should have an action of detinue for that point. For the loss of the seal, however, and the misordering of the deed, which is something else in itself, he shall have an action on the case for this something else. And whereas it was said that the party's fault was only nonfeasance, for which he shall not have an action on the case, to this they said that the maxim held place [only] if this nonfeasance amounted only to *nudum pactum*. For instance, if I promise to make you a house by a certain day, and I do not do so, this is only *nudum pactum*, on which [you] shall not have an action on the case; and [you are] not wronged as a result of this nonfeasance. If [you were] wronged by it, it would be otherwise. For instance, if I am bound in a bond in £100 to pay £20 by such and such a day, and I deliver the £20 to a stranger and he promises to deliver it [to the obligee] before the day, and he does not pay it before the day, so that I have forfeited my bond, I shall there have an action on the case for the nonfeasance; for he has wronged me.[13] The law is the same if I give certain money to someone to make me a house by a certain day, and he does not make it by the day, there that is a consideration why I shall have an action on my case for the nonfeasance.

The same law was in experience, and agreed by the justices in the Common Bench,[14] where a man recovered in ancient demesne and gave certain money to the clerk to make an entry of his matter thus recovered, and he did not do it; there it was agreed that he should

11 The person to whom the bond was payable.
12 J.C.P. 1526–1537. The reporter (Roger Yorke) died in 1536, so the case must have occurred between 1526 and 1536.
13 Such a case is *Gybbes v Wolston* (1483) CP 40/883, m. 355, where the plaintiff recovered 20 marks (£13. 6s. 8d.) for failing to pay £17 to a creditor. It is not clear why the damages were less than the debt.
14 The case is identifiable as *Ewer v Elys* (1522) CP 40/1033, m. 304; Selden Soc. vol. 94, p. 241; reported in Spelman, *Reports*, p. 3, pl. 2.

have an action on his case for the nonfeasance. But if he died his heir would not have this action which his father could have had, for it is a personal action and dies with the person.

SUKLEY v WYTE (1542)

Gell's reports, LC MS. Acc. LL 52960,
Pas. 34 Hen. VIII, fo. 12v.

In an action on the case brought by one Sukley,[15] of London, against Wyte, the plaintiff declared that the said defendant came to him on 1 May [1540], when the said plaintiff was one of the sheriffs of London, with a *capias*, and prayed that the writ should be served on one John Style;[16] to which the plaintiff said that the said John Style was a burgess of parliament, and so he could not serve it; and the defendant said to him that he would save him harmless if he would arrest him; and by virtue of this the plaintiff, being then sheriff, arrested the said John Style, then being a burgess of parliament; and for this arrest he was put in the Tower and lost his office, and so was greatly damaged by this arrest; on which facts he had conceived his action.

Bromley. It seems to me that the action does not lie, and the reason is because his action is based on a bare promise, and there is no specialty, nor any money given in covenant, but it is only a promise, on which promise he cannot have an action.

Hales to the contrary. As it seems to me, the action lies. It is not correct to say that a man cannot have an action on a promise; for if I promise my brother Saunders that I will make him a house, and I make part of it but not the whole, he may have an action on his case against me. Or if the house is not as long as I promised, he may have his action. Or if a smith promises me to shoe my horse, without being paid money beforehand, and he injures it with a nail, I shall have an action on my case. Or if a surgeon undertakes to make my disease better, and does not make me better but brings on other diseases, I shall have an action on my case against him. Also, if I sell my horse to John Noke for a certain sum of money, and there is a stranger with him, and I say that I do not trust him for the sum of money, and the stranger undertakes that if John Noke does not pay he will pay the sum; and the vendee dies before he pays the

15 Henry Suckley.
16 Actually George Ferrers of Lincoln's Inn, page of the chamber, and M.P. for Plymouth. For the details of this case, see S. T. Bindoff (ed.), *The House of Commons 1509–1558* (1982), vol. II, p. 130.

sum, and the stranger appoints his executors and dies, and the vendor brings an action on the case against the executors; and the action was well maintainable.[17] Likewise here.

SHELLEY J. That last case is a doubtful case, and it seems to me that the action on the case does not lie against executors on a promise made by their testator.

This was in effect affirmed by the whole court, but query.

WILLOUGHBY J. It seems to me that the action at the bar is well maintainable, for I will show you a case which is more like it; and it is in a book. If a sheriff takes the beasts of one John Style in withernam, and the said John Style says to the sheriff that if he will deliver the beasts back to him he will save him harmless, and he delivers them, and later the sheriff is amerced, he may in this case have an action on his case against him.

SHELLEY J. This is a good case and much learning may arise from it, for strong arguments can be made on both sides. For on one side one could say that this action is not maintainable, because the defendant undertook to save the plaintiff harmless for nothing other than what he could lawfully do, that is, the arrest: for the arrest was good, and one may arrest a burgess of parliament and the arrest is good, even though he can avoid it by *supersedeas* or by plea, and so bar him without making answer. It follows that if the defendant undertook to save him harmless for something which was lawful, that is no cause of action against him. But notwithstanding those reasons I will not say precisely that the action does not lie, but will be advised hereof; for it is a doubtful case. (So query.)

Then it was adjourned.

17 This seems to be a reference to *Cleymond v Vincent* (1520), p. 446, below, which had been attacked by Fitzherbert J.: see p. 448, below.

16   Assumpsit in lieu of debt

ORWELL v MORTOFT (1505)

(a) The record: CP 40/972, m. 123.

Norfolk. William Mortoft, late of East Dereham in the aforesaid county, mercer, was attached to answer Thomas Orwell...[1] And thereupon the same Thomas, by William Knyghtley his attorney, complains that, whereas the aforesaid Thomas on 20 April [1503] in the eighteenth year of the reign of the present lord king had bought 60 quarters of barley from the said William [Mortoft] at Aylsham for a certain sum of money (namely £6) agreed upon between them, and the same William had undertaken, covenanted and bargained to deliver the aforesaid barley there within a certain time now elapsed (namely, before the feast of All Saints then next following): the aforesaid William, scheming fraudulently and craftily to defraud the said Thomas, wholly converted the aforesaid 60 quarters of barley to his own use and did not deliver it within the aforesaid time. And thereby he says he is the worse and has damage to the extent of £20. And thereof he produces suit etc.

And the aforesaid William, by John Brampton his attorney, comes and denies the force and wrong when etc. And he says that the aforesaid Thomas did not buy from the selfsame William the aforesaid 60 quarters of barley or any part thereof in the way that the same Thomas above supposes by his aforesaid writ and count; and of this he puts himself upon the country; and the aforesaid Thomas likewise. Therefore the sheriff is commanded to cause to come here on the morrow of the Ascension 12 etc. by whom etc. who neither etc. to make recognition etc. because both etc.

---

1   The record here sets out the terms of the writ, which are repeated in the count.

Afterwards the process between the aforesaid parties in the plea aforesaid was continued, by the juries between them therein being put in respite here until this day, namely a fortnight from Michaelmas then next following, unless the lord king's justices assigned to take the assizes in the aforesaid county by the form of the statute etc. should first have come to Norwich in the aforesaid county on the Monday [21 July 1505] next after the feast of St James the Apostle last past. And now here at this day come both the aforesaid Thomas Orwell and the aforesaid William Mortoft, by their aforesaid attorneys. And the said justices of assize, before whom etc., have sent in their record in these words:[2]

Afterwards, at the day and place contained within, before Sir John Fyneux and Sir [Robert] Rede, the lord king's justices assigned to take the assizes in the county of Norfolk by the form of the statute etc., come both the within-named Thomas Orwell, by William Knyghtley his attorney, and the within-named William Mortoft, by John Brampton his attorney; and the jurors of the jury mentioned within, having been called, likewise come and are chosen, tried and sworn to say the truth concerning the matters contained within. And thereupon the aforesaid Thomas shows in evidence to the same jurors here in court that he bought the within-mentioned 60 quarters of barley from the aforesaid William Mortoft for the within-mentioned £6, in the way that the aforesaid Thomas supposes within by his writ and count. And thereupon the aforesaid William Mortoft says that the aforesaid evidence given and alleged above by the said Thomas is insufficient in law to prove and maintain the within-mentioned action and issue, and that he need not and is not bound by the law of the land to answer that evidence given in form aforesaid. And so he prays judgment whether upon that evidence the aforesaid Thomas can maintain or ought to have his aforesaid action etc. And the aforesaid Thomas, since he has given sufficient evidence to the aforesaid jurors to maintain his action and the within-mentioned issue, which evidence he is ready to verify, and which the aforesaid William Mortoft does not deny or in any way answer, prays judgment and that the aforesaid jurors should be charged to enquire of the damages etc. Whereupon the aforesaid jurors (being charged to enquire of the damges etc. if the aforesaid matter in law should be adjudged in favour of the aforesaid Thomas) say upon their oath that the aforesaid 60 quarters of barley are worth £6 if the aforesaid Thomas cannot have that barley, and assess the damages of the selfsame Thomas by reason of the withholding of that barley (besides the value of the same, and the outlay and costs expended by him about his suit in that behalf) as £4, and assess the outlay and costs as £4. Thereupon a day is given to the aforesaid parties before the within-

---

2 This *postea* records a demurrer to the evidence at Norwich assizes. Since the evidence added nothing to the facts alleged in pleading, it had much the same effect as a demurrer to the declaration, and this may explain why in Keil. 69 it is referred to as a 'demurrer in law'.

mentioned justices of the Bench at the within-mentioned day, for hearing their judgment therein, inasmuch as etc.

And because the justices here wish to be advised of and upon the foregoing before they give judgment, a day is given to the aforesaid parties here until the octaves of St Hilary for hearing their judgment therein, inasmuch as the justices here are not yet [advised] etc . . .

There are similar continuances for advisement until Michaelmas term 1506, but no judgment is entered.

(b) Report: Y.B. Mich. 20 Hen. VII, fo. 8, pl. 18.[3]

A man brought an action on his case, namely, that whereas he had bought from the defendant 20 quarters of malt, to be delivered to the plaintiff at a certain day, the defendant converted the said quarters to his own use, whereby an action accrued to him.

KINGSMILL. This action does not lie, but he must have an action of debt: for the property is not changed by the bargain, because it is unascertained (*en non certenté*) and he must have it by delivery from the defendant; and it is at the defendant's pleasure what grain he will pay him, for if he buys 20 quarters from someone else [afterwards] he may pay the plaintiff with them . . . It is not like the case where I bail goods to be looked after, and the bailee converts them to his own use: there an action on the case lies,[4] for the property is in me. But in this case at the bar, he shall recover damages in debt for the wrongful withholding of the grain.

FISHER and VAVASOUR were of the same opinion.

FROWYK [C.J.] thought the contrary. It has been argued that the plaintiff cannot take the 20 quarters, and has no property in them by the bargain; but this does not matter, for [the defendant] has done something to determine my[5] bargain, and has deceived me, whereby I am caused loss: and so it is right that he should be punished for this wrongdoing (*misdemener*) by an action on the case. If I sell £10 worth of land, parcel of my manor, and covenant further to make an estate[6] by a certain day, and before the day I sell the whole manor to someone else: in this case an action on the case lies against me. Likewise, if I sell ten acres in my wood, and then I sell the whole wood to someone else. Of if I covenant, in return for

3   Also reported by Caryll, in Keil. 69, 77 (correctly dated Mich. 21 Hen. VII).
4   See pp. 524–528, below.
5   Frowyk C.J. here begins to argue as if he were the plaintiff.
6   I.e. execute a conveyance.

money, to make a house by a certain day, and do not do it, an action on the case lies for the nonfeasance. Here, then, he has sold 20 quarters of malt to the plaintiff to be delivered at a certain day, and has not done this, but has converted them to his own use; and so it is right that he should be punished by an action on the case. And even though he could have debt, it does not follow that he cannot have this action. For if I bail money to be bailed over, and he converts it to his own use, I can have an action of account, or debt, or an action on the case. Likewise detinue: where a thing is bailed to be looked after, and he converts it to his own use, detinue lies; and so does an action on the case, as appears in the previous case of *Cheseman*.[7] But it would be a good thing to consider this present case further, and be advised.

Thereupon they were adjourned.

(On another day:) KINGSMILL. The action does not lie, but he shall be driven to his action of debt. Every bargain shall be interpreted equally as between the parties, and not more in favour of one than the other. (It is otherwise of a gift.) Therefore, since the vendor may not take his money for the thing sold, no more may the buyer take the thing (when it is unascertained, as here), especially when the bargain is that the seller should deliver it—but even if that term were left out he can not take the corn, for it must be measured out. Suppose the seller did not have corn at the time of the bargain, but bought some afterwards; or that he sold the corn which he had at the time of the bargain, but later bought other corn, which he could deliver on the day: this is good, which proves that the buyer had no interest in the grain at the time of the bargain, and is therefore to demand it by debt. (If, however, I sell the grain in my barn or house,[8] I may not deliver other grain; for it may be that there is no grain as good in the whole neighbourhood.) So it seems that debt lies. And where a general action lies, a special action on the case does not. Thus, where an assize of nuisance lies, a special action on the case does not.[9] An action on the case [sometimes] lies for not doing something: as where an attorney does not execute his office, or a

---

7 *Bourghchier v Cheseman* (1504) Mich. 20 Hen. VII, fo. 4, pl. 13; KB 27/972, m. 88. Two bags of jewels had been entrusted to a bailee, who died; they came into the defendant's hands; and the defendant *vi et armis* broke the bags open and converted the jewels to his own use. The defendant denied the conversion, and the jury found for the plaintiff with £220 damages. The question reported in the Y.B. is not whether detinue was more appropriate, but whether the defendant could traverse the conversion rather than the breaking of the chest. Fyneux C.J. thought he could.

8 In Keil. 69, Kingsmill J. said his decision would have been different if the barley had been in sacks.

9 See pp. 581–586, below.

labourer does not do his service in tilling and manuring my land, for I am damaged thereby and no general action lies.

FISHER and VAVASOUR to the same effect . . .

FROWYK to the contrary. Everyone must be punished according to his fault. Therefore, although debt lies for the grain, nevertheless because the defendant has deceived him this is a greater wrong than the withholding of the grain or the non-payment, and he can not be punished for it in any other action than this action.[10] If I deliver money to someone to deliver over to my attorney, for my costs in some suit, and he delivers it to my adversary, in this case this delivery is a greater damage to me than the non-delivery [to my attorney], and yet debt lies against the bailee: but, even though debt lies, the action on the case lies for the wrongdoing. Thus these actions are taken upon separate causes. And where I am bound[11] upon condition to pay a lesser sum, and I deliver the lesser sum to my servant to pay it, and he does not pay it, in this case debt lies (or account) for the non-payment: but because I have forfeited my bond by the non-payment I have [suffered] a greater wrong, and for that I shall have an action on the case. Likewise in this case, because the plaintiff is deceived by the conversion of the grain to the defendant's own use, he thereby has a greater damage than the non-delivery thereof; and for that cause, as I understand it, the action lies here. As for Kingsmill's argument that an action on the case does not lie where [an assize of] nuisance lies, I quite agree; for one is real and the other is purely personal, and such actions may not stand together. But it is otherwise here. Suppose I covenant to enfeoff a man with an acre which is part of my manor, and I sell the whole manor to someone else: here an action on the case lies for this deceit. Likewise in this case at the bar, inasmuch as he sold the plaintiff 20 quarters of barley and then converted them to his own use, which is a deceit and wrongdoing for which an action lies.[12]

---

10 Cf. Keil. 69: '. . . In my view the reason why this action is maintainable is that the plaintiff is damaged by the non-delivery at the time mentioned in the bargain; and even though the plaintiff could have an action of debt for the barley, he is nevertheless not thereby satisfied for being damaged'.

11 I.e. in a conditional money-bond.

12 Cf. a further reason in Keil. 77: '. . . If I covenant with a carpenter to make me a house, and pay him £20 to make the house by a certain day, and he does not make the house by the day, I shall have an action on my case because of the payment of my money: and yet it sounds only in covenant, and without payment of the money in this case there is no remedy. If he makes the house, but badly, an action on my case lies; and for the nonfeasance also, if the money has been paid, an action on my case lies. Likewise, it seems to me, in the case at the bar: the payment of the money is the cause of the action on the case, without any alteration of property'. There is no explicit statement in the record, however, that Orwell had paid Mortoft.

(*Reporter*. Coming from Westminster, I heard my lord Fyneux[13] say that in his view an action of debt would lie, in which he would recover damages for all this wrongdoing; but not this action.)

PYKERYNG v THURGOODE (1532)

Record: K B 27/1073, m. 70; Selden Soc. vol. 94, p. 247. Richard Pykeryng, a London brewer, brought an action on the case against John Thurgoode, yeoman, of Hitchin, Hertfordshire, and declared that, whereas on 30 October 1531 the defendant had bargained and sold to the plaintiff 40 quarters of malt for £5. 13s. 4d. then paid in cash and another £5. 13s. 4d. to be paid on delivery, at the feast of the Purification (2 February 1532); and the defendant had then and there promised and undertaken to deliver the malt accordingly; and that, relying on this promise, the plaintiff had made lesser provision of malt for his brewing: the defendant, scheming to cause the plaintiff loss in his trade as a brewer, did not deliver the malt on time or at all, so that the plaintiff had no malt for his brewing but was forced to buy it from others at a much higher price. The defendant pleaded *Non assumpsit*, and on 5 July 1532 at the Guildhall, London, before Fitzjames C.J., the jury found for the plaintiff with £9 damages and 40s. costs.

Spelman, *Reports*, p. 4, pl. 5.

... The plaintiff prayed judgment; and the other party, by his counsel *Cholmeley* and *Hynde* Sjts., alleged in arrest of judgment that this action does not lie, since an action of debt lies: and where a general action lies, a special action on the case does not lie in the same case.

SPELMAN J. It seems that the action on the case does lie. For where a man has a wrong done to him, and has suffered damage, he must have an action. Now, because the defendant has broken his promise and undertaking, he has wronged the plaintiff; and the plaintiff has suffered damage through the non-delivery of the malt: ergo, the law gives him an action. And no action lies on this but an action on the case; and so the action lies. Although in some books[14] a distinction has been drawn between nonfeasance and malfeasance, so that an action of covenant lies on the one and an action on the case on the other, this is no distinction in reason. If a carpenter covenants for £100 to make me a house, and does not make it before the appointed day, so that I lack somewhere to live, I shall have an action on my case for this nonfeasance just as well as if he had made it badly. And although Pykeryng could have an

---

13 Sir John Fyneux (C.J.K.B. 1495–1525).
14 See pp. 378–405, above.

action of debt, that is immaterial; for the action of debt is founded on the *debet et detinet*, whereas this action is founded on another wrong, namely, the breach of the promise. If a man sells me his land for £100 and promises to convey it to me before a certain day, and then enfeoffs someone else, I shall have an action on my case for his deceit; and yet covenant lies, because he has not performed any part of his promise. But the action of covenant is based on the covenant broken, while the action on the case is based on the deceit in enfeoffing someone else. If, in the same case, he had taken back an estate and enfeoffed me before the day, the action on the case would still lie if he had warranted [for] him and his assigns, for by taking the estate he is in of another estate, and so the warranty is void with respect to me.[15] If a man bails goods to look after, and the bailee converts them to his own use, in this case the bailor may have an action on the case upon this misdemeanour; and yet he could have had an action of detinue, but that would have been based on the bailment and the detaining. It was so [held] in the case between *Bourgchier* and *Cheseman*[16]. . . he had judgment to recover, and yet he could have had an action of detinue; but that was immaterial, for the reason given.

PORT J. thought the contrary. This promise is part of the contract,[17] and it is all one. There is no act done by the defendant, but merely the non-delivery, for which detinue[18] lies.

CONINGSBY J. and FITZJAMES C.J. It seems that the action lies, and it is at the plaintiff's election to take either action, for they are based on different points—as Spelman has said. If a man bails money to be handed over to another, and he does not hand it over, it is at the bailor's pleasure whether to bring debt, account, or an action on his case; for the actions are based on different points. Or, if a man bails to me his robe to look after, and by my neglect (*sufferance*) the robe becomes moth-eaten, he shall have an action on his case for this negligence and ill-keeping, though he could also have had a writ of detinue at his pleasure: and although I lose by [his choice of an action on the case], since I could have waged my law in detinue but not in the action on the case, this is immaterial, because in *Cheseman's Case* (above), which is good law, he was ousted from his law which he could properly have had in an action of detinue. There are many precedents where a man has bailed goods to look after, and the bailee converted them to his own

---

15   Cf. *Doige's Case* (1443), p. 392, above.
16   (1504); see 409, fn. 7, above.
17   A variant text reads 'his covenant'.
18   Perhaps a slip for 'debt'.

profit, or looked after them badly, and the bailor had an action on his case; and yet he could have had an action of detinue, in which the bailee could have waged his law. (So it seemed to them that the plaintiff ought to have his judgment to recover.)

Later in the same term judgment was given for the plaintiff to recover his damages.

The record confirms that judgment was entered this term for £9 damages, and £4 costs (increased by the court).

HOLYGRAVE v KNYGHTYSBRYGGE (1535)

Record: KB 27/1094, m. 30d; Selden Soc. vol. 94, p. 256. John Holygrave brought a bill against Henry Knyghtysbrygge complaining that, whereas he had recovered £6. 15s. against one Oliver Tateham in the Sheriffs' Court of London, and had Tateham imprisoned in the Bread Street Compter in execution for this judgment-debt, the defendant had asked the plaintiff to let Tateham go free, and had undertaken and promised to pay the debt himself; and the plaintiff had thereupon released Tateham and discharged the debt: nevertheless the defendant, little regarding his promise and undertaking, had not paid the debt. The defendant pleaded *Non assumpsit*, and on 8 May 1535 at the Guildhall, London, before Luke J., the jury found for the plaintiff with £7. 5s. damages.

The Y.B. adds some details which are not in the record: that the plaintiff (whom it calls 'Jordan') gave evidence at the trial that the undertaking was actually made to his wife, while he was away, and that she had later told him about it, and he had then released Tateham. The defendant objected that this evidence was insufficient, because the wife could not be party to the undertaking without the prior assent of her husband. The objection was overruled, and the defendant took the very unusual course[19] of praying a bill of exceptions. Such a bill was duly sealed, and it was argued in banc that it was invalid, because the procedure was not available in such a case. The better view seems to have been against allowing the bill, and that is doubtless why it was not entered of record. The argument on this point, and on the wife's agency, is here omitted.

Y.B. Mich. 27 Hen. VIII, fo. 24, pl. 3; collated with
LC MS. Acc. LL 52960, 27 Hen. VIII, fo. 42.[20]

... *Knightley*. It seems that this action does not lie, for he could have had an action of debt on this matter, and therefore should not

---

19   The usual procedure would have been to demur to the evidence: cf. *Orwell v Mortoft* (1505), p. 407, above.

20   Also reported in Spelman, *Reports*, p. 7, pl. 8. Spelman makes no mention of the bill of exceptions or of 'Jordan'.

have a writ on his case: for he should not have that unless there is no remedy by another writ.[1]

THE WHOLE COURT. That is not so, for in many cases a man shall have an action on his case where he might have had another remedy. With respect to that reason, then, the action is good.

LUKE[2] ... As to the argument that the plaintiff should have had a writ of debt, and not this action, it seems to me the contrary: for I think that a man shall not have a writ of debt except where there is a contract. The defendant has no *quid pro quo*, but this action is founded only on the undertaking, which sounds wholly in covenant. If it had been by specialty, the plaintiff would have had an action of covenant; but since there is no specialty he has no other remedy, it seems to me, than an action on his case. A case was adjudged here since I have been a judge here, which was that a stranger went with a man to a London baker and said to the baker, 'Deliver to this man as much bread as he wants, and if he does not pay you I will', and the baker delivered a certain amount of bread to the man, and the man did not later pay the baker, and so the baker brought his action on the case on his special matter against the stranger; and the stranger demurred, and it was clearly adjudged that the action lay, and the baker recovered.[3] Likewise here, it seems.

SPELMAN to the same effect ... Admitting the undertaking is good, what action should the plaintiff have? It seems to me that it is at the plaintiff's election to bring a writ of debt or this action, or some other action; for in several cases the law gives two ways for a man to attain his remedy. For instance, if I bail goods to you and you burn them, or else allow them to become moth-eaten, it is in my election to bring either action (that is, a writ of detinue or an action on my case) at my pleasure; and because I shall have one it is no proof that I shall not have the other.[4] And, if I am disseised, I may choose whether to bring a writ of entry *sur disseisin* or a writ of right. Thus it seems to me that it is in the plaintiff's election to bring either action; and therefore it seems to me that the plaintiff should recover.

---

1 Cf. Spelman's report: 'The defendant alleged in arrest of judgment that debt lay and not this action, for there is here a contract between the plaintiff and defendant whereby he promises to pay the plaintiff if he lets Tateham out of prison ... which is like the case where I promise a surgeon 100s. to cure the son of John at Style of an illness ...'
2 MS. Misprinted as 'Brooke'.
3 *Squyer v Barkeley* (1533) KB 27/1085, m. 32d (Selden Soc. vol. 94, p. 253); Spelman, *Reports*, p. 7, pl. 7.
4 MS. The passage is very garbled in print.

PORT . . . argued in the same way as SPELMAN.

FITZJAMES [C.J.] to the same effect . . . Shall he have an action of debt, or this action? It seems to me that he shall not have an action of debt, for there is no contract here, and the defendant did not have *quid pro quo*; and so he has no other remedy but an action on his case. Likewise, if a stranger buys a piece of cloth in London, and I say to the merchant, 'If he does not pay you by such and such a day, I will pay', here is no contract between the merchant and me, and he shall not have the action of debt against me[5]. . .

Afterwards the plaintiff had judgment to recover.

The record confirms that in Trinity term 1535 judgment was entered for the plaintiff for £7. 5s. damages and £2. 15s. costs.

ANON. (1542)

LC MS. Acc. LL 52960, Pas. 34 Hen. VIII, fo. 15
(C.P.).

An action on the case was brought, and the plaintiff declared that he had delivered to the defendant 20 quarters of barley, and that the defendant undertook to deliver 20 quarters of malt to the plaintiff in return for the 20 quarters of barley, before a certain day; and because the day was past, and he had not done this, he brought his action. Against this the defendant came and said that the plaintiff, at a certain place in another county, sold the said 20 quarters [of malt] to a stranger,[6] and he [the defendant] delivered them to him, and demanded judgment *Si action etc.*

Townshend. This is no plea, for two reasons. One is because it is a foreign plea, which cannot be tried where the action was brought. Another is because it is no discharge for him to say that he delivered the 20 quarters to a stranger. For if I bail my goods to someone, [who is] to rebail them to me again, and the bailee bails them over, or they are taken out of his possession, these special facts are no plea in an action brought against him; for he may have his action against the second bailee, or against the person who took them.

SHELLEY J. It seems to me that there is another point in the case, for I believe the action does not lie here. An action on the case does not lie in any case except where the plaintiff is without other action.

5 The same argument is reported in closely similar terms by Spelman, who evidently disagreed and thought debt was here available.
6 Apparently the plaintiff had resold before delivery, although this assumes that the malt was a specific chattel.

But here he could have an action of detinue. I perceive your purpose however. You brought this action because he shall not wage his law in this action, as he could in an action of detinue. Nevertheless, if we suppose that the action does lie, I am of the same opinion as you that the plea is not good.

This was agreed by WILLOUGHBY J.

ANON. (1572)

Dalison 84, pl. 35; BL MS. Add. 24845, fo. 88v.

In an action on the case brought in the King's Bench upon an *assumpsit*, the plaintiff declared that 'whereas the defendant was indebted to the plaintiff, he undertook in return for 12d. to pay [the debt]'.

Manwood took exception to the count, because he had not shown what the defendant was indebted for—such as money lent, or merchandise[7] bought, or the like. Also, he should have said that he undertook 'afterwards'; for if he undertook at the time of the contract debt lies on it, and not *assumpsit*, whereas if he undertook subsequently to the contract, then an action lies on the undertaking, but otherwise not.

This was agreed by WHIDDON and SOUTHCOTE JJ., in the absence[8] of CATLYN C.J.

EDWARDS v BURRE (1573)

Dalison 104, pl. 45; BL MS. Add. 24845, fo. 101; LI MS. Maynard 87, fo. 155; CUL MS. Ll. 3. 8, fo. 169v; HLS MS. Acc. 704755, fo. 144v.

William Edwards brought an action on the case against Edmund Burre[9] and Margaret his wife, administratrix of the goods and chattels of John Sidwell,[10] late her husband, and counted that the testator, in consideration that the plaintiff had lent the testator 40s., undertook to pay him 40s. The defendant pleaded *Non assumpsit modo et forma*. The plaintiff submitted evidence that he lent the 40s. to the testator.

WRAY J. said to the jury: if it be true that the plaintiff lent the

---

7   MS. Blank in print.
8   MS. Misprinted as 'ove lassent de'.
9   Reads 'Bury' in LI MS. and CUL MS.
10   Reads 'Snow' in LI MS. and CUL MS.

said sum, you must find for the plaintiff; for the debt is an undertaking in law.

But note that it was said that this is by reason of the custom of the King's Bench; for in the Common Pleas he would have to prove the undertaking, and it would not be sufficient to prove the debt alone. For he should have an action of debt for the debt, and not an action on the case, because the common law will not suffer a man to have an action on the case where he could have another remedy; and also because the debtor could have his law, if there is no specialty, and by an action on the case he would be prevented from having it, which is not right. Therefore in the Common Pleas he has to prove the undertaking.[11]

NORMAN v SOME (1594)

Were's reports, CUL MS. Ee. 3. 2, fo. 34;
BL MS. Hargrave 7(1), fo. 37 (C.P.).

Note, *per curiam*, that an action of debt shall not be converted into an action on the case unless the plaintiff has sustained more than ordinary damage: as where wares or grain are sold and not delivered, and the markets rise; for in such special cases of extraordinary damage sustained, debt may be converted into *assumpsit*.

Kingsmill, who moved this case, cited 20 Hen. VII[12] according.

ANON. (1596)

CUL MS. Ii. 5. 12, fo. 88 (C.P.).[13]

If a man sells me ten bushels of corn for a certain sum, an action of debt in the *detinet* lies for the corn, even though no property is there altered, because it is a plain bargain between the parties. And if the vendor is outlawed before the delivery of the corn, he shall forfeit it, and not the vendee. And an action on the case does not lie here, because *casus dicitur a cadendo*,[14] and therefore it only lies

11 The HLS MS. ends with the name 'Rookeby'.
12 *Orwell v Mortoft* (1505); see p. 406, above.
13 Probably the same as *Frisland's Case* (1596) BL MS. Hargrave 51, fo. 66v; MS. Harley 1631, fo. 210; where Walmsley J. says, '. . . he ought to have shown some extraordinary damage, for instance if through non-delivery of the wheat his children were starved'.
14 I.e. case is so called from *cadendo* (falling).

where something more than ordinary falls out: as where the vendee has been half starved for want of the delivery.

Note this, per WALMSLEY and BEAUMONT JJ.

TURGYS v BECHER (1596)

Record: KB 27/1334, m. 606. The plaintiff (an administrator) complained that, whereas the defendant was indebted to the intestate in £55 still unpaid for wheat sold and delivered to him in his lifetime, the defendant in consideration thereof undertook and promised to pay the plaintiff £55. The plaintiff recovered £60 damages; and on 25 January 1596 the court received a writ of error for removing the record into the Exchequer Chamber, where the following discussion occurred in Trinity term following.

Were's reports, BL MS. Hargrave 7(1), fo. 204;
LI MS. Misc. 490, fo. 706v.[15]

Becher brought a writ of error in the Exchequer Chamber against Turgys upon a judgment given in the Queen's Bench. The case was that a man had brought an action on the case upon an *indebitatus assumpsit* for money due to the plaintiff from the defendant upon a contract for wheat. And the question was whether he could have this action in this case.

All the justices of the Common Pleas, and all the barons of the Exchequer (except CLARKE B., who hesitated somewhat), delivered their opinions severally and confidently that this action did not lie, but an action of debt on the contract, in which the defendant should have had his law, whereof he would be ousted in the other action. And we must adjudge it thus, for otherwise the whole course of the common law would be overturned on this point.

ANDERSON C.J. would not hear argument on the contrary side, for he said there could be no reason whatever made in support of it.

OWEN J. said he had spoken with Wray C.J.Q.B. (who was the chief supporter of that error) and had pointed out to him the inconvenience that if a man bought wares from a merchant, and paid him for them, and they continued to buy from and sell to each other over a period of many years (as many do here in London), and afterwards the merchant brings an action on the *assumpsit* for all the contracts between them, if the defendant were not received to wage his law he would be in great mischief; for it is not usual for merchants to give an acquittance, and he cannot prove payment, and cannot deny the contract. Thereupon Wray said that he would

15   Also reported, very briefly, in Moo. K.B. 694, pl. 962.

never again maintain this action afterwards; and truly he never did adjudge it afterwards.

Afterwards the aforesaid judgment was reversed by consent of all ... but if it had been a promise made after the bargain or contract, then WALMSLEY J. and others thought the law would have been otherwise in the principal case.

Other manuscript reports of the case show that the judges also relied on the argument that there was no consideration: (1) 'This is *nudum pactum*, in that he who made the promise had no benefit from it' (BL MS. Harley 1697, fo. 107v; CUL MS. Gg. 3. 25, fo. 80; MS. Gg. 6. 29, fo. 133). (2) 'The debt being due beforehand, it was a thing executed, per ANDERSON C.J. Similarly, if I promise you £10 for the service you have done me, an action on the case does not lie; otherwise if it is for service to be done' (BL MS. Lansdowne 1084, fo. 120v). (3) 'When he promised to pay upon the contract, this was no more than what the law willed without the promise; and one is not to have a remedy by action on the case except where the law has not provided any other remedy: but here it has' (CUL MS. Ii. 5. 13, fo. 59).

DUPPA v JONES (1602)[16]

(a) YLS MS. G. R29.6, fo. 151 (C.P.).

Duppa, a petty servant of the king, arraigned someone in the Marshalsea Court, and from thence it was removed into this court ... and he declared in nature of an action on the case upon *assumpsit solvere.*

And the justices thought that the action could not be maintained, for an action of debt properly lies; but an action on the case is maintainable only where deceit or fraud is supposed. Nowadays they put the words *in deceptione* and *fraudulenter* into the declaration when the facts are quite otherwise. For what fraud can there be if the debtor does not pay the money he borrowed at the day? The purpose of this action, however, is solely to stop the defendant from waging law ...

(b) BL MS. Lansdowne 1074, fo. 413; LI MS. Maynard 87(2), fo. 309; HLS MS. 704774, p. 107 (untr.).

Whereas the defendant was found in arrearages upon an *insimul computavit*, in consideration that the plaintiff would give day until (etc.) he promised to pay it.

ANDERSON C.J. and WALMSLEY J. Clearly the action will not lie, for the debt is hereby not changed. And these new devices of

16   In Trinity term, the term before the judgment in *Slade's Case*: see p. 437, below.

actions of the case cannot be maintained, for there ought to be no actions of the case but grounded upon some fraud: for so are the words of the writ, *machinans* etc. What fraud was here committed? And they gave day for the defendant to imparl.

SLADE v MORLEY (1602)

Record: KB 27/1336, m. 305; 4 Co. Rep. 91. John Slade brought a bill against Humfrey Morley in Michaelmas term 1595 complaining that, whereas he possessed a close called Rack Park in Halberton, Devon, and on 10 November 1594 sowed it with wheat and rye; and on 8 May 1595 the defendant, in consideration that the plaintiff (at the defendant's request) had bargained and sold to him all the ears of wheat and corn then growing on the close, excepting the tithes due to the rector, undertook and faithfully promised the plaintiff to pay him £16 on 24 June 1595: nevertheless the defendant, little regarding his undertaking and promise, but scheming and intending subtly and craftily to deceive and defraud the plaintiff of the £16, did not and still has not paid it, though often requested to do so. The defendant pleaded *Non assumpsit*, and on 8 March 1596 at Exeter assizes (Walmsley J.C.P., Fenner J.Q.B.) the jury found this special verdict: 'The said Humfrey Morley did buy the wheat and rye growing in ears on the said close from the said John Slade for £16 to be paid on the feast of St John the Baptist [24 June] then next following, as is stated in the declaration; but there was no undertaking or promise between the said John Slade and the said Humfrey Morley besides the bargain aforesaid'. The damages were assessed at £16, if the court held this to be a verdict for the plaintiff. The first reported discussion was in November 1597, by which time it had been referred to all the justices of England in the Exchequer Chamber.[17]

(a) Exchequer Chamber, Mich. 1597:
Dodderidge's speech from LI MS. Maynard 55, fo. 246; and
BL MS. Harley 6809, fo. 45 (untr.);
Coke's reply from BL MS. Hargrave 5, fo. 67v.[18]

... After the record was read, [*John Dodderidge*], utter-barrister, opened the case ... and said that he took it (under their lordships' favour) that it was no sufficient promise to maintain the said action upon the case. In proof whereof he said that he would hold this course, viz. he would present unto the consideration of the court three several reasons in maintenance of his opinion, which reasons

17   I.e. not the court of error, but an informal assembly. The case was continued on the rolls of the Queen's Bench.
18   There are at least 11 different reports of this debate in MS. Dodderidge's speech circulated in English, and may have been put out by the speaker himself, following the precedent set by Coke with *Shelley's Case* (1581), p. 143, above.

he would confirm and enlarge with authority of book-learning: wherein he said, for that his time of premeditation was very short, he would not be long.

The first reason, he said, was drawn from the nature of writs of debt and that upon the case. The second reason was drawn from the sufficiency of the trial by *ley gager* in cases where the law alloweth it, and wherein he would speak of the injury offered unto the defendant by ousting him of his law by this devised action. The third and last reason was drawn from the nature of the contract that begetteth the debt, wherein he said he would discourse whether in every contract whereupon an action of debt might be brought there was not included an *assumpsit* and sufficient promise to maintain an action upon the case.

I As concerning the first reason, he said that he must first call to remembrance before he would enter into it that there are two efficient causes of all actions, *et tanquam parentes unde concipiuntur: injuria et damnum*, the injury done and the hurt and damage sustained. And touching the sundering of these is bred that disputation *de damno absque injuria, et injuria absque damno.* The action which ensueth of these is defined by Bracton to be nothing else than *jus prosequendi in judicio quod alicui debetur.*[19] This is brought to pass and deduced to judgment *per istius modi juris formulas quae brevia nuncupantur. Brevia sunt quae rem est et intentionem petentis breviter enarrat.*[20] Writs (as concerning the purpose I now have in hand) are of two kinds. Some are of form and framed certain; some are without form, uncertain, and varying with the case. My reason, then, (said he), is this: where there is a ready framed writ of form in the register, sufficiently able to deduce to judgment the wrong and the damage, and thoroughly to punish the one and to satisfy the other, there shall the party plaintiff never have recourse to the writ without form to satisfy the same damage and punish the same wrong. But here is a ready framed writ in the register: the action of debt, the natural remedy, the writ of form. Therefore here is no place for the action upon the case, the writ without form, the usurped remedy. The second part of this argument cannot be denied, for no man can deny but the action of debt [is a writ of form][1] and the action of debt most properly lieth in this case. It is the former part that needeth proof.

I speak not therein without authority. In the *Lord Mounteagle's*

---

19 *Bracton*, vol. II, p. 282 (fo. 98b).
20 *Bracton*, vol. II, p. 318 (fo. 112). Cf. vol. I, p. 167; vol. IV, p. 285.
1 Conjectural insertion.

Case for the trover and conversion of the chain,[2] it is said and affirmed as a rule that where a man hath an ordinary framed writ in the register for to serve his case the action upon the case lieth not; for he shall never have no other form of writ.[3] In 14 Hen. VIII, the last case of the year and the last words of the case,[4] Broke [J.] saith that the action upon the case lieth not where other remedy is provided. Again, an action upon the case is not maintainable where there is other remedy. In the case argued upon the sale of corn in 20 Hen. VII,[5] the most notable case in the law touching the matter in hand, and yet not ruled but left at large, all those judges that hold the side that I do maintain take this for the root of all their reasons: that the action upon the case lieth not where there is another framed and provided remedy. He said that it would be tedious to trouble them with repetition of all the places in the law where that allegation is affirmed; therefore he would surcease with these few, for that he well remembered (as he said) where he was and that he was well understood at a word. But general rules are much impeached, for *non est regula quin fallit*. And although the saying aforesaid were somewhat contradicted somewhere,[6] yet is that contradiction no older than our fathers' memory. But yet he said that he had laid the first proposition of his former reason in such ground and had so hedged it with such limitations as that it could not be much impeached. For he did not deny but that a man might have two actions (and those of several natures) upon one and the self-same fact, crime or offence; but yet in these cases the things deduced into judgment were divers, for either the wrong or the damage (being the grounds of those actions as aforesaid) do differ, and the one action is larger and of more scope than the other:

If a man do enter into my lands and do disseise me, I have an assize or a writ of right. The fact is one; but those actions deduce divers things to judgment. The assize is possessory and of mine own possession; but the writ of right is not only of mine own right but the mere right and possession of him in whom the seisin is alleged (if the demi-mark be tendered).

If a man take away my goods, I may have an action of trespass, a replevin, or an appeal of robbery, if I will. The act done is one; the actions are divers, for they deduce divers things to judgment. The trespass only punisheth the taking, disaffirmeth property, and

2   (1555); see p. 531, below.
3   *Bracton*, vol. IV, p. 284 (fo. 413 cited in margin of MS.).
4   See p. 587, below.
5   *Orwell v Mortoft* (1505); see p. 406, above.
6   *Holygrave v Knyghtysbrygge* (1535), p. 413, above (cited in margin of MS.).

recovereth damages only. The replevin affirmeth the property, requireth the deliverance of the thing and damages for the taking and detaining. The appeal is criminal, seeketh a revenge of blood for the violence and villainy done.

If I deliver unto John Style money to be delivered to John Dale or to merchandise for me, I may have an action of debt or an account. Yet the matter is but one that maintaineth the actions; but the demand is different and divers things are deduced to judgment. By the action of debt I do demand the money delivered and my damages for the withholding thereof. But in the action of account I do demand the profit of the money gotten by the use and traffic therewith, for so is the express reason made 28 Hen. VIII, Dyer 22, *Core's Case.*[7]

If I deliver money to bail over to another, and the bailee converteth the same to his own use, I may have an action of debt, an action upon the case, and an action of account. The fact is one, the actions are divers: debt for the money, an action upon the case for the conversion, and an action of account for the increase and profit of the money.

If I promise unto John Style £20 to marry my daughter, and he doth so accordingly, an action of debt lieth for the money, for the money is a duty arising upon the contract.[8] And therefore an action of debt lieth. Also an action upon the case lieth of an *assumpsit*, but yet upon an actual promise, for the promise in this case is not implied, but expressed.

And were it that the action of the case argued in 20 Hen. VII were ruled (which is this: a man did sell corn for £20 and after the vendor converteth the corn to his own use in deceit of the bargainee, and he brought an action upon the case): allow, I say, that it were adjudged that this action would lie (whereas the case is left at large), yet the same would not impeach mine assertion. For the action upon the case there brought is grounded upon another wrong, namely the deceit which is wrought by the conversion of the corn by the vendor to his own use. But if the vendor had brought an action upon the case for his money, without any actual promise, then had it been more near, nay our case in effect.

But to return to the case in question, from whence we have digressed. The case here is of no more value than is the action of debt, neither can it bring to judgment any other thing touching the wrong and damage in this case sustained than the action of debt doth. For by the action of debt the plaintiff shall recover his money

7   *Core v May* (1536); see p. 243, above.
8   *Anon.* (1458); see p. 236, above.

due and his damages for the detainer. In the action of the case he shall recover all in damages, which shall be no more than the value of the debt and damages for the detainer. There is no more wrought by the one than by the other. In vain, then, it is to have liberty of choice where there is no choosing for the better. Therefore, where the home-made and free-born will serve the turn, let the stranger and late-made denizen be excluded.

That reason, would it should be so, see otherwise a mischief: if the action upon the case have thus encroached upon the action of debt, why should it not encroach hereafter upon the other actions of form, and so make a confusion of the register, which is said in the *Commentaries*[9] to be for such matters of writs the foundation and grounds of the law. And here let me speak somewhat of the antiquity of the register and the use thereof. I do suppose that in ancient time the forms of writs were devised by counsel, as are now the pleas; for that divers of the writs in Glanvill (in the time of King Henry II) vary in form from many of those which Bracton hath, and those which he hath do vary from the register. But in King Edward I's time it is likely they came in to be registered. For that king, as saith Prysot C.J. in 35 Hen. VI,[10] caused divers books of the law to be written and purposed to have reformed the law, as it were the English Justinian. Because, therefore, it is a matter of no small moment to begin well, and that the writ is the foundation of the future action, the policy of England hath from this time which I speak of cast this care upon him that is great next the greatest,[11] adjoining unto him a college of clerks (whom the register calleth sometimes *clerici de cursu*) for the framing and bringing into form of those *formulae juris*: whereof some of them (in a memorial of those discreet men that devised and framed them) have annexed unto them in the register a note of their authors' names, and carry it in their forehead as a mark by whom they were devised. This seemeth to resemble the ancient policy of the Romans, who cast the care of those *formulae juris* upon their *pontifices* and that college at whose hands their lawyers received them, as we do of the Chancery, and at length were collected into a volume by Gnaeus Flavius, which volume thereof was afterwards called *Lex Flaviana*.[12]

9 Plowd. 77, 228v.
10 Y.B. Hil. 35 Hen. VI, fo. 42, pl. 2.
11 Presumably meaning the lord chancellor, but perhaps the master of the rolls. Bacon L.K. had formed the cursitors into a company in 1573, but Dodderidge is here speculating about the medieval Chancery.
12 Actually *Jus Flavianum*: D.1.2.6, 7. This occurred in or shortly before 304 B.C.: see H. F. Jolowicz, *Historical Introduction to the Study of Roman Law* (3rd ed., 1972), p. 91.

Thus you see the propositions proved, and thereof do observe the conclusion. And thus much for the first reason.

II The second reason is the consideration of the efficacy of *ley gager*, which I will consider in parts.

1 First, it is right worthy of observation which is spoken 33 Hen. VIII, Brooke [Abr.], *Trialls*,[13] that the trials of law are dispatched by a complete number: 12 judges to try and determine matters in law, 12 jurors to try matters in fact, and *ley gager* is determined by 12 (viz. *duodena manu*, every of which must swear: 9 Hen. III, Fitz. [Abr.], *Ley*, 78). And in 33 Hen. VI, where it is debated whether non-summons (which is usually tried by *ley gager*) should be tried by pais, it is said in express terms that *ley gager* is equivalent unto the trial by jury, for that the one and the other is *duodena manu*;[14] and therefore in presumption of law the trial by *ley gager* is as effectual, as satisfactory, and ordained to breed such content, as the trial by country. For *ley gager* is not allowed in every action, nor for every defendant, nor against every plaintiff; and therefore bounden within his limits it is in all presumption of law as sufficient, as full, and as convenient, as the other trial, that is by the country.

2 Secondly, how the law esteemeth of *ley gager* and of what benefit it is appeareth partly hereby. If a man bring an action of debt upon a contract, the defendant shall not traverse the contract, for that he may wage his law. But in those actions of debt, detinue or account in the which he cannot wage his law, he shall not answer to the point of the writ (for that he is ousted of his benefit by *ley gager*) but shall traverse the conveyance,[15] which otherwise is not traversable, for the law taketh from him no benefit but giveth him as good. For taking from him his *ley gager* it doth allow him to traverse the conveyance, which otherwise is not traversable.

3 Thirdly, how much the law esteemeth the loss of *ley gager* where it is due it may thus appear. The queen in her excellent estate of highness for the care of the common-wealth cast upon her and in ease of that burthen is enriched above all others with many favours of the law. And yet nevertheless where otherwise her poor subject should be put from his law by her prerogative, she shall lose her highness's benefit rather than he shall sustain such hard measure: for if a man be outlawed, and have many men indebted unto him upon simple contracts, the queen shall not have these debts, for if she should then should the party be put from his law (for none can

13 Presumably Brooke Abr., *Trialls*, pl. 143, which does not mention the number 12.
14 Y.B. Hil. 33 Hen. VI, fo. 8, pl. 23.
15 I.e. the introductory recital.

wage his law against the queen), the which rather than it should be suffered the crown shall lose the benefit of those debts.

4   Lastly, I do observe that it hath been attempted in ancient times to put defendants from their law by divers devices, but none have long stood in favour. First, they used to bring supposed actions of debt upon arrearages of an account, until the statute of [5] Hen. IV[16] ordained this examination. Also, they used to bring a *quominus* in the Exchequer, supposing themselves to be indebted to the queen to the intent to participate with her prerogative and to oust the defendant of his law,[17] but these were devised and endured but their time.

And thus much for the second reason.

III   As to the third reason, we are to consider whether in every contract whereupon an action of debt doth lie there be included an assumption or promise, and whether such a promise be sufficient to maintain an action of debt. True it is that is said in the *Commentaries*, in *Rede and Norwood's Case*,[18] that in every contract is included a promise: but will that promise maintain an action upon the case? I verily think no, for many reasons.

1   First, as hath been said, actions are grounded upon wrongs and injuries. But included, implied or imaginary wrongs are no causes of action. They must be actual, real and express. An action upon the case upon the *assumpsit* is grounded upon the *assumpsit*, upon the promise. But in our case the jury have found no actual promise, but an implied and included promise; therefore no sufficient promise, for that injuries whereof actions do arise ought to be imminent and evident.

2   Secondly, there is nothing found but the contract, but the bare stipulation (as Bracton,[19] borrowing the word out of the civil law, calleth it): that is, I agree you shall have my wares, and you agree that I shall have your money. This is nothing but the very contract itself, out of which resulteth properly the action of debt, which is the only legitimate son of that marriage. For there is no case where the action of debt lieth more properly, more peculiarly. For the stipulation is the contract, which is said of *contraho*, and is *quasi actus contra actum*. Therefore the action upon the case in this case intrudeth upon the proper inheritance of another.

3   Thirdly, that your action upon the case lieth not without an actual promise may be proved by the declaration. For every

16   5 Hen. IV, c. 8.
17   Y.B. Trin. 11 Hen. VII, fo. 26, pl. 9. See also p. 218, fn. 10 below.
18   *Norwood v Norwood and Rede* (1557); see p. 448, below.
19   *Bracton*, vol. II, pp. 284–285 (fo. 99b).

declaration containeth two parts, the cause of grief and the damage. And when you come to set forth your damage in such actions (for there is your recovery, for you recover all in damages) you ground not yourself upon the contract but upon the deceit: *fidem adhibens promissioni*, which must be an actual promise whereunto you gave credit and some other thing than the contract out of which ariseth only the debt in his proper kind.

4 Lastly, it is evident that those actions upon the case which are grounded upon an actual promise in case where the debt doth lie are nothing in effect but the debt. They go no further than the debt. For a bar by *ley gager* in the action of debt is bar in such actions upon the case: as 33 Hen. VIII is in Brooke [Abr.], *Action sur le case*.[20] Which is a proof that they are but of one effect, for otherwise the bar in the one would not be a bar in the other. As, a bar in detinue by the *ley gager* is no bar in account thereof: 2 Ric. III.[1] But the cause why in the one case the action upon the case doth lie, and not in the other, is the actual promise.

And so, upon all the whole matter, it seemeth that the action will not lie.

Coke Att.-Gen. to the contrary. It has been said that this action on the case is an imaginary and a deformed action, and a usurper. I will maintain that it is a regular and ancient action. But first I will confute the other side, and then confirm my own side.

1 He who has just argued drew his first argument from *Lord Mounteagle's Case* in 3 Mar., but the book is adjudged against that argument, and is thus a plain authority in my favour. In 14 Hen. VIII, fo. 31, it is said that an action on the case lies for stopping a way in part; and yet the assize of nuisance lies . . . And an action on the case is a formal action, for it is in the register. And the register was not made in Edward I's time, for many writs are there expressed which were made after Edward I's time. [Prysot C.J. in] 35 Hen. VI meant Britton, not the register. The register, however, does mention an action on the case on a promise.

2 The second reason advanced on the other side is *petitio principii*, for if the action on the case lies in law it follows that it does not deprive the defendant of any benefit. For trespass to goods a man may have an action of trespass, or a replevin, upon which wager of law does not lie; but in detinue it does lie. So if the plaintiff here has an election to have which action he wishes,

---

20 Brooke Abr., *Action sur le case*, pl. 105.
1 Mich. 2 Ric. III, fo. 14, pl. 39.

nothing is taken from the defendant. The benefit of the queen will take it away: for 8 Hen. V, [Fitz. Abr.], *Ley*, 10, and temp. Hen. VIII,[2] hold that in *quominus* for debt the defendant shall not wage his law, for the bringing of such an action takes it away. And the queen shall have debt on a contract upon a forfeiture: and that is the experience, if it is something certain it shall be forfeited, otherwise if it is uncertain. Hence that is no reason.

3　For the third reason which has been put forward: here this is a real and actual promise. But this action will lie on a promise in law.

Now to my own argument. I hold that this action lies. My reason is that here is an express promise, for that is my case and I shall have an action on it. Here it is said, 'You shall have my money': that is a promise, for put it in writing and covenant lies on it.[3] Promise and agreement are all one, for every agreement executory is a promise. A man shall not have an action on the case for nonfeasance without consideration, but it is otherwise for misfeasance; for if a man undertakes to build a house without consideration, and spoils it, an action on the case lies for that.

Now for authorities in this case[4]... Moreover, precedents[5] have always been respected, and here in this case there are many precedents in books of entries and elsewhere ... In *ejectione firmae* a man could not recover possession until 14 Hen. VII,[6] but now it is allowed without any question, inasmuch as there are many precedents in point.

Thus, for these reasons, he concluded that judgment ought to be given for the plaintiff.

(b) Serjeants' Inn, Mich, 1598:
BL MS. Add. 25203, fo. 12.

Before all the justices of England, assembled at Serjeants' Inn, *Tanfield* ... prayed judgment for the plaintiff.

2　*Anon.* (1535); see p. 448, below.
3　Cf. report of the same speech in IT MS. Petit 516.5, fo. 121: 'When the plaintiff said, "You shall have my corn" and the other said, "You shall have so much money for your corn", these were express promises. These words *assumpsit, promisit* and *agreavit* are all synonymous and of one signification. Would you have every plain man use the proper words "I assume" or "I take upon myself"? It is unnecessary. If he says "I promise" or "I agree" it is tantamount, and all one. If you will deny that there was any promise here, there is no contract either, for in every contract there is a reciprocal agreement: *actus contra actum*'.
4　These reported cases are discussed below.
5　'Precedents' here means records, rather than reports.
6　See pp. 179–180, above.

First, I must answer the objections which have earlier been made against my side. First, it has been said that there is no express promise in this case, and therefore the action on the case does not lie. As to this, I will demonstrate what an assumption is. As I have learned, an assumption is nothing other than a mutual agreement between the parties for something to be performed by the defendant in consideration of some benefit which must depart from the plaintiff, or of some labour or prejudice which must be sustained by the plaintiff. It suffices if some benefit leaves the plaintiff, whether it goes to the defendant or to a stranger, for it shall be presumed to have been at the defendant's request. For example, if a man undertakes to do something in consideration that I will give £20 to John Style, that is a good *assumpsit*. Likewise, in consideration that I will go to York for the defendant, he undertakes to do something, that is a good *assumpsit*: for it is a labour to me. In the same way, if, in consideration that I forbear my debt, he undertakes, for that is a prejudice. And in our case the undertaking comes within this definition, and so I hold it to be good.

Although countrymen do not always use apt words, the construction of the law will make them effectual.[7] For this see 5 Hen. VII,[8] where a man (being indebted to another) licensed the debtee to take his gold chain and to retain it until he paid the money: although no apt words had been used there, the law says that it is a pledge. It is similarly held there that if a man licenses me to enter into his land and occupy it for one month, this is a lease and not a licence, and it must be pleaded as such. Here, in our case, countrymen do not know what are the apt words to use; for it is not usual among them to say 'in consideration that you will do such and such a thing, I undertake to pay you such and such a sum'. Nevertheless the law will make their words effectual. For this see 21 Hen. VII,[9] where Frowyk C.J. put the case of a man having a rent-charge who commanded the tenant to pay someone else, and he paid it; and this payment is no bar in an avowry, but the party is driven to bring his action on the case: and that must be an action on the case on a promise, and although there are no words expressly proving the promise the law makes it a sufficient undertaking.

Another matter has been objected: that a man shall not have two actions upon one wrong where both reduce the same thing to

---

7 Cf. CUL MS. Dd. 8.48, fo. 33: 'Although there was no express promise *quoad verba*, yet the matter was so and it should be pleaded as an *assumpsit*'.
8 *Lord Dudley v Lord Powles* (1489) Y.B. Mich. 5 Hen. VII, fo. 1, pl. 1.
9 *Abbot of Ramsey v Prior of Anglesey* (1506) Y.B. Hil. 21 Hen. VII, fo. 12, pl. 13.

judgment, but in the action of debt and in the action on the case the same thing is reduced in judgment, and so the action on the case does not lie. This objection, however, is not true. For in the action of debt the debt itself is to be recovered, but in the action on the case only damages. And it may be that the jury would give less damages than the sum to which the debt amounts, and if they do so no attaint lies for giving too little in damages. Thus the actions do reduce several things in judgment.

Another matter has been objected: that where a man has a proper action framed in the register he must not resort to an action on the case. As to this, however, the law is contrary. For sometimes one may have an action on the case where one could have an assize of novel disseisin (being a real action), as appears in 4 Edw. IV.[10] Likewise in 21 Hen. VII in *Lord Grey's Case*,[11] if someone makes a trench whereby the water running to another person's mill is put out of its course, the party aggrieved may have an action on the case or an assize of nuisance. And the case in 20 Hen. VII[12] was that a man bought 20 quarters of barley to be delivered at a place and day, and the vendor did not perform the contract, and an action on the case was maintainable. And although in the book at large some opinion seems to impugn this, yet by the record the rule is thus,[13] and so it is cited by Fitzjames C.J. in the case between *Core and Woddy*.[14] And in the book of 20 Hen. VII, Frowyk C.J. puts the case, if I deliver money to someone to deliver over to my attorney, and he delivers it to my adversary, an action on the case lies.[15] In 33 Hen. VIII[16] it is held that if a man brings a writ of debt and is barred by wager of law, and then brings an action on the case for the same money, the defendant may plead that he had already barred the plaintiff by wager of law. So it is not doubted that an action on the case lies. In 2 and 3 Phil. and Mar., between *Peck and Redman*,[17] the case was that two bargained together that one would deliver to the other 20 quarters of barley every year during their

---

10 Y.B. Pas. 4 Edw. IV, fo. 2, pl. 2.
11 (1505); see p. 586, below.
12 *Orwell v Mortoft* (1505); see p. 406, below.
13 This seems to be incorrect; see p. 408, above. Cf. CUL MS. Dd. 8.48, fo. 33: 'And ... whereas the [year] book says that three justices were against the action and one for, he cited Mr. Carril's reports that afterwards judgment was given in favour of the action in accordance with Frowyk's opinion'. Caryll's report is in Keil. 69, 77, which supports the Y.B.
14 *Core v May* (1536); see p. 245, above.
15 See p. 410, above.
16 Brooke Abr., *Action sur le case*, pl. 105.
17 (1555) Dyer 113.

lives, and that the plaintiff would pay four shillings for each
quarter; and there it is doubted, in an action on the case brought
for the non-performance of this bargain, whether the plaintiff
should recover damages for the entire bargain or only in recompense for what was past. But it was not questioned that the action
well lay.

Moreover there are various precedents in this case on my side,
and I vouch several in the King's Bench: in Trinity term 12 Hen.
VIII, roll 78;[18] Hilary term 22 Hen. VIII, roll 66;[19] Trinity term 22
Hen. VIII, roll 64;[20] 32 Hen. VIII and 30 Hen. VIII, and various
others.[1] All of which were ruled upon this reason, inasmuch as the
law gives the party his double remedy. This action on the case was
brought into use once men were found too unreliable (*dangerous*)
in taking their oath. Moreover, since the course of the court has
been thus for so long a time, it would seem hard if all their
precedents should be overturned; for it has always been usual for
one court to yield to the customs of another . . . So I think that in
our case the party has two remedies, and therefore he may make
election as to which he will use . . . And so, for these reasons, I pray
judgment for the plaintiff.

Bacon to the contrary.[2]

(c) Serjeants' Inn,[1] 13 May 1602:
BL MS. Add. 25203, fo. 496.

Before all the justices of England assembled at Serjeants' Inn on
Ascension Day, 13 May, *Bacon* recited the case . . . and it seemed to
him that the action on the case does not lie. And in arguing this he
proved his point by three arguments. First, that there wants
substance and matter here on which to base an action on the case.
Secondly, that the action lacks form; and therefore where there is a
writ in the register framed and formed for this case, this action on

---

18 *Blanke v Spinula* (1520) KB 27/1036, m. 75. The plaintiff sued on an *assumpsit* to
    pay £150 in Flemish money in exchange for £100 in English money paid by him
    to the defendant, and recovered £104 damages.

19 *Turnor v Nelethropp* (1531) KB 27/1078, m. 66. An action of *assumpsit* for the
    price of goods and services: see [1971] C.L.J. 58, fn. 43.

20 *Whitehed v Elderton* (1530) KB 27/1076, m. 64. This was an *indebitatus assumpsit*
    for the price of goods, though the declaration avoided reciting a sale: [1971]
    C.L.J. 58, fn. 44.

1   According to CUL MS. Dd. 8. 48, fo. 33: '. . . he cited about 30 precedents
    between 21 Hen. VII and the present time, that an action on the case brought
    for a debt will lie . . .' For examples of such precedents, see Selden Soc. vol. 94,
    pp. *275–281.*

2   Bacon's argument is not given in this text. A brief summary of it is printed in
    [1971] C.L.J., at 59–60. His points were made more fully in the argument which
    follows.

the case does not lie. Thirdly, the subject is hereby ousted from the benefit of law if an action on the case should be maintained, and so on account of this mischief he ought to sue an action of debt.

As to the first reason, a contract is no basis for an action on the case. For an action on the case must be based on deceit or breach of promise, whereas in debt on a contract no deceit or breach of promise is supposed. A bargain, of whatever kind, is something executed and not executory (as an *assumpsit* is); for a bargain changes the property on each side. Therefore in an action of debt it is alleged that the defendant withholds the money or thing demanded as if it were his already: in other words, that the plaintiff had the property thereof by reason of the contract. For this reason Bracton says that *contractus est permutatio rerum*. When, therefore, the plaintiff only demands what was already his, it cannot be said that he has been deceived by the defendant, but only that the defendant withholds something whereof the property was in the plaintiff. In 3 Hen. VI[3] and 11 Hen. IV[4] an *assumpsit* is called a parol covenant. Thus when a man covenants by writing to pay a sum of money, the person to whom the covenant is made shall have an action of debt and not an action of covenant, since the deed is a pure obligation. Likewise, on the other side, when this covenant is made by parol it sounds only in the nature of a contract and not in the nature of a promise, and therefore the plaintiff shall be put to his action of debt and be ousted from the action on the case. Suppose a man, in consideration of certain corn delivered to him by the plaintiff, acknowledges himself to be indebted in £20: those are the usual words of a bond, and it is clear that had they been put into writing no action except an action of debt could have been maintained upon them. For the same reason, when such a promise or acknowledgment is made by parol, without any writing, it is nevertheless solely in the nature of a debt and therefore no other action lies for it than a writ of debt. In 45 Edw. III[5] it is said that upon a broken promise a man shall have suit in Court Christian *pro laesione fidei*; but it is clear that if a man makes a contract with another, then even if the money is not paid at the day no suit *pro laesione fidei* lies for this in Court Christian. And in 21 Hen. VII[6] it is held that if a man promises to enfeoff me with certain land and does not do so accordingly, I shall have an action on the case or a *subpoena* in Chancery at my election; and by the one I shall recover

3   *Watkins' Case* (1425); see p. 380, above.
4   See p. 379, above.
5   Untraced.
6   Fyneux C.J.'s dictum of 1499; see p. 401, above.

damages, and by the other the chancellor will compel the party by imprisonment to execute the feoffment. But if a man contracts with another to give him a certain sum of money in return for a certain quantity of corn, and the money is not paid, nevertheless no *subpoena* lies to compel the defendant to pay the money, but he must sue for it by writ of debt.

Thus it appears that there is a great difference between the nature of the action of debt and the nature of an action on the case. For the action on the case implies a wrong, bad conscience, and deceit, and therefore in 20 Hen. VII Frowyk C.J. calls it a misdemeanour.[7] And the action on the case is an action of trespass, and for that reason the law does not allow the defendant to wage his law in this action. Thus, when the nature and basis of these actions is so different, it is not right that an action on the case should be maintained on a contract, for which properly an action of debt lies.

He said, however, that sometimes when a contract is mixed with collateral matter an action on the case shall be maintained upon it. For instance, if a man contracts to pay me £10 in angels or crowns, or in some other special coin, I may have an action on the case, since it is not here a bare contract but is mixed with some other collateral circumstance. Similarly, if I sell a horse to someone else, he shall have an action of debt for the horse; but if it be added on to the contract that the horse shall be broken and taught ready for the field, there he shall have an action on the case. Likewise if a special place of delivery or payment is added to the contract, namely that the defendant must deliver the thing or pay the money at such and such a place, an action on the case lies. For in a writ of debt the plaintiff shall recover the money, but neither the place nor the other collateral circumstances just mentioned shall be regarded in the action of debt. It also seemed to him that if a contract is broken down and divided into several days [of payment], an action on the case shall lie perfectly well. And these distinctions, he said, will reconcile all the cases objected on the opposing side. Such as the case in 21 Hen. VI,[8] for there was a contract for two pipes of wine, and this was to be delivered at a certain place. And in *Norwood's Case*,[9] there was a place appointed for the delivery of the corn, and also the contract was broken down into several days. And in *Peck and Redman's Case*,[10] the barley was to be delivered to the plaintiff annually, so that there was again a breaking down of the contract.

---

7   See p. 408, above.
8   *Tailboys v Sherman* (1443); see p. 395, above.
9   *Norwood v Norwood and Rede* (1557); see p. 448, below.
10 *Peck v Redman* (1555) Dyer 113; see p. 430, above; p. 440 below.

The same reasons can be attributed to 5 Mar., Brooke [Abr.], *Action sur le case*, pl. 108, for there the marriage-money was to be paid over four years. But it seems that if a man contracts to pay money at one day, even if a certain time is limited, this is not so forcible to change the nature of the action as the limiting of the place or the breaking down of the contract into several days. The reason why the law allows an action on the case in those cases is that it will not put him to two actions, namely the action of debt to recover the money and then the action on the case [to recover damages] because it was not paid at the due place.

And so he concluded his first argument, that the matter is insufficient to bring an action on the case.

As to the second, it seemed to him that the action is not maintainable because it wants form. The law favours order and abhors confusion. Therefore the register must not be confounded, but men must sue by the writs in the register and not frame actions out of their own heads. So when the register appoints debt as a proper action to give the plaintiff a remedy for his grievance, he must not pursue an action on the case. He agreed that often a man can, at his election, sue several actions for one same thing; for, as is commonly said, *bonum est simplex et malum est multiplex*. Therefore the same act can in several respects give cause for several actions. But he said that no action on the case lies where there is any other remedy. For it is only a supplemental action, and for that reason it does not lie in cases where there is a proper action: unless the matter digresses in some way from the nature of the proper action. For instance, 11 Hen. IV and 33 Hen. VI,[11] if a man stops my way I shall have an assize of nuisance, but if he narrows the way and does not stop it completely, an action on the case lies, since this digresses somewhat from the nature of the assize of nuisance. In the case of the stopped way, if it is done by a stranger and not by the terre-tenant no assize lies, and therefore I shall have an action on the case.

He also agreed that sometimes an action on the case lies in cases where there is also a formal writ in the register. But that is where the writ in the register is of a higher nature and more penal to the defendant than an action on the case. For the law will not compel any man to pursue his wrong in extremity, but (if he will) he may well refuse the remedy which is more penal to the defendant and pursue a milder action. Therefore, when a man has cause to pursue an appeal of mayhem, he may have an action on the case. Similarly,

11   Y.B. Trin. 11 Hen. IV, fo. 82, pl. 28; Trin. 33 Hen. VI, fo. 26, pl. 10; see p. 584, below.

where he has cause to sue a writ of rescue he may well have an action on the case. Likewise, where he can have an assize of nuisance or trespass *quare vi et armis*, he may waive it and take an action on the case. In these cases the other actions are greater and higher than an action on the case. But an action on the case is greater and higher, and more penal to the defendant, than an action of debt. For in an action of debt the defendant wages his law, but not in an action on the case: which proves that it is the higher action. Also, an action on the case supposes a wrong and a deceit in the defendant. Therefore, although the plaintiff may forego his right in taking his remedy by an inferior action, he may nevertheless not at his pleasure use an action superior to that which is proper to his case.

As to the last reason, he objected that the action on the case does not lie because then the defendant would be ousted from his law, which is a defence whereof the law is very tender. Therefor he observed three reasons why the law principally allows the defendant to discharge himself of a debt by doing his law. The first is for expedition, for several matters are briefly determined by wager of law which would depend longer if they were tried by inquest. The second reason is so that the defendant shall not be surprised in his proof. For contracts are often made in secret, and it would be most inconvenient if for every private bargain between men they were compelled to call unto them a notary or witnesses to prove the bargain. Therefore the law has allowed the defendant in such cases to discharge himself by his oath. The third reason is that such private contracts are difficult to be tried by juries. And the law has great regard of this, for trials by inquests are in our law stricter than trials in any other law. An inquest must necessarily give a verdict, and (whether or not the parties give evidence) it cannot say 'it does not appear'. Secondly, a majority of voices does not carry the verdict, but it behoves them all to agree in their verdict or else it is not good. Thirdly, the jurors are in duress until they have given their verdict. When all these matters are considered, it is a strong argument for providing that as far as may be all the issues to be tried by juries should be on plain and clear matter. Therefore the law allows a man to discharge himself of these secret contracts by wager of law rather than put him upon trial by an inquest. For even if the contract was made in the presence of witnesses, the proof of it is nevertheless dangerous and uncertain, when the wresting or mistaking of a word may alter the whole substance of the contract. Therefore it is very reasonable to submit this to the oath of the party himself. That accords with the law of God, for *finis omnis*

controversiae est juramentum.[12] And whereas it is said that this trial
by wager of law is an occasion of much perjury, when the party for
his own profit is tempted to speak contrary to the truth, surely the
mischief is not so great on this side as on the other? For whereas by
wager of law the defendant himself may be perjured, the trial of
such secret matters by inquest gives occasion for 12 jurors and also
several witnesses to be forsworn. For these reasons the law gives
much favour to trial by wager of law. Therefore the queen's
prerogative shall not oust a man from his law, as appears from 49
Edw. III, 16 Edw. IV and 9 Eliz. Dyer 262:[13] if I am indebted to
someone else upon a simple contract, and the debtee commits
suicide or is outlawed, the debt shall nevertheless not be forfeited,
because the debtor must not be ousted from his law.

POPHAM C.J.Q.B. That is not law.

WALMSLEY J.C.P. Nevertheless, it is what the books say.

POPHAM C.J.Q.B. The books are against law. (To which several
other justices assented.[14])

Bacon. And it is no wonder that this trial has obtained such
respect in law, being as indifferent as it is. The law has provided
that it shall be done by the oath of a true and credible person, for
one who has been attainted of a false oath by writ of attaint shall
not be received to do his law: as in 33 Hen. VI.[15] Also it must be
done *duodena manu*, for the oath of the party himself is not
sufficient, but he must be sworn with 11 others who will swear that
they think the oath of the party himself is true. Thus it seems, in
respect of the mischief which would ensue to the defendant in this
case by being ousted from his wager of law, that the action on the
case does not lie.

As to the precedents, he confessed that several had been shown
him, of which the oldest are in 8 Hen. VI, and after. But all the
precedents until 22 Hen. VIII are on an *assumpsit* to deliver, and
not on an *assumpsit* to pay. After 22 Hen. VIII, however, there
have been several precedents that an action on the case has been
maintained on an *assumpsit* to pay; but these have been adjudged
solely in the King's Bench, and also several of them may be
answered with the distinctions set out before, such as where a place
of payment was appointed or where the contract was broken down
into several separate days of payment.

---

12   *Hebrews*, VI, 16.
13   Y.B. Hil. 49 Edw. III, fo. 5, pl. 8; Pas. 16 Edw. IV, fo. 4, pl. 9; *Anon.* (1567)
      Dyer 262, §31; see pp. 425, 428, above.
14   Coke (4 Co. Rep. 95) said it had been recently resolved in the Exchequer that
      such debts are forfeited.
15   Y.B. Mich. 33 Hen. VI, fo. 32, pl. 6.

So he concluded that the action on the case did not lie.

(d) Queen's Bench, 9 November 1602:
BL MS. Add. 25203, fo. 607.

Remember that on 9 November this term, *Coke* A.-G. moved the case . . . and since the case had depended a long time, and had been argued and debated in this court and also so often before all the justices of England and the barons of the Exchequer, who had conferred about it amongst themselves, he prayed their resolution and judgment in the case.

POPHAM C.J. answered that they had conferred and advised concerning the case, and that they had resolved it, and were agreed:

First, that every contract executory implies in itself a promise or *assumpsit*.

Secondly, that although an action of debt lies upon such a contract to recover the duty, the plaintiff may nevertheless have an action on the case upon the *assumpsit*.

He said they had resolved this not only upon the precedents of this court, but also upon reason, and upon the precedents of all the courts which the queen has: for there are several precedents both in the Common Bench and in the Exchequer which concur with this resolution. (But whether an action on the case would lie on such an *assumpsit* against the executors of him who made it, he said they were not resolved.)

All this that was delivered by the Chief Justice was affirmed by the other justices to have been so agreed.

So POPHAM C.J., *ex assensu sociorum*, commanded judgment to be entered for the plaintiff.

The record shows that judgment was given this term for the £16 damages and 20s. costs assessed by the jury, and an additional £9 costs assessed by the court, making £26 in all.

(e) Coke's retrospective summary: 4 Co. Rep. 92;
collated with Coke's autograph report,
BL MS. Harley 6686, ff. 526–530v.

John Slade brought an action on the case in the Queen's Bench against Humphrey Morley . . . and against the maintenance of this action various objections were made by *John Dodderidge*, of counsel with the defendant:

1   That the plaintiff upon this bargain could have an ordinary remedy by an action of debt, which is an action formed in the register; and therefore he should not have an action on the case, which is an extraordinary action and not limited within any certain

form in the register. For *ubi cessat remedium ordinarium ibi
decurritur ad extraordinarium, et nunquam decurritur ad extraordinarium ubi valet ordinarium*: as appears by all our books.[16] *Et nullus
debet agere actionem de dolo ubi alia actio subest.*[17]

2 The second objection was that the maintenance of this action
takes away the defendant's benefit of wager of law, and so bereaves
him of the benefit which the law gives him, which is his birthright.
For peradventure the defendant has paid or satisfied the plaintiff in
private between them, and he has no witness of this payment or
satisfaction, and therefore it would be mischievous if he should not
wage his law in such a case. And that was the reason (as it was said)
why debts by simple contract were not to be forfeited to the king by
outlawry or attainder, because then by the king's prerogative the
subject would be ousted from his wager of law, which is his
birthright: as is held in 40 Edw. III, fo. 5; 50 [Lib.] Ass., [pl.] 1; 16
Edw. IV, fo. 4; and 9 Eliz. Dyer 262. And if the king should lose the
forfeiture and the debt in such a case, and by the judgment of the
law the debtor should rather be discharged of his debt than
deprived of the benefit which the law gives him for his discharge,
even if in truth the debt was due and payable: a fortiori, in the case
at bar, the defendant should not be charged in an action in which
he would be ousted from his law, when he may charge him in an
action in which he could have the benefit of it.

As to these objections the courts of King's Bench and Common
Pleas were divided. For the justices of the King's Bench held that
the action was maintainable, notwithstanding such objections; and
the justices of the Common Pleas held the contrary. And for the
honour of the law, and for the repose of the subject to put an end to
this difference of opinion, *quia nil in lege intolerabilius est eandem
rem diverso jure censeri*,[18] the case was openly argued before all the
justices of England and barons of the Exchequer, namely SIR JOHN
POPHAM C.J. of England, SIR EDMUND ANDERSON C.J.C.P., SIR
WILLIAM PERYAM C.B. of the Exchequer, CLARKE B., GAWDY
J.Q.B., WALMSLEY J.C.P., FENNER J.Q.B., KINGSMILL J.C.P.,
SAVILE B., WARBURTON J.C.P., and YELVERTON J.Q.B.,[19] in the

16 Coke MS. cites only Dyer 121.
17 This is not in Coke MS.
18 'Nothing in law is more intolerable than to decide the same thing according to
    different rules': The maxim is not in Coke MS.
19 These names were added in print, and are not a correct list of the judges in 1597,
    when Coke argued against Dodderidge, but are a list of the judges in 1602. It
    seems from MS. reports of other cases that Anderson C.J., Peryam C.B.,
    Walmsley and Kingsmill JJ. and Savile B. were against the action on the case, so
    the majority was probably only 6:5.

Exchequer Chamber, by the queen's attorney general for the plaintiff and by *John Dodderidge* for the defendant; and at another time the case was argued at Serjeants' Inn before all the said justices and barons, by the attorney general for the plaintiff and by *Francis Bacon* for the defendant.

And after many conferences between the justices and barons it was resolved[20] that the action was maintainable and that the plaintiff should have judgment. And in this case these points were resolved:

I That although an action of debt lies upon the contract, the bargainor may nevertheless have an action on the case or an action of debt at his election, and that for three reasons or causes:

1 In respect of infinite precedents (which George Kemp, esquire, secondary of the prothonotaries of the King's Bench showed me)[1] both in the Court of Common Pleas and in the Court of King's Bench, in the reigns of King Henry VI, Edward IV, Henry VII and Henry VIII, by which it appears that the plaintiffs declared that the defendants, in consideration of a sale to them of certain goods, promised to pay so much money etc., in which cases the plaintiffs had judgment.[2] To which precedents and judgments, being so great in number, in so many successions of ages, and in the several times of so many reverend judges, the justices in this case gave great regard. And so did the justices in olden times, and from time to time, both in matters of form and in deciding doubts and questions of law (both at common law and in construing acts of parliament) . . .[3] so that in the case at bar it was resolved that the multitude of the said judicial precedents in so many successions of ages well proved that in the case at bar the action was maintainable.

2 The second cause of their resolution was various judgments and cases resolved in our books where such an action on the case on an *assumpsit* has been maintainable, when the party might have had an action of debt . . .[4]

3 It was resolved that every contract executory imports[5] in itself an *assumpsit*. For when one agrees to pay money or to deliver something, he thereby assumes or promises to pay or deliver it.

---

20   This expression was objected to by the judges who dissented: see p. 442, below.
1   Words in parentheses added in print.
2   Scholars have been unable to find any such precedents before the time of Henry VIII.
3   Here follows a lengthy discourse on the value of precedents (i.e. of entries on the plea rolls).
4   These are fully discussed above.
5   Altered in MS. from 'implies'.

Therefore, when one sells any goods to another, and agrees to deliver them at a day to come, and the other in consideration thereof agrees to pay so much money at such and such a day, in that case both parties may have an action of debt or an action on the case upon *assumpsit*, for the mutual executory agreement of both parties imports in itself reciprocal actions on the case as well as actions of debt. Therewith agrees the judgment in *Rede and Norwood's Case*, Plowd. 182.[6]

4   It was resolved that the plaintiff in this action on the case upon *assumpsit* should recover damages not only for the special loss which he has suffered (if any) but also for the entire debt; so that a recovery or bar in this action would be a good bar in an action of debt brought on the same contract, and so *vice versa* a recovery or bar in an action of debt is a good bar in an action on the case on the *assumpsit* . . .

5   In some cases it would be mischievous if an action of debt only should be brought, and not an action on the case. For instance, in the case between *Redman* and *Peck* (2 & 3 Phil. & Mar.), Dyer 113, they bargained together that for a certain consideration Redman should deliver to Peck 20 quarters of barley yearly during his life, and it was adjudged that an action well lay for non-delivery in one year, for it would otherwise be mischievous to Peck: for if he should be driven to his action of debt, then he himself could never have it, but his executors or administrators, since debt does not lie in such a case until all the days have been incurred, and that would be contrary to the bargain and intention of the parties, for Peck provides it yearly for his necessary use . . . Also, it is good nowadays to oust the defendant from his law whenever it may be done by law and to try it by the country, for it would otherwise occasion much perjury.[7]

6   It was said that an action on the case on an *assumpsit* is just as well formed an action and contained in the register as an action of debt; for its form there appears. It appears also in various other cases in the register that an action on the case will lie even though the plaintiff may have another formed action in the register . . . and therefore it was concluded that in all cases when the register has two writs for one and the same case, it is at the party's election to take the one writ or the other. But the register has two several actions, namely an action on the case on an *assumpsit* and also an action of debt; and therefore the party may elect the one or the other.

6   (1557); see p. 448, below.
7   In the MS., this sentence is added in the margin.

And as to the objection which has been made, that it would be mischievous to the defendant that he should not wage his law, since he might pay it in secret: to that it was answered that it should be accounted his folly that he did not take sufficient witnesses with him to prove the payment which he made. But the mischief would rather be on the other side, for experience now proves that men's consciences grow so large that the respect of their private advantage rather induces men to perjury, and principally those with declining estates. For *jurare in propria causa* (as someone said) *est saepenumero hoc saeculo praecipitium diaboli ad detrudendas miserorum animas ad infernum.* For this reason, in debt, or other actions where wager of law is admitted by the law, the judges without good admonition and due examination of the party do not admit him to it . . .

And note, reader, this resolution agrees with the judicial law of God, on which our law is in every point founded. For it appears from the 22nd chapter of *Exodus*, verse 7, 'If a man shall deliver unto his neighbour money or stuff to keep, and it be stolen out of the man's house, if the thief be found he shall pay double'. And verse 10, 'If a man deliver to his neighbour an ass, or an ox, or a sheep, or any beast, to keep, and it dies or is hurt or driven away, no man seeing it, the oath of the Lord shall be between them both whether he hath not put his hand unto his neighbour's goods; and the owner thereof shall accept it, and he shall not make restitution'. From which it appears that it is in the plaintiff's election either to charge the defendant by witnesses, if he will, and to oust him from his law, or to refer it to the defendant's oath: for the text says, 'no man seeing it'. Similarly by our law, in the same case as is put in the text, the owner has an election either to bring an action on the case in which the defendant cannot wage his law, or an action of detinue in which he may: *et jusjurandum in hoc casu est finis*, for the plaintiff is bound thereby and it is the end of the controversy. And I am surprised that in these days so little consideration is given to an oath, as I observe from day to day . . .

WRIGHT v SWANTON (1604)

Record: CP 40/1716, m. 544. Daniel and Alice Wright brought an action on the case against William Swanton and declared that, whereas on 24 June 1601 at Hartest, Suffolk, in consideration that Alice (who was then single) would bring and deliver 12 cartloads of wood to the defendant's house, the defendant undertook and promised to pay her 5s. 6d. for each load; and afterwards on 20 August she delivered 12 loads: nevertheless the defendant, scheming to defraud her, did not pay the 66s., although requested to do so on 1 October. The defendant, protesting that he did not make the undertaking, pleaded that Alice did not deliver the wood. On 11 July 1604 at Newmarket assizes (Popham C.J., Clarke B.) the jury found for the plaintiffs with £4 damages and 5s. costs.

(a) BL MS. Hargrave 29, fo. 94.

Note, by WALMSLEY J. this term, that a man shall not have an action on the case where he might have an action of debt. The first reason is because the defendant is by that means ousted from the benefit of his law, which has always been allowed. The second reason is because in an action on the case the plaintiff shall recover everything in damages; and that is uncertain, because the jury may give him a greater or lesser sum in damages, while in an action of debt he shall recover the debt certain. Thus by such means the law is reduced from certainty to uncertainty: which had been seen several times this term upon error brought in respect of judgments given in the King's Bench. It seems to me that this is a great mischief, and it is apparent what will ensue. As for the case of *Slade v Morley*, which is reported by the attorney general,[8] it was not resolved upon argument or reasons delivered;[9] but the justices were assembled and each was asked for his opinion, and thus it was resolved by the opinion of the greater number.

(b) HLS MS. 2069, fo. 20v.

Action on the case upon *assumpsit* was brought in respect of a simple contract, and it was found for the plaintiff.

Croke demanded judgment, according to the resolution in *Slade v Morley* . . . which was agreed by all the justices of England.

WALMSLEY J. denied that it was agreed by them in the Exchequer [Chamber]; but their opinion was asked in Serjeants' Inn, without any argument[10]. . . and as to the policy, which was to prevent wagers of law, he said that men ought to trust in wager of law where the law willed it.

ANDERSON C.J. said it lay [only] where no other action would lie; and by this means all actions could be made actions on the case.

The other justices seemed to be of the same opinion.

---

8   Coke's report (printed in 1604) is abstracted at pp. 437–441, above.
9   This refers to formal speeches by the judges.
10   I.e. of the judges: cf. fn. 9, above.

(c) CUL Cholmondeley (Houghton) MSS.
Pell Papers 7(1), fo. 14v.

. . . It was now moved in arrest of judgment that . . . an action on the case does not lie, but an action of debt.

On the first motion, the opinion of the court was in accordance; for by this means the subjects would be ousted from their law, which would be a great inconvenience: for where a man has paid his debt and has no witness thereof, he shall be compelled to pay it again by this action of *assumpsit*. And they denied the case of *Slade v Morley*, and said that it was never resolved, but only the opinion of the judges given obiter at Serjeants' Inn.

ANDERSON C.J. said that actions on the case were not at common law, but were first given by the Statute of Westminster II, c. 24[11]. . . . from whence it appears that an action on the case does not lie except in cases where the law is defective of a remedy and where there is no writ in the register: then an action on the case lies, but not otherwise.

So they were for giving judgment that the plaintiff take nothing by her writ; but by reason of the case of *Slade v Morley* they would be advised.

At another day, however, when it was moved again, the opinion of all the justices (except WALMSLEY J.) was that the plaintiff should have her judgment: for this is not a perfect bargain and contract whereon an action of debt lies, but only an *assumpsit*. For it is in consideration that she should bring and deliver, so that the carrying is a labour and charge, and the money is to be paid for the carriage as well as for the cartloads of wood; and she should have recompense for it . . .

WALMSLEY J. . . . was strongly of opinion that the action on the case did not lie in the [present] case; for this putting in of [the words] 'should bring and deliver' was only a device to take away actions of debt and wager of law, which is a benefit to which every subject is born. And he said that the money was given principally for the wood, and not for the bringing and delivery thereof, and therefore it is a good bargain.

Notwithstanding his opinion, however, judgment was given that the plaintiff should recover . . .

The record confirms that judgment was entered for the plaintiffs in Michaelmas term 1604 for £4 damages and £6. 10s. costs. Anderson C.J. died the following August, and (although Walmsley J. survived until 1612) there is little doubt that thereafter the Common Pleas gave way to the

---

11 Cf. p. 590, below.

majority view in *Slade's Case*.[12] The one remaining problem was whether the action lay against executors; see pp. 446–457, below.

ANON. (1672)

Treby's reports, MT MS., p. 747 (untr.).

In this case tried before HALE C.J. he said an executor was charged in his own right upon a promise pretended to be made by him, without any cause or truth. He said he would always require marvellous strong evidence for such a promise and charge; for it was become a great grievance, two men could hardly talk together but a promise is sprung. He said it were well if a law were made that no promise should bind unless there were some signal ceremony,[13] or that wager of law did lie upon a promise. For the common law was a wise law, that men should wage their law in debt on a contract, and if they proved their reputation *duodena manu*[14] should be discharged, that so things might be reduced to writing and brought to certainty. And *Slade's Case*, which was hardly brought in (for it was by a capitulation[15] and agreement among the judges) has done more hurt than ever it did or will do good.[16]

In *Buckeridge v Sherly* (1671), at p. 651 of the same reports, HALE C.J. said: '... actions on the case are become one of the great grievances of the nation; for two men cannot talk together but one fellow or other who stands in a corner swears a promise and cause of action. These catching promises must not be encouraged. It were very well if a law were made whereby some ceremony, as striking hands etc., were required to every promise that should bind'. In that case William Buckeridge had been awarded £200 damages against Ralph Sherly at Abingdon assizes (before Turnor C.B. and Archer J.) for breach of an *assumpsit* to pay that sum in consideration of marriage. Judgment was later entered for the plaintiff, with £15 costs: KB 27/1919, m. 608. It will be noticed that promises in consideration of marriage, and promises by executors (as in the principal case) were both expressly included in the provisions of the Statute of Frauds.

---

12 See Ibbetson, 4 *Oxford Journal of Legal Studies*, at 304–305.
13 Cf. *Anon.* (1672), at p. 775 of the same reports: '... It were very well that some solemnity, as the delivery of a piece of money or something like livery of seisin, were requisite to the making [of] every promise. It was the wisdom of the law to require a solemnity in contracts (as well as marriages), which if not observed the party should have liberty to wage his law'.
14 I.e. with 12 hands (with compurgators).
15 I.e. treaty.
16 Cf. *Edgcomb v Dee* (1670) Vaugh. 89, at 101, per Vaughan C.J.C.P.; p. 224, fn. 20, above.

THE STATUTE OF FRAUDS (1677)

29 Car. II, c. 3;
Statutes of the Realm, vol. V, p. 840 (untr.).

For prevention of many fraudulent practices which are commonly endeavoured to be upheld by perjury and subornation of perjury, be it enacted by the king's most excellent majesty, by and with the advice and consent of the lords spiritual and temporal and the commons in this present parliament assembled, and by the authority of the same . . .

4 . . . that from and after the said four and twentieth day of June [1677] no action shall be brought whereby to charge any executor or administrator upon any special promise to answer damages out of his own estate; or whereby to charge the defendant upon any special promise to answer for the debt, default or miscarriages of another person; or to charge any person upon any agreement made upon consideration of marriage; or upon any contract or sale of lands, tenements or hereditaments, or any interest in or concerning them; or upon any agreement that is not to be performed within the space of one year from the making thereof: unless the agreement upon which such action shall be brought, or some memorandum or note thereof, shall be in writing and signed by the party to be charged therewith, or some other person thereunto by him lawfully authorised . . .[17]

17 And be it further enacted by the authority aforesaid, that from and after the said four and twentieth day of June no contract for the sale of any goods, wares and merchandises for the price of ten pounds sterling or upwards shall be allowed to be good, except the buyer shall accept part of the goods so sold and actually receive the same, or give something in earnest to bind the bargain, or in part of payment, or that some note or memorandum in writing of the said bargain be made and signed by the parties to be charged by such contract, or their agents thereunto lawfully authorised . . .

17 For ss. 5–8, see p. 131, above.

17　Assumpsit against executors for money

CLEYMOND v VYNCENT (1520)

Record: KB 27/1037, m. 40. Oliver Cleymond brought a bill of 'trespass and deceit' against Robert and Tamsin Vyncent complaining that, whereas a discussion took place on 20 February 1519 in Cornhill between himself and Roger Penson for the sale to Roger of six barrels of salted salmon worth £6, and Tamsin's former husband Robert Penson[1] spontaneously requested Oliver to deliver the salmon to Roger, promising that if Roger did not pay within a year he (or his executors) would; and whereas Oliver, trusting in Robert's promise, sold and delivered the salmon to Roger for £6, which he did not pay:[2] nevertheless Tamsin, as Robert's executrix, had not paid the £6 as promised. The defendants pleaded *Non promisit*, and on 27 November 1520 at the Guildhall, London, before Fyneux C.J., the jury found for the plaintiff with £6 damages and £1. 6s. 8d. costs

(a)　Y.B. Mich. 12 Hen. VIII, fo. 11, pl. 3.

... The question of law was, shall he have this action against the executors or not? It was adjudged by all the justices that he should recover by this action, for two reasons: (1) because he has no other remedy at common law save by this action; and (2) because the plaintiff delivered the goods upon the testator's promise, and it is not right that the testator's soul should be in danger if he had sufficient to pay him, since the plaintiff was prejudiced by relying on his promise.

And thus was judgment given.

1　Port (see p. 447, opposite) says that he was Roger's father, a fact not mentioned in the record.
2　The Y.B. says he died unable to pay, another fact not mentioned in the record.

FYNEUX [C.J.] said that this is outside the principle *Actio moritur cum persona*, for that is where the hurt or damage is corporal. For if someone beats me and dies, my action is gone—or, if I die, my executors shall have no action—because the party cannot be punished when he is dead. In this case, however, the plaintiff can have what he would have had if the party had been alive, namely the price of his goods; and therefore this action does not die, for each party may have his remedy. It is not so in battery, because the writ cannot say that the executors beat him and they shall not answer for another's act.

(Query: if the testator had been alive, would the plaintiff have had this action against him, or could he have waged his law in this case?)

(b) John Port's notebook, HEHL MS. HM 46980, fo. 21v.

... Exception was taken, that these facts would not have been sufficient at common law to maintain this action without specialty if the father had been alive, because the father had no recompense and did not make the contract. A fortiori the action does not lie against his executors.

MORE J.K.B. said that in London a writ of covenant lies without specialty. And by the custom there executors may in some cases wage their law ...

This action was maintained, and the plaintiff had his judgment to recover.

The record shows that judgment was given on 24 January 1521 for £6 damages and £3 costs, the latter having been increased by the court after the motion in arrest of judgment. For a criticism of this decision by Sir Anthony Fitzherbert, who had been counsel for Cleymond, see p. 448, below; and for doubts expressed by Shelley J., see *Sukley v Wyte* (1542), p. 404, above.

ANON. (1535)

Y.B. Trin. 27 Hen. VIII, fo. 23, pl. 21;
LC MS. Acc. LL 52960, 27 Hen. VIII, fo. 40v.

Knightley asked FITZHERBERT: if a man is indebted to me because he made a simple contract with me, and he dies, leaving assets to his executors, shall I—after the debts which the executors are chargeable to pay have been paid, and the legacies performed—have an action on the case against the executors? Since the executors have assets in their hands of the testator's goods, it is right that they should pay their testator's debts: for even though the testator is dead, the indebtedness still remains as it was before, and they have the goods to the use of the testator.

FITZHERBERT. You shall not have any action on the case, or any other remedy; for, once the testator is dead, this debt which was due by reason of a simple contract is dead also.

Knightley. The reason why no writ of debt lies against executors is because the testator could have waged his law, and the executors cannot do his law, and therefore they are not chargeable. In the Exchequer it is a common practice for the king's [debtors][3] to have *quominus* against the executors of their own debtors (who are indebted to them by simple contract), supposing that they have not been paid and thereby the king cannot have his debts.[4]

FITZHERBERT. That is not so, for there is no such practice in the Exchequer. The law is quite otherwise. In Michaelmas in the twelfth year of the present king:[5] I was of counsel with one Cleymond[6] of London in an action on the case brought against executors in a similar matter, and the case was adjudged in my favour by Fyneux [C.J.] and Coningsby [J.], against the executors. But I hold that the law is clearly otherwise, and that they acted without taking any advice, but only on their own opinions.

Someone told him that the case was reported in the twelfth year of the present king.

FITZHERBERT. Put that case out of your books, for it is not law without doubt. (Note that.)

NORWOOD v NORWOOD AND REDE (1557)

Record: KB 27/1182, m. 188; Plowd. 180v. Richard Norwood brought a bill of trespass on the case against Thomas Norwood, the elder, and Edward Rede, executors of Thomas Gray, complaining that, whereas on 2 April 1556, in the parish of St Sepulchre, London, he had delivered 40s. to Thomas Gray at his request, and in consideration thereof Gray had faithfully promised and undertaken that he, his executors or assigns would deliver to the plaintiff at Ramsgate, Kent, 50 quarters of wheat for £33. 6s. 8d., to be delivered and paid for in two instalments (in December and March): nevertheless Gray, wickedly scheming to defraud the plaintiff, did not deliver the wheat or any part thereof in his lifetime, though the plaintiff often requested delivery and was ready with the money at the appointed

3 Both texts read 'debtees'.
4 The last clause is garbled in print, but correct in MS.
5 *Cleymond v Vyncent* (1520); see p. 446, above.
6 Reads 'Clement' in print, 'client' in MS.

times and places; and the executors, having assets to satisfy the plaintiff and pay all the testator's debts, did not deliver the wheat either; and as a result the plaintiff was damaged in his credit with various persons, especially Ralph Mannings and Christopher Stransham, to whom he had resold the wheat; to his damage of 200 marks. The defendants demurred to the declaration.

Plowd. 181v.

. . . And it was argued in Michaelmas term in the fourth and fifth years of the present king and queen [1557], by *Lovelace* and *Gerrard* on behalf of the defendants, and by *Fosset*[7] and *Manwood* on behalf of the plaintiffs—as I heard, for I was not present throughout—whether or not the action on the case lay against executors upon such an undertaking by the testator. On behalf of the defendants it was said that this undertaking was nothing other than a simple contract, and if executors should be charged by such a contract they should for the same reason be charged by any contract executory, both for debt and for other things. For every contract executory is an undertaking in itself. And it would be unfitting to charge them by contracts made in pais by word of mouth, as well as by specialties, for they cannot have knowledge of [the former]. It was further said that there are various precedents in the court here which have been shown to you, my lords the judges, that in such actions brought against executors as ours is here, the executors have pleaded in bar and when the pleas were found in favour of the plaintiffs they have recovered. Nevertheless, this does not prove the law to be against us in our case here, where we have demurred in law . . . There is but one case touching our matter which has been ruled. That is the case in 12 Hen. VIII[8] . . . As to that, however, it does not appear there whether it was demurred in judgment or not, and perhaps the party pleaded in bar[9] . . . And even if judgment was given upon demurrer, may it please you to hear what Fitzherbert J. said in 27 Hen. VIII[10] concerning the said case . . . Thus (it was said) the authority of that case is impeached by Fitzherbert J., who had been of counsel on behalf of the plaintiff for whom the judgment was given, and who as a judge of great reputation held it to be erroneous. And it was in

---

7   Sic. Probably Richard Forsett, reader of Gray's Inn.
8   *Cleymond v Vyncent* (1520); see p. 446, above.
9   The record shows that the defendant did plead in bar.
10 See p. 448, opposite.

fact contrary to the principles of the law, because such an undertaking is but a contract in pais, as a contract of debt is . . .[11]

But it was said on the other side that in this case the testator
could not have waged his law; and where he could not have done so
the action lies against executors by the rule of the common law: for
it is not right that, if they have assets to pay the debts and legacies
and also to satisfy the plaintiff, they should retain the residue of the
goods for their own use. And there is no prejudice in paying this,
but it is charitable, and beneficial to the testator's soul; whereas to
leave it unpaid is no good to anyone except the executors, and they
ought not to have the benefit of it, for that was not the testator's
intent; for they are but ministers and distributors of the goods of
the deceased, and in taking a benefit themselves they break the
trust of the deceased. And the judgment in 12 Hen. VIII, given by
the court, is not to be so easily rejected by the dictum of Fitzherbert . . .

All the justices agreed that the declaration was good, and that
the executors should be charged to the plaintiff. And so, without
solemn argument,[12] they gave judgment for the plaintiff and that he
should have a writ to inquire of the damages . . .[13]

The record shows that judgment was given accordingly in Michaelmas term
1557.

ANON. (1571)

BL MS. Add. 25211, fo. 100.

Note that the Lord DYER C.J.C.P. would not allow trespass on the
case against executors on an *assumpsit* of the testator; and he said
that Mountague C.J.[14] had first allowed them in the Common
Bench, and that he brought the course with him when he was
removed here out of the King's Bench.

---

11 Counsel then attacked the declaration for not saying that the executors had
assets to pay legacies as well as debts.
12 I.e. without a full speech from each judge.
13 Plowden adds at the end: 'It has been greatly doubted since the ruling in the
said case of 12 Hen. VIII whether the action will lie here by the law, and
whether the said case in the year 12 Hen. VIII was well adjudged or not. And it
seemed to many wise men who were well learned in our law that by the old law
the action was not maintainable against executors in the above case; but that
conscience had encroached this case on the common law. But it seems that this
is not so . . .' Such doubts in the 1540s are noted in Brooke Abr., *Action sur le
case*, pl. 4, 106.
14 Sir Edward Mountague (d. 1557), C.J.K.B. 1539–45, C.J.C.P. 1545–53.

COTTINGTON v HULETT (1587)

Record: KB 27/1301, m. 186. Margery Cottington, widow, brought a bill of trespass on the case against Anne Hulett, widow and executrix of Robert Hulett, complaining that, whereas the deceased, on 25 March 1576 at Wells, Somerset, in consideration that the plaintiff had lent him £200 at his request, undertook to pay her back at the next Lady Day: nevertheless neither he nor his executrix had paid back the £200. The defendant pleaded *Non assumpsit*; and on 7 August 1587 at Taunton assizes (Anderson C.J.C.P., Gent B.) the jury found for the plaintiff with £200 damages. The defendant moved in arrest of judgment the following Michaelmas term.

HLS MS. 16, fo. 401v; CUL MS. Ii. 5. 38, fo. 249.[15]

It was moved whether the plaintiff in an action on the case against executors upon their testator's *assumpsit* ought to aver that they have assets to discharge all other debts and legacies. And it was in effect agreed that he need not aver that they have assets to discharge legacies; but it was doubted whether or not he ought to aver that they have assets to discharge other debts as well.

Coke. Conscience has encroached the whole of this action upon the common law,[16] for such an action did not lie under the old law. And (according to him) it is not like the case of an action of debt against an heir, for there the action is in the *debet et detinet* and there is no need to aver assets . . . In the case of 12 Hen. VIII[17] there was an averment of assets to content him and also to pay other debts . . .

WRAY C.J. The assets are not traversable; and what mischief is there for the defendant? For he may plead Nothing in hand, or Fully administered; and if he pleads *Non assumpsit*, still the judgment shall be in respect of the testator's goods.

Coke. He has no title without assets.

WRAY C.J. If they do not have assets, they may plead Nothing in hand.

GAWDY J. thought he ought to aver assets, to the intent that it may appear to the court that he has a cause of action.

Coke. At common law one could not have an action on the case if he could have a remedy by some other action; but that old law is now altered, and it is now taken to be a rule that for matters whereupon he can have his bill and *subpoena* in the Chancery, he can now have an action on the case upon *assumpsit* at common law.

15 Anonymous here, but identified from the shorter report in Cro. Eliz. 59.
16 A quotation from Plowden; see p. 450, fn. 13, opposite.
17 *Cleymond v Vyncent* (1520); see p. 446, above.

Tanfield said he had the report of a case which was in 19 Eliz., and as he believed a distinction was there taken that in an action on the case against executors upon their own promise he ought to aver assets, for otherwise there is no cause of action, whereas [in an action] against the executors on the testator's promise he need not aver assets. But he said he did not well remember the case, and therefore he wished to refer to his book for it.

Coke. 34 Hen. VI,[18] debt against executors upon their testator's deed, they plead *Non est factum*, and [it is held that] judgment shall be in respect of the testator's goods.

Godfrey. There are other books contrary to that.

And, although it was moved in arrest of judgment that he had not averred assets, later in this term judgment was entered nevertheless.

The record confirms that judgment was entered for the plaintiff this term. In the margin is written *Breve erroris allocatur*, but no Exchequer Chamber proceedings are entered.

WOLMAN v SIDNEY (1589)

HLS MS. 1057, fo. 211 (C.P.).

An action on the case was brought by Wolman against Sidney, executor of Sidney, and he declared on a contract made between him and the defendant's testator, whereby the testator undertook to pay so much to the plaintiff.

Shuttleworth moved whether this action lay against an executor, and said that in the Queen's Bench it has always been taken to lie perfectly well.

PERYAM J. And that is the reason for us to take here.

WYNDHAM J. agreed (ANDERSON C.J. being in the Star Chamber).

Shuttleworth. Then I think, sir, that we may plead Fully administered.

PERYAM and WYNDHAM JJ. granted this, for then [judgment] shall only be in respect of the testator's goods.

This departure from the 1571 opinion (see p. 450, above) may have been an aberration. Certainly, after the Exchequer Chamber began to find its teeth in the 1590s, the Common Pleas judges in that court consistently reversed Queen's Bench judgments against executors: e.g., *Griggs v Helhouse* (1595); *Mathew v Mathew* (1595); *Stubbings v Rotherham* (1595); *Jordan v Jordan*

18   Y.B. Mich. 34 Hen. VI, fo. 22, pl. 42.

(1596) (see p. 454, below); *Serle v Rosse* (1596) Cro. Eliz. 459. In 1601, Gawdy J.Q.B. said in such a case, 'if we give judgment for the plaintiff it will be reversed in the Exchequer Chamber' (BL MS. Add. 25201, fo. 285). According to the brief report in Yelv. 20, it was decided by *Slade's Case* (1602) that *assumpsit* did not lie against executors upon a contract made by the testator. But the fuller reports (see p. 437, above) do not bear this out. The Common Pleas held to its old view until at least 1605: *Anon.* (1605) CUL MS. Gg. 5. 6, fo. 34v.

ANON. (1602)

CUL MS. Gg. 2. 31, fo. 440v, pl. 33 (untr.).

My Lord Keeper [EGERTON] said in Trinity term 44 Eliz. that he would relieve one upon a simple contract against an executor, upon a bill exhibited containing the matter [and] averring that there is assets sufficient. And this my lord said, he would relieve the party although he had formerly brought his action in the King's Bench and had declared upon an *indebitatus assumpsit solvere*, and there after recovery by a writ of error the judgment is reversed in 'Chequer Chamber; yet notwithstanding after the plaintiff had thus attempted the law, and so far, yet my lord said he would receive his bill if he exhibited it in Chancery and pray[ed] there to be relieved.

ANON. (*c.* 1602)

CUL MS. Gg. 2. 31, fo. 459v, pl. 179 (untr.).

If one would be relieved [in Chancery] against an executor upon a simple contract made by his testator, or an *assumpsit*, or such like, let the plaintiff well take heed that the contract or *assumpsit* be well grounded and upon good groundwork; for if there be usury, or any patching or paltering chevisance in the case, my lord will not [relieve][19] it: for my lord is very tender to relieve any such plaintiff in any case, though the cause be never so good, for my lord's reason is because that as the cause of suit ariseth upon an *assumpsit*, parol or simple contract, or an account, so there may be a discharge of these matters between the plaintiff and the defendant by parol, whereof the executors may be ignorant; and therefore it is good to be tender in relief of such cases.

---

19 Reads 'believe' in MS.

MAINE v PEACHER (1610)

CUL MS. Gg. 4. 9, fo. 38; MT MS., fo. 124v.[20]

The plaintiff declared in the King's Bench that, whereas he had sold various parcels of wares (which he set out in detail) to the defendant's testator, the testator promised to pay the plaintiff £5, which he had not paid. Judgment was thereupon given for the plaintiff against the executor, in an action on the case. And now the executor had brought [error][1] upon this judgment, supposing that he should not be charged upon a simple contract.

COKE C.J.C.P. For my part, I will not have this judgment reversed unless more of us agree to its reversal than there were judges in the King's Bench who gave the judgment. For there are only seven of us here, and if four of us (being the majority) reverse what has been done judicially by five, it would be mischievous, save in cases where manifest error has intervened.

[WALMSLEY J.C.P. For my part I would reverse it.

TANFIELD C.B. That is your opinion, but you stand alone and our opinion is to the contrary.

COKE C.J. to WALMSLEY J. One Kercher, my chaplain, had such a suit against him in the Common Pleas recently,[2] and you gave judgment against him in my absence one day when I was in the Star Chamber. Upon what reason do you think the law is now altered, unless you want to be against the opinion of the others?

And no one but WALMSLEY J. inclined to reverse the judgment.][3]

It was said by counsel that a judgment such as this had been reversed in *Jordan and Jordan's case*, Hil. 38 Eliz.;[4] and another was reversed in Mich. 37 & 38 Eliz.[5] And it was ordered that the record of *Kercher's case* should be looked at.

Later, on another day in the term, the judges were moved in the said case of *Maine* and *Peacher*; and they were shown that such a judgment was reversed here in Pas. 37 Eliz. between *Mathew* and

---

20   Lane's reports, but not in the printed version. Also noted, sub nom. *Meane v Peacher*, in 1 Rolle Abr. 14, line 8.
1   Reads 'action' in MS.
2   Reported in Godb. 176; cited in 2 Bro. & Golds. 41. Coke's chaplain was Dr. Robert Kercher.
3   Passage omitted in CUL MS.
4   (1596) KB 27/1330, m. 334; Owen 57.
5   Probably *Griggs v Helhouse* (1595); cited in Cro. Eliz. 455, Moo. K.B. 691; reported in MS.

Mathew, roll 155;[6] and *Rotherham's case*, Trin. 36 Eliz., roll 551,[7] another such judgment was reversed.

Despite this, the judges thought to affirm the judgment. Since, however, it is *vexata quaestio*, they appointed that the case should be argued in Michaelmas term next by all the judges of England.

TANFIELD C.B. It has always been conceived that if a man declares on a sale, an action on the case lies against executors as aforesaid, if there is any collateral matter such as marriage. The authority of . . . 12 Hen. VIII[8] and *Norwood and Rede's case*[9] moves me greatly and strongly . . . And Sir John Fyneux was a profound judge of great experience, and at the time of the said judgment he was 106 years old.

This case was not debated afterwards in Michaelmas term . . .

PYNCHON v LEGAT (1611)

Record: KB 27/1415, m. 533; Co. Entr., fo. 1. Sir Edward Pynchon and Sir Richard Weston, executors of Sir Jerome Weston, executor of Rose Pynchon, brought a bill of trespass on the case against Thomas Legat, esquire, executor of John Legat, esquire, complaining that, whereas on 7 February 1595 at Writtle, Essex, Rose had lent John £200, and the same John in consideration thereof undertook and promised Rose that he would repay her, her executors or administrators on request: nevertheless John (and after his death the defendant), little regarding the promise and undertaking, but scheming to defraud Rose and her executors, had not paid the £200, though often requested to do so. The bill alleged that the defendant had assets both to pay debts and funeral expenses and to satisfy the plaintiffs, and that as a result of not being paid the £200 the plaintiffs lost the profit they would have made in trading with it, to their damage of £240. The defendant pleaded *Non assumpsit*, and on 24 July 1609 at Chelmsford assizes (Walmsley and Croke JJ.) the jury found for the plaintiffs with £300 damages.

(a) King's Bench: LI MS. Hill 122, fo. 80v.

. . . *Stevens* moved that the action does not lie, because (1) it is upon a simple contract without specialty, and (2) because it is not averred that the defendant had assets to pay all legacies besides

---

6 (1595) KB 27/1333, m. 155; cited in Moo. K.B. 702; reported in MS.

7 *Stubbings v Rotherham* (1595) KB 27/1330, m. 551; Cro. Eliz. 454; Moo. K.B. 691.

8 *Cleymond v Vyncent* (1520); p. 446, above.

9 (1557); see p. 448, above.

this. But, notwithstanding both these exceptions, it was ruled by
YELVERTON and WILLIAMS JJ. (alone in banc) that the plaintiff[s]
should recover, and that without argument. (It was an Essex case,
and *Courtman* was for the plaintiff[s].)

The record shows that judgment was given for the plaintiffs on 23 January
1611. The technical problem that the jury had awarded more than the
plaintiffs claimed was resolved by the plaintiffs waiving £60 of the damages,
so that judgment was entered for £240, with £13 costs. On 20 April 1611 a
transcript of the record was sent to the Exchequer Chamber upon a writ of
error brought by Legat.

(b) Exchequer Chamber: 9 Co. Rep. 86.[10]

... the principal error which was assigned was that no action upon
the case upon *assumpsit* for payment of the said debt lies against
executors. And it was argued for the plaintiff in the writ of error
that the action did not lie; for it is a maxim in law that executors
shall not be charged with a simple contract, and that for two
reasons. One because by the presumption of law they cannot have
knowledge either of the beginning of the debt (being made by word
without writing) or of the continuance of it, because the testator
might pay it privately between themselves ... and if an action on
the case would lie against executors it would impugn the said
maxim of the common law, for every contract executory implies an
assumpsit in law, and by consequence the executors would be
charged with every contract executory, which would be directly
against the said maxim. Another reason was added, that this action
on the case upon *assumpsit* is *actio personalis, quae moritur cum
persona*; for the entry in this case is 'in a plea of trespass on the
case'; and therefore it does not lie against executors...
   And this case depended in consideration for several terms, and
after many arguments on both sides and conferences had amongst
the judges—namely, COKE C.J.C.P., TANFIELD C.B., WARBURTON
J., SNIGGE B., ALTHAM B., FOSTER J. and BROMLEY B.[11]—it was
resolved by them all and with one voice (*nullo contradicente*) that
the action on the case against the executors in the case at the bar
well lay: and that not only without impugning any rule or reason of
law, or any book resolved in the point, but also well warranted and
confirmed by various authorities in law, judgments, and resolu-

10   Also reported in Cro. Jac. 294; 2 Bro. & Golds. 137.
11   The name of Walmsley J. is, significantly, missing from this list.

tions, both recent and ancient . . .[12] As to the other objection, that this personal action of trespass on the case dies with the person: although it is termed 'trespass', in respect that the breach of promise is alleged to be mixed with fraud and deceit to the special prejudice of the plaintiff, and for that reason it is called 'trespass on the case', yet that does not make the action so annexed to the persons of the parties that it shall die with the persons—for then if he to whom the promise is made dies, his executors should not have any action, which no man would affirm . . .[13] So that, upon all these authorities, judgments and resolutions, and for the reasons aforesaid . . . it was unanimously, upon long and mature deliberation, adjudged that the judgment given in the King's Bench should be affirmed . . .[14]

The record shows that the judgment was affirmed by the Exchequer Chamber on 19 October 1611, and the plaintiffs' costs increased by £5.

12 A number of Y.B. cases to the effect that debt would not lie against executors, without specialty, are next explained on the ground that wager of law was available. But in cases where wager of law was not available *inter vivos* (as in debt for a labourer's salary) the action always lay against executors. Coke concluded that the effect of the decision in *Slade's Case* was therefore to enable *assumpsit* (in which there was no wager of law) to be brought against executors in all cases, and 'no birthright or privilege of the subject is taken away by this resolution, but thereby justice and right is advanced, since the creditor shall be paid his just and true debt'.

13 Coke then discusses *Norwood v Norwood and Rede* (see p. 448, above) and *Cleymond v Vyncent* (see p. 446, above), which 'remaining yet of record in full force ought not to be discredited or disgraced by the bare saying of a judge upon a sudden motion at the bar'. Various precedents are also considered.

14 According to Croke's report, Coke C.J. 'willed the students to observe that this is now adjudged by all the judges and barons of all the courts'.

18 Various developments of the money counts

(1) Actions on bills of exchange

WOODFORD v WYATT (1626)

HLS MS. 106, fo. 263 (Exchequer Chamber).

An action on the case upon an *assumpsit* was brought by Woodford against Wyatt, grounded on a bill of exchange. Judgment was given in the King's Bench, and upon a writ of error brought [these] errors were assigned:

1 It was laid to be a custom of the city of London that if any merchant in London sent his bill of exchange to a merchant in parts beyond the sea, and that merchant accepted and subscribed it, this amounted to an *assumpsit*: whereas the custom of London can only extend to London, and not to any place beyond the sea. But this was not allowed, for this action is founded on a particular promise made by Wyatt and not on the custom of merchants.

2 The custom is laid as extending to places beyond the sea, but the execution of this custom is laid at Hamburg in the parish and ward of Cheap, London, which is not a place in parts beyond the sea. But this was not allowed, for it is so laid for necessity of trial, according to the books . . .[1]

3 The *assumpsit* is laid 'that if D. E. did not pay, he would pay', and D. E. is not any known name. But this was not allowed, for he ought to be named in the same way as he is named in the promise.

---

1 E.g., Y.B. Pas. 20 Hen. VI, fo. 28, pl. 21 (bond made in Paris); Mich. 15 Edw. IV, fo. 14, pl. 18 (Calais in Kent). See also Hil. 48 Edw. III, fo. 2, pl. 6 (Harfleur in Kent).

And [so] the judgment was affirmed in the Exchequer Chamber.

BROWNE v LONDON (1671)

Record: KB 27/1919, m. 523. In Michaelmas term 1669 Alexander Browne brought a bill of trespass on the case against William London, merchant. The first count set out the custom of merchants that the acceptor of a bill of exchange was chargeable (*onerabilis*) with the payment of the sum mentioned in the bill; and that on 18 January 1668 the defendant accepted a bill drawn by Philip Willimson, merchant, at Newcastle, requesting him to pay £53. 4s. 8d. to the plaintiff; and that in consideration thereof the defendant undertook to pay that sum to the plaintiff. The second count set out more generally—omitting the custom—that the defendant was on 1 May 1668 indebted to the plaintiff in £53. 4s. 8d. unpaid upon another[2] bill of exchange drawn by Willimson and accepted by him according to the custom of merchants, and in consideration thereof undertook to pay. London pleaded *Non assumpsit*, and on 2 August at Newcastle assizes (Christopher Turnor and Littleton BB.) the jury found for the plaintiff on the second count, with £59. 4s. 8d. damages. The defendant moved in arrest of judgment in Michaelmas term 1670.

1 Mod. 285, pl. 32 (untr.).[3]

Indebitatus assumpsit for £53 due to the plaintiff upon a bill of exchange drawn upon the defendant, and accepted by him according to the custom of merchants. After a verdict for the plaintiff, it was moved in arrest of judgment that, though an action upon the case does well lie in such case upon the custom of merchants, yet an *indebitatus* may not be brought thereupon . . .

RAYNSFORD J. This is the very same with *Milton's Case*,[4] lately in the Court of Exchequer, where it was adjudged that an *indebitatus assumpsit* would not lie. In this case he added that the verdict would not help it; for though [Hale] C.B. said it were well if the law were otherwise, yet he and we all agreed that a bill of exchange accepted was indeed a good ground for a special action upon the case, but that it did not make a debt. First, because the acceptance is but conditional on both sides: if the money be not received it returns back upon the drawer of the bill; he remains liable still, and this is but collateral. Secondly, because the word 'chargeable'

---

2 Plainly a fiction, designed to prevent recovery on both counts.
3 Also reported this term in 2 Keb. 695, 713; 1 Lev. 298; (Pas. 1671) 2 Keb. 758; (Mich. 1671) 2 Keb. 822; 1 Vent. 152.
4 (1668); see p. 248, above. It was actually an action of debt, but the point was the same.

(*onerabilis*) doth not imply debt. Thirdly, because the case is *primae impressionis*; there is no precedent for it . . .

Judgment was given for the defendant (Twisden J. hesitating) in Michaelmas term 1671: record; 2 Keb. 822; 1 Vent. 152. But it was agreed that if money had been paid to the acceptor, the payee could have brought *indebitatus* for money had and received.

SARSFIELD v WITHERLEY (1689)

Record: KB 27/2056, mm. 645–646. Francis Sarsfield brought a bill in the King's Bench against Hamond Witherley and set out the custom among merchants and other persons living and trading (*negotiantes*) in Paris and London respectively that if such a person made a bill of exchange in Paris directed to another such person in London, and the payee indorsed it to another, who in turn indorsed it to another, and notice of the indorsements was given to the drawee, and the drawee did not pay the second indorsee, the latter could protest the bill according to the custom of merchants; and if the first indorsee then paid the sum in the bill the drawer became chargeable to him in that sum. The bill then alleged that the defendant, on 5 August 1677 at Paris (in the parish of St Mary-le-Bow, London), drew a bill on Thomas Witherley M.D. in London, requiring him to pay £74 to William Ellis, merchant; that Ellis on 10 August indorsed the bill to order of Francis Sarsfield, merchant (the plaintiff), and that on 1 September Sarsfield indorsed it to John Comyn, merchant; that the sum was not paid to Comyn, who protested the bill; that on 20 September 1681 Sarsfield paid Comyn himself, as a result of which the defendant became chargeable to him in £74; and that the defendant, in consideration thereof, undertook on 20 September to pay him. The bill also contained a count in *indebitatus assumpsit* for £74 as money laid out to the plaintiff's use. The defendant pleaded that he was the son and heir apparent of Dr. Witherley, who was never a merchant, and that at the time in question he was travelling abroad as an English gentleman in order to see foreign parts and people and to note and understand their customs and languages, and was at Paris as a gentleman traveller, without this that he was ever a merchant. The plaintiff demurred, and on 12 February 1687 the King's Bench gave judgment for the defendant. Sarsfield brought a writ of error, and in May the record was removed into the Exchequer Chamber.

1 Show. K.B. 125 (untr.).[5]

. . . I[6] argued for the plaintiff that this plea was ill, because it did amount to the general issue . . . Besides, the matter of the plea is ill, for it is repugnant in itself, for he admits himself to have drawn the

---

5   Also reported in Comb. 152; 2 Vent. 292. Abridged in Holt 112.
6   Sir Bartholomew Shower, the reporter.

bill, and yet traverses that he never was a merchant, whereas the bare negotiating of a bill of exchange makes him a merchant for that purpose. The very act of taking up moneys in a foreign country, and undertaking for the repayment here by bill of exchange, is such an act of merchandise as you will take notice of. Moneys are now become merchandise, and some men's business is wholly in its exchange . . . Besides, the inconveniency will be great both at home and abroad and work a manifest wrong. If a bill be payable to him he has the advantage of it, though a gentleman, and by the same argument he ought to be bound. If a traveller's bill, drawn beyond sea, shall not enforce a payment upon a protest, our English gentry must suffer in their credit . . .

Hoyle to the contrary. By their own showing he must be a merchant, else not within the custom; and [the defendant] traversed that, and they have confessed it by their demurrer.

[POLLEXFEN C.J.][7] It is not every plea that amounts to a general issue that is ill; and the custom is the foundation, and the plea is an answer to that, and therefore well enough. But this drawing a bill must surely make him a trader for that purpose; for we all have bills directed to us, or payable to us, which must be all avoidable if the negotiating a bill will not oblige . . .

And so we had judgment reversed . . .

The record shows that the judgment was reversed on 23 November 1689. After a writ of inquiry as to the damages, judgment was signed in the King's Bench the following term for £128. 14s. 7d. damages and £38. 5s. 5d. costs.

CLERKE v MARTIN (1702)

2 Ld Raym. 757 (untr.).[8]

The plaintiff brought an action upon his case against the defendant upon several promises; one count was upon a general *indebitatus assumpsit* for money lent to the defendant; another count was upon the custom of merchants as upon a bill of exchange, and showed that the defendant gave a note subscribed by himself by which he promised to pay [a certain sum] to the plaintiff or his order. Upon *Non assumpsit* a verdict was given for the plaintiff, and entire

---

7 The report says Holt, who was C.J.K.B. It must have been Pollexfen C.J.C.P. who gave judgment in the Exchequer Chamber: cf. Comb. 152.

8 Also reported in 1 Salk. 129, 364.

damages. And it was moved in arrest of judgment that this note was not a bill of exchange within the custom of merchants, and therefore the plaintiff (having declared upon it as such) was wrong; but that the proper way in such cases is to declare upon a general *indebitatus assumpsit* for money lent, and the note would be good evidence of it.

But it was argued by *Sir Bartholomew Shower* the last Michaelmas term for the plaintiff, that this note—being payable to the plaintiff or his order—was a bill of exchange, inasmuch as by its nature it was negotiable; and that distinguishes it from a note payable to John Style or bearer, which he admitted was not a bill of exchange because it is not assignable nor indorsable by the intent of the subscriber ... There is no difference in reason between a note which saith, 'I promise to pay John Style or order etc.', and a note which saith, 'I pray you to pay John Style or order etc.': they are both equally negotiable. And to make such a note a bill of exchange can be no wrong to the defendant, because he by the signing of the note has made himself to that purpose a merchant (*Sarsfield v Witherley*[9]), and has given his consent that his note shall be negotiated, and thereby has subjected himself to the law of merchants.

But HOLT C.J. was *totis viribus* against the action, and said that this note could not be a bill of exchange; that the maintaining of these actions upon such notes were innovations upon the rules of the common law; and that it amounted to the setting up a new sort of specialty, unknown to the common law, and invented in Lombard Street—which attempted in these matters of bills of exchange to give laws to Westminster Hall; that the continuing to declare upon these notes upon the custom of merchants proceeded from obstinacy and opinionativeness, since he had always expressed his opinion against them, and since there was so easy a method (as to declare upon a general *indebitatus assumpsit* for money lent.) As to the case of *Sarsfield v Witherley*, he said he was not satisfied with the judgment of the King's Bench and that he advised the bringing of a writ or error ...

And judgment was given that the plaintiff take nothing by his bill, by the opinion of the whole court.

As a consequence of this and similar pronouncements by Holt C.J. against

9 (1689); see p. 460, above.

the actionability of promissory notes in this manner, Parliament enacted in 1705 (3 & 4 Ann., c. 8/9) that notes should be negotiable and actionable in the same manner as bills of exchange.

(2) Quantum meruit

SHEPHERD v EDWARDS (1615)

Cro. Jac. 370, pl. 4 (untr.).

Error of a judgment in Exeter, before the mayor and bailiffs there. The error assigned was because that Edwards the plaintiff declared that, he being a professor of physic and surgery,[10] and so having been for divers years, and the defendant being troubled with a disease called a fistula and in danger of his life by reason of that disease, the defendant on 26 March 1603 in consideration that the plaintiff at the defendant's request would with his best skill apply wholesome medicines for the curing the defendant of his disease, and would also give and bestow his labour and counsel to the said defendant in that behalf, assumed and promised to pay to him upon request 'such a sum of money as the plaintiff should deserve for his labour and counsel in and about the cure of the aforesaid disease'; and alleges in fact that the plaintiff on the said 26 March 1603 and on various other days and occasions betwixt the said 26 March and the last of February following, according to his best skill, caused to be applied divers medicines for cure of the said disease, and gave his counsel and bestowed his labour in that behalf throughout that time; and that the defendant, as well by the means of the said medicines as by the labour and counsel of the plaintiff, was by the said last of February [1604] well cured of the said disease and made whole; and he saith in fact that 'he well deserves £100 for his labour and counsel bestowed about the curing of the said disease', and that the defendant, although he had been required, had not paid the said £100 or any part thereof. The defendant pleaded *Non assumpsit*, and it was found against him, and thereupon the plaintiff had judgment; although it was objected that 'as much as he should deserve' (*quantum mereret*) is insufficient and uncertain.

---

10 See p. 648, below.

(3) The general *indebitatus* count

WOODFORD v DEACON (1608)

Cro. Jac. 206, pl. 2 (untr.).

Error in the Exchequer Chamber of a judgment in the King's Bench. The error assigned because the plaintiff in an *assumpsit* declares that the defendant, being indebted unto him, assumed to pay etc., and doth not shew for what cause the debt grew: viz. for rent, or by specialty, or by record; and if by any of those means, a general *assumpsit* lies not.

And for this cause all the judges and barons held it to be error. But if it had been, that he 'being indebted for divers wares sold' (or for such like contract) assumed to pay etc., it had been good enough for the generality thereof. And because a recovery in this action should be a bar of such a debt, therefore for this reason it was reversed; although it was objected that there be many precedents of such actions in the King's Bench.

The like judgment was given between *Fayreclough* and *Seed*. And Mich. 6 Jac. *Buckingham v Costerden, quod vide postea.*[11]

(4) Goods sold

BELLINGER v GARDINER (1614)

1 Rolle Rep. 24, pl. 1; LI MS. Maynard 22, fo. 76.[12]

An action on the case was brought in the King's Bench upon a promise, and the plaintiff declared that the defendant, being indebted to him 'both for depasturing [his beasts in the plaintiff's ground] and for wheat and various other merchandises bought'

---

11   Cro. Jac. 213 (K.B.). See also *Tirwhit v Kynaston* (1607) CUL MS. Gg. 5. 6, fo. 56v; Noy 146; *Ivers v Ingram* (1609) ibid.; *Limbey v Hemmurse* (1610) 1 Buls. 67; *Paschall v Russell* (*c.* 1610), cited in Palm. 171; *Occould's Case* (1612) Godb. 186; *Beckingham v Vaughan* (1616) 1 Rolle Rep. 391; *Barker v Barker* (1621) Palm. 171; *Mayor v Harre* (1622) Cro. Jac. 642; *Anon.* (1624) Hetley 107; *Holme v Lucas* (1625) Cro. Car. 6; *Foster v Smith* (1626) Cro. Car. 31; *Hern v Stubbs* (1627) Godb. 400; *Cooke v Samburne* (1664) 1 Sid. 182; *Moore v Lewis* (1669) 1 Vent. 27; *Wise v Wise* (1675) 2 Lev. 152; *Potter v James* (1693) Comb. 187, 12 Mod. 16, 1 Show. K.B. 347.

12   Also reported in Hob. 5, where there is an incorrect plea roll reference.

undertook to pay this money. Upon this judgment was given, and it was now assigned as error [in the Exchequer Chamber] by *Coventry* that 'for various merchandises' is uncertain, and so the declaration wants substance; just as an action on the case upon a general *indebitatus assumpsit* is ill.

But it was resolved that the declaration here is good enough.

ALTHAM B. If a man brings debt on an *insimul computaverunt*, it is too general and uncertain; but if he says that the defendant accounted 'for various sums of money' it is good enough. And in our case some things are specified, and therefore it is good enough.

TANFIELD C.B. The reason why a general *indebitatus assumpsit* is not good was always given in the King's Bench, when I was a practitioner there, to be that it might be he was indebted for rent— which is real [and not][13] personal—because you ought not to put them in hotchpot together. But here it is apparent that all are personal, for 'merchandises' imports as much: though if he had said 'for various things' I think it would not have been good.

The judgment was affirmed by them all.

(5) Money had and received

BECKINGHAM AND LAMBERT v VAUGHAN (1616)

It seems from the two reports that the declaration was to the effect that, whereas the defendant was indebted to the plaintiffs in various sums amounting in all to £24 which were received by him by the hands of various persons to the use of the plaintiffs: the defendant, in consideration thereof, undertook to pay the £24 to the plaintiffs, but did not do so. The jury found for the plaintiffs.

1 Rolle Rep. 391, pl. 11.[14]

It was moved in arrest of judgment by *Harris* that the declaration is not good. The case is as follows: a man delivers money to my use, may I have an action on the case for it? It seems not, because I shall not have an action of debt for it, but account; as in 41 Edw. III[15]. . .

---

13 MS. Garbled in print.
14 Also reported in Moo. K.B. 854.
15 See p. 291, above.

COKE C.J. thought the contrary, and that he may have debt or account at his election ...

But *Harris* took another exception: namely that the declaration says, 'whereas the defendant was indebted for various sums received by him by the hands of various persons', without stating what persons.

COKE C.J. and HOUGHTON J. thought it sufficient, since this is not traversable.[16]

And judgment was given for the plaintiff.

But *Harris* said that this[17] is to be proved by evidence.

ARRIS v STEWKLY (1677)

Record: E13/706, m. 17. Thomas Arris, sen., M.D., and Thomas Arris, jun., brought a bill of *quominus* in the Exchequer against Scipio Stewkly in an action of *indebitatus assumpsit* for £200 had and received to the plaintiffs' use at Totnes, Devon, on 10 July 1676. The defendant pleaded *Non assumpsit*, but failed to appear at the trial. On 24 March 1677 the jury at Exeter Castle (before Jones J.) found a special verdict: that by letters patent dated 17 August 1660 the king granted John Holle and the defendant the office of comptroller of the port of Exeter, during pleasure; that Holle died in 1669, and the defendant continued to execute the office and receive fees; and that after Holle's death the king by letters patent granted the office to the plaintiffs; but whether upon the whole matter the defendant *assumpsit* in the manner alleged, the jurors did not know. They assessed the damages as £100, in case this should be adjudged a verdict for the plaintiff. The first question argued in banc was whether the later patent was valid; but counsel for the defendant also questioned the form of action.

2 Mod. 260, pl. 148 (untr.).

... *Pollexfen*, for the defendant. A general *indebitatus assumpsit* will not lie here for want of a privity, and because there is no contract. It is only a tort, a disseisin, and the plaintiff might have brought an assize for this office, which lies at the common law, ... [or] an action on the case against the defendant for disturbing of him in his office; and that had been good, because it had been grounded on the wrong. In this case the defendant takes the profits against the will of the plaintiff, and so there is no contract. But if he had received them by the consent of the plaintiff, yet this action would not lie, for want of privity. It is true, in the case of the king, where his rents are wrongfully received, the party may be charged

---

16   Cf. Moo. K.B.: '... because it is a consideration executed, and so not traversable ...'
17   I.e. the receipt of money from various people.

to give an account as bailiff; so also may the executors of his accountant, because the law creates a privity; but it is otherwise in the case of a common person . . . because in all actions of debt there must be a contract, or *quasi ex contractu . . .*

Winnington S.-G. and *Sawyer*, to the contrary, said that an *indebitatus assumpsit* would lie here; for where one receives my rent, I may charge him as bailiff or receiver; or if anyone receive my money without my order, though it is a tort, yet an *indebitatus* will lie, because by reason of the money the law creates a promise. And the action is not grounded on the tort, but on the receipt of the profits in this case.

THE COURT. An *indebitatus* will lie for rent received by one who pretends a title; for in such case an account will lie.[18] Wherever the plaintiff may have an account, an *indebitatus* will lie . . .

And in the Michaelmas term following the court gave judgment for the plaintiff.

The record confirms that in Michaelmas term 1677 the court gave judgment for the plaintiffs, to recover £100 damages and £25 costs. It also shows that on 27 November the defendant obtained a writ of error, and that on 9 February 1678 in the Council Chamber[19] (in the presence of Raynsford C.J.K.B. and North C.J.C.P.) the judgment was affirmed.

MARTIN v SITWELL (1691)

1 Show. K.B. 156, pl. 123 (untr.).[20]

Indebitatus assumpsit for £5 received by the defendant to the plaintiff's use. *Non assumpsit* pleaded. Upon evidence it appeared that one Barksdale had made a policy of assurance upon account for £5 premium in the plaintiff's name, and that he had paid the said premium to the defendant, and that Barksdale had no goods then on board, and so the policy was void and the money to be returned by the custom of merchants.

At the trial I[1] urged these two points. First, that the action ought to have been brought in Barksdale's name, for the money was his: we received it from him, and if the policy had been good it would have been to his advantage; and upon no account could it be said

18 Cf. *Tottenham v Bedingfield* (1572); see p. 295, above.
19 I.e. the statutory court of error erected by 31 Edw. III, stat. 1, c. 12. It is usually referred to as the Exchequer Chamber, though the statute refers to 'any council chamber near the Exchequer' and this terminology is followed in the record.
20 Also reported in Holt 25.
1 Sir Bartholomew Shower, the reporter.

to be received to Martin's use, it never being his money. Besides, here may be a great fraud upon all insurers, in this, that an insurance may be in another man's name, and if a loss happen then the insurer shall pay for that some cestuy que trust had goods on board: if the ship arrive, then the nominal trustee shall bring a general *indebitatus* for the premium as having no goods on board.

To all which HOLT C.J. answered that, the policy being in Martin's name, the premium was paid in his name and as his money; and he must bring the action upon a loss, and so upon avoidance of the policy for to recover back the premium. And as to the inconveniences, it would be the same whosoever was to bring the action; and therefore the insurers ought with caution to look to that beforehand.

Then, secondly, I urged that it ought to have been a special action of the case upon the custom of merchants; for this money was once well paid, and then by the custom it is to be returned upon matter happening *ex post facto*. I argued, if the first payment were made void, then the law will construe it to be to the plaintiff's use, and so an *indebitatus assumpsit* will lie. But when a special custom appoints a return of the premium, an *indebitatus* lies not as for money received to the plaintiff's use, but a special action of the case upon that particular custom.

To which HOLT C.J. answered me with the case adjudged by Wadham Wyndham J.[2] of money deposited upon a wager concerning a race, that the party winning the race might bring an *indebitatus* for money received to his use, for now by this subsequent matter it is become as such. And as to our case, the money is not only to be returned by the custom, but the policy is made originally void, the party for whose use it was made having no goods on board; so that by this discovery the money was received without any reason, occasion or consideration, and consequently it was originally received to the plaintiff's use.

And so judgment was for the plaintiff against my client.

ANON. (1695)

Comb. 341 (untr.): *nisi prius* at Guildhall, London,
14 June 1695.

An *indebitatus assumpsit* was brought for money had and received to the plaintiff's use, and the plaintiff gives in evidence that he is a burgess of Westminster and the defendant bailiff there, and that

2   J.K.B. 1660–68.

the plaintiff gave the defendant £9 to be excused from fines for non-appearance at the court and from the offices of constable and scavenger,[3] which the defendant took, promising to excuse him; and at the next court the plaintiff was fined.

HOLT C.J. Away with your *indebitatus*, 'tis but a bargain.

Shower, for the plaintiff. Where a Custom House officer hath taken a bribe not to make a seizure, it hath been often ruled that an *indebitatus* lieth.

HOLT C.J. Never by me. I think it hath been carried too far, and I will retrench them. I confess, where a man is overreached upon an account etc. and pays more than is due, it hath prevailed that an *indebitatus* lieth: and that is as far as it ought to go. I would discourage such foolish bargains as this.

Shower. It hath been resolved that if A. pays money to B. to the use of C., and B. fails to pay it over, either A. or C. may bring an *indebitatus*.

HOLT C.J. Aye, but that's not like this case. I have known an *indebitatus* brought 'for various amercements'; but 'tis most certain no *indebitatus* lieth for a duty.

Plaintiff non-suited.

ANON. (1697)

Comb. 446 (untr.): *nisi prius* at Guildhall, London,
22 June 1697.

HOLT C.J. An *indebitatus assumpsit* hath been carried too far. There was one before me for money received to the plaintiff's use, and it appeared it was upon a bond, and the plaintiff would suggest the contract was usurious: but I would not allow it. Where, upon a reckoning, a man receives more from me than he ought, an *indebitatus* will lie; nay, it hath prevailed further, where money [was] paid for fees which were not justly due (though it is hard to maintain that). But where there is a bargain, though a corrupt one, or where one sells goods that were not his own, I will never allow an *indebitatus*.

HUSSEY v FIDDALL (1699)

12 Mod. 324, pl. 558 (untr.).[4]

Error of a judgment in the Common Pleas, in an *indebitatus*

---

3 See pp. 476–477, below.
4 Also reported in 3 Salk. 59; Holt 95.

assumpsit by the assignee of a commissioner of bankrupt[cy]. The exception was that it was for goods sold after the bankruptcy committed, and the action should be trover; and debt would not lie therefor, because trover might be brought for it again.

HOLT C.J. They may avoid the sale, if they will, and bring trover for the goods; but if they bring the one, they shall not afterwards bring the other . . . And without doubt the action well lies here, and even a general *indebitatus* would have done.

Northey, at the bar. If a man receives a thing to my use, I may say that it was received to my use, and bring the proper action in such case; or, without any such suggestion, bring trover.

HOLT C.J. *Indebitatus* was brought for money received upon a usurious contract, but it was held that it would not lie.[5] And Kelyng C.J.[6] would allow it against a receiver or factor, but Hale C.J.[7] would not. By my consent it shall go as far as it has gone, but not a step further. It has been held to lie for a fine by custom;[8] but surely that was hard, for it was to leave matter of law to a jury.

But *Northey* said, some strains had been in favour of remedy; and he said that if a man, pretending title to my land, receive my rent, and get my tenants to attorn to him, an *indebitatus* had been maintained for the money.

Which HOLT C.J. agreed; but said that had been very hard too.

LAMINE v DORRELL (1705)

2 Ld Raym. 1216 (Q.B.).

In an *indebitatus assumpsit* for money received by the defendant to the use of the plaintiff as administrator of J.S., on *Non assumpsit* pleaded, upon evidence the case appeared to be that J.S. died intestate possessed of certain Irish debentures, and the defendant (pretending to a right to be administrator) got administration granted to him, and by that means got these debentures into his hands and disposed of them; then the defendant's administration was repealed, and administration granted to the plaintiff, and he brought this action against the defendant for the money he sold the debentures for. And, it being objected upon the evidence that this action would not lie, because the defendant sold the debentures as one that claimed a title and interest in them, and therefore could

5   *Tomkins v Bernet* (1693) 1 Salk. 22.
6   Sir John Kelyng, C.J.K.B. 1665–71.
7   Sir Matthew Hale, C.J.K.B. 1671–76.
8   *Shuttleworth v Garnett* (1689); p. 480, below.

not be said to receive the money for the use of the plaintiff which indeed he received to his own use, but the plaintiff ought to have brought trover or detinue for the debentures: the point was saved to the defendant. And now the court was moved, and the same objection made.

POWELL J. It is clear the plaintiff might have maintained detinue or trover for the debentures; but when the act that is done is in its nature tortious, it is hard to turn that into a contract, and against the reason of *assumpsit*. But the plaintiff may dispense with the wrong[9] and suppose the sale made by his consent, and bring an action for the money they were sold for as money received to his use. It has been carried thus far already. *Howard v Wood*[10] is as far: there the title of the office was tried in an action for the profits.

HOLT C.J. These actions have crept in by degrees. I remember, in the case of Mr. Aston,[11] in a dispute about the title to the office of clerk of the papers in this court, there were great counsel consulted with; and Sir William Jones and Mr. Saunders were of opinion, an *indebitatus assumpsit* would not lie, upon meeting and conferring together and great consideration. If two men reckon together, and one overpays the other, the proper remedy in that case is a special action for the money overpaid,[12] or an account; and yet in that case you constantly bring an *indebitatus assumpsit* for money had and received to the plaintiff's use. Suppose a person pretends to be guardian in socage, and enters into the land of the infant and takes the profits, though he is not rightful guardian, yet an action of account will lie against him. So, the defendant in this case pretending to receive the money the debentures were sold for in the right of the intestate, why should he not be answerable for it to the intestate's administrator? If an action of trover should be brought by the plaintiff for these debentures after judgment in this *indebitatus assumpsit*, he may plead this recovery in bar of the action of trover . . . This recovery may be given in evidence upon

9 I.e. 'waive the tort'.
10 (1680); see p. 478, below.
11 *Woodward v Aston* (1676) KB 27/1974, m. 153; reported in 1 Mod. 95; 1 Vent. 296; 1 Freem. 429. Francis Woodward brought *indebitatus assumpsit* against Richard Aston for £10 had and received to the plaintiff's use at the parish of St Clement Danes on 4 February 1676. Both parties are named as clerks of Robert Henley, chief clerk of the King's Bench, but there is no mention of the office of clerk of the papers. Aston pleaded *Non assumpsit*, and we know only from the reports that the dispute about the clerkship emerged in evidence at the trial. Although nothing is recorded beyond the *venire facias*, the reports indicate that the plaintiff was successful; but there was no discussion of the propriety of the form of action.
12 Presumably a special *indebitatus*, setting out the overpayment in the count.

Not guilty in the action of trover, because by this action the plaintiff makes and affirms the act of the defendant in the sale of the debentures to be lawful, and consequently the sale of them is no conversion.

Afterwards, the last day of the term, upon motion to the court, they gave judgment for the plaintiff.

And HOLT C.J. said that he could not see how it differed from an *indebitatus assumpsit* for the profits of an office by a rightful owner against a wrongful, as money had and received by the wrongful officer to the use of the rightful.

(6) Money laid out and work done

WIDDRINGTON v GODDARD (1664)

Bill of complaint, from KB 27/1865, m. 778;
A. Vidian, *The Exact Pleader* (1684), p. 12 (omitting
the names). The bill contains both a special *assumpsit*
(including a *quantum meruit* claim) and an *indebitatus*.

Cambridgeshire. Ralph Widdrington, S.T.P., complains against Guybon Goddard,[13] esquire, in the custody of the marshal etc., that, whereas the same Ralph on 21 February [1660] in the twelfth year of the reign[14] of the lord Charles the second now king of England etc. and continually from thence until 1 March [1661] in the thirteenth year of the reign of the said present lord king has been and still is one of the fellows of Christ's College in the university of Cambridge, being apt and able by the laws and statutes both of the aforesaid university and of the aforesaid college to undertake the care, tuition and instruction of the young students dwelling and studying in the college and university aforesaid, as the tutor of such students, and (the said Ralph thus being, as before mentioned, a fellow of the aforesaid college and being apt and able as aforesaid) the same Guybon afterwards, namely on the aforesaid 1 March in the above-mentioned thirteenth year, at Cambridge aforesaid in the county aforesaid, in consideration that the same Ralph at the special instance and request[15] of the selfsame Guybon had for the space of one year (between 21 February in the above-mentioned twelfth year and the

---

13 Bencher of Lincoln's Inn; serjeant at law 1669; d. 1671.
14 *De jure*, but before the restoration on 29 May 1660.
15 This insertion of a request prevented any objection that the consideration was past.

aforesaid 1 March in the above-mentioned thirteenth year) at Cambridge aforesaid in the county aforesaid undertaken the care, tuition and instruction of a certain Thomas Goddard, son of the aforesaid Guybon and a young student in the college aforesaid during the aforesaid period, as tutor of the selfsame Thomas, and had bestowed his labour and worked to instruct and help the selfsame Thomas in his studies during the aforesaid period, and had laid out and disbursed various sums of money amounting in all to £9[9]. 1s. 1d. of lawful money of England for the instruction of the selfsame Thomas in music, for food and drink, books, clothing and other things apt, necessary and suitable for the same Thomas according to the degree and quality of the selfsame Thomas, did take upon himself and then and there faithfully did promise the same Ralph that he the same Guybon would well and faithfully pay and content the same Ralph both the aforesaid £9[9]. 1s. 1d. and all such sums of money as the same Ralph reasonably deserved[16] to have for the tuition and instruction of the aforesaid Thomas during the period aforesaid; and the same Ralph says in fact that he the same Ralph reasonably deserves to have £8 of lawful money of England for the tuition and instruction of the aforesaid Thomas during the aforesaid period:

[17]Whereas also the aforesaid Guybon afterwards, namely on 2 April [1661] in the aforesaid thirteenth year, at Cambridge aforesaid in the county aforesaid, was indebted to the said Ralph in another £99. 1s. 1d. of similar money, both for his labour in the tuition of the aforesaid Thomas Goddard, son of the selfsame Guybon Goddard, bestowed by him the said Ralph before that time at the special instance and request of the selfsame Guybon, and for various sums of money before that time laid out and disbursed for the necessary and suitable learning and upkeep of the aforesaid Thomas at the like special instance and request of the selfsame Guybon; and, being so indebted, the same Guybon in consideration thereof afterwards (namely on the same day and in the same year) at Cambridge aforesaid in the county aforesaid took upon himself and then and there faithfully promised the same Ralph that he the same Guybon would well and faithfully content and pay the same Ralph the aforesaid £99. 1s. 1d.:

[18]Nevertheless the aforesaid Guybon, little regarding his several

16   *Quantum meruit.*
17   Alternative count in *indebitatus assumpsit* for labour and money laid out. The words 'another £99. 1s. 1d.' only thinly conceal a fiction. The practice of joining alternative counts in this way seems to have begun in the 17th century: the next case is another example.
18   Assignment of breach in respect of both counts.

promises and undertakings aforesaid, but scheming and fraudulently intending wickedly and craftily to deceive and defraud the same Ralph, has not yet paid the aforesaid several sums of money (amounting in all to £198. 2s. 2d.) or any penny thereof to the same Ralph, nor contented him for the same, although the same Guybon was afterwards (namely on 1 May [1662] in the fourteenth year of the reign of the said present lord king), at Cambridge aforesaid in the county aforesaid, often requested to do it; whereby the same Ralph says he is the worse and has damage to the amount of £100. And thereof he produces suit etc.

The record shows that on 10 June 1664 the defendant pleaded *Non assumpsit* and a jury was summoned. No more is entered.

R. v W. (c. 1670)

The Clerk's Manual (1678), p. 83.

This precedent illustrates three common counts laid as alternative claims in a King's Bench bill. A wigmaker sues for her charges (1) in an *indebitatus assumpsit* for work done, (2) on a *quantum meruit*,[19] and (3) on an *insimul computassent* or account stated.

Middlesex. Eleanor R. complains of Robert W., in the custody of the marshal etc., for this:

[1: *indebitatus for work done*]

Whereas the aforesaid Robert on 1 February [1668] in the twentieth year of the reign of the present lord King Charles II, at the parish of St Margaret's, Westminster, in the aforesaid county, was indebted to the aforesaid Eleanor in £3 of lawful money of England for her work and labour in making various periwigs (*capillamenta vocata* perrywigs) for the aforesaid Robert; and, being so indebted, the aforesaid Robert afterwards (namely on the same day in the same year) at the aforesaid parish of St Margaret's, Westminster, in the county aforesaid, in consideration thereof, took upon himself and then and there faithfully promised the same Eleanor that he the same Robert would well and faithfully content and pay the aforesaid £3 to the same Eleanor when he should be thereafter requested to do so;

---

19 Cf. T. Wood, *Institute of the Laws of England* (1724 ed.), p. 536: 'where a *quantum meruit* is laid, you need not prove any price agreed on ... so that in an action for goods sold or work done it is the best way to lay a *quantum meruit* with an *indebitatus assumpsit*; for if you fail in the proof of an express price agreed you will recover the value'.

[2: *quantum meruit*]

And whereas the aforesaid Eleanor, before the aforesaid 1 February [1668] in the twentieth year of the reign of the said lord king that now is, at the special instance and request of the aforesaid Robert, made and wove various periwigs for the aforesaid Robert; and the aforesaid Robert afterwards (namely on the aforesaid 1 February in the aforesaid twentieth year), at the aforesaid parish of St Margaret's, Westminster, in the county aforesaid, in consideration thereof, took upon himself and then and there faithfully promised the same Eleanor that he the same Robert would well and faithfully content and pay the same Eleanor as many sums of money as the aforesaid Eleanor should reasonably deserve to have for the same, when he should be requested to do so; and the same Eleanor says in fact that she reasonably deserved to have £3 of lawful money of England from the said Robert for the same;

[3: *account stated*]

And whereas also the aforesaid Eleanor and Robert afterwards, namely on 1 February [1668] in the aforesaid twentieth year of the reign of the said lord king that now is, at the aforesaid parish of St Margaret's, Westminster, in the county aforesaid, accounted together for various sums of money owed by the said Robert to the same Eleanor and not paid before that time; and upon that accounting the same Robert was then and there found to be in arrears as against the said Eleanor in another £3 of lawful money of England; and (being thus in arrears) the aforesaid Robert afterwards (namely on the same day in the same year), at the aforesaid parish of St Margaret's, Westminster, in the county aforesaid, in consideration thereof, took upon himself and then and there faithfully promised the same Eleanor that he the same Robert would well and faithfully content and pay the same Eleanor the aforesaid £3 last mentioned, when he should be requested to do so:

[*Assignment of breach*]

Nevertheless the aforesaid Robert, little regarding his several promises and undertakings,[20] but scheming and fraudulently intending wickedly and craftily to deceive and defraud the same Eleanor of the aforesaid sums of money, has not paid the aforesaid sums of money or any penny thereof to the aforesaid Eleanor according to his several promises and undertakings aforesaid,

---

20 The printed precedent ends here with an 'etc.' and refers generally to previous precedents. What follows is adapted from the precedent on p. 72 of *The Clerk's Manual* (1678).

though often requested by the aforesaid Eleanor to do so (namely on etc., at etc. in the county aforesaid), but until now has utterly refused to pay them to her and still refuses to do so. And thereby she says she is the worse and is damaged to the amount etc. And thereof she produces suit etc.

HIBBERT v COURTHOPE (1693)

Carthew 276 (untr.).[1]

Assumpsit etc., and judgment against the defendant by default. And now upon a writ of error brought, the error insisted on was that the declaration was general, namely, that the defendant was indebted to the plaintiff in so much money 'for the work and labour of the selfsame plaintiff before that time done and performed for the aforesaid defendant at the special instance and request of the aforesaid defendant', without setting forth what manner of work it was, so that it might appear to the court to be lawful—for it might be about some unlawful matter for which the law will not imply any promise etc.

But this was not accepted; for, *per curiam*, the only reason why the plaintiff is bound to shew wherein the defendant is indebted is that it may appear to the court that it is not a debt on record or specialty, but only upon a simple contract; and any general words by which that may be made to appear are sufficient.

The judgment was affirmed.

(7) Customary dues

CITY OF LONDON v GORAY (1676)

Record: KB 27/1972, m. 636. In Hilary term 1675 the mayor of London brought a bill of trespass on the case against Nicholas Goray.[2] The first count recited the custom of the city of London to receive a toll called

---

1 Also reported, sub nom. *Hebbert v Corsthorp*, in Skin. 409, where (in the previous term) another objection was taken: that the sum (£12) was expressed in figures as 'xii'. This was held not to be error, though it was said that '12' in Arabic numerals would have been.

2 Spelt 'Goree' in the report. He had previously been sued in debt for the same scavage, but in that case some problem arose concerning the city charter: KB 27/1965, m. 199 (undetermined demurrer).

scavage (or shewage)[3] on the goods of alien merchants brought into the port of London; and said that the defendant, an alien merchant, claimed 8,718 lb. of wrought silks (worth £17,436) brought into the port at Southwark; and that scavage was due on this merchandise at the rate of 1d. per 20s., that is, £72. 13s.; and that Goray, being so indebted, undertook in consideration thereof to pay the £72. 13s. on request. The second count was that on 1 January 1675 the defendant, being indebted to the mayor in another[4] £72. 13s. for scavage due upon merchandise, undertook in consideration thereof to pay the sum. On 24 January 1676 the defendant pleaded *Non assumpsit*, and on 6 March 1676 at Southwark assizes in Surrey (Twisden J., Pemberton Sjt.) the jury found for the defendant on the first count; and on the second count found a special verdict setting out the custom and circumstances in terms closely similar to the wording of the first count, so as to show that the £72. 13s. was due, but concluding that there was no 'actual' promise to pay. The case was argued in banc in Michaelmas term 1676.

3 Keb. 677, pl. 52 (untr.).[5]

... *Simpson*, for the plaintiff: that in *Carpenter's Case* here, and for the duty of water-bailage, *indebitatus* lieth.

And, by RAYNSFORD C.J.: in the Exchequer on argument it was adjudged that *indebitatus* lay upon acceptance of a bill of exchange.[6] And on a policy of assurance *indebitatus* lieth ... And all the actions for wharfage, cranage and duties of the city are thus: and in *Bradshaw v Proctor* for fees as judge of the Sheriffs' Court; and this term in *Woodward v Aston*,[7] *indebitatus* by one clerk against the other for fees. And the reason of *Slade's Case*[8] was not on the wager of law, but because he was not indebted. And by the act of parliament confirming the custom, this is a duty that ariseth *ex quasi contractu* and not *ex delicto*, though it were originally but a charge upon the subject; for, it being agreed that debt lieth, a fortiori an *indebitatus*.

Judgment for the plaintiff.

The record confirms that on 26 October 1676 judgment was given for the plaintiff, with £5. 6s. 8d. damages and £20. 3s. 4d. costs. It is not clear why the jury assessed the damages at such a low figure.

---

3 Keble says 'duty of waiage', which is perhaps a misprint. For scavage, see the statute 19 Hen. VII, c. 8.
4 Evidently a fiction: cf. *Browne v London* (1671), p. 459, above.
5 Also reported in 1 Freem. 433; 2 Lev. 174.
6 The contrary was held in *Milton's Case* (1668), p. 248, above. The mistake was doubtless the reporter's: cf. Raynsford J., p. 459, above.
7 (1676); see p. 471, fn. 11, above.
8 (1602); see p. 420, above.

HOWARD v WOOD (1680)

Record: KB 27/1987, m. 573. Sir Robert Howard and his son Thomas brought *indebitatus assumpsit* against Henry Wood, gentleman, for 60s. received to the plaintiffs' use on 2 April 1677, and for 100s. similarly received on 17 May 1677. Wood pleaded *Non assumpsit*; and on 1 February 1678 the jury at bar in Westminster Hall (before Raynsford C.J.) found the following facts by special verdict: the honour of Pontefract had in 1619 been leased in trust for Prince Charles, who became King Charles I in 1625; in 1629 the lease was assigned to trustees for Queen Henrietta, and in 1640 they granted the stewardship of the honour to the earl (later to become the duke) of Newcastle; and in 1660 the lease was reassigned in trust for Queen Henrietta for life and then for King Charles II; and in 1672 (after the queen mother's death) the king and the lessees granted the stewardship in reversion to the plaintiffs; later in 1672 the lease was reassigned to trustees for Queen Catherine, and in 1676 the queen and her trustees sub-let the honour to the above-mentioned duke of Newcastle, who further sub-let it to one Richard Mason; and Mason granted the stewardship to Henry Wood during pleasure; and after the death of the duke of Newcastle (in 1676) Wood, claiming the stewardship, had taken the sums of money as due to the steward. The principal question was whether the stewardship belonged to the plaintiffs or the defendant, but it was also argued that the form of action was inappropriate to try such a title.

(a) Mich. 1678: 2 Show. K.B. 21, pl. 14 (untr.).

. . . The next point is if the plaintiff, having a right to the place, can have an *indebitatus assumpsit*.

It was argued[9] that he might, because it is his money, and he has a right to it, and by construction of law the defendant received it to his use; and then the plaintiff, by bringing his action, gives his subsequent assent thereto. In the case of *Tottenham v Bedingfield*,[10] it is agreed that if one receives my rents I may implead him in a writ of account; and then by the bringing of my action there is privity. For I may make a privity by my own consent, and I may as well bring case as an account: and so is the case of *Lady Cavendish v Middleton*.[11] And for late authorities there have been two known cases express in the point: as that of *Arris v Stukely*[12] in the Exchequer, about a year since, . . . There was also in this court the cause of *Aston v Woodward*;[13] the two present clerks of the papers, concerning that office, tried at this bar in this action . . .

Mr. Bigland to the contrary. An assize properly lies of an office.

9 By Holt: 1 Freem. 473.
10 (1572); see p. 295, above.
11 (1628); see p. 523, below.
12 (1677); see p. 466, above.
13 (1676); see p. 471, fn. 1, above.

The books are full thereof. A special action of the case will lie, but not a general *indebitatus assumpsit*. There must be a contract or agreement of the parties before ever the law will raise a promise; therefore he thought the action would not lie. The declaration ought to be according to the fact. It is laid that the defendant received the fees 'to the use and profit of the plaintiff', whereas in truth he received them to his own use. This course will turn out assizes, and ejectments too, for they will now try all such titles by this action: nay, they may by the same reason try titles to land by bringing this action for the profits thereof . . .

(b) Hil. 1679: 2 Show. K.B. 24, pl. 14 (untr.).

SCROGGS C.J., in Hilary term following, delivered the opinion of the court: we have considered of the case by ourselves, and discoursed it together, and are agreed on both points. First, whether an *indebitatus assumpsit* lies against a man who receives the profits of an office, claiming a right. If this were now an original case, we are agreed it would by no means lie; for nothing then which might not be tried by itself. But because judgments have been upon it, and that on solemn arguments, and many judgments—though some passed *sub silencio*, yet others have been debated and settled, and particularly in the Exchequer[14]—we are therefore willing to go the same way, and are of an opinion that it is better to comply with things once used, that are not of very pernicious consequence, than to make one court thwart and contradict another in its judgments: and certainly the inconvenience is not so very great, since the title must be given in evidence, and so is well tried. We do upon that account adjudge that the action doth well lie . . .

[But at the importunity of *Jones* A.-G., to be further heard in this case, it was adjourned.][15]

T. Jones 125 reports that in Hilary term 1680 it was 'resolved by the whole court that the action lay, for it is an expeditious remedy, and facilitates the recovery of just rights; and this manner of action hath now prevailed for a long time, and the point hath been ruled often by the judges in their circuits, and actions frequently brought in this manner . . .'. The record confirms that in January 1680 judgment was entered for the plaintiffs to recover 21s. damages and £58. 19s. costs.

---

14 *Arris v Stewkley* (1677), p. 466, above. In *Woodward v Aston* (1676), p. 471, fn. 11, above, the point passed *sub silencio*.

15 From the different report in 2 Lev. 245 (dated Pas. 1679).

SHUTTLEWORTH v GARNETT (1689)

Record: KB 27/2068, m. 965. Lady Katharine Shuttleworth, widow and administratrix of Sir Richard Shuttleworth, brought a bill against John Garnett complaining that, whereas the defendant (being tenant of certain customary tenements in the manor of Barbon, Westmorland, the inheritance of which had descended to Sir Richard) was indebted to Sir Richard in £27 for a reasonable customary fine payable by him for the tenements which he had held of Sir Richard's father, and on 1 June 1686 in consideration thereof undertook to pay the £27; and whereas he was indebted in another £27 for a similar fine,[16] and on 20 June 1687 undertook to pay it: nevertheless the defendant, little regarding his undertakings, but scheming to defraud Sir Richard and his administratrix, had still not paid. Garnett pleaded *Non assumpsit*; and on 25 August 1688 at Appleby assizes (Wright C.J.K.B., Jenner J.C.P.) the jury found for the plaintiff with £27 damages and 40s. costs.

1 Show. K.B. 35, pl. 34 (untr.).[17]

. . . [*Thompson*][18] moved in arrest of judgment that the action doth not lie, because it savours of the realty; no more than *indebitatus* will lie for rent . . .

Against this it was argued by *Hoyle* and *Levinz* that this is a flower fallen. It is debt, and why should not an *assumpsit* lie? If reasonable, it is a contract; if unreasonable, it is void. Debt hath been held to lie. It is after a verdict. This is no more than a contract. If I agree to give my tenant a freehold estate, and he agree to give me a fine for it, an action on the case lies; so it does for the purchase money upon sale of lands. It will not lie for rent, because it is entirely in the realty. This is but a contract . . . In the case of *Howard v Wood*,[19] an *indebitatus* for the profits of an office, there they founded a contract upon a wrong. In the case of *The Mayor and Commonalty of London v Gory*,[20] an *indebitatus* was held to lie for scavage money. Where money is due, the law doth imply a contract . . .

16 This looks like a fiction: cf. pp. 459, 473, 474, 477, above, for alternative counts. Probably there were two undertakings to pay the same fine.
17 Also reported in 3 Lev. 261; Carthew 90; Comb. 151; 3 Mod. 239.
18 Cf. Comberbach's report '*Thompson* moved in arrest of judgment (the last term) that the action did [not] lie. That this fine don't arise by contract of the party, but by custom out of the land . . . An *indebitatus assumpsit* don't lie on a policy of assurance or bill of exchange. That no *indebitatus assumpsit* lieth where the cause of action is grounded on a custom'.
19 (1680); see p. 478, above.
20 (1676); see p. 476, above. Holt C.J. said of this (Carthew 92): 'the cases are not parallel, for the duty of scavage doth arise out of things in the personalty; but the duty in the principal case issued out of the realty'.

EYRE J. Debt lies for a copyholder's fine, and for scavage. And a stronger case than this is the case of the Lord North,[1] for moneys due for the value of a marriage, where the register gives a writ *de valore maritagii*. This is a sum in gross, a fruit fallen, a duty.

HOLT C.J. *Indebitatus* lies where wager of law will lie,[2] but this seems of an higher nature, so that wager of law would not lie if debt were brought . . . *Indebitatus* lies upon a personal contract for a sum in gross . . . if a man grants his land for a year and the party agrees to pay so much for it: this is a sum in gross for which an *indebitatus* lies. But here both the custom and tenure appear, and it is of an higher nature, so as the action will not lie.

DOLBEN J. It is a sum in gross, and a duty, for which the administrator of the heir to whom it was due upon the death of the lord hath no other remedy but this or debt . . .

GREGORY J. After a verdict we must intend a promise, and then it lies.

EYRE J. I think the action lies, it being a fruit fallen, and a duty.

And so, by three judges, judgment for the plaintiff (HOLT C.J. dissenting).

(8) Use and occupation of land

LEWIS v WALLACE (1752)

F. Buller, *Nisi Prius* (1768), p. 195 (K.B.).

In case for use and occupation of an house by permission of the plaintiff, the defendant pleaded *Nil habuit in tenementis*; and upon demurrer the court held it not a good plea, as it would be upon a lease at common law, because there an interest is supposed to have passed from the lessor; but here the court must take it that there was an express promise, and therefore if the plaintiff had an equitable title, or no title at all, yet if the defendant have enjoyed by permission of the plaintiff it is sufficient, and it is not necessary for the plaintiff to say it is his house—any more than in *assumpsit* for goods sold to say they were the goods of the plaintiff.

---

1   (1588) 2 Leon. 179.
2   Cf. Comberbach's report (per Holt C.J.): 'It doth not follow that an *indebitatus* lies because debt lies; where wager of law doth not lie, there an *indebitatus* don't lie, and it is mischievous to extend it further than *Slade's Case*: for an *indebitatus* is laid generally, and the defendant can't tell how to make his defence, but debt is laid more particularly'.

19 Consideration

GREGORY ADGORE'S READING ON USES (*c.* 1490)

Reading on 1 Ric. III, c. 1, in the Inner Temple:
CUL MS. Hh. 3. 10, fo. 19; UCO MS. 162, fo. 102;
LI MS. Maynard 3, fo. 191v; there is a fourth text in
KU MS. D127.

It is to be observed that four things are requisite to a bargain: a vendor, a buyer (*achatour*), a thing, and a price . . .

There must be a price or else the bargain is void.[1] A sale of land [for money] to be paid at the will of the vendee is void; but otherwise if it is at the will of the vendor, for then it is a duty immediately . . . [but] a sale for so much as shall be assessed by A. and B. is void, even if it is in writing, on account of the uncertainty; and therefore this is no price. But a sale for so much as another person has sold his manor for seems to be good, if his manor has in fact been sold; but if the sale is for so much as a particular manor shall be sold for it is void. (Note that.) A sale for £100 and as much more as shall be assessed by another man is void. A sale whereby the vendor shall have a certain sum which a stranger owes the vendee is good, if it is by specialty; but not otherwise, because otherwise he has no remedy. A sale [in return] for having the profits for 20 years of certain land whereof the vendor is seised, namely etc., seems to be good by specialty; but not otherwise. Also a sale for £100 which the vendor owes the vendee is good by specialty, [since it is] like a release. A sale by executors for a certain sum which their testator owed the vendee upon a simple contract seems to be good by specialty, for they were bound in conscience to pay it

---

1 Cf. *Bracton*, fo. 61b (based on Justinian's *Institutes* 3.23), which nevertheless does not have all the cases put here.

even though the law does not compel them to do so. A bargain because the vendee has performed good service for the vendor is not good; for even if he has performed such service, it is nevertheless at the vendor's pleasure whether to reward him or not. (But he may do it by way of covenant.) A bargain to pay so much as [the land] is worth by the year, according to 30 years' purchase, is good; but if it is according to the value as assessed or examined by the vendor or the vendee, it is void. A sale for a certain sum, where no day is expressed, is good [if it is] by specialty. A bargain where the sum and the day are expressed, but no money is paid, is void; for part must be paid as earnest ...

J. RASTELL, EXPOSITIONES TERMINORUM
(*c.* 1525)

Sig. B4v (untr.).

'Contract' is a bargain or covenant between two parties where one thing is given for another, which is called *quid pro quo*; [as, if I sell my horse for money, or if I make you a lease of my manor of Dale in consideration of £20 that you shall give me, these are good contracts because there is one thing for another];[2] for if a man make a promise to me that I shall have 20s. and that he will be debtor to me thereof, and after I ask the 20s. and he will not deliver it, yet I shall never have no action for to recover this 20s., for that this promise was no contract, but a bare promise: *et ex nudo pacto non oritur actio*. But if anything was given for the 20s., though it were not but to the value of a penny, then it was a good contract.

C. ST GERMAN, DOCTOR AND STUDENT (1531)

Dialogue II, c. 24:
Selden Soc. vol. 91, pp. 228–233 (untr.).

What is a nude contract or naked promise after the laws of England, and whether any action may lie thereupon.

Student ... It is not much argued in the laws of England what diversity is between a contract, a promise, a gift, a loan, a bargain, a covenant, or such other; for the intent of the law is to have the effect of the matter argued and not the terms. And a nude contract is where a man maketh a bargain or a sale of his goods or lands

2 Insertion in 1579 ed., fo. 47v.

without any recompense appointed for it. As, if I say to another, 'I sell thee all my land (or all my goods)', and nothing is assigned that the other shall give or pay for it, that is a nude contract and (as I take it) it is void in the law and conscience. And a nude or naked promise is where a man promiseth another to give him certain money such a day or to build him a house, or to do him such certain service, and nothing is assigned for the money, for the building, nor for the service. These be called naked promises, because there is nothing assigned why they should be made. And I think no action lieth in those cases, though they be not performed. Also, if I promise to another to keep him such certain goods safely to such a time, and after I refuse to take them, there lieth no action against me for it; but if I take them and after they be lost or impaired through my negligent keeping, there an action lieth . . .[3] And therefore, after divers that be learned in the laws of the realm, all promises shall be taken in this manner, that is to say: if he to whom the promise is made have a charge by reason of the promise, which he hath also performed, then in that case he shall have an action for that thing that was promised, though he that made the promise have no worldly profit by it. As, if a man say to another, 'Heal such a poor man of his disease', or 'Make such a highway, and I shall give thee thus much', and if he do it I think an action lieth at the common law. And, moreover, though the thing that he shall do be all spiritual, yet if he perform it I think an action lieth at the common law. As, if a man say to another, 'Fast for me all the next Lent and I shall give thee £20', and he performeth it, I think an action lieth at the common law. And in like wise if a man say to another, 'Marry my daughter and I will give thee £20', upon this promise an action lieth if he marry his daughter. And in this case he cannot discharge the promise, though he thought not to be bound thereby; for it is a good contract, and he may have *quid pro quo*— that is to say, the preferment of his daughter—for his money. But in those promises made to a university or such other [charitable promises], that is to say, to the honour of God, or to the increase of learning, or such other like, where the party to whom the promise was made is bound to no new charge by reason of the promise made to him but as he was bound before, there they think that no action lieth against him though he perform not his promise; for it is no contract . . .

3 There follows here a lengthy dialogue on the binding force of naked promises in conscience. The doctor speaks of a vow to God, a promise upon past consideration, and a charitable promise as being obligatory in conscience. But where there was 'no manner of consideration' the promise would be presumed to have been made in error.

Doctor. But what hold they if the promise be made for a thing past? As, if I promise thee £40 for that thou hast builded me a house: lieth an action there?

Student. They suppose nay. But he shall be bound in conscience to perform it after his intent, as is aforesaid.

Doctor. And if a man promise to give another £40 in recompense for such a trespass that he hath done him: lieth an action there?

Student. I suppose nay. And the cause is, for that such promises be no perfect contracts. For a contract is properly where a man for his money shall have by assent of the other party certain goods or some other profit at the time of the contract or after. But if the thing be promised for a cause that is past, by way of a recompense, then it is rather an accord than a contract. But then the law is that upon such accord the thing that is promised in recompense must be paid or delivered in hand; for upon an accord there lieth no action . . .[4]

LUCY v WALWYN (1561)

Record: KB 27/1198, m. 183. Thomas Lucy brought an action on the case against Simon Walwyn, gentleman, and complained that, whereas King Philip and Queen Mary I by letters patent dated 5 March 1555 demised the manors of Hampton Bishop and Hatton, in Warwickshire, to John Swyfte for 16 years; and the plaintiff desired to purchase them, and had great faith in the defendant because of the long fellowship and familiarity between them, and knew that the defendant was also a great friend of Swyfte: the plaintiff, on 12 February 1556 at Charlecote, Warwickshire, earnestly requested the defendant to do his utmost to purchase Swyfte's interest for a reasonable sum of money; and then and there promised (*pollicitatus fuit*) the defendant, for his labour to be bestowed in procuring the interest, to pay all his expenses and give him a gelding worth 100s. (or 100s. in cash) immediately upon the purchase of the interest; and thereupon the defendant afterwards (on the same day) in consideration that the plaintiff would pay all his expenses and give him a gelding or 100s., as aforesaid, faithfully promised the plaintiff and undertook that he would do his utmost to obtain Swyfte's interest as quickly as he could; nevertheless the defendant did not perform this undertaking, but purchased the manors for himself on 1 March 1556. Walwyn pleaded that on 13 February 1556, in the parish of Christ

---

4 Cf. p. 502, below. There follows a further discussion of conscience, and of the effect of an oath. The student asserts that prohibition or *praemunire facias* lay against the church courts if they entertained an action on a promise concerning a temporal matter, even if it was a case where there was no remedy at common law. The doctor thought this 'marvellous'.

Church, in the ward of Barnard's Castle, London, and always thereafter until 1 March, he did all he could to obtain the manors for the plaintiff, but Swyfte utterly refused to grant them to the plaintiff; and that on 1 March Swyfte sold his interest to the defendant, so that he could not possibly obtain it for the plaintiff from Swyfte. To this plea the plaintiff demurred.

Gell's reports, MS. at Hopton Hall, ff. 154v, 158v.

. . . *Bromley*, for the plaintiff, said that this plea in bar is not good because of its form and the manner of pleading (and this for various reasons[5]) . . . And he said that the bar was not good in substance, for by the bar it is confessed that he obtained the thing himself, which proves that he did not do as much as he could . . .

Thomas Nicholls to the contrary, and that the action does not lie . . . It seems to me that the defendant shall not be bound by this undertaking, because in itself it is no undertaking. First, because it appears from the pleading that the words and discussion between the plaintiff and defendant were on 12 February, and the pleading further says that 'afterwards on 12 February' in return for such and such a thing, he undertook; and this undertaking cannot be good, for the talking was at one time and the promise at another, and therefore they did not make an undertaking . . . The undertaking is not good for another reason; for in an action on the case there must always be a consideration, in fact or in law. For instance, if a man menaces my villeins of my manor of Dale, so that they flee from it, I shall have an action on the case because it is a wrong and against the law and reason, and this makes a consideration in law. Likewise for slandering me, this is a consideration in law. But if there is no consideration in fact or in law, no action on the case lies. For this reason the book is agreed in 11 Hen. IV,[6] where someone started a school which was to the nuisance of another, and yet no action on the case against the person who started it. So it is of a mill and a fair, agreed in the same case that no action on the case lies. And here in our case there is no consideration in fact or in law, for the party who undertook to obtain the lease was to have nothing

5 These were: (1) he pleaded that he did all he could from 13 February, whereas he had undertaken on 12 February, and so (since he did not start trying on the latter day) he had not done everything possible; (2) he said he had laboured 'always' since 13 February, which is impossible, since he could only do it at reasonable times. (The reporter says he believed Bromley made some other points, but he did not hear them because he missed the end of the argument.) Nicholls replied to these formal objections that it was reasonable to take a day to go from Warwickshire to London, and that it was for the plaintiff to set out in reply in what respect the defendant had not acted with all speed.

6 See p. 613, below.

before obtaining it, and so there was no *quid pro quo*, but only *nudum pactum*, upon which there can be no undertaking...

Onslow to the contrary, and that the action lies. He argued as to the exception to the pleading in bar... (And he argued much on the other exceptions to the pleading, as I heard from others; but I did not hear him, for I came late.) As to the undertaking, he said it was good. It has been said that the undertaking is not good because the discussion was alleged to have been on 12 February, and afterwards on the said day the defendant undertook... but in our case the discussion and the undertaking and the promise are all one, and there are words in the pleading which make this clear (as it seems to me), namely 'and thereupon the defendant promised and undertook to obtain the lease', which [means] 'upon the discussion', and the one refers to the other. There must necessarily be a distance of time between the discussion and the undertaking, for when one has spoken the other answers him afterwards: and that is 'afterwards' even if it is all in the same hour. So this is immaterial, and the undertaking is good. It has been said that there ought to be *quid pro quo* in an undertaking, and that the undertaking was that if he laboured and obtained the lease he would have a gelding, and so if he did not obtain the lease it could be said that he would not have a gelding, and therefore no undertaking. But that is not so, for the gelding is not only in return for the obtaining but for the labour mixed with the obtaining...

Plowden argued to the contrary; and the main reason he advanced was that which Onslow answered on *quid pro quo*.

No more is reported. The record shows that the court took further advisement until Trinity term 1562, and then held the plea insufficient and gave judgment that the plaintiff recover his damages. An inquest upon a writ of inquiry assessed the damages as £100, but the court took further advisement until Easter term 1563 and thereafter no more was entered.

AN INNER TEMPLE MOOT (1562)

Gell's reports, MS. at Hopton Hall, fo. 198.[7]

Note that *Keilwey* said that if I give someone else 20s. or a penny, in consideration that he to whom the gift is made shall make me an assurance of his manor of Dale for the sum of £20 to be paid later, and he takes the money but makes no assurance, the other may

---

7 Richard Onslow, who argued for Lucy, above, was autumn reader of the inn this year. Thomas Bromley, his junior, was a member of the same inn.

have an action on the case and recover damages to the value of the land, because it was a contract and there was *quid pro quo.*

Thomas Gawdy said that even if no money was paid, but someone promised another to enfeoff him of his manor of Dale before a certain day, and the other promised to pay him £20 for it, if the feoffor did not make the feoffment the other could have an action on the case even though no money had been paid.

But *Keilwey* denied this, and said that it is only *nudum pactum,* whereupon *non oritur actio,* without *quid pro quo.*

(And see Lucy's case, above,[8] well argued in a similar action on the case.)

SHARINGTON v STROTTON (1565)

Record: KB 27/1212, m. 253; Plowd. 298. Henry Sharington, esquire, and Gabriel Pledal, gentleman, brought a bill of trespass against Thomas Strotton and six others for entering their wood in Bremhill, Wiltshire, on 20 March 1564, and cutting and carrying away 200 cartloads of timber worth £40. The defendants pleaded that the wood was part of the manor of Bremhill, of which Andrew Baynton, esquire, was seised; and that on 3 July 1560, at Salisbury, Baynton had covenanted by indenture with his brother Edward that, since Andrew had no male issue and wished his manors to descend to such as were of the name and blood of the Bayntons, and 'for the good will and brotherly love and favour which he had borne towards both his brother Edward Baynton and his other brothers', he or his feoffees would stand seised of the manors to the use of himself for life, remainder to Edward and his wife for lives, with various other remainders; that Andrew had died, and Edward and his wife entered and were seised (by the operation of the Statute of Uses); and that they (the defendants) had entered and taken the trees as servants of Edward and his wife. The plaintiff demurred. The principal question was whether the covenant of 1560 was made for sufficient consideration to raise the uses under which the defendants justified.

Plowd. 301.

... *Fletewoode* and *Wray*, for the plaintiffs ... The consideration ought to be to him who is seised of the land, for if he has no recompense there is no cause why the use of his land should pass. None of the considerations contain recompense here: for the continuance of the land in his blood and the name of the Bayntons is no recompense to him, nor a worthy cause to raise a use, any more than the fraternal love and favour which he bore towards Edward Baynton or his other brothers. Although these causes

8   See p. 485, above.

induce affection, not every affection is sufficient to alter the use. For if I grant to John Style, in consideration of his long acquaintance, or of great familiarity with him, or that they were schoolboys together in their youth, or such like considerations, that he will stand seised of his land to the use of him, this will not change the use, for such are not taken to be considerations worthy in law to make a use, for they are of no value or recompense. For if upon consideration that you are on terms of great familiarity or acquaintance with me, or that you are my brother, I promise to pay you £20 at such a day, you shall not have an action on the case or an action of debt for it, for it is but a naked and barren pact, and *ex nudo pacto non oritur actio*, for the cause is not sufficient. Nothing is done or given on one of the sides, for you were my brother before and would be afterwards; and you were of my acquaintance before and would be afterwards. Thus nothing new is here done on one side or the other, as is requisite in contracts and also in a covenant upon consideration. For instance, if I sell my horse to someone for money, or for some other recompense, here is a thing given on both sides (namely, one gives the horse and the other the money or other recompense), and therefore it is a good contract. Likewise in the case of the covenant upon consideration: for instance, if I covenant with you that if you marry my daughter you will have my land, or I will be seised to your use, here is an act on each side (namely, you shall marry my daughter, and in return for that I grant you the use). Thus there is an act done and a fresh cause arising from each side. But in the principal case there is no such cause, for the issue male of Andrew Baynton would be his issue male, and his name and blood would be his name and blood, and his brothers would be his brothers and there would be fraternal love between them, even if this covenant or grant had not been made. Thus all was before the indenture or covenant, and would be after the time of the indenture and covenant, just as if the indenture or covenant had not been made. So there is nothing new done or any new cause for one of the parties here, and there is no cause here but what would have been even if no covenant or indenture had been made. The common law, however, requires a new cause, whereof the country may have intelligence or knowledge for trial if need be; and thus it is necessary for the public good ...

[*Plowden*, for the defendants] ... If I make a contract with another that if he will marry my daughter I will give him £20, in this case if he marries her he shall have an action of debt for the £20 in our law, according to 22 Edw. III in the book of assizes.[9] And yet I

9   22 Lib. Ass., pl. 70. Cf. pp. 236, 242, above.

have nothing thereby; and if one were to have no regard to nature it would be said *nudum pactum, et ex nudo pacto non oritur actio*. But sir, my daughter is hereby advanced, and that is consideration enough to me. Thus consideration proceeding from nature is a sufficient consideration in our law. From which reasons and cases it is made manifest that things proceeding from nature are respected not only in philosophy but also in our law, and have efficacy and vigour in our law, and are thereby taken to be sufficient consideration. From whence it follows that the consideration of Andrew Baynton here expressed for the provision of his issue male is good consideration to change the use. The second consideration is for the continuance of the land in the name of the Bayntons, and this seems a good consideration to raise a use. For by the continuance in the name of the Bayntons he intended to exclude all females from inheriting this land, and to place it in the heirs male: for a female by marriage changes her surname into her husband's surname and loses her father's name, whereas the male continues his first name. Sir, various good reasons might move him to do that. For God has divided reasonable creatures into two sexes, namely male and female. The male is the superior (*soveraigne*), the female inferior (*pluis base*). Aristotle in his *Politics* says, *Mas est praestantior; deterior fœmina*. Also men are for the most part more reasonable than women, and have more discretion in guiding things than women have; for men are more apt than women in all government and direction ... and perhaps Andrew Baynton was thinking of this and felt that the profits of his inheritance would not be so well spent or employed by females as they would be by males, nor the lands so well ordered by woman as by man, nor hospitality so well kept by one as by the other, nor that there would be so great a stay or comfort to his race or class, his allies or friends or acquaintances, and the country generally where he and his parents have lived, if this inheritance should come to females; which is something a man cannot think without grief ... Also by establishing the inheritance in the heirs male having the name of Baynton, Andrew would thereby obtain fame and memory with his posterity: and every man has an appetite for fame after his death, and this appetite urges many to perform notable acts or things in their lifetimes which shall be monuments to them long after their death; which appetite is laudable. And to establish a great inheritance (as this is) in one name is a feat which begets great fame with his posterity, and he deserves to be called founder of the family ... And in 17 Edw. IV[10] it is taken by several speakers that if I promise

10   See p. 242, above.

a certain sum to a surgeon to cure such a poor man, or if I promise certain money to a labourer to repair such a road which is a highway, he shall have an action of debt for it, for it is a thing of charity and I deserve thanks from them for it, and therefore it shall not be said to be *nudum pactum*. Likewise here, Andrew Baynton deserves thanks and requital for his generosity from all those named Baynton who inherit the land or who are relieved by reason of the establishing of such manors and lands in the name of the Bayntons... Sir, the law of the land has two ways of making contracts or agreements for land or chattels. One is by words, which is the lower, and the other is by writing, which is the higher. And because words are often spoken or uttered by a man without great advisement or deliberation, the law has provided that a contract by words shall not bind without consideration. Thus, if I promise to give you £20 to rebuild your hall, here you shall not have an action against me for the £20, as is affirmed in the said case in 17 Edw. IV, above, for it is a naked pact, *et ex nudo pacto non oritur actio*. And the reason is because the agreement is by words, which pass from men lightly. But where the agreement is made by deed there is more stay. For when a man passes something by deed there is first the determination of the mind to do it, and thereupon to cause it to be written, and that is one part of the deliberation, and then to put his seal to it, and that is another part of the deliberation, and thirdly he delivers the writing as his deed, and that is a consummation of his resolution. And by the delivery of the deed from him who made it to him to whom it is made, he gives his assent that he parts willingly with the thing contained in the deed to him to whom he delivers the deed; and this delivery is like a ceremony in law, plainly signifying his good will that the thing in the deed should pass from him to the other. Thus there is great thought and deliberation in the making of deeds, and therefore we receive them as a final tie of the party and adjudge them to bind the party without thinking what cause or consideration there was for making it. Therefore, in the case of 17 Edw. IV, suppose I promise you by deed to give you £20 to rebuild your hall, you shall have an action of debt upon this deed and the consideration is not examinable; for in the deed there is a sufficient consideration, namely the will of the party who made the deed. Likewise where a carpenter by word, without writing, undertakes to build a new house, and for not doing it the party in 11 Hen. IV brought an action of covenant[11] against the carpenter, and it did not appear that he was to have anything for building the house, and it was there adjudged that the

---

11 Action on the case: see p. 379, above.

plaintiff should take nothing by his writ. But if it had been by specialty, it would have been otherwise ... So, where it is by deed, the cause or consideration is not enquirable and is not to be thought of, but he must only answer the deed; and if he confesses that it is his deed he shall be bound. For every deed imports in itself a consideration, namely the will of the maker of the deed. Therefore it shall never be said *nudum pactum* where the agreement is by deed ...

After these arguments the court took deliberation until Hilary term, and from thence until Easter term, and from thence until this Trinity term in the eighth year of the present queen [1566]; and the defendants now pray their judgment.

CORBET J. said that he and all his companions had resolved that judgment should be given that the plaintiffs be barred; for it seemed to them that the considerations of continuance of the land in the name and blood, and of fraternal love, were sufficient to make the uses as limited. But he said, because my lord chief justice is not now present, move it again when he is present and you will have judgment.

Later, on another day, when CATLYN C.J. was present, [*Plowden*] prayed judgment. And CATLYN C.J. and the court were agreed that judgment should be entered against the plaintiffs, and commanded *Heywood*,[12] the prothonotary, to enter it.

[*Plowden*]. May it please you, my lord, for the sake of our learning, to show us the reasons of your judgment?

CATLYN C.J. It seems to us that the affection of the said Andrew for the provision for his heirs male whom he should beget, and his affection that he had that the land should remain to the blood and name of the Bayntons, and the fraternal love which he bore to his brothers, were causes quite sufficient to make the uses in the land ...

(Note that *nudum pactum* is defined by the civil law as follows: a naked pact is where there is no cause (*causa*) apart from the agreement. But where there is a cause there is an obligation, and an action will lie ...).

LORD GREY'S CASE (1567)

HLS MS. 2071, fo. 18v; Bod. Lib. MS. Rawlinson C.
112, fo. 292; CUL MS. Ll. 3. 8, fo. 51v (C.P.).

An action on the case against Arthur, Lord Grey, that, whereas the defendant's father was indebted to the plaintiff, the defendant in

12   Richard Heywood, joint chief clerk of the King's Bench 1548–68.

consideration thereof and of two[13] shillings paid to him by the plaintiff took upon himself to pay the same debt.

Gawdy Sjt. asked the court whether the consideration of two shillings was traversable; or, if we traverse [generally] *Non assumpsit modo et forma*,[14] whether the plaintiff ought to prove the consideration.

DYER C.J. No; for it is only alleged as a matter of course. It is now alleged so frequently in the Queen's Bench that it would be hard to stop it there.[15]

Gawdy. Then we suffer a mischief, for he has no other consideration to charge us; for the son is not chargeable with his father's debt. I think, however, that whenever an undertaking is the cause of a debt the action lies well. For instance, where there is discussion (*communication*) of a bargain between them, and they agree on the bargain (namely, the sum and the day of payment) but one of them mistrusts the other's credit, if I say, 'Do not doubt: if he does not pay at the day, I will', this is a good undertaking and a good consideration to charge me; for perhaps the other would not have given credit to the vendee but for my promise. But when a debt was already due, it seems to me that it is not right to charge a man upon such words without any consideration, which ought to be proved.

DYER C.J. The case which you have put is much clearer than the other case. Likewise, if a man is in execution at your suit, and I say, 'Discharge him, and if he does not pay you I will', this is a good consideration (if you discharge him) to charge me in an action on the case; for in this case you have discharged him from the execution by reason of my promise: as in Tateham's case, 27 Hen. VIII.[16] It seems to me also that it shall be likewise where there was a debt already in existence, for the discharge and ease of my friend is a good consideration to charge me without more. Therefore if my kinsman, brother or friend is indebted to you, and I say to you that if he does not pay you I will, here if you forbear to sue in respect thereof and to charge my friend, this is a good consideration to charge me; for what goes in ease and for the benefit of my friend is my ease and benefit also.[17]

WESTON J. agreed.

---

13 Or 'seven' (CUL MS.).
14 I.e. he did not undertake in the manner and form alleged by the plaintiff.
15 This sentence is omitted from the HLS MS., and is corrupt in the others.
16 See p. 413, above.
17 Cf. the different report (sub nom. *Anon v Watton*) in CUL MS. L1. 3. 14, fo. 145; YLS MS. G. R29.2, fo. 84v.; '... DYER C.J. was in doubt ... and he said that Tateham's case in 27 Hen. VIII was against law; and he said that no action on the case lay on a promise in law, but only on a promise in fact'. The name 'Watton' was perhaps a mistake for [Lord Grey of] Wilton.

HUNT v BATE (1568)

Dyer 272 (C.P.).

The servant of a man was arrested and imprisoned in the London compter[18] for a trespass, and he was let to mainprise by the manucaption of two London citizens (who were well acquainted with the master) in consideration that the master's business should not go undone; and afterwards, before judgment and condemnation, the master upon the said friendly consideration promised and undertook to one of the mainpernors to save him harmless against the party plaintiff in respect of all damages and costs, if any should be adjudged, as happened afterwards in fact; and thereupon the surety was compelled to pay the condemnation, namely £31. And thereupon he brought an action on the case, and the undertaking was traversed by the master, and found in London at *nisi prius* against him. Now it was moved in arrest of judgment that the action does not lie.

And by the opinion of the court it does not lie in this matter, because there is no consideration why the defendant should be charged for the debt of his servant, unless the master had first promised to discharge the plaintiff before the enlargement and mainprise of his servant; for the master never requested the plaintiff to do it, on behalf of his servant, but he did it of his own head.

But in another like action on the case brought upon a promise of £20 made to the plaintiff by the defendant in consideration that the plaintiff, at the special instance of the said defendant, had taken to wife the defendant's kinswoman, that was good cause, even though the marriage was executed and past before the undertaking and promise, because the marriage followed the request of the defendant. And land may also be given in frankmarriage with the donor's kinswoman as well after the marriage as before, because the marriage may be intended the cause.

Therefore the opinion of the court in this case this term was that the plaintiff should recover upon the verdict. And so note the difference between the aforesaid cases.

WEST v STOWELL (1577)

Record: CP 40/1346, m. 719. Thomas West brought an action on the case against John Stowell and declared that, whereas on 25 September 1573 there was a shooting match at the pricks between Sir Charles Howard, Lord

18 A London prison.

Effingham, and the defendant, at Salisbury, to see which of them should win the match by gaining the first 15 shots of the other: the defendant, in consideration that the plaintiff promised him that if he (Stowell) won he would pay him £10, promised the plaintiff and undertook that if Lord Effingham won he would pay the plaintiff £10; and although Lord Effingham won the match, the defendant (little regarding his promise, but wickedly scheming to defraud the plaintiff) has not paid the £10.

2 Leon. 154, pl. 187 (untr.).[19]

... It was moved that here is not any sufficient consideration; for the promise of the plaintiff to the defendant *non parit actionem*,[20] for there is not any consideration upon which it is conceived, but [it] is only *nudum pactum*, upon which the defendant could not have an action against the plaintiff: and then here is not any sufficient consideration for the promise of the defendant.

MOUNSON J. conceived that here the consideration is sufficient, for here this counter-promise is [a] reciprocal promise, and so a good consideration: for all the communication ought to be taken together.

MANWOOD J. Such a reciprocal promise betwixt the parties themselves at the match is sufficient, for there is consideration good enough to each: as, the preparing of the bows and arrows, the riding or coming to the place appointed to shoot, the labour in shooting, the travail in going up and down between the marks. But for the betters by there is not any consideration, if the better doth not give aim.[1]

MOUNSON J. A cast at dice alters the property, if the dice be not false. Wherefore, then, is there not here a reciprocal action?

MANWOOD J. At dice the parties set down their moneys, and speak words which do amount to a conditional gift: namely, if that the other party cast such a cast he shall have the money.

SIDENHAM v WORLINGTON (1585)

2 Leon. 224, pl. 286 (untr.); Godb. 31;
LI MS. Misc. 361, fo. 52v (C.P.).[2]

In an action upon the case upon a promise the plaintiff declared that

---

19 Dated Mich. 20 Eliz., which (it seems from the record) should be Mich. 19 & 20 Eliz. (1577).

20 I.e. does not beget an action.

1 Cf. the brief report in CUL MS. Ll. 3. 14, fo. 249v: '... MANWOOD J. The consideration is naught. DYER C.J. That remains to be seen; for the archers may have an action of debt, but it is to be considered whether the betters may'.

2 Also reported in Cro. Eliz. 42.

he, at the request of the defendant, was surety and bail for John Style, who was arrested into the King's Bench, upon an action of £30, and that afterwards for the default of John Style he was constrained to pay the £30; after which the defendant, meeting with the plaintiff, promised him for the same consideration that he would repay that £30; which he did not pay, upon which the plaintiff brought the action. The defendant pleaded *Non assumpsit*, upon which issue was joined, which was found for the plaintiff.

Walmsley Sjt., for the defendant, moved the court that this consideration will not maintain the action, because the consideration and promise did not concur and go together; for the consideration was long before executed, so as now it cannot be intended that the promise was for the same consideration. As, if one giveth me a horse, and a month after I promise him £10 for the said horse, he shall never have debt for the £10 nor *assumpsit* upon that promise, for there it is neither contract nor consideration, because the same is executed.

ANDERSON C.J. This action will not lie, for it is but a bare agreement, and *nudum pactum*, because the contract was determined and not *in esse* at the time of the promise. (But he said it is otherwise upon a consideration of marriage of one of his cousins, for marriage is always a present consideration.)

WYNDHAM J. agreed with ANDERSON C.J. . . .

PERYAM J. conceived that the action did well lie. And he said that this case is not like unto the cases which have been put of the other side. For there is a great difference betwixt contracts and this case. For in contracts upon sale the consideration and the promise and the sale ought to meet together; for a contract is derived from *con* and *trahere*, which is a drawing together, so as in contracts everything which is requisite ought to concur and meet together: viz. the consideration of the one side, and the sale or the promise on the other side. But to maintain an action upon an *assumpsit* the same is not requisite, for it is sufficient if there be a moving cause or consideration precedent, for which cause or consideration the promise was made. And such is the common practice at this day. For in an action upon the case upon a promise the declaration is laid that the defendant, for and in consideration of £20 to him paid, *postea* (that is to say, at a day after) *super se assumpsit*, and that is good; and yet there the consideration is laid to be executed. And he said that the case in Dyer, 10 Eliz. 272,[3] would prove the case . . .

RODES J. agreed with PERYAM J. And he said that if one serve me

---

3   *Hunt v Bate* (1568) Dyer 272; p. 494, above.

for a year, and hath nothing for his service, and afterwards at the end of the year I promise him £20 for his good and faithful service ended, he may have and maintain an action upon the case upon the same promise, for it is made upon a good consideration. But if a servant hath wages given him, and his master *ex abundanti* doth promise him £10 more after his service ended, he shall not maintain an action for that £10 upon the said promise, for there is not any new cause or consideration preceding the promise. (Which difference was agreed by all the justices.)

And afterwards, upon good and long advice and consideration had of the principal case, judgment was given for the plaintiff. And they much relied upon the case of *Hunt* and [*Bate*] (10 Eliz.), Dyer 272.

MEGOD'S CASE (1586)

BL MS. Add. 25195, fo. 61v; HLS MS. 16, fo. 338
(Q.B.).[4]

Megod brought an action on the case against two persons, and the case was as follows. One Mounson had enfeoffed the two [defendants] of land, with the intention that they should convey it to whomever he should later sell it to; and he sold it to the plaintiff; and they did not convey it to him accordingly: and therefore he brought this action.

It was argued for the defendants that the action did not lie, inasmuch as there was no consideration between the plaintiff and the defendants, but only between the said Mounson and the defendants.

GAWDY J. No one is damaged except the plaintiff.

SHUTE J. There is no consideration from him, for when they were enfeoffed it was not known to whom it would be sold; and it would be hard to raise a consideration by matter *ex post facto* between him and the defendants, when they were uncertain to whom it would be sold.

On another day, *Rokeby* (for the plaintiff) said: the benefit is not reserved[5] to the feoffor himself, but to the person to whom he sells. Moreover, they have a good consideration, for they shall take profits in the mean time before he bargains and sells, and that is a good consideration.

4 Briefly reported in Godb. 64, pl. 77.
5 BL MS. Reads 'referré' in HLS MS.

Godfrey. The consideration does not arise between the plaintiff and the defendants, and therefore the action does not lie. I concede that the bargain and sale made by the feoffor to the plaintiff is a good consideration between them, but not between the plaintiff and the defendants.

SHUTE J. There is no consideration between the plaintiff and the defendants to raise the action, and so it does not lie.

GAWDY and CLENCH JJ. There is a trust reposed in them; ergo it is a good consideration. For they take this [land] in trust for whomever he should sell it to, and thereupon they may have a *subpoena*; and therefore it is good consideration.

Afterwards, in Michaelmas term 28 & 29 Eliz. [1586], the case was moved again. This time WRAY C.J. held with GAWDY and CLENCH JJ. that the action lay perfectly well. For he said it was a consideration, since there was a trust reposed in them that they would convey to the [plaintiff]; and where there is a good consideration in the Chancery an action on the case will lie upon it here. And judgment was entered that it was a good consideration and that the action well lay. (Note that.)

(In Corderay's reports[6] the defendants made a promise to the plaintiff to convey; but query, for that would seem contrary to the arguments and reasons advanced here.)

STONE v WITHIPOLE (1589)

(a) YLS MS. G. R29.6, fo. 81 (Q.B.).[7]

Stone, of Cheapside, brought a writ *sur assumpsit* against Dorothy Withipole and counted that Paul Withipole, esquire, bought velvet from Stone to the value of £100 and various other merchandise amounting in all to the value of £4, and promised the said Stone to pay this; and that he made the said Dorothy his executrix and died;[8] and Stone went to Dorothy and demanded it, and she undertook to pay it at Michaelmas if he would forbear accordingly;

---

6   William Corderay was called to the bar by Lincoln's Inn in 1584. His reports have not been identified, though a set was sold at the Umfreville sale in 1758 (lot 195).

7   Also reported in 1 Leon. 113 (below); Owen 94; Cro. Eliz. 126; Dyer 272 (in the margin).

8   Paul Withipole of Ipswich, Suffolk, died in 1585, unmarried and aged about 21. His executrix Dorothy was his widowed mother, a daughter of Lord Wentworth. (See 5 *Miscellanea Genealogica et Heraldica* (5th Series), 381.) Leonard's report must be in error in stating that she was sued as executor of her husband. Her husband was also called Paul, but he died in 1579 aged around 40.

and because this was not performed he brought this action. To this the defendant pleaded that the testator at the time of the sale, and of the promise, was under age. Thereupon the plaintiff demurred.

It was argued by *Egerton*, S.-G., that the action was well maintainable. And he relied principally on three judgments. [The first was] 15 & 16 Eliz. between Pitcher and Bonde, where an executor undertook to pay the testator's debt (which was upon a simple contract), and it was held a good promise. The second: Edmonds, a Master of Arts in Cambridge, was bound with an infant, and at full age the infant promised to pay the debt (for it was the infant's debt) and to save him harmless, and he died, and Edmonds (having been compelled to pay the debt) recovered on this promise against Barton, the infant's administrator.[9]

WRAY C.J. said he did not remember this case as having been decided, and would not grant it as law. Nevertheless it differed from this case, because the bond is not made void, as where there is no deed.

The third case was that of Lord Grey of Wilton,[10] who undertook to pay his father's debt upon a contract, and he was only his heir (having land in fee simple descended); and it was held a good *assumpsit* even though he was never chargeable.

This case was utterly denied by advice of the whole court.

It was held by the court that all effectual considerations ought to be beneficial to the party who promises or [a loss] to the party to whom the promise is made, or else they are invalid. And because here the defendant had no benefit nor the plaintiff any loss by the delay, because the defendant was not chargeable to him in any action, it was awarded that the plaintiff take nothing by his writ.

(b) 1 Leon. 113, pl. 156 (untr.).

... *Egerton* S.-G. for the plaintiff. As I conceive, these contracts made by the plaintiff are not merely[11] void; so that if an action of debt or upon the case had been brought against the testator himself he could not have pleaded upon the matter *Nihil debet*, or *Non assumpsit*, or *Non est factum*, but he ought to avoid the matter by special pleading. And therefore here it is a good consideration. And I conceive that if the testator at his full age had assumed to pay the debt, that that promise would have bound him ... And

---

9 Cited in 1 Leon. 114 as of Mich. 28 & 29 Eliz. I (1586). Cro. Eliz. 127 says the court agreed with this case, which was in the Queen's Bench.

10 (1567); p. 492, above.

11 I.e. absolutely.

also here the defendant is to have ease, and shall avoid trouble of suits, for perhaps if she had not made such promise the plaintiff would have sued her presently, which should be a great trouble unto her; and therefore it is a good consideration.

Coke [to the] contrary. No consideration can be good if not that it touch either the charge of the plaintiff or the benefit of the defendant.[12] And none of them is in our case. For the plaintiff is not at any charge for which the defendant can have any benefit, for it is but the forbearance of the payment of the debt which she was not compellable to pay. And as to the suit of the Chancery,[13] the same cannot make any good consideration, for there is not any matter in the case which gives cause of suit in Chancery; for they will not order a matter there which is directly against a rule and maxim of the common law. As, if a feme covert be bound etc., and the obligee bring her into the Chancery. And if a man threaten me that if I will not pay to him £10 he will sue me in the Chancery, upon which I promise to pay it to him, no action will lie. And an infant is not chargeable upon any contract but for his meat, drink, and necessary apparel: 19 Edw. IV, 2.[14] And in debt upon such necessary contract the plaintiff ought to declare specially, so as the whole certainty may appear upon which the court may judge if the expense were necessary and convenient or not, and upon the reasonableness of the price; for otherwise, if the necessity of the thing and reasonableness of the price doth not appear, the chancellor himself would not give any remedy or recompense to the party.

WRAY C.J. conceived that the action would not lie, for the contract was void, and the infant in an action against him upon it may plead *Nil debet* ...

RETCHFORD v SPURLINGE (1591)

Record of first action: KB 27/1314, m. 701. John Retchford brought a bill against Henry Spurlinge complaining that, whereas on 20 March 1589 he had delivered £6 of his own money to the defendant to the use of Henry Glanfeyld (to whom he was indebted in £6), with the intention that Spurlinge should pay the £6 to Glanfeyld in discharge of the plaintiff's debt,

---

12 In Cro. Eliz. 127, Coke says 'no case can be put out of this rule'. Cf. Owen 94: 'The consideration is the ground of every action on the case, and it ought to be either a charge to the plaintiff or a benefit to the defendant. 17 Edw. IV, 5'. For the case of 1477, see p. 242, above.
13 This answers an argument, not reported in 1 Leon., that 'admitting the executor be not chargeable by law, yet in equity and conscience he is chargeable in Chancery' (Owen 94); 'and this matter will maintain suit in Chancery' (Cro. Eliz. 126).
14 *Recte* Y.B. Pas. 18 Edw. IV, fo. 2, pl. 7, per Vavasour '*in secreto* a Littleton'.

and Spurlinge on this consideration undertook to pay the money to Glanfeyld and to save the plaintiff harmless (i.e. indemnify him) against Glanfeyld: nevertheless Spurlinge, scheming to defraud the plaintiff, did not pay the £6 to Glanfeyld or save the plaintiff harmless, though requested to do so on 10 May 1589, but the plaintiff was compelled to pay Glanfeyld and to spend £5 defending the suit by Glanfeyld, and had lost any profit from the £11 so spent. Spurlinge pleaded *Non assumpsit*, and on 31 July at St Alban's assizes (Clarke B., Puckering Sjt.) the plaintiff failed to appear and judgment was entered by default for the defendant. The reports which follow apparently relate to a second action in the same form, in which the defendant demurred.

(a) HLS MS. 16, fo. 315v.

. . . Two objections were alleged. The first point was that, since one could have an action of account, ergo no action on the case. The other was that there is no consideration to charge Spurlinge, for he took no benefit from the money, which he was to deliver to someone else.

But it was adjudged that the action on the case lay; for in account one shall not recover damages, whereas in an action on the case damages are to be recovered. And the court said that having the money in his hands for only a day, or an hour, is such a profit to Spurlinge that it shall be called sufficient consideration to have an action on the case . . .

(b) CUL MS. Ii. 5. 16, fo. 97v.

. . . The defendant demurred to the count.

Spurling thought the action would not lie, for 17 Edw. IV[15] [says] that in every undertaking there must be a consideration whereon to ground the *assumpsit*, and that is wanting in this case.

Coke to the contrary; for it has been adjudged in this court, where goods were delivered to one Barker and in consideration thereof he undertook to redeliver them to the plaintiff on request, and *assumpsit* was brought, and it was maintainable. So it is if a man promises to make me a house without consideration, an action nevertheless lies. Likewise if he misuses my timber, an action lies.

Gawdy J. I deny your case where a man promises to make you a house without consideration: no action lies. 3 Hen. VI[16] is thus, concerning a mill. But if he misuses your timber an action on the case lies.

15 See p. 242, above.
16 See p. 380, above.

Fenner. According to 9 Edw. IV[17] if a trespasser agrees to deliver the goods to the owner, and does so, this accord is no plea in trespass without some act done by the defendant, such as carrying the goods to some place, or labour by the defendant. Likewise in this *assumpsit* there ought to be consideration.

The next term, upon the motion of Mr. *Coke*, the court thought there was consideration, for it may be that the defendant was to pay certain money at a certain hour and could not provide, but borrowed the said money to save his bond. Therefore a day was given to have judgment, unless the defendant showed some other matter. Later judgment was entered the next term for the plaintiff. (There is no judgment entered on the roll, for the money was paid and so the party saved the charge of entering the judgment—as the attorneys told me. Wingate of Staple Inn was for the plaintiff, and Cobb of Barnard's Inn was for the defendant. I have seen the roll.)

LEVET v HAWES (1599)

(a) Mich. 1598: Cro. Eliz. 619, pl. 8 (Q.B.) (untr.).[18]

Assumpsit, and declares, in consideration that the plaintiff agreed with the defendant that John Levet, son and heir of the plaintiff, should espouse Constance, the defendant's kinswoman, and in consideration that the plaintiff agreed to assure to the said Constance lands of £10 *per annum* for her jointure, that the defendant assumed to the plaintiff to give to John Levet the son in marriage with the said Constance £200; and allegeth *in facto* that the marriage took effect, and that the plaintiff had assured such land for the jointure, and that the defendant had not paid to his son the £200. Whereupon the father brought the action, and upon *Non assumpsit* issue; and found for the plaintiff.

It was moved in arrest of judgment that the action ought not to have been brought by the father, for the son only is to have advantage thereof.

But it was said on the other side that the promise is only made with the father, and all the considerations arise on his part, and the son is a stranger thereto; and therefore the son cannot maintain the action, but the father.

But the court doubted thereof; *et adjournatur.*

---

17 Y.B. Trin. 9 Edw. IV, fo. 19, pl. 21, per Choke J. See also *St German*, p. 485, above.

18 Also reported, sub nom. *Lever v Heys*, in Moo. K.B. 550; and sub nom. *Hadves v Levit* in Hetley 176.

(b) Hil. 1599: Cro. Eliz. 652, pl. 11 (untr.).

The case was now moved again.

And POPHAM C.J. was of opinion that the action ought to have been brought by the son, and not by the father. For the promise is made to the son's use, and the ordinary covenants of marriage are with the father to stand seised to the son's use, and the use shall be changed and transferred to the son as if it were a covenant with himself. And the damage for non-performance thereof is to the son.

And of that opinion was FENNER J., but CLENCH J. doubted. (GAWDY J. was absent.)

And *Towse*, of counsel with the plaintiff, cited a case adjudged in this court between Cardinal and Lewes, where in consideration of marriage betwixt the defendant's son and the plaintiff's daughter the defendant assumed to give a stock of £100 to his son; and for non-performance of that promise the father brought the action, and [it was] adjudged maintainable.

And the court willed him to show that precedent; *et adjournatur.*

And it was afterwards adjudged for the defendant.

GILBERT v RUDDEARD (1607)

Dyer (1688 ed.) 272 (in the margin); collated with
HLS MS. 105, fo. 88 (K.B.).

An action on the case upon *assumpsit*, and [the plaintiff] declared that, whereas a certain Arthur Tempest was indebted to the plaintiff, and the said Tempest had appointed the said defendant and delivered to the defendant £50 to pay to the plaintiff in part-payment of his aforesaid debt, whereupon the plaintiff came to the defendant and asked for the £50, and he answered and said he was then busy, but if he would come back on such and such a day he would pay him; and the plaintiff came on that day, and the other refused to pay, to his damage etc.

Dale moved that the action does not lie, because the plaintiff is a stranger to the delivery of the money. And in support of this it is said in Dyer 21[19] that debt does not lie in a case like this.

POPHAM C.J. When the debtor delivers the money to the defendant to deliver to the plaintiff, there is implied (*includé*) an agreement by the defendant to deliver it to the plaintiff, which

---

19 *Core v May* (1536); see p. 243, above.

agreement will bind him in *assumpsit* to the person who ought to receive the money. See 4 Co. Rep. 83.[20]

TANFIELD J. agreed, that where there is some precedent matter which causes the delivery, as in our case the debt, then the delivery cannot be countermanded; otherwise he may revoke it. But here there is another consideration besides the debt due to the plaintiff, for he is to come to the defendant's house to fetch the money; and that is a good consideration in itself.

YELVERTON J. agreed.

So it was adjudged that the plaintiff should recover, FENNER and WILLIAMS JJ. being absent.

HODGE v VAVISOUR (1616)

3 Buls. 222 (untr.).[1]

In an action upon the case for a promise, the plaintiff delivered certain cloths to the defendant for so much, and was thus indebted to him in so much; the defendant afterwards, in consideration thereof, did assume and promise to pay this a year after; for not payment thereof the action brought; upon *Non assumpsit* pleaded, a verdict was given for the plaintiff.

It was moved for the defendant in arrest of judgment that this promise should not bind him, it being said 'that afterwards, in consideration thereof', he assumed to pay this: which promise is grounded upon a consideration that is past, and so not good to raise a promise. And here he may have debt for his goods.

CROKE J. If a man owes to another so much for certain goods, and he demands of him when he will pay him for them, who answers 'at such a time', and the other agrees unto it, this is good; and the law will here imply a tacit consideration by the law annexed unto it.

HOUGHTON J. In consideration that the plaintiff hath built a house for the defendant, he did assume and promise to pay him so much, this is executed; here the *assumpsit* is for money; this is to be paid upon request; here the defendant is clogged with a debt continually, and therefore this is here a good consideration to raise a promise.[2]

---

20   *Southcote v Bennet* (1601); see p. 274, above.
1   Also reported in 1 Rolle Rep. 413.
2   Cf. 1 Rolle Rep.: '... the continuance of the debt at the time when the promise was made is a good consideration continuing till the promise to raise the action...'

DODDERIDGE J. Here is a promise made for the payment at a day certain, till which time the same was forborne, and therefore this is a good consideration. Here the express promise shall not take away the action upon the case implied: namely, if for fear he will pay here the action upon the case for the first contract still remains. For if one be indebted to another in a sum of money, and saith unto him, if he will forbear till Christmas he will then pay this to him, this is good. But if he arrest him before this, what remedy shall he have? No action upon the case for this. The debt here always continues, and no discharge can be made of this, but by the payment of it.

The court therefore overruled the exception as being of no force, and declared the promise to be grounded upon a good consideration. And therefore by the rule of the court judgment was given for the plaintiff.[3]

3　1 Rolle Rep. adds: '... Query this case, for it seems that there is here no consideration for a new promise, since no forbearance is promised; for it has been held that a consideration to forbear for a little while is not good, because notwithstanding this he may sue him; ergo it is the same in our case...' (As to forbearance for a short while, see *Lutwich v Hussey* (1583) Cro. Eliz. 19; *Sackford v Phillips* (1594) Cro. Eliz. 455, Owen 109; *Purslowe v Tisdale* (1600) Cro. Eliz. 758.)

20 Actions on the case for deceit

FERRERS v JOHN, VICAR OF DODFORD (1307)

Select Cases in the Court of King's Bench, III,
Selden Soc. vol. 58, p. 179.

Northamptonshire. John, the vicar of Dodford church, in mercy
for several defaults. The same John was attached to answer John de
Ferrers concerning a plea why, whereas the king recently by his
letters ordered his beloved and faithful John de Ferrers to come
quickly with horses and arms to [join] him on his Scottish campaign to help with his aforesaid campaign, and the same John,
preparing to travel to the aforesaid parts, at Dodford bought a
certain horse for a certain great sum of money from the aforesaid
John, the vicar of Dodford church, trusting in the words of the
same John who exposed that horse for sale under guarantee,
affirming by corporal oath taken before trustworthy men at
Dodford that the same horse was sound in all its members and not
maimed, and the said John de Ferrers, having paid the aforesaid
John, the vicar, the aforesaid sum of money for the aforesaid horse
and had it taken to his manor of Bugbrooke, found the aforesaid
horse to be maimed in its left shoulder, by reason of which maim
and defect of that horse the aforesaid John de Ferrers came too late
to the said parts of Scotland to help with the king's said campaign,
nor did he get any benefit from the aforesaid horse, as the king
understands from the same John de Ferrer's complaint, to the
grave damage and deceit of that John and the manifest deceit of
[the king] himself.[1]

---

1 It was no doubt the king's interest that brought this case into the king's court
when trespass actions which did not allege breach of the king's peace were not yet
regularly admitted and not yet distinguished as 'on the case'.

And thereupon he complained that the aforesaid John, the vicar, on the Thursday next before the feast of St Barnabas the Apostle in the thirty-fourth year of the present king's reign, did him the aforesaid trespass, by which he says he is the worse and has damage to the amount of £100. And thereof he produces suit etc.

And the aforesaid John, the vicar, comes and denies all wrong and deceit and whatever etc. And he says that he sold no horse to the aforesaid John nor made any contract with him nor is he in any way guilty of the aforesaid trespass and deceit. And concerning this he puts himself on the country . . .

GARROK v HEYTESBURY (1387)

Y.B. Trin. 11 Ric. II, p. 4, pl. 2.

(a) The count: CP 40/506, m. 116d.

Kent. Godfrey Heytesbury in mercy for several defaults. The same Godfrey was attached to answer William Garrok concerning a plea . . . And thereupon the same William, by Thomas Kenefeld his attorney, says that, whereas on the Saturday [8 September 1386] next before the feast of the Exaltation of the Holy Cross in the tenth year of the reign of the present lord king, he made a bargain with the aforesaid Godfrey at Canterbury to buy [a certain] horse from him: the same Godfrey, knowing that it was disabled by a certain infirmity, falsely and fraudulently sold the aforesaid horse to the same William at that place for a large sum of money (namely, five marks) by warranting it to be sound and suitable; and the aforesaid horse died of the infirmity within eight days next following; whereby he says he is the worse and has damage to the amount of 20 marks. And thereof he produces suit etc.

(b) The Y.B. report.

. . . *Lokton.* Sir, you clearly see how he has counted concerning a sale of a horse which we are supposed to have warranted, and this in effect sounds in covenant, for which he should have a writ of covenant. We demand judgment of the writ.

Rikhill. Since this action is brought on our case, namely that we bought a horse with warranty, and to this you answer nothing, and since we cannot have an action of covenant without a deed, therefore [we pray judgment and our damages].

Lokton objected that he ought not to have this action without a deed. (This was not accepted). Then he said: sir, you plainly see how he has counted that the horse had a certain infirmity, and has not counted with certainty what infirmity it had; and since no one can have knowledge of what was inside it, [we demand judgment].

Rikhill. Since we have said that you knew the horse was inwardly[2] full of infirmity, and that you sold it to us by deceit, we pray judgment and our damages.

Then *Lokton* asked leave to imparl.

Afterwards he came back and said: sir, we sold him the horse hale and sound, without this that we warranted it in the way he has said; ready to do our law.

Rikhill. You shall not reach that issue, for we have counted in effect of a deceit, and in no action of deceit shall a man have his law. So we pray judgment.

Lokton. Do you, then, refuse the [wager of] law?

Rikhill. Yes.

So *Lokton* demanded judgment how they ought to leave the matter. And then he did not dare to demur on the point that he ought to have his law, but said that he did not warrant the horse in the way the plaintiff had counted; ready etc.[3]

The other side *econtra.*

The record shows that the defendant, not admitting that the horse was disabled by any infirmity at the time of sale or that it died of any infirmity within the period mentioned, pleaded that he sold the horse by a bargain made between them simply, without this that he warranted the horse upon the bargain to be sound and suitable. Issue was joined on the warranty, but no verdict is recorded.

FITZWILLIAM'S CASE (1406)

Y.B. Pas. 7 Hen. IV, fo. 14v, pl. 19; BL MS. Harley
5144, fo. 41v; MS. Hargrave 1, fo. 56v.

Henry FitzWilliam brought a writ of trespass against one J. of S. and counted that the said J. sold him a tun of unwholesome wine, knowing the wine to be unwholesome, to his damage.

Skrene. Sir, the defendant gave him a taste of the wine, and at that time he accepted the said wine as good and suitable. [We pray] judgment *Si action.*

Hill. We accepted the wine as good, but on condition that it would [still] be good after it was brought to our house; (saying all the rest as before).

---

2 The count as entered does not specify whether the infirmity was internal or external.
3 This formula indicates an offer of jury trial.

Skrene. He agreed to the sale and accepted the wine as good, without this that there was such a condition; ready etc.

The other side *econtra*.

DREW BARANTINE'S CASE (1411)

Y.B. Mich. 13 Hen. IV, fo. 1, pl. 4; LI MS. Hale 189,
fo. 110 (dated Hil. 13 Hen. IV, i.e. 1412).

Drew Barantine brought a writ of deceit against one E. C. of Chichester, upon this matter: whereas the same Drew bargained with the said E. C. at London to buy from him 50 sacks of wool for a great sum of money, the aforesaid E. C. knowing certain sarplers to contain only 46 sacks [sold them to the said Drew] warranting them [to contain 50] . . .

Skrene. We say that after the bargain was made the plaintiff sent to us at Chichester J.C. and R.G., his servants, who were merchants, and they had a look at the same wool out of the sarplers; and then they packed the wool into 46 [sacks], and we carried them to the king's weighhouse in the same town, and by the same they were weighed as containing 50 sacks of wool and accepted by his aforesaid servants; and we paid custom and tronage at the rate for 50 sacks, and forthwith delivered them at that place to the said servants, who took them from thence to the sea and took them overseas. And we demand judgment *Si action* . . .

HANKFORD. If a man sells me a blind horse and warrants it sound in all its parts, I shall not have an action of deceit against him afterwards, because I could have looked at it. But if it is sick inside its body, I shall have such an action, because I could not have known of that illness. Likewise in the case here, if he bailed the sarplers to the plaintiff with such a warranty, where they had never been weighed, the plaintiff should not have an action of deceit, because he could have weighed them.

THIRNING [C.J.] If I buy a horse from you in some place other than where the horse is, by reason of the trust which I place in you, and you warrant it sound in all its parts, whereas in truth it is blind, I shall have a good action of deceit against you . . .

ANON. (1430)

Y.B. Mich. 9 Hen. VI, fo. 53v, pl. 37; corrected from
Fitz. Abr., *Action sur le case*, pl. 5.

A writ of deceit on the case, *quare cum* etc., was brought by A.

Caunt against B. and C., alleging in the writ that 'whereas the aforesaid A. bargained to buy a certain butt of rumney wine[4] from the aforesaid B. and C., the aforesaid C., knowing it to be unwholesome and unsuitable, warranted it to be suitable (*habilem*) and wholesome, and sold it for a certain sum of money'.

Rolf. [We pray] judgment of the writ; for the writ says *habilem* (with an *h*), whereas it should be *abilem* (without an *h*), and so it is false Latin, or no Latin.

BABINGTON [C.J.] Some of the Chancery clerks say it should be written with an *h*, and some say the contrary, so leave that point.

[*Rolf.* The writ does not specify the sum for which the wine was sold.

The court said that the writ went 'for a certain sum of money', and the details appear in the count; so answer.][5]

Rolf. Still [we pray] judgment of the writ, for he has not alleged that we warranted the wine to be good, and [if it is not to his taste] it shall be adjudged his own foolishness.

MARTIN [J.] The warranty is irrelevant, for it is enacted[6] that no one should sell unwholesome food.

COTTESMORE [J.] That is [enforced by] *actio popularis.*[7]

BABINGTON. The warranty, as Martin has said, is irrelevant. If I go into a tavern to eat, and the taverner gives and sells me unwholesome drink or meat, whereby I am made extremely sick, I shall clearly have an action on my case; and yet he made no warranty to me.

Godered. It was recently adjudged in the King's Bench that where someone sold a piece of woollen cloth, knowing it to be rotten and not well fulled, this [action] was adjudged good without a warranty.

Then *Heuster*[8] pointed out that the writ did say 'warranted', as indeed it did.

Rolf (smiling): while making protestation that the plaintiff is a wine-drawer and knows nothing about wine, we say for our plea on behalf of B. that at the time of the sale the wine was sufficient and suitable; ready etc.

THE WHOLE COURT: you must traverse the plaintiff.

Then *Rolf* said, 'and not unwholesome'; and the other side *econtra.*

---

4 A sweet wine of Greek origin. The name is associated with Romania.
5 Passage in Fitz. Abr. only.
6 Probably a reference to *Judicium pillorie*, in *Statutes of the Realm*, vol. I, p. 202.
7 I.e. a presentment.
8 Conjectural emendation of 'West' in the printed Y.B. Thomas Heuster was the chief prothonotary.

Rolf. And on behalf of C. we say that he sold the wine to the plaintiff through the aforesaid B., as his servant, without this that he sold it to him in any other manner.

MARTIN. Then by your own confession you have deceived him.

Rolf. If I have a servant who trades on my behalf, and he goes to a fair with a defective horse or other merchandise, and sells it, shall the other party have an action of deceit for this against me? (Implying that he would not.)

MARTIN. What you say is true, for you did not command [the servant] to sell the thing to him, or to any other particular person. But if your servant, with your collusion and by your command, sells some unwholesome wine, the buyer shall have an action against you; for it is your own sale. If the case is that you did not command your servant to sell the wine to this plaintiff, then you may say that you did not sell it to the plaintiff.

Rolf. It would be very dangerous to put that in the mouths of the lay people,[9] because it is a question of law.

ANON. (1471)

Y.B. Trin. 11 Edw. IV, fo. 6, pl. 10.

An action of deceit was brought by someone against another for this: whereas the plaintiff bought from the defendant in London certain pieces of cloth, the defendant warranted them to be of a certain length, whereas they were only of such and such a length. The defendant said that long before the said sale one B. was possessed of the said pieces of cloth as of his own goods, and (being so possessed) the said defendant as the said B.'s servant sold them in his house, as alleged above, without this that he sold to him in the manner alleged.

The court said that he must say that the said B. sold them through the defendant as his servant.

Pigot. It is all the same, for it is common to say that I paid such money by my master's command, and I shall not be compelled to say that my master paid through me.

Fairfax. It seems that the plea is not good; for even if the property is B.'s, it does not matter, for he has shown that the sale was in a place which is market overt, and therefore the property in such a case is immaterial; for if they belonged to a stranger he would be barred by this sale, and therefore when he sets out that the defendant sold them he does not deny that he warranted as

9 I.e. have it tried by jury.

above. Therefore it is right that such an action should be maintained against him.

Pigot. If the defendant, in such an action of deceit in respect of a sale or bargain with warranty, traverses the bargain, that goes to everything. Now, we have shown here that we ourselves did not sell, but that it was B.'s sale, and the defendant was only an instrument and a minister; for it is the master who shall have an action of debt for the money for which the cloths were sold. Therefore the buyer shall not have an action of deceit for a servant's warranty made upon the master's sale.

CHOKE. If a man sells me something, and someone else (a stranger) warrants to me that it is good and sufficient, I shall not have an action of deceit on this parol warranty, though if it were by deed I should have an action of covenant. Therefore the bargain must be part of the contract, or else I shall not have an action of deceit against the person who made the warranty. Here, then, the sale is the master's sale, and the warranty is the servant's act, and so upon this warranty I shall not have an action against the servant. If a man undertakes to cure me of a certain illness, and he gives me medicines which make me worse, I shall have an action on my case against him; but if he makes the same undertaking, and then sends his servant to give me medicine, and he applies medicine which makes me worse, I shall not have an action against the servant, but against the master. Likewise if someone undertakes to shoe my horse, and instructs his servant, who injures it with a nail, the action lies against the master.

LITTLETON. Even though this sale is the master's sale, yet it is made by the servant, and perhaps if he had not warranted the thing the plaintiff would not have bought it. Therefore, since he made the warranty and the sale was made by him, it is right that if the plaintiff is deceived he should have an action of deceit. Sir, if my servant sells my horse to a man in this way, 'Sir, you shall give my master £20 for the horse and 20s. to me', in this case the servant shall have an action of debt for the 20s.

BRYAN [C.J.] The 20s. might be for his labour. But, sir, it seems here that the action of deceit does not lie in this case; for it is the master's sale and not the servant's (as has been argued). In some cases the warranty is traversable and in some cases not. If I sell a man 20 sheep for slaughter, and they are unwholesome, nevertheless if I warrant them he shall not have an action of deceit on the warranty and it shall not be traversed; for [until] they are dead I cannot know that they are unwholesome. When I place trust and confidence in you, and I am deceived, I shall have an action of deceit. [So] if I sell mutton for eating which is unwholesome, he shall have an action of deceit even if I do not warrant it.

NEELE. In your case the reason is that it is prohibited by the law for a man to sell unwholesome victuals.

BRYAN. If a man sells me seed and warrants to me that it is good, and it is bad, or warrants that it is seed from a certain part of the country, and it is not, I shall have an action of deceit; for I cannot know these facts, whereas the seller can. But if he warrants to me that the seed will grow, such a warranty is void; for it is not his place to warrant to that, but it is in the power of God. If a man sells me a horse and warrants that it has two eyes, and it has not, I shall not have an action of deceit, because I could have known of that at the outset.

LITTLETON. Perhaps you had a good look at him at the time of the bargain. And the bargain is good even if the horse is defective. So it is where a man sells pieces of cloth, which are perhaps beyond the seas, and warrants that they are of such and such a length: if they are not, I shall have an action of deceit. The warranty is perhaps the cause of the bargain.

CHOKE. If I sell a horse and warrant that he will go 30 leagues in a day, and he does not, [there will be no] action of deceit. The warranty is void, for one must warrant something which exists at the time of the warranty: one may not warrant something yet to come.

Fairfax. If I buy something from a man with warranty, and the warranty concerns something which I could discover at the outset by my five senses, and things are not as warranted, I shall not have an action. For instance, if he sells me murrey cloth and warrants that it is blue; for I could have known that by looking when it was sold to me.

BRYAN. If the buyer in your case was blind, he would have an action of deceit.

Fairfax. If a man sells me certain pieces of cloth and warrants to me that they are of a certain length, and they are not, I shall have an action of deceit; for I could not know the length by looking, but only by a collateral proof (namely, by measuring). Therefore, when I have believed you that they are of a certain length, and you have deceived me, it is right that I should have an action of deceit.

JOHN SARGER'S CASE (1481)

Y.B. Pas. 21 Edw. IV, fo. 22, pl. 6.

A man sued an action on his case in the King's Bench against

Sarger, one of the officers of the same bench,[10] supposing by his bill that, whereas the plaintiff affirmed a plaint of debt against one B. in London, the said Sarger purchased a *supersedeas* out of this bench, under the seal of the said bench and directed to the sheriffs of London, reciting that the said B. was the said Sarger's servant and in attendance on him (whereas he was not), commanding them to surcease; by force of which writ the plaint was discontinued and the said B. set at large, to the wrong and damage of the plaintiff. The said Sarger pleaded to issue, and it was found against him.

The plaintiff prayed his judgment.

Tremayle. You ought not to go to judgment, for it appears that he has assigned the defendant's fault to be that the plaint was discontinued by the *supersedeas*; and that, sir, is not the defendant's act but the act of the king...

HUSSEY [C.J.] Show me the difference from this case, which has been adjudged: in a *praecipe quod reddat* the tenant purchases a protection, reciting that he has been retained to go across the sea, when he has not been retained (or does not go); and by putting forward the protection the suit in the *praecipe quod reddat* is adjourned *sine die*. In that case it has been adjudged that ... he shall have a writ of deceit. And yet that case is stronger than yours is, for your writ was under the seal of this court, whereas the protection is under the great seal. And that was adjudged in the year 20 Hen. VI, in deceit brought by the abbot of Selby.[11]

It was moved at the bar, that if two people conspire or procure to indict (or to sue an appeal against) a man, this procurement or conspiracy is the cause of the action.

FAIRFAX [J.] said that what is done by virtue of a verdict is well done; and if jurors indict someone, he shall never have an action upon that, even though he is aggrieved by this verdict... But, sir, I would make this distinction in this case: where the information on which the *supersedeas* is granted is the act of the defendant, and of him who gave the information, and where it is the court's fault. For instance, if a clerk tells us that a poor man has been arrested in London, and that he was previously arrested here for surety of the peace, or that an action was depending against him here before the arrest in London, and prays a *habeas corpus* for him, and we award it upon this information, and thereby the party is removed and set at large: there is here no remedy against the clerk who gave the

10   John Sarger was filazer for Gloucestershire and Herefordshire. The filazers and their servants had the privilege of being sued (in personal actions) only in the King's Bench.

11   *Abbot of Selby v Stillington* (1441) Y.B. Mich. 20 Hen. VI, fo. 10, pl. 11.

information, because it was our fault in not looking up our records to see whether what he informed us was true before we awarded the writ. It is otherwise, however, where one of the clerks comes to us and shows us that one of his servants who is attendant upon him has been arrested in London, and prays a writ of privilege ... because it is his fault to give this information on behalf of someone who was not in fact his servant, for we cannot know how many servants the clerks of this court have, or who they are, without information. So in this case this action shall be well maintained against the defendant, because the writ of privilege was granted on his information, which was his act alone; and since the verdict has passed, we will have regard to the verdict and to the facts. And so I advise you who are pleaders that if we pay more attention to these actions on the case, and maintain the jurisdiction of this and other courts, *subpoenas* would not be used as often as they are at present.

And so, on another day, the justices held the matter previously alleged to be of no effect in preventing judgment ...

ANON. (1491)

Caryll's reports, BL MS. Harley 1624, fo. 12v;
LI MS. Maynard 86, fo. 17v.

In a writ of deceit the plaintiff counted through *Jay* that, whereas on a certain day in a certain year in a certain parish and ward in London the defendant had sold the plaintiff for a certain sum of money a certain butt of malmsey, knowing the wine to be stale, he warranted the same to be good and drinkable, to the wrong and damage of the plaintiff.

Kebell pleaded that the defendant did not warrant the wine in the manner and form alleged.

And the plaintiff rejoined that he did.

Later *Jay* came back and moved the court that the issue had been misjoined, because the warranty in this case is not traversable.

And it was said by the whole court that if a man sells me cloth, or a horse, with a warranty, and it has a hidden defect, the warranty is traversable. But in the present case the warranty is immaterial, because the statute[12] prohibits anyone from selling bad victuals.

So *Kebell* said that, after the sale and before the delivery of the wine referred to by the plaintiff, the defendant at St Alban's in the county of Middlesex[13] delivered to the plaintiff a butt of good and

12 Probably *Judicium pillorie*: see p. 510, above.
13 *Sic.* It is not clear whether this is a mistake by the reporter, or a deliberate legal fiction for venue purposes.

sufficient wine according to the bargain, and demanded judgment *Si action*.

Jay. In what way have you answered us?

Kebell. Well enough; for if we have performed the bargain with good wine, then even if we afterwards gave you a butt of bad wine you shall not have an action for it. If, on the other hand, we traversed 'without this that we gave you the stale wine whereof you speak', it would be found against us. So it seems the plea is good. If I give you a horse or something else which has a hidden defect, you shall not have an action for it. And I would suppose that if I sold you 20 quarters of good corn for a certain sum of money, and delivered to you 20 quarters of bad corn, I should not have an action of debt for the money, because the bargain was for good corn, which is not performed by the delivery of bad corn; and so it is the delivery of good corn which causes you to be charged.

NOTE (*c.* 1505)
Caryll's reports, Keil. 91, pl. 16.

Note, per FROWYK [C.J.C.P.], that no man may justify the selling of corrupt victual, but an action on the case lies against the vendor whether or not the victual is warranted to be good. But if a man sells me cloth or something else which he knows is bad, now I am deceived to his own knowledge, and in this case because of the fact that he was *sciens* and sold it—albeit that the sale was without warranty—he shall nevertheless be punished by a writ on my case. But if he is not *sciens*, he shall not be punished without having warranted the thing to be good. And in this case the writ on the case, and all writs on the case (which do not follow any course, but are made to suit the case), must be as certain as the count save for the time and place: and therefore in 9 Hen. VI[14] *Rolf* challenged the writ in the case of corrupt wine because one word had a letter too many.

TAYLOUR v TRERICE (1511)
Record: KB 27/999, m. 5.

London. Nicholas Taylour, by his attorney, offered himself on the fourth day[15] against Ralph Trerice, late of London, cooper, in a

---

14 See p. 510, above.
15 See p. 390, above.

plea why, whereas he the said Nicholas (at London in the parish of St Martin in Vintry Ward) was desirous of buying 20 butts of wine called rumney[16] and 15 butts of wine called bastard,[17] and told the aforesaid Ralph that he did not know how to assess the quality (*bonitas*) of those kinds of wine, the aforesaid Ralph there asserted to the aforesaid Nicholas that he was an expert connoisseur of such wines (*in cognitione bonitatis hujusmodi vinorum se ipse valde sciens*), and the same Ralph in return for a certain sum of money there agreed between him the said Ralph and Nicholas, and there paid in advance by the same Nicholas to the same Ralph, there took upon himself to buy for the aforesaid Nicholas 20 butts of good and merchantable rumney wine, fit for human consumption, and 15 butts of good and merchantable bastard wine, fit for human consumption: nevertheless the aforesaid Ralph, scheming fraudulently to deceive the selfsame Nicholas, chose 12 butts of rumney wine and 4 butts of bastard wine and there asserted [and] warranted to the said Nicholas that they were good and merchantable, and fit for human consumption; as a result of which the same Nicholas, because of the great confidence which he then reposed in the said Ralph, there bought those wines for £32; which wines were spent, unmerchantable and unfit for human consumption, and were then so bad, stale and feeble that the wines within 20 days next following at that place became utterly sour (*penitus acerba*); to the damage of him the said Nicholas £40, as he says . . .

There is no record that the defendant ever appeared.

KINGE v BRAINE (1596)

Owen 60; collated with HLS MS. 110, fo. 227, and retranslated.

A man sold certain sheep, and warranted that they were sound and that they would remain sound for the space of a year; and upon this warranty an action on the case was brought. And it was moved that it does not lie, since this warranty is impossible for the party to perform, because whether or not they remain sound for a year is the act of God alone.

But CLENCH and FENNER JJ. thought the contrary, for it is no more impossible than if I warrant that such a ship will return safely from Bruges; and it is the usual course between merchants to warrant the safe return of ships.

16 A sweet wine of Greek origin: cf. p. 510, above.
17 A sweet wine of Spanish origin, similar to muscatel.

(See 11 Edw. IV, fo. 6, per Choke, a warranty that a horse will carry me 30 miles a day is void.[18])

CHANDELOR v LOPUS (1604)

Cro. Jac. 4, pl. 4 (untr.).

Action upon the case. Whereas the defendant, being a goldsmith and having skill in jewels and precious stones, had a stone which he affirmed to Lopus to be a bezoar stone[19] and sold it to him for £100, whereas in truth it was not a bezoar stone; the defendant pleaded Not guilty; and verdict was given and judgment entered for the plaintiff in the King's Bench.

But error was thereof brought in the Exchequer Chamber, because the declaration contains not matter sufficient to charge the defendant, namely that he warranted it to be a bezoar stone, or that he knew that it was not a bezoar stone; for it may be, he himself was ignorant whether it were a bezoar stone or not.

And all the justices and barons (except ANDERSON C.J.) held that for this cause it was error: for the bare affirmation that it was a bezoar stone, without warranting it to be so, is no cause of action. And although he knew it to be no bezoar stone, it is not material;[20] for everyone in selling his wares will affirm that his wares are good, or the horse which he sells is sound, yet if he does not warrant them to be so it is no cause of action. And the warranty ought to be made at the same time of the sale... Wherefore, forasmuch as no warranty is alleged, they held the declaration to be ill.

ANDERSON C.J. to the contrary; for the deceit in selling it for a bezoar, whereas it was not so, is a cause of action.

But notwithstanding it was adjudged to be no cause, and the judgment was reversed.

LOPUS v CHANDLER (no. 2) (1606)

(a) The bill: KB 27/1391, m. 265.

London. Jerome Lopus, a foreign merchant, complains of Robert Chandler, goldsmith, being in the custody of the marshal of the

---

18   See p. 513, above.
19   A calculus found in the stomach of certain oriental animals, and believed to be an antidote to poison.
20   Cf. 2 Rolle Rep. 5, where it is said that the reason for the reversal was that no knowledge was alleged.

lord king's marshalsea before the king himself, on the grounds that, whereas the same Robert is and for ten years last past has been a goldsmith, and during all that time had the knowledge and understanding of the natures and qualities of gems and precious stones, and could distinguish and tell the difference between the natures, qualities and prices of such precious stones, and during all that time he had gained and acquired his living by way of buying and selling precious stones and gems; and whereas the aforesaid Robert, on 1 October [1597] in the thirty-ninth year of the reign of the lady Elizabeth late queen of England, at London, namely in the parish of St Mary-le-Bow in the ward of Cheap, London, was possessed of a certain stone which the same Robert then and there asserted and affirmed unto the same Jerome to be a true and perfect precious stone called 'a beazers stone' (a bezoar stone) and of the true nature and quality thereof, as of his own goods, and the same Jerome was then possessed of a gold ring with a certain precious stone called a diamond fixed into the same ring (value £100), as of his own goods; and, the selfsame Jerome being thus possessed of the aforesaid gold ring with the precious stone called a diamond fixed into the same, and the aforesaid Robert being likewise possessed of the aforesaid stone which the same Robert (as is stated above) asserted and affirmed to be a precious stone called a bezoar stone, the same Jerome on the aforesaid 1 October in the above-mentioned thirty-ninth year, at London aforesaid in the parish and ward aforesaid, made a bargain with the said Robert to buy from the same Robert the aforesaid stone of the selfsame Robert, which the same Robert then and there asserted and affirmed to the same Jerome was a precious stone called a bezoar stone, and of the true nature and quality thereof: the aforesaid Robert, then and there knowing that the aforesaid stone of the selfsame Robert was not a true precious stone called a bezoar stone, nor of the nature and quality thereof, but a false and counterfeit bezoar stone, then and there affirmed the same stone of the selfsame Robert to be a true precious stone called a bezoar stone and of the nature and quality thereof; and on the aforesaid 1 October in the above-mentioned thirty-ninth year, at London aforesaid in the parish and ward aforesaid, the same Jerome being then entirely ignorant of the goodness of the aforesaid stone of the selfsame Robert, [the aforesaid Robert] falsely and fraudulently sold the same stone to the same Jerome in return for the aforesaid gold ring with the aforesaid precious stone called a diamond fixed into the same, and for £10 to be paid to the same Robert by the same Jerome when he should be thereunto requested; to the damage of him the said Jerome £200. And thereof he produces suit etc.

In Trinity term 1606 the defendant prayed judgment of the bill as being insufficient in law, and the plaintiff joined in demurrer.

(b) Report in YLS MS. G. R29.17, fo. 157v;
MS. G. R29.18, fo. 123v; HLS MS. 118, fo. 114v;
HLS MS. 1180 (2), fo. 127v; IT MS. Barrington 7, fo. 215v.

[Hil. 1606]

... *Hele* prayed judgment for the plaintiff, and said that in all bargains the law requires plainness and will punish deceit in the vendor if he affirms more than is true of his wares, even if he does not warrant them. As in the case of 9 Hen. VI, fo. 53,[1] one shall have an action on the case against someone who sells bad wine even though there is no warranty in the bargain, if he knows that it is bad. The same case is in 22 Hen. VII, Croke[2] 91, that this action lies on the deceit, even though there is no warranty, if the defendant knows the wares to be corrupt. And in 42 [Lib.] Ass. pl. 8, an action on the case was brought against someone because he had stolen cattle and sold them to the plaintiff as his own; and it was adjudged that it lay.[3] And I have seen a case where someone had forged a lease, and (knowing it to be forged) sold it to someone else as a good and sufficient lease: an action on the case lay, even though there was no warranty. And it seems to me that these words 'asserted and affirmed' amount to a warranty, since the defendant knew that the stone was false; though if the vendor had been ignorant of this, doubtless no action would lie.

Goldsmith to the contrary. Where it is mentioned in the count that the defendant was a goldsmith and lapidarist, this is irrelevant in this case; for a bezoar stone is a drug and belongs to the knowledge of the apothecaries, not lapidarists. And when someone is selling wares it is lawful for him to speak the best of them that he can, in order to raise the price; and even though the vendee buys it at his price, if there is no warranty or at least reliance (*fidem adhibens*) on his promises or prices, an action on the case does not lie, even though he is deceived: for *caveat emptor*. In the book 42

1 See p. 509, above.
2 I.e. Caryll's reports (p. 516, above), edited by John Croke (1602). Beale (*Harvard Law Review*, vol. VIII, p. 293) mistook this to indicate the beginning of a speech by Croke.
3 *Adam Brown's Case* (1368), apparently at Essex assizes, where it was argued unsuccessfully in abatement of the bill that 'this suit is more naturally given by way of detinue of chattels than trespass'.

[Lib.] Ass. pl. 8, the book expressly says 'the plaintiff trusting in the defendant's loyalty'. As for the book of 9 Hen. VI, fo. 53, that was for wine, which is corrupt victual prohibited by the law to be sold, knowing it to be thus corrupt, so that even if it is not warranted, and the vendee does not put his trust in him, nevertheless an action on the case lies; but for any other commodity, which is not victual, it does not lie without a warranty or at least reliance (*fidem adhibens*). And (as is said in 6 Edw. VI, Dyer fo. 76, pl. 28[4]) there cannot be deceit without a precedent trust. But here in our case there is no trust. And if there is a warranty in cases where the vendee can judge by his own eyes of the imperfections, the action does not lie; for it shall be presumed that no one was deceived or put his trust [in the vendor] when he saw it [for himself]. (For that, see 20 Hen. VI, fo. 35, a query by Paston.[5]).

Trin. 1606.

Afterwards, in Trinity term in the fourth year, this case was argued again by *Hele* for the plaintiff, as above in effect.

FENNER J. If someone purchases a protection to delay a suit, and does not go [on service] according to the protection, an action on the case lies for the deceit.[6]

TANFIELD J. That is for the deceit to the king's court. And it is not in vain that in all our books, in actions on the case like this action a warranty is always expressed; and that must be annexed to the bargain, or else no action lies (unless it be for victual). An action does not lie in respect of an earlier discussion (*communicatio*), but for the warranty in the contract. If someone negotiates with me to buy my horse as it stands in the stable, and asks me whether it ambles or trots, and I say that it ambles, whereas in truth it trots, and we bargain, shall this man have an action? It seems not, for it was his own overcredulity which deceived him.

POPHAM C.J. This case is a dangerous case, and may be the cause of a multitude of actions if it be understood that a bare affirmation by the seller causes this action. But that is not so. There must be knowledge in the vendor that the vendee will not have the effect of his bargain, together with the intention of deceiving him. For instance, if I have a horse which is privily wounded, so that it cannot live more than a day or two, and I (knowing this) sell it to John Style, and the horse afterwards dies, John Style shall have an

---

4 *Andrew v Boughey* (1552), where the plaintiff counted on a warranty of goods made by the seller at the time of delivery, the sale having been concluded a month earlier.

5 *Doige's Case* (1442); see p. 394, above. Cf. p. 513, above.

6 See p. 514, above.

action on the case against me, because I sold him a thing whereof I knew he could not have the benefit. But if John Style resells the horse, and affirms it to be sound, and then it dies, the second vendee shall not have an action, because his vendor did not know that it was thus mortally and privily wounded. If someone sells goods to which he knows he has no title, and they are [taken by the owner] (*evict*), the vendee shall have an action; but if the vendee resells them without knowing of this, an action does not lie against him, even though the second buyer is deceived. Likewise in the case at bar. The principal matter is that the defendant, knowing the stone to be counterfeit, sold it to the plaintiff as a bezoar stone, when to the vendor's knowledge he could not have the profit thereof. And it is immaterial whether he is a lapidarist or goldsmith, or not, for the cause of action is the defendant's knowledge that the stone was not a bezoar stone and the selling it with intent to deceive him. And it seems to me that the law can be gathered from these distinctions; but I will be advised concerning the present matter, for it may arise many times.

Mich. 1606.

And in Michaelmas term in the fourth year this case was moved again by *Hele*, who argued much the same as above in effect, and no one answered him.

POPHAM C.J. said that this case was of importance, and he thought it good that it should be considered by all the justices of England; for if it were found in favour of the plaintiff it would affect all the contracts in England, which would be dangerous. Therefore he would procure all the justices to consider it. And for the better argument thereof before the justices, he said that the questions in the case are whether or not he shall be charged upon his own knowledge and affirmation of the sale, without a warranty. As to this, if I have a commodity which is corrupt, be it victual or something else, and, knowing that it is corrupt, I sell it as good, and so affirm it, it seems to me that an action on the case lies for the deceit. But even though it is corrupt, an action will not lie if I do not know that, even if I affirm it to be good, so long as I do not warrant it to be good. That distinction will reconcile all the books; and it is reasonable that it should be so, for not everyone knows the corruption of goods which are to be bought and sold. If someone sells a horse which he has wrongfully taken from another, and the horse is afterwards taken back, the vendee shall have an action on the case; but if the vendee sells the horse to someone else, and he is evicted, the second vendee shall not have an action against the first if he had no knowledge of the first wrong. And if someone forges a lease of my land and sells it, the vendee shall have an action on the case; but if the vendee resells it, as above, an action on the case does not lie. In these cases there is no need for any affirmation that they are the vendor's own goods, for that is implied in the sale. And if someone sells corrupt wine and has no knowledge thereof, an action does not lie against him without a warranty. I would have these cases considered upon seeing the books, and furnished [to] those who are to argue before all the justices.

TANFIELD J. I will reserve my opinion as to the principal case. But without doubt—and it is agreed by everyone—if the words 'the defendant, knowing (*sciens*)' were omitted, the plaintiff would not recover; for that, if anything, is what entitles him. But the count would have been better if it had mentioned that the defendant sold it to the plaintiff *pro bono et vero*; whereas that is omitted.

LADY CAVENDISH v MIDLETON (1628)

Record: KB 27/1562, m. 243. Lady Cavendish[7] brought a bill of trespass on the case against Richard Midleton, and complained that, whereas on 1 July 1623 at Derby, through her bailiff Francis Bucke, she bought 12 oxen from the defendant for £80 payable in one month; and whereas Bucke paid the defendant £80 at the end of the month with the plaintiff's money, according to the bargain, and then died on 20 November: after Bucke's death, on 1 June 1624 at Derby, the defendant fraudulently and deceitfully demanded £60 (part of the £80 aforesaid), alleging that it had not been paid, whereupon the plaintiff (trusting the defendant) on 30 November paid the £60 by the hand of Thomas Challenor; and so she was defrauded of the £60. The defendant pleaded Not guilty, and on 28 July 1628 at Derby assizes (Richardson C.J., Hutton J.) the jury found for the plaintiff with £60 damages.

Cro. Car. 141, pl. 18 (Mich. 1628) (untr.).[8]

... *Serjeant Crewe* moved in arrest of judgment ... that this action lies not; but she ought to have brought an action of account as for money unduly received.

But all the court conceived that the action well lies, although the plaintiff might have brought an action of account.

Whereupon it was adjudged for the plaintiff.

The record shows that judgment was entered to recover £60 damages and £9 costs. On 24 January 1629 Midleton brought a writ of error, but he defaulted on 12 February.

7 Grace, widow of Sir Henry (d. 1616).
8 Also reported in 1 Rolle Abr. 106, line 18; Wm Jones 196.

21   Actions on the case for conversion

(1)   Conversion by a bailee

RILSTON v HOLBEK (1472)
(a) Record: CP 40/844, m. 332.

Yorkshire. William Holbek late of York, merchant,[1] was attached to answer William Rilston, executor of the testament of Henry Brounflete, knight, late Lord Vessy,[2] in a plea why, whereas the same Henry [on 10 August 1460] at Wymington in Bedfordshire had delivered to a certain Richard Burton, chaplain, and Benet Malyok ten table-cloths, 32 towels, a linen cloth called a cupboard-cloth, and 15 linen cloths called napkins, to keep safely and securely; and whereas the said Richard and Benet [on 20 February 1461] had there delivered the same table-cloths, towels and cloths to a certain John Clifford,[3] knight, to keep safely and securely to the use of the said Henry; and whereas afterwards [on 28 February 1461] the same John at Doncaster in Yorkshire had delivered the said table-cloths, towels and cloths to the said William Holbek, to keep safely and securely to the use of the said Henry: the same William Holbek [on 10 April 1469] at Doncaster, after the death of the said Henry, occupied, broke and tore the aforesaid table-

---

1 A prominent merchant and alderman, four times mayor of York (d. 1477): Surtees Soc. vol. 79, p. 32n.
2 Seated in Yorkshire and at Wymington, Bedfordshire (d. 16 January 1469). Will printed in Surtees Soc. vol. 1, p. 53.
3 'The family of Rilston was for several generations most intimately connected with the great house of Clifford, under the shadow of whose lordly castle they were so long resident': Surtees Soc. vol. 30, p. 87n.

cloths, towels and cloths (which were in his keeping by reason of the aforesaid bailment made to him) in such a way that those table-cloths, towels and cloths (which at the time of the said bailment thereof made to the said William Holbek were worth £40) were well-nigh destroyed by that occupying, breaking and tearing, and are now worth only 40s.; which hampered the execution of the aforesaid testament, to the damage of the said executor of £40 . . .[4]

And the aforesaid William Holbek, by Leonard Knyght his attorney, comes and denies the force and wrong when etc. And he says that he did not occupy, break or tear the aforesaid table-cloths, towels and cloths in the form in which the aforesaid William Rilston above complains against him. And of this he puts himself upon the country; and the aforesaid William Rilston likewise. Therefore the sheriff is commanded to cause 12 men to come here in the octaves of Hilary . . .

Process to summon a jury is continued without effect until Easter term 1475. There were other actions pending between the parties. On m. 334 of the same roll is an action of detinue founded on the bailment by Lord Vessy to Burton and Malyok, on 10 August 1460 at Wymington, of various curtains and bedding, including a green and red counterpane embroidered with griffins and a green worsted counterpane embroidered with vine leaves; the count alleges that the bailees lost the chattels, and that they came to the defendant's possession by trover on 28 February 1461 at York; the defendant pleads *Non detinet*, and process to summon a jury is likewise continued until Easter term 1475. On m. 335d is a closely similar action of detinue in respect of a cloth of gold 'bawdekyn' (counterpane), a tarterin counterpane embroidered with the arms of Lord Vessy, a large cloth of gold counterpane embroidered with the arms of Lord Willoughby, and other valuable cloths. The Y.B.s also report a detinue action in which the plaintiff counted not only on the bailment to Burton and Malyok, but also on the sub-bailment to Clifford; and the defendant pleaded that Clifford had bailed the chattels to him to deliver to the abbot of York, which he had done: Y.B. Mich. 12 Edw. IV, fo. 11, pl. 2; and fo. 14, pl. 14. All the actions seem to relate to the contents of the manor-house at Wymington, which Lord Vessy had directed his executors to sell, and which in 1472 passed on the death of Jacquetta duchess of Bedford to her son Sir Richard Wydeville: *Victoria County History of Bedfordshire*, vol. III, p. 118. The entry on m. 335d enables the case to be identified with the case of cloth of gold cited in 1478 (see p. 527, below).

(b) Report: Y.B. Mich. 12 Edw. IV, fo. 13, pl. 9;
BL MS. Add. 37493, fo. 27v.

This term an action was brought in this form: whereas the plaintiff

---

4 Count omitted: dates from count inserted in square brackets.

had bailed certain goods to Lord Vessy[5] to look after, and he bailed them to the defendant to keep to the use of the plaintiff, the defendant had wasted and used the goods so that they were impaired etc., to the damage etc.

BRYAN [C.J.] said that it seemed to him that the action did not lie, because this defendant is a stranger to the first bailment. Likewise, if I bail my horse to a farrier to shoe, and he bails it to another farrier who injures the horse with a nail, an action does not lie against him.

But the other justices were of the contrary opinion.

CALWODELEGH v JOHN (1479)

Record: CP 40/868, m. 428. Thomas Calwodelegh brought an action on the case against David John of Exeter, and declared that, whereas on 14 July 1469 he had delivered two silver-gilt cups of his to one Robert Reynell at Tiverton, Devon, to keep safely to his use and return on request; and Robert on the same day delivered them to Hugh Germyn at Tiverton to keep safely to the plaintiff's use and return to him on request; and Hugh on the same day delivered them to the defendant on the same terms: the defendant on 20 January 1478 broke the cups at Exeter and made them into various kinds of silver vessel, and converted them to his own uses. The defendant pleaded that, before the plaintiff had any property in the cups, they had belonged to Hugh Germyn; and a certain Walter Reynell had taken them from Hugh's possession and delivered them to the plaintiff to keep to the use of Walter; and the plaintiff delivered them to Robert Reynell, who delivered them to Hugh; and Hugh, being so possessed, gave them to the defendant, who broke and converted them as his own goods. The plaintiff traversed the property in Hugh Germyn, and issue was thereupon joined.

Y.B. Hil. 18 Edw. IV, fo. 23, pl. 5.

In an action on the case the plaintiff declared that he bailed certain silver cups to the defendant to keep safely, and the defendant broke them and converted them to his own use.

Tremayle. It seems that the action does not lie, for it appears that he could have a writ of detinue: for the property is not altered, and even though he cannot recover the very things he can still recover damages for them.

[*Catesby*][6] thought the contrary. It would be against reason to

---

5 Omitted in MS. and clearly wrong.
6 Reads 'Choke' in print. But it appears from the order of speeches, and from the mention of Catesby in the following speech, that Choke and Catesby have been transposed.

force him to pursue an action of detinue, for when he brings it he cannot have the effect of his suit and therefore it is in vain. For the nature of an action of detinue is to recover the very thing in demand, or the value in damages if it cannot be found: but here it appears to you that he shall never recover the very thing in demand. Moreover, there was a similar action sued here recently, and the plaintiff counted that he bailed certain cloth of gold to the defendant, who made clothes from it; and the action was maintainable, because it appeared to the court that he could not recover the thing itself.[7]

[CHOKE.][8] It seems that he may choose to have either action. Similarly, if I deliver £20 to Catesby to deliver to Pigot, he may choose whether to have a writ of account against Catesby or a writ of debt. Also, if [I] lend [you my] horse to ride to York, and you ride on to Carlisle, I shall have a writ of detinue and recover the horse; and then I shall have my action on the case and recover damages for the overworking of my horse beyond the provisions of the agreement. In the same way, if I bail to you my robes to look after, and you make use of them so that they wear out, I shall have an action of detinue—for in all these cases the property is unaltered—and then I shall have an action on my case and recover damages for the loss sustained by the using of the robes. Likewise here, he may choose either [action].

BRYAN [C.J.] It seems that he shall have an action of detinue in this case, and no other action. As to the argument that [in the case of the money delivered to Catesby] he shall have an action of debt or of account, I say that he shall have an action of account and not an action of debt. What would his action of debt be based on? He cannot declare on a contract, on a sale or on a loan; and so that action fails. As to the other point, I pose you this question: if I bail to you my cup to look after, and you break it into four pieces and keep them in your chest, is the property changed or altered, or not? (It was said that it was not.) Then it is clear that he shall have an action of detinue, if the property is in him so that he can recover the thing itself. And I have understood it to be clear law that one shall never have an action on the case where one can recover the thing itself. Moreover, the defendant in an action of detinue may wage his law; and by the plaintiff's action in this case he would be ousted from that. (So note that in his opinion he would recover damages for the breaking, or for the impairment of his robes, but [must use

---

7 See *Rilston v Holbek* (1472), p. 525, above. No judgment was entered.
8 Reads 'Catesby' in print. See p. 526, fn. 6, opposite.

detinue] where the whole value is to be recovered in damages, the goods being entirely destroyed.

ANON. (1510)

The following discussion may have arisen in an action commenced the previous term, in which the plaintiff declared that he had bailed a deed to the defendant, who had kept it so carelessly that the seal came off. The declaration alleged that great trust (*magna confidencia*) had been placed in the defendant, but did not mention any undertaking. The defendant demurred to the declaration, and the case was continued for advisement until Trinity term 1513, with no judgment being entered: *Hayden v Ragge-lond* (1510) CP 40/992, m. 451. There may also have been discussion of the boundary between case and detinue in another case the same year, where the plaintiff declared that the defendant had bought plate knowing it to have been stolen from the plaintiff, melted it down, and converted it to his own use. The defendant, protesting that the declaration was insufficient, denied the conversion. No more is recorded beyond the joinder of issue: *Astley v Fereby* (1510) CP 40/993, m. 512.

Caryll's reports, Keil. 160, pl. 2.

In the Common Pleas, *More* Sjt. suggested a distinction between where a man should have an action on the case and where an action of detinue. If I bail goods to a man to keep safely, and he undertakes to do so (with or without reward), and through his fault the goods perish, I shall have an action on my case in this case. For if I were to bring an action of detinue—as I could, if I wished—I would recover the thing as it is; and it would be foolish of me to bring such an action where I could have a better. If, however, in such a case he sold the goods to someone else, I should have an action of detinue against my bailee and not an action on my case.

Several of the justices said that, in the latter case, the party should have an action on the case against his bailee, for he had misconducted himself in selling my goods to someone else; and the action on the case is always based on such misconduct by the bailee, even though the party might have had an action of detinue if he wished.

FAIRFAX J. said that if I bail a chest to someone, and the bailee breaks the chest, I shall have a general action of trespass against him. (This was not denied.)

REDE C.J. said that if someone robbed me of my goods, and someone else robbed him of the same goods, I should have an appeal of robbery against the first robber (who robbed me) and also against the second, because the property of the goods remained in me at all times. And the person who robbed me shall be indicted in each county where he went with my goods, 'for that he has feloniously robbed me'.

WARTON v ASHEPOLE (1524)

Spelman, *Reports*, p. 4, pl. 4.

Warton brought an action on his case against Ashepole for this: he delivered a horse to the defendant to look after and return to him on request, and the defendant undertook to do so in return for 40d., and the defendant had used the horse and converted it to his own use.

The court said that the defendant could not traverse the undertaking, since it is immaterial. The cause of action is the delivery and the conversion to his use.

So the defendant traversed the delivery, and they were at issue upon that.

ANON. (1576)

KU MS. D127, *Action sur le case*, pl. 10 (C.P.).

If I bail to you a horse for one day, and you keep it for two days, or convert it to your own use, no action on the case [lies] for this conversion. For an action of detinue lies: and then, if [you] can have the horse back, [you] shall have damages for the conversion; [or], if not, you shall have the whole in damages. But if, after the bailment, the bailee kills the horse, then—because it is obvious that the bailor cannot have the horse back—the action on the case lies; for it then appears upon his own showing that he cannot have the thing bailed. If, however, I bail goods to you and you allow them to be spoiled—for instance, if I bail cloth and it is spoiled by moths, or wine is spoiled by your negligence—then, even though I shall have them back in my action of detinue or replevin, and damages for the detaining, I shall nevertheless have damages for impairing them, which is your own default. And for this special wrong, which would not be satisfied in my common action, I am driven to my action upon the special wrong.

But in the King's Bench they are accustomed to admit such actions; and if a man has my goods by bailment or finding, and uses them, this is a conversion, whether he destroys them or sells them. And there the conversion is not traversable, but ought to be proved in evidence. (In the Common Bench, however, if the action is brought there, the conversion is traversable.)

GUMBLETON v GRAFTON (1600)

YLS MS. G. R29.14, fo. 99v;
LI MS. Misc. 492, fo. 56; HLS MS. 2076, fo. 47;
BL MS. Add. 25203, fo. 243.[9]

Gumbleton brought an action on the case against Grafton, and declared that he delivered to the defendant certain pieces of cloth to look after, and that the defendant had converted them to his own use. The defendant pleaded Not guilty, which was found against him at *nisi prius* in Wiltshire.

Godfrey moved in arrest of judgment . . .[10] that the action on the case does not lie, but he must have a writ of detinue, since the property remained in the plaintiff (for anything which is shown[11]). And so is 18 Edw. IV, fo. 23,[12] to be understood.

GAWDY and FENNER JJ. thought the action lay perfectly well, for the conversion takes the property in the pieces of cloth away from the plaintiff. For this GAWDY J. vouched 2 Hen. VII, fo. 11,[13] if a man bails sheep to someone to look after, who by his negligence allows them to perish, an action on the case lies. And so it is taken in 28 Hen. VIII, Dyer 22b, *Core's Case*,[14] if a man bails plate to someone who breaks it up or alters it, an action on the case lies, even though the defendant in these cases had the goods by delivery from the plaintiff.

Godfrey agreed to these cases; for in these cases, since the thing bailed is lost, the property must of necessity be out of the bailor, and he cannot recover the things themselves by a writ of detinue. A bare conversion, however, does not disprove the property.

But GAWDY and FENNER JJ. held as above; and so, in the absence of POPHAM C.J. and CLENCH J., they awarded judgment for the plaintiff.

---

9 Also reported in Cro. Eliz. 781; Moo. K.B. 623.
10 After a technical objection to an error in the process against the jury, which the court held had been cured by the Statute of Jeofails. This is the only point reported in Moore.
11 Cf. Croke: 'because he allegeth not that he lost them'.
12 See p. 526, above.
13 See p. 398, above.
14 See p. 243, above.

(2) Trover and conversion

NOTE (1484)

Y.B. Mich. 2 Ric. III, fo. 15, pl. 39.

... It was said by someone that if a person loses his goods, and someone else finds them, the person who lost them may have a writ of trespass if he wishes, or a writ of detinue. But if the goods so lost were in any danger, then [the finder] may well justify on grounds of saving them: per *Donington*.[15]

The first action on the case for conversion against a finder to have come to light in the King's Bench rolls is *Wysse v Andrewe* (1531) KB 27/1081, m. 78. Wysse declared that he had lost a purse, which came to the defendant's hands by finding; and that the defendant had refused to give it up, and (scheming to defraud the plaintiff of the contents) had taken out the contents, feloniously sold them, and converted the proceeds. The defendant pleaded that he had bought the goods in market overt in London, but the jury found for the plaintiff. (There may have been earlier precedents in the Common Pleas: see Selden Soc. vol. 94, p. *251*, n. 9. There are also earlier precedents of actions for converting lost goods which were traced by various means into the defendant's hands: ibid., pp. *251–252*.)

LORD MOUNTEAGLE v COUNTESS OF WORCESTER (1555)

Common Pleas: record printed in Benl. 41, pl. 73. Thomas Stanley, Lord Mounteagle, brought an action on the case against Elizabeth, countess of Worcester, and declared that, whereas he was possessed of a gold chain (price 100 marks), and being so possessed on 26 March 1534 he accidentally lost the chain at London in the parish of St Mary-le-Bow, which chain afterwards came into the hands and possession of the countess by finding: the same countess, knowing the chain to belong to the plaintiff, and wickedly scheming to defraud and deceive the same plaintiff of the chain, there sold the chain to various persons unknown to the plaintiff, for various sums of money, and received the money for the same and converted it to her own use, and refuses to make satisfaction to the plaintiff for the chain or its value; to his damage of 100 marks. The countess pleaded that she did not sell the chain in the manner and form supposed in the writ and count: 'and this she is ready to aver; wherefore she prays judgment whether the

---

15 William Donington (d. 1485), bencher of Lincoln's Inn.

aforesaid Thomas ought to have his aforesaid action against her etc.' To this plea the plaintiff demurred, in Hilary term 1555.

Dyer 121; augmented from
BL MS. Harley 1691, fo. 94.[16]

... It seemed to *Rokeby* that this was no plea, but that the issue should be Not guilty; which would answer all the misdemeanours in the writ and count ... Also, she ought not to have concluded in her plea 'Judgment *Si action*', but ought to have put herself upon the country, since it was a direct negative and a traverse to the affirmative supposed by the plaintiff. Also, it seems that the plaintiff had a choice whether to have this special action on the case or an action of detinue, since a misdemeanour is supposed.[17]

[*Dyer.*][18] It seems to me that the contrary is the case. First, the form of the writ and count is not good by reason of the word 'price', whereas it should be 'value', since it is a dead chattel ... Also, it says that 'being possessed of the chain he accidentally lost it', which is *quasi impossibile*, as I believe, since there is no interval of time. (Nevertheless query that.) Then, he has supposed fraud and deceit in the defendant, whereas it appears that she came to the chain by finding, and therefore without any delivery or privity; and there was no credit or trust between them beforehand. Also, the action on the case will not lie, since it appears that the plaintiff could well maintain an action of detinue; and where a man has an ordinary writ ready framed in the register for his case he shall not pursue some other novel form of writ. Here nothing is alleged whereby the writ of detinue is altered in its nature to an action on the case, since no property is changed by the sale; for it was not made in market overt, and even though London has been held to be a market overt every day by prescription, this ought to be specially alleged. See 18 Edw. IV.[19] And [see] 5 Hen. VII: in trespass for boots, slippers and shoes seized by the person who was the owner of the leather from which they were made, since it cannot be

---

16   Also reported in 1 And. 20; Benl. 41.
17   Cf. MS. Harley 1691: '... *Rokeby* first argued in favour of maintaining the action, because although he could have a writ of detinue, this misdemeanour afterwards gives him an action on the case, and he may have that or a writ of detinue at his pleasure ... That he took to be the better opinion in 18 Edw. IV, fo. 24 ...'
18   MS. Harley 1691. Not named in his own report.
19   *Calwodelegh v John* (1479); see p. 526, above.

identified.[20] Moreover, there is no privity destroyed here, as in the case of the sheep drowned by a shepherd through negligent keeping, 2 Hen. VII[1] ... Also, the defendant in any case of misdemeanour may say generally Not guilty, or traverse the point of the writ (for instance, *Ne forgea pas, Non ejecit, Non rapuit, Non manutenuit,* and so forth). Now, as to the conclusion of the plea, it seems good enough. Even if there would have been a better form of pleading (as Rokeby has said), a good issue may well be joined on this plea if the plaintiff replies that the defendant did sell, and so maintains his writ and count.

[Some of the justices argued that the action well lies, because there is no other remedy ... And the opinion of BROOKE C.J. was that this bar was not good, because of the conclusion; otherwise it would have been good.][2]

Dyer notes in the margin that the plea was adjudged bad because of the conclusion, but does not mention the judicial opinion on his own argument that case did not lie. The brief reports in Anderson and Bendlowes are to the same effect but in the margin of Bendlowes is the note: 'This was an action of detinue in its nature, and not an action on the case, and so this action does not lie. And see Hil. 26 Eliz. in the Common Bench, held accordingly by the justices'.

ANON. (1579)

LI MS. Misc. 488, p. 64 (Q.B.).

An action on the case was brought, and the plaintiff declared that he lost his horse and that it came into the defendant's hands by finding, and the defendant sold it and converted the proceeds of sale to his own use. The defendant pleaded Not guilty, and the jury found these facts specially: the plaintiff lost the horse, and it came to the defendant's hands, but he did not sell it or take money for it, or convert the money to his own use. And they further found that

---

20 *Vanellesbury v Stern* (1490) Y.B. Hil. 5 Hen. VII, fo. 15, pl. 6; CP 40/913, m. 310. Arnold Vanellesbury brought trespass against Thomas Stern for taking 200 pairs of shoes, 100 pairs of slippers, 100 pairs of thigh-boots (*ocreae*), 100 pairs of 'buskyns' and 100 pairs of 'pynsons' on 17 September 1489. Stern pleaded that he had been possessed of dickers of leather which came into the plaintiff's possession, and the plaintiff made them into the shoes etc., and he seized them. According to the report, the court held the plea bad; but the record has an undetermined demurrer.

1 See p. 398, above.

2 MS. Harley 1691.

the defendant is now in possession of the horse and ready to deliver it up.[3]

Now *Aunger* moved the matter at the bar, and said that the plaintiff should not have judgment; for nothing charges the defendant except the sale and conversion to his use, and that is found for the defendant. The residue (namely, the trover) is not traversable. Thus is the book in 27 Hen. VIII.[4]

But GAWDY, SOUTHCOTE and AYLOFFE JJ. (WRAY C.J. being then in the Chancery) thought the contrary. For they said that the sale and conversion to the defendant's use is only a matter of form, and if for that reason they did not give judgment for the plaintiff in this case they would overturn a thousand precedents, and all actions on the case for trover.

GAWDY J., however, said that the course in the Common Bench was contrary: for Dyer C.J. would have the plaintiff prove that [the defendant] sold the horse and converted it to his own use. So in that court it seems to be a matter of substance and not merely of form.

The following day the case was moved again, and it was held by WRAY C.J. as above, and that the detaining and using of the horse was in law a converting to the defendant's use.

ANON. (1582)

HLS MS. Acc. 704755, fo. 106 (C.P.).

An action on the case was brought, and the count was for trover of certain cloths of the plaintiff's, and that he requested redelivery and the defendant refused and detained them until they perished for want of good keeping. And it was found[5] that the defendant had sold them etc.

Walmsley Sjt. prayed judgment.

And all [the justices] were of the opinion that he should not have it; for this action is based on the misuse of goods, and is not like detinue (in which action judgment would have been given in this case). And although other courts do the opposite, they themselves were unwilling to pervert actions from their natural gist (*gittes*).

---

3 In detinue the defendant could discharge his liability by bringing the chattel into court. It was disputed for another century and more whether this was so in case: *Anon.* (1601) Goulds. 155, pl. 83; *Farrell's Case* (1700) 12 Mod. 398; *Huxser v Gapan* (1723) 8 Mod. 176.

4 See p. 272, above (an action of detinue).

5 Presumably by special verdict.

(Note well this case. And see a case in Edw. IV[6] where one may have an action on the case for misusing one's thing and nevertheless have detinue afterwards for the thing itself.)

But WYNDHAM J. said that if he had counted that they had perished by fire, and it was found to have been by water, this would not have been material; for in substance they are all one. But it is not so here.

ANDERSON C.J. [spoke] contrary to the opinion in *Townesend's Case*[7] in the new reports.

SANDS v SCAGNARD (1587)

2 Leon. 37, pl. 50 (C.P.) (untr.).

In an action upon the case the plaintiff declared that he was possessed of certain chattels which came to the defendant by trover. The defendant pleaded that heretofore the plaintiff brought debt against the now defendant, and demanded certain moneys, and declared that the defendant bought of him the same goods whereof the action is now brought, for the sum then in demand, to which the then defendant waged his law and had his law; by which *Nihil capiat per breve etc.*[8] was entered; and demanded judgment if etc.

And, by WYNDHAM and RODES JJ., the same is no bar in this action; for the waging of the law, and the doing of it, utterly disproves the contract supposed by the declaration in the said action of debt, and then the plaintiff is not bound by the supposal of it, but is at large to bring this action.

And so judgment was given for the plaintiff.

GALLYARD v ARCHER (1589)

Record: CP 40/1476, m. 1529. Cornelius Gallyard brought an action for trover and conversion against Edward Archer of Epping, Essex, in respect of 50 yards of 'tuffed taffeta' lost in London on 1 August 1588, which came to the defendant's possession on 1 September, and which the defendant (knowing it to be Gallyard's taffeta) sold to persons unknown to Gallyard. The defendant pleaded that one Thomas Copland was possessed of the taffeta and on 1 September 1588 at London sold it to him for £15, as a result

6 *Calwodelegh v John* (1479) (p. 527, above), per Choke J.
7 Unidentified, but perhaps a slip for *Mounteagle v Worcester* (1555), p. 532, above. Dyer's report of that case was first printed in 1582.
8 I.e. judgment for the defendant: '[that the plaintiff] take nothing by his writ etc.'

of which he was possessed; and, before he had any notice or knowledge that it belonged to Gallyard, the defendant sold and delivered it to third parties as his own goods. To this plea the plaintiff demurred, in Trinity term 1589.

LI MS. Misc. 791, fo. 113; YLS MS. G. R29.6, fo. 5v.[9]

... *Fenner* moved the court that [Archer's plea] is no answer, for the plaintiff complains in respect of *his* goods, and to this he has made no answer; and therefore he ought to have taken the general issue, Not guilty.

ANDERSON C.J. and WYNDHAM J. agreed, for (by them) an action lies against him even though he sold them before notice.

But PERYAM and WALMSLEY JJ.[10] to the contrary. And PERYAM J. said that detinue lay, but not an action on the case, for that lies solely against the finder. Therefore he asked: if he recovered against the vendee, and afterwards brought an action against the finder, how would he be helped? For he shall not plead a recovery against the other, to whom he is a stranger.

To this *Fenner* answered that he can.

The case was moved again, and ANDERSON C.J. held strongly that either is punishable in an action on the case, and so the plea is nought; and he should have pleaded Not guilty.

But the other three justices held the plea good, and a sufficient confession and avoidance, because this action supposes a fraudulent conversion, and here he justifies by a lawful conversion: for they held the law to be that an action on the case lies against a finder, and detinue against the possessor, but no action on the case against a person who is their grantee.

Afterwards it was adjudged for the plaintiff that the bar is not good.

No judgment is entered. The record ends with the adjournment to Michaelmas term 1589. Cf. *Vandrink v Archer* (1590) 1 Leon. 221, an action with a closely similar plea and demurrer, in which judgment was given for the plaintiff. The reporter above may have confused the two cases. In the second

9   The LI MS. attributes these reports to Edward Henden (1558–1644), who was admitted to Gray's Inn in 1586. Also reported in 1 Leon. 189.

10   Cf. different report in HLS MS. 110, fo. 5v: '... Note that WALMSLEY J. said that in detinue or in an action on the case upon trover it is no plea that before the action brought he had delivered over the goods or lost them; but it is a good plea to plead a bailment to him by a stranger, to be returned, and that he had returned them before the action was brought, for he was compellable to do that'. And see 1 Leon. 189: '... by some, the defendant, having the goods by sale, might traverse the finding... and, by WYNDHAM J., the defendant may traverse the property of the goods in the plaintiff...'

case, Anderson C.J. and Wyndham J. said the plea confessed the conversion without avoiding it by showing good title; Peryam J. doubted, but thought that neither the property nor the knowing was traversable, and that such things should be given in evidence under Not guilty; while Walmsley J. thought the sale of the goods here was not a conversion. There seems to have been considerable vacillation.

EASON v NEWMAN (1596)

Record: KB 27/1332, m. 460. John Eason, executor of John Pepper, brought a bill in the Queen's Bench against Richard Newman, complaining that, whereas on 12 October 1587 John Pepper was possessed at Throwley, Kent, of three joined bedsteads, a joined press, two joined stools, a joined form, three chests, a pewter dish, a leather bottle, a brass mortar, a great joined chair, three tubs, a cauldron, a brass pot, a kettle, two spits, one 'pair of irons to make cakes withall', six trugs 'to put milk in', three painted cloths, a bed mat, three latten candlesticks, an iron 'peele', two stocks of bees, a cupboard, a table, and a bed pan, and on 31 October 1590 accidentally lost them, and on 10 November 1590 they came into Newman's possession by finding: nevertheless Newman, knowing them to belong to Pepper in his lifetime and to his executors after his death, did not give them back, but on 1 November 1593 converted them to his own use. On 23 January 1595 Newman pleaded Not guilty, and at Maidstone assizes on 14 July (GAWDY J.Q.B., OWEN J.C.P.) the jury found him not guilty as to some of the goods; as to the others they found specially that they came to him by finding, and that he 'utterly refused to deliver them and still withholds the same goods and chattels' in his own keeping, concluding that they did not know whether this *denegatio et detentio* should be adjudged in law a conversion. The case was argued in banc in October 1596.

HLS MS. 110, fo. 218v.[11]

... FENNER J. When someone comes to goods by finding, this is by act of the law; because, as they are out of the owner's possession, it is quite permissible for anyone to take them and keep them to the owner's use. But according to 33 Hen. VI,[12] if a man finds my goods and I request the party to give them up, and he refuses, an action of trespass lies against the party, because he relinquishes the act which the law gives him by way of justification and betakes himself to wrong. But in this case now in question, the goods were lost by the testator, and so the present plaintiff cannot have trespass for the refusal, since here the act began to be wrongful *ab initio*.

---

11 Also reported in Cro. Eliz. 495; Moo. K.B. 460; Goulds. 152; 1 Rolle Abr. 5, line 43.
12 *Carles v Malpas* (1455) Y.B. Trin. 33 Hen. VI, fo. 26, pl. 12.

Nevertheless the denial and withholding are a conversion, and are like a using of the goods . . .

GAWDY J. Although the opinion of the Common Bench is that if a man can take the proper action to recover damages or the thing in demand he shall not have this action, it is nevertheless not right that if the defendant commits a further wrong to the thing the plaintiff should not have this action also, or the proper action, at his election. Thus in 2 Hen. VII, fo. 12,[13] if John Style receives my goods delivered by me to keep in the same way as his own goods, and he allows moths to ruin them, or allows some other damage to spoil them, although upon the delivery I may have an action of detinue, it is nevertheless right that for this negligent tort and wrong I should maintain an action on my case. To this same effect is 20 Hen. VII, fo. 8[14]. . . The law is the same in this case now in question: although the plaintiff could have had an action of detinue for the goods, whereby he could recover the things themselves, nevertheless the withholding and refusing to deliver them is another wrong, properly to be punished by this action. And so it seemed to him that this refusal was a conversion.

CLENCH J. was also of this opinion.

But GAWDY J. doubted whether the plaintiff here ought to recover or not, because the jury have found the defendant guilty only of the conversion. (Query, because I do not understand him.)

[. . . being afterwards moved again, POPHAM C.J. held it to be no conversion. But it was cited at the bar that [in] 23 Eliz. in this court it was ruled to the contrary.

And it was adjourned.][15]

The record shows that on 8 October the court gave judgment for the plaintiff on the special verdict, with £3. 18s. damages and £8. 10s. costs.

WATSON v SMITH (1599)
Cro. Eliz. 723, pl. 16 (C.P.) (untr.).

Action for trover and conversion of an obligation.

WALMSLEY, GLANVILL and KINGSMILL JJ. held that it lies not: for if he finds the obligation and cancels it, trespass *vi et armis* lies, for he destroys the thing found; and if he receive the money, and deliver the obligation to the obligor, account lies, and not this action.

13   See p. 398, above.
14   *Orwell v Mortoft* (1505); see p. 406, above.
15   From Cro. Eliz. 495.

HALLIDAY v HIGGES (1600)

Record: KB 27/1349, m. 336. Leonard and William Halliday in Michaelmas term 1597 brought a bill in the Queen's Bench against Robert Higges, and complained that, whereas on 31 August 1597 they had lost £120 in coin in the parish of St Mary-le-Bow, London, and on 8 September it came into the defendant's possession by finding: nevertheless the defendant, knowing the money to belong to the plaintiffs, did not deliver it when requested on 20 September but on 23 September converted it to his own use. On 3 May 1598 Higges pleaded Not guilty, and on 21 October 1598 at the Guildhall, London, before POPHAM C.J., a special verdict was found: Higges was the plaintiffs' servant and factor, and had received from them 200 quarters of grain to sell for them, and he sold some for £25, which he received and took away and, instead of paying it over to the plaintiffs, converted to his own use. As to the other £95, they found him not guilty. The case was argued in banc in 1599 (see Cro. Eliz. 638, 661), and on 25 April judgment was given for the plaintiff to recover £25 damages with £8. 13s. 4d. costs. A writ of error was immediately purchased, and the case was reargued in the Exchequer Chamber.

BL MS. Add. 25203, fo. 147v; YLS MS. G. R29.14,
fo. 15v; abridged in Cro. Eliz. 746, pl. 2.

... When the case was moved last Michaelmas term [1599], ANDERSON C.J. thought that the property in the money was never in the master, but in the servant; for if a man bails money the property therein is in the bailee, since the money cannot be identified. Therefore he ought to have a writ of account.

The others agreed, except for CLARKE B.

WALMSLEY J. said that the writ of account itself proves that the property of the money is in the plaintiff, since the writ supposes the defendant to be receiver of the plaintiff's money. But he said that the declaration was invalid; for it expressly alleges that the plaintiff accidentally lost the money out of his possession, and when he has lost the possession of it he has also lost the property (for the reason given by ANDERSON C.J.) Therefore he cannot have an action on the case, because at the time when the money was found it was not his. It is otherwise where a man bails money. (The reason behind his distinction, as I conceive, was that the bailee's possession is the master's possession, and so it is not like the case of finding.)

It was adjourned until this term, and now *Stevens* moved that the action does not lie; for it appears that Higges was Halliday's bailee of his wheat, and therefore he ought to have had a writ of account, in which the bailee would have an allowance for his expenses; whereas if this action were to lie, the defendant would lose all these allowances. And in truth when the defendant received the wheat he was under age, and so he cannot be charged in an account; and therefore they have devised this shift to deprive him of the benefit of his nonage.

This time they all agreed clearly that the action did not lie, for the reason given by WALMSLEY J. last term ... Therefore they all agreed that the judgment should be reversed.

Cf. Cro. Eliz. 661; 'all the justices and barons resolved that this action lies not for money found, unless it be in a bag or chest'. The King's Bench record does not contain this judgment. The particular point was overruled by the Exchequer Chamber in *Kynaston v Moore* (1627); see p. 545, below.

BYSSHOPPE v VISCOUNTESS MOUNTAGUE (1604)

Record: CP 40/1640, m. 733 (Pas. 1600). Richard Bysshoppe and William Jorden, executors of John Bysshoppe, brought an action on the case against Magdalene, viscountess Mountague, for trover and conversion of five oxen at Ewhurst, Sussex, on 21 March 1596. The viscountess pleaded Not guilty, and in Easter term 1601 the jury found her not guilty as to three oxen; and as to the other two found specially that she was seised of the manor of Battle for life, that the testator died possessed of the oxen on 4 March 1596, that the plaintiffs were possessed of the same oxen as executors after his death, and that Anthony Loe as bailiff of the manor took the oxen as heriot due to the viscountess (having no title to do so), and the viscountess later agreed to the taking and converted the oxen to her own use; and that Loe had died before the writ was brought. The first motion in banc is reported in the same term as the special verdict in banc.

(a) Pas. 1601: Cro. Eliz. 824, pl. 1 (untr.).

... And whether this action lies, or that he should have brought a general action of trespass, was the question.

WALMSLEY and KINGSMILL JJ. held that this action lies not, for when the bailiff took them tortiously the property and the possession is divested out of the plaintiff, so that he cannot suppose that he was possessed of them until he lost them and until they came to the defendant's hands. And the defendant, by assenting to the taking, is a trespasser *ab initio* ... Therefore, where he might have had a general writ of trespass, he cannot have any other manner of action: especially not this action, which differs from it in nature and quality.

ANDERSON C.J. and WARBURTON J. to the contrary. They agreed that an assent before or after the taking of the goods made her trespasser *ab initio*, and to be punished as a trespasser; but not an assent after to a battery formerly done, or to that which is a tort and punishable by the statute law (as, an assent to a riot or forcible entry after it be done, shall not make him punishable). But although trespass lies, yet he may have this action if he will, for he hath his election to bring either. And, as he may have detinue or replevin for goods taken by a trespass, which affirms always property in him at his election, so he may have this action; for one may qualify a tort, but not increase a tort. So he hath election to make it a tortious prisal or not: which is the reason that if goods be taken by a trespasser, yet if the party from whom they were taken be attainted of felony he shall forfeit them, for the right and property remain in him, and the law shall adjudge them in him until he makes his election to the contrary by bringing a writ of trespass. Wherefore here he might maintain the one writ or the other, at his election.

(b) Mich. 1604: Cro. Jac. 50, pl. 21; corrected from
HLS MS. 105, fo. 116.

... *Foster*, for the plaintiff, argued that this action well lay; for it is at his election whether he will admit himself to be out of possession or not, for he might have had a replevin if he would; and in this action the trover is not traversable, but the conversion only is material.

Herne to the contrary, because the property is gone by the taking, so as he cannot dispose of them ... And here the proper action is trespass.

WALMSLEY J.[16] agreed; for trespass and trover are contrary actions: for it cannot be that he should have property and no property at one and the same time. And there is not any word of the writ true, for he hath not any property at the time of the conversion ...

And of that opinion was DANIEL J.

But ANDERSON C.J., WARBURTON[17] and KINGSMILL JJ. to the contrary, and that he had election to bring either of the actions at his pleasure.

Wherefore it was adjudged for the plaintiff.

The record shows that judgment was entered in Michaelmas term 1604 for £7 damages and £20 costs (increased by the court from 12d.).

ISAACK v CLARK (1615)

Record: KB 27/1440, m. 1100. Thomas Isaack brought an action on the case

16 MS. The printed text interchanges Walmsley and Warburton.
17 MS. See fn. 16, above.

against James Clark for trover and conversion of a bag of money at Tavistock, Devon, in February 1609. The defendant pleaded Not guilty, and the jury found a special verdict: that one Richard Adams had recovered a debt against one William Lewes in the Guildhall Court of Exeter, and a writ of *capias ad satisfaciendum* had been awarded against Lewes, and the writ came to the defendant as serjeant at mace, who returned it *non est inventus*; a writ of *fieri facias* was then awarded against one of Lewes's pledges; and the plaintiff, to prevent three butts of sack being sold in execution, pawned the bag of money to Clark, to retain until the next court-day as a pledge for the redelivery of the wine to Clark if the surety failed in the interim to obtain Adams's leave to stay execution; that the surety did not obtain this leave; but the plaintiff requested the defendant to return the bag of money, which he refused to do.

2 Buls. 306 (untr.).[18]

... HOUGHTON J. In this case judgment ought to be given for the defendant, there being no cause here for the plaintiff to have this money. There is no conversion here; nor is there any trover in the case. The matter upon which this action is grounded is not the trover, but the conversion to his use: this is the trespass. As this case here is, if there had been a conversion the action would have held, though no trover. Here he came to these goods by bailment ... and many times in detinue or trover the bailment comes not in question, nor is material, if the conversion be actionable. As to the verdict here, the jury find nothing of the trover, because he came unto the goods by bailment and therefore not guilty as to this; but though the action is here brought for a trover and conversion, and no trover in the case because he had the goods by bailment, yet if there be a conversion the court shall judge upon this ... Here is no sufficient cause or ground for an action of trover by the plaintiff. It is only found that he did request him to deliver this money, and that he refused to do it, and so much is in every action of detinue: *contradixit et adhuc contradicit*, this is the point of the action of detinue; but this is not conversion. He may require him to make delivery thereof in one place, and the goods may be in another place: shall this denier here by a conversion? It shall not, but of necessity there ought to be some user of it to make a conversion. If he keeps this in his chest, this is no conversion. The denier here is but the not doing of an act, and this shall make no conversion ...

DODDERIDGE J. In this case these things are considerable: (1) what action this plaintiff here shall have, and whether this verdict

18   Also reported in 1 Rolle Rep. 59 (Mich. 1614), 126; Moo. K.B. 841 (who says it was first argued in Trin. 1614). There is another full report in HLS MS. 109, ff. 49v–54.

will maintain his action, [i.e.] whether he is here to have an action of detinue or an action upon the case; (2) if an action upon the case, then whether an action upon the case for a trover and conversion: (3) and if so, then whether there be any conversion found, or not. For the first, he may have an action upon the case, as this case here is, but not an action upon the case for a trover and conversion, but a special action on the case upon his case. But if he might have an action upon the case for a trover and conversion, then I should hold that here is a good and sufficient conversion found. And therefore it is good advice for all counsellors to show unto their clients their proper actions, which they are to have suitable to their cause or complaint and as the same shall require ... As to the conversion, whether here be any or not is the question. I agree that a denier to deliver doth not in every case make a conversion, as in detinue there is a denier (*et adhuc detinet*); but when an action is framed by one upon his case (as here it is), a denier will make a conversion ...[19]

CROKE J. Judgment ought to be given in this case for the defendant, in regard that the plaintiff here hath no cause of action. This money here, which was thus bailed or pledged, ought not to be delivered until the three butts of sack are delivered ... Here an action upon the case for a trover and conversion is brought by the plaintiff, for the not delivery of this pledge, the debt not being discharged: and this ought to be first done, and the serjeant here ought not to make any demand to have delivery made unto him of three butts of sack. A bare denial shall not make a conversion; neither shall there be any conversion so long as the privity of the bailment remains. But destroy this, and then otherwise it shall be. The bailee here is as a possessor *bonae fidei*. To make a conversion there ought to be a pertinacy and also a contumacy in the manner of the denier, namely '*contradixit et adhuc contradicit*'. We are to see and to examine when the wrong begins to the party. The wrong begins by the denier. By this denier he is possessor *malae fidei*. By this denier the privity of bailment is altogether destroyed, if they are *bona peritura*: as sour wine, corn musty. This denier keeps the party from his possession, and this is a wrong ... Here in this case, the condition annexed unto the pledge is not performed; and until performance of which the same is not to be delivered. And so the

---

19 He based the remainder of his judgment on *Eason v Newman* (1596); see p. 537, above. Cf. Rolle Rep. '... it was said at the bar, and by COKE C.J., that they had a report of this case in which the court was divided; but it was afterwards adjudged [for the plaintiff], as appears by the record, as has been alleged. COKE C.J. said that the reason given by those who held the denial to be a conversion was that he came to the goods by trover, and the denial of them afterwards made him a trespasser *ab initio*: which cannot be law, this being merely nonfeasance ...'

plaintiff hath no cause of action. Judgment is therefore to be given against him.

COKE C.J. In this case the judgment ought to be 'that the plaintiff take nothing by his bill'. Divers things in this case are considerable. Here is an action upon the case brought upon a trover and conversion. The jury find that these goods came to his hands by bailment. This action upon the case is a magistral action: he ought to comprehend his case in the action upon the case. He comes to these goods by the privity of bailment. The second point considerable is what he is to recover in the action upon the case, whether anything in special or the whole value. And in this, the third thing, whether the property be changed. By the judgment and execution the property is changed. The fourth thing considerable is this: a man finds my goods, if he remove the possession, whether he shall then be chargeable or not. The fifth and last matter is touching the conversion, and whether here be any conversion in this case or not . . .

What shall make a conversion? As to this, there ought to be an act done, to convert one thing to another. And whether a denier only shall make a conversion? By this you will confound all form: for then, [in] this way, every action of detinue shall be an action upon the case upon a trover, because there is a denier. If this should be so, there would be a double conversion, namely a denier and a request. In no case you shall have a man to be a trespasser upon the case without some act done . . . 'He converted and disposed to his own use': these are the words that make a conversion. And therefore it shall be very absurd if every denier should be said to be a conversion. The party makes a request to have his goods, the other doth not deliver them: it should be a hard case to make him by this to be a trespasser, and subject unto an action upon the case for a trover and conversion only by his denier to deliver them (being demanded); but there ought to be some other act done by him to make him thereby to be such a trespasser as that 'he converted and disposed to his own use' . . . I agree that in some cases a denier to deliver the same shall make a conversion, as if it be of money which cannot be known from other money (as if it be out of a bag), thereupon his refusal to deliver the same (being demanded), for this an action upon the case sur trover lieth: but if it be for money in a bag, there upon his denier no trover lieth, but an action of detinue . . . Here [the defendant] is a serjeant at mace, not a serjeant at law: he did not know whether the condition was performed or not. So this refusal is good evidence to a jury, but no good conversion in point of law.[20] As to the verdict, and the exceptions taken to it, which have been well and truly taken (concerning the finding and the conversion): they find the defendant guilty, and upon the whole matter he is not guilty of the finding, for they find 'that he pledged [the goods]'. Herein I agree in opinion that this finding of theirs is not material ... juries are to meddle with matters of fact, but not with the matter here of a conversion, being matter in law: this is only to be determined by the judges.[1] I agree also in this, that until the three butts of sack are delivered to him the plaintiff is not to have his money ... So that in this case we do all of us agree in this, that prima facie a denier upon a demand is a good evidence to a jury of a conversion; but if the contrary be showed, then the same is no conversion.

And so the judges all agreed in this case, upon the whole matter to them appearing, for the defendant and against the plaintiff, that he had no just cause of action. And, according to this, the judgment of the court was pronounced, and so entered: 'that the plaintiff take nothing by his bill'.

KYNASTON v MOORE (1627)

Record: KB 27/1553, m. 850. Thomas Kynaston brought an action on the case against George Moore for trover and conversion of a pack of flax and £196 in coin, in London. The defendant pleaded Not guilty, and on 10 February 1627 at the Guildhall, London, before Hyde C.J., the jury found for the plaintiff with £199. 5s. damages. Judgment was given accordingly, and in April Moore brought a writ of error in the Exchequer Chamber.

Cro. Car. 89, pl. 14 (untr.).

... The error was assigned, because trover and conversion cannot be of money out of a bag.[2]

---

20 Cf. Rolle Rep.: '... HOUGHTON J.... A conversion is in the use of the thing, though delivery of it to someone else (or such like) may be a conversion. I agree, however, that a denial is good evidence to the jury that he has converted it: which was agreed by the whole court. For when he refuses it shall be presumed that he has converted it to his use, and therefore "it shall stand presumed until the contrary has been proved" (as COKE C.J. said). But since the jury has found only a denial upon request, and no other conversion, the court cannot adjudge it to be a conversion, this being only a nonfeasance'.

1 Coke here cites a maxim of which he was very fond: *ad quaestionem facti non respondent jurisperiti* [or *judices*], *ad quaestionem juris non respondent juratores.* He attributed it to Bracton, but is suspected of having invented it: Pollock and Maitland, *History of English Law*, vol. II, p. 629, n. 3.

2 I.e. money not in a bag.

But all the justices and barons agreed that it well lies: for although it was alleged that money lost cannot be known (and so whether it was the plaintiff's money, whereof the trover and conversion was, as is the charge of this action), yet the court said, it being found by a jury that he converted the plaintiff's money (for the losing is but a surmise and not material . . .), the plaintiff had good cause of action.

Wherefore the judgment before well given was now affirmed.

The justices and barons said that this action lies as well for money out of a bag as of corn, which cannot be known.

The record shows that judgment was affirmed in the Exchequer Chamber on 24 November 1627.

PUTT v RAWSTORNE (1682)

Record: KB 27/2020, m. 442. Samuel Putt and William Hardy brought a bill in the King's Bench against Sir William Rawstorne, Sir Thomas Beckford and Miles March, esquire, complaining of a trover and conversion of numerous items of furniture, bedding and other household goods in May 1680. The defendants pleaded that an action of trespass *vi et armis* had been brought for the same goods, alleged to have been taken by them and disposed of to their own use in April 1678, and a judgment had been given in their favour; and that the cause of action was one and the same. The plaintiffs demurred.

T. Raym. 472 (untr.).[3]

. . . And adjudged for the plaintiff[s], in this action of trover, because trover and trespass are actions sometimes of a different nature. For trover will sometimes lie where trespass *vi et armis* will not lie: as, if a man hath my goods by my delivery to keep for me, and I afterwards demand them and he refuses to deliver them, I may have an action of trover but not trespass *vi et armis*, because here was no tortious taking. And sometimes the case may be such that either the one or the other will lie, as where there is a tortious taking away of goods and detaining them the party may have either trover or trespass; and in such case judgment in one action is a bar in the other. And the rule for this purpose is that wheresoever the same evidence will maintain both the actions, there the recovery or judgment in one may be pleaded in bar of the other; but otherwise

---

3 Sub nom. *Put v Rawsterne*. Also reported in Pollex. 634; 2 Show. K.B. 211; 2 Mod. 318; 3 Mod. 1.

not ... This judgment was given positively by PEMBERTON C.J., JONES J. and myself,[4] DOLBEN J. *haesitante.*

The record shows that in Michaelmas term 1682, after a writ of inquiry as to the damages, judgment was entered for the plaintiffs for £600 damages and £29 costs.

ARMORY v DELAMIRIE (1722)

1 Stra. 505, at *nisi prius* before Pratt C.J.K.B. in
Middlesex (untr.).

The plaintiff, being a chimney-sweeper's boy, found a jewel and carried it to the defendant's shop (who was a goldsmith)[5] to know what it was and delivered it into the hands of the apprentice, who under pretence of weighing it took out the stones and, calling to the master to let him know it came to three-halfpence, the master offered the boy the money, who refused to take it and insisted to have the thing again; whereupon the apprentice delivered him back the socket without the stones. And now in trover against the master these points were ruled:

1 That the finder of a jewel, though he does not by such finding acquire an absolute property or ownership, yet he has such a property as will enable him to keep it against all but the rightful owner; and consequently may maintain trover.

2 That the action well lay against the master, who gives a credit to his apprentice and is answerable for his neglect.

3 As to the value of the jewel, several of the trade were examined to prove what a jewel of the finest water that would fit the socket would be worth. And [PRATT] C.J. directed the jury that, unless the defendant did produce the jewel and show it not to be of the finest water, they should presume the strongest against him and make the value of the best jewels the measure of their damages: which they accordingly did.

HARTOP v HOARE (1743)

2 Stra. 1187 (K.B.) (untr.).[6]

In trover for jewels, the jury found this special verdict: that the

---

4 Sir Thomas Raymond J.K.B.
5 Paul Lamerie (as he is now better known) was one of the leading goldsmiths of the time.
6 Also reported in 1 Wils. K.B. 8; and very fully in 2 Atk. 44 (where numerous authorities are considered).

plaintiff, being owner of the jewels, lodged them in the hands of Seamer (a goldsmith) for safe custody only, enclosed in a paper sealed up, and that also enclosed in a bag sealed up with the plaintiff's seal, and took a receipt from him for the same; that Seamer broke the seals and carried the jewels to the defendants' open shop in Fleet Street,[7] where they traded in jewels and often lent money on the security of jewels, and there borrowed of them £300 and deposited the jewels as his own, by way of security, at the same time giving his note for the money; that Seamer had no authority from the plaintiff to sell, order, pawn or dispose of the jewels; and that the defendants have converted them to their own use.

This cause was twice solemnly argued at the bar: the first time by Sjt. *Prime* and Mr. *Mildmay*, and the second time by myself[8] and Mr. *Bootle*.

And this term [LEE] C.J. delivered the resolution of the court as follows. The general question in this case is whether the property found to be originally in the plaintiff is divested by any act found to have been done in this case. In order to consider this, it will be proper to see (1) how Seamer stands with regard to the plaintiff, and (2) with regard to the defendants. (1) As to the plaintiff he is a mere bailee for safe custody only, without any authority to open the bag the jewels were in; and he was a trespasser in so doing[9]. . . (2) As to the defendants, though they came honestly by them, yet they are within the general rule of *caveat emptor*, unless something appears particularly to exempt them. What they rely upon is that they are purchasers of them in a market overt, it being found that they bought them in an open shop where they dealt in jewels, which according to the custom of London is a market overt for that purpose. To this it was properly answered by the plaintiff that this custom not being found the court cannot judicially take notice of it; and in all cases these customs are pleaded or found . . . Another, and we think also a proper answer was likewise given, that if we could take notice of the custom yet that extends only to the case of a sale and not of a pawn . . . It is a rule that all customs must be taken strictly, and not extended to similar cases . . . but here a pawn is not a similar case: sales in market overt are encouraged, because

---

7 Sir Richard Hoare (d. 1754), was grandson of Sir Richard Hoare (d. 1718), who founded the merchant bank.

8 Sir John Strange K.C.

9 Cf. Wilson's report: '. . . We are of opinion that Seymour [Seamer] had no property general or special; it is true they originally came by right to him, but when he broke the seal he became a possessor *malâ fide*'.

it is a circulation of property, whereas pawning is *pro tempore* a locking of it up ... We are all of opinion, the plaintiff must have judgment.

COOPER v CHITTY (1756)

1 Burr. 20 (K.B.).[10]

This cause was twice argued. It came first before the court on Monday 9 June 1755, and again upon Tuesday the 10th instant [November 1756]. It was an action of trover brought by the assignees of William Johns, a bankrupt, against the sheriffs of London, who had taken and sold the goods of Johns in execution under a *fieri facias* which had issued against Johns at the suit of one William Godfrey. On the trial, a special case was settled,[11] which case states: that Johns was regularly declared a bankrupt on 8 December 1753, and as to the rest the following times and facts were stated: viz. that on 5 December 1753 one Godfrey obtained judgment in the Common Pleas against the said Johns; and on the same day (5 December 1753) execution upon the said judgment was taken out against him by Godfrey, and the goods seized by the sheriffs under it; that Johns committed the act of bankruptcy on 4 December 1753, and on the 8th of the same December a commission of bankruptcy was taken out against him; and on the very same day the commissioners of bankruptcy executed an assignment; and afterwards, viz. on 28 December, a bill of sale of the goods was made by the sheriffs. The plaintiffs are the assignees under the commission; the defendants are the sheriffs of London who seized the goods under the execution. The point was, whether the assignees under the commission of bankruptcy can maintain an action of trover against the sheriffs, who executed this process under a regular judgment and execution, for seizing the goods under a *fieri facias* issued and executed after the act of bankruptcy was committed, and selling them after the assignment was executed ...

And now (Tuesday 23 November 1756) LORD MANSFIELD C.J. delivered the opinion of the court, and said they were all agreed, as

---

10 Also reported in 1 Wm. Bla. 65; 1 Kenyon 395.

11 There is no mention of this in the record (KB 122/261, m. 869), which contains an action of trover in common form by Francis Cooper and Henry Read, as assignees of William John, against Thomas Chitty and Matthew Blakiston, for various domestic chattels; a plea of Not guilty; and process against the jury to Trin. 1754 only.

well his two brethren then present in court as his Brother WILMOT J. who was at present engaged in another place, in their opinion. There are few facts essential to this case, and it lies in a narrow compass. (He then stated the case ... and was very particular in specifying the dates of the several transactions.) The general question is: whether or not the action is maintainable by the assignees against the defendants, the sheriffs, who have taken and sold the goods. It is an action of trover. The bare defining the nature of this kind of action, and the grounds upon which a plaintiff is entitled to recover in it, will go a great way towards the understanding, and consequently towards the solution, of the question in this particular case. In form it is a fiction: in substance a remedy to recover the value of personal chattels wrongfully converted by another to his own use. The form supposes the defendant may have come lawfully by the possession of the goods. This action lies, and has been brought in many cases where, in truth, the defendant has got the possession lawfully. Where the defendant takes them wrongfully, and by trespass, the plaintiff (if he thinks fit to bring this action) waives the trespass and admits the possession to have been lawfully gotten. Hence, if the defendant delivers the thing upon demand, no damages can be recovered in this action for having taken it. This is an action of tort, and the whole tort consists in the wrongful conversion. Two things are necessary to be proved to entitle the plaintiff to recover in this kind of action: first, property in the plaintiff, and secondly, a wrongful conversion by the defendant.

As to the first, it is admitted in the present case that the property was in the plaintiffs as on and from 4 December (which was before the seizure), by relation ...

Secondly, the only question then is, whether the defendants are guilty of a wrongful conversion. That the conversion itself was wrongful is manifest: the sheriffs had no authority to sell the goods of the plaintiffs, but of William Johns only ... It is admitted on the part of the defendants that the innocent vendee of the goods so seized can have no title under the sale, but is liable to an action; and that Godfrey the plaintiff would have no title to the money arising from such sale, but if he received it would be liable to an action to refund. If the thing be clearly wrong, the only question that remains is whether the defendants are excusable ... The fallacy of the [defendant's argument] turns upon using the word 'lawful' equivocally in two senses. To support the act, it is not lawful; but to excuse the mistake of the sheriff through unavoidable ignorance, it is lawful. Or, in other words, the relation introduced by the statutes binds the property; but men who act innocently at the time are not made criminals by relation, and therefore they are excusable from being punishable by action or indictment as trespassers. What they did was innocent, and in that sense lawful; but as a ground to support a wrongful conversion by sale, after a commission publicly taken out and an actual assignment made, it was not lawful . . .

Judgment for the plaintiffs.

22 Actions on the case for negligence

(1) Custom of the realm: innkeepers

NAVENBY v LASSELS (1368)

(a) Record: KB 27/428, m. 73;
Selden Soc. vol. 82, pl. 152

Huntingdonshire. Walter Lassels of Huntingdon and William of Stamford, ostler of the aforesaid Walter, were attached to answer both the lord king and Thomas of Navenby, the king's under-escheator in the county of Northampton, concerning a plea ... to the damage and in contempt of the lord king and to the no small expense and burden of the selfsame Thomas, and against the peace etc. And thereupon the same Thomas of Navenby, who sues for the king as well as for himself, by William of Stathern his attorney, complains that, whereas according to the law and custom of the king's realm innkeepers who keep common inns in order to accommodate men travelling through the places where such inns are, and lodging in the same, are bound to keep their goods (which are inside those inns) day and night without any removal or loss, so that damage does not befall such travellers in any way through the fault of the said innkeepers or their servants: certain wrongdoers on Tuesday [5 October 1367] before the feast of St Denys in the forty-first year of the reign of the present lord king, with force and arms (namely, with swords etc.),[1] broke by night into a certain chamber wherein the aforesaid Thomas was lodged in the aforesaid Walter's inn at Huntingdon, while he was coming to London on the king's business, and took and carried away goods and chattels

---

1 Note that the force is alleged in the wrongdoers, not in the defendant.

of the same Thomas to the value of £4, namely one belt, a seal with a silver chain, one sword with a buckler, linen and woollen cloths, and one baselard, and also £9 of the king's money which was in the same Thomas's keeping, through the fault of the same Walter and William, against the peace; whereby he says he is the worse and has damage to the extent of £15. And thereof he produces suit etc.

And the aforesaid Walter Lassels and William of Stamford, by John of St Neot's their attorney, come and deny the force and wrong when etc., and whatever [is against the peace] etc., and make protestation that they do not confess that Thomas has lost any goods or chattels as he complains. And the aforesaid Walter Lassels says that at the time when the same Thomas supposes the aforesaid trespass to have been done to him, and before and after that, he was out of the area (that is to say, he was in the county of Essex), and so the aforesaid Thomas was not lodged there by him, the said Walter, and did not lose any chattels through his fault. And of this he puts himself upon the country etc. And the aforesaid William says that the aforesaid Thomas, at the aforesaid time etc., was lodged by the selfsame William, and the same William delivered to the same Thomas and his servants a certain room with a sufficient lock, and they were at the time content with this room; and he says that the security (*claustura*) of the said inn was sufficient, and therefore the aforesaid Thomas did not lose any goods or chattels through his fault, as he complains. And of this likewise he puts himself upon the country etc.

The parties were adjourned from Gloucester, where the King's Bench was sitting, to Westminster; and in Easter term 1368 the plaintiff demurred specially, on the grounds that Walter had not denied that he kept a common inn and that William was his ostler, nor that Thomas was lodged in the inn by William, who received his goods into the inn, nor that Thomas lost his goods there.

(b) Report: 42 Lib. Ass., pl. 17.[2]

. . . William came and pleaded that the plaintiff was not damaged through his fault.

Childrey. You shall not get to that, since he has not denied that he is a common innkeeper or that the plaintiff was lodged with him; and so long as that is so, he comes under your protection and safeguard. We demand judgment whether he can succeed in saying that the plaintiff was not damaged through his fault. And we pray that he be convicted.

---

2   Also reported, on another point, in Y.B. Pas. 42 Edw. III, fo. 11, pl. 13.

The other side to the contrary; inasmuch as the plaintiff did not say that the damage was done by the defendant, he demands judgment.

KNYVET [C.J.] and INGLEBY, by the advice of their fellows, and of the serjeants, awarded that the plaintiff recover the principal and his damages taxed by the court at [£]15. For KNYVET said that a similar case had previously been adjudged in the Council, and the cause of the judgment was that an innkeeper should answer for himself and his household in respect of the rooms and stables . . .

The record shows that in Michaelmas term 1368 the court gave judgment for the plaintiff to recover £13 for the chattels and 40s. damages, taxed by the court.

HORSLOW'S CASE (1443)

Y.B. Mich. 22 Hen. VI, fo. 21, pl. 38.

A writ of trespass on the case was brought against W. Horslow, labourer, for this: that the common law of the land is that innkeepers who keep common inns ought to keep safely the goods of those lodged in their inns, so that no damage should befall them by persons unknown; and the plaintiff showed how certain of his goods (and he set out which) were taken out of his possession in the defendant's house by persons unknown.

Prysot. [We demand] judgment of the writ; for the writ says 'whereas according to the law and custom of the realm', and in that case it appears that the aforesaid matter lies in custom, which shall not be understood as the common law.

NEWTON [C.J.] What is the custom of the [realm][3] but the law of the land? So, as to that, answer . . .

Prysot. Again [we demand] judgment of the writ, for the custom is recited in respect of common inns, and by the writ and count it is not shown that the defendant's house (in which the goods were taken) is a common inn: so it may be that it is not a common inn. If someone is lodged with me, or in the house of a husbandman (which is not a common inn), even though his goods are taken out of his possession his action fails.

NEWTON. The exception is good, and we will be advised. On another day, *Markham* would not waive this writ and take another.

Browne.[4] This writ is good, and the course is not otherwise. (And he showed two or three precedents.)

3 'land'.
4 Thomas Browne, the second prothonotary.

Prysot. All those writs are *pone etc.* such and such, 'innkeeper', and it cannot be otherwise presumed than that his house is a common inn. But in the case at the bar the defendant is not named 'innkeeper', but 'W. Horslow, labourer'.

Browne. No addition need be given in this action, because process of outlawry does not lie in the said action.[5]

NEWTON. A labourer may keep a common inn; and, conversely, an innkeeper may have other houses for lodging [people] by his licence and good will . . .

On another day the writ was adjudged good.

Prysot. You ought not to have the action, for we ourselves delivered to the plaintiff a room and a key thereto, to have and to hold in his keeping, to keep his goods safely; and we say that the plaintiff brought certain unknown persons into his room, who took the aforesaid goods; judgment *Si action* etc.

Markham. That plea amounts to nothing other than that the goods were [not] taken through your fault.

NEWTON. The plea is good if he names those who took the goods, for to him they are persons unknown and the law excuses him in respect of this taking.

Prysot showed their names: Thomas T. and W. Liere.

Markham. The said T. and W., whom we brought with us into the room, did not take away the goods.

NEWTON. That is a negative pregnant[6]. . .

Prysot. To prevent ambiguity, we say that the goods were not taken through our default.

FULTHORPE. That is no issue.

Browne. Such an issue has been taken and entered before now.

Afterwards *Prysot* pleaded the former bar, as above.

Markham. We did not bring the said W. and T. with us into the room; ready . . .

It later became a common form of pleading that the defendant had given the plaintiff a key to his room, and that the plaintiff had himself let in the person who took the goods: e.g., *Kyrkeham v Jenkyns* (1502) CP 40/959, m. 158 (goods taken by plaintiff's servant); *Robyns v Dyngley* (1505) CP 40/974, m. 353 (goods taken by labourer to whom plaintiff's servant gave the key). There were also attempts to plead that the goods were brought into the inn at the plaintiff's own risk (in other words, that the custom could be overridden by contract): see Selden Soc. vol. 94, p. *228*. In *Sanders v Spencer* (1567) Dyer 266; LI MS. Maynard 77, fo. 3; it was held a good plea that the innkeeper had offered to put the goods in a safe store, with a key, but that

5 See p. 342, above.
6 See Selden Soc. vol. 94, p. *150*.

the plaintiff had left them lying in the courtyard, where they were taken by evil persons through the plaintiff's own fault. And in *Windham v Mead* (1586) 4 Leon. 96; HLS MS. 16, fo. 345v; it was held a good plea that the innkeeper put the plaintiff's horse out to pasture at the plaintiff's command, and it was stolen in the field.

JELLEY v CLARKE (1607)

Record: KB 27/1396, m. 254; abstracted in Kiralfy, *Source Book*, p. 205. William Jelley brought an action on the case against Philip Clarke on the custom of the realm concerning innkeepers, for the loss of a hamper containing nine felt hats (worth £4) from the defendant's common inn, the White Hart at Uxbridge, Middlesex, on 26 May 1605. The defendant pleaded Not guilty, and the jury found a special verdict: the plaintiff brought the hamper into the defendant's inn, but went away for two days leaving the hamper in the defendant's care; and the defendant undertook to look after it until the plaintiff's return; but it was stolen while the plaintiff was away.

HLS MS. 1058(2), fo. 58v.[7]

. . . *Foster* Sjt. prayed judgment for the plaintiff.

Harris against him.

WILLIAMS J. When gentlemen come to London many of them will not lodge in an inn, but set their horses there and provide their lodgings in other places. Suppose, then, that their horses are stolen from the inn in the interim: shall not the host be charged? (Implying that he shall.)

Foster. Although the defendant promised that the hamper would be safe, there is nevertheless no consideration for this promise; and so I agree that no action lies on *assumpsit*. Nor does any action other than that which is brought here.

FENNER J. When a man [goes out and] returns to his inn at night, he continues a guest; but here he was not to return at night, and if the host shall preserve them for two days he would be compelled by the same reason to preserve them for two years.

WILLIAMS J. If there was a valid consideration to ground the promise, then this action would not lie. But on the [present facts] (*matter*) I would draw this distinction (and it has been so held before this time): namely, when the host has no benefit from the goods which are left with him, and the owner is not his guest at the time—as he is not a guest in our case—the owner shall not have any action against the host; but if the host had reaped some advantage

7   Also reported in Cro. Jac. 188; Noy 126; 1 Rolle Abr. 3.

by having the goods—for instance, if it was a horse, he would have money for its fodder—there, even though the owner was not his guest at the time when the horse was stolen, the host shall be charged. We are living at Serjeants' Inn[8] and our horses stand in an inn in Fetter Lane: if they are stolen, shall not my host be charged? It is clear that he shall. If a man comes to an inn he is not bound to continue there all day: he may go to his counsel, or his merchant, and if he returns at night he is a guest . . .[9] When the term was kept at Hertford,[10] various people left their horses at Ware and lodged themselves at Hertford. One of them had his horse stolen in the interim, at Ware, and brought an action against his host in the Common Pleas; and as far as I remember he recovered.

It was awarded in the principal case (FLEMING C.J. being absent) that the plaintiff should take nothing by his bill *nisi* etc.

No judgment was entered. Noy's report confirms that the plaintiff lost.

(2) Custom of the realm: fire[11]

BEAULIEU v FINGLAM (1401)

Y.B. Pas. 2 Hen. IV, fo. 18, pl. 6.

Someone brought this writ: 'If William Beaulieu [shall make you secure of pursuing his claim], put [by gage and safe pledges] Roger Finglam [that he be before our justices of the Bench etc. to show] why, whereas according to the law and custom of our realm of England until now obtaining everyone in the same realm should keep, and is bound to keep, his fire safely and securely so that no damage befall any of his neighbours in any wise through his fire, the aforesaid Roger kept his fire at Carlyon[12] so negligently that for want of due keeping of the aforesaid fire the goods and chattels of the selfsame William to the value of £40 (being in the houses there) and the aforesaid houses were then and there burned by the fire, to the damage of the selfsame William etc.'

And he counted accordingly.

Hornby. Judgment of the count. For he has counted on a custom

8   Williams J. was a member of the Chancery Lane inn.
9   Yelverton and Croke JJ. deliver concurring opinions, and then Williams J. speaks again.
10   Because of plague.
11   For other actions for fire, not based on the custom of the realm, see pp. 304, 320, above; pp. 565, 569, below.
12   'Carlion': probably Carlyon in Cornwall rather than Caerleon, Monmouthshire.

of the realm and has not said that this custom has been used since time immemorial.

To this the whole court said: move on, for the common custom of this realm is common law.

THIRNING [C.J.] said that a man should answer for his fire which by misfortune burns another's goods.

And some were of opinion that the fire could not be called 'his fire', because a man cannot have property in fire: but that opinion was not allowed.

MARKHAM. A man is bound to answer for his servant's act, as for his lodger's act, in such a case. For if my servant or lodger puts a candle on a wall and the candle falls into the straw[13] and burns the whole house, and also my neighbour's house, in this case I shall answer to my neighbour for the damage which he has suffered.

The court granted this.

Hornby. Then he ought to have had a writ *quare domum suum ardebat* or *exarsit.*

Hill. It would be against all reason to put blame or fault on a man where there is none in him; for his servant's negligence cannot be said to be his doing.

THIRNING. If a man kills or slays another man by misfortune, he shall forfeit his goods; and he must have his charter of pardon by way of grace.

The court agreed with this.

MARKHAM. I shall answer to my neighbour for anyone who enters my house by my leave or with my knowledge, or is my guest or my servant's guest, if he does something with a candle (or whatever) by which my neighbour's house is burned. But if a man outside my house, against my will, sets fire to the thatch of my house, or elsewhere, so that my house is burned and my neighbours' houses also, I shall not be bound to answer to them for it, since it cannot be said to be ill-doing on my part when it is against my will.

Hornby. This defendant will be undone and impoverished for ever if this action is maintainable against him, for then 20 other suits will be brought against him for the same matter.

THIRNING. What is that to us? It is better that he should be utterly undone than that the law should be changed for him.

Then they were at issue that the plaintiff's house was not burned by the defendant's fire; ready; and the other side *econtra.*

---

13 It was the custom to cover floors with straw or rushes.

ANON. (1584)

LI MS. Misc. 488, p. 115 (Q.B.).

An action on the case was brought in the King's Bench and the plaintiff declared against the defendant upon the general custom of the realm for negligently keeping the defendant's fire so that the plaintiff's house was burned. The defendant came in and said for a plea (*protestando* that he kept the fire well) that the plaintiff's house which was so burned was a good way away from the defendant's house—namely, three houses or ten yards away—and when the defendant's house was burning a gust (*tempest*) of wind arose, which blew the fire on to the plaintiff's house, whereby the plaintiff's house was burned against his will. And he prayed judgment *Si action.*

WRAY C.J. That is no plea, for you must at your own peril keep your fire so well that no damage ensues therefrom to anyone.

Therefore he gave the defendant a peremptory day[14] to plead a good plea.

TURBERVILE v STAMPE (1697)

Record: KB 27/2121, m. 359; 3 Ld Raym. 250. Thomas Turbervile, esquire, brought a bill against John Stampe, gentleman, complaining that, whereas according to the custom of the realm of England every man is bound to keep his fire safely and securely day and night, lest for want of due keeping any damage should befall anyone: the defendant on 6 April 1697 was possessed of a heath at Stoke, Dorset, adjoining the plaintiff's heath, and so negligently and improvidently kept his fire in the said heath that the plaintiff's heath and furze was burned to the value of £40. The defendant pleaded Not guilty, and on 22 July 1697 at Dorchester assizes (Ward C.B., Rokeby J.) the jury found for the plaintiff with £18 damages and 40s. costs. The motion in arrest of judgment was heard in Michaelmas term 1697.

(a) 1 Ld Raym. 264 (untr.).[15]

... *Gould,* king's serjeant, moved in arrest of judgment that this action ought not to be grounded upon the common custom of the realm, for this fire in the field cannot be called 'his fire'; for a man has no power over a fire in the field, as he has over a fire in his house. And therefore this resembles the case of an innkeeper, who must answer for any ill that happens to the goods of his guest so

---

14 A day after which judgment would be entered by default if he failed to plead.
15 Also reported in Carthew 425; Comb. 459; Comyns 32; Holt 9; 1 Salk. 13; Skin. 681.

long as they are in his house; but he is not answerable if a horse be stolen out of his close.[16] And in fact in this case the defendant's servant kindled his fire by way of husbandry, and a wind and tempest arose and drove it into his neighbour's field, so that it was not any neglect in the defendant, but the act of God.

But this was not accepted: for, *per curiam*, as to the matter of the tempest, that appeared only upon the evidence and not upon the record, and therefore the King's Bench cannot take notice of it; but it was good evidence to excuse the defendant at the trial.

Then, as to the other matter, per HOLT C.J., ROKEBY and EYRE JJ., a man ought to keep the fire in his field as well from the doing of damage to his neighbour as if it were in his house. And it may be as well called 'his', the one as the other, for the property of the materials makes the property of the fire. And therefore this action is well grounded upon the common custom of the realm.

But TURTON J. said that these actions grounded upon the common custom had been extended very far. And therefore (by him) the plaintiff might have case for the special damage, but not grounded upon the general custom of the realm.

But by the other justices judgment was given for the plaintiff . . .

HOLT C.J. If a stranger set fire to my house, and it burns my neighbour's house, no action will lie against me. (Which all the other justices agreed.) But if my servant throws dirt into the highway, I am indictable: so, in this case, if the defendant's servant kindled the fire in the way of husbandry, and proper for his employment, though he had no express command of his master, yet his master shall be liable to an action for damage done to another by the fire; for it shall be intended that the servant had authority from his master, it being for his master's benefit.

(b) 12 Mod. 152 (untr.).

. . . TURTON J. There is a difference between fire in a man's house and in the fields. In some countries[17] it is a necessary part of husbandry to make fire in the ground, and some unavoidable accident may carry it into a neighbour's ground and do injury there; and, this fire not being so properly in his custody as the fire in his house, I think this is not actionable as it is laid.

But, by HOLT C.J., ROKEBY and EYRE JJ., every man must so use his own as not to injure another. The law is general. The fire which a man makes in the fields is as much 'his fire' as his fire in his house: it is made on his ground, with his materials, and by his order, and

---

16   See pp. 555–556, above.
17   I.e. parts of the country.

he must at his peril take care that it does not through his neglect injure his neighbour. If he kindle it at a proper time and place, and the violence of the wind carry it into his neighbour's ground and prejudice him, this is fit to be given in evidence. But now here it is found to have been by his negligence; and it is the same as if it had been in his house.

Judgment was given for the plaintiff.

The record shows that judgment for the plaintiff was signed on 23 November 1697, for £31, the court having increased the costs by £11.

(3) Custom of the realm: carriers

RICH v KNEELAND (1613)

Record: KB 27/1440, m. 1549; abstracted in Kiralfy, *Action on the Case*, p. 224, and in Hob. 17. John Rich brought an action on the case against Arthur Kneeland and declared that, whereas the defendant was a common hoyman and carrier by water (*communis nauta et vector*) and used to carry goods for hire between Milton, in Kent, and London; and whereas by the custom of the realm of England common hoymen and carriers ought to keep the goods and chattels delivered to them on their boats without loss, so that they should not be lost or spoiled through the fault of such common hoymen or carriers or their servants; and whereas the plaintiff on 20 January 1612 delivered to the defendant a portmanteau with £50 in it, to be carried, and gave him twopence: the defendant suffered the goods to be lost, through the fault of him and his servants, on 25 January. The defendant pleaded that on 21 January the plaintiff discharged him of the keeping of the goods. The plaintiff traversed this, and the defendant demurred. Judgment was given for the plaintiff, and the defendant brought a writ of error in the Exchequer Chamber.

Cro. Jac. 330, pl. 9 (untr.).[18]

... A writ of error being brought, it was assigned: first, because this action lies not against the common bargeman without special promise.

But all the justices and barons held that it well lies, as against a common carrier upon the land.

Secondly, they held that the traverse was good.[19]

---

18 Also reported in Hob. 17; sub nom. *Keeling v Rich*, 1 Rolle Abr. 2.
19 The point (according to Hobart) was that the defendant did not plead a discharge of the *carrying*.

Wherefore the judgment was affirmed.[20]

SYMONS v DARKNOLL (1628)

HLS MS. 106, fo. 187; abridged in Palm. 523.

Action on the case. The plaintiff declares that, whereas by the common law every lighterman ought so to guide and govern his lighter that the merchants' goods carried therein should not perish, and showed that the plaintiff was a merchant and the defendant a lighterman who had carried goods in his lighter from A. to B. for hire, and that he had goods from the plaintiff (namely, etc.) to carry to C. in return for so much money, and that he so negligently governed his lighter that the lighter thereby took in water and thus spoiled his goods, to the damage of the plaintiff etc.

And although there was no promise,[1] it nevertheless seemed to the court that the plaintiff should recover.

Not alleging that he was a *common* lighterman did no harm: though this exception was taken.

HYDE C.J. The very delivery of the goods makes the contract.

WHITELOCKE J. This action is *ex maleficio*, and not *ex contractu*.

DODDERIDGE J. said that a carrier ought to provide tarpaulins[2] and the like defence to protect the goods, by the common law . . .

And the exception that he did not allege specially how he had spoiled the goods was also overruled.

Cf. the *Humber Ferry Case* (1348), p. 358, above, where no custom was alleged.

E. R. v J. P. (*c.* 1675)

King's Bench bill, in *The Clerk's Manual* (1678), p. 70.

Middlesex. E. R. complains of J. P., in the custody of the marshal etc., that, whereas according to the law and custom of the realm of England until now used and approved[3] every person called a carter is bound while leading or driving any horse or horses which are pulling any cart or waggon so exactly to govern, rule and lead the horse, horses and other beasts pulling the cart or waggon that no

---

20 Hobart mentions a third point: '. . . and it was resolved that, though it was laid as a custom of the realm, yet indeed it is common law'.

1   For *assumpsit* against a bargeman see p. 399, above.

2   'tarclothes', misprinted in Palmer as 'cartclothes'.

3   This alleged custom of the realm seems never to have been judicially recognised. See the comments by M. J. Prichard [1964] C.L.J., at p. 236.

damage or hurt should in any way befall any one of the people of the said lord king, through default in the good keeping and governing of the same: yet the aforesaid J., little regarding the same laudable laws and customs, but wholly neglecting and thinking little of them, on etc. at etc., so negligently, improvidently and inadvisedly drove and governed three horses drawing a cart called a dung-cart that the aforesaid horses, through the fault of the said J., then and there vehemently drew the cart on top of a sow (price 50s.) belonging to him the said E., and so hurt and injured the aforesaid sow with the cart that the aforesaid sow afterwards, namely on the same day and year at etc., died. Whereupon the said E. says that he is the worse, and has damage to the amount of £10. And thereof he produces suit etc.

(4) Bailment or lease but no express undertaking[4]

BLUET v BOULAND (1472)

(a) Record: CP 40/844, m. 346 (Mich. 1472).

The vill of Southampton. John Bouland, late of Hursley in the county of Southampton, husbandman, was attached to answer Robert Bluet of the vill of Southampton, merchant, in a plea why . . .[5] whereas on the seventeenth day of August [1471] in the eleventh year of the reign of the present lord king he had bailed (*tradidisset*) a certain horse of his to the said John at Southampton, for a certain sum of money (namely 6s. 8d.) paid in advance to the same John, to look after (*custodiendum*) until a certain date (namely the twentieth day of September then next following): the same John so negligently kept the horse within the period aforesaid that on the fifteenth day of September in the above-mentioned year the horse (price £10) died for want and neglect of due keeping by him the said John; to the damage of the selfsame Robert of £20. And thereof he produces suit etc.

And the aforesaid John, by John Uffenham his attorney, comes and denies the force and wrong when etc. And he prays leave to imparl therein here until the octaves of St Hilary; and has it etc. The same day is given to the said Robert, here etc.

Nothing is recorded in the roll beyond this imparlance.

---

4 Cf. the case of the sheep (1487), p. 398, above, where it is not clear whether an *assumpsit* was alleged or not.

5 Recital of writ, the substance of which is repeated in the count.

(b) Report: Y.B. Mich. 12 Edw. IV, fo. 13, pl. 10;
BL MS. Add. 37493, fo. 27v.

An action on the case for this: that, whereas the plaintiff had bailed a horse to the defendant to keep safely, in return for a certain sum of money paid beforehand, the defendant so negligently kept the horse that for want of good keeping it died. The defendant said that the same plaintiff had previously sued a writ of detinue in respect of the same bailment of the same horse, and the defendant had said that he did not detain it, and waged his law on that, whereby the plaintiff was barred; and he demanded judgment whether [this action lay], contrary to this matter of record.

Catesby. That is no estoppel, for it is not in respect of the same thing for which our action is conceived. This action is only for the defendant's negligence, as a result of which the horse died; whereas the writ of detinue [was] brought for the detaining, and thereby he ⁶was to recover⁶ the horse. Therefore, although he is barred in a writ of detinue, he shall not be barred in this action for a wrong done to him ...

Jenney. It seems the plea is good, for by this action he is to recover the value of the horse, and by the judgment in the writ of detinue he is estopped from claiming the horse itself ...

And the justices rose.

MOSELEY v FORCETT (1598)

Record: KB 27/1347, m. 183. Francis Moseley, a King's Bench clerk, brought a bill of privilege against Edward Forcett and John Sherston; and complained that, whereas on 26 May 1597 he had delivered a gelding worth £5 to the defendants at St Clement Danes, London, to pasture and to keep safely and to be returned on request, in return for two shillings a week to be paid to them: nevertheless the defendants, neglecting the faithful trust to redeliver the gelding, so negligently put it to pasture on 12 June that by their carelessness and negligence and for want of good keeping it was taken away by unknown wrongdoers to a place unknown to the plaintiff; as a result of which the plaintiff was not only defrauded of the gelding but also deprived of all easement and profit of the gelding in riding about his arduous business affairs. The defendants, making protestation that the plaintiff did not deliver the gelding to them, demurred to the declaration.

Moo. K.B. 543, pl. 720.

... The justices were divided two against two.

Popham C.J. and Fenner J. said that the action does not lie

6   Or 'demanded' (MS.).

without alleging a request for redelivery, and showing how the horse was removed, or how it died or was lost.

GAWDY and CLENCH JJ. to the contrary, because the action is based on the negligence and the special undertaking[7] to keep safely.

But they all agreed that without such special undertaking the action would not lie.

The record shows that the suit was continued until Michaelmas term 1600, when the plaintiff consented to its being discontinued.

COUNTESS OF SHREWSBURY v CROMPTON
(1600)

The countess of Shrewsbury brought an action on the case in the Queen's Bench against Richard Crompton, a bencher of the Middle Temple, and counted that she had leased a house to him at will, and that he had so negligently and improvidently kept his fire that the house was burned down. Crompton pleaded Not guilty, and the jury found for the plaintiff.

(a) HLS MS. 2076, fo. 60.[8]

... *Warburton* prayed judgment for the plaintiff ... for when a tenant at will by his negligence allows the house to be burned, an action on the case well lies. Similarly, if a man bails goods to another, and he by his negligence loses them, an action on the case lies. And 12 Edw. IV, fo. 13,[9] is that if a man bails a horse to another to keep safely, and for want of good keeping he allows the horse to perish, an action on the case lies. And 21 Hen. VI, fo. 15,[10] if a father puts his child to nurse, and she does not keep the child well, the father shall have an action on the case.

Snigge to the contrary. A tenant at will is not punishable for any waste, or for such negligence; but for voluntary waste done by him, in felling timber or pulling down a house, an action of trespass lies.[11] The reason of which is, that by doing such an act (which a tenant at will may not do) he explains his intent to be to waive his estate at will; and so this act done by him is like an act done by a stranger.

Tanfield to the contrary. First, it is not in doubt that an action will lie for a negligent act as well as for a voluntary act ... But the

---

7 No *assumpsit* is laid. The term as to keeping safely is laid merely as a qualification of the original delivery, and later recited as a 'trust' in the clause alleging the negligence. Perhaps this was the reason for the disagreement.

8 Also reported in Cro. Eliz. 777, 784.

9 *Bluet v Bouland* (1472); see p. 564, opposite.

10 Mich. 21 Hen. VI, fo. 15, pl. 29, per Fulthorpe J.

11 See *Anon.* (1374), p. 304, above.

most probable reason which can be advanced why the action shall
not be maintained is because the defendant is in by the plaintiff's
will, and by her lease, and so it shall be reckoned to be her own
foolishness that she did not provide by some covenant or collateral
assurance at the making of the lease that the defendant should keep
the house in a good state. That, however, is no reason; for it is
agreed by those on the other side (and Mr. Littleton also[12]) that if a
tenant at will commits voluntary waste he shall be punished for it,
and yet he comes in by the lessor's act just as in this case. And the
case vouched in 12 Edw. IV proves it also, for there the defendant
had the horse by delivery from the plaintiff. And I think that if the
bailiff of a manor by his negligence allows the house to be burned
down, an action on the case lies.

FENNER J. denied that ...

Croke to the same effect [as Tanfield]. And he vouched Mich. 12
Hen. VII, rot. 320;[13] [and another case] between Nicholas and
[*blank*][14] where in an action on the case the plaintiff declared that he
was tenant for life of a house, reversion to the queen, and made a
lease at will to the defendant, who by his negligence allowed the
house to be burned down; and there the defendant took issue that it
was not burned through his fault or negligence, and so it appears
that if it is burned through the fault of the lessee at will an action
on the case shall be maintained.

GAWDY J. It seems that the action does not lie for this negligent
waste. But I allow that if a tenant at will burns or pulls down a
house voluntarily a general action of trespass lies ... And 2 Hen.
VII, fo. 11,[15] if a man bails sheep to a shepherd, who by his
negligence suffers them to be drowned, an action on the case lies;
but that is because he undertook the charge of looking after the
sheep by accepting them in his charge. But in this case the tenant at
will does not undertake any such charge, but takes it only to
occupy and use, and is to pay his rent for that to the lessor, but to
no other intent. No one would say that if a tenant at will suffered
the house to fall down for want of repair, without giving notice to
the lessor that it was in decay, an action would lie. (*Tanfield*
conceded this, because the lessee at will is not charged with doing
repairs.) Likewise here.

12 Littleton, *Tenures*, s. 71.
13 *Critoft v Emson and Nicols* (1506) CP 40/978, m. 320; cited in Cro. Eliz. 777;
    Herne, *The Pleader*, p. 162; an action by the executor of a lessee from King's
    College, Cambridge, against an under-lessee for years of three mills in
    Horstead, Norfolk.
14 The text is here corrupt. The reporter has apparently confused the previous case
    with *Earl of Oxford v Manning* (1511), cited in Cro. Eliz. 777.
15 See p. 398, above.

FENNER J. agreed with him, and took the same distinction between voluntary and permissive waste.

CLENCH J. and POPHAM C.J. also assented.

POPHAM C.J. said that there is a distinction between interest and authority. For if a man has authority to do something, and abuses it, a general action of trespass lies; but when a man has an interest, his misfeasance during his interest cannot be punished by a general action of trespass. Nevertheless, as has been said, if a tenant at will fells timber or pulls down houses, a general action of trespass lies, for his interest is thereby determined and he has become a stranger . . . And so he concluded that the action did not lie.

And in accordance with this it was ordered that judgment be entered against the plaintiff.

(b) 5 Co. Rep. 13.

. . . And the reason of the judgment was that at common law no remedy lay for waste, whether voluntary or permissive, against a lessee for life or years, because the lessee had an interest in the land through the lessor's act, and it was the lessor's own foolishness to make such a lease and not to restrain the tenant by covenant, condition or otherwise that he should not commit waste. Likewise, and for the same reason, a tenant at will shall not be punished for permissive waste . . . But it was agreed that in some cases, where a trust is put in the party, the action on the case will lie for negligence even though the defendant came into possession through the plaintiff's act. For instance, 12 Edw. IV, fo. 13, where a man bails a horse to someone to keep safely, and the defendant so negligently kept the horse that it died for want of good keeping, the action on the case lies for this breach of the trust. Likewise 2 Hen. VII, fo. 11, if I trust my shepherd with my sheep, and by his negligence they are drowned or otherwise perish, an action on the case lies. But in the case at the bar there was a demise at will made to the defendant, and no trust reposed in him.

So it was awarded that the plaintiff take nothing by her bill.

(5) No custom of the realm, bailment or undertaking

LOGHTON v CALYS (1473)

Record only: CP 40/847, m. 382.

Middlesex. Richard Calys of the parish of St Clement Danes

without the bar of the New Temple, London, in the county aforesaid, brewer, was attached to answer Richard Loghton and Joan his wife in a plea why...[16] whereas the aforesaid Richard Calys on the fifth day of June [1472] in the twelfth year of the reign of the present lord king, at the parish aforesaid, negligently put up in his soil (namely in a garden adjacent to the king's highway there) a heap or pile of logwood which was in danger of falling into the same way: the same Richard Calys, knowing the aforesaid heap or pile to be on the point of collapse (*in articulo corruendi*) into the said way, and on that account to be a grave risk to the lord king's lieges passing along that way, permitted the same heap or pile to stand in that manner without any rearrangement for a long time, namely from the aforesaid fifth day until the thirty-ninth [*sic*] day of September then next following, when (through the default of the selfsame Richard) the heap or pile fell upon the aforesaid Joan, who was passing along the aforesaid way and unaware of the aforesaid danger, and crushed the same Joan and wounded her in many ways so that the same Joan wholly lost the strength of her limbs; to the damage of them the said Richard and Joan Loghton of £40. And thereof they produce suit etc.

And the aforesaid Richard Calys comes in his own person and denies the force and wrong when etc. And he says that the aforesaid Richard and Joan Loghton ought not to have their aforesaid action against him, because he says that he put up the aforesaid pile well, sufficiently and firmly, and kept it so put up until on the day and in the year above mentioned the pile was constrained to fall upon the aforesaid Joan by the vehemence of a great storm of wind; without this, that the aforesaid pile fell upon the aforesaid Joan by reason of the negligent and tumbledown construction of the pile, as the aforesaid Richard and Joan Loghton allege above. And this he is ready to aver; and so he prays judgment whether the aforesaid Richard and Joan Loghton ought to have or maintain their aforesaid action against him etc.

And the aforesaid Richard and Joan Loghton say that they ought not to be barred by anything previously alleged from having their aforesaid action, because they say that the aforesaid pile fell upon the aforesaid Joan by reason of the negligent construction of the pile in the way which the same Richard and Joan above suppose. And they pray that this may be enquired into by the country; and the aforesaid Richard Calys likewise. Therefore the sheriff is ordered to cause 12 men to come here in the octave of Michaelmas...

16   Recital of writ omitted.

The process continues to one month from Michaelmas, but no trial is recorded.

ANON. (1582)
Cro. Eliz. 10, pl. 5 (C.P.) (untr.).

Snagg moved this case, and demanded the opinion of the judges in it: John Style[17] with a gun at the door of his house shoots at a fowl, and by this fireth his own house and the house of his neighbour; upon which he brings an action on the case generally, and doth not declare upon the custom of the realm (as 2 Hen. IV[18]), viz. for negligently keeping his fire. The question was, if this action doth lie?

And all the court held it did. For the injury is the same, although this mischance was not by a common negligence but by misadventure. And if he had counted upon the custom of the realm, as 2 Hen. IV, the action had not been well brought. Yet the custom of the realm is common law.

WALGRAVE v OGDEN (1590–91)[19]
(a) Mich. 1590: 1 Leon. 224, pl. 305 (untr.).

An action upon the case was brought upon a trover [20]and conversion[20] of 20 barrels of butter, and declared that by negligent keeping of them they were become of little value; upon which there was a demurrer in law.

And by the opinion of the whole court upon this matter no action lieth. For a man who comes to goods by trover is not bound to keep them so safely as he who comes to them by bailment.

WALMSLEY J. If a man find my garments and suffereth them to be eaten with moths by the negligent keeping of them, no action lieth; but if he weareth my garments it is otherwise, for the wearing is a conversion.

(b) Hil. 1591: sub nom. *Mulgrave v Ogden*,
Cro. Eliz. 219, pl. 20 (untr.).

Action sur trover of 20 barrels of butter, and counts that he so

17 Not a real name.
18 *Beaulieu v Finglam*: see p. 557, above.
19 The plea roll cited in some of the reports (C.P., Hil. 32 Eliz. I, m. 2529) is no longer extant.
20 This seems to be a mistake, and is not mentioned in the other reports. If conversion had been alleged, the question would not have arisen.

negligently kept them that they became of little value. Upon this it was demurred; and held by all the justices that no action upon the case lieth in this case, for no law compelleth him that finds a thing to keep it safely. As, if a man finds a garment and suffers it to be moth-eaten; or if one finds a horse and giveth it no sustenance. But if a man find a thing and useth it, he is answerable, for it is conversion. So if he of purpose misuseth it: as, if one finds paper and puts it into the water, and so forth. But for negligent keeping no law punisheth him.

And it was adjourned.[1]

(c) Pas. 1591: sub nom. *Algar's Case*, HLS MS. 110,
fo. 46v; BL MS. Lansdowne 1073, fo. 122.

Action on the case; and he counted that he lost certain barrels of butter, and the defendant found them, and so badly, negligently and improvidently preserved them that they became worthless. Upon this there was a demurrer.

And it was said that if a man finds cloth and keeps it, and it is wasted by moths, nevertheless no action lies. And if a man finds a horse, and so negligently keeps it that it wanders away, or is stolen, or keeps it so that it dies of hunger, still no action lies.[2] But if the defendant had put the butter or wool in a place where he knew the rain would ruin it, or on purpose put the horse in a place to starve it, perhaps an action would lie. Without an act done by him, however, for the purpose of harming the things, no action lies; for it is not right to find him guilty when no act is done.

BLYTH v TOPHAM (1607)

(a) Cro. Jac. 158, pl. 11 (K.B.) (untr.).

Action on the case, for that he digged a pit in such a common, by occasion whereof his mare (being straying there) fell into the said pit and perished. The defendant pleaded Not guilty, and it was

---

1 Cf. Owen 141 (same term), corrected from YLS MS. G. R29.3, fo. 290 (sub nom. *Malgrave v Ogden*): '. . . The court held clearly that the action would not lie, for he who finds goods is not bound to preserve them from putrefaction; but it was agreed that if goods [found] were used [and worn] and [so] by usage made worse, the action would lie'.

2 An abridged version of the same report in BL MS. Lansdowne 1067, fo. 146, stops here, adding: '. . . unless such negligence is *de male purpose*, in which case an action lies'.

3 By preventing judgment being entered for the defendant upon the verdict.

found for him. The plaintiff, to save costs,[3] now moved in arrest of judgment upon the verdict that the declaration was not good; for when the mare was straying, and he shows not any right why his mare should be in the said common, the digging of the pit is lawful as against him; and although his mare fell therein, he hath not any remedy, for it is *damnum absque injuria*, wherefore an action lies not by him.

The whole court was of that opinion. It was therefore adjudged upon the declaration that the bill should abate, and not upon the verdict.

(b) HLS MS. 105, fo. 82v.

. . . *Dyott* moved the case to be as follows. The defendant, as a trespasser, dug a pit in the waste of A., 30 feet from the highway; the mare of the plaintiff, who had no common or anything to do with the waste, escaped from him and went wandering into the waste, and fell into the pit and broke its neck; whereupon the plaintiff brought this action against the defendant who dug the pit.

POPHAM C.J. and FENNER J. There is a difference between this case and the case of 27 Hen. VIII, fo. 27,[4] where Fitzherbert said that if a man made a ditch across a highway, and someone received a particular damage thereby, he should have an action on the case against the person who made the ditch; because the highway is open to all liege-subjects, whereas the plaintiff here had nothing to do in the waste, but only in the highway, which was 30 feet off.

And it was adjudged (the court being full) that the action did not lie.

Herne, *The Pleader*, p. 162, notes in the margin a record of 1621, where an action on the case was brought against a Derbyshire miner 'for his negligence in digging a pit for lead etc. in such a place that it was not easily discoverable, wherein the plaintiff's horse perished', and the defendant pleaded Not guilty (Trin. 19 Jac. I, m. 577).

---

4 Y.B. Mich. 27 Hen. VIII, fo. 27, pl. 10. Baldwin C.J. advanced the view (found in earlier Y.B.s) that no private action lay for a public nuisance, which was an offence against all the king's subjects and punishable in the court leet. But Fitzherbert J. argued that an action lay if someone had 'greater hurt or inconvenience from it than everyone has': as where someone riding in the highway fell into a ditch. Fitzherbert's view was followed in *Serjeant Bendlowes v Kemp* (before 1584), cited in Cro. Eliz. 664; and this view has been accepted ever since.
5 The bill is entered as 'a plea of trespass on the case'.

MITCHELL v ALLESTRY (1676)

(a) The bill: KB 27/1973, m. 1283.[5]

Middlesex. James Mitchell and Mary his wife, by Henry Wynne their attorney, complain of William Allestry, esquire, and Thomas Scrivener, in the custody of the marshal of the marshalsea of the lord king before the king himself, for that on the first day of June [1673] in the twenty-fifth year of the reign of the lord Charles II now King of England etc., in the parish of St Clement Danes in the aforesaid county in a certain public and open place there called Little Lincoln's Inn Fields,[6] where all day and every day various subjects of the lord king have constantly walked about and gone (and been accustomed to go) in and about their necessary business, the same William and Thomas,[7] improvidently, rashly and without due consideration of the unsuitability of the place for the purpose, drove and exercised two wild and untamed mares pulling a coach, in order to break and tame the same mares for pulling coaches, the aforesaid place being inapt and unsuitable for that purpose by reason of the throng of many subjects then and there walking about; and the mares, because of their wild nature (inasmuch as the same mares could not be ruled or governed in this wise), then and there ran upon her the said Mary and there threw her to the ground with great force and ran over her with the aforesaid coach, so that the same Mary was so seriously crushed and broken in her body and limbs that by reason thereof she became lame and mutilated and cannot now be restored to perfect health. Whereupon the same James and Mary say that they are the worse and have damage to the extent of £200. And thereof they bring suit.

This action was commenced in Michaelmas term 1675. In Hilary term 1676 the defendants pleaded Not guilty, and on 5 May 1676 at *nisi prius* in Westminster Hall (before Raynsford C.J.) the jury found for the plaintiff with damages of 40 marks.

(b) 3 Keb. 650, pl. 2 (untr.).[8]

Simpson excepted in arrest of judgment, in action upon the case for bringing horses wild to tame in Little Lincoln's Inn Fields, being an open public place where people are all the day passing and repassing, because it is not said to be any highway, nor said that the

---

6 A public square to the south-east of Lincoln's Inn Fields, including what is now New Square and part of Portugal Street.

7 The reports reveal that Scrivener was Allestry's servant—his coachman—and that Allestry was not present when the accident occurred.

8 Also reported in 2 Lev. 172.

defendant knew them to be wild, nor was there negligence in the coachman (who was thrown out and hurt).

But, by *Saunders*, an action upon the case well lay. As, by Smith of Westminster, for not penning an ox but setting a dog on him, whereby he ran into Palace Yard and hurt him. So where a monkey escaped and did hurt by default of the owner.[9]

And, *per curiam*, it is at the peril of the owner to take strength enough to order them. And the master is as liable as the servant, if he gave order for it.[10] And the action is generally for bringing them thither, which is intended personal.

And judgment for the plaintiff.

The record confirms that judgment was given for the plaintiff, with £12. 6s. 8d. costs.

(c) 1 Vent. 295 (untr.).

... Upon Not guilty pleaded, and a verdict for the plaintiff, it was moved by *Simpson* in arrest of judgment that here is no cause of action. For it appears by the declaration that the mischief which happened was against the defendant's will, and so *damnum absque injuria*. And then not shown what right the king's subjects had to walk there: and if a man digs a pit in a common, into which one that has no right to come there falls in, no action lies in such case.[11]

Curia contra. It was the defendant's fault to bring a wild horse into such a place where mischief might probably be done by reason of the concourse of people. Lately in this court an action was brought against a butcher who had made an ox run from his stall and gored the plaintiff, and this was alleged in the declaration to be in default of penning of him.[12]

WILDE J. said: if a man hath an unruly horse in his stable, and leaves open the stable door, whereby the horse goes forth and does mischief, an action lies against the master.

TWISDEN J. If one hath kept a tame fox, which gets loose and grows wild, he that kept him before shall not answer for the damage the fox doth after he hath lost him and he hath resumed his wild nature...[13]

Judgment for the plaintiff.

9 Perhaps 'Andrew Baker's case, whose child was bit by a monkey that broke his chain and got loose': M. Hale, *History of the Pleas of the Crown* (1736), vol. I, p. 430.
10 Cf. 2 Lev. 'and it shall be intended the master sent the servant to train the horses there'.
11 *Blyth v Topham* (1608); see p. 570, above.
12 *Smith's Case*, cited by Saunders (above).
13 The reporter cites *Weaver v Ward* (1616); see p. 351, above.

(d) ECO MS. 178, p. 183 (untr.).

... *Simpson*. This is a case, I think, *primae impressionis*; and, they not having laid (1) that the place *in quo* is a public highway, (2) that the defendants did know them to be untamed mares, (3) nor that the defendants did negligently suffer them to run upon her—nay indeed the plaintiff by his own declaration has excused them from that, for he says that on account of their ferocity they could not govern them, but that they did run upon her—[we pray judgment for the defendants].

Saunders to the contrary. As to (1), we say 'in a public place, where every day the king's people continually [pass] etc.' And suppose the defendants had brought his coach and mares into Westminster Hall ... that is no highway, yet sure if the mares did any hurt an action would lie. And he remembered the court of a late case against a butcher for not pinioning his ox. As to the second, we say that the defendants brought their mares into the place *in quo* to tame them, and then they must needs know that they were not tamed before.

Jeffreys on the same side. As to the third, we had formerly brought an action in this case, and then we had laid it that the defendants 'did negligently permit etc.'; but, coming to trial before my lord Hale [C.B.], the evidence as to the negligence seeming against us, we were non-suit. And my lord Hale did in a manner direct this action, and [said] that it would lie without laying it to be done negligently.

WILDE J. Suppose I have a wild horse, and I put him in my stable, and do not lock the door, and he gets loose and does mischief, an action will lie.

TWISDEN J. I am of another opinion, for when I put him in my stable I do a lawful action, and I am not bound to put a lock upon my door if I will venture my goods without one.

RAYNSFORD C.J. The law does preserve places frequented, and punishes more severely anything done to disturb them. And if one throws a stone into a market and kills one, it is murder.

WILDE and TWISDEN JJ. remembered a case where one was sued for that his monkey broke loose and hurt some children, but it was referred.[14]

THE COURT. Let the plaintiff have his judgment *nisi*.

The defendant brought a writ of error in 1677: IND 1/6062, citing Trin. 28 Car. II, m. 857 (recognisance). No further proceedings have been noticed.

14 I.e. to arbitration. See p. 573, fn. 9, above.

BROWNE v DAVIS (1705)

Queen's Bench bill in Lilly, *Entries* (3rd ed.), p. 38;
collated with W. Bohun, *Declarations and Pleadings*
(1733), p. 211.[15]

Middlesex. William Browne complains of John Davis, in the custody of the marshal etc., for this: namely that, whereas the said William, on the sixth day of March [1705] in the fourth year of the reign of the lady Anne now queen of England etc., in the parish of Chelsea in the county aforesaid, was lawfully possessed of a certain flat-bottomed boat then laden with dung, and riding at anchor in the River Thames within the parish aforesaid, as of his own proper boat; and whereas the said John Davis was then and there master and pilot of a certain barge then sailing in the River Thames aforesaid, within the parish aforesaid, towards the city of London: the said John Davis then and there so negligently, carelessly and unskilfully steered and governed his said barge that for want of good and sufficient care and steerage thereof the said barge then and there fouled the selfsame William's said boat, so laden as aforesaid, and broke and sank the said boat; by reason whereof the said William not only wholly lost his aforesaid dung, which was loaded in the said boat, but likewise lost the whole use, profit and benefit of his said boat for the space of six[16] days then next following, and also expended and laid out large sums of money in and about the raising, recovering and repairing of his said boat. And thereby the said William says he is the worse, and has damage to the amount of £30.[17] And thereof he produces suit etc.

The availability of such an action against the master of a ship seems to have been recognised for at least 40 years previously: see *Martin v Green* (1664) 1 Keb. 730; *Mustard v Harnden* (1680) T. Raym. 390; and p. 375, above.

SCARBORROW v HAMBLETON (1732)

J. Mallory, *Modern Entries* (1734), vol. I, p. 158
(an English translation from the Latin record).

Middlesex. James Hambleton, late of the parish of St Andrew's, Holborn, coachman, was attached to answer to John Scarborrow of a plea of trespass upon the case. And [thereupon] the said John, by Robert Martin his attorney, declares that, whereas on the first

---

15 These are two different English translations from the Latin. The present text is slightly reworded from both.

16 Reads 'fourteen' in Bohun, *Declaration and Pleadings* (1733).

17 Reads '£40' in Bohun, *Declaration and Pleadings* (1733).

day of September in the year of our Lord 1721, at the parish of St
John, Hackney, in the king's highway there, he the said John was
journeying in a chaise, and he the said James was at the same time
there driving a coach; and the said John in fact avers that the said
James then and there so improvidently and carelessly managed his
cattle[18] that were then and there drawing the said coach that the
said cattle drew the said coach upon the said chaise in which the
said John was so journeying, so that the said chaise then and there
by the negligence of the said James was overturned by the said
coach and the said [John] was much bruised thereby. And whereas
also afterwards,[19] that is to say, the same day and year above, at
Hackney aforesaid in the said county, he the said John was driving
another chaise in the said king's highway in the said parish of St
John, Hackney, in the county aforesaid, and then and there a
certain person unknown to the said John, who at that time was a
servant to the said James, was driving another coach of and
belonging to the said James; and the said John doth in fact aver
that the said servant of the said James then and there drove and
whipped his cattle drawing the said coach in such a negligent and
careless manner that the same cattle drew the said coach upon the
last-mentioned chaise, in which the said John was then and there as
aforesaid, so that the said chaise last mentioned was then and there
overturned, by means whereof the said John was grievously bruised
and wounded. Whereupon the said John saith that he is injured
and endamaged to the value of £50. And therefore [he produces
suit] etc.

'This declaration was perused and settled by Mr. Serjeant Hawkins, but the
cause was never tried. However, I was informed that the defendant's
attorney, upon advice and counsel, was told the declaration was well
drawn': note at end, by Mallory.

BOYD v ROBINSON (1738)[20]

HLS MS. Notebook 155
(notes of evidence at Northumberland assizes).

Christopher Boyd, plaintiff.   William Robinson, defendant.

---

18   Presumably a translation of *averia*, which included horses.
19   In so far as this is laid as a separate event it is fictional. A note in the margin
     reads: 'The plaintiff not knowing whether it was the defendant himself, or one of
     his servants, here is another charge upon the servant of the like nature'.
20   This is inserted to show the course of a trial at *nisi prius*.

Action upon the case against the defendant as a farrier for negligence in the making of a rowel[1] in plaintiff's horse.

Plea: Not guilty.[2]

[Witnesses for the plaintiff:]

Mrs Boyd. Did not observe it worsted at all—a small scratch on the forehead—the next morning his eye appeared something full—defendant sent for to wash the wound and put a plaster to keep out the cold—defendant cut the horse on the throat—he said if the horse died he would pay for it—died in the stable . . .

Alexander Constable. A little cut, but no damage at all—saw the horse every day—gave his water—the horse ate and drank very well—the rowel put into his throat Thursday—the horse died the Saturday after—defendant made use of a pen-knife in making the rowel and found some difficulty in pushing the rowel in—the horse never rose and stood upon his legs after the cutting in his throat for making the rowel—worth six guineas—the defendant came to him the Friday, and nothing was afterwards done till the Thursday following—the swelling increased and it was bigger the Thursday than before—plaintiff not present when the rowel was put on.

John M'Afour.[3] A farrier 28 years—saw the horse the Saturday—his eye was open—a cut on the eye—the skin only cut—he would have put a rowel behind his ears to direct the humour—on opening the rowel he found blood in the wound—caused by his instrument—his not eating caused by the rowel, and the rowel the cause of his death—worth six guineas—caked or coagulated blood in the wound. He took out the rowel—never knew an horse die of such a fall or bruise as this horse had—says defendant is a good farrier.

Henry Corbet. Value of the horse six guineas . . . opened it in a proper manner—put in his finger—shows how far—and took out a great deal of coagulated blood—proceeded from cutting the wound too deep—the rowel was put too far in, and he thinks it was the occasion of his death.

For the defendant:

Mr. Robert Barwyes. Saw the horse after the fall—it was cut in a most desperate manner—it swelled near as big as his fist—the rowel was put in the place where it was usual to put a rowel—says

---

1 A circular piece of leather or other suitable material, with a hole in the centre, inserted between the flesh and the skin of a horse in order to cause a discharge of humours.
2 This shows that it was not an *assumpsit* action.
3 Referred to below as 'McFall'.

McFall told him that the rowel would do him no hurt—the swelling over the eye appeared to be large and all jellied at the side of his cheek—believes he died of a hurt by the fall, and not from the rowel—neither windpipe nor weezle (*wyzell*) were cut.

Mr. Blamire. Was called about two days after the horse died—defendant told him he was blamed for killing the horse—the horse was covered with mould—probed the hole with his finger—the head was swelled and the rowel was put there to draw off the humour—the stoprell[4] was properly placed—he saw nothing damnified—saw nothing cut but what is common—saw no cakes of blood—the swelling appeared on the side of his head—thinks the stoprell under his jaw—could do the horse no hurt—witness would have put a stoprell under his jaw to draw the humour from the swelling. This witness not called in till next day after the horse died.

Daniel Mathews . . . the plaintiff came while defendant was doing it—found no fault—the plaintiff further said, 'Why don't you do it?'—the eye and side of his head badly swelled—the horse did not drop down the time he was there.

Thomas Mark. To put a rowel in the cheek blade if it can be come at, if not under the jaw—thinks it must die of the fall—witness mentions his knowing a like case—died of the eye.

Isaac Marks. Hath known a rowel to be put under the throat with success—if care be taken of the knife, damage may happen—might die of the hurt on his eye—master farrier—known 23 or 24 years—McFall an ill farrier—would not trust him with an horse of that value—thinks his judgment of no value, but thinks he would not perjure himself—hath employed defendant seven years and he hath behaved well, and takes him to be a good farrier. As to [plaintiff's][5] first witness—plaintiff's mother—'Are you going to serve me with an action as you have Robinson? I'll swear myself to the Devil before you shall get that action'.

Verdict for the defendant.

THE LAW RELATIVE TO TRIALS AT NISI PRIUS
(*c.* 1750)[6]

From the 1st ed. (1768), pp. 35–37, 98, 103.

Of injuries arising from negligence or folly.
Every man ought to take reasonable care that he does not injure his

4 Not in the *New English Dictionary*.
5 Reads 'defendant's', presumably a slip.
6 Formerly attributed to Sir Francis Buller (d. 1800), who edited later editions. He was a special pleader in 1768, but was not called to the bar until 1772. Selwyn, another editor, identified it as the work of Lord Bathurst (1714–94), probably written in the 1740s. There is a MS. version in LI MSS. Hill 99–101.

neighbour. Therefore wherever a man receives any hurt through the default of another, though the same were not wilful, yet if it be occasioned by negligence or folly the law gives him an action to recover damages for the injury so sustained. As in the case mentioned in the third chapter,[7] where the defendant, by uncocking his gun, accidentally wounded the plaintiff who was standing by to see him do it. If a man ride an unruly horse in any place much frequented (such as Lincoln's Inn Fields) to break and tame him, if the horse hurt another, he will be liable to an action; and it may be brought against the master as well as the servant, for it will be intended that he sent the servant to train the horse there; or it may be brought against the master alone.[8] The servants of a carman ran over a boy in the streets and maimed him by negligence; an action was brought against the master, and the plaintiff recovered.[9] And note that in such case the servant cannot be a witness for his master without a release, because he is answerable to him.[10] So in the case above-mentioned, if one whip my horse, whereby he runs away with me and runs over a man, the man may bring an action against such person; for the whipping my horse was an act of folly, and therefore he ought to be answerable for the consequence of it. A fortiori I might maintain an action if I received any hurt from my horse's running away, because the consequence is more natural. However it is proper in such cases to prove that the injury was such as would probably follow from the act done: as, that many people were assembled together near the place at the time of his whipping the horse, or that the person run over was standing near and within sight. Yet as the defendant is only to answer *civiliter*, and not *criminaliter*, it does not seem absolutely necessary to give such proof: though to be sure such circumstances will have weight in diminishing or increasing the quantum of the damages... So if a surgeon undertake to cure a person, and by his negligence and unskilfulness miscarry, an action will lie. But if the person undertaking to make the cure be not a common surgeon, there must be an express promise, because if it were not his profession it was the folly of the plaintiff to trust him, unless he were deceived by an express promise; and the law in such case will not raise a promise. The defendant may in either case give in evidence that the plaintiff did not follow his directions...[11]

---

7   *Underwood v Hewson* (1724) 1 Stra. 596, before King C.J. at the Guildhall.
8   *Mitchell v Allestry* (1676); see p. 572, above.
9   *Anon.* (before 1710) 1 Ld Raym. 739; Salk. 441; before Holt C.J. at the Guildhall.
10   *Jarvis v Hayes* (1737) 2 Stra. 1083, before Lee C.J. at the Guildhall.
11   The only authority cited on the surgeon's liability is 1 Danv. 177, a translation (1705) of 1 Rolle Abr. 91, which does not draw all these distinctions.

Of case for misbehaviour in an office, trust or duty.

... For misbehaviour in a trust or duty an action on the case will likewise lie, for whosoever undertakes to do a thing for another ought to do it faithfully, else he is answerable for the damages arising from his negligence or misbehaviour. Therefore if a man deliver goods to a common carrier to carry, and the carrier lose them, an action on the case will lie against him; but if there appear to be no default in the defendant, the plaintiff shall be non-suited. As, if an action were brought against a carrier for negligently driving his cart so that a pipe of wine burst and was lost, it would be good evidence for the defendant that the wine was upon the ferment and when the pipe burst he was driving gently.[12] So where the defendant's hoy, coming through [a] bridge, by a sudden gust of wind was drove against the bridge and sunk, Pratt C.J. held the defendant not liable, the damage being occasioned by the act of God, which no care of the defendant could foresee or prevent. And as to the evidence given by the plaintiff, that if the hoy had been better it would not have sunk with the stroke received, the chief justice said no carrier was obliged to have a new carriage for every journey: it is sufficient if he provide one which without any extraordinary accident (such as this was) will probably perform the journey.[13] But nothing is an excuse except the act of God and the king's enemies; and therefore in an action against such a carrier, where the goods were spoiled by water, the defendant proving that when the goods were put on board the ship was tight and that the hole through which the water came had been made by a rat eating out the oakum, was holden to be no exception.[14]

... And note that in all cases where a damage accrues to another by the negligence, ignorance or misbehaviour of a person in the duty of his trade or calling, an action on the case will lie. As, if a farrier kill my horse by bad medicines, or refuse to shoe him, or prick him in the shoeing. But it is otherwise where the law lays no duty upon him: as, if a man find garments, and by negligent keeping they be spoiled.[15]

---

12   *Farrar v Adams* (1711), before Holt C.J. at the Guildhall; cited from Serjeant Salkeld's manuscript.
13   *Amies v Stevens* (1718) 1 Stra. 457.
14   *Dale v Hall* (1750) 1 Wils. 281. This was an *assumpsit*, though it was said that a common carrier's liability in tort was the same.
15   Walgrave v Ogden (1591); see p. 569, above.

23 Actions on the case for nuisance

(1) Establishment of actions on the case to supplement or supplant the assize

RIKHILL'S CASE (1400)

Y.B. Mich. 2 Hen. IV, fo. 11, pl. 48; corrected from
LI MS. Hale 189, fo. 93v; CUL MS. Hh. 3. 5, fo. 82v;
BL MS. Hargrave 1, fo. 10; MS. Harley 5144, fo. 7v;
MS. Harley 5145, fo. 21v (C.P.).

Sir William Rikhill, justice, Sir William Brencheley, [justice], and
William Makenade,[1] before now sued a writ of trespass against two
parsons of Barham,[2] and their writ comprised this matter: whereas
the plaintiffs were seised of 14 acres of land in the manor of
Barham,[2] and of a certain quantity of meadow in the same vill,
from which lands the plaintiffs (and those whose estate they have in
the same land and meadow) from time immemorial have had and
ought to have a way across three [and a half][3] acres of the
defendants' land leading to their said meadow: yet the defendants
have maliciously hindered them, to their damage of 40s. And they
were at issue, as appears last term, whether or not the plaintiffs
(and those whose estate they have etc.) have had such a way across
the land from time immemorial. And this term the jury came to the

---

1 Recorder of London 1392–94, J.P. for Kent (d. 1407). The plaintiffs were Kentish
 lawyers, and in the next case in the Y.B. (pl. 49) are said to have been feoffees to
 uses.
2 So spelt in MS. Harley 5145 (pl. 49); reads Barom, Boram, Borham, in other
 MSS., 'Bromaye' in print. There was a manor of Brome in Barham, Kent.
3 MSS. only

bar and were charged, and found for the plaintiffs with half a mark damages.

At another day, THIRNING [C.J.] said to *Tyrwhit*, who was with the defendants: do you know of anything to say why the plaintiffs should not have their judgment?

Tyrwhit Yes, sir . . .[4]

THIRNING. That matter is not much to the purpose. But let us see whether this action is maintainable or not; namely, whether this tillage (*mainour*)[5] which is done by the defendants on their own freehold, by ploughing their own soil, can be said to be an impediment to or disturbance of the plaintiffs' way; and whether it can be redressed or amended[6] by this action. That would be good matter to talk about.

MARKHAM. If a man puts up a hedge or ditch across my way, I shall have an assize of nuisance for it, and not this writ.

Skrene. This writ is not *contra pacem*, but a writ on our case. If they had hindered me with force (for instance, by sword or staff, or other arms) I should have been able to make a good declaration against them *contra pacem*, [as I have done here *contra pacem*],[7] and I would have been well able to maintain that upon my matter.

THIRNING. That could well be in your example, for the trespass supposed in your example is not something incident or pertaining to freehold. But see whether this tillage[8] which pertains to freehold—which the law allows him to till as his own soil—can be said to be such a hindrance to you that you ought to be able to maintain such an action.

MARKHAM. If you have common of pasture on my land, and I cause all my land to be ploughed up so that your beasts cannot be pastured, shall you there have a good writ of trespass upon your case (*matier*)? (As if to say, no.) But I know full well that you shall have a good assize. And it may well be that the way which you claim, and in which you allege the nuisance, is not so advantageous to you as it was, by reason of such ploughing; but it seems to me that such an action as this is not maintainable for it.

Rede. If a watercourse runs to your mill, and I make part of this water take another course into my own soil so that your mill—

4　Moves in arrest of judgment on the ground that the defendants had pleaded several tenancies, but the damages had not been severed.
5　Most MSS.; reads 'maile' in LI MS., 'mat[er]' in print.
6　I.e. remedied by amends, or compensation in damages.
7　All MSS.; meaning unclear, and omitted in print.
8　Reads 'mat[er]' in print.

which used to grind two[9] quarters a day—will no longer grind one quarter a day, you shall have such a writ.[10]

MARKHAM. You shall not; but you shall have the assize. Likewise, if you have reasonable estovers in my wood, and I fell all the timber so that you cannot have them, you shall have the assize and no other remedy.

Hill.[11] If your close between you and me is not fenced, and you ought to fence it, I shall have a writ *de curia claudenda*. And in the case put by Mr. [Justice] Markham I shall have a *quominus*.[12]

HANKFORD. It is true; this *quominus* is an assize. But, as you well know, it cannot be treated like your case of fencing; for the law is not all one where I ought to do a thing and do not, and where I do it and more, or do it otherwise than I ought: for not doing (*non fesance*) and overdoing (*pluis fesance*) are not all one.

Tyrwhit. If I have a right to fish in your pond, and you break the whole pond so that no water remains and all the fish are gone, I shall have a writ of trespass for this although it was done in your own soil.

Skrene. [Here] the way still remains, but it is not so advantageous as it was before. Therefore if you had brought the assize, all would have been amended and the nuisance ended (*ousté*)[13] at the defendants' cost; but that cannot be in this case.

Hill. Sir, where the thing [alleged to be a] trespass is continuing, it seems to me that it would be good to bring the assize: as where a ditch or hedge is set up across a way, the wrong is continuing all the time and the plaintiff is in effect deprived of his way. In this case, however,[14] he is in possession of the way, albeit not so advantageously as he was: and so, for a trespass which has been done to him in disturbing his advantage, it seems right that he should recover by such a writ founded on his case.

THIRNING. You say well. But if a nuisance is done to you, and you yourself cause the nuisance to be abated, you shall never have an action for the trespass done to you; for you could have brought the assize[15] of nuisance and recovered, and even if the defendant had put right or made amends for the nuisance while your suit was

9   MSS. Reads 'ten' in print.
10 Such a case was then pending, in a *quod permittat*: *Bishop of Winchester v Abbot of Hyde* (1400) Y.B. Mich. 2 Hen. IV, fo. 13, pl. 55.
11 LI MS. Reads 'Rikhill' in print, and in most MSS., perhaps misreading 'R. Hill'. He is 'R. Hill' at his next appearance in print, but Rikhill again in some MSS.
12 Not the Exchequer writ: Selden Soc. vol. 80, p. cxcvii; vol. 96, p. xxix.
13 MSS. only.
14 In the printed version this distinction is lost and the two cases are confused.
15 Reads 'your writ of nuisance' in MS.

pending your writ would nevertheless have been good and you would have recovered such damages as the law gives you. If someone disseises you, and you oust him again, you shall never have the assize of novel disseisin, for by your entry you have purged the disseisin; and you shall never have a writ of trespass afterwards for the entry which the disseisor committed against you by the disseisin: for you could have had a good action for that had you wished, but when you have re-entered (*rentrastez*)[16] and been your own judge you have lost your action.

And afterwards, by the consent of all the justices (except the plaintiffs Rikhill and Brencheley), their writ was abated by judgment.

RIGHT'S CASE (1455)
Y.B. Trin. 33 Hen. VI, fo. 26, pl. 10.

John Right sued a writ on the case against several Londoners, and the writ would have it shown why, whereas John had a certain way to the church by reason of his tenure, the defendants built a certain wall whereby he could not have his way . . .

MOYLE. It seems the plaintiff shall not have such a writ on his case in this manner, but he should have an assize of nuisance; for the writ says that the defendant has built a certain wall so that the plaintiff cannot use his way, which proves a disseisin of his way. If the way had been narrowed or made worse than it was before, then he could have had such a writ on his case; but where it is stopped completely, so that he cannot use the way, it is a disseisin.

PRYSOT [C.J.]. Where a way is narrowed the party shall have an action on his case *quare viam arctavit*, and where it is completely stopped he shall have an assize, as you say; but this can only be where the freehold tenants do it. If I have a way from my house across your land as far as a certain pasture of mine, and you stop the way, I shall have an assize if you are tenant of the freehold of the way; but if some stranger does the like, of his own wrong,[17] I shall have a writ on the case. And it is so here.

MOYLE. Still the writ is not good, because it does not appear by the writ who is the freeholder of the way where the nuisance is supposed; for it might perhaps be the highway, in which case no action of any kind lies, for it is *actio popularis* and he who has thus stopped the king's highway should be presented at the leet and fined, but no common person can have an action against him;[18]

16   MSS. Misprinted as '*refusastez*'.
17   I.e. not by command of the freeholder.
18   Cf. p. 571, above.

though it is lawful for anyone to break down the wall where the nuisance is if it is a common nuisance. And so he ought to show who has the freehold, or else it shall be understood by us that it is the highway.

DANVERS. It is good on the face of it, and if what you say is true the party may raise it by plea.

PRYSOT. In an assize of nuisance, or *quod permittat*, the plaintiff must show who has the freehold, for all the freeholders ought to be named. Thus, if I have a way coming out of my land across Walter Moyle's land and across Robert Danby's land and across various other people's land to my freehold, and Walter Moyle stops his land so that I cannot pass over it, I shall have an assize against him and against all the other tenants of the freehold in which I have the way.

DANBY. In that case you are only hindered in your way by Walter Moyle, and so it would be against reason to have an assize against the others.

PRYSOT. If Walter Moyle builds a wall so that I cannot pass over his land, I am stopped from passing over the others' land as well.

DANBY. But you are not kept from your way by the others.

PRYSOT. The writ is repugnant in itself, for it says, 'whereas he has a certain way to the church by reason of his tenure' the defendants 'built a certain wall, as a result of which wall he cannot have his way': and so he sets up in the preamble how he has a way, but then states at the end that he cannot have the way.

Several held this bad.

Wangford. It could be that we are still seised of the way but perhaps the wall is built two or three feet high, in which case we can get over the wall . . .

PRYSOT. The writ says, 'so that he cannot have his way'. I think the writ is not good.

INNER TEMPLE MOOT (*c*. 1494)

BL MS. Harley 1691, fo. 64; MS. Hargrave 87, fo. 119.

Note, by VAVASOUR,[19] that if a neighbour puts up a dunghill on his soil to the nuisance of another neighbour, an action on the case lies and not an assize of nuisance; for it is not properly a thing annexed to the freehold, as it is where a wall or house is built on one man's

---

19 John Vavasour, serjeant at law 1478, J.C.P. 1489–1506, a former bencher of the inn. The dictum was probably at Richard Sutton's reading (Lent 1494) on the Statute of Westminster II, c. 24.

freehold to the nuisance of another's freehold. But the smell of the dunghill is a nuisance to the person, and not properly to the freehold.[20] Likewise where a smith sets up a forge, the sound of the hammer-blows is a nuisance and discomfort to the person, but not to the freehold; and for this reason no assize lies, but an action on the case. And this he said was adjudged in the time of Edward IV, and he showed between which parties.

LORD DE GREY'S CASE (1505)
Y.B. Mich. 21 Hen. VII, fo. 30, pl. 5.

An action on the case was brought against someone by Henry, lord de Grey, and he counted that, whereas he had a mill in T. and from time immemorial there had been water flowing from the vill of A. as far as his mill: the defendant had made a trench there to let the water out of its course, and so an action accrues to the plaintiff.

Pigot demanded judgment of the writ, because he could have had an assize of nuisance:[1] for one shall never have an action on the case where he can have another action at common law. . .

And the opinion of the court was that the action on the case lay well enough.

So *Pigot* went on to say that the plaintiff leased the mill to one T. for a term of years which is still running; judgment etc.

And it was held that such an action on the case lies just as well for not doing as for doing ill.

The decision seems to reflect contemporary practice in both benches. Precedents of successful actions on the case for diverting water from mills are: *Gilbert v Franke* (1472) CP 40/844, m. 126 (plaintiff claims by prescription to have half the water from a watercourse divided in two by two great bole-stones, and says the defendant removed the stones and diverted all the water to his own mill; defendant justifies as servant of the prior of Totnes, who claims all the water; plaintiff recovers 26s. 8d.); *Debenham v Bateman* (1491) KB 27/921, m. 75 (plaintiff recovers £6 for want of defence); *Scrop v Leventhorp* (1507) KB 27/983, m. 70 (plaintiff complains that defendant dug a trench in a bank and diverted the water so that for a time his mill would not grind; the jury awards £10 damages; the court takes advisement for a term before entering judgment); *Bishop of Exeter v Ackelond* (1518) CP 40/1020B, m. 321 (for setting up a new mill and

---

20 According to a different report of the same moot by John Port, it was agreed that if a dunghill was left so long that it damaged the freehold, or infected a well, an assize of nuisance would lie: HEHL MS. HM 46980, fo. 154v.

1   A precedent of a successful assize for diverting water is *Duke of Exeter v Hengescote* (1473) CP 40/848, m. 508.

diverting water, so that the bishop's productivity was halved). The difficulty probably came to a head in *Beaumont v Benet* (1519–25) CP 40/1024, m. 345, where there was a demurrer but no judgment, and the next case.

ANON. (1522)

Y.B. Pas. 14 Hen. VIII, fo. 31, pl. 8.

One John brought an action on the case against S. for this: whereas the river S. had run through such a vill, he had set up a mill so that the river did not run as well as it used to; and he showed that the defendant had made floodgates so that the river ran into the meadows and flooded the land.

Rowe. It seems that here he should have had an assize of nuisance, and not an action on the case. Likewise if you stop a conduit, I shall have an assize of nuisance.

POLLARD. There is a distinction between the case where he stops all your way so that you cannot pass, for there you shall have an assize of nuisance, and where he stops part so that you can pass, albeit narrowly, for there you shall have an action on your case. And so there is a distinction between restraining part and restraining the whole.

All the justices agreed with this.

BROKE. An action on the case lies where there is no other action provided for such remedy.

YEVANCE v HOLCOMBE (1566)

Record: CP 40/1238, m. 1552; Co. Entr., fo. 11v, pl. 10. John Yevance brought an action on the case against John Holcombe and complained that, whereas the late duke of Suffolk[2] was seised of a messuage and land called 'Birches' in Coldridge, Devon, and he and all those whose estate he had were accustomed from time immemorial to have a way for themselves, their farmers and tenants, with their carriages, in and over the defendant's land, called Southmore and Northmore, from their messuage and land to Coldridge Park; and whereas the duke on 16 November 1552 demised the messuage and land to the plaintiff for life, and the plaintiff was and is seised, and had 20 cartloads of wood lying in the park which he intended to cart along the way to his messuage: the defendant, being not unaware of the foregoing, in order to prevent the plaintiff using his way, on 20 January 1562 stopped up the way so that the plaintiff could not use it. The defendant pleaded that he was seised of Southmore and Northmore, and enclosed them, as well he might; without this that the duke and others had the way as

2   Henry Grey, 12th duke of Suffolk, executed in 1554.

alleged. The plaintiff maintained the prescription, and a jury was summoned. According to Dyer 250, the jury found for the plaintiff.

Assembled from 3 Leon. 13; 4 Leon. 167, 224 (untr.).[3]

... It was moved by *Carus* that no action on the case lies on this matter, but an assize, because the freehold of the house is in the plaintiff and the freehold of the land over which the way is claimed is in the defendant. But if the plaintiff or defendant had but an estate for years, then an action on the case would lie and not an assize. And it is not material if the plaintiff has but an estate for years in the park.

All this was granted by the court ...

ANON. (1587)

HLS MS. 16, fo. 401v, pl. 71 (Q.B.).

According to *Coke* an assize of nuisance is only to be brought against the tenant of the freehold where the nuisance is set up, and if such nuisance is set up by a stranger there ought to be an action on the case.

And *Houghton* moved that someone had stopped the whole of a way with a hedge, and an action on the case was brought for it, whereas he ought to have had an assize of nuisance inasmuch as he has stopped the whole of his way; though where he has stopped only part it ought to be an action on the case.

But it was held by the court that he can have the one or the other at his pleasure. And the exception was disallowed, against divers books.

There is a report in the same MS., fo. 355, pl. 59, of what may be the same case. Cowper took exception to an action on the case *quod viam penitus obstupavit* because an assize lay: 'yet the justices held that he could have the one or the other at his pleasure, and risk a demurrer that the distinction [between a partial and a complete stoppage] is invalid'. The Queen's Bench consistently rejected the Common Pleas view formulated in the previous case: see *Sly v Mordant* (*c.* 1580) 1 Leon. 247; *Aston's Case* (1586) and *Villet v Parkhurst* (1586) noted in Treby's edition of Dyer, at p. 250, which may be the case here; *Leverett v Townsend* (1590) Cro. Eliz. 198; *Alston v Pamphyn* (1596) Cro. Eliz. 466*, *Beswick v Cunden* (*no. 2*) (1596) Cro. Eliz. 520.

CANTRELL v CHURCHE (1601)

Record: KB 27/1359, m. 473. John Churche brought a bill against Ralph

3   All versions of the same report. More briefly reported in Dyer 250.

Cantrell complaining that, whereas the plaintiff was seised of land in Hemingstone, Suffolk, and he and all those whose estate he has were accustomed to have common of pasture in a certain piece of land: the defendant (scheming to hinder the plaintiff of his common, and of the profits and easements thereof) on 15 August 1588 enclosed the piece of land with various ditches, hedges, posts and gates, and kept it enclosed until the purchase of the bill on 20 November 1599, so that the plaintiff could not use the pasture and lost all the profit and easements which he could have had. Cantrell pleaded Not guilty, and on 24 February 1600 at Bury St Edmund's assizes (Popham C.J., Clarke B.) the jury found for the plaintiff with 20s. damages. Judgment was entered the following term, with £7 costs. On 31 May 1600 the record was removed into the statutory Exchequer Chamber by writ of error.

LI MS. Misc. 492, fo. 224v.[4]

(a) Easter term 1601.[5]

... The defendant brought a writ of error, and assigned the error in the body of the matter: that no action on the case lies here. And that, I conceive, was the majority opinion of the justices and barons; for it was said that in this case the plaintiff could have had an assize of common.

And WALMSLEY J. thereupon cited 2 Hen. IV.[6] If a man has common in another's soil, and he who is seised of the land encloses it so that the commoner loses his common, he shall not have an action on the case but an assize of common ...

(b) October 1601.

... This case was often argued, once last Trinity term, and twice this term.

Hitcham moved that the action lay well. And the distinction is that when the common or way is enclosed by the owner of the soil an action on the case does not lie, but an assize of common or assize of nuisance, while if a stranger does it an action on the case lies. And this distinction is taken in 22 Hen. VI, fo. 15, and 33 Hen. VI, fo. 26.[7]

But the opinion of the justices and barons upon the two first motions was strong that the action on the case did not lie.

ANDERSON C.J. said that even if the law is admitted to accord with the distinction taken by Hitcham, nevertheless in this case the declaration is insufficient: for it is not enough to say that it does not

---

4 Also reported in Cro. Eliz. 845; Noy 37.
5 Another copy in HLS MS. 2076, fo. 127.
6 See p. 582, above, per Markham J.
7 *Prior of St Neot's v Weston* (1443) Mich. 22 Hen. VI, fo. 14, pl. 23; *Right's Case* (1455); see p. 584, above.

appear in the record that the defendant was interested in the soil, but it behoves the plaintiff if he wishes to maintain his action to show it in his bill. For in every action on the case the plaintiff ought to make it appear to the court that he has no remedy by any ordinary suit at common law. And therefore if the action is to lie in this case, it is for the plaintiff to show in his bill that the defendant is a stranger. For by the common law there were no actions on the case, but everyone had to sue by the writs in the register; and if the register had no writ for his case, he was without remedy. But the action on the case is based on the Statute of Westminster II,[8] *Concordent clerici* etc.

And WALMSLEY J. said that it is clear that if the way or common is stopped it is a disseisin of the commoner, whereupon he may have an assize of common; and even if it is done by a stranger, still no action on the case lies, but an assize against him who made the enclosure and the tenant of the freehold. Similarly, if I distrain for rent, and a stranger makes rescue, I shall have an assize against the tenant and the rescuer.

With this opinion many of the justices agreed. And some of them said that if a stranger encloses the common with a ditch and hedge this is a disseisin of the freehold tenant, and he has thereby gained the interest in the soil, so that an assize of common lies against him. WARBURTON J. was of this opinion.

But it was said by PERYAM C.B. and WALMSLEY J., and not denied by anyone, that if my way is stopped and then the nuisance is abated, I shall still have an action on the case for the first wrong, since I have no other remedy for it: for, the nuisance being abated, and I being in possession of my way again, no assize of nuisance lies.[9]

But later, after looking at the books and good advice had in the case, it was agreed by ANDERSON C.J., CLARKE and SAVILE BB., and KINGSMILL J., that the action lay.

And ANDERSON C.J. said that in this case it would not be right to compel the plaintiff to sue an assize of common, in which the freehold-tenant should be named, since he has done no wrong. And SAVILE B. said it would be mischievous to bring an assize against [the tenant], for then he should pay damages without having done any wrong. But WALMSLEY J. denied this, for the freehold-tenant is named not on account of any injury done by him, but because the

8   The *In consimili casu* provision of c. 24.
9   Another distinction, in Cro. Eliz. 845, was that case would lie if the way was only partially obstructed, whereas here it is '*totaliter*': '. . . but they conceived it not to be any difference'.

nature of the action is such that it only lies against the freehold-tenant; and therefore all the damages will fall on the disseisor, and not on him.

And SAVILE B. relied much on the case of Lord Grey,[10] which (as he observed) was resolved in the Common Bench . . .

KINGSMILL J. said that if it had appeared in the principal case that the freehold-tenant had been alive, so that the plaintiff could have had an assize of common against him and the disseisor, it would be more doubtful whether the action on the case would lie. But it does not appear at all that he is alive, nor in whom the freehold is, and so this action on the case ought to be maintained.

And for these reasons they resolved the judgment given in the Queen's Bench to be good.

PERYAM C.B. and WALMSLEY J. were of a contrary opinion, *sed non multum contradixerunt*. WARBURTON J. was absent. And so a day was given to the plaintiff in the writ of error, to shew better matter on the following Saturday, or else the judgment would be affirmed.

And note that after the judgment given openly in the Exchequer Chamber in this case, because no other error had been assigned on behalf of the plaintiff [in error] at the appointed day, *Goldsmith* came before the justices and barons at Serjeants' Inn on the following Wednesday, and there assigned another error: that the declaration was uncertain . . . But [the justices] all said that they would not hear any other error assigned, for although the judgment has not yet been entered it was nevertheless pronounced in open court at a time when the plaintiff did not see fit to assign this error or any other. Therefore they would not hear any speech against their judgment, for if they did they would never make any end of causes. Therefore they said to the plaintiff that if he wished he could seek his remedy in parliament. And they commanded judgment to be entered according to their first agreement.

The record shows that the Exchequer Chamber affirmed the judgment on Saturday, 31 October 1601, and increased the costs by £6. Despite this clear ruling, the objection was still occasionally raised in the time of James I: e.g., *Gainsford's Case* (1605) 1 Rolle Abr. 104; *Pollard v Casy* (1610) 1 Buls. 47; *Kirbie's Case* (1612) 1 Rolle Abr. 104; *Collocote v Tucker* (1613) ibid. 104, 109. But the point seems never again to have been taken with success.

10   See p. 586, above.

(2) The balancing of interests

JEFFREY'S CASE (*c.* 1560)
Cited by Coke in *Aldred's Case* (1610), as reported in
BL MS. Add. 25209, fo. 211v; HLS MS. 2069, fo. 206v.

Serjeant Jeffrey, before he was a serjeant,[11] had a house in London
where many clients came to him. And someone came and hired a
room beneath his study and kept a school there, so that by reason
of the jabbering of the boys he could not study. And he wished to
have an action on the case; but he could not, for it is lawful to keep
school anywhere.[12] So he changed his study to another part of his
house.

HALES' CASE (1569)
(a) Printed in English as *A briefe declaration for
what manner of speciall nusance a man may have his
remedy* (1636), pp. 1–24.[13]

Hales brought an action on the case in the Queen's Bench and counted that,
whereas he had an ancient house in London which from time immemorial
had received light through its windows, and from time immemorial the
defendant had had no house near the plaintiff's house: nevertheless the
defendant had built a new house which stopped the plaintiff's lights on the
south side of his house. The defendant pleaded a custom of London for
freeholders to build new houses which stopped their neighbours' lights at
the side of their houses.

Mounson. A man hath a house, and the windows thereof open on
to another man's house: whether he may build a house so as to stop
up the same lights, or not? Concerning which, I purpose to show
you my opinion, and likewise to show unto you the necessity and
use of houses.

The first and chief use of an house is to defend man from the
extremity of wind and weather; and by the receipt of comfortable
light and wholesome air into the same to preserve man's body in
health. Therefore who so taketh from man so great a commodity as

---

11 John Jeffrey was created serjeant in 1567, and was later Chief Baron (d. 1578).
He had been admitted to Gray's Inn in 1544, which fixes the *terminus a quo*.
12 See the *Case of Gloucester School* (1410), p. 613, below.
13 No law French text has been found. (The only known manuscript, KU MS.
D152(5), is also in English). The date is indicated by report (b), which is almost
certainly of the same case.

that which preserveth man's health in his castle or house doth in a manner as great wrong as if he disseised him altogether of his freehold. As, if I have a mill, and another will turn away the water running to the same, I may bring an assize against him. So, if I have a pipe which conveyeth water unto my house through the ground of another, and he will cut my pipe, I shall have an action against him. In like manner who so stoppeth my light is the cause that no air can enter into my house, without which no man can live, and a house lacking light is rather a dungeon than a house. If one who hath a horrible sickness be in my house, and will not depart, an action will lie against him: and yet he taketh not any air from me, but infecteth that which I have. So if one cast filth near unto my house, I may bring my action against him. If a man build so high that his house droppeth on my house, I shall have remedy against him.

And though light and air be common, yet if by any man's own act they be made private, they may not then be taken from him, and if they be he shall not be without remedy. This appeareth by hawks and deer, which be *ferae naturae*, yet if by man's industry they are made tame the owner will thereby gain property in them. But peradventure it will be said, the soil is his own, and it is *damnum absque injuria*. What then? Though it be his own, he must so use it that he hurt not his neighbour. As, if a man had a pond of water, and will suffer it to drown his neighbour's land, he shall have remedy against him. If a man be bound to repair the banks of the sea, that it drown not the land adjoining, and so doth not, but the land is drowned, an action lieth against him. You may perhaps say [that] there is plenty of light remaining: this notwithstanding, our action will lie very well for the taking away or impairing part thereof, as [where] an action was brought *quare arctavit [viam]*; and 2 Hen. IV, where a man had a way and another ploughed the same, and it was thought there that an action would very well lie, and yet the way remained . . .[14]

As touching your custom, whereby a man may stop his neighbour's lights, I think this is rather *malus usus* than any custom; for, as I have learned of Mr. Hales, a custom is thus defined, *consuetudo est jus non scriptum nunquam repugnans rationi naturali*, and therefore if any custom swerve from reason and natural equity it is but *malus usus*, and for that to be abolished[15]. . .

Plowden. Albeit it hath been alleged that the windows have

14 See p. 581, above.
15 Littleton, *Tenures*, s. 212 (*malus usus abolendus est*).

been time out of memory there, and the lights ancient, it is all one as if the house had been built at this day. Put the case there is a pale betwixt your ground and mine, and you build to the uttermost part of mine, by your first building I am bridled and stopped of my building. And in the country who so maketh a hedge will make a ditch in the uttermost part upon his own land . . .

But you aid yourself with a prescription that you have had light time out of mind. This is no good prescription, for a prescription must be against some party, but this is against God. You say further, that the other had no house, which is not good, for a prescription must be in the affirmative, and this is in the negative; and so saith Prysot Sjt. in 22 Hen. VI,[16] that a man cannot prescribe in the not having a house. But, admitting it to be the usage, an usage is general and a constitution special. In 12 Edw. IV[17] a diversity is taken between usage and custom, for that a custom is a thing disagreeing from the common law but not contrary. And also it would not be beautiful that cities should have any void places in them, and it would be most honourable that they should be populous; and therefore was there a statute made, 27 Hen. VIII, c. 1, that there should not be any void places in divers cities. Also houses are necessary for the sustenance of man . . . And therefore upon the whole matter I think the plaintiff ought not to recover in this action.

Wray. I think the contrary, and first I will consider these four things: (1) whether such buildings *ex opposito* be a nuisance by the common law, (2) whether this custom be a good custom, (3) whether such kind of buildings be for the beautifying of the city, and (4) whether the said confirmation by parliament make this custom good, or not.

As touching the first matter, the nuisance which is supposed to be in stopping up of windows in the south part of an house, I conceive is a nuisance by the common law. For by the common law one shall not hurt the freehold of another, and no greater hurt, grievance or damage can be done to any man's freehold than to take away the light and air thereof, which is comfortable and commodious for him; for when this light and air are taken from him, his house remaineth as a dungeon. And divers cases there be where a man taketh away from another not the thing itself but the commodity of the thing, and for that he shall have his remedy by action; as, if I have a water running through your ground unto my

16   *Prior of St Neot's v Weston* (1443) Y.B. Mich. 22 Hen. VI, fo. 14, pl. 23.
17   Perhaps a gloss on *The Prior of Llanthony's Case* (1472) Y.B. Pas. 12 Edw. IV, fo. 1, pl. 3; and fo. 8, pl. 22 (custom to hold a market every day).

mill, and you will turn away the course thereof or stop the same, I may bring an assize ...

As touching the second matter, whether this custom be a good custom or not? And I think the same is no good custom; for a custom is not against law and reason, but this custom of yours is against reason, and is in effect as if a man should take my life from me, for these be the instruments to maintain and preserve man's life. And the law saith, *sic utere tuo ut alienum non laedas.* Therefore a custom against this precept is *malus usus,* and therefore *abolendus* ...

For the third point, this is no beautifying at all to the city. In our case Mr. Hales's house is an ancient house, and therefore against reason that by later building the commodity and use of the same should be taken away. You say also that it is a thing honourable to have buildings in cities. This I grant, and I think no man will deny it; but by building of one to impair a better house, this is not any beautifying or honour at all to a city, but rather the contrary.

For the fourth matter, if the custom be not good, the confirmation cannot make it good ...

As this custom of yours, that a man should stop his neighbour's lights, is altogether unlawful and unreasonable, therefore the plaintiff ought not thereby to be barred of his action.

Manwood. Here be two matters chiefly to be considered. Whether by the common law this be a nuisance, to stop up part of a man's light? Then, if the common law seem to be doubtful, whether the custom will help us, or not?

Divers cases have been put, when a man toucheth not the freehold of another but on his own land doth wrong unto another man's. But all these cases do vary from our case, for they are where a man hath a private profit in a thing, and another by doing an act upon his own land taketh away the same, wherefor an action will lie. As the case in 46 Edw. III,[18] where the abbot of Buckfast had salmon coming in at a sluice from the sea, and a stranger stopped the same so that they could not come, and he had his action. So it is where one taketh away my way, because this is a thing local. And so of water running to my mill, if one miscarry the same. Generally wheresoever I have a private profit or interest, and one bar me of the same, it is an injury. But the air is not any element local, neither may any man miscarry it, for it suffereth nothing to be void. Also light and air be not things of necessity, but of pleasure, and be not any profit *in certo loco,* and therefore not like unto other cases of things both profitable and also necessary ... Your case was also

18 *Abbot of Buckfast v Dean and chapter of Exeter* (1372) Y.B. Mich. 46 Edw. III, fo. 23, pl. 7 (assize of nuisance).

compared to the case in 4 Edw. III[19] where the assize was maintained, not for that the plaintiff was annoyed by the smell of the smoke, but because his apple trees and other his fruits were destroyed by the same, and this is a good reason for that it is to his disinheritance. As for the case of the limehouse at Ratcliffe, and the smoke of the smiths' houses which cast many unsavoury smells, it is *damnum absque injuria*. And I myself was by a smith annoyed by the smell of his smoke, but yet might I not have any action against him ... I will agree with you, that if all your windows were stopped an action will lie. And where you say *sic utere tuo ut alienum non laedas*, this is not meant of things of pleasure but of things of profit.[20] And here is not any part of your house consumed, but herein a let of your pleasure only, for which your action is not maintainable ... If one house should not be adjoining unto another it would be a great deformity, and if Cheapside were so built it would be a strange Cheapside. And the civil laws say, that two lights on the former part and back of an house are sufficient. And if you make your windows into our garden, this is a wrong done unto us, for by this means I cannot talk with my friends in my garden but your servant may see what I do;[1] and so the wrong first begun in Mr. Hales ...

But if the common law would not help us, yet custom will. And whereas it hath been said that it is against natural reason and law, it is not so. *Consuetudo ex rationabili causa privat communem legem*,[2] and unless it do *privare communem legem* it is no custom. As, that an infant of 15 years' age may alien; for at this age he may consent to marriage, therefore in as great reason may he alien his lands. And in some places any infant of nine years may bind himself apprentice, which is a good custom and standeth with reason ...

This city is the greatest city, and most populous in this realm, and the more populous the more honourable, and the more buildings the more populous and honourable it will be. And therefore

---

19 *Dalby v Berch* (1330) Y.B. Trin. 4 Edw. III, fo. 36, pl. 26; 4 Lib. Ass. 3. Dalby complained that Berch's father had set up a lime-kiln near his house and garden, and that the smoke rendered the house uninhabitable and had also singed and desiccated the fruit trees in the garden so that they would not bear fruit. The discussion relates more to points of pleading than of principle, and does not fully bear out Manwood's interpretation.

20 For the background to this distinction between things of pleasure and of profit, see Selden Soc. vol. 94, pp. *35–36*.

 1 In 1512 Fyneux C.J. referred to a custom of London that none should make a window to see into his neighbour's garden: Spelman, *Reports*, p. 17.

 2 Littleton, *Tenures*, s. 169.

building is to be favoured. And by this building all his light is not stopped, but parcel; and Mr. Hales thereby loseth not any great commodity, but is restrained of a little pleasure, for which he cannot maintain his action . . . So our custom is for the maintenance of the city, neither is it against the common law directly, neither hereby any offence or hurt is done unto Mr. Hales, for his house is not thereby impaired. And therefore I think his action will not lie.

(b) LI MS. Maynard 87, fo. 51 (Trin. 1569).

The case was this: a man was seised of a house in London which had five lights on the south side and various other lights in other parts of the house, and then another man built a new house and stopped the five lights on the south side; and thereupon he brought an action on the case, and according to the better opinion it lay.

CATLYN C.J. said that the law is grounded on three things, namely, *honeste vivere*, *alienum non laedere*, and *reddere cuique quod suum est*.[3] And here that which was wrong to another, by taking away his air and the prospect and light of the soil, was not good. And that is proved by the cases in 4 Lib. Ass.[4] . . . 22 Hen. VI[5] . . . and 11 Hen. IV.[6] Also he compared the house to the quality of a man, in which the head is the principal member; and if one hurt any member thereof, as by putting out the eyes, an action lies: and so here. And he said that various nuisances contained in the declaration do not make it double.

BLAND v MOSELEY (1587)

Record: KB 27/1302, m. 253; abstracted in Kiralfy, *Action on the Case*, p. 213. Thomas Bland brought an action on the case against Thomas Moseley and declared that, whereas he was the tenant of an old house in York, and from time immemorial the freehold tenants thereof had been accustomed to have necessary easements and advantages of air and light for themselves and their tenants through seven windows or lights called 'clerestories' over against an adjacent piece of land: the defendant, intending to deprive the plaintiff of the whole easement and advantage of the seven lights, on 20 November 1586 built a new building on the adjacent piece of land and obstructed and stopped up the seven lights, so that the plaintiff lost

---

3 Ulpian's precepts: cf. Justinian's *Institutes* 1. 1. 3; *D*. 1. 1. 10; *Bracton*, fo. 3 (Thorne ed., vol. II, pp. 24, 25). Cf. *Bracton*, fo. 3b (*justicia tribuit cuique quod suum est*).

4 *Dalby v Berch* (1330); see p. 596, fn. 19, above.

5 *Prior of St Neot's v Weston* (1443) Y.B. Mich. 22 Hen. VI, fo. 14, pl. 23.

6 See p. 434, above.

the advantage and easement of the lights and the greatest part of his house was cast into terrible darkness (*horrida tenebritate obscurata fuit*). The defendant pleaded that the plaintiff had other lights, and alleged a custom of the city of York that anyone having land facing another's windows might build so as to obstruct the lights. The plaintiff demurred.

(a) HLS MS. 16, fo. 402; CUL MS. Ii. 5. 38, fo. 249.

... *Coke*, upon a demurrer to this plea, argued for the plaintiff; and according to him no custom can enable the defendant to build so as to stop the plaintiff's light. As to this, he first examined it at common law, as to which he believed that light and sweet air were as necessary as pure and wholesome water ... And in 27 Eliz. at Exeter assizes, before Manwood C.B., an action on the case or an assize of nuisance was brought for stopping light, [and the defendant justified] by a custom of Exeter, but the lord chief baron held that he could not, for one custom cannot bar another custom. Moreover, every custom must rest upon usage, and that cannot be applied to a new thing: but here he prescribes in a new building, to which a custom cannot be extended. If I have a custom which is as old as yours is, then (being of equal antiquity) they are of equal dignity; and therefore the rule is, *in aequali jure melior est conditio possidentis*[7] ... [And] in our case here the old rule holds place, *sic utere tuo ut alienum non laedas*. If I prescribe to have a way to my house, can you prescribe to build over it? Certainly not; for a custom which is against a custom is not good, because *consuetudo privat communem legem* [*sed*] *non aliam consuetudinem* ...

Godfrey against him. He conceded that nuisance lay at common law; but the question is whether such building can be supported by the custom. As to what you say about your prescribing to have lights, I say that lights belong to you of common right [and not by custom, for common right][8] being founded on common law may be taken away by custom ...

WRAY C.J. It is a hard prescription to stop up lights, for that is a great benefit to the house, and windows have three advantages: prospect, air and light. One may build in restraint of another's prospect, air or light, but not so as to take away (*toller*) his light: though he may diminish it, so long as he leaves sufficient light for the house.

Later, on another day, judgment was given for the plaintiff. (And whereas *Godfrey* moved that the plaintiff had not shown that the defendant had stopped all his light, *Coke* [said] he had declared

7 Cf. Plowd. 296 (1565). The ultimate source of this maxim is *D*. 50. 17. 128.
8 Omitted by haplography in CUL MS.

as much, *quod horrida tenebritate opplebatur domus*: therefore the judgment was not stayed.)

(b) Cited by Coke, 9 Co. Rep. 58.[9]

... It was adjudged by SIR CHRISTOPHER WRAY C.J. and the whole court of King's Bench that the bar was insufficient in law to bar the plaintiff from his action, for two reasons: (1) when a man has a lawful easement or profit by prescription from time immemorial, another immemorial custom cannot take it away, for the one custom is as old as the other... (2) it may be that before time of memory the owner of the said piece of land granted to the owner of the said house to have the said windows without any stopping thereof, and so the prescription may have a lawful beginning.

And WRAY C.J. then said that an action lies for stopping the wholesome air as well as light, and damages shall be recovered for them, for both are necessary. For it is said, *et vescitur aura aetheria*.[10] And the said words *horrida tenebritate etc.* are significant, and imply the benefit of the light. But he said that no action lay for stopping a prospect, which is a matter only of delight and not of necessity, and yet it is a great commendation of a house if it has a long and large prospect, whence it is said, *laudaturque domus, longos qui prospicit agros*.[11] But the law does not give an action for such things of delight ...

ALDRED v BENTON (1610)

Record: CP 40/1825, m. 2802; Co. Entr., fo. 19, pl. 16; Herne, *The Pleader*, p. 179.[12] William Aldred brought an action on the case against Thomas Benton, and complained that, whereas on 29 September 1608 the plaintiff was seised in fee of a house and a parcel of land next to the hall and parlour of the house, in Harleston, Norfolk; and whereas the defendant was possessed of a small garden on the east side of this parcel of land and contiguous with it: the defendant, maliciously scheming and intending to hinder and deprive the plaintiff of the easement and profit of the house and parcel of land, on 29 September 1608 constructed a pile of wood ('a woodstacke') near the plaintiff's parcel of land and raised it so high that it stopped the windows and lights in the plaintiff's hall and rooms, and

---

9   Coke's contemporary note of this case is in BL MS. Harley 6687, fo. 734v.

10 'And he feeds on the air of heaven': Vergil, *Aeneid*, I, line 546.

11 'And praised is the mansion which looks out on distant fields': Horace, *Epistles*, 1. 10. 23.

12 Herne (ibid., at p. 180) also cites the record of a later Common Pleas case (1619) in which the defendant, sued as here for erecting a pig-sty, justified it by prescription.

stopped up the door of the hall, so that the plaintiff's lost all the advantage, easement, use and profit of the land and of the windows, lights and doors from 29 September 1608 to 25 March 1609; and the defendant, further scheming and maliciously intending to harm the plaintiff and deprive him of the whole advantage, easement, use and profit of the whole messuage, on 29 September 1608 set up a pig-sty ('the hogges' coate') in the said garden, and put in sows and hogs and kept them there from 29 September 1608 till 25 March 1609, so that by the fetid and unwholesome stink of the dirt of the defendant's aforesaid sows and hogs, seeping and flowing into the hall and chamber (*conclave*) and other parts of the plaintiff's messuage, the plaintiff and his servants and other persons living in his house could not stay there without danger of infection; as a result of which the plaintiff lost all the advantage, easement, use and profit of the greatest part of the messuage for the time aforesaid. The defendant pleaded Not guilty, and on 30 July 1609 at Norwich assizes (Coke C.J., Williams J.) the jury found for the plaintiff with 1d. damages and 20s. costs.

(a) HLS MS. 2069, fo. 206v;
BL MS. Add. 25209, fo. 211v.

... *Houghton* moved in arrest of judgment that the action does not lie, for it is lawful for anyone to make a hog-sty, even in a market town, for one cannot be so tender-nosed ... And if someone sets up a starch-house next to [another's] house, no action lies.

COKE C.J. A man builds (1) for habitation, (2) for health, (3) for ornament. If a man does anything which hinders [another's] inheritance[13] or health an action lies; but not if he hinders his pleasure. In this case he hurts the air. If someone makes a lime-kiln whereby my apple trees are parched or the wind carries the smoke to my house so that I cannot live there, I shall have an action for it: 4 Edw. III[14]. ...

FOSTER J. to the same effect. (But they both denied the case of the starch-house clearly.)

WARBURTON J. I do not see the difference between a stable and a hog-sty, but I will be advised.

On another day it was resolved *per curiam* that judgment should be given for the plaintiff ... [for] we must presume that everything [alleged by the plaintiff] is true, because it is found by verdict ... that he could not live in his house for fear of evil smells and annoyance ... But they all held that a man may make his hog-sty adjacent to his neighbour's house if he keeps it clean ...

(b) 9 Co. Rep. 57.

... And now it was moved in arrest of judgment that the building

13 Perhaps a slip for 'habitation'.
14 *Dalby v Berch* (1330); see p. 596, fn. 19, above.

of the hog-sty was necessary for the sustenance of man, and one ought not to have so delicate a nose that he cannot bear the smell of hogs; for *lex non favet delicatorum votis.*

But it was resolved that the action for it is well maintainable in this case; for four things are desirable in a house, *habitatio hominis, delectatio inhabitantis, necessitas luminis, et salubritas aeris*: and for a nuisance done to three of these an action lies[15]... And if the stopping of the wholesome air gives a cause of action, a fortiori an action lies in the case at the bar for infecting and corrupting the air ...

The record shows that judgment was entered for the plaintiff, the award for costs being increased by £8. 19s. 11d., making £10 in all.

JONES v POWELL (1629)

(a) HLS MS. 1083, fo. 50v (K.B.).[16]

Jones brought an action on the case against Powell, and showed that he had a house in which he and his household lived, and how he was registrar to the court of the bishop [of Gloucester] and used to keep his records and papers in his house, and that the defendant had built a common brewhouse close to his house in which he used to burn a large amount of sea-coal, by the smoke whereof the air is corrupted so that he and all the inhabitants of his house are deprived of their health and by the said continual smoking his records and papers are putrefied and spoiled,[17] to the grave damage etc. To this the defendant pleaded Not guilty, and a verdict was given against him.

And afterwards it was moved in arrest of judgment by *Noy* at the bar, that this action does not lie. First, because an action does not lie in general for building a brewhouse, for it is a thing necessary for the common wealth inasmuch as man cannot live without drink. And in whatsoever case a thing is necessary for the public good a person shall not have an action for particular damage done to himself. It could be objected that, although a brewhouse is a thing necessary for the public good, nevertheless the burning of sea-coal whereby neighbours are annoyed is not a necessary thing, since other fuel could be used such as wood and charcoal, and then

15 The three things disturbed here were habitation, light and the flow of wholesome air. For the last, reference was made to *Bland v Moseley* (1587); see p. 597, above.
16 Also reported in Palm. 536; CUL MS. Dd. 12. 48, fo. 115v. These give in addition the argument of Berkeley Sjt. for the plaintiff.
17 The declaration also complained of the setting up of a stinking privy, but most of the arguments were addressed to the smoke.

a brewhouse would not be so noisome. As to that, he said that sea-coal is the ordinary fuel of the realm and is necessarily to be used because wood in recent times has become so scarce that there is no sufficient stock of it in the realm. Therefore sea-coal is necessary to be burned; and therefore this is no objection. And for this reason he prayed that the judgment be arrested.

WHITELOCKE J. was of opinion that judgment should be arrested, for the action does not lie. For without question a brewhouse is a necessary thing. And there is no difference between public and private, for both are necessary. But the chief question in the case seems to be whether the burning of sea-coal causes the action to lie. I am of opinion that it does not, for this is the common and principal fuel of the realm; and if subjects were to be compelled to brew with any other fuel, then on account of the scarcity and expense thereof no one would do it, and then great prejudice would accrue to the common wealth. And what is necessary for the common wealth shall never be called a nuisance to any private person. [*Privata debent cedere publicis.*[18]] As to that which he shows in his declaration about his papers being spoiled, it is better that they should be spoiled than that the common wealth stand in need of good liquor.[19] In every nuisance we ought principally to pay regard to the public good. It is true that an action on the case will lie for erecting a lime-kiln, because that is not quite so necessary for the common wealth, and also it is more noisome than other things. So he concluded that the action does not lie, and thus the judgment should be arrested.

JONES J. to the contrary. He said that the action lies, and so judgment is to be given for the plaintiff. It is not the building of a brewhouse which is punishable but the nuisance in using it, namely the burning of coals. It is true that the moderate burning of sea-coal is not actionable, because as has been said it is the common fuel of the realm and necessarily to be used; and the moderate use thereof is not so noisome that it should be a nuisance. But the immoderate and continual use thereof in great measure is noisome and shall be called a nuisance. In an action on the case for nuisance, this rule is general: that in every case where one could be indicted an action also lies for a particular wrong.[20] For I have

---

18 CUL MS.
19 This should not be read anachronistically as an indication that judges were prepared to put pleasure before business. Beer and ale were common beverages for all classes in 1629 because drinking water was dangerous.
20 See p. 571, fn. 4, above.

known someone indicted for making candles, namely for using the trade of tallow-chandler, whereby he annoyed his neighbours;[1] and yet that is a trade necessary for the common wealth, but because it was so obnoxious to men and so noisome, being in an inapt place for such a trade, he was indicted. Yet that is a lawful trade, and just as lawful as the brewing trade. But one may use a trade that is lawful in itself in such a way that it shall be noxious and unlawful. Thus, if a butcher (which is a trade lawful and necessary for the public good) uses his trade in Cheapside, certainly an action lies against him by those who live there. There is a lawful place for such noisome trades, such as the Shambles at Newgate, and therefore no action lies against a butcher who occupies his trade there, since it is a proper place for it. The makers of hats and beavers have a lawful trade; yet one was indicted for setting up and using such a trade at Ludgate Hill. But we all know that on the back side of Bridewell there is a great number of this trade; and surely they may lawfully use it there. The setting up of a lime-kiln is a lawful thing, but it has been adjudged that an action lies for using it near a man's house, who thereby suffers great prejudice from the smoke and smell thereof. Likewise in our case, true it is that brewing is a trade necessary and beneficial for the common wealth, and that sea-coal is the ordinary fuel for it; but if one erects a brewhouse and thereby annoys his neighbours, so that they incur great prejudice, in such a case an action on the case lies. And it would be a hard case if it did not lie, for otherwise a man might erect a brewhouse adjoining anybody's house and thereby spoil the light and gardens so that the house would be uninhabitable and the owner of the said house would be without remedy, which is a cause without a reason as I conceive: for I might thereby spoil the house of anyone's seat in the world, who lives near me, and he shall be without remedy. For these reasons, I conceive that an action on the case lies if someone suffers a special prejudice from the erecting of a brewhouse, as Jones has in this case—for his air is corrupted, which is a prejudice to his body, since his health is thereby taken away; and his papers

---

1 Perhaps 'Tohayle's case, who erected a tallow-furnace across the street from Denmark House in the Strand, and it was found a nuisance upon the indictment and adjudged to be removed': cited in Cro. Car. 510. Jones J. added that there had been indictments in London for burning sea-coal, and also alum: CUL MS. In the later case of *Morley v Pragnel* (1638) 1 Rolle Abr. 88, a Basingstoke innkeeper recovered damages against a chandler who had driven away his custom by melting stinking tallow nearby. Cf. *Rankett's Case* (1605) 2 Rolle Abr. 139: 'If a man makes candles in a town, whereby he causes a noisome smell to the inhabitants, yet it is no nuisance, for the needfulness of them dispenses with the noisomeness of the smell'.

and writings are spoiled, so that he (being a registrar) is deprived of his maintenance and livelihood. So judgment should be given for the plaintiff.

DODDERIDGE J. to the contrary. For he thought the action did not lie, and therefore judgment ought to be arrested. [A house is not only for habitation, but to have the concomitants of life, such as salubrity for health, and light, which is the comfort of life.][2] And, as to that, he took a distinction between an old brewhouse and a brewhouse newly erected. In the one case, where it is an old brewhouse which has continued for a long time, the neighbours next adjoining cannot have an action on the case for any prejudice accrued to them by using it.[3] But in the other case, if a brewhouse is newly erected, and thereby the neighbours receive great prejudice, there is a doubt whether the action will not lie. And that is our case. [In these matters the law is like clothing, which alters with the times.][4] Let us see, then, in what scarcity the realm is come for lack of fuel, so that today there is not a tenth part of the timber in England that there was a hundred years ago. Therefore the principal fuel used today is charcoal, for at the present time the greater part dress their meat with it. For we know that the glass-house has destroyed much,[5] [and] therefore they themselves are compelled to burn sea-coal. Now, if sea-coal is necessary, what reason is there for someone to have an action on the case against another for using the common fuel of the realm? Surely, no reason. Therefore, if this be so, this action does not lie. For the reason why the damages accrue to the plaintiff is given by the burning of sea-coal, the smoke whereof putrefies the air and spoils the papers and writings. And if this action should lie, no man would burn any sea-coal in his kitchen without being liable to actions on the case; for certainly the smoke of sea-coal burning in a kitchen would cause some prejudice to his neighbours by spoiling linen and killing young plants or flowers in gardens and the like. [And if a man is so tender-nosed that he cannot endure sea-coal he ought to leave his house.][6] And so, upon all the matter, he thought the action does not lie, and that judgment should be arrested.

2 From Palm. 538.
3 The argument, as reported in Palmer, is that one who comes to live near an existing brewhouse should be content to take it as he finds it.
4 From Palm. 538, substituted here for a vague sentence in the MS.
5 Cf. CUL MS.: 'by [reason of] the patent for melting glass much wood was spent and consumed, but now they use sea-coal...'. Hyde C.J. said the erection of a glass-house (i.e. furnace) was a nuisance: Palm. 539.
6 From Palm. 538. Cf. CUL MS.: 'one ought not to be so fine-nosed that he cannot abide the smell of it'.

HYDE C.J. *econtra*. For he held that the action lay, and so judgment should be given. And he said it is true that sea-coal is the ordinary fuel, yet by burning it a cause of action may accrue, for a special prejudice may thereby come for which an action lies. So much is alleged in our case, namely that the air is corrupted so that it is obnoxious to health and that his papers and writings are spoiled, whereby his maintenance and livelihood is gone. But not every erecting of a brewhouse and burning of sea-coal is actionable, unless there be apparent and special prejudice accruing from it. The trade of tanning is a lawful and necessary trade, but if one erected a tanhouse in Cheapside this would surely be actionable;[7] or otherwise the neighbours would lose the profits of their houses, which pay great rents and profits, and would be remediless. And so he concluded, with Jones J., that the action lay; so that judgment should be given for the plaintiff.

(b) Hutton 136 (untr.).

... By which cases it appeareth that although sea-coal be a necessary fuel to be used, and that brewhouses are necessary, yet the rule in law is: *sic utere tuo ut alienum non laedas*.[8] And chimneys, dye-houses and tan-vats are also necessary; but so to be used that they be not prejudicial to their neighbours.

And in this case the jury found that this new brewhouse and privy was maliciously erected to deprive the plaintiff of the benefit of his habitation and office, and that the plaintiff was hereby damnified, as in the declaration is alleged.

And upon conference and consideration of the case, all the judges did concur that judgment should be given for the plaintiff.[9]

Although no judgment seems to have been entered, the judges in the end agreed on the principle but differed as to its application. They would not hold certain trades or processes unlawful, but each case would be governed by the local circumstances. The judges were not slow to suppress brewhouses in London. Since 1606 they had allowed indictments against brewers who burned sea-coal within half a mile of the king's palace of Whitehall: Palm. 538, and CUL MS. Dd. 12. 48, ff. 118, 119, per Jones and Dodderidge JJ. And about ten years after the present case one Lewis Young began

---

7 Cf. *Smyth v Moxam* (1607) in Co. Entr., fo. 17v: in an action for setting up tanvats and lime-pits for tanning within 12 feet of the plaintiff's house in a Somerset village, whereby the water and air were infected, the plaintiff recovered 12d. damages and 2d. costs (which the court increased to £11).

8 This maxim (as to which, see p. 595, above) was cited in argument by Berkeley Sjt.: Palm. 536.

9 Palmer, however, says the difference was unresolved, *et sic pendet*.

brewing with sea-coal in the Whitefriars, next to Serjeants' Inn, thereby incurring the combined wrath of the judges and serjeants and the benchers of the Inner Temple. That dispute was settled: Young moved elsewhere, but had to complain to the House of Lords that he had not received his agreed compensation: *House of Commons Journals*, vol. 2, p. 156; Historical MSS. Commission, *Fourth Report*, p. 67.

(3) The standard of liability

EDWARDS v HALINDER (1594)

Edwards was tenant from week to week, at will, of a cellar in London. Halinder had a lease from the same lessor, on similar terms, of the warehouse immediately above the cellar. The day after the lease was made, Halinder put such a quantity of merchandise upon the floor of the warehouse that the floor collapsed and the merchandise fell on three butts of sack which Edwards had stored in the cellar. Halinder pleaded that before the event the floor had borne a similar weight, and that the lessor had demised the warehouse for storing 30 tons, whereas the merchandise in question weighed only 12 or 14 tons; and that the damage occurred because the floor was rotten before the lease, and the supporting walls were likewise rotten, for want of repair by those who were bound to repair. To this plea the plaintiff demurred.

(a) In the Exchequer: 2 Leon. 93, pl. 116 (untr.).

... It was argued by *Godfrey* for the plaintiff. Where injury or wrong is done unto any, the law gives remedy to the party grieved; and although the shop was let unto him to lay wares there, which he hath done, and that it was not his intent to surcharge the said warehouse, although the event be contrary, yet forasmuch as by the laying of wares there a wrong and damage follow to the plaintiff, the defendant shall be punished; for the rule is, *sic utere tuo ut alienum non laedas*... Also it is alleged in our declaration that the defendant, intending to hurt and spoil the plaintiff's wines, did lay such a weight etc., and the defendant answers thereunto that the floor fell in default of repairing of the walls of the cellar, or for the ruinousness of them, where he ought to have pleaded further, *absque hoc* that the shop was surcharged with the intent to hurt the plaintiff's wines...

Dalton [to the] contrary. Where in doing of a lawful act by a mishap a damage cometh to another, against the will of the doer, no punishment shall follow. See the case cited by the other side in 6 Edw. IV, 7.[10] If he might have done more than he had done to have

10 *Case of Thorns* (1466); see p. 327, above.

prevented the mischief, he should be punished; but if he could not have done more than he hath done, or otherwise than he hath done, to prevent it, he is dispunishable. And he may *uti jure suo*, although it be to the prejudice of another: see 12 Hen. VIII, 2, *Harecourt's Case*,[11] if I cannot otherwise let the water out of my land I may justify the letting of it in your land which is adjoining, although your land be drowned thereby. Sometimes ignorance of the party shall excuse the offence: as, if my dog worry your sheep, if I do not know of such ill quality in him I shall not be punished for the same.[12] And it doth not appear that the defendant had notice of the ruinousness of the walls, although now it appeareth that they were ruinous, and for that cause the floor fell; for the defendant said that the walls were ruinous *in occultis et absconditis partibus ipsorum*. And here needs not any traverse, for it is confessed that the floor of the shop was surcharged, but the same is avoided and excused because that the walls were ruinous *in occultis et absconditis ipsorum partibus*; and forasmuch as our landlord (who is also the landlord of the plaintiff) hath let to us the shop to lay there the weight of 30 ton, so as the defendant hath good right as to such weight against the lessor of the plaintiff and all others claiming under him . . .

[At another day:]

Atkinson . . . We who are the lessee are not bound to repair, for if the ground timber be in decay and so the house ruinous at the time of the lease, it is a good plea in an action of waste if the house fall in such defect, for the lessee is not bound to such reparation, namely for great timber, which was rotten at the time of the lease . . .

MANWOOD C.B. The defendant hath pleaded that the fall of the floor was *eo quod* the walls were ruinous *in partibus occultis*, which was a secret thing and unknown to the defendant, upon which the plaintiff hath demurred and so confessed the plea of the defendant to be true; and that he was ignorant of the feebleness of the walls, and therefore he needs not any traverse. And here the defendant hath pleaded that the shop was demised to him for greater carriage.

GENT B. was of opinion that the defendant had not fully answered the declaration, for he is charged with the laying of so much weight upon the floor there so as *vi ponderis* it fell down; to which the defendant hath said that the walls were ruinous *in occultis partibus*, and doth not answer to the surcharging (namely, *absque hoc* that he did surcharge it).

---

11 *Harecourt v Spycer* (1520) Y.B. Trin. 12 Hen. VIII, fo. 2, pl. 2; Trin. 13 Hen. VIII, fo. 15, pl. 1; CP 40/1027, m. 428.
12 See, e.g., Dyer 25.

CLARKE B. It is a general rule that every material thing alleged in the pleading ought to be traversed [or] confessed and avoided, which the defendant hath not done here; but he would excuse himself through the default of another, and answer nothing to that with which he himself is charged.

And afterwards judgment was given in the Court of Exchequer for the plaintiff. Whereupon afterwards the defendant brought a writ of error in the Exchequer Chamber, where the case was argued again . . .

(b) In the Exchequer Chamber: Poph. 46 (untr.).

. . . and the error assigned was, that the judgment ought to have been given for the defendant because that now it appeareth that there was not any default in the defendant, for he was not [bound] to repair that which was so ruinous at the time of his lease, and therefore if it did bear so much lately before it cannot fall by the default of the defendant in the weight put upon it, but by the ruinousness of the thing demised.

And yet, by the advice of the justices, the judgment was this term affirmed; for the plaintiff hath alleged expressly that the floor brake by the weight of the merchandise put upon it, which ought to be confessed and avoided, or traversed; whereas here he answers but argumentatively, to wit that it did bear more before, therefore that he did not break it by this weight, or that it was so ruinous that it brake, ergo not by the weight; whereas here it is expressly alleged that it brake by the weight put upon it, and if lesser weight had been put it would not have broken. And he who takes such a ruinous house ought to mind well what weight he put into it at his peril, so that it be not so much that another shall take any damage by it. But if it had fallen of itself without any weight put upon it, or that it had fallen by the default only of the posts in the cellar which support the floor, with which the defendant had nothing to do, there the defendant shall be excused . . . so there is a diversity where default is in the party, and where not. So here, the defendant ought to have taken good care[13] that he did not put upon such a ruinous floor more than it might well bear; and if it would not bear anything he ought not to put anything into it to the prejudice of a third person, and if he does he shall answer to the party his damages.

---

13 'Good care' may here denote strict liability.

BRADSHAWE v NICHOLSON (1601)

HLS MS. 2076, fo. 66; BL MS. Add. 25203, fo. 266v;
YLS MS. G. R29.14, fo. 118.

Bradshawe brought a writ of error in the Exchequer Chamber against Nicholson and Yates upon a judgment given against him in the King's Bench.

Tanfield assigned for error that no action on the case can be maintained for such nonfeasance. And the case is nothing other than that a man having a kitchen above his shop leased the shop to someone for years, and then leased the kitchen to another at will (for so it must be understood, because no certain estate is alleged which the defendant has in the kitchen); and the tenant at will[14] suffered his kitchen to fall into disrepair so that water descended out of it into the shop. Does an action on the case lie, or not? Surely it will not, for a tenant at will is not bound by the law to make any repairs; and when the law does not compel him to do it, he shall not be constrained to do it by a collateral action on the case.

But *Hele* said that, if the case be admitted to be such, although a tenant at will is not bound to repair vis-à-vis his lessor, nevertheless in respect of a stranger to whom he causes annoyance by not repairing an action on the case lies.

WALMSLEY J. agreed with *Tanfield* that the action did not lie, for two reasons. First, because there is here no act done, but there is only a nonfeasance; and this action on the case is in the nature of an assize of nuisance, which does not lie for a nonfeasance. The second reason was because no prescription is alleged why the defendant should be bound to repair as against the plaintiff.

But ANDERSON C.J., CLARKE and SAVILE BB., to the contrary.

Afterwards, in Hilary term 43 Eliz., the case was mentioned again by *Tanfield*. And he moved that no action on the case lies here for this nonfeasance, unless a prescription had been alleged that the defendant ought to keep his house in good repair; and it does not appear what water it was that descended upon the plaintiff's clothes, so that it could be that it was only the rain, and the defendant shall not be bound to protect the plaintiff from rain without a prescription.

WALMSLEY J. conceded this, and likewise it seemed also to the other justices and barons. So they awarded that if nothing should be said to the contrary on Wednesday next the judgment should be reversed; at which day nothing was spoken, and so the judgment was reversed.

---

14   I.e. Bradshawe.

In Michaelmas term 1602, Bradshawe brought an action against Nicholson: CP 40/1691, m. 2907; Herne, *The Pleader*, p. 104. The declaration is to the effect that one Edward Kympton on 27 November 1590 (being a lessee for 24 years of a kitchen in Bread Street) leased the kitchen to the plaintiff for 21 years; and the defendants possessed a shop and entry adjoining, part of which was directly beneath part of the kitchen (which was supported by a brick wall in the shop and a timber partition on the wall); and the defendants, scheming to deprive the plaintiff of the profit of the kitchen, on 13 August 1592 took away the wall, partition and post, whereby the kitchen floor sank down and was in danger of collapsing. The record ends with an imparlance.

24 Actions on the case for various kinds of economic loss

PRIOR OF COVENTRY v GRAUNTPIE (1309)

Y.B. 2 & 3 Edw. II. Selden Soc. vol. 19, p. 71.

The prior of Coventry brought his writ of trespass[1] against W[illiam] Grauntpie and others; and counted that, whereas the said prior ought to have, and all the same prior's predecessors from time immemorial have been accustomed to have, their market in the town of Coventry in a certain place that people call Priorshalf on Friday in each week throughout the year, so that no merchant in the same town should sell his merchandise in any place in the same town other than in the said place, there have the aforesaid William and the others named in the writ lately come and wrongfully sold their wares and merchandises, namely cloth, fine linen, silk and other kinds of wares and merchandises, elsewhere in the same town in a certain place that people call Erlestrete, from [such a date] until the purchase of this writ; and by reason of this the prior has lost profit from the letting of stalls etc., wrongfully and to [the prior's] damage [of £200].

Malberthorpe . . . In counting you give the loss of profit from [the letting of stalls etc.] as the reason for recovering damages; and of this your writ makes no mention. [We ask] judgment of the writ.

Herle. Our writ alleges that you have lately come and [sold goods and exposed them for sale] in the same town [outside our

---

1 Phrases like 'trespass on the case' were not yet in use. But actions such as this were later called by that name, e.g. Y.B. Hil. 11 Hen. VI, fo. 19, pl. 13 and Pas. 11 Hen. VI, fo. 25, pl. 2.

market]; and it is by this trading that we are damaged. [We ask] judgment whether our writ is not good enough.

Friskeney. You cannot say that you suffer loss by reason of our trading, but only that you have lost [profit from the letting of stalls etc.] of which you make no mention in your writ. [We ask] judgment.

BEREFORD. The substance of his action is that you have been selling outside his market, from which he has lost profit. And so the trading is the substance from which his action arises.

Herle. If I have a market in a certain town and another sets up a market near that town to the nuisance of my market, I shall bring a writ of nuisance and will say in my writ 'he wrongfully set up a certain market to the nuisance of my free market'; and I shall not specify any further how I am damaged, and the writ will be good. So here.

Malberthorpe. We still ask judgment of this writ, because this writ is brought against various persons alleging an equal wrong [by each]; and so [the prior] will recover equal damages [from each], whereas it may be that some committed a greater, others a lesser wrong. [We ask] judgment.

BEREFORD. Even though he has counted [against all the defendants] in common, you can give separate answers; and each will be punished according to [the wrong] of which he is found guilty. So say something else.

Malberthorpe. Whereas he says that he and his predecessors have had the market, and that no merchandises should be sold outside the Priorshalf on Fridays throughout the year, and that we have, so he says, lately infringed this right, we tell you that we and our ancestors and the predecessors in title of our lands have from time immemorial sold and been used to sell all kinds of merchandise, namely silks, fine linen etc., in that part of Coventry known as Erlestrete on every day of the week at our pleasure as well on Fridays as on other days without coming to the prior's market if that seemed good to us.

The Y.B. reports further argument, but the record (CP 40/174, m. 151) shows that the prior denied the defendants' selling from time immemorial, and issue was joined on this. The jury found that goods had not been sold on Fridays outside the prior's market until recently, and put the prior's damages at £60. Besides these damages, the judgment included a specific order prohibiting the defendants from so selling in future.

CASE OF GLOUCESTER SCHOOL (1410)

Y.B. Hil. 11 Hen. IV, fo. 47, pl. 21; BL MS. Harley
5144, fo. 136v; MS. Harley 5145, fo. 117;
MS. Hargrave 1, fo. 167.

Two masters of a grammar school brought a writ of trespass
against another master, and counted that, whereas the collation[2] to
the grammar school of Gloucester belonged from time immemorial
to the prior of Llanthony near Gloucester,[3] and the said prior had
made collation to the said plaintiff to have the governance of the
scholars and to teach the children and others: the defendant had set
up school in the same town, as a result of which the plaintiffs—who
had been accustomed to take 40d. or two shillings a quarter from
each child—now took only 12d.; to their damage etc.

Horton made a full defence.[4]

Tildesley. [Truly],[5] his writ is invalid.

Skrene. It is a good action on the case, and the plaintiffs have
shown sufficient matter and have shown how they are damaged.

HANKFORD. *Damnum* may be *absque injuria*. For instance, if I
have a mill and my neighbour sets up another mill, so that the
profit from my mill is reduced, I shall have no action against him;
and yet it is damaging to me.

THIRNING [C.J.] agreed, and said that teaching children is a
spiritual matter.[6] And if a man retains a master in his own house to
teach the children, although it would damage the common schoolmaster of the town, I believe he shall not have an action.

Skrene. The masters of St Paul's School claim that there shall be
no other schoolmasters in the whole city of London except them.

Then *Horton* demanded judgment whether the court would take
cognisance.[7]

Skrene. You have passed that [step].[8]

Then *Horton* demurred, that the action was not maintainable.

Skrene. Since we will aver the prior's title, as above, and that we
are damaged by reason that he has drawn away our schoolboys—

---

2 I.e. appointment. The term was normally used of spiritual benefices.

3 The school was confirmed to the priory by King John in 1199, and by King Edward
III in 1340. It was later known as the King's School. See *Victoria County History
of Gloucestershire*, vol. I, p. 314.

4 By making a 'full' defence—i.e., without a saving clause—the defendant waived
the right to challenge the jurisdiction.

5 Hargrave MS.

6 I.e. within the jurisdiction of the ecclesiastical courts.

7 This indicates a tentative plea to the jurisdiction.

8 Reads 'pas' in MS. Harley 5144, 'paas' in MS. Harley 5145, 'pais' in Hargrave
MS.; omitted in print.

so that where we used to take 40d. or two shillings from each schoolboy for the quarter we now take only 12d.—we demand judgment, and pray our damages.

HILL. In this there is lacking a foundation to support an action, because the plaintiffs have no estate, but only a ministry for the time being. And if another person, who is as well learned in the faculty as the plaintiffs are, comes to teach the children, this is a virtuous and charitable thing and [needful][9] to the people, and for that he shall not be punished by our law.

THIRNING. This court cannot take cognisance whether the prior can have such collation of schools or not, because the teaching and instruction of children is a spiritual matter. It seems to me that, since the plaintiffs have claimed the school by the prior's collation, and have based their action on that, which is accessory to and dependent on the prior's title, which is the principal matter, and since that is a spiritual matter, this action cannot be tried in this court.

Skrene. If a market is set up to the nuisance of my market, I shall have an assize of nuisance. And in a common case, if those coming to my market are hindered or beaten, whereby I lose my tolls, I shall have a good enough action on my case. Likewise here.

HANKFORD. It is not comparable, because in your example you have a freehold and an inheritance in the market. Here, however, the plaintiffs have no estate in the schoolmastership, save for an uncertain time. And it would be against reason for a master to be prevented from holding school wherever he pleases, unless in the case of a university which has been incorporated, or schools founded in ancient times. In the case of a mill, as I said before, if my neighbour sets up a mill, and others who used to grind at my mill go to the other mill, so that my toll is reduced, I shall not for this reason have an action. If, however, a miller prevents the water from running to my mill, or commits some nuisance of that kind, I shall have such action [against him][10] as the law gives.

And the opinion of the court was that the writ did not lie. So it was awarded that they take nothing by their writ etc.

COPLEY v FITZWILLIAM (1571)

HLS MS. Acc. 704755, fo. 12v.

An action on the case was brought in the King's Bench, and it was moved by *Flowerdew* apprentice: one Copley had brought this

9   Reads 'bosoignous' in MSS., 'ease' in print.
10   Hargrave MS.

action against one Fitzwilliam, because the said Fitzwilliam with [the connivance of] one Harvey,[11] alias Clarenceux King of Arms, by falsehood between them, had taken a leaf out of Clarenceux's book [of pedigrees][12] and put in others, and thus by falsehood had made out the said Fitzwilliam to be a descendant of the ancient house of Fitzwilliam, whereas he was from a more junior (*puisné*) [branch], by force whereof the said Fitzwilliam brought formedon against him in the Common Bench and recovered; to the plaintiff's wrong and damage.

And it seemed at this time that the action did not lie, and the justices willed *Flowerdew* to demur upon it. (Query the reason why it would not lie.)

The justices said that the book of Clarenceux King of Arms is not a record and is of no force in law; but he could have this pedigree made by Clarenceux King of Arms disproved if he would: for it is not an estoppel against him.

No more was said to this today.

J. G. v SAMFORD (1584)[13]

(a) Record: Cory's entries,
BL MS. Hargrave 123, fo. 168v.

[The plaintiff, by his attorney, complains] that, whereas the same plaintiff[14] is a clothier, and for 12 years past at T. in the county aforesaid used the art and mystery [of making][15] woollen cloths called Reading kerseys, 'halfes' cloths and Bridgwaters, and during all that time all such cloths as he made at T. aforesaid were good and substantial without any fraud or deception in that behalf; and for the whole of the aforesaid time he was accustomed to mark[16] such cloths with the two letters 'J. G.' and with a sign called a tucker's handle; and the same plaintiff sold the same cloths, thus

---

11 William Harvey (d. 1567), Clarenceux King of Arms 1557–67.

12 Probably an heraldic visitation. In Harvey's visitation of Bedfordshire (1566) there is a pedigree of Fitzwilliam of Kempston, which purports to trace that branch of the family back to Norman times: *The Visitations of Bedfordshire* (F. A. Blaydes, ed., 1884) Harleian Soc. vol. 19, p. 27.

13 Briefly noted, sub nom. *Samforde*, in CUL MS. Ii. 5. 38, fo. 132, which states the case accurately but ends 'Query concerning this action'. Cited as *Sandforth's Case* in HLS MS. 2074, fo. 84v. The plaintiff's initials are from the abstract of the record.

14 In this abstract, the plaintiff is simply *q[uerens]* and the defendant *d[efendens]*.

15 Reads '*custodiendi*', perhaps a slip for '*conficiendi*'.

16 See p. 618, fn. 20, below.

made and marked, through the whole of the aforesaid time, at T. aforesaid and at C. in the aforesaid county and in various other places within this realm of England, and likewise at M. in Wales and in various other places in parts beyond the seas, as well to various merchants and other subjects of this realm of England as to various other merchants and foreigners; and the buyers thereof were accustomed for eight years last past to buy those cloths well and substantially made and from wool marked as above said, from the same J.G. at all the aforesaid several places, and to pay for the same cloths as for good and substantial cloths (the same cloths in truth being good and substantial), upon the affirmation of the same plaintiff and his servants and factors that the same cloths were good and substantial, without any inspection or contradiction of the same cloths; and by reason thereof the same plaintiff through-out the aforesaid time lawfully and honestly obtained and acquired much gain and profit from the making and selling of such cloths, for the further support and living of the same plaintiff and his whole family: [nevertheless] the defendant, being not unaware of the foregoing, scheming and plotting to hinder the same plaintiff in selling such cloths of his and to take away and worsen the opinion and esteem which the aforesaid merchants and subjects had con-cerning the cloths of the same plaintiff, for the space of two years now last past at T. aforesaid made various woollen cloths called etc. which were ill, insufficient and unmerchantable; and deceitfully marked the same cloths with the aforesaid letters 'J.G.' and with the aforesaid mark called a tucker's handle; and exposed for sale the same cloths, so insufficiently and deceitfully made and marked as aforesaid, in the aforesaid several places, as the cloths of the same plaintiff and under the aforesaid mark and letters, in the name of the selfsame plaintiff, whereupon various merchants and other subjects who were buyers and had previously been accus-tomed to buy the same plaintiff's cloths, trusting to the aforesaid words and [seeing][17] the aforesaid cloths marked with the aforesaid letters 'J.G.' and the aforesaid mark called a tucker's handle, bought the same cloths (deceitfully and insufficiently made by the defendant as aforesaid) from the same defendant, without further inspection or contradiction of the same cloths, as being good and substantial cloths such as the cloths of the same plaintiff had used to be, and as being the same plaintiff's cloths; and the aforesaid buyers, when they later inspected the aforesaid cloths deceitfully sold by the aforesaid defendant as aforesaid, and found the aforesaid cloths to be deceitful, insufficient and unmerchantable,

17   Reads '*vendent*' for '*videntes*'.

both in length and width and in quality and substance of the same cloths, not only completely reversed the opinion and esteem which they had previously had of the same cloths but also gave notice to many other merchants and subjects of the deceitful and insufficient making of the aforesaid cloths; and as a result of this the same plaintiff, when he recently desired to sell certain good and substantial cloths of his (marked in form aforesaid) at the aforesaid places, and there exposed the same cloths for sale, could not sell those good and substantial cloths (marked in form aforesaid) by reason of the deceit committed and used by the aforesaid defendant as set out above, but the merchants and subjects aforesaid who previously used to buy such cloths from the same plaintiff refused to buy the same cloths from him by reason of the aforesaid deceit; to the damage etc.

(b) HLS MS. 2071, fo. 86.[18]

J. S., being a clothier who made good cloth, used (*donast*) a mark; and J. D., being also a clothier but who made bad cloth, used another mark; then J. D. set J. S.'s mark on his [own cloth], and by means thereof obtained good business (*utterance*); but [J. D.'s] cloth was found upon trial to be bad, and by reason thereof J. S.'s cloth was discredited and he could not have as good business afterwards as he had before. Upon all this matter J. S. brought an action on the case against J. D.

ANDERSON C.J. It seems the action lies, because J. S. is damaged by J. D. using his mark.

PERYAM J. said there was no law against anyone using whatever mark he wished; and when J.D. used the mark which J. S. used he did no wrong to J. S., it being a lawful act. And even though J. S. was thereby damaged, he shall not have an action on the case for it, because it is *damnum absque injuria*.

ANDERSON C.J. said if someone has a house he may lawfully burn it if he wishes; but if by its being burned someone else's house is burned, the latter shall have an action on the case: and yet it was a lawful act.

(c) HLS MS. Acc. 704755, fo. 118v.

Note, by *Fletewoode*, that an action on the case lies by the custom

18 Also cited by Dodderidge J. in *Southern v How* (1618) Cro. Jac. 468, at 471; and in Poph. 144. The former citation is very inaccurate, and says the action was brought by the *buyer* of the bad cloth for deceit. The case was known to posterity only from these imperfect citations (see *Blanchard v Hill* (1742) 2 Atk. 484), and Holdsworth was misled by preferring Croke's version: *History of English Law*, vol. XV, p. 41

of London for counterfeiting another's mark. And he put this case when the following matter was moved by *Fenner*: 'a clothier did give the mark of another clothier, but with a little difference hardly to be perceived, and set that on bad and false cloths, whereby the cloths of the other (which made good) were after discredited'.[19] And it was demanded whether an action on the case lay.

ANDERSON C.J. said it did.

WYNDHAM J. agreed, if the statute enacted that no clothier shall give the mark of another.[20]

Fletewoode. In 5 Mar. it was adjudged in one Longe's case accordingly in parliament, and the counterfeiter was [a member] of the house and for this reason was put out and paid the other £300.[1]

PERYAM and MEAD JJ. said that anyone may give what mark he will, and it is *damnum absque injuria* to the other; and deceit does not lie against him who does a wholly lawful act for his own profit.

FARMOUR v BROOKE (1589)

Sir George Farmour brought an action on the case in the Queen's Bench, setting out an immemorial custom that all lands and tenements in Towcester, Northamptonshire, were part of the manor of Towcester, of which he was lord; and that the lords of the manor were accustomed to have a bakehouse and a baker in Towcester, to bake sufficient white bread and horse-bread for all the inhabitants, and for strangers passing through the town, and that this bread had been sold at reasonable prices; and that from time immemorial no other person had used a bakehouse or sold bread in Towcester except by licence from the lord; and yet the defendant had started a bakehouse there, to the nuisance of the plaintiff. The defendant pleaded that at the time in question there were three bakers in Towcester, that he himself was an apprentice to the trade, and that he had set up the bakehouse for the benefit of all persons, as was lawful for him to do. To this justification the plaintiff demurred.

1 Leon. 142, pl. 199 (untr.).

. . . *Morgan.* The matter only is, if this prescription made by the plaintiff be good or not. It is to be considered if all prescriptions at

19 Passage in English
20 A statute of 1536 (27 Hen. VIII, c. 12) required every clothier to 'weave or cause to be woven his or their several token or mark in all and every cloth . . . made and wrought to be uttered or sold'; and by this and another statute (3 & 4 Edw. VI, c. 2) the clothier was also required to 'set his seal of lead' to the cloth. The present case probably refers to the woven mark, and Wyndham J. may be reflecting on the word 'several'.
1   This must refer to the 1558 session; but there is no reference to this case in the *House of Commons Journals*.

the common law are one, and if all prescriptions be guided by one rule and line. And I conceive that prescription at the common law is but one. And there are two points in prescriptions, usage and reasonableness, but they are not guided by one line: for some prescriptions are against strangers, and then there ought to be consideration and recompense, [and] some prescriptions [are] against privies (as between lord and tenant, for there the tenure is sufficient, and *volenti non fit injuria*) ... And see Fitz. N.B. 122b, [the writ of] *secta ad furnum*.[2] And although such a manner of prescription should bind a stranger, yet here our case is stronger, for the defendant is our tenant. And Hil. 15 Eliz. rot. 166, an express judgment was given in such case for the plaintiff.

Buckley, contrary. Although that here be a loss to the plaintiff, yet there is not a wrong. As the case in 12 Hen. VIII, fo. 3, if I have an acre of land adjoining to your acre, and my acre is drowned,[3] I may make a sluice to carry away the water, and although that by so doing your acre is drowned, yet I shall not be punished for it, because it is lawful for me to make a trench in my own land; and then if it be any nuisance to you, you may make a trench in your ground, and so carry away the water until it come to a river or ditch.[4] See the case 11 Hen. IV, of schoolmasters;[5] [no action], for it is *damnum absque injuria*. And it is against the liberty of the common wealth that liberty of contracts be not free but restrained with privileges to one only ... and God forbid that bread, and the baking of it, should be restrained to any special person, especially in a market town ...[6]

Leonard does not report the outcome, but three other reporters agree that the prescription was upheld and judgment given for the plaintiff: Cro. Eliz. 203; 8 Co. Rep. 125; Owen 67.

DAMPORT v SYMPSON (1596)

Cro. Eliz. 520, pl. 8 (untr.).[7]

The plaintiff complained that he had brought a former action against one

---

2 A. Fitzherbert, *Novel Natura Brevium*, fo. 123 B. This was a *praecipe*: 'Command D. justly and without delay to do suit to the bakery (*furnum*) of P. in A., which he owes and is accustomed to do, as is said ...'. It was a variant of the writ for mill-suit.
3 I.e. flooded.
4 *Harecourt v Spycer* (1520) Y.B. Trin. 12 Hen. VIII, fo. 2, pl. 2; Trin. 13 Hen. VIII, fo. 15, pl. 1; CP 40/1027, m. 428.
5 See p. 613, above.
6 There follows a brief discussion of monopolies.
7 Also reported in 2 And. 47; Owen 158.

Spilman for conversion, on the grounds that he had delivered a silver fountain worth £500 to Spilman to sell overseas, and that Spilman had sold it to Sympson. In that action, Spilman had pleaded Not guilty, and Sympson had given evidence that the fountain was worth only £200. The jury awarded Damport £200, and he now brought an action on the case against Sympson for the £300 he had lost by reason of the false oath.

... And it was moved in arrest of judgment that the action lay not, for the law intends the oath of every man to be true; and therefore, until the statute of 3 Hen. VII, c. 1, which gives power to examine and punish perjuries in the Star Chamber, there was not any punishment for any false oath of any witness at the common law. And now there is a form of punishment for perjury provided by the statute of 5 Eliz., c. 9; and if this action should be allowed, the defendant might be twice punished—namely, by the statute and by this action—which is not reasonable.

And of that opinion were WALMSLEY, BEAUMONT and OWEN JJ., that this action lies not; for at the common law there was not any course in law to punish perjury, but yet before the statute of 3 Hen. VII, c. 1, the king's council used to assemble and punished such perjuries at their discretion. And if he should be punished in law by this action, there would be some precedent of it before this time: but being there is not any precedent found thereof, it is a good argument that the action is not maintainable ... and here they would in this action draw in question the intent of the jurors, what greater damages they would have given unless for this oath, which is secret and cannot be tried; and therefore to punish a man for his oath upon a secret intent would be hard, and if this might be suffered every witness would be drawn in question.

Wherefore, upon these reasons, they held that this action lay not, and gave judgment for the defendant (against the opinion of ANDERSON C.J., who conceived the action was maintainable).

WALLEY v RICHMOND (1603)

Record: CP 40/1673, m. 3272; abstracted in Herne, *The Pleader*, p. 161. Thomas Walley, a skinner of London, brought an action on the case against Henry Richmond, yeoman, and declared that, whereas he was a citizen and skinner living in St Martin's parish in the Vintry, and on 24 September 1597 retained one Thomas Roper as his apprentice for nine years, and entrusted £1000 worth of merchandise to Roper to sell on his behalf, and Roper served faithfully until 20 March 1599: nevertheless the defendant, well knowing these facts and scheming to deprive the plaintiff of Roper's service and of his money, on 20 March 1599 and other days between then and March 1601 instigated, incited and procured Roper to absent himself from the plaintiff's service, and to embezzle sums of money totalling £100 belonging to the plaintiff, in order to play with the defendant at unlawful games (namely cards, tables and dice); and the defendant falsely and fraudulently acquired the said sums from Roper; by virtue whereof the plaintiff lost Roper's services and was defrauded of his money. Richmond pleaded Not guilty, and a jury was summoned. No more is recorded beyond Trinity term 1602, but it appears from the reports that a verdict was given for the plaintiff.

(a) LI MS. Maynard 66, fo. 291v.

. . . It was argued by *Hele* that the action does not lie; for upon such matter all improvident sons, and men who misspend their time and money in play, might be called embezzlers of others, who were so full of themselves as to play without winning.[8] And although Fitzherbert puts the case that if a man gains money with false dice an action on the case lies,[9] nevertheless if a man plays with another and wins his money with good dice no action lies.

Herne Sjt. to the contrary. And he said that the whole effect of the action is that the plaintiff, being the apprentice's master, has lost the service of his servant and has had his goods embezzled from him by the defendant's procurement, and it is not for winning the money in play. An action lies for mistreating my servant so that I lose his service: 20 Hen. VII.[10]. . . And 19 Ric. II, tit. *Briefe*,[11] if a man disturbs my bailiff in collecting my rents an action lies for me. And 21 Hen. VI,[12] for threatening my tenants at will . . . And since the action is maintainable for some of the matters in question it suffices, even if the other matters will not maintain the action: as was adjudged in Bradley and Brian's case, 28 Eliz.

And upon this reason of Herne's argument, namely, concerning the embezzling and loss of service, the action lay well.[13]

(b) CUL MS. Gg. 5. 6, fo. 1v; MS. Mm. 1. 21, fo. 1.

. . . According to WARBURTON and WALMSLEY JJ. the action does not lie for the master for winning the money from his apprentice, for a gamester is not bound to take notice whether the other party has a lawful property in the money or not. But it lies for the procurement to play, if that is alleged as the substance of the action,

---

8 Sentence garbled in MS.
9 See p. 344, above.
10 Mich. 20 Hen. VII, fo. 5, pl. 15.
11 Pas. 19 Ric. II, Fitz. Abr., *Briefe*, pl. 927.
12 Hil. 21 Hen. VI, fo. 31, pl. 18.
13 The brief report in CUL MS. Gg. 2. 5, fo. 331, confirms that it was adjudged that the action lay. But no judgment is entered.

for thereby he loses his service; and perhaps in the absence of the procurement the apprentice would have attended the shop and the plaintiff's business. It is otherwise if the procurement is alleged solely by way of recital (*conveyance*). Likewise, if a man arrests me by the procurement of John Style, an action lies against John Style for the procurement.

25 Actions on the case for defamation

(1) Spiritual matters

ROSHALE v THORNE (1382)

KB 27/483, m. 44; Selden Soc. vol. 88, p. 22.

Middlesex. Master John Thorne, notary, was attached (together with William Wakelyn) to answer John Roshale in a plea of falsehood and deceit by bill. And there are pledges for prosecuting, namely Stephen del Falle and John Wynchecombe. And thereupon the same John Roshale, in his own person, complains that the aforesaid Master John (together etc.) on Monday [20 January 1382] after the feast of St Hilary in the fifth year of the reign of the present king, at Westminster, falsely and deceitfully plotting to separate the selfsame John Roshale from Angharad,[1] his wife, and utterly to ruin him with respect to his goods and chattels, made and caused to be made a certain false instrument which states that the same John Roshale had made a precontract of matrimony with a certain woman named Isabel, by words of espousal; and the same John Thorne, notary, promised the said Angharad that he would effect a divorce between the said John Roshale and the selfsame Angharad, in the same Angharad's absence; and by virtue of this instrument and promise the same Angharad withdrew herself from the company of the selfsame John Roshale, her husband, together with his goods and chattels (namely, woollen and linen cloths, gold and silver rings and brooches, and other jewels) to the value of £200; and the same John Thorne put the said John Roshale to much labour and expense in searching for his wife and goods, to

---

1 Or 'Ancret' in English (*Ankeretta* in Latin).

the damage of the selfsame John Roshale of £300. And thereof he produces suit etc.

Thorne pleaded Not guilty, and on 21 February 1382 the jury at bar in Westminster Hall found for the plaintiff with 200 marks damages. Judgment was given accordingly. It will be noted that only one month elapsed between the tort complained of and the verdict.

ANON. (1497)

Y.B. Trin. 12 Hen. VII, fo. 22, pl. 2 (K.B.).

A citation was sued in the spiritual court against a single woman for slander, and the party's libel proved to be true, whereupon the court awarded the party a certain sum for his costs and for the defamation. Then the woman married, made her husband her executor, and died; and after her death a citation was sued against the husband, as his wife's executor, to satisfy the party in respect of the same sum; and thereupon a prohibition was sued. Now a consultation was prayed.

Coningsby. It seems to me that no consultation should be granted; for, although at first the case was spiritual, once a duty[2] is adjudged to the party by the spiritual court this indebtedness is purely temporal. Now, when it appears that a lay person is sued in a spiritual court for a temporal cause, the court grants a prohibition, because otherwise it is in derogation of the king...

Frowyk. I think the contrary: for, just as the common law ought to entertain pleas concerning things which are temporal, by the same argument the spiritual law should have jurisdiction over spiritual things. Now, it appears here that the cause is spiritual, and cannot be punished by the law of land; and it follows that all acts and things done by reason of that cause shall follow its nature and shall be of the same condition as the cause is...

Mordaunt. I think the contrary; for, although at the outset the defamation was a spiritual thing and ought to be punished by a spiritual court, nevertheless once a judgment has thereupon been given whereby something is owed to the party by reason thereof— which is a temporal thing—it is now temporal. Therefore it has been said in our books that if a man promises on his faith to pay a certain sum of money by a certain day, and at the day he does not pay, and is sued by the party in a spiritual court for breach of faith (*laesio fidei*), a prohibition has been granted, because they will not absolve him unless he will satisfy the party, and in that way they

2   I.e. debt.

meddle with temporal things at the suit of a party. But it would be otherwise, in my view, if the spiritual court wished to punish him *ex officio*[3]...

REDE. It seems to me that a consultation shall be granted. The matter is spiritual at the outset, and is determinable by the spiritual law and not elsewhere. Then, when judgment is given that the party should have compensation for his costs (namely, a certain sum of money), that sum is not demandable as a debt at common law...

TREMAYLE to the same effect...

FYNEUX [C.J.] There are several things which it would be well to look into: whether or not the prohibition was properly granted in the first place; whether or not a married woman may appoint executors; and, if so, in respect of what goods. In the first place, a prohibition shall be granted in [some] cases where the matter is spiritual and they proceed to judgment on a temporal matter... [For example,] in the case which has been put where someone is sued in a spiritual court for breach of faith where he was to pay a certain sum at a certain day, and judgment is given for the party: the court shall grant a prohibition because this indebtedness was a temporal matter demandable by temporal law, which is not for them to meddle with... But here in the case at the bar it is quite otherwise, for the cause of defamation is a wholly spiritual offence, which may not be punished elsewhere ... and it therefore follows that when they proceed thereon and give judgment as they have, it is a spiritual judgment; for it was not an indebtedness demandable or determinable by the common law in the first place. Moreover, an offence cannot be more suitably compensated than by money...

A consultation was granted.

OLD NATURA BREVIUM

Translated from the 1528 ed., fo. clxxxv

Note that the spiritual court should have jurisdiction in causes of defamation, subject to a qualification: for there are two kinds of defamation, one of which is an offence under the spiritual law and the other under the temporal law. For instance, if a man slanders another by saying that he committed fornication or adultery, he may be sued for that in the spiritual court. The law is the same if he defames another in respect of simony, or not paying his tithes, or eating flesh on a fast day (as in Lent), or not being confessed for a

---

3 I.e. by a criminal procedure, not at the suit of a party.

year, or not receiving the body of Our Saviour, and such like. But it is otherwise with such defamations as concern purely temporal matters which are punishable by temporal law. For instance, if someone defames another in respect of treason, murder, felony or such like, even though these also sound to the displeasure of God, yet in no way and in no part are they punishable by spiritual law; for, if they were, the party so defamed would have to make his purgation, and thus he would purge something which ought to be purged by the law of the realm. The law is the same if the defamation concerns outlawry, murder, conspiracy, forgery and publication of deeds, and such like, for they shall be punished by actions on the case in the temporal law. (Nevertheless, query the law as to both matters just mentioned.) But plaintiffs who bring their actions on the case for the matters just mentioned must say that they were damaged by the defamation: for instance, by saying that because the defendant defamed him of felony a merchant would not deal with him, or that through suspicion arising from these words he was arrested on suspicion of felony. But the issue shall not be on the damages, but on the speaking of the words, as it is said.[4]

ANON. (1535)

Y.B. Trin. 27 Hen. VIII, fo. 14, pl. 4;
LC MS. Acc. LL 52960, fo. 30 (C.P.).

An action on the case was brought because the defendant had called the plaintiff a heretic, and one of the new learning.

Willoughby asked whether this action lay here, since it is a spiritual matter.

FITZHERBERT and SHELLEY. It is clear that this action does not lie here, for it is purely spiritual. If the defendant wanted to justify, by alleging that the plaintiff is a heretic and stating in what respect, we could not discuss whether that is heresy or not. If, however, it were something where we could determine the principal matter, such as 'thief' or 'traitor', or such like, an action would lie for the words here; for we have knowledge of what things are treason or felony. But where it is for calling him an adulterer, or as the case is here, no action lies, for the aforesaid reason.

FITZHERBERT. Some things are mixed, and punishable under

4   See p. 348, above.

both laws—for instance, if one says that another keeps bawdery[5] or something like that—and for those one may elect where he will bring his case . . .

Cf. the King's Bench case of *Howard v Pynnes* (1537) KB 27/1105, m. 11. The defendant was found to have said that the plaintiff and another broke their fasts on the eve of St Thomas and the ember days 'like heretics', and the court entered judgment for the plaintiff. (See, however, the opinion of James Hales in his Gray's Inn reading in the same year, to the contrary: p. 348, above).

DAVYES v GARDINER (1593)

Record: KB 27/1325, m. 323d. Anne Davyes brought an action on the case against John Gardiner and complained that, whereas she was a virgin of good fame, free of all suspicion of incontinency, and whereas Anthony Elcocke, a London mercer worth £3,000, wanted to marry her and had spoken to her father about it: the defendant, being not unaware of the foregoing, and intending to dissuade Elcocke from proceeding with the match, spoke these words, 'I know Davyes' daughter well (*innuendo*, the aforesaid Anne); she dwelt in Cheapside, and there was a grocer that did get her with child'; and the defendant, after being warned to take care what he said about Anne, further said of her, 'I know very well what I say; I know her father and mother and sister, and she is the youngest sister and had the child by the grocer'; and by reason of these words Elcocke utterly refused to marry Anne. The defendant pleaded Not guilty, and at Buckinghamshire assizes the jury found for the plaintiff with 200 marks damages.

4 Co. Rep. 16v.[6]

. . . It was now moved in arrest of judgment by the defendant's counsel that the said defamation of incontinency concerned the spiritual and not the temporal jurisdiction. Therefore, just as the offence should be punished in court christian, so her remedy for such defamation should be there also; for *cognitio causae non spectat ad forum regium*. Likewise if a man is called a bastard, heretic, miscreant, or adulterer; since these belong to the ecclesias-

---

5 Bawdy behaviour was punishable in the spiritual court, but keeping a bawdy house or being a common bawd was an indictable nuisance at common law. In 1598, however, an action on the case was brought by a woman against the portreeve of Gravesend, Kent, for saying 'Thou keepest a house of bawdery'; and the Common Pleas would not enter judgment for the plaintiff, despite a verdict for 4d. damages, 'but bid her go to the Bawdy Court, which understood what bawdery was, for they did not': BL MS. Lansdowne 1074, fo. 282v. See also *Dymmock v Fawcett* (1635) Cro. Car. 393.

6 Also reported in Poph. 36. Coke's autograph first version is in BL MS. Harley 6686, fo. 79.

tical jurisdiction no action lies at common law. And in proof thereof were cited 12 Hen. VII, fo. 22;[7] and 27 Hen. VIII, fo. 14.[8]

But it was answered by the plaintiff's counsel, and resolved by the whole court, that the action was maintainable, for two reasons. First, because if the woman had a bastard she was punishable by the statute of 18 Eliz., c. 3, . . . Secondly, it was resolved that if the defendant had charged the plaintiff with bare incontinency the action would still have been maintainable, for in this case the ground of the action is temporal: namely, that she was to be advanced in marriage, and she was defeated of it, and the means by which she was defeated was the said slander, which means (tending to such an end) shall be tried by the common law. Likewise, if a divine is to be presented to a benefice, and in order to defeat him someone says to the patron that he is a heretic, or a bastard, or that he has been excommunicated, so that the patron refuses to present him (as he well might, if the imputations were true), and he loses his preferment, he shall have an action on the case for these scandals tending to such an end. And if a woman is bound [by deed] that she shall live continent and chaste, or if a lease is made to her *quamdiu casta vixerit*, in these cases incontinency shall be tried by the common law . . .

BARNABAS v TRAUNTER (1640)

1 Rolle Abr. 37, pl. 15 (K.B.).

In an action on the case the plaintiff declared that, whereas he was a parishioner of S., the defendant (being vicar there), with the intention of slandering the plaintiff and drawing a bad opinion of the plaintiff amongst his neighbours, so that they would withdraw from his company as a man excommunicate, of no faith and not worthy of credit, and of unjustly excluding the plaintiff from the church and for a long time depriving him of the benefit of hearing divine service in the said church: the defendant, during divine service in the church, in the hearing of the parishioners, maliciously pronounced the plaintiff to be excommunicated by virtue of a certain instrument received by him from the ordinary, where there was no such instrument of excommunication and he was not excommunicated; and also on another occasion . . . in the hearing of the parishioners, maliciously pronounced the plaintiff excommunicated and refused further to celebrate divine service until the

7 See p. 624, above.
8 See p. 626, above.

plaintiff left the church; as a result of which the plaintiff was compelled to go out of the church, though he was not excommunicated, whereby he was slandered and prevented from hearing divine service for a long time, and had been at great pains and had been forced to lay out vast sums of money in clearing this slander and [establishing] his innocence therein, to his extreme impoverishment and greatest ignominy. [And it was adjudged by the court, when this was moved in arrest of judgment,][9] that this action lies, even though he does not set out that anyone did avoid his company or would not trade or deal with him, nor any temporal or special loss. For this is a great slander and malicious, even though it be to his soul and [therefore] spiritual.

For a celebrated parallel over a century earlier, which resulted in an undetermined demurrer, see *Hunne v Marshall* (1513) KB 27/1006, m. 36; 76 E.H.R. 80. Perhaps it was to avoid the difficulty about the legality of the excommunication that Barnabas emphasised the non-existent instrument: a triable question of fact.

(2) Establishment of the action on the case

HAUKYNS v BROUNE (1477)

Record: KB 27/862, m. 30; abridged in Rastell, *Collection of Entrees*, fo. 287. Thomas Broune, a London draper, brought an action on the case in the Common Pleas against Richard Haukyns for claiming him as his villein and lying in wait to seize him, so that he did not dare to go about his business. The defendant pleaded that he was a villein, the plaintiff replied that he was a free man; at Royston assizes in June 1476 (before Bryan C.J.) the jury found for the plaintiff with £110 damages. Haukyns thereupon brought a writ of error in the King's Bench, and alleged (i) that a writ of trespass did not lie on these facts 'without some other trespass punishable by law being mentioned', and (ii) 'that it is not permitted in law for someone to recover damages for business undone by reason of the fear of some bodily harm being done to the person, unless some actual threats were made first'. A preliminary discussion on a point of pleading is reported in Y.B. Trin. 15 Edw. IV, fo. 32, pl. 15.

Y.B. Trin. 17 Edw. IV, fo. 3, pl. 2.

... *Wode*. It seems to me that the judgment should be reversed, because it seems to me that the matter in itself is not sufficient to maintain the action. For I have learned it as a maxim (*grounde*)

9 Transposed from end of entry.

that a man shall not have an action for something which depends solely on someone's state of mind, for that cannot properly be tried. For instance, if I say that I will knock your house down, and later I approach your house but do nothing, you shall not have an action; and yet perhaps it was my intention to carry out what I had said before. A fortiori in the case at bar, for it is lawful for me to claim someone as my villein when I think he is so; and likewise to claim a ward, or a servant. And I shall not be punished for this claiming to take him, without an act done. Moreover, as it seems to me, the lying in wait shall not be presumed to be for the same cause unless it is so stated in fact (which it is not); for if I bring a writ of trespass and recite in my writ that I am seised of the manor of Dale with wreck of sea, the wreck shall not be presumed to be appendant to the manor unless this is set out in fact; likewise here.

Sulyard to the contrary. I think you would all agree that if Haukyns had threatened to take and imprison him, and for fear of that he did not dare to go about his business, he would have had an action for that. And likewise here. I shall prove that all of that is included here; for the claim includes a threat in itself, and his subsequent demeanour well proves that that is what he intends by the claim. Similarly where a man distrains my horse, and then sells it or kills it, [this subsequent conduct shows the taking to have been a trespass *ab initio*.] The like is proved by the lying in wait in our case. A man may be threatened even though he is not present; and he may avoid a deed by reason of such a threat. Also, an assault may take place even though the parties are not together: for instance, if I am riding along the road, and someone comes up and says, 'Take good care of yourself, for someone has just told me that he was riding after you and that if he could catch you he would kill you', and for fear of this I ride more quickly to escape and kill my horse by overworking it, I shall here have an action on my case.

That was denied by the whole court.

Townshend to the contrary. The facts in this action are wholly self-contradictory. If I send my horse to a smith to be shod, and by his negligence he kills it, and so I bring an action on my case reciting the special facts and conclude that he killed the horse with force and arms, I shall take nothing by my writ: for I have put two causes of action into one writ, namely, facts appropriate to an action on the case and facts appropriate to a general writ of trespass. Likewise here, in this action on the case, there are later in the writ the words 'he lay in wait with force and arms', so that together with the preceding matter the writ includes two actions of different natures. Also, the substance of the action is not good, for neither of the articles by itself is sufficient to have an action: that is, neither the claiming nor the lying in wait. It follows that taking them together does not make the action more maintainable. As to the first, namely the claim, that is merely defamatory (*un infamy*); and if a man calls me a thief, that gives rise to no action in our law. As to the second, namely the lying in wait, he did not thereby commit any wrong; for without an act done it is more reasonable to adjudge it to have been done from good will than from ill.

Jenney to the contrary. Although he cannot have an action in respect of the claiming, when the defendant lay in wait in pursuit of his claim, and by reason of that the plaintiff did not dare to go about his business, that gives him a cause of action. Similarly, if someone lurks in the high street and says he will beat me if I come to Westminster Hall, and someone (as my friend) tells me this, so that I dare not come here to plead, shall I not have an action? (Meaning, that he should.) And yet he did not say a single word to me . . . And as to the argument that a man cannot have an action in respect of a claim, that is not so: especially in respect of such a thing as this, which will cause a man and all his blood to be corrupted.

Digas to the contrary. A man shall never have an action in our law without an act done . . . And the matter is insufficient for another reason: for there is a distinction between threatening battery and threatening imprisonment. For by battery a man shall be put in danger of his life, which a man would not wish for all the treasure in the world; whereas for lucre a man would undergo imprisonment and recover damages in a writ of false imprisonment, and would also have a writ *de homine replegiando*; but for battery it is impossible for a man to have amends. I believe that if a man were to demand surety of the peace before you against someone else for no other cause than that he fears the other might take and imprison him, you would not grant it.

The court agreed.

Pigot to the same effect. In the case between my lord of Salisbury and Lord Egremont, when there was a great crowd of people on both sides in warlike array,[10] nevertheless it should not have been adjudged to be any assault unless some of them shot with their bows. Thus, in order to commit an assault, a man must

10 This probably refers to the 'battle' of Stamford Bridge in 1454, which was the culmination of a feud between the Percys and the Nevilles. The two leaders were Sir Thomas Percy, Lord Egremont, and Sir John Neville (son of the earl of Salisbury), and the confrontation resulted in legal proceedings: see R. A. Griffiths, 43 *Speculum*, at pp. 621–623.

speak or extend his arms, so that his intentions can thereby be known. If a man brings a writ of trespass against me *quare clausum fregit* 'with the intention of taking his goods', everything after the words 'with the intention' is completely void, and he shall have damages only for the breaking of the close. Thus the intention of a man, without any act done, is by itself irrelevant.

FAIRFAX to the contrary. I agree that the claim and the lying in wait alone do not give rise to a cause of action; but when he goes on to say, 'whereby he did not dare to go about his business', everything together constitutes a good matter for having an action. I agree that the words do not matter, for a man shall have an action on his case where no words have been spoken: for instance, if I write on a slip (*scrowe*) that I will beat John Style if he comes out of his house, and then throw this slip into John Style's house so that he does not dare to come out on business, he shall in this situation have an action on his case, and yet no word has been spoken.

NEDEHAM, and BILLING C.J., to the contrary. When neither the claim nor the threat give any cause of action (as is agreed), and that is the antecedent, how can the consequence give rise to an action? (Implying that it cannot.) For it shall be reckoned the plaintiff's foolishness that he did not go out on business. There are various cases in our law where a man shall have *damnum absque injuria*: for instance, defamation in calling a man a thief or a traitor, which is a damage but not a wrong in our law. And if two people conspire to indict a man, he shall have no remedy unless he was in fact indicted and also acquitted thereof. Likewise in our case. But because this is the first time that this matter has been argued, we will be advised hereof.

No later report has been found. Nedeham J. died in 1480, and Billing C.J. in 1481. Then, in November 1483, the King's Bench (under Hussey C.J.) affirmed the judgment. After this, judgments were frequently given in both central courts: e.g., *Baude v Kendale* (1489) KB 27/913, m. 32 (£10 recovered); *Fox v Wykam* (1495) CP 40/932, m. 338 (£120 recovered after advisement); *Smyth v Prior of St Neot's* (1509) CP 40/989, m. 419 (£340 recovered). Cf. Keil. 40, pl. 1 (1501): 'Note that it was clearly stated and agreed by all the bar and all the bench that if I threaten to seize a man as my villein, this is no cause of action without more: namely, an act in fact such as lying in wait to take and seize him, or something similar'.

SPAROWE v HEYGRENE (1508)

KB 27/986, m. 55d.

Norfolk. William Sparowe, by his attorney, offered himself (*optulit se*) on the fourth day against Richard Heygrene, late of Wretton in the aforesaid county, husbandman, in a plea why, whereas the same William was of a good and honest bearing and condition, and was so esteemed, called and reputed among good and serious men: the aforesaid Richard, scheming wrongfully to trouble the said William, and to harm, worsen and withdraw from him his name and estate, accused the same William of the crime of larceny, and at Wretton openly and publicly said, related and published that the selfsame William was a common thief and robber (*latro et fur*); as a result of which the same William is in many ways harmed and worsened in his estate and name, and in his business, wherein he is accustomed to buy and sell and make lawful bargains with honest persons; to the damage of him the said William £20, as he says.

In this early precedent from the King's Bench rolls there is no record of the defendant's appearance. In a similar action the next year, issue was joined, but the suit was discontinued in 1510: *Glover v Wenmar* (1509) KB 27/991, m. 7; KB 27/997, m. 28d. This simple form was still in use a generation later (e.g., *Fylehode v Godwyn* (1529) CP 40/1061, m. 540d), but the trend was for writs and declarations to become more detailed, setting out the words alleged and adding particulars of the plaintiff's condition (such as offices held) and of his special damage.

RUSSELL v HAWARD (1537)

Record: CP 40/1091, m. 326. Christopher Russell brought an action on the case against George Haward, clerk, for speaking the following words at Buckingham on 11 April 1535: 'I will abide by it that Christopher Russell was and is a false thief, and was at my door in the sessions day at night between one and two of the clock after midnight, and would have robbed me, and did break open my doors and did put me in jeopardy of my life'. The defendant pleaded in bar that the plaintiff was not damaged by virtue of the speaking of the words, in the form which he supposed by his writ and count. The plaintiff demurred, and the court took advisement till Hilary term 1537.

Dyer 26.

... And by the opinion of the court the plea was clearly invalid,[11] for he had confessed the speaking of the words aforesaid but had said the plaintiff was not thereby damaged: yet what could be more grievous damage than such a report of him?

They were in opinion to give judgment for the plaintiff, unless

---

11 Cf. *Natura Brevium*, p. 626, above; James Hales' Gray's Inn reading, p. 348, above.

the defendant said something by Monday next; and at that day, by the opinion of the whole court, a writ of inquiry as to the damages was awarded without any argument.

The record confirms that in the octave of Hilary the court held the plea insufficient and awarded a writ of inquiry. Nothing further is entered.

HAMOND v COCKE (1544)

LC MS. Acc. LL 52960, Trin. 36 Hen. VIII, fo. 39v
(C.P.).

An action on the case was brought by one Hamond against Cocke, of the guard, and the plaintiff supposed by his writ that the defendant on such a day, in such a year, and at such a place, spoke the following words to the great damage of the plaintiff: 'Thou, John Hamond, art a thief, and hath stolen my fish'. Upon this matter the plaintiff based his action. Evidence was given for the plaintiff by three witnesses that the defendant said to the plaintiff, 'Thou hast robbed me'.

When the evidence had been given on both sides, SHELLEY J. summed up (*reherce*) the evidence to the jurors and said: 'You (who are jurors) see that evidence has been given here on behalf of the plaintiff, namely, three people have deposed that the defendant said that the plaintiff had robbed him. If you find that the defendant said that the plaintiff had robbed him, you will assess damages ...'.

Query concerning this point, as put by SHELLEY J., for some books say that if a man calls another a thief and does not say what he has stolen, no action lies. Likewise here, even if it is proved by evidence that the defendant said the plaintiff had robbed him, he did not say of what he robbed him.

ANON. (1564)

Dalison 63, pl. 23; BL MS. Add. 24845, fo. 74v
(C.P.).

An action on the case for that the defendant called the plaintiff's father a bastard. It was tried at Warwick, and the plaintiff had judgment to recover.

DYER C.J. said it would be the same if he called the plaintiff himself a bastard.

But BROWNE J. doubted this, because they could not try the bastardy of the plaintiff himself;[12] though it is otherwise of a stranger. He also said that it was as reasonable to have an action on the case where a man called the bastard eigné a lawful son, whereby the younger son is debarred from having the inheritance. Likewise, according to him, the action lies well enough for this.

And it seemed likewise to be the opinion of the court that an action on the case was well maintainable for the words 'knave, mongrel, half a Guisian and no mere[13] Englishman', because at that time the duke de Guise was reputed as an enemy to the realm—and therefore in Pole's indictment he was named 'the greatest enemy of the lady queen and an enemy to the realm'.[14] Likewise, if someone calls another an alien, he ought to have an action on the case, for he stands to lose thereby various liberties and freedoms which he ought to have by the law of the land.

UTTING'S CASE (1566)

HLS MS. 2071, fo. 8v (C.P.).[15]

An action on the case by Thomas Utting against N. B. for these words: 'Thomas Utting is a traitor and worthy to be hanged, for he said that money was fallen a noble[16] in the pound'. The defendant denied the words, and they were at issue thereon, and it was found for the plaintiff.

Harpur, then serjeant, alleged in arrest of judgment that an action did not lie on the words. For an action well lay on the first words, but when he went on 'for he said that money was fallen etc.' this is an explanation of his meaning, that that was the reason why he called him a traitor; and that was no cause for which the plaintiff could be impeached of treason . . .

---

12 Cf. 4 Co. Rep. 17, per Popham C.J.: '. . . 25 Eliz. in the King's Bench, between Banister and Banister, it was resolved that where the defendant said of the plaintiff (being son and heir to his father) that he was a bastard, an action on the case lay; for it tends to his disherison of the land which descends to him from his father'.

13 I.e. pure.

14 Edmund and Arthur Pole, nephews of Cardinal Pole, were convicted of treason in 1563 for plotting to obtain aid from the duke de Guise in support of Mary queen of Scots.

15 Printed from a different text in Selden Soc. vol. 101, p. 76. Differently reported in LI MS. Maynard 87, fo. 48.

16 6s. 8d.

DYER C.J. agreed.[17]

BROWNE J. I well agree that the action is not maintainable in this case for the first words, 'a traitor', since he has explained his meaning by the other clause ('for he said etc.'). But if the words had been in the copulative, namely, 'Thomas Utting is a traitor *and* he said that money etc.', there an action would well lie for the first words, because the latter clause there does not explain the former but adds another clause. There was such a case before me and my lord chief justice in our circuit in Bedfordshire, where someone said 'John Style is a thief and he keepeth 200 marks from me which I should have had after the death of my father'; and there we held that the action lay well for the first words. It is otherwise here, however, for the above reason. But in this case it seems to me that the action lies well for the latter words, and the plaintiff should recover. For we have seen that by such bruits and reports of inflation (*fall de money*) the common weal has been greatly disturbed and the price of all things much enhanced; and various persons who have first started such reports have been taken and suffered corporal punishment for it . . .

WALSH J. It seems to me that the action lies well for the first words, notwithstanding the latter clause 'for he said etc.'; for the first words are too heinous, and such as cannot by any means be taken in a good sense, and the defendant cannot temper or qualify them from their own nature by any words which he speaks afterwards . . .

According to the HLS MS., the court gave judgment for the defendant, even though the two elements were each actionable separately, because by combining the two the plaintiff had brought an action in the wrong form. He should have brought 'an action for defaming him and putting him in danger of losing his goods and being bodily punished as a result of the report that money had fallen 6s. 8d. in the pound'.

HOUSDEN v STOYTON (1568)

LI MS. Maynard 87, fo. 87v.

In London, between Housden of the Belle Sauvage Inn in Fleet Street, and Stoyton, an action on the case was brought by Housden because Stoyton said that he had had the plague in his house and buried in his garden some people who had died of the plague.

And it was maintainable, by the opinion of the justices of the Common Pleas before the matter came in question.

17 So did Weston J., according to the LI MS.

ANON. (1575)

LI MS. Maynard 77, p. 339 (C.P.).

An action on the case for these words 'Thou art a rogue and a false thief'. They were at issue, and the jury found that the defendant called the plaintiff a rogue (but not a false thief) and assessed damages. This matter was now objected in arrest of judgment, in that the entire issue was not found for the plaintiff...

But the court was in doubt whether the word 'rogue' would bear an action on the case, or not. Some said it was a new-found term, unknown and not in use until the last ten years;[18] and so they said they wished to be advised until the next term.

MANWOOD J. said that parliament had taken notice of the term, and expounded what a rogue was,[19] and enjoined so severe a punishment against such persons that it was right to maintain an action for the slander.

(3) Construction *in mitiori sensu*

CARPENTER'S CASE (1558)

Gell's reports, MS. at Hopton Hall, fo. 49v.

... DYER J. I think these actions on the case for words are too (*plus*) common, and it is not good to allow an action on the case for every trifling word. In the register, which is the foundation of our writs, it appears that such new actions were not there so common as they are today...

ANON. (1565)

LI MS. Maynard 87, fo. 34 (C.P.).

Someone brought an action on the case because he had named another 'murderer'. And it was held that the action did not lie unless he said it in malice; for the speaking of words in anger, without intending to defame the plaintiff by virtue thereof, does not cause the plaintiff to have any cause of action. Thus, if someone calls another 'false knave' in sport, no action lies; but if it

---

18 The etymology of the word is uncertain, and the earliest instance cited in the *New English Dictionary* is in 1561.

19 In 1572: 14 Eliz. I, c. 5, s. 5.

were in malice and displeasure, and with intent to defame the plaintiff, then the action lies perfectly well.[20] (Note that.)

ANON. (1575)

LI MS. Maynard 77, p. 313 (C.P.).

An action on the case for these words: 'Thou art false in all thy doings'.

[*Counsel.*] If someone published of another that he is false in something which concerns his trade, a good action on the case lies. For instance, if someone says to [*sic*] a brewer that he is false in the measure of his barrels, or to a grocer that he uses false weights, a good action on the case lies. Or if someone says of a merchant that he is bankrupt, an action lies. And when someone says of another that he is false in all his doings, this shall be understood principally to mean in his trade: for instance, if he is an attorney, in obtaining a writ. And that is a great defamation of the party and a great hindrance, since many people will have nothing to do with him as a result of such a sinister report. Therefore it is right to give him a remedy by action.

MOUNSON J. agreed, if it was something concerning his trade.

DYER C.J. It seems the words proceeded rather from anger than from any defamation, since he did not charge him with any specific falsehood.

But he said this, it seemed, on account of the little favour which he showed to these actions: for he then said that he wished such actions would go to the further end of the Hall (meaning the Queen's Bench).

ANON. (1580)

LI MS. Misc. 488, p. 76 (Q.B.).

Judgment was prayed by *Fuller* in an action on the case brought in London, in which the issue had been found [for the plaintiff]. The facts were that the defendant said to the plaintiff that she was a witch, and that he would prove it in various ways.

And it was held by WRAY C.J. and GAWDY J. that these words

---

20   Cf. *Anon.* (1558) Gell's reports, MS. at Hopton Hall, fo. 32v, where Brooke C.J. and Browne J. held 'false knave' actionable, but Dyer and Staundford JJ. held it was not, because it was neither a punishable offence nor a reflection on the plaintiff's calling.

would not maintain an action, for it is common speech among men to call old women witches.[1] Actions on the case are so common that they are not to be favoured. It has been held that 'rogue' will not maintain an action.[2]

Fuller. If a man is called 'bankrupt', or an attorney is called 'ambidexter', these will maintain an action.

WRAY C.J. If a merchant is called 'bankrupt' an action on the case will lie, because his credit is his entire livelihood, or the greater part of it. It is otherwise of a gentleman or anyone else.[3]

GRAY'S CASE (1582)

LI MS. Misc. 488, fo. 106 (Q.B.).

An action on the case was brought against Gray, and the plaintiff declared that the defendant spoke various slanderous words of him, namely, 'Thy conscience (*innuendo*, the plaintiff's) can inform thee how unable thou art to satisfy thy creditors, and how thou hast suborned witnesses, and how thou hast dealt in ill causes'.

Gawdy Sjt. for the defendant. It seems to me that these words will not bear an action. As for the first words and the third sentence, they are too general and do not much discredit the plaintiff. As to the second words (that he has suborned witnesses), they are also too general and uncertain, for they do not imply whether he procured witnesses to lie on oath, or without an oath. Moreover, he does not speak these words directly of him, but only said that his conscience could accuse him.

WRAY C.J. and GAWDY J. As the law is now understood at the present day we will not favour actions on the case, but will take and

---

1 Cf. *Thompson v Baines* (1572) KB 27/1243, m. 127, where a woman recovered 60s. damages for the words 'Alice Thompson is a witch'. (This was brought to our notice by Professor R. H. Helmholz.) And see p. 644, below, for calling a man a witch.

2 Cf. *Anon.* (1575), p. 637, above and *Anon.* (1579) LI MS. Misc. 488, p. 48, per Wray C.J.: '. . . at this day these actions on the case are so increased and so common—for one cannot say any word which slightly discredits any other but he will bring an action on it—that it is good to restrict them as much as we can, and by that means to abridge the multitude of suits which there would otherwise be here. For this reason it has recently been held in this court that if a man calls another a "rogue", "cozener" or "false knave", or such like, the action on the case shall not be given for it . . . and he further said that these words "knave", "rogue", and so forth, are words more of anger and for the most part spoken hastily and without any advisement . . . and it seemed to him to be good to reduce [these actions] *ad pristinum statum* and not to give any favour to these actions'. By their pristine condition he evidently meant the law as stated in *Haukyns v Broune* (1477); see p. 629, above.

3 Note also that only merchants were subject to proceedings under the Bankruptcy Act (1571), 13 Eliz. I, c. 7.

record them strictly against the plaintiff. The reason is that these actions are so common, and are usually based wholly on malice and not on righteous causes. Therefore we will not give actions on the case in various cases where they have been taken before. As to the case now in question, we think that (as has been said) the words are too general, and are such words as do not plainly, perfectly or directly discredit the plaintiff. Therefore, as we are now advised, they will not maintain an action.

Gawdy Sjt. The truth of the matter is that the defendant did not speak these words spontaneously, but wrote them in a letter at the command and entreaty of someone else, and in his name; and after he had written them he read the letter (including these words) to him, and not otherwise.

WRAY C.J. That does not appear to us.

STANHOPE v BLYTHE (1585)

Record: KB 27/1292, m. 545; Co. Entr., fo. 21. Edward Stanhope brought a bill against William Blythe and complained that, whereas he was learned in the law[4] and retained of counsel with various great men and other subjects of the queen, and was of good name and reputation, without any stain of falsehood or perjury; and whereas he was surveyor of the duchy of Lancaster in Nottinghamshire, and a justice of the peace there and in Lincolnshire, and had been a member of the previous parliament, and had remained in all these offices without perjury: nevertheless the defendant, scheming to deprive the plaintiff of his good name and to lose him his clients and public offices, on 20 July 1583 at Bingham, Nottinghamshire, maliciously and devilishly said in the presence of many people, 'What is he (*innuendo*, the plaintiff)? He (*innuendo*, the plaintiff) hath nothing but what he hath gotten by swearing and forswearing'; and by reason of these words the plaintiff was harmed in his reputation and in great danger of losing his offices, fees and clients. Blythe pleaded Not guilty; and on 19 March 1585 at Nottingham assizes (Dyer C.J.C.P., Mead J.K.B.) the jury found for the plaintiff, with £66. 13s. 4d. damages.

4 Co. Rep. 15; autograph notebook, BL MS. Harley 6686, fo. 112v.

. . . And it was adjudged that the said words were not actionable. First, because they were too general; and words which shall charge someone with an action in which damages shall be recovered must

---

4   He was a bencher of Gray's Inn.

have suitable certainty. Secondly, the defendant does not charge the plaintiff with swearing or forswearing, for he may recover or obtain a manor by swearing or forswearing even though he did not procure or assent to it.[5] And words which maintain an action must be applied directly to the plaintiff, and not by collection or inference; for the damages must be given to the plaintiff in respect of the damage which he has by the scandal. Thirdly, if someone charges another that he has forsworn himself, that is not actionable, for two reasons: (1) because he may be forsworn in ordinary speech, *quia benignior sentencia in verbis generalibus seu dubiis est praeferenda*;[6] (2) it is a usual expression of passion and anger to say to another that he has forsworn himself. Similarly, if one says to another that he is a villain, a rogue, or a varlet, or such like, these and the like [expressions] will not bear an action: for *boni judicis interest lites dirimere*.[7] But if one says of another that he is perjured, or that he has forsworn himself in such and such a court, an action will be maintainable for such words; for by these words it appears that he has forsworn himself in a judicial proceeding. *Sed haec ita in promptu sunt, ut res probatione non egeant*;[8] for all these cases have been often adjudged.

And WRAY C.J. said that, although slanders and false imputations are to be suppressed, because many times *a verbis ad verbera perventum est*,[9] nevertheless he said that the judges had resolved that actions for scandals should not be maintained by any strained construction or argument, nor any favour extended in supporting them, since nowadays they abounded more than in times past, and the intemperance and malice of men had increased: *et maliciis hominum est obviandum*. And in our books *actiones pro scandalis sunt rarissimae*; and those which are brought are for words of eminent slanders and of great import.[10]

At the end of his collection of slander cases, Coke wrote: 'These brief

---

5 Cf. the report in BL MS. Lansdowne 1067, fo. 96: 'For instance, if a man recovers land by a false verdict it may be said to him that this land which he has, he has by forswearing, though this does not refer to him but to the jury'.
6 Because in general or doubtful words the milder sense is to be preferred.
7 A good judge is concerned to make an end of lawsuits.
8 But these things are so apparent that they do not need proof.
9 Words turn to blows.
10 The report in CUL MS. Ii. 5. 38, fo. 182, sets out the arguments of Popham for the plaintiff, and Egerton for the defendant, and ends: '... The justices said that they would not allow actions grounded on implied meanings (*intendments*), and for these trifling causes, which anyone might speak to others in anger'.

resolutions and the reason thereof, being well understood and observed, will perhaps give great direction and instruction for many others, and will deter men from subjecting themselves to actions in which damages and costs are to be recovered . . . for words, which are but wind' (4 Co. Rep. 20).

JEAMES v RUTLECH (1599)

4 Co. Rep. 17 (Q.B.).

The plaintiff counted that the defendant and one John Bonner were discussing the plaintiff, and the defendant said of the plaintiff, to the said John Bonner, these words: 'Hang him (*innuendo*, the aforesaid John Jeames), he is full of the pox (*innuendo*, the French pox). I marvel that you (*innuendo*, the aforesaid John Bonner) will eat or drink with him (*innuendo*, the aforesaid John Jeames). I will prove that he is full of the pox (*innuendo*, the French pox)'. The defendant pleaded Not guilty, and it was found for the plaintiff, and damages assessed. And it was moved in arrest of judgment that the said words were not actionable.

It was resolved that in every action on the case for slanderous words, two things are requisite: (1) that the person who is scanda-lised is certain; (2) that the scandal is apparent from the words themselves. Therefore if someone says, without any previous discussion, that one of the servants of John Style (who has several) is a notorious felon or traitor, no action lies here on account of the uncertainty of the person; and an *innuendo* cannot make it certain. So it is if someone says generally, 'I know one near about John Style that is a notorious thief', or such like. But where the person is once named with certainty, as where two persons are talking together about John Style and one says, 'He is a notorious thief', there John Style may set out in his count that there was talk of him between the two of them, and that the one said of him, 'He (*innuendo*, the aforesaid John Style) is a notorious thief'. For the office of an *innuendo* is to contain and designate the same person who was named with certainty before, and in effect stands instead of 'aforesaid'. But an *innuendo* cannot make a person certain who was uncertain before . . . Here, in the case at the bar, when the defendant and Bonner were speaking about the plaintiff, and the defendant said 'Hang him', the *innuendo* will denote the same person named before . . .

As to the second point, just as an *innuendo* cannot make the person certain who was uncertain before, neither can it alter the matter or sense of the words themselves. Therefore when the defendant in the case at the bar said of the plaintiff that he was 'full of the pox (*innuendo*, the French pox)', this *innuendo* does not perform its proper office; for it strives to extend the general words 'the pox' by imagination of an intent which is not apparent from any preceding words to which the *innuendo* refers. And the words themselves shall be taken *in mitiori sensu*.[11]

HOLT v ASTGRIGG (1607)

Cro. Jac. 184, pl. 4 (K.B.) (untr.).

Action upon the case for words: 'Sir Thomas Holt struck his cook on the head with a cleaver, and cleaved his head; the one part lay on the one shoulder and another part on the other'. The defendant pleaded Not guilty, and [it was] found against him; and now moved in arrest of judgment that these words were not actionable: for it is not averred that the cook was killed, but *argumentativè*.

And of that opinion was the court (FLEMING C.J. and WILLIAMS J. *absentibus*), for slander ought to be direct, against which there may not be any intendment. But here, notwithstanding such wounding, the party may yet be living, and it is then but trespass.

---

11 The distinction between allegations of having small pox (not actionable) and the French or great pox, i.e. syphilis (actionable), had been drawn for at least a quarter of a century: see *Anon.* (1572), p. 644, below; *Boxe's Case* (1582) Cro. Eliz. 2. According to another report of the above case in BL MS. Add. 25203, fo. 90v, the reason was that, since small pox was infectious, it was permissible for a man to warn friends to refrain from the company of an infected person. Popham C.J. had taken the view, contrary to the above case, that 'to say "Thou hast the pox" or "Thou art a pocky knave" should be understood as the French pox, because men do not use to speak such words to those who have the small pox': *Hilliard's Case* (1595) BL MS. Lansdowne 1076, fo. 156. But the year before that, it was held not actionable to say 'Thou art a pocky fellow, for thou hast lost the hair of thy head and beard and hast a picked clout on thy head and lookest as white as thine arse': *Anon.* (1594) CUL MS. Ll. 3. 9, fo. 402v. The following expressions, nevertheless, were held to be actionable (because they indicated the French pox): *Anon.* (1588) BL MS. Lansdowne 1067, fo. 97 ('Thou art a pocky knave and I will prove thou wast laid of the pox in Spain'); *Levet's Case* (1592) Cro. Eliz. 289 ('Thy wife was laid of the pox'); *Davies v Taylor* (1599) Cro. Eliz. 648 ('Thou art rotted with the pox'); *Brooke v Wye* (1602) BL MS. Add. 25203, fo. 471 ('The pox hath eaten off her nose'); *Miles v Bland* (1609) 1 Rolle Abr. 67, line 14 ('Thou art a pocky whore and the pox have eaten out the bottom of thy belly that thy guts are ready to fall out'); *Prekington's Case* (1610) 1 Rolle Abr. 66, line 53 ('The pox haunts thee twice a year'). It was also actionable to say that someone had submitted to medical treatment associated with French pox: *Browne v Charnocke* (1595) BL MS. Harley 1631, fo. 138v (Fowler's tub); *Anon.* (*temp.* Jac. I) CUL MS. Gg. 2. 5, fo. 136v (Cornelius's tub, 'who was notoriously known to be a curer of French pox').

Wherefore it was adjudged for the defendant.[12]

(4) Construction in an ordinary or bad sense

ANON. (1568)

HLS MS. 1180(1), fo. 334v.

An action on the case lies for calling the plaintiff 'conjurer' generally, so it seems. Likewise for calling him a witch,[13] or maintainer of causes, generally; for it cannot be understood *in bonam partem*, prima facie.

ANON. (1572)

CUL MS. Gg. 5. 2, fo. 109 (C.P.).

... MANWOOD J. I have known an action on the case to be brought in the King's Bench for these words, 'Thou art a pocky merchant', and it was held there that the action lay perfectly well and £50 was given in damages, even though it could mean the small pox; for it was presumed *in malam partem*...[14]

GASTRELL v TOWNSEND (1591)

Cro. Eliz. 239, pl. 8 (Q.B.) (untr.).

Action for words: 'Thou has sought the blood of thy husband and wast his death, for if thou hadst been an honest woman he had been alive yet'. And avers *in facto* that her husband was killed.

It was moved [that] the action lieth not, for it is not said she did any unlawful act. And it was cited to be adjudged, Mich. 18 & 19 Eliz., that for these words, 'Thou wert the death of John Style', an action lieth not; for it may be by grief.

---

12   Cf. another report, sub nom. *Holt v Astricke*, HLS MS. 1058(2), fo. 54: '... and because the plaintiff did not lay that his cook was dead, *Stapleton* prayed that the plaintiff should take nothing by his bill. And it was adjudged accordingly by FENNER, YELVERTON and CROKE JJ., being alone in court, for if [the cook] is not dead the other is but a trespasser'.

13   Cf. p. 638, above. In *Netlingham v Ode* (1578) KB 27/1266, m. 779; Selden Soc. vol. 101, p. 61, a man recovered £6 damages for the words, 'If there were ever any witch, thou art one'.

14   For construction *in malam partem*, see also *Utting's Case* (1566), p. 636, above, per Walsh J.; *Prowse v Carey* (1588) Cro. Eliz. 93.

But it was ruled here that the action lieth, for they shall be taken to be spoken *in malam partem*;[14] and it was adjudged for the plaintiff.

LEWES v ROBERTS (1661)

Hardres 203, pl. 1.

Action upon the case for these words: 'You and your crew brought the late king to death'. The words were spoken at an election of knights of the shire to serve in parliament. After a verdict found for the plaintiff, and £200 damages, it was now moved for the defendant in arrest of judgment that the words are not actionable; for that they ought to be taken *in mitiori sensu*, and they may be understood that he attended the king to his death.

But, *per curiam*, the words sound in scandal; and in common acceptation and construction they amount to this: that the plaintiff put the king to death, or had a hand in his death.

HARRISON v THORNBOROUGH (1714)

Gilb. Cas. 114 (Q.B.).[15]

In an action for words the plaintiff declared that, whereas he was a dyer, and there was a suit depending between him and B., and a trial was had, at which one Bell was a witness, and the defendant on a certain day in a certain year when talking with a certain Hugh Raw of the trial and Bell's evidence, and of the plaintiff, said these words: 'Harrison got a poor fellow, Bell, to forswear himself (*innuendo*, at the trial). You (*innuendo*, Hugh Raw) or he (*innuendo*, the plaintiff) hired him (*innuendo*, Bell) to forswear himself'; and, when having another talk, he said, 'Two dyers (*innuendo*, two persons exercising the art or mystery of dyers) [are gone off][16] (*innuendo*, bankrupt), and that for anything that I know Harrison will go off before this time 12 months.' Verdict for the plaintiff, and entire damages.

Mr. Solicitor[17] and *Lutwyche* moved in arrest of judgment that the action did not lie; that the first words, 'Harrison got a poor fellow to forswear himself', does not import a charge of subornation, for though it was alleged that they were spoke with relation to

15 Also reported in 10 Mod. 196.
16 From 10 Mod. 196.
17 Sir Robert Raymond.

the evidence he gave at the trial, yet it was not shown that the evidence was material, and if he did forswear himself in an immaterial matter that would not be perjury in him, and consequently not subornation in the plaintiff. But they insist that if these words taken by themselves would be actionable, yet the subsequent words (which appear to be spoken at the same time) had rendered them wholly uncertain ... It was objected to the second count that the words 'gone off' were uncertain, and did not import bankruptcy; for a man might be said to go off upon divers accounts. But, if they should be so taken, yet the latter words did not charge the plaintiff, but at most did only express suspicion of him. That to tie up the meaning of the first words to bankruptcy the plaintiff had laid an *innuendo*, but that could not carry the words beyond their strict meaning for want of an averment to which that *innuendo* might refer: 4 Co. Rep. 20.[18]

But the court held that the first exception to the first count was only an exception to the form of laying the slander ... As to the second count, they held that 'gone off', as understood in common parlance, applied to the plaintiff here as a tradesman, mean bankruptcy; and that the rule now was that words shall be taken in the sense that the hearers understood them, and not *in mitiori sensu* as formerly. Therefore no *innuendo* was necessary. But, if it were, it was well laid in this place, and that an averment is only necessary where the *innuendo* concerns some new fact, and not where it is brought in to explain for the sense of the words.

Per curiam. Judgment for the plaintiff.

Some things were said in general at the bench of these actions for words, and all the judges agreed that they ought not to be discouraged.

PARKER C.J. remembered a saying of Treby C.J.[19] that people should not be discouraged that put their trust in the law, for if men could not have a remedy at law for such slanders they would be apt to carve it for themselves; which would let in all the ill consequences of private revenge.

And POWYS J. said that the latter judgments had been right in denying the rule of taking words *in mitiori sensu*, because it left a liberty for men to defame others provided they did it with a little caution; and it had been known that people had taken advice of counsel upon a sheet of paper full of scandalous words in order to know which they might out with safety.

18   *Barham v Nethersall* (1602): the words 'Mr. Barham did burn my barn' could not be extended by *innuendo* to mean 'barn with corn', so as to make it an accusation of felony. See also *Jeames v Rutlech* (1599), p. 642, above.

19   Sir George Treby (d. 1700), C.J.C.P. 1692–1700.

Chesshyre Sjt., for the plaintiff, cited these authorities of uncertain slanders held actionable: 1 Sid. 227 ('I dreamed you stole a horse'); 2 Lev. 277 ('I heard a bird sing you committed felony'); Style 130, 141 ('He is a bankrupt, for ought I know'); Cro. Jac. 407 ('I think in my conscience, if he might have his will, he would kill the king'); 2 Keb. 718, Raym. 207 ('I believe all is not well with the plaintiff: many merchants have failed of late, I expect no better of him'); Dyer 72 ('He will be a bankrupt within three weeks').

(5) Libel

ANON. (1562)

Gell's reports, MS. at Hopton Hall, fo. 198v (C.P.).

An action on the case was brought against another because the defendant had said in writing that the plaintiff had taken many bribes, whereby the Lord Arundel and the Lord Lumley had had great losses and damage from their tenants.

Carus moved whether these words are a cause of an action on the case, and said that *Bendlowes* had demurred upon this writ.

DYER C.J. It seems to me that the action will not lie upon such matter, for two reasons. First, because the words were in writing, and that cannot be a declaration by words: neither *dixit* nor *propalavit*. And there was a case here between the Lord Stourton and another, and a demurrer in law thereon, where someone brought an action on the case against Lord Stourton because he wrote a letter to the plaintiff saying that he was a traitor; and it was agreed that no action on the case lay upon this matter, because the letter (which was written between the defendant and the plaintiff) was neither published nor made known to others, and if the plaintiff had not declared what the letter was others could not [have known], and therefore it was no slander to the plaintiff except by his wish. So it was agreed in that case that no action lay there; and likewise here. And the action does not lie for another reason: the words are no cause of action unless the defendant were a great officer, such as a judge, justice of the peace, or in commission, in which case to say that one took bribes is a good cause of action; or if someone is a great officer to a nobleman, such as his steward, receiver or auditor, and the defendant says he took bribes, it is a good cause of action. But if he says to someone who is not such an officer, but a common person, that he took bribes, no action on the case.

EDWARDES v WOOTTON (1607)

Hawarde, *Cases in Camera Stellata*, p. 343
(Star Chamber) (untr.).[20]

This day [27 November 1607] also a cause was heard between Thomas Edwardes, a physician of Exeter, plaintiff,[1] and Dr. Wootton,[2] a physician, Norris's wife, an apothecary, one other physician, and an apothecary, defendants. The offence was a libel made by Dr. Wootton and by him and the rest published in the manner ensuing. Edwardes and Dr. Wootton falling out and using bitter terms, Dr. Wootton writes a letter and begins, 'Mr. Docturdo and fartardo . . .', more than two sides of paper full of vile matter, ribaldry and defamation, and encloseth it as a letter, and subscribes it, and sends it to Mr. Edwardes, and keeps a copy thereof and afterwards publisheth the same and delivers copies to divers, who likewise read and publish the same to divers, and say that Dr. Edwardes will forswear them and bear them out in it, howsoever or whatsoever it cost him. This was greatly to the defaming and damnifying of the plaintiff, Edwardes, being brought up as an apothecary and allowed a physician by the College of Physicians in London upon examination had, and otherwise reputed a very honest and discreet man. The defendant, Dr. Wootton, pretended that the plaintiff himself had first published this libel, but made no proof of it; and had ministered 80 interrogatories (four yards of parchment, by the measure of the lord chancellor) against the plaintiff, thereby examining all the principal men of those countries touching the honesty, credit, reputation and carriage of the plaintiff (a very dangerous precedent and not to be suffered, for the plaintiff can have no knowledge thereof before publication), yet they all did generally with one consent approve the sufficiency, honesty and good course and carriage of the said complainant, and no one witness accused or touched him with any blemish in any kind.

The question was, whether this was a libel or no. And resolved by the judges and all the court that it was a libel; for if a man will write a private letter defamatory and not otherwise publish it, either before or after the writing, he shall not have an action of the case, but forasmuch as the same doth provoke malice and breach of the peace and revenge it shall be punished in this court and nip it *dum seges in herba*. For being a letter only kept close it giveth no

---

20   Also reported in 12 Co. Rep. 35.
1   See the action by him for fees (1615), p. 463, above.
2   Probably Henry Wootton, M.D. (Oxon.) 1567.

cause of action, because he hath no damages; and this being an offence that doth provoke revenge, bring danger to the state and common weal, *et interest reipublicae*, and therefore an offence in this court to be severely punished.

Therefore the Lord COKE [C.J.C.P.] began a sharp sentence, and the greatest number agreed thereunto. The defendant, Dr. Wootton, in regard of his degree, he would spare for corporal punishment, but he fined him £500; and the other three defendants £40 a piece; and £200 damages to the plaintiff (the other three to pay £10 a piece, and the doctor the rest) ... And the doctor at a public market at the next general assizes at Exeter should be set in some eminent place, and wear about his neck for a tippet the four yards of interrogatories, and confess his fault; and then the interrogatories to be returned to the court, and to be defaced and cancelled; the doctor to be imprisoned and bound to his good behaviour.[3]

By the LORD CHANCELLOR.[4] It did appear that there was an ancient law that the slanderer should be let blood in the tongue, and he that would hear libels should be let blood in the ears.[5] He vouched *Pickering's Case*,[6] [and] Vicar Bruerton's letter,[7] and agreed in his sentence with the Lord Coke.

W. HUDSON, TREATISE OF THE COURT OF STAR CHAMBER (1621)

From *Collectanea Juridica* (F. Hargrave, ed., 1792), vol. II, pp. 100–104, (untr.).

In all ages libels have been severely punished in this court; but most especially they began to be frequent about 42 & 43 Eliz. when Sir Edward Coke was her attorney general ... Libels are of several kinds: either by scoffing at the person of another in rhyme or prose, or by the personating him, thereby to make him ridiculous; or by setting up horns at his gate, or picturing him or describing him; or by writing of some base or defamatory letter and publishing the same to others, or some scurvy love-letter to himself, whereby it is not

3 This is inconsistent with what Coke C.J. is reported to have said, and is perhaps the suggestion of another member of the court. Coke's own report does not mention the sentence.
4 Lord Ellesmere.
5 Coke (12 Co. Rep. 36) said this was the law of the Lydians.
6 *A.-G. v Lewis Pickering* (1605), in Hawarde, *Cases in Camera Stellata*, p. 222; sub nom. *De Libellis Famosis*, 5 Co. Rep. 125. This was a libel on the late Archbishop Whitgift (d. 1604).
7 *Lloide v Breverton*; see p. 650, below.

likely but he should be provoked to break the peace; or to publish disgraceful or false speeches against any eminent man or public officer. Of each of these I shall only remember an example or two, and then leave it to the search of infinite precedents.

For a libellous rhyme, *Bland v Davies and others* was an unhappy libel in verse against the plaintiff and his wife, which Davies took upon him to make, being a barber in London, and was justly sentenced to be whipped for helping himself (for assuredly he was not able to have written such a line), for which he was sentenced about 1 Jac. . . . The personating of the earl of Lincoln in a play was severely punished . . .

Picturing or setting up horns at a man's gate was severely punished in the case of *Horsey v Astley*, 33 & 34 Eliz. And in the great libel of Wells, there being a fame against a townsman that he lived incontinently with the wife of the plaintiff Hole, in a May game used yearly in that town they brought a man riding with a board before him on which was a pair of nine-holes, one riding at the one side saying, 'He holes for a groat', the defendants (being many in number) were severely punished for this pastime.[8]

And for scandalous letters the precedents are infinite. One of the first sent to the person himself was *Lloide*, register of the bishop of St Asaph, against *Peter Breverton*, clerk, sentenced Mich. 2 Jac.: and yet the defendant would have undertaken to have proved the contents of the letter to have been true, he thereby charging him with bribery and extortion in his place. Then was *Sir William Hall's case* against *Ellis*, a scoffing letter, and severely punished. A scurrilous letter from one mean man to another was Mich. 12 Jac. sentenced at the suit of *Barrows* against *Luelling*;[9] and the same only sent to the party himself. Nay, *Norton v Roper*, 1 Jac., [he] was sentenced for writing a scoffing letter by one rival to another. But if the letter be written to a man in authority, as in Trin. 32 Eliz., *Hide v Smalley*, for writing a letter to the mayor of the borough of Wallingford charging him with injustice, that was severely punished. And [for] a letter written by Booth to Sir Edward Coke, charging him with some cautelous courses in prosecuting a forgery, [Booth] was sentenced to the pillory. Nay, disgraceful words and speeches against eminent persons have been grievously punished in all ages. In 8 Hen. VIII one Scott, a justice of peace of Surrey, was

---

8　Rustic customs of teasing cuckolded or hen-pecked husbands survived until the last century, and one is described in Hardy's *The Mayor of Casterbridge*. They were held to be actionable at common law in *Bodily v Lawme* (1662), cited in 6 Mod. 56, otherwise *Lumley v Baddenly*, cited in T. Raym. 401; *Mason v Jennings* (1680) T. Raym. 401. For other cases, see p. 655, below.

9　Sub nom. *Barrow v Lewellin* (*c.* 1614) Hob. 62.

punished for speaking certain words against the lord cardinal. And in the same year one Knivett, and one called Long James, for using uncivil words to the sheriff of London in the wrestling-place at Clerkenwell. And 12 Hen. VIII one Saye was sentenced for raising a false report of the Lord Dacre of the South. And in 7 Hen. VIII Lucas, a privy councillor, was sentenced for speaking scandalous words against the lord cardinal.[10] And in the days of Queen Elizabeth one [was] sentenced to the pillory for saying the Lord Dyer was a corrupt judge. And *George Vernon's case*, at the suit of Mr. Serjeant Crewe, for speaking against Sir Henry Townsend.

And the publishers of libels are as severely punished as the makers. Therefore it is usually said that it were a punishment to a libeller if no man would publish it. Therefore to hear it sung or read, and to laugh at it and to make merriment with it, hath ever been held a publication in law.

There are two gross errors crept into the world concerning libels: one, that it is no libel if the party put his hand unto it, and the other, that it is not a libel if it be true, both which have been long since expelled out of this court. For the first, the reason why the law punisheth libel is for that they intend to raise the breach of the peace, which may as well be done (and more easily) when the hand is subscribed than when it is not. And for the other, it hath ever been agreed that it is not the matter but the manner which is punishable. For libelling against a common strumpet is as great an offence as against an honest woman, and perhaps more dangerous to the breach of the peace. For, as the woman said she would never grieve to have been told of her red nose if she had not one indeed, neither is it a ground to examine the truth or falsehood of a libel . . .[11]

In this court a libel made against a dead man shall be punished, as *Lewis Pickering's Case* for his scornful libel against that reverend prelate archbishop Whitgift.[12] But whether only in this court, or by

---

10 Scott and Lucas were both benchers of the Inner Temple. For other examples of clashes between Wolsey and members of the legal profession, see Selden Soc. vol. 94, pp. *77–78.*

11 Lord Hardwicke C.J.K.B. considered that this principle extended even to civil actions for libel. In *R. v Roberts* (1735) Selw. N.P., ch. xxvi, n. (6), he said (obiter): 'It is said, that if an action were brought, the fact, if true, might be justified; but I think that is a mistake . . . I never heard such a justification in an action for a libel even hinted at. The law is too careful in discountenancing such practices. All the favour that I know truth affords in such a case is that it may be shewn in mitigation of damages . . .'. It is doubtful whether this position was generally accepted: certainly it was not law by the end of the century.

12 *Case de libellis famosis* (1605) 5 Co. Rep. 125; Hawarde, *Cases in Camera Stellata*, p. 222.

indictment at the common law also, I am doubtful. For as a trespass to the party it cannot be, and as a scandal to him that is dead in his public service it hath been adjudged that words of imputation against a great judge after his death should not be examined, lest the public justice might receive prejudice when he is gone, that should make it appear to be false and scandalous: which was the judges' opinions in *Strowd's Case*. And yet surely the king may punish the detraction of his public justice? But this is left to the discretion of good and temperate times.

And I desire to observe one difference, which standeth with the rules of law and reason, and which (under favour) I have ever conceived to be just: that upon the speaking of words, although they be against a great person, the defendant may justify them as true. As in all actions *de scandalis magnatum*, which are as properly to be sued in the Star Chamber as in any other court, and he shall be there received to make the truth appear. But if he put the scandal in writing, it is then past any justification, for then the manner is examinable and not the matter . . .

KING v LAKE (1667)

Record: E13/667, mm. 34–37; Kiralfy, *Source Book*, p. 154. Edward King brought a bill of *quominus* against Sir Edward Lake Bt., and complained that, whereas the plaintiff was a faithful subject, of the king and prepared with all his power for the Restoration, and had always been of good name and reputation, and was a barrister at law of Gray's Inn and retained of counsel with many subjects of the king; and whereas on 14 November 1666 the plaintiff presented to a parliamentary committee a petition of grievances against the defendant, as official of the bishop of Lincoln, and his ministers, who had vexed and oppressed the plaintiff and his tenants in that diocese by unlawful citations, excommunications, extortions and exactions,[13] connected with the oath *ex officio*: the defendant on appearing before the committee made no answer but, scheming maliciously to deprive the plaintiff of his good name, he caused to be printed and published on 7 January 1667 a false libel containing the words set out in the report below, by reason of which the plaintiff was in danger of incurring the king's displeasure and had been injured in his good name, to his damage of £5,000. The defendant pleaded Not guilty, and on 22 May at the Guildhall, London, before Hale C.B., the jury found a special verdict setting out the full text of Lake's tract, the material part of which is paraphrased in the report below.

13 Lake (d. 1674) fought on the king's side and was made chancellor of Lincoln in 1660. The feud between the parties seems to have begun in the ecclesiastical courts. For a previous suit between the parties, see *King v Lake* (1664) Hardres 364, 388 (two prohibitions to stay excommunications).

Damages of £150 were awarded in case this should be held to be a verdict for the plaintiff.

Hardres 470, pl. 5 (Exchequer Chamber) (untr.).

In an action upon the case for printing and publishing a false and malicious libel against the plaintiff, containing amongst other things these words and matters in an answer to a petition preferred by the plaintiff to the House of Commons against the defendant:[14]

The prosecutor is Mr. King, whose violence both formerly and lately is very notorious, to say nothing before His Majesty's happy restoration, of which much might be said too horrid to be related, which this respondent passeth by in regard of the Act of Oblivion, though the three years therein mentioned are long since elapsed; and also said in the consistory court in Lincolnshire with a loud voice, in the presence of many people, that he would strike at the root; whereas this respondent conceives (always referring himself to the judgment of this honourable House) that there is no root under God of ecclesiastical government but the king himself (*and in the margin, with an asterisk, are these words*: at least with respect to coercive power); and that the plaintiff's petition is stuffed with illegal assertions, ineptitudes, imperfections, clogged with gross ignorances, absurdities and solecisms.

By reason of which words and libel he is damnified in his good name and credit, and profession of a barrister at law, £5,000. Upon Not guilty pleaded ... a special verdict finds those words in the margin (omitted in the declaration), and this clause also: 'always referring himself to the judgment of this honourable House'.

Sir Robert Atkyns, for the plaintiff, cited Yelv. 152 and Hob. 180.[15]

Stevens, for the defendant, insisted that the words as recited were too general to ground an action upon.

HALE C.B. There is no material variance betwixt the declaration and the special verdict; and although such general words spoken once, without writing or publishing them, would not be actionable, yet here (they being writ and published—which contains more malice than if they had but been once spoken) they are actionable.

And, the court being all of that opinion, judgment was given for the plaintiff, unless cause be shown.

The record shows that judgment was entered for the plaintiff. (The judgment is said to have been affirmed by a writ of error: see p. 655, below). Lake retaliated with an action in the King's Bench for an alleged libel contained in King's petition: *Lake v King* (1668) KB 27/1897, m. 1179, printed in A.

14 Paraphrased in the report from the full text in the record.
15 *Higges v Austen* (1609) Yelv. 152; *Sydenham v May* (1615) Hob. 180.

Vidian, *The Exact Pleader* (1684), p. 36; reported in Wms Saund. 120; 1 Lev. 240; 1 Sid. 414; 1 Mod. 58; 2 Keb. 361, 462, 496, 659, 664, 801, 832. The case was fully argued on the question whether parliamentary privilege extended to the printing of petitions, and after some judicial hesitation[16] judgment was given for King in 1671. King then brought a Common Pleas action for libel against Lake, in respect of a letter written to his client the countess of Lincoln saying he was a griping lawyer and would milk her purse. King again succeeded, despite a vigorous dissent from Vaughan C.J. on the ground that actions for words ought to be discouraged: '. . . the growth of these actions will spoil all communication; a man shall not say such an inn, or such wine, is not good . . .' (2 Vent. 28; 1 Freem. 14).

AUSTIN v CULPEPER (1683)

2 Show. K.B. 313, pl. 322 (K.B.) (untr.).[17]

Case, wherein the plaintiff declares that, whereas there was a cause depending in the Court of Chancery between the said parties, and witnesses sworn and examined on the behalf of the plaintiff: the defendant, to scandalise the plaintiff, did forge and counterfeit an order of the said Court of Chancery that Sir John Austin should stand committed unless cause [be shown], and this did cause to be written and published as an order of the said court; and afterwards, namely the same day, did make the picture or representation of a pillory, and under the same did write these words: 'For Sir John Austin and his suborned, forsworn witnesses' etc.

Mr. Pollexfen moves in arrest of judgment. This declaration consists of two parts, namely the forgery of the order, and the figure with the words underwritten; and the damages are entire. Now, if either of them be not actionable, the plaintiff ought not to have judgment . . . Then for the words themselves, if they had been spoken, they had not been actionable: for to call a man 'forsworn' is not actionable unless it appear that it was in a court of justice. Now the forgery itself is not actionable, for he lays no damage or trouble accrued to him thereby.

Mr. Holt to the contrary. It is all but one complicated act, and the action is for libelling him in that manner. Now, supposing the

16 E.g. Saund., at 132: '. . . it was said that although the exhibiting of the said petition was lawful, yet the printing of it was a publication of it to all the world, which is not lawful to be done in any case. And of such opinion KELYNG C.J., in his lifetime, seemed to be strongly. But TWISDEN J. was of a contrary opinion, because it is no more than if the defendant had employed several clerks to write as many copies as he has now printed . . .'.

17 Also reported in Skin. 123, which says the jury awarded £500 damages to the plaintiff.

words themselves were not actionable, yet, being published by way of libel, they are so. There was the case of *Colonel King v Lake*,[18] before lord Hale, where the action was for printing a petition which he delivered to several members of the House of Commons (having a complaint there against him) containing scandalous matter concerning him, as that he was dishonest and unjust and had abused him; and although none of these words printed would have borne an action if spoken, yet the action was held to lie: and judgment was affirmed upon a writ of error. An action lies for a libel as well as an indictment; and a libel may be either by writings or by signs (*per signa*). And here was the case of *Mingey v Moodie*, where an action was brought for riding skimmington (as it is called).[19]

Per curiam. It is but one complicated act; and an action lies for scandalising a man by writing those words, which will not, being spoken, bear an action. Here was the cause of *Sir William Bolton v Deane*, for carrying a fellow about with horns, and bowing at his door etc.

And, by the whole court, judgment was given for the plaintiff.[20]

In *Bradley v Methwyn* (1736) Selw. N.P., ch. xxvi, n. (2), an action on the case, Lord Hardwicke C.J.K.B. said, 'the present case is not for words, but for a libel, in which the rule is different; for some words may be actionable (or prosecuted by way of indictment) if reduced into writing, which would not be so if spoken only. For the crime in a libel does not arise merely from the scandal, but from the tendency which it has to occasion a breach of the peace by making the scandal more public and lasting, and spreading it abroad'.

18 (1667); see p. 652, above.
19 A noisy procession, usually with effigies and a pair of stag's horns, intended to ridicule an ill-treated husband or wife. The word is first noticed in the 17th century, but its etymology is uncertain. See also p. 650, above.
20 Cf. Skinner's report: '... And 'twas said, that to say of anybody that he is a dishonest man is not actionable; but to publish so, or put it up upon posts, is actionable. So the plaintiff had his judgment by the unanimous opinion of the court'.

Index of names

This index does not include surnames without Christian names, except in the case of lawyers, or Christian names without surnames; fictitious people (such as John Style) or places; references to kings and saints for dating purposes; or general references to London and Westminster. Lawyers are identified with their Christian names, dates of death (where known) and inns or professional titles; but only titles and ranks relevant to their appearances in this volume are noted.

Index of subjects

maxims and aphorisms—*continued*
  usus est dominium fiduciarium, 127
    fn. 7
  volenti non fit injuria, 619
mayhem, 334, 362
medical practitioners
  actions against, for negligence, 340–
    341, 360–367, 384, 397, 404, 579
  actions by: assumpsit, 463; debt, 239;
    defamation, 648–649
  expert evidence by, 334
merchants
  custom of, 249, 458–462, 468
  defamation of, 626, 638, 639
  do not usually give acquittance, 418
  duty imposed on, 477
merger of estates, 87
mill, nuisance to, 582–583, 586–587, 593,
  594–595, 613
miller
  accused of taking excessive tolls, 349
  competition by, 486
  nuisance by, 587, 614
mill-maker, action against, 380–383
miner, negligence by, 571
'misdemeanour': breach of contract as,
    408, 412, 433; tort as, 320, 532–533
misfeasance, 356, 401, 428
  see also under assumpsit
mistake, overpayment by, 469, 471
money
  exchanged by Lombards, 294
  inflation, 635–636
  noble, 635
  ownership of, 245, 246, 267, 290–291,
    539
  paid into court, 293
  payment countermanded, 504
  portugals, 246
  receiver of *see under* account, action of
  special coin, payment in, 433
  sum in gross severed from realty, 480–
    481
  trover for, 539–540, 542, 544, 545–546
  see also account; assumpsit for money;
    debt
money had and received, count, 465–
    472, 523
money laid out, count, 472–476
monk, incapacity of, 73, 83, 256
monopoly, 611–614, 618–619
mort d'ancestor, assize of, 25–30, 53, 55,
    200
mortmain, 10, 139–140

motion *see* arrest of judgment
murder, accusation of, 626, 637
name, initials treated as, 458
necessity, 311–312, 316–317, 335, 607
negligence
  alleged in trespass vi et armis, 303–
    304, 307
  care: 'all diligence', 362; 'good care',
    608; 'reasonable care', 578; 'utmost
    care', 374
  common, and gross neglect, 373
  deceit, as, 376
  duty of care, 356–357, 578–579
  evidence of, 576–578, 579–580
  'male purpose', 570 fn. 2
  relevance in trespass vi et armis, 333
  'sufferance', 412
  see also neighbour
negligence, actions on the case for, 358–
    377, 552–580
  against bailee, 306, 398 fn. 18, 412,
    414, 529, 530
  against finder of goods, 569–570
negotiable instruments *see* bill of
  exchange; promissory note
negotiorum gestio, 316–317
neighbour, duty not to injure, 356 fn. 13,
  560–561, 578–579
niggard, 349
non est factum, plea of, 256, 452
nonfeasance, 345–348, 356, 411–412,
  428, 583, 586, 609
  see also under assumpsit
nonsuit, by consent, 221, 222, 223, 225,
    574
novel disseisin, 1–4, 19, 30–36, 38–41,
    45–46, 53–56, 199, 298, 430, 584
nuisance
  action on the case for, 355, 430, 434,
    581–610
  assize of, 328, 409, 410, 430, 434, 435,
    581–591; for common, 589–591; for
    diverting water, 586 fn. 1
  public (common): action for, 571, 584,
    602; indictment for, 560, 603, 605;
    presentment for, 584
  varieties of: excessive weight, 606–608;
    infection, 593, 600–605; interference
    with market, 612, 614; noise, 586,
    592; not removing hay, 347; not re-
    pairing partition, 607–609; obstruct-
    ing light, 328, 592–599; overhanging
    trees, 328–329; removing support,
    610; smell, 585–586, 596, 600–605

words and phrases—*continued*
  scintilla juris, 141, 152
  secundum aequm et bonum, 206
  solamen et consortium, 308, 309
  tail, 52
  termes (year books), 235
  trespass as nomen collectivum, 351
  use is as clay in the hands of the
    potter, 137
  vagabond, 349
  see also maxims and aphorisms
work done, count for, 472–476
writs, judicial, *see* process
writs, original
  affirmed by view, 65
  bad Latin in, 510
  changes in formulae, 424
  invention of, 427, 434
  kinds of, 421, 434–435

writs, original—*continued*
  need for, 4
  specimens: assumpsit and deceit, 385,
    390; assumpsit for nonfeasance,
    343; case against innkeeper, 343;
    case for deceit, 506, 516–517; case
    for defamation, 632–633; case for
    using false dice, 344; case on custom
    of realm concerning fire, 557; eject-
    ment, 179; formedon, 50; right, 13,
    16
  see also register of writs

year books
  'auncient ans', 107
  'put that case out of your books', 448
  'termes', 235
  to be referred to, 452